Property Law: Fundamental Principles and Moral Concerns
Published by:

Esq.

ESQUIRE BOOKS, INC.
www.esqbooks.com

Esquire Books, Inc., is a publishing corporation specializing in law and business textbooks. Please visit **www.esqbooks.com** to purchase books of interest or to submit your manuscript for consideration for publication.

****

D1602046

This book is intended for educational and thought provoking purposes only, and it is not legal advice. The accuracy and completeness of the subjects is not guaranteed and the reader hereby waives the right to pursue claims in reliance on this material. Please consult an attorney prior to acting in reliance on this information.

ISBN 978-0-578-12198-7

Copy on file at the Library of Congress.

Esq. ESQUIRE BOOKS, INC.

Better books for better minds

Esquire Books, Inc., is a publishing corporation specializing in law and business textbooks. Please visit www.esqbooks.com to purchase books of interest or to submit your manuscript for consideration for publication.

PROPERTY LAW

FUNDAMENTAL PRINCIPLES AND MORAL CONCERNS

IRA L. SHAFIROFF
PROFESSOR OF LAW
SOUTHWESTERN LAW SCHOOL

To Cindy and Hannah

v

Esq.

ESQUIRE BOOKS, INC.
www.esqbooks.com

TABLE OF CONTENTS

ACKNOWLEDGMENTS

I owe a debt of gratitude to numerous people who made this book possible.

First, I want to thank the many students at Southwestern Law School who, through the years, used this casebook in its non-published form in my property classes. Their enthusiasm and charity allowed me to experiment with this book and revise it, to get it into its present structure.

I also want to thank Southwestern Law School for its support of this project.

I owe many thanks to the Editorial and Advisory Board of Esquire Books for the many helpful suggestions and comments that they made. These few words of thanks are merely a token of my deep felt appreciation to Benjamin Harrel, Esq., Kirkland & Ellis LLP; Shannon Travis Harrel, Esq., Information Law Group; Professor Jeffrey Jones, Lewis & Clark Law School; Benjamin Julius, Esq., Godwin Lewis PC; Professor Vada Lindsey, Marquette University Law School; and Professor Chad J. Pomeroy, St. Mary's University School of Law.

I am especially grateful to Matt Berger, Editor, Esquire Books, for guiding this book to completion.

Saving the best for the last, I want to thank my wife and daughter for their support for this book and all my writing projects. Thank you, Cindy and Hannah, thank you.

INTRODUCTION

Property is a wonderful course. Am I biased? To answer that question, allow me to say that I began teaching property in 1986, and I continue to enjoy every moment of it. Thus, I stand guilty as charged. Nonetheless, there actually are less personal reasons for my enthusiastic claim.

First, we live in a capitalist society. In this country, people own property, real and personal. As such, it is fascinating, if not necessary, to learn about the driving force of our economy—ownership and property rights—and the impact that it has on our own individual lives. Second, every case that we read in property has a story behind it—a human story. People shape the law, and nowhere is this better exemplified than in the law of property. "It's mine!" is a recurring theme. Consequently, property law is an absorbing study of people as much as it is the study of the law. Third, moral concerns regularly influence the formation of legislation and judicial decisions, and our study of property law will cause us regularly to delve into these important considerations. Finally, the study of property law often requires that we study history—and history (contrary to what you may have experienced in high school and college) is nothing if not captivating. We cannot understand where we are unless we understand from where we came. In the property course, we will touch on feudal times, the American Revolution, slavery, the Great Depression, World War II, as well as other topics in history.

To facilitate your study, I have created this casebook, which is in the format of the traditional law school casebook—a book of cases that teaches fundamental principles. Indeed, the study of appellate cases is how lawyers traditionally have learned the law. When appropriate, I have severely edited the cases to provide you with just a few sentences of relevant black-letter law. Nonetheless, there are other cases that I barely touched in the editing process because they are so rich with reasoning—which is the heart of legal education and what law students must learn to do if they want to become lawyers.

I have omitted many footnotes from the opinions, except for those footnotes that I believe add to your understanding. My own footnotes, added for further elucidation, are easily distinguished from the court's footnotes: mine are in brackets [in this manner].

Moreover, while this text is traditional in the sense that it is in the form of an orthodox casebook, it also is novel because of the many sections and subsections in each chapter. Each section and subsection heading, corresponding to rules and elements, clearly indicates the narrow topic (a particular rule or element of a rule) at hand. Thus, when you read a given case in this text, you will clearly understand how that case fits into the seamless web and (sometimes) the puzzle of the law. Further, perusing these sections and subsections in the table of contents before classes start will enable you to get a very good overview of the course and show you where our journey will take us.

Finally, because no lawyer ever reads a case out of context, I have provided you with something unique among casebooks: a short summary preceding virtually all sections, subsections, and cases, to give you a better focus of what lies ahead.

I hope you enjoy this casebook and the study of property law.

IRA L. SHAFIROFF
July 2013

CHAPTER 1
ACQUIRING RIGHTS TO
PROPERTY BY POSSESSION

§ 1.1 Discovery

Possession, as you will see in this and other chapters, is an important concept in the law of property. Indeed, possession alone may bestow ownership. (You soon will learn that there may be a difference between "possession" and "ownership.") In this regard, we start with "ancient" history —how discovery of the New World by various explorers gave their sponsoring nations rights to what ultimately became the United States.

Johnson v. McIntosh
21 U.S. 543 (1823)

The background to this case was that Indian tribes conveyed certain land to "A" and the United States subsequently conveyed the same land to "B." A now seeks to eject B from the land. The United States Supreme Court, therefore, must decide who owns the land—A or B. The court will hold that B owns the land. What you should try to determine is the reasoning of the court: the basis for the holding that B prevails over A.

This was an action of ejectment for lands in the State and District of Illinois, claimed by the plaintiffs under a purchase and conveyance from the Piankeshaw Indians, and by the defendant, under a [subsequent] grant from the United States. * * *

Mr. Chief Justice MARSHALL delivered the opinion of the Court.

The plaintiffs in this cause claim the land, in their declaration mentioned, under two grants, purporting to be made, the first in 1773, and the last in 1775, by the chiefs of certain Indian tribes, constituting the Illinois and the Piankeshaw nations; and the question is, whether this title can be recognised in the Courts of the United States?

The facts, as stated in the case agreed, show the authority of the chiefs who executed this conveyance, so far as it could be given by their own people; and likewise show, that the particular tribes for whom these chiefs acted were in rightful possession of the land they sold. The inquiry, therefore, is, in a great measure, confined to the power of Indians to give, and of private individuals to receive, a title which can be sustained in the Courts of this country.

* * *

On the discovery of this immense continent, the great nations of Europe were eager to appropriate to themselves so much of it as they could respectively acquire. Its vast extent offered an ample field to the ambition and enterprise of all; and the character and religion of its inhabitants afforded an apology for considering them as a people over whom the superior genius of Europe might claim an ascendency. The potentates of the old world found no difficulty in convincing themselves that they made ample compensation to the inhabitants of the new, by bestowing on them civilization and Christianity, in exchange for unlimited independence. But, as they were all in pursuit of nearly the same object, it was necessary, in order to avoid conflicting settlements, and consequent war with each other, to establish a principle, which all should acknowledge as the law by which the right of acquisition, which they all asserted, should be regulated as between themselves. This principle was, that discovery gave title to the government by whose subjects, or by whose authority, it was made, against all other European governments, which title might be consummated by possession.

* * *

* * * [T]he rights of the original inhabitants were, in no instance, entirely disregarded; but were necessarily, to a considerable extent, impaired. They were admitted to be the rightful occupants of the soil, with a legal as well as just claim to retain possession of it, and to use it according to their own discretion; but their rights to complete sovereignty, as independent nations, were necessarily diminished, and their power to dispose of the soil at their own will, to whomsoever they pleased, was denied by the original fundamental principle, that discovery gave exclusive title to those who made it.

While the different nations of Europe respected the right of the natives, as occupants, they asserted the ultimate dominion to be in themselves; and claimed and exercised, as a consequence of this ultimate dominion, a power to grant the soil, while yet in possession of the natives. These grants have been understood by all, to convey a title to the grantees, subject only to the Indian right of occupancy.

The history of America, from its discovery to the present day, proves, we think, the universal recognition of these principles.

Spain did not rest her title solely on the grant of the Pope. Her discussions respecting boundary, with France, with Great Britain, and with the United States, all show that she placed in on the rights given by discovery. Portugal sustained her claim to the Brazils by the same title.

France, also, founded her title to the vast territories she claimed in America on discovery. * * *

* * *

Thus, all the nations of Europe, who have acquired territory on this continent, have asserted in themselves, and have recognised in others, the exclusive right of the discoverer to appropriate the lands occupied by the Indians. Have the American States rejected or adopted this principle?

By the treaty which concluded the war of our revolution, Great Britain relinquished all claim, not only to the government, but to the 'propriety and territorial rights of the United States,' whose boundaries were fixed in the second article. By this treaty, the powers of government, and the right to soil, which had previously been in Great Britain, passed definitively to these States. We had before taken possession of them, by declaring independence; but neither the declaration of independence, nor the treaty confirming it, could give us more than that which we before possessed, or to which Great Britain was before entitled. It has never been doubted, that either the United States, or the several States, had a clear title to all the lands within the boundary lines described in the treaty, subject only to the Indian right of occupancy, and that the exclusive power to extinguish that right, was vested in that government which might constitutionally exercise it.

* * *

The United States, then, have unequivocally acceded to that great and broad rule by which its civilized inhabitants now hold this country. They hold, and assert in themselves, the title by which it was acquired. They maintain, as all others have maintained, that discovery gave an exclusive right to extinguish the Indian title of occupancy, either by purchase or by conquest; and gave also a right to such a degree of sovereignty, as the circumstances of the people would allow them to exercise.

The power now possessed by the government of the United States to grant lands, resided, while we were colonies, in the crown, or its grantees. The validity of the titles given by either has never been questioned in our Courts. It has been exercised uniformly over territory in possession of the Indians. The existence of this power must negative the existence of any right which may conflict with, and control it. An absolute title to lands cannot exist, at the same time, in different persons, or in different governments. An absolute, must be an exclusive title, or at least a title which excludes all others not compatible with it. All our institutions recognise the absolute title of the crown, subject only to the Indian right of occupancy, and recognise the absolute title of the crown to extinguish that right. This is incompatible with an absolute and complete title in the Indians.

We will not enter into the controversy, whether agriculturists, merchants, and manufacturers, have a right, on abstract principles, to expel hunters from the territory they possess, or to contract their limits. Conquest gives a title which the Courts of the conqueror cannot deny, whatever the private and speculative opinions of individuals may be, respecting the original justice of the claim which has been successfully asserted. The British government, which was then our government, and whose rights have passed to the United States, asserted title to all the lands occupied by Indians, within the chartered limits of the British colonies. It asserted also a limited sovereignty over them, and the exclusive right of extinguishing the title which occupancy gave to them. These claims have been maintained and established as far west as the river Mississippi, by the sword. The title to a vast portion of the lands we now hold, originates in them. It is not for the Courts of this country to question the validity of this title, or to sustain one which is incompatible with it.

Although we do not mean to engage in the defense of those principles which Europeans have applied to Indian title, they may, we think, find some excuse, if not justification, in the character and habits of the people whose rights have been wrested from them.

The title by conquest is acquired and maintained by force. The conqueror prescribes its limits. Humanity, however, acting on public opinion, has established, as a general rule, that the conquered shall not be wantonly oppressed, and that their condition shall remain as eligible as is compatible with the objects of the conquest. Most usually, they are incorporated with the victorious nation, and become subjects or citizens of the government with which they are connected. The new and old members of the society mingle with each other; the distinction between them is gradually lost, and they make one people. Where this incorporation is practicable, humanity demands, and a wise policy requires, that the rights of the conquered to property should remain unimpaired; that the

5

new subjects should be governed as equitably as the old, and that confidence in their security should gradually banish the painful sense of being separated from their ancient connections, and united by force to strangers.

When the conquest is complete, and the conquered inhabitants can be blended with the conquerors, or safely governed as a distinct people, public opinion, which not even the conqueror can disregard, imposes these restraints upon him; and he cannot neglect them without injury to his fame, and hazard to his power.

But the tribes of Indians inhabiting this country were fierce savages, whose occupation was war, and whose subsistence was drawn chiefly from the forest. To leave them in possession of their country, was to leave the country a wilderness; to govern them as a distinct people, was impossible, because they were as brave and as high spirited as they were fierce, and were ready to repel by arms every attempt on their independence. What was the inevitable consequence of this state of things? The Europeans were under the necessity either of abandoning the country, and relinquishing their pompous claims to it, or of enforcing those claims by the sword, and by the adoption of principles adapted to the condition of a people with whom it was impossible to mix, and who could not be governed as a distinct society, or of remaining in their neighbourhood, and exposing themselves and their families to the perpetual hazard of being massacred.

* * *

That law which regulates, and ought to regulate in general, the relations between the conqueror and conquered, was incapable of application to a people under such circumstances. The resort to some new and different rule, better adapted to the actual state of things, was unavoidable. Every rule which can be suggested will be found to be attended with great difficulty.

However extravagant the pretension of converting the discovery of an inhabited country into conquest may appear; if the principle has been asserted in the first instance, and afterwards sustained; if a country has been acquired and held under it; if the property of the great mass of the community originates in it, it becomes the law of the land, and cannot be questioned. So, too, with respect to the concomitant principle, that the Indian inhabitants are to be considered merely as occupants, to be protected, indeed, while in peace, in the possession of their lands, but to be deemed incapable of transferring the absolute title to others. However this restriction may be opposed to natural right, and to the usages of civilized nations, yet, if it be indispensable to that system under which the country has been settled, and be adapted to the actual condition of the two people, it may, perhaps, be supported by reason, and certainly cannot be rejected by Courts of justice.

* * *

So far as respected the authority of the crown, no distinction was taken between vacant lands and lands occupied by the Indians. The title, subject only to the right of occupancy by the Indians, was admitted to be in the king, as was his right to grant that title. The lands, then, to which this proclamation referred, were lands which the king had a right to grant, or to reserve for the Indians.

* * *

After bestowing on this subject a degree of attention which was more required by the magnitude of the interest in litigation, and the able and elaborate arguments of the bar, than by its intrinsic difficulty, the Court is decidedly of opinion, that the plaintiffs do not exhibit a title which can be sustained in the Courts of the United States; and that there is no error in the judgment which was rendered against them in the District Court of Illinois.

Judgment affirmed, with costs.

§ 1.2 Capture

Yet again, we will see the importance of possession in the law of property. This time it is in the realm of capture.

Pierson v. Post

2 Am. Dec. 264 (Supreme Court of N.Y. 1805)

In this case, "A" is chasing a fox when "B" suddenly comes on the scene and actually kills the fox. The court must decide, as between A and B, who owns the fox? The court will hold that B owns the fox. Why does the court award B the fox?

The declaration stated that *Post,* being in possession of certain dogs and hounds under his command, did, "upon a certain wild and uninhabited, unpossessed and waste land, called the beach, find and start one of those noxious beasts called a fox," and whilst there hunting, chasing and pursuing the same with his dogs and hounds, and when in view thereof, *Pierson,* well knowing the fox was so hunted and pursued, did, in the sight of *Post,* to prevent his catching the same, kill and carry it off. * * *

TOMPKINS, J. delivered the opinion of the court.

This cause comes before us on a return to a *certiorari* directed to one of the justices of *Queens* county.

The question submitted by the counsel in this cause for our determination is, whether *Lodowick Post,* by the pursuit with his hounds in the manner alleged in his declaration, acquired such a right to, or property in, the fox, as will sustain an action against *Pierson* for killing and taking him away?

The cause was argued with much ability by the counsel on both sides, and presents for our decision a novel and nice question. It is admitted that a fox is an animal *feræ naturæ,* and that property in such animals is acquired by occupancy only. These admissions narrow the discussion to the simple question of what acts amount to occupancy, applied to acquiring right to wild animals?

If we have recourse to the ancient writers upon general principles of law, the judgment below is obviously erroneous. *Justinian's Institutes,* lib. 2. tit. 1. s. 13. and *Fleta,* lib. 3. c. 2. p. 175. adopt the principle, that pursuit alone vests no property or right in the huntsman; and that even pursuit, accompanied with wounding, is equally ineffectual for that purpose, unless the animal be actually taken. The same principle is recognised by *Bracton,* lib. 2. c. 1. p. 8.

Puffendorf, lib. 4. c. 6. s. 2. and 10. defines occupancy of beasts *feræ naturæ,* to be the actual corporal possession of them, and *Bynkershoek* is cited as coinciding in this definition. It is indeed with hesitation that *Puffendorf* affirms that a wild beast mortally wounded, or greatly maimed, cannot be fairly intercepted by another, whilst the pursuit of the person inflicting the wound continues. The foregoing authorities are decisive to show that mere pursuit gave *Post* no legal right to the fox, but that he became the property of *Pierson,* who intercepted and killed him.

It therefore only remains to inquire whether there are any contrary principles, or authorities, to be found in other books, which ought to induce a different decision. Most of the cases which have occurred in *England,* relating to property in wild animals, have either been discussed and decided upon the principles of their positive statute regulations, or have arisen between the huntsman and the owner of the land upon which beasts *feræ naturæ* have been apprehended; the former claiming them by title of occupancy, and the latter *ratione soli.* Little satisfactory aid can, therefore, be derived from the *English* reporters.

Barbeyrac, in his notes on *Puffendorf,* does not accede to the definition of occupancy by the latter, but, on the contrary, affirms, that actual bodily seizure is not, in all cases, necessary to constitute possession of wild animals. He does not, however, *describe* the acts which, according to his ideas, will amount to an appropriation of such animals to private use, so as to exclude the claims of all other persons, by title of occupancy, to the same animals; and he is far from averring that pursuit alone is sufficient for that purpose. To a certain extent, and as far as *Barbeyrac* appears to me to go, his objections to *Puffendorf's* definition of occupancy are reasonable and correct. That is to say, that actual bodily seizure is not indispensable to acquire right to, or possession of, wild beasts; but that, on the contrary, the mortal wounding of such beasts, by one not abandoning his pursuit, may, with the utmost propriety, be deemed possession of him; since, thereby, the pursuer manifests an unequivocal intention of appropriating the animal to his individual use, has deprived him of his natural liberty, and brought him within his certain control. So also, encompassing and securing such animals with nets and toils, or otherwise intercepting them in such a manner as to deprive them of their natural liberty, and render escape impossible, may justly be deemed to give possession of them to those persons who, by their industry and labour, have used such means of apprehending them. * * * The case now under consideration is one of mere pursuit, and presents no circumstances or acts which can bring it within the definition of occupancy by *Puffendorf,* or *Grotius,* or the ideas of *Barbeyrac* upon that subject.

The case cited from 11 *Mod.* 74--130. I think clearly distinguishable from the present; inasmuch as there the action was for maliciously hindering and disturbing the plaintiff in the exercise and enjoyment of a private franchise; and in the report of the same case, 3 *Salk.* 9. *Holt,* Ch. J. states, that the ducks were in the plaintiff's decoy pond, and *so in his possession,* from which it is obvious the court laid much stress in their opinion upon the plaintiff's possession of the ducks, *ratione soli.*

We are the more readily inclined to confine possession or occupancy of beasts *feræ naturæ,* within the limits prescribed by the learned authors above cited, for the sake of certainty, and preserving peace and order in society. If the first seeing, starting, or pursuing such animals, without having so wounded, circumvented or ensnared them, so as to deprive them of their natural liberty, and subject them to the control of their pursuer, should afford the basis of actions against others for intercepting and killing them, it would prove a fertile source of quarrels and litigation.

However uncourteous or unkind the conduct of *Pierson* towards *Post,* in this instance, may have been, yet his act was productive of no injury or damage for which a legal remedy can be applied. We are of opinion the judgment below was erroneous, and ought to be reversed.

* * *

§ 1.3 Find

We have all heard the silly rhyme, "Finders keepers, losers weepers." Many a five-year old has chanted this on the playground. Yet, it actually has a basis in the law of property, as you will now find out.

§ 1.3.1 In General

Finding a "chattel" (what does this mean?) may give the finder great rights to the property. In this regard, the next case is a classic.

Armory v. Delamirie
1 Strange 505 (King's Bench 1722)

The court must decide who owns a jewel: the one who found the jewel, a chimney sweep's boy, or a goldsmith, to whom the boy gave the jewel for purposes of securing an appraisal. The court will find that the boy has better rights to the jewel than the goldsmith. Consider why the court holds for the boy.

The plaintiff being a chimney sweeper's boy found a jewel and carried it to the defendant's shop (who was a goldsmith) to know what it was, and delivered it into the hands of the apprentice, who under pretence of weighing it, took out the stones, and calling to the master to let him know it came to three halfpence, the master offered the boy the money, who refused to take it, and insisted to have the thing again; whereupon the apprentice delivered him back the socket without the stones. And now in trover[1] against the master these points were ruled:

1. That the finder of a jewel, though he does not by such finding acquire an absolute property or ownership, yet he has such a property as will enable him to keep it against all but the rightful owner, and subsequently may maintain trover.

* * *

3. As to the value of the jewel several of the trade were examined to prove what a jewel of the finest water that would fit the socket would be worth; and the Chief Justice directed the jury, that unless the defendant did produce the jewel, and shew it not to be of the finest water, they should presume the strongest case against him, and make the value

---

[1] [Trover was the common law action for damages based on the defendant's conversion of the plaintiff's goods. Conversion is the unauthorized exercise of possession of the personal property of another.]

of the best jewels the measure of their damages: which they accordingly did.

Clark v. Maloney
3 Harr. 68 (Del.Super. 1840)

In Armory v. Delamirie, *we have seen that finding property can bestow ownership rights on the finder. What we now deal with is a series of finders—F1 and F2. F1 finds and acquires possession of certain logs found adrift in a bay, but then loses possession. Later, F2 finds the logs and acquires possession over them. The question is, as between F1 and F2 (the true owner, "O," is not in the picture), who has better rights to the logs?*

Bayard, Chief Justice, charged the jury:

The plaintiff must show *first*, that the logs were his property; and *secondly*, that they were converted by the defendants to their own use. In support of his right of property, the plaintiff relies upon the fact of his possession of the logs. They were taken up by him, adrift in the Delaware bay, and secured by a stake at the mouth of Mispillion creek. Possession is certainly prima facie evidence of property. It is called *prima facie* evidence because it may be rebutted by evidence of better title, but in the absence of better title it is as effective a support of title as the most conclusive evidence could be. It is for this reason, that *the finder of a chattel, though he does not acquire an absolute property in it, yet has such a property, as will enable him to keep it against all but the rightful owner.* The defense consists, not in showing that the defendants are the rightful owners, or claim under the rightful owner; but that the logs were found by them adrift in Mispillion creek, having been loosened from their fastening either by accident or design, and they insist that their title is as good as that of the plaintiff. But it is a well settled rule of law that the loss of a chattel does not change the right of property; and for the same reason that the original loss of these logs by the rightful owner, did not change his absolute property in them, but he might have maintained trover against the plaintiff upon refusal to deliver them, so the subsequent loss did not divest the *special* property of the plaintiff. It follows, therefore, that as the plaintiff has shown a special property in these logs, which he never abandoned, and which enabled him to keep them against all the world but the rightful owner, he is entitled to a verdict.

Verdict for the plaintiff.

§ 1.3.2 Place of Find Decisive

In determining the rights of finders of property, it may well be that the place where the chattel is found can govern who owns the property, as the next case illustrates.

Hannah v. Peel
[1945] K.B. 509, King's Bench Division

Hannah v. Peel *is another classic; it is in virtually every property casebook. Here are the facts: During World War II, the British government requisitioned the house of one Major Peel (who, the court will point out, never lived in the house). While stationed on duty in the house, one Corporal Hannah found a brooch in the crevice of a window frame. The question before the court is, who owns the brooch? Is it Major Peel or Corporal Hannah? The court will hold that it is Corporal Hannah. As you read the case, try to determine the reasoning of the court.*

ACTION tried by Birkett J.

On December 13, 1938, the freehold of Gwernhaylod House, Overton-on-Dee, Shropshire, was conveyed to the defendant, Major Hugh Edward Ethelston Peel, who from that time to the end of 1940 never himself occupied the house and it remained unoccupied until October 5, 1939, when it was requisitioned, but after some months was released from requisition. Thereafter it remained unoccupied until July 18, 1940, when it was again requisitioned, the defendant being compensated by a payment at the rate of £250 a year. In August, 1940, the plaintiff, Duncan Hannah, a lance-corporal, serving in a battery of the Royal Artillery, was stationed at the house and on the 21st of that month, when in a bedroom, used as a sick-bay, he was adjusting the black-out curtains when his hand touched something on the top of a window-frame, loose in a crevice, which he thought was a piece of dirt or plaster. The plaintiff grasped it and dropped it on the outside window ledge. On the following morning he saw that it was a brooch covered with cobwebs and dirt. Later, he took it with him when he went home on leave and his wife having told him it might be of value, at the end of October, 1940, he informed his commanding officer of his find and, on his advice, handed it over to the police, receiving a receipt for it. In August, 1942, the owner not having been found the police handed the brooch to the defendant, who sold it in October, 1942, for £66., to Messrs. Spink & Son, Ltd., of London, who resold it in the following month for £81. There was no evidence that the defendant had any knowledge of the existence of the brooch before it was found by the plaintiff. The defendant had offered the plaintiff a reward for the brooch, but the plaintiff refused to accept this and maintained throughout his right to the possession of the brooch as against all persons other than the owner, who was unknown. By a letter, dated October 5, 1942, the plaintiff's solicitors demanded the return of the brooch from the defendant, but it was not returned and on October 21, 1943, the plaintiff issued his writ claiming the return of the brooch, or its value, and damages for its detention. By his defence, the defendant claimed the brooch on the ground that he was the owner of Gwernhaylod House and in possession thereof.

* * *

BIRKETT J.

There is no issue of fact in this case between the parties. As to the issue in law, the rival claims of the parties can be stated in this way: The plaintiff says: "I claim the brooch as its finder and I have a good title against all the world, save only the true owner." The defendant says: "My claim is superior to yours inasmuch as I am the freeholder. The brooch was found on my property, although I was never in occupation, and my title, therefore, ousts yours and in the absence of the true owner I am entitled to the brooch or its value." Unhappily the law on this issue is in a very uncertain state and there is need of an authoritative decision of a higher court. Obviously if it could be said with certainty that this is the law, that the finder of a lost article, wherever found, has a good title against all the world save the true owner, then, of course, all my difficulties would be resolved; or again, if it could be said with equal certainty that this is the law, that the possessor of land is entitled as against the finder to all chattels found on the land, again my difficulties would be resolved. But, unfortunately, the authorities give some support to each of these conflicting propositions.

In the famous case of Armory v. Delamirie, the plaintiff, who was a chimney sweeper's boy, found a jewel and carried it to the defendant's shop, who was a goldsmith, in order to know what it was, and he delivered it into the hands of the apprentice in the goldsmith's shop, who made a pretence of weighing it and took out the stones and called to the master to let him know that it came to three-halfpence. The master offered the boy the money who refused to take it and insisted on having the jewel again. Whereupon the apprentice handed him back the socket of the jewel without the stones, and an action was brought in trover against the master, and it was ruled "that the finder of a jewel, though he does not by such finding acquire an absolute property or ownership, yet he has such a property as will enable him to keep it against all but the rightful owner, and consequently may maintain trover." The case of Bridges v. Hawkesworth is in process of becoming almost equally as famous because of the disputation which has raged around it. The headnote in the Jurist is as follows: "The place in which a lost article is found does not constitute any exception to the general rule of law, that the finder is entitled to it as against all persons except the owner." The case was in fact an appeal against a decision of the county court judge at Westminster. The facts appear to have been that in the year 1847 the plaintiff, who was a commercial traveller, called on a firm named Byfield & Hawkesworth on business, as he was in the habit of doing, and as he was leaving the shop he picked up a small parcel which was lying on the floor. He immediately showed it to the shopman, and opened it in his presence, when it was found to consist of a quantity of Bank of England notes, to the amount of £65. * * *

It is to be observed that in Bridges v. Hawkesworth which has been the subject of immense disputation, neither counsel put forward any argument on the fact that the notes were found in a shop. * * * Patteson J. never made any reference to the public part of the shop and, indeed, went out of his way to say that the learned county court judge was wrong in holding that the place where they were found made any legal difference.

Bridges v. Hawkesworth has been the subject of considerable comment by text-book writers * * *. * * * Sir Frederick Pollock, whilst he agreed with Mr. Justice Holmes that Bridges v. Hawkesworth was properly decided wrote: "In such a case as Bridges v. Hawkesworth, where a parcel of banknotes was dropped on the floor in the part of a shop frequented by customers, it is impossible to say that the shopkeeper has any possession in fact. He does not expect objects of that kind to be on the floor of his shop, and some customer is more likely than the shopkeeper or his servant to see and take them up if they do come there." He emphasizes the lack of de facto control on the part of the shopkeeper.

* * *

With regard to South Staffordshire Water Co. v. Sharman, the first two lines of the headnote are: "The possessor of land is generally entitled, as against the finder, to chattels found on the land." I am not sure that this is accurate. The facts were that the defendant Sharman, while cleaning out, under the orders of the plaintiffs, the South Staffordshire Water Company, a pool of water on their land, found two rings embedded in the mud at the bottom of the pool. He declined to deliver them to the plaintiffs, but failed to discover the real owner. In an action brought by the company against Sharman in detinue it was held that the company were entitled to the rings. Lord Russell of

Killowen C.J. said: "The plaintiffs are the freeholders of the locus in quo, and as such they have the right to forbid anybody coming on their land or in any way interfering with it. They had the right to say that their pool should be cleaned out in any way that they thought fit, and to direct what should be done with anything found in the pool in the course of such cleaning out. It is no doubt right, as the counsel for the defendant contended, to say that the plaintiffs must show that they had actual control over the locus in quo and the things in it; but under the circumstances, can it be said that the Minster Pool and whatever might be in that pool were not under the control of the plaintiffs? In my opinion they were. . . . * * *

* * *

A review of these judgments shows that the authorities are in an unsatisfactory state, * * *. The general principle is that the first finder of a thing has a good title to it against all but the true owner, even though the thing is found on the property of another person," and he cites Armory v. Delamirie and Bridges v. Hawkesworth in support of that proposition. Then he continues: "This principle, however, is subject to important exceptions, in which, owing to the special circumstances of the case, the better right is in him on whose property the thing is found," and he names three cases as the principal ones: "When he on whose property the thing is found is already in possession not merely of the property, but of the thing itself; as in certain circumstances, even without specific knowledge, he undoubtedly may be." The second limitation Sir John Salmond puts is: "If anyone finds a thing as the servant or agent of another he finds it not for himself, but for his employer." Then: "A third case in which a finder obtains no title is that in which he gets possession only through a trespass or other act of wrongdoing." It is fairly clear from the authorities that a man possesses everything which is attached to or under his land. Secondly, it would appear to be the law from the authorities I have cited, and particularly from Bridges v. Hawkesworth, that a man does not necessarily possess a thing which is lying unattached on the surface of his land even though the thing is not possessed by someone else. A difficulty however, arises, because the rule which governs things an occupier possesses as against those which he does not, has never been very clearly formulated in our law. He may possess everything on the land from which he intends to exclude others, if Mr. Justice Holmes is right; or he may possess those things of which he has a de facto control, if Sir Frederick Pollock is right.

There is no doubt that in this case the brooch was lost in the ordinary meaning of that term, and I should imagine it had been lost for a very considerable time. Indeed, from this correspondence it appears that at one time the predecessors in title of the defendant were considering making some claim. But the moment the plaintiff discovered that the brooch might be of some value, he took the advice of his commanding officer and handed it to the police. His conduct was commendable and meritorious. The defendant was never physically in possession of these premises at any time. It is clear that the brooch was never his, in the ordinary acceptation of the term, in that he had the prior possession. He had no knowledge of it, until it was brought to his notice by the finder. A discussion of the merits does not seem to help, but it is clear on the facts that the brooch was "lost" in the ordinary meaning of that word; that it was "found" by the plaintiff in the ordinary meaning of that word, that its true owner has never been found, that the defendant was the owner of the premises and had his notice drawn to this matter by the plaintiff, who

13

found the brooch. In those circumstances I propose to follow the decision in Bridges v. Hawkesworth, and to give judgment in this case for the plaintiff for £66.

Judgment for plaintiff.

§ 1.3.3 Nature of the Property Decisive

In Hannah v. Peel, *you saw that as between the owner of the place where the property was found and the finder, the place of the find can be decisive in deciding who owns the chattel. We now come to another line of cases that teach another principle: that the nature of the found property itself can be decisive with respect to ownership rights of chattels. What we mean by "nature of the found property itself" becomes clearer when you read the next several cases.*

McAvoy v. Medina
93 Mass. 548 (1866)

A patron in a barbershop found a pocketbook on a table. The court must decide, as between the finder and the owner of the barbershop, who owns the pocketbook. The court will hold for the owner of the barbershop.

DEWEY, J.

It seems to be the settled law that the finder of lost property has a valid claim to the same against all the world except the true owner, and generally that the place in which it is found creates no exception to this rule. 2 Parsons on Con. 97. *Bridges v. Hawkesworth,* 7 Eng. Law & Eq. R. 424.

But this property [a pocketbook] is not, under the circumstances, to be treated as lost property in that sense in which a finder has a valid claim to hold the same until called for by the true owner. This property was voluntarily placed upon a table in the defendant's [barber]shop by a customer of his who accidentally left the same there and has never called for it. The plaintiff also came there as a customer, and first saw the same and took it up from the table. The plaintiff did not by this acquire the right to take the property from the shop, but it was rather the duty of the defendant, when the fact became thus known to him, to use reasonable care for the safe keeping of the same until the owner should call for it. In the case of *Bridges v. Hawkesworth* the property, although found in a shop, was found on the floor of the same, and had not been placed there voluntarily by the owner, and the court held that the finder was entitled to the possession of the same, except as to the owner. But the present case more resembles that of *Lawrence v. The State,* 1 Humph. (Tenn.) 228, and is indeed very similar in its facts. The court there take a distinction between the case of property thus placed by the owner and neglected to be removed, and property lost. It was there held that "to place a pocket-book upon a table and to forget to take it away is not to lose it, in the sense in which the authorities referred to speak of lost property."

We accept this as the better rule, and especially as one better adapted to secure the rights of the true owner.

In view of the facts of this case, the plaintiff acquired no original right to the property, and the defendant's subsequent acts in receiving and holding the property in the manner he did does not create any.

Exceptions overruled.

Michael v. First Chicago Corp.

139 Ill.App.3d 374 (1985)

This case builds on McAvoy v. Medina *by introducing you to new terms: abandoned, lost, and mislaid property. We then learn the rights that a finder has for each of these categories of property.*

* * *

Plaintiffs' alternative contention is that the certificates of deposit are abandoned property, rather than lost or mislaid property, which the finder is entitled to keep. Both parties cite *Paset v. Old Orchard Bank & Trust Co.* (1978), 62 Ill.App.3d 534, 19 Ill.Dec. 389, 378 N.E.2d 1264, as the leading case in Illinois which sets forth the distinctions between the terms abandoned, lost, and mislaid property. Mislaid property is that which is intentionally put in a certain place and later forgotten; property is lost when it is unintentionally separated from the dominion of its owner; and property is abandoned when the owner, intending to relinquish all rights to the property, leaves it free to be appropriated by any other person. (62 Ill.App.3d 534, 537, 19 Ill.Dec. 389, 378 N.E.2d 1264.) A finder of property acquires no rights in mislaid property, is entitled to possession of lost property against everyone except the true owner, and is entitled to keep abandoned property. 62 Ill.App.3d 534, 537, 19 Ill.Dec. 389, 378 N.E.2d 1264.

* * *

Herron v. Whiteside

782 S.W.2d 414 (Mo.App. 1989)

This case builds on Michael v. First Chicago Corp. *by examining in some depth the nature of abandoned property.*

* * *

Abandonment is the voluntary relinquishment of ownership so that the property ceases to be the property of any person and becomes the subject of appropriation by the first taker. *Wirth v. Heavey,* 508 S.W.2d 263, 267 (Mo.App.1974). Abandonment of property requires intent plus an act. *Id.* A sufficient act is one that manifests a conscious purpose and intention of the owner of personal property neither to use nor to retake the property into his possession. *Id.* Intention to abandon may be inferred from strong and convincing evidence and may be shown by conduct clearly inconsistent with any intention to retain and continue the use or ownership of the property. *Wilson v. Wheeler Farms, Inc.,* 591 S.W.2d 287, 289 (Mo.App.1979); *Wirth,* 508 S.W.2d at 267; *see Russell v. Allen,* 496 S.W.2d 290, 294 (Mo.App.1973). The reasons for abandoning property and the motives inducing the abandonment are not an element or factor thereof, and in this sense the abandoning owner's intentions are not material. 1 C.J.S. *Abandonment* § 5 (1985); The abandonment is complete at the moment the intention to abandon and the relinquishment of possession unite. *Id.* at § 4; 1 AM.JUR.2d *Abandoned, Lost, and Unclaimed Property* § 16 (1962). Abandonment may be declared as a matter of law where all the essential facts are admitted or indisputably proved and the inferences to be drawn from them are certain and free from doubt. 1 C.J.S. *supra* § 11; 1 AM.JUR.2d *supra* § 39.

* * *

§ 1.3.4 Nature of the Relationship Decisive

In Hannah v. Peel, *when analyzing* South Staffordshire Water Co. v. Sharman, *the court made passing reference to the nature of the relationship between the litigants as decisive in determining ownership rights.* Morrison v. United States, *which follows, makes this point abundantly clear.*

Morrison v. United States
492 F.2d 1219 (Ct. Cl. 1974)

An American soldier, on a so-called search and destroy mission in South Vietnam during the Vietnam War, found $150,000 in American currency in a cave. The soldier, Morrison, brought an action against the United States to recover the currency he had found. The basis of Morrison's claim was that he was a finder of abandoned property and, therefore, the owner. The Court of Claims held that the soldier was not a "finder" under Anglo-American common law because Anglo-American common law is not the applicable body of law. What is the applicable body of law?

***

Plaintiff asserts that the $150,000 in United States currency constitutes 'treasure trove' and from his capacity as a 'finder' claims the right to its possession against all the world other than the true owner. The law of 'finders' does not apply to this money. Plaintiff's rights are determined by statute and duly authorized administrative regulation. It is not necessary to resort to the ancient arcane principles that were developed in the Common Law of England prior to the American Revolution to determine the rights of a squad leader in the United States military forces to 3,000 United States $50 bills that were located in a cave in the Central Highlands of South Vietnam in the course of a search-and-destroy patrol.[2]

---

[2] The doctrine of 'treasure trove' is of ancient origin and stems from the situations involved in the discovery of gold and silver coin, bullion, and plate that had been concealed in the ground by Roman conquerors when they were driven from the British Isles. Modern cases in the United

* * *

Plaintiff's claim is disposed of by the nature of plaintiff's mission at the time the discovery was made. Seizure of the currency was plaintiff's military responsibility, and possession of the currency was taken as an agent of the United States [under the Uniform Code of Military Justice]. Plaintiff can assert no right to possession. This case is not concerned with, and no decision is made as to, what the result would be if plaintiff were not on a combat mission and acting well within the scope of his assigned official duties. Nor is this case concerned with a 'finding' made by a member of an army of occupation or by military personnel in pursuit of wholly personal activities that lay outside the scope of assigned official responsibilities.

CONCLUSION OF LAW

Upon the findings of fact and the foregoing opinion, which are adopted by the court and made a part of the judgment herein, the court concludes as a matter of law that plaintiff is not entitled to recover, and the petition is dismissed.

§ 1.4 Bailment

Bailment is an important legal relationship in the law of personal property and ties into the law of finders, as you will now learn.

§ 1.4.1 In General

In the next case, you will learn what a bailment is. By way of introducing you to the concept, bear in mind that, for example, when you bring your car to a repair shop to get it fixed, you have created a bailment relationship with the owner of the shop. More specifically, this would be a voluntary bailment and you would be the bailor; the shop owner would be the bailee.

States hold that the law of treasure trove has been merged with that of lost goods generally, at least insofar as the rights of the finder are concerned. 'Lost' property is defined as that which the owner has involuntarily parted with, through neglect, carelessness, or inadvertence. 'Mislaid' property is property which the owner intentionally places where he can again resort to it and then forgets. 'Abandoned' property at common law was property voluntarily and unilaterally relinquished with no intent to reclaim. If concealed intentionally and deliberately, there could be no abandonment. The facts in this case show that the money was carefully placed in the cave. These common law concepts, applied to the facts of this case, would find that the $150,000 was 'mislaid' and not 'lost' or 'abandoned.' Schley v. Couch, 155 Tex. 195, 284 S.W.2d 333 (1955); Jackson v. Steinberg, 186 Or. 129, 200 P.2d 376 (1948), rehearing denied, 186 Or. 129, 205 P.2d 562 (1949); see also 1 Am.Jur.2d, Abandoned, Lost, Etc. Property §§ 4—5, 12, 15, 18—19, 21 (1962).

Broaddus v. Commercial Nat. Bank of Muskogee
113 Okla. 10 (1925)

A tenant, behind in rent, claims that cash was taken from the office safe (coincidentally, the same amount owed the landlord). The tenant seeks to hold the landlord liable on the basis of a bailment relationship (with the tenant being the bailor and the landlord the bailee). Importantly, while the landlord had access to the tenant's office, the tenant, too, always retained access. The court will hold that the landlord is not liable to the tenant on the basis of bailee liability.

MASON, J.

The Commercial National Bank, of Muskogee, Okl., and Johnella P. Barnes, as plaintiffs, commenced this action by filing their petition in the district court of Muskogee county, Okl., alleging, in substance, that the defendants B. Broaddus and C. A. Ambrister were indebted to said plaintiffs in the sum of $115 as rent for space occupied by them in an office building owned by the plaintiffs in the city of Muskogee, known as the Commercial National Bank building, or the Barnes building. For convenience, the parties will be referred to as they appeared in the trial court.

The defendants admitted that they had been tenants in said building for a number of years, and that they had been paying $80 per month as rent, and that they were indebted to the plaintiffs in the sum of $115.

Further answering, and by way of cross-petition, the defendants alleged that a part of the consideration for the space occupied in the building of the plaintiffs was the janitor service, heat, light, and safety from burglary or fire.

The defendants further alleged that on the 1st day of July, 1922, they placed $90 in currency in a safe belonging to said defendants and situated in the space occupied by them in said building; that said safe was a combination safe and filing cabinet composed of steel, and that said safe had a combination lock thereon; that, after said money had been placed in said safe, the bolts to the lock were thrown, but that said defendant did not remember whether the combination was turned or not, but was of the opinion that said door was not locked; that, when said defendants returned Monday morning to said office, the said money was gone, by reason of the negligence of the servants and employees of the plaintiffs, in either appropriating the money to themselves or in leaving the door unlocked so that other parties could come into said office and secure the property located therein; that said defendants and their stenographer were the only persons having a key to said office, except the keys which were held by the plaintiffs or by their servants and employees; that, when said office was left by the defendants, the same was securely locked, and, when they returned Monday morning, the doors had not been broken into or the persons entering same had not done so by way of the transom.

The defendants further alleged that on Saturday, the 11th day of August, 1922, they placed in said safe situated in said office the sum of $25, which was received after banking hours, and that the same was found missing on Monday morning when the defendants opened their office. The defendants further alleged that the doors did not appear to have been broken, and that entrance was not made by way of the transom. It was further alleged that, by reason of the carelessness of the plaintiffs, their servants, and employees, the defendants had lost the total sum of $115.

18

* * *

For reversal it is first contended that the relation of bailor and bailee existed between the cross-petitioners and the plaintiffs at the time of the occurrence in question, and that the trial court erred in refusing to submit this theory of the case to the jury.

Bailment is defined as follows:

"A delivery of goods in trust, upon a contract, expressed or implied, that the trust shall be executed and the goods restored by the bailee, as soon as the purpose of the bailment shall be answered." 2 Kent's Comm. 559.

"A bailment may be defined as a delivery of personalty for some particular purpose, or on mere deposit, upon a contract, express or implied, that after the purpose has been fulfilled it shall be redelivered to the person who delivered it, or otherwise dealt with according to his directions, or kept until he reclaims it as the case may be." 5 Cyc. 161.

The rule is elemental that, in order to constitute a transaction in bailment, there must be a delivery to the bailee, either actual[3] or constructive.[4] It has been held that such a delivery of property must be made to the bailee as will entitle him to exclude for the period of the bailment the possession thereof, even of the owner. Fletcher v. Ingram, 46 Wis. 191, 50 N. W. 424.

The defendants' theory of this case is that their offices and contents were delivered to the plaintiffs and their agents at all times, except during office hours; that the plaintiffs and their agents possessed keys to said offices and had access thereto at such times for the purpose of performing janitor service; and that thereby the duty of a bailee devolved on the plaintiffs during such times.

The evidence, however, discloses that each of the defendants and their stenographer had a key to said offices and access thereto at all times. Therefore one of the necessary elements of a contract for bailment is fatally absent, to wit, such a delivery to the bailees as would entitle them to exclude for the period of the bailment the possession thereof, even of the owner.

In 6 C. J. 1103, the rule is stated as follows:

"Such a full delivery of the subject-matter must be made to the bailee as will entitle him to exclude for the time of the bailment the possession of the owner, as will make him liable as its sole custodian to the latter in the event of his neglect or fault in discharging his trust with respect to the subject-matter, and as to require a redelivery of it by him to the owner or other person entitled to receive it after the trusts of the bailment have been discharged," citing Bertig v. Norman, 101 Ark. 76, 141 S. W. 201, Ann. Cas. 1913D, 943; Atlantic Coast Line R. Co. v. Baker, 118 Ga. 809, 45 S. E. 673; Wentworth v. Riggs, 159 App. Div. 899, 143 N. Y. S. 955, 957; Fletcher v. Ingram, 46 Wis. 191, 50 N. W. 424.

In the note to Zeterstrom v. Thomas, 92 Conn. 702, 104 Atl. 237, in 1 A. L. R. 392, it is said:

"On the question of fact whether or not there is a sufficient delivery in any given case, the general rule is that, in order to constitute such a delivery, there must be a full

---

[3] [An actual delivery arises when the property itself is transferred from the bailor to the bailee.]

[4] [As to what constitutes a constructive delivery, see *Carson v. Bankers Trust Company* and *Scherer v. Hyland*, infra.]

transfer, either actual or constructive, of the property to the bailee, so as to exclude the possession of the owner and all other persons, and give to the bailee for the time being the sole custody and control thereof."

[Based on the definition of bailment, the court found that no bailment was created.]

* * *

We have examined all the instructions given to the jury by the trial court, and are of the opinion that they were probably more favorable to the defendants than they should have been.

Finding no reversible error, the judgment of the trial court is affirmed.

NICHOLSON, C. J., and PHELPS, LESTER, RILEY, and CLARK, JJ., concur.

§ 1.4.2 Classification of Bailments

Traditionally, we classify voluntary bailments (are there involuntary bailments?) as bailments for the sole benefit of the bailor, sole benefit of the bailee, mutual benefit bailments, and bailments for hire. Godfrey v. City of Flint *explains these types of voluntary bailments.*

Godfrey v. City of Flint
284 Mich. 291 (1938)

One Godfrey leased an airplane to Helm, who stored it on City's property. City workers later damaged the airplane. The question before the court is whether a "bailment for hire" exists between Helm and City (which Godfrey would have standing to enforce). The court, after explaining the various types of bailments, holds that a bailment for hire may well have existed and remands back to the trial court to resolve the matter.

SHARPE, Justice.

This is an action instituted by plaintiff to recover damages for the loss of an airplane stored in a hangar at the City of Flint Airport. Plaintiff had verdict, but defendant's motion non obstante veredicto was granted. Plaintiff appeals.

In April, 1933, plaintiff was the owner of a three passenger commercial airplane which he leased to Gordon Helm, who stored the same in the airport at Flint. In October, 1933, Helm was engaged by the City of Flint to operate the airport. He was paid $50 per month, had the use of the field for commercial flying, and was permitted to store his airplane in the hangar. His duties were to take care of the airport, look after the beacon light, keep a log of incoming and outgoing airplanes, telephone weather reports to other airports, and collect rentals and remit the same to the city treasurer.

In December, 1933, the City of Flint received aid from the federal government for the improvement of the airport. Helm was transferred to the CWA[5] pay roll and worked

---

[5] [The CWA (Civil Works Administration) was one of many public works programs created in 1933 during the early days of President Franklin Roosevelt's "New Deal" administration. The

24 hours per week. He continued to store his airplane in the city hangar, to keep the beacon lighted at night, to make a log of incoming and outgoing planes, to telephone weather reports, and to collect rentals. He was never instructed by the City of Flint to discontinue these services nor was he authorized to continue the same.

On January 30, 1934, while the CWA project was still in progress, Helm had the airplane stored in one of the city hangars at the airport. The City of Flint owned a tractor and stored the same in the hangar directly under the left wing of the airplane. On the morning in question, a mechanic employed by the City of Flint was instructed to go to the airport for the purpose of starting the tractor. The principal trouble was that the tractor had sticking valves. In attempting to start the motor, the oil was drained from the motor into an open bucket 12 or 14 inches in diameter which was placed under the motor and gasoline was poured into the priming cups. The motor was primed several times by two different employees of the city and in this process gasoline leaked upon the wooden floor. In the process of starting the motor, it backfired through the carburetor, igniting the gasoline. The fire spread to the gasoline and oil on the floor, then to the airplane, which was destroyed. Upon two other occasions the motor had been found difficult to start and had backfired, but no fire had resulted.

Before the cause was submitted to the jury, defendant made a motion for a directed verdict which was reserved. The court instructed the jury that there was no bailment for hire in this case; and submitted the case to them on the second count in plaintiff's declaration, namely, that of a gratuitous bailment. He instructed them that plaintiff must prove defendant's employees were grossly negligent in the attempt to start the tractor and that this gross negligence was the cause of the loss of the airplane. The jury returned a verdict for plaintiff, but the court granted defendant's motion non obstante veredicto.

Plaintiff appeals and contends that the trial court was in error in his refusal to submit the cause to the jury upon the first count in the declaration, namely, that a mutual benefit bailment existed between plaintiff's lessee and the defendant, and defendant was liable for the destruction of plaintiff's property through ordinary negligence of defendants' employees; and that there was ample evidence to sustain the jury's verdict that the defendant's employees were guilty of gross negligence.

It is conceded that a bailment relation exists between the parties in this case.

In 6 Amer.Juris. p. 145, § 14, it is said that:

'* * * bailments are now generally classified under three heads: (1) Those for the sole benefit of the bailor; (2) those for the sole benefit of the bailee; and (3) those for the benefit of both parties.'

'Bailment for the benefit of both parties thereto has been defined as one wherein a person gives to another the temporary use and possession of property, other than money, for a reward, the latter agreeing to return the same to the former at a future time.' 8 C.J.S. Bailments, p. 243, § 8.

'To ascertain the rights, duties, and liabilities of the parties, it is usually necessary to determine whether a bailment is lucrative, for the mutual benefit of both parties, or

---

purpose of these public works programs was an attempt to alleviate the 25% unemployment rate created by the worldwide Great Depression that started with the stock market crash of 1929.]

whether it is for the sole benefit of one party, the other remaining uncompensated.' 6 Amer.Juris. p. 147, § 18.

'In determining whether or not there is a lucrative bailment, the nature and amount of the compensation are immaterial, as the law will not inquire into its sufficiency or the certainty of its being realized by the bailee.' 6 Amer.Juris. p. 149, § 21. For cases holding that the bailment was mutual see: Knights v. Piella, 111 Mich. 9, 69 N.W. 92, 66 Am.St.Rep. 375; Henry v. Salomon, 148 Mich. 467, 111 N.W. 1035; Fraam v. Grand Rapids & Indiana Railway Co., 161 Mich. 556, 126 N.W. 851, 29 L.R.A.,N.S., 834, 21 Ann.Cas. 96; Vigo Agricultural Society v. Brumfiel, 102 Ind. 146, 1 N.E. 382, 52 Am.Rep. 657; Perera v. Panama-Pacific International E. Co., 179 Cal. 63, 175 P. 454; Isreal v. Uhr, Sup., 164 N.Y.S. 50.

Prior to December 9, 1933, when Helm was taken off the city pay roll, there was a specific agreement between the City of Flint and plaintiff's lessee whereby he was to manage the airport and render the services above mentioned. In return Helm was paid $50 per month, given the use of the flying field for commercial flying, and the use of defendant's hangar for the storage of plaintiff's airplane. When Helm was transferred from the city pay roll to the CWA pay roll, the relationship of master and servant between Helm and the city ceased, but it does not follow that the relationship of bailor and bailee ceased to exist. Helm continued to perform the same services for the City of Flint that he had prior thereto. The record shows that he was not notified to discontinue his services as manager of the airport; that the federal regulations required that someone be in charge of the field; that on the date of the fire Helm was the only person in charge of the field; that the city permitted Helm to continue the storage of his airplane at the city airport; and that the city through its city treasurer and superintendent of public works had knowledge of and accepted the services of Helm in the collection of rentals for planes stored at the airport. In our opinion there was evidence from which a jury could find that the relationship between plaintiff's bailee[6] and the city of Flint was for the mutual benefit of both parties.

'It is clear from the decisions that matters of form are usually of slight significance as far as the validity of a contract of bailment is concerned. So long as the lawful possession of property is in the bailee, under circumstances which impose upon him the duty to return or account for it, there appears to be no disposition on the part of the courts to regard it as any the less a bailment because the agreement was informal in character, oral or implied in fact or in law.' 6 Amer.Juris. p. 206, § 81.

The degree of care required where the bailment is for the benefit of both parties is well stated in Hofer v. Hodge, 52 Mich. 372, 18 N.W. 112, 113, 50 Am.Rep. 256, where we said: 'The bailment being beneficial to both parties, the duty of the defendant in keeping the property was substantially the same as in a bailment for hire. He was bound to keep and preserve the property with ordinary care--that care which a prudent man ordinarily takes of his own property.'

And in Fraam v. Grand Rapids & Indiana Railway Co., 161 Mich. 556, 126 N.W. 851, 853, 29 L.R.A.,N.S., 834, 21 Ann.Cas. 96, where we said: 'The contract of bailment here under consideration is one for the mutual benefit of the parties, and the bailee thereunder was bound to exercise ordinary care of the subject-matter of the bailment, and

---

[6] [The court actually means to state, "plaintiff's lessee."]

is liable for ordinary negligence. Ordinary care means such care as ordinarily prudent men, as a class, would exercise in caring for their own property under the like circumstances, and whether it is exercised or not is a question of fact for the determination of the jury, under proper instructions.'

The trial court was in error in not submitting to the jury the issue presented by the first count in plaintiff's declaration.

Judgment is reversed and a new trial granted. Plaintiff may recover costs.

WIEST, C. J., and BUTZEL, BUSHNELL, POTTER, CHANDLER, NORTH, and McALLISTER, JJ., concur.

§ 1.5 Gifts of Personal Property

We now proceed to another aspect of personal property—gifts.

§ 1.5.1 Gifts Inter Vivos

We begin with gifts inter vivos, that is, gifts made by the donor (transferor) during the donor's lifetime.

Johnson v. Hilliard
113 Colo. 548 (1945)

This excerpt tells you the elements for a gift inter vivos. Note especially that the property that is the subject of the gift must be "delivered."

* * *

A gift inter vivos, as we understand it, is one in which the donor parts with all present and future dominion over the property given. The subject of the gift must be delivered to the donee, or someone for him, and the gift must be absolute and irrevocable without any reference to taking effect at some future period. Thomas v. Thomas, 70 Colo. 29, 197 P. 243; Hardy v. Carrington, 87 Colo. 461, 288 P. 620; 24 Am.Jur. 732, 38 C.J.S., Gifts, § 3, p. 781; Thornton on Gifts and Advancements, p. 2; 2 Schouler's Personal Property (2d Ed.) p. 73 et seq. * * *
* * *

Ray v. Leader Federal Sav. & Loan Ass'n
40 Tenn.App. 625 (1953)

There are several ways to make a "delivery," as the Ray *case states.*

* * *

Symbolical or constructive delivery of a gift may be made and thereby complete the delivery factor as legally as if actual physical delivery had occurred. The general rule is stated in 24 Am.Jur. 744-5, and is as follows:

'As a general rule, where an actual manual delivery of property cannot be made, the donor may do, that which, under the circumstances, will in reason be considered equivalent to an actual delivery. In such cases the delivery may be symbolical or constructive, although in all cases it must be as nearly perfect and complete as the nature of the property and the attendant circumstances and conditions will permit. Thus, in some cases, an unequivocal declaration of gift accompanied by a delivery of the only means by which possession of the article given can be obtained, is held to be sufficient, and the general rule prevails where the article intended to be given is incapable of manual delivery, that a symbolical delivery of a fund may be made by delivery of the instrument making an appropriation of the fund.'

* * *

Carlson v. Bankers Trust Co.
242 Iowa 1207 (1951)

This case explains the meaning of a "constructive delivery."

* * *

Where the things intended to be given are not present or are incapable of manual delivery because of size or weight, delivery of a key which gives access to them is frequently held to be a valid constructive or symbolical delivery. Thus delivery of the key to a safety deposit box is often held a sufficient delivery of its contents unless the circumstances are such that they might be then and there actually delivered. See Braum v. Brown, 14 Cal.2d 346, 94 P.2d 348, 127 A.L.R. 773, and Ann. 780; Oliver v. Crook, 321 Ill.App. 55, 52 N.E.2d 453, and citations; In re Stevenson's Estate, 79 Ohio App. 315, 69 N.E.2d 426; 38 C.J.S., Gifts, § 83, page 904; 24 Am.Jur., Gifts, section 28. And see Iowa cases cited last above.

* * *

Hill v. Baker
48 Del. 305 (Del. Super. 1953)

One Landreth Hill executed a will leaving all of his property to a nephew, Charles Lewis Hill, the plaintiff in this case. Landreth had another nephew, J. Clyde Baker, the defendant. Landreth and Clyde were close. Before Landreth died, Clyde paid Landreth a visit. The question before the court is whether, during that visit, Landreth made an inter vivos gift of $840 to Clyde. Because a will passes property a person owns at death, if Landreth had made an inter vivos gift to Clyde, then the $840 belongs to Clyde, not Charles (because then Landreth would have died without owning the $840 in question). The court will ultimately hold that Landreth made an inter vivos gift to Clyde.

RICHARDS, President Judge.
* * * [O]n Sunday, March 30, 1952, the defendant, J. Clyde Baker, and Mabel B. Baker, his wife, Mildred E. Morris and Ronald E. Morris, her husband, visited Landreth Hill at his house and found him unwell but able to be up and around the house; that while

Mrs. Morris and Mrs. Baker were out in the yard with the children, Landreth Hill insisted that Ronald E. Morris and the defendant, J. Clyde Baker, go upstairs with him, and when they got upstairs he went to a room opposite his bed room, unlocked a bureau drawer and took from it a pocketbook which he handed to J. Clyde Baker saying, 'this is yours, take it with you'; that Clyde took the pocketbook and he and Landreth Hill counted the money found in it; that after they had finished counting the money they both said that it amounted to $840; that Clyde asked Landreth Hill if he could keep the money where it was, and Hill then gave him the key to the bureau drawer and told him to keep it; that Clyde then put the pocketbook and money back in the bureau drawer from which Landreth Hill had taken it, locked the drawer with the key which he had given him and put the key in his pocket; that on the following Friday, being April 4, 1952, Landreth Hill died; that after learning of his death J. Clyde Baker went to his house, unlocked the drawer in the bureau in which he, Clyde, had put the pocketbook and $840, with the key which the deceased have given him, and took out said pocketbook and $840.

The plaintiff contends that the pocketbook and money in question were in the possession of Landreth Hill at the time of his death, and became a part of his estate which at the time of his death passed, under the terms of his will, to his nephew, Charles Lewis Hill.

The plaintiff further contends that the conversations which the deceased had with his sister, Mary J. Baker, and the other members of his family, including the conversation and what took place between him and the defendant, J. Clyde Baker, on March 30, 1952, were not sufficient to support a donatio inter vivos or a donatio causa mortis,[7] because there was no delivery of the property to the donee, either actual or constructive.

The defendant takes the position that the evidence in this case not only supports a gift inter vivos, but that based upon the authorities cited in his brief, it is sufficient to constitute a gift causa mortis.

* * *

Every voluntary transfer of property from one person to another, without any consideration therefor constitutes a gift. Vol. 24 Am.Jur., p. 730, § 2.

Generally speaking gifts are classified as gifts inter vivos and gifts causa mortis. A gift inter vivos is usually defined as one between living persons, consisting of a voluntary transfer of property from one living person to another without any valuable consideration perfected and made absolute during the lifetime of the parties. A gift causa mortis is usually defined as a gift of personal property made in expectation of the donor's death but which may be revoked by him, upon condition that the donee shall be entitled to the property if the donor dies as expected and the donee survives him. 24 Am.Jur., p. 732, § 4.

The principle is well established by the authorities, that there must be an actual or constructive delivery of the property to the donee, in order for a gift inter vivos or causa mortis to be valid and effective. * * *

The deceased was not well on Sunday, March 30, 1952, when he insisted that the defendant, J. Clyde Baker, and Ronald E. Morris go upstairs with him while they were visiting him at his house, at which time he unlocked a bureau drawer, and taking from it a pocketbook handed it to J. Clyde Baker saying, 'this is yours take it with you,' but there

---

[7] [The gift causa mortis is discussed in the next section.]

is nothing in the evidence to indicate that he was in extremis, or that he was in expectation of death. This being the case, I am convinced that what took place at that time cannot be classed as a gift causa mortis.

For a period of four or five years before his death Landreth Hill had been telling his sister, Mary J. Baker, that he wanted J. Clyde Baker, the defendant, to have what was in the bureau drawer. Similar statements were made by him prior to his death to other members of his family. These conversations were an indication that he wanted the defendant to have what was in the bureau drawer. On March 30, 1952, he showed clearly what he wanted said defendant to have by taking a pocketbook from the bureau drawer and handing it to him, in the presence of Ronald E. Morris, with the remark, 'this is yours take it with you.' After the deceased and the defendant counted the money found in the pocketbook and agreed that it amounted to $840, the defendant retained possession of it. When the defendant later asked the deceased if he could leave it there, the deceased handed the defendant the key to the drawer, and putting the pocketbook and money back in the drawer, the defendant locked the drawer with the key which the deceased had given him and put the key in his pocket. This amounted to a delivery of the pocketbook and money to the defendant. The fact that the defendant left the pocketbook and money at the home of deceased does not prove that he relinquished his possession of the property, or that the property was still in the possession of the deceased. As a matter of fact, it remained where the defendant put it until he took it out of the drawer after Landreth Hill died. During the time it remained in the drawer it was under the defendant's control as he had the key with which he locked the drawer in which he put it.

The plaintiff calls attention to the fact that the deceased had made his will in 1943, by which no money was bequeathed to the defendant. Reliance is placed upon the circumstance that during the conversations which the deceased had with his sister and other members of his family, he never mentioned his will, or told them how much money he had, but simply referred to the money which he had in the bureau.

The contention is made that the deceased knew how to make a gift at the time he had these conversations and had already made his will by which he had named the person whom he desired to have his property.

It is well established that a will does not become effective until after the death of the person by whom it is executed. Property disposed of by will may be sold or given away at any time before the death of the person who disposes of it in this manner. In other words, it does not become his will until his death.

Title to property bequeathed or devised by will does not pass until the death of the person in whose will it is included.

* * *

The conversation between the deceased and the defendant at the home of the deceased on March 30, 1952, the act of the deceased by which he gave the defendant the pocketbook and contents, and what transpired between them thereafter, constituted a gift inter vivos.

The deceased did not die until five days after that date and his will did not take effect until that time.

Having arrived at this conclusion, I am of the opinion that the property involved in this litigation belongs to the defendant, J. Clyde Baker.

Judgment for the defendant for costs.

§ 1.5.2 Gifts Causa Mortis

A gift causa mortis is a gift made in contemplation of imminent death. The elements for a gift causa mortis are the same as for a gift inter vivos with one additional element: the donor of the gift must be in contemplation of imminent death (and must die soon thereafter).

Scherer v. Hyland

75 N.J. 127 (1977)

The decedent, Catherine Wagner, endorsed a check received from an insurance company because of injuries she suffered in an accident. She then put the endorsed check in a place where her boyfriend, with whom she lived, would necessarily find it. There was no issue of fraud or mistake. Catherine then committed suicide. There are two questions before the court: (1) Did Catherine make a constructive delivery? (2) Is suicide a death that will sustain a gift causa mortis?

PER CURIAM.

Defendant, the Administrator ad litem of the Estate of Catherine Wagner, appeals from an Appellate Division decision, one judge dissenting, affirming a summary judgment by the trial court holding that Ms. Wagner had made a valid gift causa mortis of a check to plaintiff. We affirm.

The facts are not in dispute. Catherine Wagner and the plaintiff, Robert Scherer, lived together for approximately fifteen years prior to Ms. Wagner's death in January 1974. In 1970, the decedent and plaintiff were involved in an automobile accident in which decedent suffered facial wounds and a broken hip. Because of the hip injury, decedent's physical mobility was substantially impaired. She was forced to give up her job and to restrict her activities. After the accident, plaintiff cared for her and assumed the sole financial responsibility for maintaining their household. During the weeks preceding her death, Ms. Wagner was acutely depressed. On one occasion, she attempted suicide by slashing her wrists. On January 23, 1974, she committed suicide by jumping from the roof of the apartment building in which they lived.

On the morning of the day of her death, Ms. Wagner received a check for $17,400 drawn by a Pennsylvania attorney who had represented her in a claim arising out of the automobile accident. The check represented settlement of the claim. Plaintiff telephoned Ms. Wagner at around 11:30 a.m. that day and was told that the check had arrived. Plaintiff noticed nothing unusual in Ms. Wagner's voice. At about 3:20 p.m., decedent left the apartment building and jumped to her death. The police, as part of their investigation of the suicide, asked the building superintendent to admit them to the apartment. On the kitchen table they found the check, endorsed in blank, and two notes handwritten by the decedent. In one, she described her depression over her physical condition, expressed her love for Scherer, and asked him to forgive her "for taking the easy way out." In the other, she indicated that she "bequeathed" to plaintiff all of her possessions, including "the check for $17,400.00 * * *." The police took possession of the check, which was eventually placed in an interest-bearing account pending disposition of this action.

Under our wills statute it is clear that Ms. Wagner's note bequeathing all her possessions to Mr. Scherer cannot take effect as a testamentary disposition.[8] N.J.S.A. 3A:3-2. A donatio causa mortis has been traditionally defined as a gift of personal property made by a party in expectation of death, then imminent, subject to the condition that the donor die as anticipated. Establishment of the gift has uniformly called for proof of delivery.

The primary issue here is whether Ms. Wagner's acts of endorsing the settlement check, placing it on the kitchen table in the apartment she shared with Scherer, next to a writing clearly evidencing her intent to transfer the check to Scherer, and abandoning the apartment with a clear expectation of imminent death constituted delivery sufficient to sustain a gift causa mortis of the check. Defendant, relying on the principles established in Foster v. Reiss, 18 N.J. 41, 112 A.2d 553 (1955), argues that there was no delivery because the donor did not unequivocally relinquish control of the check before her death. Central to this argument is the contention that suicide, the perceived peril, was one which decedent herself created and one which was completely within her control. According to this contention, the donor at any time before she jumped from the apartment roof could have changed her mind, re-entered the apartment, and reclaimed the check. Defendant therefore reasons that decedent did not make an effective transfer of the check during her lifetime, as is required for a valid gift causa mortis.

The majority and dissenting opinions in Foster v. Reiss contain thorough analyses of the evolution of the delivery requirement of the gift causa mortis. See also Mechem, "The Requirement of Delivery in Gifts of Chattels and of Choses in Action Evidenced by Commercial Instruments," 21 Ill.L.Rev. 341, 457, 568 (1926); Burton, "The Requirement of Delivery as Applied to Gifts of Choses in Action," 39 Yale L.J. 837 (1930). For commentary on Foster v. Reiss, see Bordwell, "Testate and Intestate Succession," 10 Rutgers L.Rev. 293, 297 (1955); Note, 10 Rutgers L.Rev. 457 (1955); Note, 54 Mich.L.Rev. 572 (1956). We see no need to retrace that history here.

There is general agreement that the major purpose of the delivery requirement is evidentiary. Proof of delivery reduces the possibility that the evidence of intent has been fabricated or that a mere donative impulse, not consummated by action, has been mistaken for a completed gift. Since "these gifts come into question only after death has closed the lips of the donor," the delivery requirement provides a substantial safeguard against fraud and perjury. See Keepers v. Fidelity Title and Deposit Co., 56 N.J.L. 302, 308, 28 A. 585 (E. & A.1893). In Foster, the majority concluded that these policies could best be fulfilled by a strict rule requiring actual manual tradition of the subject-matter of the gift except in a very narrow class of cases where "there can be no actual delivery" or where "the situation is incompatible with the performance of such ceremony." 18 N.J. at 50, 112 A.2d at 559. Justice Jacobs, in his dissenting opinion (joined by Justices Brennan and Wachenfeld) questioned the reasonableness of requiring direct physical delivery in cases where donative intent is "freely and clearly expressed in a written instrument." Id. at 56, 112 A.2d at 562. He observed that a more flexible approach to the delivery

---

[8] [This means that the note is not a will, which passes property at death.]

requirement had been taken by other jurisdictions and quoted approvingly from Devol v. Dye, 123 Ind. 321, 24 N.E. 246, 7 L.R.A. 439 (Sup.Ct.1890). That case stated:

"(G)ifts causa mortis * * * are not to be held contrary to public policy, nor do they rest under the disfavor of the law, when the facts are clearly and satisfactorily shown which make it appear that they were freely and intelligently made. Ellis v. Secor, 31 Mich. 185. While every case must be brought within the general rule upon the points essential to such a gift, yet, as the circumstances under which donations mortis causa are made must of necessity be infinite in variety, each case must be determined upon its own peculiar facts and circumstances. Dickeschild v. Bank, 28 W.Va. 341; Kiff v. Weaver, 94 N.C. 274. The rule requiring delivery, either actual or symbolical, must be maintained, but its application is to be militated and applied according to the relative importance of the subject of the gift and the condition of the donor. The intention of a donor in peril of death, when clearly ascertained and fairly consummated within the meaning of well-established rules, is not to be thwarted by a narrow and illiberal construction of what may have been intended for and deemed by him a sufficient delivery * * *."

The balancing approach suggested in Devol v. Dye has been articulated in the following manner:

"Where there has been unequivocal proof of a deliberate and well-considered donative intent on the part of the donor, many courts have been inclined to overlook the technical requirements and to hold that by a "constructive" or "symbolic" delivery is sufficient to vest title in the donee. However, where this is allowed the evidence must clearly show an intention to part presently with some substantial attribute of ownership." (Gordon v. Barr, 13 Cal.2d 596, 601, 91 P.2d 101, 104 (Sup.Ct.Cal.1939)).

In essence, this approach takes into account the purposes served by the requirement of delivery in determining whether that requirement has been met. It would find a constructive delivery adequate to support the gift when the evidence of donative intent is concrete and undisputed, when there is every indication that the donor intended to make a present transfer of the subject-matter of the gift, and when the steps taken by the donor to effect such a transfer must have been deemed by the donor as sufficient to pass the donor's interest to the donee. We are persuaded that this approach, which does not minimize the need for evidentiary safeguards to prevent frauds upon the estates of the deceased, reflects the realities which attend transfers of this kind.

In this case, the evidence of decedent's intent to transfer the check to Robert Scherer is concrete, unequivocal, and undisputed. The circumstances definitely rule out any possibility of fraud. The sole question, then, is whether the steps taken by the decedent, independent of her writing of the suicide notes, were sufficient to support a finding that she effected a lifetime transfer of the check to Scherer. We think that they were. First, the act of endorsing a check represents, in common experience and understanding, the only act needed (short of actual delivery) to render a check negotiable. The significance of such an act is universally understood. Accordingly, we have no trouble in viewing Ms. Wagner's endorsement of the settlement check as a substantial step taken by her for the purpose of effecting a transfer to Scherer of her right to the check proceeds. Second, we note that the only person other than the decedent who had routine access to the apartment was Robert Scherer. Indeed, the apartment was leased in his name. It is clear that Ms. Wagner before leaving the apartment placed the check in a place where Scherer could not fail to see it and fully expected that he would take actual possession of the check when he entered. And, although Ms. Wagner's subsequent suicide does not itself constitute a component of the delivery of this gift, it does provide persuasive evidence that when Ms. Wagner locked the door of the apartment she did so with no expectation of returning. When we consider her state of mind as it must have been upon leaving the apartment, her surrender of possession at that moment was complete. We find, therefore, that when she left the apartment she completed a constructive delivery of the check to Robert Scherer. In light of her resolve to take her own life and of her obvious desire not to be deterred from that purpose, Ms. Wagner's failure manually to transfer the check to Scherer is understandable. She clearly did all that she could do or thought necessary to do to surrender the check. Her donative intent has been conclusively demonstrated by independent evidence. The law should effectuate that intent rather than indulge in nice distinctions which would thwart her purpose. Upon these facts, we find that the constructive delivery she made was adequate to support a gift causa mortis.

Defendant's assertion that suicide is not the sort of peril that will sustain a gift causa mortis finds some support in precedents from other jurisdictions. E. g., Ray v. Leader Federal Sav. & Loan Ass'n, 40 Tenn.App. 625, 292 S.W.2d 458 (Ct.App.1953). See generally Annot., "Nature and validity of gift made in contemplation of suicide,"60 A.L.R.2d 575 (1958). We are, however, not bound by those authorities nor do we find them persuasive. While it is true that a gift causa mortis is made by the donor with a view to impending death, death is no less impending because of a resolve to commit suicide. Nor does that fixed purpose constitute any lesser or less imminent peril than does a ravaging disease. Indeed, given the despair sufficient to end it all, the peril attendant upon contemplated suicide may reasonably be viewed as even more imminent than that accompanying many illnesses which prove ultimately to be fatal. Cf. Berl v. Rosenberg, 169 Cal.App.2d 125, 336 P.2d 975, 978 (Dist.Ct.App.1959) (public policy against suicide does not invalidate otherwise valid gift causa mortis). And, the notion that one in a state of mental depression serious enough to lead to suicide is somehow "freer" to renounce the depression and thus the danger than one suffering from a physical illness, although it has a certain augustinian appeal, has long since been replaced by more enlightened views of human psychology. In re Van Wormer's Estate, 255 Mich. 399, 238 N.W. 210 (Sup.Ct.1931) (melancholia ending in suicide sufficient to sustain a gift causa mortis). We also observe that an argument that the donor of a causa mortis gift might have changed his or her mind loses much of its force when one recalls that a causa mortis gift, by definition, can be revoked at any time before the donor dies and is automatically revoked if the donor recovers.

Finally, defendant asserts that this gift must fail because there was no acceptance prior to the donor's death. Although the issue of acceptance is rarely litigated, the authority that does exist indicates that, given a valid delivery, acceptance will be implied if the gift is unconditional and beneficial to the donee. See, e. g., Sparks v. Hurley, 208 Pa. 166, 57 A. 364, 366 (Sup.Ct.1904); Graham v. Johnston, 243 Iowa 112, 49 N.W.2d 540, 543 (Sup.Ct.1951). The presumption of acceptance may apply even if the donee does not learn of the gift until after the donor's death. Taylor v. Sanford, 108 Tex. 340, 344, 193 S.W. 661, 662 (Sup.Ct.1912) (assent to gift of deed mailed in contemplation of death but received after grantor's death should be presumed unless a dissent or disclaimer appears). A donee cannot be expected to accept or reject a gift until he learns of it and unless a gift is rejected when the donee is informed of it the presumption of acceptance is not defeated. See id. at 344, 193 S.W. at 662. Here the gift was clearly beneficial to Scherer, and he has always expressed his acceptance.

Judgment affirmed.

§ 1.6 Adverse Possession

One also may acquire rights to property by adversely possessing it. Because the subject is somewhat complex, the next entire chapter is devoted to the subject.

CHAPTER 2
ADVERSE POSSESSION

§ 2.1 Introduction

By the act of possession, an "adverse possessor" may actually wrest title from the true owner. Securing title in this manner, however, is not as easy as it sounds—as the materials that follow make clear.

Fraley v. Minger
829 N.E.2d 476 (Ind. 2005)

This case simply explains the history of adverse possession and provides, as a broad overview, the elements that must be satisfied for the adverse possessor to secure this new title.

* * *

Common Law Adverse Possession

The common law doctrine and application of adverse possession has a long history. As early as 2250 B.C. the Code of Hammurabi discussed adverse possession and the misuse of land, including provisions that punished land waste, rewarded long-term development, and allowed one who worked the land of another for three years to take and keep the land. * * *

With the western migration of pioneers, the federal government initially prohibited settlement of the western lands unless purchased from the government, but that requirement was gradually relaxed; anti-squatting prohibitions were abandoned, recognition of preemptive purchase rights were extended, and land was distributed to military veterans. *See* John G. Sprankling, *The Antiwilderness Bias in American Property Law,* 63 U. Chi. L.Rev. 519, 528-29 (1996). Eventually, with the 1852 passage of the Homestead Act, land was freely available to such settlers. *Id.* At the same time, whereas the courts had originally followed the English example of requiring that the adverse possessor engage in activities giving notice to an inspecting owner such as residence, cultivation, fencing, and other improvements, American courts began to focus upon acts by the adverse possessor in keeping with the nature and character of the land involved. *Id.* at 538-39. The policy behind favoring adverse possession was the same as that of land distribution: favoring the productive use of the land. *Id.* at 534-40; *see also* Netter at 219 (adverse possession rewards the use of land and punishes those who sit on their rights). Claims of adverse possession were litigated in Indiana from the early years of statehood. * * * During the latter nineteenth century, many of the Indiana adverse possession cases began to articulate specific elements required to establish adverse possession. *See, e.g., Hargis v. Inhabitants of Congressional Township,* 29 Ind. 70, 71 (Ind.1867) (requiring the claimant be "in actual, open, notorious, and exclusive possession thereof, claiming to be the owner in fee"). A relatively consistent list of similar elements of common law adverse possession developed and is found thereafter even in more recent cases. Citing *Penn Central Transportation Co. v. Martin,* 170 Ind.App. 519, 353 N.E.2d 474 (1976), the parties each assert that to establish title by adverse possession, the claimant has the burden of proving the possession was: (1) actual; (2) visible; (3) open and notorious; (4) exclusive; (5) under claim of ownership; (6) hostile; and (7) continuous for the statutory period. Brief of Appellant Fraley at 5, Brief of Appellees Minger at 4. *See also Marengo Cave Co. v. Ross,* 212 Ind. 624, 630, 10 N.E.2d 917 (Ind.1937). Later cases from this Court have used a slightly different formulation that omits "visible" and "hostile" but adds "adverse," and substitutes "claim of right" for "claim of ownership." This Court's opinions in *Beaver v. Vandall,* 547 N.E.2d 802, 804 (Ind.1989), and *McCarty v. Sheets,* 423 N.E.2d 297, 300 (Ind.1981), state that adverse possession is established by "open, continuous, exclusive, adverse and notorious possession of property under a claim of right for the statutory period." As authority for this statement, *McCarty* cited *Worthley v. Burbanks,* 146 Ind. 534, 45 N.E. 779 (1897). But *Worthley* lists the "five indispensable elements" of adverse possession as "1, It must be *hostile and under a claim of right;* 2, it must be *actual;* 3, it must be *open and notorious;* 4, it must be *exclusive;* and 5, it must be *continuous.*" 146 Ind. at 539, 45 N.E. at 781 (emphasis in original). * * *

* * *

§ 2.2 Burden of Proof

In most civil cases, the claimant must prove his or her case by a mere "preponderance" of the evidence. In adverse possession cases, however, the burden of proof is otherwise, as the next case makes clear.

Barley v. Fisher
267 Mich. 450 (1934)

* * *

* * * The determination of what acts or uses are sufficient to constitute adverse possession depends upon the facts in each case; yet it was said in Yelverton v. Steele, 40 Mich. 538, at page 541: 'The doctrine which sanctions the divestiture of the true owner * * * is to be taken strictly, and the case is not to be made out by inference, but by clear and cogent proof.'

* * *

§ 2.3 Actual Entry

We now proceed to examine all of the elements in some depth. The first element is the "actual entry" requirement.

Roy v. Kayser

501 So.2d 1110 (Miss. 1987)

This case explores how a fence around the property may satisfy the "actual entry" requirement. As you read it, try to understand why fencing the subject property constitutes an actual entry. As importantly, you also should try to determine what exactly an actual entry is.

* * *

The mere existence of a fence around the property for a period of at least fifty five years offers this Court a substantial basis for its holding [that plaintiffs established ownership by adverse possession]. In *Cole v. Burleson,* 375 So.2d 1046, 1048 (Miss.1979), we stated, "If a fence encloses the property for ten years, under a claim of adverse possession, title vests in the claimant and possessor, even though the fence was subsequently removed or fell into disrepair." This is consistent with 7 Powell and Rohan, *Powell on Real Property,* § 1013[h][ii] (1984), which states that "fencing is one of the strongest indications of adverse possession." Indeed, at the conclusion of the trial, the Chancellor stated, "[T]he fence obviously has been in the same location for many years. I would say during our lifetimes, but at least for 30 years or so. I think that complainants were charged with notice of the fence and the use being made of that fence."

Additionally, the Court has rendered other decisions where the presence of a fence helped to demonstrate title to land by adverse possession: *Trotter v. Gaddis and McLaurin, Inc.,* 452 So.2d 453 (Miss.1984) (fence, raised crops, pastured cattle, and cut timber); *McSwain v. B.M. Stevens Co.,* 247 So.2d 707 (Miss.1971) (fence and garden); *Casey v. Valentour,* 218 So.2d 863 (Miss.1969) (fence and church, holding regular services); *Kuhn v. Gabriel Cemetery Assn.,* 202 So.2d 634 (Miss.1967) (fence and cemetery, containing fresh graves); *Berry v. Houston,* 195 So.2d 515 (Miss.1967) (fence and garden); *Bounds v. Davis,* 253 Miss. 849, 179 So.2d 566 (1965) (fence, raised crops, and pastured cattle); *Bickham v. Bates,* 246 Miss. 171, 150 So.2d 138 (1963) (fence, pastured cattle, cut timber, and paid taxes). *See also, Hewlett v. Henderson,* 431 So.2d 449, 452 (Miss.1983); *Hardy v. Lynch,* 258 So.2d 414, 417 (Miss.1972); *Manar v. Smith,* 236 Miss. 192, 196-99, 109 So.2d 652, 653-55 (1959); *Avera v. Turner Lumber Co.,* 230 Miss. 123, 130, 92 So.2d 458, 461 (1957); *Broadus v. Hickman,* 210 Miss. 885, 892-893, 50 So.2d 717, 720 (1951); *Kelly v. Wilson,* 204 Miss. 56, 65, 36 So.2d 817, 820 (1948); *Henritzy v. Harrison County,* 180 Miss. 675, 695, 178 So. 322, 326 (1937); *Gillespie v. Magruder,* 92 Miss. 511, 515-16, 46 So. 77, 78 (1908); *Jones v. Gaddis,* 67 Miss. 761, 767, 7 So. 489, 490 (1890).

Several of the acts mentioned in the preceding paragraph are also present here, and likewise demonstrate that the Balls manifested the elements of adverse possession within the now disputed tract prior to 1953, sufficient to vest title in them and their successors, the Roys. Consequently, we reverse the Chancellor as a matter of law, and render judgment for the Roys.

Hayes v. Cotter
439 So.2d 102 (Ala. 1983)

Yet another means of satisfying the actual entry requirement is by cultivating the land. Again, you should be trying to determine what an actual entry is.

* * *

The plaintiffs in the instant case produced numerous witnesses who testified that the Hayes family and their tenants cultivated the disputed strip continuously from 1923 until 1979. Cultivation by a coterminous landowner up to a turnrow is a sufficient possessory act to constitute adverse possession. *Cambron v. Kirkland,* 287 Ala. 531, 535, 253 So.2d 180, 183 (1971); *Withers v. Burton,* 268 Ala. 365, 371, 106 So.2d 876, 880-881 (1958).

Three witnesses testified on behalf of the defendants. John Morgan sold the property to Cotter. Morgan testified that he had not farmed the land for fifteen to twenty years before he sold it and that he did not know exactly where the line was. Cotter himself knew nothing of the history of the land. When Veston Bush, the surveyor hired by Cotter, was asked whether, in his professional judgment, he saw any evidence of adverse possession when examining the property, he replied "[nothing] except the plowed field was being used."

* * *

Burkhardt v. Smith
17 Wis.2d 132 (1962)

In Burkhardt v. Smith, *the adverse possessor, among other activities, built a cottage on the claimed property but did not occupy the whole of the property. The court will nonetheless find that the claimant made an actual entry (what the court calls an actual occupancy) and acquired title by adverse possession. By now, you should have a reasonable idea of what constitutes an actual entry.*

* * *

HALLOWS, Justice.

The only question is whether the finding of the trial court that the defendant acquired ownership of parcel X8 by adverse possession is contrary to the great weight and clear preponderance of the evidence. Since Smith is not claiming title founded upon a written instrument or a judgment or any color of title,[1] his claim of title by adverse possession must meet the call of sec. 330.10, Stats., which requires adverse possession for 20 years. To sustain such a claim, only the land actually occupied is considered to be

---

[1] [Color of title is discussed later in this chapter.]

held adversely,[2] and by sec. 330.09, Stats., land is deemed to have been possessed and occupied adversely when it has been protected by a substantial enclosure or when it has been usually cultivated or improved. No claim is made that lot X8 has been protected by a substantial enclosure for 20 years. The issue is whether the evidence shows the defendant usually cultivated or improved tract X8 within the meaning of the statute.

On July 3, 1938, shortly after the defendant purchased the lots, he commenced building a cottage which he thought was on the boundary line between his two lots but, in fact, was on the boundary line between his easterly lot No. 1 and parcel X8 and extended onto parcel X8 a distance of some 13 feet on the north side and five feet on the south. He did not discover this error for some four or five years. The cottage was completed in the summer of 1938 and a septic tank installed. In the same year Smith cleaned up his lots including lot X8 by cutting out all dead trees and all the bramble and wild bushes which he stacked and burned. He also dug up and burned all of the dead stumps. At the time of purchase, the land was wild, unimproved, and the surface was sandy with only a few patches of grass. He spaded up the entire area which was covered with weeds, raked it and seeded it with blue grass.

After completing the cottage, Smith married and lived there continuously with his wife during 1938 and for some years thereafter, then later used it for a summer place. These acts of Smith in 1938 are the only ones performed prior to 20 years before the commencement of this suit and must be considered as the indicia of his actual occupancy. During the subsequent years, Smith used lot X8 in various ways in keeping with the usual occupancy of a lakeshore cottage. In 1939 he built up the soil, reseeded the area, and planted trees in the northeast corner of lot X8 and along the north line and even extending over the boundaries of X8. He built a fence partly around the lawn on the north and on the east. The following year, 1940, he planted other trees in the area, added a terrace, walk and rock garden on the east side of the cottage. At various times in subsequent years, he had built on X8 a fireplace, fences approximately along the east line of X8, a rock garden, flower bed, clothes line, and swings for his children. For some period of time he had two cabins and a movable fishing shack. The cabins were sold to the YMCA and removed. During the time they were on parcel X8 the cabins were used either by the defendant, his relatives, or rented.

* * *

In the instant case, the several acts of the defendant would indicate to any stranger that lot X8 was usually being used as an owner would use such land in that lake resort area and thus proclaimed he asserted exclusive ownership. We consider the acts of the defendant, in building his cottage, in removing the dead trees and brush, and in putting in a lawn, extended substantially over the whole tract of X8 and was sufficient to plant the defendant's 'flag of hostility.' The defendant used lot X8 and exercised such acts of ownership over it as was necessary to enjoy the ordinary use of which it was capable. Adverse possession without enclosure need not be characterized by a physical, constant, visible occupancy or improved by improvements of every square foot of the land. The

---

[2] '330.08. *Extent of possession not founded on writing, judgment, etc.* When there has been an actual continued occupation of any premises under a claim of title, exclusive of any other right, but not founded upon any written instrument or any judgment or decree, the premises so actually occupied, and no other, shall be deemed to be held adversely.'

argument that one claiming adverse possession must actually lay his hands, so to speak, upon the entire lot and keep them there as if covering the premises with a mantle was soundly rejected by this court in Illinois Steel Co. v. Jeka (1905), 123 Wis. 419, 101 N.W. 399. Actual occupancy is not limited to structural encroachment which is common but is not the only physical characteristic of possession. Actual occupancy means the ordinary use to which the land is capable and such as an owner would make of it. Any actual visible means, which gives notice of exclusion from the property to the true owner or to the public and of the defendant's domination over it, is sufficient.

§ 2.4 Open and Notorious

The next element that the adverse possessor has to satisfy is that the possession must be "open and notorious." The next several cases examine this element and explain what open and notorious means.

Tanner v. Thompson
376 So.2d 697 (Ala. 1979)

* * *

* * * Appellant also did not show openness, notoriety or exclusiveness of possession. The only evidence presented is that appellant had some refrigerator compressors on the land and that appellant had a bathroom in the store and the door opened up onto the [claimed] land. This is not such openness, notoriety and exclusiveness as the law requires. Moreover, appellant did not claim the disputed land for the requisite period.

* * *

Striefel v. Charles-Keyt-Leaman Partnership
733 A.2d 984 (Me. 1999)

* * *

The following summary of the facts is largely from the court's opinion: The claimants, the MacLeod family, who claimed title by adverse possession, used the disputed property as a driveway, lawn, and garden. They raked and mowed the parcel, trimmed bushes and lilacs, maintained a compost pile, and formed a rock garden. Claimants' father stored wood and building materials on the parcel, and plowed or shoveled the parking area in the winter. Her mother planted forsythia bushes. When claimant was in high school, her family stored a twelve-foot sailboat on the parcel. They often kept a picnic table there. The claimants played with their dog and walked it on the parcel. The claimants' children and their neighborhood friends played on the parcel, and skated on it when it froze in the winter. Did the claimants satisfy the open and notorious requirement? The court will hold in the affirmative.

"Open" means without attempted concealment. *See, e.g., Foot v. Bauman,* 333 Mass. 214, 129 N.E.2d 916, 919 (1955); *Hindall v. Martinez,* 69 Ohio App.3d 580, 591 N.E.2d 308, 310 (1990). "Visible" means capable of being seen by persons who may view the premises.[3] *See* Gaudio, *American Law Of Real Property* § 11.02[3] at 11- 20 to - 21 (1994). "Notorious" means known to some who might reasonably be expected to communicate their knowledge to an owner maintaining a reasonable degree of supervision over his property.[4] *See, e.g., Foot,* 129 N.E.2d at 919; *Hindall,* 591 N.E.2d at 310. The purpose of these three requirements is to provide the true owner with adequate notice that a trespass is occurring, and that the owner's property rights are in jeopardy. *See Emerson,* 560 A.2d at 2-3. Hence, a claimant will fail to satisfy the requirements of openness, visibility, and notoriety unless the possession and use were sufficiently apparent to put the true owner on notice that the claimant was making an adverse claim of ownership. *See id.; Maine Gravel Servs., Inc.,* 1998 ME 18, ¶ 3, 704 A.2d at 418. "Such notice need not be actual; it is sufficient to prove acts so open[, visible,] and notorious that the owner's knowledge of them and of their adverse character may be presumed." *Emerson,* 560 A.2d at 3. (citations omitted); *see also Estate of Stone,* 621 A.2d at 854.

The MacLeod family's possession and use of the parcel were sufficiently apparent to put the true owner on notice that they were making an adverse claim of ownership. *See Emerson,* 560 A.2d at 3. First, the record does not indicate, nor does Striefel [the owner of record title] assert, that the MacLeods attempted to conceal their possession and use of the parcel (*i.e.,* that the possession and use were not "open"). Second, Brignull [one of the MacLeod family members] testified that, throughout the limitations period, neighbors and passersby on the bordering municipal street were able to clearly observe her family's possession and use of the parcel (*i.e.,* the possession and use were "visible"). Third, the record indicates that the possession and use were "notorious" because, *inter alia,* the families of the neighborhood children who played on the parcel with the MacLeod children might reasonably have been expected to communicate their knowledge of the possession and use to a true owner maintaining a reasonable degree of supervision over its property. The record supports the trial court's finding that the MacLeod family's possession and use were "open," "visible," and "notorious" throughout the limitations period.

* * *

---

[3] An adverse possession claimant would fail to satisfy the visibility element if the encroachment covered a relatively small portion of the adjoining owner's land and the fact of the intrusion was not readily apparent to the naked eye, but would require an on-site survey to discern (*e.g.,* in urban areas where boundary lines are infrequently delineated by markers). *See, e.g., Mannillo v. Gorski,* 54 N.J. 378, 255 A.2d 258, 263 (1969). In such circumstance, "[t]he only method of certain determination would be by obtaining a survey each time the adjacent owner undertook any improvement at or near the boundary, and this would place an undue and inequitable burden upon the true owner." *Id.* at 263-64. However, the MacLeod family's encroachment was readily apparent to the naked eye.

[4] According to BLACK'S LAW DICTIONARY 1063 (6th ed.1990), "notorious" possession and use are "so conspicuous that [they] are generally known and talked of by the public or the people in the neighborhood."

Mannillo v. Gorski

54 N.J. 378 (1969)

The claimants (defendants) built some stairs to their house that extended over to their neighbor's property by 15 inches. The court must address whether such an encroachment satisfies the open and notorious element. The court holds that it may—but pay attention to the reasoning of the court.

HANEMAN, J.

Plaintiffs filed a complaint in the Chancery Division seeking a mandatory and prohibitory injunction against an alleged trespass upon their lands. Defendant counterclaimed for a declaratory judgment which would adjudicate that she had gained title to the disputed premises by adverse possession under N.J.S. 2A:14-6, N.J.S.A., which provides:

'Every person having any right or title of entry into real estate shall make such entry within 20 years next after the accrual of such right or title of entry, or be barred therefrom thereafter.'

* * *

The facts are as follows: In 1946, defendant and her husband entered into possession of premises in Keansburg known as Lot No. 1007 in Block 42, under an agreement to purchase. Upon compliance with the terms of said agreement, the seller conveyed said lands to them on April 16, 1952. Defendant's husband thereafter died. The property consisted of a rectangular lot with a frontage of 25 feet and a depth of 100 feet. Plaintiffs are the owners of the adjacent Lot 1008 in Block 42 of like dimensions, to which they acquired title in 1953.

In the summer of 1946 Chester Gorski, one of the defendant's sons, made certain additions and changes to the defendant's house. He extended two rooms at the rear of the structure, enclosed a screened porch on the front, and put a concrete platform with steps on the west side thereof for use in connection with a side door. These steps were built to replace existing wooden steps. In addition, a concrete walk was installed from the steps to the end of the house. In 1953, defendant raised the house. In order to compensate for the resulting added height from the ground, she modified the design of the steps by extending them toward both the front and the rear of the property. She did not change their width.

Defendant admits that the steps and concrete walk encroach upon plaintiffs' lands to the extent of 15 inches. She contends, however, that she has title to said land by adverse possession. N.J.S.A. 2A:14-6, quoted above. Plaintiffs assert contrawise that defendant did not obtain title by adverse possession as her possession was not of the requisite hostile nature. They argue that to establish title by adverse possession, the entry into and continuance of possession must be accompanied by an intention to invade the rights of another in the lands, i.e., a knowing wrongful taking. They assert that, as defendant's encroachment was not accompanied by an intention to invade plaintiffs' rights in the land, but rather by the mistaken belief that she owned the land, and that therefore an essential requisite to establish title by adverse possession, i.e., an intentional tortious taking, is lacking.

The trial court concluded that defendant had clearly and convincingly proved that her possession of the 15-inch encroachment had existed for more than 20 years before the institution of this suit and that such possession was 'exclusive, continuous, uninterrupted, visible, notorious and against the right and interest of the true owner.' There is ample evidence to sustain this finding except as to its visible and notorious nature, of which more [will be discussed] hereafter. However, the judge felt impelled by existing New Jersey case law, holding as argued by plaintiffs above, to deny defendant's claim and entered judgment for plaintiffs. 100 N.J.Super, at 150, 241 A.2d 276. * * *

* * *

[The court first addressed the issue of claim of right. That part of the opinion is reproduced later in this chapter. The second issue was whether the fifteen-inch encroachment was open and notorious. The court stated:]

However, this conclusion [on the issue of the claim of right] is not dispositive of the matter Sub Judice. Of equal importance under the present factual complex, is the question of whether defendant's acts meet the necessary standard of 'open and notorious' possession. It must not be forgotten that the foundation of so-called 'title by adverse possession' is the failure of the true owner to commence an action for the recovery of the land involved, within the period designated by the statute of limitations. The justifications for the doctrine are aptly stated in 4 Tiffany, Real Property (3d ed. 1939) § 1134, p. 406 as follows:

'The desirability of fixing, by law, a definite period within which claims to land must be asserted has been generally recognized, among the practical considerations in favor of such a policy being the prevention of the making of illegal claims after the evidence necessary to defeat them has been lost, and the interest which the community as a whole has in the security, of title. The moral justification of the policy lies in the consideration that one who has reason to know that land belonging to him is in the possession of another, and neglects, for a considerable period of time, to assert his right thereto, may properly be penalized by his preclusion from thereafter asserting such right. It is, apparently, by reason of the demerit of the true owner, rather than any supposed merit in the person who has acquired wrongful possession of the land, that this possession, if continued for the statutory period, operates to debar the former owner of all right to recover the land.'

See also 5 Thompson, Real Property (1957 Replacement), 497.

In order to afford the true owner the opportunity to learn of the adverse claim and to protect his rights by legal action within the time specified by the statute, the adverse possession must be visible and notorious. In 4 Tiffany, Supra (Supp.1969, at 291), the character of possession for that purpose, is stated to be as follows:

'* * * it must be public and based on physical facts, including known and visible lines and boundaries. Acts of dominion over the land must be so open and notorious as to put an ordinarily prudent person on notice that the land is in actual possession of another. Hence, title may never be acquired by mere possession, however long continued, which is surreptitious or secret or which is not such as will give unmistakable notice of the nature of the occupant's claim.'

See also 5 Thompson, Supra, s 2546; 6 Powell, Real Property, 1013 (1969).

Generally, where possession of the land is clear and unequivocal and to such an extent as to be immediately visible, the owner may be presumed to have knowledge of the adverse occupancy. In Foulke v. Bond, 41 N.J.L. 527, 545 (E. & A. 1879), the court said:

'Notoriety of the adverse claim under which possession is held, is a necessary constituent of title by adverse possession, and therefore the occupation or possession must be of that nature that the real owner is *presumed* to have known that there was a possession adverse to his title, under which it was intended to make title against him.' (Emphasis supplied.)

However, when the encroachment of an adjoining owner is of a small area and the fact of an intrusion is not clearly and self-evidently apparent to the naked eye but requires an on-site survey for certain disclosure as in urban sections where the division line is only infrequently delineated by any monuments, natural or artificial, such a presumption is fallacious and unjustified. See concurring opinion of Judge (now Justice) Francis in Predham v. Holfester, 32 N.J.Super. 419, 428-429, 108 A.2d 458 (App.Div.1954). The precise location of the dividing line is then ordinarily unknown to either adjacent owner and there is nothing on the land itself to show by visual observation that a hedge, fence, wall or other structure encroaches on the neighboring land to a minor extent. Therefore, to permit a presumption of notice to arise in the case of minor border encroachments not exceeding several feet would fly in the face of reality and require the true owner to be on constant alert for possible small encroachments. The only method of certain determination would be by obtaining a survey each time the adjacent owner undertook any improvement at or near the boundary, and this would place an undue and inequitable burden upon the true owner. Accordingly we hereby hold that no presumption of knowledge arises from a minor encroachment along a common boundary. In such a case, only where the true owner has actual knowledge thereof may it be said that the possession is open and notorious.

It is conceivable that the application of the foregoing rule may in some cases result in undue hardship to the adverse possessor who under an innocent and mistaken belief of title has undertaken an extensive improvement which to some extent encroaches on an adjoining property. In that event the situation falls within the category of those cases of which Riggle v. Skill, 9 N.J.Super. 372, 74 A.2d 424 (Ch.Div.1950), affirmed 7 N.J. 268, 81 A.2d 364 (1951) is typical and equity may furnish relief. Then, if the innocent trespasser of a small portion of land adjoining a boundary line cannot without great expense remove or eliminate the encroachment, or such removal or elimination is impractical or could be accomplished only with great hardship, the true owner may be forced to convey the land so occupied upon payment of the fair value thereof without regard to whether the true owner had notice of the encroachment at its inception. Of course, such a result should eventuate only under appropriate circumstances and where no serious damage would be done to the remaining land as, for instance, by rendering the balance of the parcel unusable or no longer capable of being built upon by reason of zoning or other restrictions.

We remand the case for trial of the issues (1) whether the true owner had actual knowledge of the encroachment, (2) if not, whether plaintiffs should be obliged to convey the disputed tract to defendant, and (3) if the answer to the latter question is in the affirmative, what consideration should be paid for the conveyance. The remand, of course, contemplates further discovery and a new pretrial.

Remanded for trial in accordance with the foregoing.

§ 2.5 Exclusive

In addition to making an actual entry that is open and notorious, the adverse possessor's occupation must be "exclusive." The next two cases consider this element.

Collins v. Smith
372 P.2d 878 (Okl. 1962)

* * *

Under the above citations, plaintiff had the burden of proving every fact necessary to prove his adverse possession. Among these elements is that of exclusiveness. In the case of Howard v. Stanolind Oil & Gas Co., 197 Okl. 269, 169 P.2d 737, this court said in the body of the opinion:

"Adverse possession, in order to ripen into title, must be exclusive. 'Exclusive possession' means that the disseizor must show an exclusive dominion over the land and an appropriation of it to his own use and benefit. * * *

"Where the possession of land is mixed, the legal seisin is according to the legal title." Deputron v. Young, 134 U.S. 241, 10 S.Ct. 539, 33 L.Ed. 923.

* * *

Rick v. Grubbs
147 Tex. 267 (1948)

The court must determine if the exclusivity requirement is satisfied when the true owner (Rick) granted a right of way across the land; sold a strip of the land; allowed a billboard on the property; and allowed the U. S. Army to conduct maneuvers on the property. The court will hold that on these facts the adverse possessor (Grubbs and Jones) did not satisfy the exclusivity requirement.

HART, Justice.

This is a suit in trespass to try title, brought by the petitioner, Leo Z. Rick, who, by stipulation of the parties is conceded to be the owner of the record title to the land in controversy, Lot No. 4 in Block 1 of the Wescalder Addition to the City of Beaumont. Petitioner purchased this lot in 1924. The respondents are W. D. Grubbs, Jr., and his grantee, T. B. Jones. The only defense raised by the evidence is the claim of title by adverse possession under the ten year statute of limitation, Article 5510, Vernon's Annotated Civil Statutes. At the conclusion of the testimony the district court instructed a verdict in favor of the petitioner on the ground that the respondents had failed to meet their 'burden of proof of open, adverse claim,' entitling them to limitation title, an judgment was entered accordingly. The Court of Civil Appeals reversed and remanded the case for a new trial on the grounds that there was an issue of fact raised by the evidence as to whether the respondents had exclusive possession of the land for the limitation period and that the re-entries made upon the land by the petitioner did not as a matter of law break the continuity of respondents' possession. 212 S.W.2d 489.

Upon a consideration of the record, we have concluded that the judgment of the district court was correct and that the Court of Civil Appeals erred in reversing it, because the evidence wholly fails to show that the respondents had adverse possession of the land, as required by Article 5510 and as defined by Article 5515, Vernon's Annotated Civil Statutes.

* * *

The evidence shows without dispute that Rick rendered Lot No. 4 for taxes and paid taxes thereon for all of the years during which Grubbs claims to have had adverse possession of it, and also that during this period Rick exercised dominion over the lot in the following ways:

(1) The parties stipulated that in May, 1932, Rick conveyed to Gulf Pipe Line Company a right of way one hundred feet wide across Lot No. 4. The evidence shows that under this grant the pipe line company laid seven pipe lines across this lot and that one of its employees entered the enclosure to make inspection trips across the lot at least once each day. Grubbs made no protest against the construction of the pipe lines across Lot No. 4 and did not interfere with the pipe line company's employees; in fact, he testified that he agreed with the pipe line company's employees that the company could put a gate in the fence so that the inspections could be made more easily, and that this gate was constructed in the fence.

(2) In August, 1939, Rick sold to the State of Texas a strip of land twenty-five feet wide along one side of Lot No. 4, which was purchased for the purpose of widening United States Highway No. 90. The fence which Grubbs had constructed along this line was torn down and moved back to the new line. Grubbs made no claim to any part of the purchase price of this strip and did not protest against the tearing down and moving of the fence. During this same time, Grubbs was engaged in a condemnation suit with Jefferson County involving a portion of Lot No. 5, which was taken for the same project, but in that lawsuit and in the settlement negotiations Grubbs asserted no claim to ownership of Lot No. 4.

(3) In 1939 Rick granted permission to a sign builder to construct and advertising sign on Lot No. 4, and under this permission a large sign was constructed on the lot within the enclosure. No protest was made by Grubbs against the construction of the sign, and it remained on the lot for over a year, until it was blown down by a storm.

(4) In 1941 Rick gave the Army permission to maneuver over Lot No. 4, and the Army maneuvered on the land under this permission, without protest from Grubbs.

* * *

An important part of the law as so stated is that the possession must be of such character as to indicate unmistakably an assertion of a claim of exclusive ownership in the occupant. It follows that the law's requisites are not satisfied if the occupancy is shared with the owner or his agents or tenants. See 2 C.J.S., Adverse Possession, § 48, page 566:

'To be effective as a means of acquiring title, the possession of an adverse claimant must be exclusive of the true owner. The owner must be wholly excluded from possession by claimant. Any sort of joint or common possession by claimant and the owner or a tenant of the owner prevents the possession of claimant from having the requisite quality of exclusiveness. In these circumstances, the law refers the possession to the person having the legal title. * * *'

In Southwestern Lumber Co. v. Allison, Tex.Com.App., 276 S.W. 418, the evidence indicated that the land in question, which had been enclosed, was used jointly by the record owner's tenants and by the defendant claiming limitation title. The Court held that such joint use could not be sufficient to entitle the defendant to a judgment on his plea of limitation, saying, 276 S.W. at page 419:

'* * * Possession in order to be adverse must be exclusive. The rule is aptly stated in the case of Wichita Valley R. Co. v. Somerville, Tex.Civ.App., 179 S.W. 671:

"The law presumes the true owner is in possession until adverse possession is proved to begin, and when two persons are in mixed possession of the same land, one by title, and the other by wrong, the law considers the one who has title as in possession to the extent of his rights, so as to preclude the other from taking advantage of the statute of limitation. 2 Corpus Juris, Adverse Possession, § 587, p. 264; Satterwhite v. Rosser, 61 Tex. 166. * * *"

In Black v. Goolsbee, Tex.Civ.App., 226 S.W. 463, writ of error dismissed the evidence [which] showed that the defendant, claiming title by limitation, had fenced and cultivated a tract of land for over ten years. During this period, however, the record owners went on the land and cut and removed timber from the tract so occupied. While this timber was being cut and removed, the defendant asserted no claim to it and did not oppose the record owners' acts in cutting and removing it. The Court held that title by adverse possession had not been established.

In analogous cases it has been held that where the record owner or persons claiming under him enter upon unenclosed land, the adverse possession of the limitation claimant is thereby restricted to the land actually enclosed and occupied by him. Evitts v. Roth, 61 Tex. 81; Evans v. Houston Oil Company, Tex.Com.App., 231 S.W. 731; Furlow v. Kirby Lumber Co., Tex.Civ.App., 53 S.W.2d 642.

The facts in the present case show that Grubbs did not have such adverse possession as the law requires in order to perfect limitation title. Under the undisputed evidence, the record owner's tenants, licensees and grantees were permitted to enter and use the land freely without any protest from Grubbs. Whenever the owner undertook to exercise any control or dominion over the land, Grubbs made no effort to interfere. At most the evidence showed a claim by Grubbs to a right to use the land jointly with the record owner and those claiming under him; it certainly did not unmistakably indicate a claim to exclusive ownership in Grubbs. The trial court was therefore correct in holding that the adverse claimant had wholly failed to sustain by proof his claim of adverse possession sufficient to show title by limitation.

* * *

The judgment of the Court of Civil Appeals is reversed and the judgment of the District Court is affirmed.

§ 2.6 Hostile

Intuitively, one may think that hostility means that the claimant must demonstrate anger of sorts. This is not the case, however, as the cases which follow make clear.

Rorebeck v. Criste
1 Ariz.App.1 (1965)

* * *

The term 'hostile' leads to some confusion, however. One dictionary definition might lead to a conclusion that a showing of 'ill will', 'malevolence' or that the plaintiff had an evil intent or desire to thwart or injure is necessary. However, this approach does not correctly show the kind or degree of 'hostility' necessary as an element of adverse possession. There need be no 'ill will' or 'evil intent'. There need be merely a showing that one in possession of the land claims the exclusive right thereto and denies (by word or act) the owner's title. Gusheroski v. Lewis, 64 Ariz. 192, 167 P.2d 390 (1946); Mittet v. Hansen, 178 Wash. 541, 35 P.2d 93 (1934); 1 Am.Jur., Adverse Possession Sec. 138, p. 873. * * *

* * *

Cluff v. Bonner County
121 Idaho 184 (1992)

* * *

This is an adverse possession case. The primary issue presented is whether there is a genuine issue of material fact concerning the improvement of the property by the adverse claimant. We conclude there is a genuine issue of material fact and vacate the trial court's summary judgment dismissing the adverse claimant's quiet title action. We also restate principles concerning adverse possession: (1) [a person may claim title not based upon a written claim], (2) continuous occupation of property for five years creates a presumption that the possession has been adverse and under a claim of right, and (3) the requirement of occupation with hostile intent merely refers to occupation without permission by the owner of the property. * * *

Lovejoy v. School Dist. No. 46 of Sedgwick County
129 Colo. 306 (1954)

* * *

The very essence of adverse possession is that the possession must be hostile, not only against the true owner, but against the world as well. An adverse claim must be hostile at its inception, because, if the original entry is not openly hostile or adverse, it does not become so, and the statute does not begin to run as against a rightful owner until the adverse claimant disavows the idea of holding for, or in subservience to another, it actually sets up an exclusive right in himself by some clear, positive and unequivocal act. The character of the possession must become hostile in order that it may be deemed to be adverse. And this hostility must continue for the full statutory period. 1 Am.Jur., p. 871, § 137. The statute begins to run at the time the possession of the claimant becomes adverse to that of the owner, and this occurs when the claimant sets up title in himself by some clear, positive and unequivocal act.

* * *

§ 2.7 Claim of Right

A good number of cases combine hostility with claim of right. That is not correct, however. The cases that follow define claim of right. In the process, you will come to see why hostility and claim of right are two distinct elements.

§ 2.7.1 In General

Peters v. Gillund *makes clear that claim of right goes to intent. As you will see in the subsections that follow, however, there are three lines of authority defining claim of right.*

Peters v. Gillund
186 S.W.2d 1019 (Tex.Civ.App.1945)

* * *

The court properly defined adverse possession as being any actual and visible appropriation of the land under a claim of right inconsistent with, and hostile to, the claim of the real owner; and defined "claim of right" as meaning that the entry of the limitation claimant must be with the intent to claim the land as his own, to hold it for himself, etc.

* * *

§ 2.7.2 Good Faith Standard

The first line of authority defines claim of right to be in "good faith." Carpenter v. Ruperto *explores what this good faith standard means—that the claimant made a good faith mistake in believing the property was his.*

Carpenter v. Ruperto

315 N.W.2d 782 (Iowa 1982)

The claimant possessed land that she knew she did not own. The question before the court was, on those facts, could she have possessed the land in question under claim of right? The court holds in the negative.

McCORMICK, Justice.

Plaintiff Virginia Carpenter appeals from an adverse decree in her action to quiet title to land adjacent to her residential premises based on a theory of adverse possession. Defendants Charles L. Ruperto, Edith C. Ruperto, and Tom McCormick cross-appeal from a portion of the decree awarding plaintiff limited relief on equitable grounds. We affirm on the merits of the appeal and dismiss the cross-appeal for want of jurisdiction.

The determinative question on the appeal is whether the trial court misinterpreted the law governing the claim of right element in finding plaintiff failed to carry her burden of proof. The determinative question on the cross-appeal is whether it was timely. Because the case was tried in equity, we find the facts anew. The evidence is largely undisputed.

Plaintiff and her husband moved in 1951 to a home which they purchased in southeast Des Moines. Plaintiff's husband subsequently died, but plaintiff has lived on the premises continuously. Her lot has a frontage of 40 feet and is 125 feet long. It is legally described as: [legal description here].

A larger undeveloped lot bounded plaintiff's property to the north. * * * Defendants and their predecessors have held record title to this lot at all material times.

The property which plaintiff claims to have acquired by adverse possession is the south 60 feet of defendants' lot. Thus, the property in dispute is a 60 by 125 foot parcel adjacent to the north boundary of plaintiff's lot.

When plaintiff and her husband moved into their home in July 1951, the lot north of their property was a cornfield. Although plaintiff was not certain of the location of the northern boundary of her lot, she knew her lot's dimensions, and she knew it did not include the cornfield. In 1952 the corn was not planted as far south on the adjacent lot. Concerned about rats and the threat of fire, and desiring additional yard for their children, plaintiff and her husband cleared several feet of the property to the north, graded it, and planted grass seed on it. Since that time plaintiff has used the land as an extension of her yard. She planted peony bushes on it during the 1950's, installed a propane tank on it approximately 30 feet north of her lot in 1964, constructed a dirt bank on the city right of way to divert water from that parcel in 1965, and put in a driveway infringing five feet onto the land in 1975.

* * *

In seeking to establish her ownership of the disputed parcel, plaintiff alleged she had "for more than thirty (30) years last past been in open, exclusive, hostile, adverse and actual possession under claim of right." The trial court held in part that she did not establish her possession was under a claim of right. The court reasoned that a claim of right must be made in good faith and that plaintiff was not in good faith because she knew someone else had title to the land.

* * *

* * * In contending the trial court erred in finding she failed in her proof of this element, she attacks the viability of the principal case relied on by the trial court, Goulding v. Shonquist, 159 Iowa 647, 141 N.W. 24 (1913). Its facts are analogous to those here.

In Goulding the individual also cleared land adjacent to his house. The land was overrun with brush and willows and was frequented by hunters. After clearing it, the individual used the land as a pasture and garden. In finding he did not establish good faith claim of right, the court said:

> When he moved into his present property, the lands in question were objectionable because they were frequented by hunters, and for that reason he and his wife thought they ought to clear them up. He says he supposed they were part of the old river bed or waste land upon which anyone could enter. No other facts are offered by defendant as a reason for entering into the possession of the land at that time. Whether the title to the land was in the state or some other person, the defendant knew that he had no title and that he had no claim of title, and no right whatever to enter into the possession, and his possession was not in good faith for that reason.

Id. at 651, 141 N.W. at 25. The court quoted a statement from Litchfield v. Sewell, 97 Iowa 247, 251, 66 N.W. 104, 106 (1896), that "that there can be no such thing as adverse possession where the party knows he has no title, and that, under the law, he can acquire none by his occupation."

* * *

* * * [T]he possessor in Goulding not only knew that he had no title but that he had no claim of title or any right to enter into possession of the property. He was a mere squatter.

* * *

We believe plaintiff failed to prove a good faith claim of right in the present case. She knew her lot did not include the cornfield north of it. She knew someone else had title to it and she had no interest in it or claim to it. This is not a case of confusion or mistake. At the time she entered possession of the disputed land, plaintiff knew she had no legal right to do so. To say that one can acquire a claim of right by merely entering possession would recognize squatter's rights. Possession for the statutory period cannot be bootstrapped into a basis for claiming a right to possession.

We hold that the trial court was right in rejecting plaintiff's claim.

II. The cross-appeal. * * * Because the cross-appeal was untimely, we did not acquire jurisdiction of it, and it must be dismissed.

AFFIRMED ON THE APPEAL; DISMISSED ON THE CROSS-APPEAL.

§ 2.7.3 Bad Faith Standard

The next line of authority defines claim of right to mean that the claimant had "bad faith"—that he knew the land was not his but he intended to take it anyway.

Mannillo v. Gorski

54 N.J. 378 (1969)

The facts in Mannillo v. Gorski *were reproduced earlier in this chapter in the section dealing with the open and notorious requirement. The first part of the opinion, dealing with claim of right, was not reproduced earlier. It is reproduced here:*

* * *

The first issue before this Court is, therefore, whether an entry and continuance of possession under the mistaken belief that the possessor has title to the lands involved, exhibits the requisite hostile possession to sustain the obtaining of title by adverse possession.

The first detailed statement and acceptance by our then highest court, of the principle that possession as an element of title by adverse possession cannot be bottomed on mistake, is found in Folkman v. Myers, 93 N.J.Eq. 208, 115 A. 615 (E. & A. 1921), which embraced and followed that thesis as expressed in Myers v. Folkman, 89 N.J.L. 390, 99 A. 97 (Sup.Ct.1916). It is not at all clear that this was the common law of this State prior to the latter case. An earlier opinion, Davock v. Nealon, 58 N.J.L. 21, 32 A. 675 (Sup.Ct.1895), held for an adverse possessor who had entered under the mistaken belief that he had title without any discussion of his hostile intent. However, the court in Myers v. Folkman, supra, at p. 393, 99 A. at p. 98, distinguished Davock from the case then under consideration by referring to the fact that 'Charles R. Myers disclaims any intent to claim what did not belong to him, and apparently never asserted a right to land outside the bounds of his title * * *.' The factual distinction between the two cases, according to Myers, is that in the later case there was not only an entry by mistake but also an articulated disclaimer of an intent by the entrant to claim title to lands beyond his actual boundary. Folkman, although apparently relying on Myers, eliminated the requirement of that decision that there be expressed an affirmative disclaimer, and expanded the doctrine to exclude from the category of hostile possessors those whose entry and continued possession was under a mistaken belief that the lands taken were embraced within the description of the possessor's deed. In so doing, the former Court of Errors and Appeals aligned this State with that branch of a dichotomy which traces its genesis to Preble v. Maine Cent. R. Co., 85 Me. 260, 27 A. 149, 21 L.R.A. 829 (Sup.Jud.Ct.Me.1893) and has become known as the Maine doctrine. In Preble, the court said at 27 A. at p. 150:

> "There is every presumption that the occupancy is in subordination to the true title, and, if the possession is claimed to be adverse, the act of the wrongdoer must be strictly construed, and the character of the possession clearly shown. Roberts v. Richards, 84 Me. 1, 24 Atl.Rep. 425, and authorities cited. 'The intention of the possessor to claim adversely,' says Mellen, C.J., in Ross v. Gould, supra (5 Me. 204), 'is an essential

ingredient in disseisin.' And in Worcester v. Lord, supra (56 Me. 266) the court says: 'To make a disseisin in fact, there must be an intention on the part of the party assuming possession to assert title in himself.' Indeed, the authorities all agree that this intention of the occupant to claim the ownership of land not embraced in his title is a necessary element of adverse possession; and in case of occupancy by mistake beyond a line capable of being ascertained this intention to claim title to the extent of the occupancy must appear to be absolute, and not conditional; otherwise the possession will not be deemed adverse to the true owner. It must be an intention to claim title to all land within a certain boundary on the face of the earth, whether it shall eventually be found to be the correct one or not. If, for instance, one in ignorance of his actual boundaries takes and holds possession by mistake up to a certain fence beyond his limits, upon the claim and in the belief that it is the true line, with the intention to claim title, and thus, if necessary, to acquire 'title by possession' up to that fence, such possession, having the requisite duration and continuity, will ripen into title. Hitchings v. Morrison, 72 Me. 331, is a pertinent illustration of this principle. See, also, Abbott v. Abbott, 51 Me. 575; Ricker v. Hibbard, 73 Me. 105.

If, on the other hand, a party through ignorance, inadvertence, or mistake occupies up to a given fence beyond his actual boundary, because he believes it to be the true line, but has no intention to claim title to that extent if it should be ascertained that the fence was on his neighbor's land, an indispensable element of adverse possession is wanting. In such a case the intent to claim title exists only upon the condition that the fence is on the true line. The intention is not absolute, but provisional, and the possession is not adverse."

This thesis, it is evident, rewards the possessor who entered with a premeditated and predesigned 'hostility'-the intentional wrongdoer and disfavors an honest, mistaken entrant. 3 American Law of Property (Casner ed. 1952), § 104, pp. 773, 785; Bordwell, 'Desseisin and Adverse Possession,' 33 Yale L.J. 1, 154 (1923); Darling, 'Adverse Possession in Boundary Cases,' 19 Ore.L.Rev. 117 (1940); Sternberg, 'The Element of Hostility in Adverse Possession,'6 Temp.L.Q. 206 (1932); Annotation, 'Adverse possession involving ignorance or mistake as to boundaries-modern views,' 80 A.L.R.2d 1171 (1961).

The other branch of the dichotomy relies upon French v. Pearce, 8 Conn. 439 (Sup.Ct.Conn.1831). The court said in Pearce on the question of the subjective hostility of a possessor, at pp. 442, 445-446:

"Into the recesses of his (the adverse claimant's) mind, his motives or purposes, his guilt or innocence, no enquiry is made. * * *
* * * The very nature of the act (entry and possession) is an assertion of his own title, and the denial of the title of all others. It matters not that the possessor was mistaken, and had he been better informed, would not have entered on the land." 8 Conn. at 442, 445-446.

The Maine doctrine has been the subject of much criticism in requiring a knowing wrongful taking. The criticism of the Maine and the justification of the Connecticut branch of the dichotomy is well stated in 6 Powell, Real Property (1969) 1015, pp. 725-28:

'Do the facts of his possession, and of his conduct as if he were the owner, make immaterial his mistake, or does such a mistake prevent the existence of the prerequisite claim of right. The leading case holding the mistake to be of no importance was French v. Pearce, decided in Connecticut in 1831. * * * This viewpoint has gained increasingly widespread acceptance. The more subjectively oriented view regards the 'mistake' as necessarily preventing the existence of the required claim of right. The leading case on this position is Preble v. Maine Central R.R., decided in 1893. This position is still followed in a few states. It has been strongly criticized as unsound historically, inexpedient practically, and as resulting in better treatment for a ruthless wrongdoer than for the honest landowner. * * * On the whole the law is simplified, in the direction of real justice, by a following of the Connecticut leadership on this point.'

Again, 4 Tiffany, Real Property (3d ed. 1939), § 1159, pp. 474-475, criticizes the employment of mistake as negating hostility as follows:

'* * * Adopting this view, it is only in so far as the courts, which assert the possible materiality of the mistake, recognize a contrary presumption, of an intention on the part of the wrongful possessor not to claim title if he is mistaken as to the boundary, that the assertion of the materiality of mistake as to boundary becomes of substantial importance. That the presumption is properly in favor of the adverse or hostile character of the possession rather than against it has been previously argued, but whatever presumption in this regard may be recognized, the introduction of the element of mistake in the discussion of the question of adverse possession is, it is submitted, unnecessary and undesirable. In no case except in that of a mistake as to boundary has the element of mistake been regarded as having any significance, and there is no reason for attributing greater weight thereto when the mistake is as to the proper location of a boundary than when it is a mistake as to the title to all the land wrongfully possessed. And to introduce the element of mistake, and then limit its significance by an inquiry as to the intention which the possessor may have as to his course of action in case there should be a mistake, an intention which has ordinarily no existence whatsoever, is calculated only to cause confusion without, it is conceived, any compensating advantage.'

Our Appellate Division in Predham v. Holfester, 32 N.J.Super. 419, 108 A.2d 458 (App.Div.1954) although acknowledging that the Maine doctrine had been severely criticized felt obliged because of stare decisis to adhere thereto. See also Rullis v. Jacobi, 79 N.J.Super. 525, 528, 192 A.2d 186 (Ch.Div.1963).

We are in accord with the criticism of the Maine doctrine and favor the Connecticut doctrine for the above quoted reasons. As far as can be seen, overruling the former rule will not result in undermining any of the values which stare decisis is intended to foster. The theory of reliance, a cornerstone of stare decisis, is not here apt, as the problem is which of two mistaken parties is entitled to land. Realistically, the true owner does not rely upon entry of the possessor by mistake as a reason for not seeking to recover possession. Whether or not the entry is caused by mistake or intent, the same result eventuates-the true owner is ousted from possession. In either event his neglect to seek recovery of possession, within the requisite time, is in all probability the result of a lack of knowledge that he is being deprived of possession of lands to which he has title.

Accordingly, we discard the requirement that the entry and continued possession must be accompanied by a knowing intentional hostility and hold that any entry and possession for the required time which is exclusive, continuous, uninterrupted, visible and notorious, even though under mistaken claim of title, is sufficient to support a claim of title by adverse possession.

* * *

§ 2.7.4 Objective Standard

The third and final line of authority defines claim of right from an objective standard. Try to figure out what this "objective standard" is in the ITT *case.*

ITT Rayonier, Inc. v. Bell
112 Wash.2d 754 (1989)

The claimant, one Bell, moored his houseboat on property owned by ITT Rayonier, Inc. After holding that the claimant's possession was not exclusive, the court discusses an alternative basis for holding against the claimant: that his possession was not under claim of right.

PEARSON, Justice.

ITT Rayonier, Inc. (ITT), plaintiff, instituted this action to quiet title to property situated in Clallam County. In addition, ITT prayed for damages for trespass and for the ejectment of defendant Arthur Bell. Bell answered, alleging ITT was not entitled to judgment in its favor by reason of Bell's adverse possession of the property for a period greater than the statutory period of 10 years. Additionally, Bell counter-claimed against ITT praying for judgment quieting title in Bell. On July 8, 1986, the trial court entered partial summary judgment, quieting title in favor of ITT. The Court of Appeals affirmed. *ITT Rayonier, Inc. v. Bell*, 51 Wash.App. 124, 752 P.2d 398 (1988).

FACTS

In 1972, Arthur Bell purchased a houseboat moored near the mouth of the Big River in Swan Bay on Lake Ozette. The property that is the subject of this action is directly adjacent to that moorage and was purchased by ITT in 1947. ITT, as owner of record, has paid the property taxes on the land in question continuously since its purchase. Bell admits that he never purchased any of the property involved in this action. Additionally, he concedes that he has never maintained any "No Trespassing" signs on the property, nor has he ever denoted any boundary with a fence or any other markers. A very rough approximation of the amount of land in question is one-half of an acre. Bell testified that he regularly occupies his houseboat in the spring, summer, and fall, and visits only occasionally during the winter months.

Bell testified that at the time he purchased the houseboat, he believed the adjacent land was owned by the State. When asked whether it was his understanding that other people could use the property, his response was, "[a]ctually when I--no, not really. When I was there they--I didn't think somebody was going to come up and go camping right there. But I suppose if they tried to, I wouldn't have said anything to them."

According to further deposition testimony of Bell, at the time he purchased the houseboat it had been moored in the same location since approximately 1962. The houseboat was moored to the land initially via a cable, and subsequently via a rope tied to two trees. The record reveals that only the following structures have been situated on the property in question for the full statutory period: a woodshed that existed prior to Bell's purchase of the houseboat, a woodshed he began building in 1978, an abandoned sauna that has existed since 1973, and the remains of an outhouse built by Bell in 1972 that has occupied numerous sites on the property.

Other than 6 weeks in the summer of 1973, when the houseboat was moored in Boot Bay, approximately 2 miles from the disputed property, the houseboat has at all times been situated adjacent to the property both Bell and ITT presently claim.

Bell's deposition testimony further reveals that he was away from the property during the 1974-75, 1975-76, and 1976-77 school years, while he was teaching school in Nanana, Alaska. During the first and third winters, he allowed friends to use the houseboat occasionally. During the 1975-76 school term, he rented the houseboat for $30 per month. Bell returned to Lake Ozette each of the three summers, personally occupying his houseboat during those months.

Bell's houseboat is not the only one in the area. Two families, the Klocks and the Olesens, have co-owned a houseboat for approximately 20 years that floats adjacent to both Bell's houseboat and the disputed property. Mr. Klock, in a sworn affidavit, stated:

"When using the houseboat, I and my family have used the adjacent land for the purpose of digging a hole for an outhouse and for other minimal uses. I do not own the land next to my houseboat but have used it permissively over the last twenty years. Arthur Bell has never attempted to exclude us from using the property nor has he attempted to claim the property as his own."

In addition, Mr. Olesen swore to an identical statement.

Gerald Schaefer, an employee of ITT, stated in his sworn affidavit that ITT owns 383,000 acres in eight counties in Washington State. Often ITT is absent from its land for long periods of time:

"In its normal management of its land, Rayonier often will not visit or use its lands for long periods of time. After property has been logged and planted, it is common for Rayonier not to visit the property for 15 years, at which point precommercial thinning occurs. After precommercial thinning, property is often left 30 to 35 years before timber becomes commercial. It is virtually impossible to patrol all of Rayonier's lands that are not undergoing logging operations."

ANALYSIS

The doctrine of adverse possession arose at law, toward the aim of serving specific public policy concerns, ["] that title to land should not long be in doubt, that society will benefit from someone's making use of land the owner leaves idle, and that third persons who come to regard the occupant as owner may be protected.["] Stoebuck, *Adverse Possession in Washington,* 35 Wash.L.Rev. 53 (1960).

In order to establish a claim of adverse possession, there must be possession that is: (1) open and notorious, (2) actual and uninterrupted, (3) exclusive, and (4) hostile. *Chaplin v. Sanders,* 100 Wash.2d 853, 857, 676 P.2d 431 (1984). Possession of the property with each of the necessary concurrent elements must exist for the statutorily prescribed period of 10 years. RCW 4.16.020. As the presumption of possession is in the holder of legal title, *Peeples v. Port of Bellingham,* 93 Wash.2d 766, 773, 613 P.2d 1128 (1980), *overruled on other grounds, Chaplin v. Sanders, supra,* the party claiming to have adversely possessed the property has the burden of establishing the existence of each element. *Skansi v. Novak,* 84 Wash. 39, 44, 146 P. 160 (1915), *overruled on other grounds, Chaplin v. Sanders, supra.*

EXCLUSIVE POSSESSION

We are asked whether summary judgment against the defendant was proper based on the defendant's failure to establish his exclusive possession of the disputed property for the statutory period. * * *

* * *

As the Court of Appeals correctly held, Bell's shared and occasional use of the property simply did not rise to the level of exclusive possession indicative of a true owner for the full statutory period. Accordingly, we affirm the Court of Appeals.

GOOD FAITH

Having affirmed the trial court's partial summary judgment against Bell, the Court of Appeals nevertheless provided an alternative ground for its decision:

> [A]nother element of adverse possession is that the party seeking to acquire title to land by adverse possession must possess the land under a good faith claim of right. Bell concedes that at no time, prior to the time he claims his possession of the property ripened into title, did he believe that he had title to this property or any claim of right to it. . . . Holding in this case, as a matter of law, that Bell did not raise a genuine issue of fact on the question of his good faith claim of right to the property is, in our judgment, consistent with *Chaplin.*

ITT Rayonier, Inc., 51 Wash.App. at 129-31, 752 P.2d 398. This portion of the Court of Appeals decision is in error.

In *Chaplin v. Sanders,* 100 Wash.2d at 855, 676 P.2d 431, this court unanimously held that the adverse possessor's "subjective belief whether the land possessed is or is not his own and his intent to dispossess or not dispossess another are irrelevant to a finding of hostility." In so doing, this court expressly overruled cases dating back to 1896.

The Court of Appeals reasoned that the *Chaplin* decision did not specifically do away with the good faith element of adverse possession, and stated, "the question of whether or not one acts in good faith is a question that can only be answered by making a judgment about the actor's subjective belief." *ITT Rayonier, Inc.,* 51 Wash.App. at 130, 752 P.2d 398. In a footnote, the court noted, "to conclude otherwise . . . we would be encouraging . . . 'squatting.' " *ITT Rayonier, Inc.,* at 130 n. 4, 752 P.2d 398.

As stated, the doctrine of adverse possession was formulated at law to protect both those who knowingly appropriated the land of others, and those who honestly held the property in the belief that it was their own. 3 Am.Jur.2d *Adverse Possession* § 142 (1986). Twenty-four years before *Chaplin,* Professor Stoebuck suggested this court should return to the original formulation of the adverse possession doctrine:

> Perhaps the reader will agree that the law would have been clearer and in the long run more useful to the people if Washington had never gone into the "subjective intent" business at all. . . . [T]he common law of England seems to have . . . had no such element to adverse possession. Adverse possession revolves around the character of possession, and it is difficult to see why a man's secret thoughts should have anything to do with it. Maybe the idea originated in a confusion of permission or agreement between owner and possessor with unilateral intent in the possessor's mind. Whatever the reason, the court could yet perform a service by doing away with any requirement of subjective intent, negative or affirmative. Since a man cannot by thoughts alone put himself in adverse possession, why should he be able to think himself out of it?

Stoebuck, *Adverse Possession in Washington,* 35 Wash.L.Rev. 53, 80 (1960).

Today, we reaffirm our commitment to the rule enunciated in *Chaplin v. Sanders, supra:*

> The "hostility/claim of right" element of adverse possession requires only that the claimant treat the land as his own as against the world throughout the statutory period. The nature of his possession will be determined solely on the basis of the manner in which he treats the property. His subjective belief regarding his true interest in the land and his intent to dispossess or not dispossess another is irrelevant to this determination. Under this analysis, permission to occupy the land, given by the true title owner to the claimant or his predecessors in interest, will still operate to negate the element of hostility. The traditional presumptions still apply to the extent that they are not inconsistent with this ruling.

(Footnotes and citations omitted.) *Chaplin v. Sanders,* 100 Wash.2d at 860-62, 676 P.2d 431. Accordingly, good faith no longer constitutes an element of adverse possession. Thus, we affirm the Court of Appeals on the basis of Bell's failure to establish exclusive possession, and reverse the Court of Appeals alternative holding that Bell failed to establish a good faith claim to the property.

CALLOW, C.J., and UTTER, BRACHTENBACH, DOLLIVER, DORE, ANDERSEN and SMITH, JJ., concur.

§ 2.8 Continuity of Possession

To obtain title by adverse possession, the claimant must possess the property continuously for the statutory period. This statutory period—the period of limitations-- varies from jurisdiction to jurisdiction, from five years to thirty years.

§ 2.8.1 In General

If, for example, the period of limitations is ten years, must the claimant possess the property for the full 3650 days? The next few cases answer this and other questions.

Kash v. Lewis
6 S.W.2d 1098 (Ky.App. 1928)

* * *

* * * A more important element is that it must be continuous. There must be no break in the possession. It must be such that if the owner of the property should desire to institute suit against him who holds possession he might do so at any time during the period required for possession to ripen into a title. The abandonment of possession for any period of time however brief interrupts the continuity and the statute of limitations commences to run from the time of the break, if he who is seeking to obtain title by adverse possession again enters on the property.

* * *

Anneberg v. Kurtz
197 Ga. 188 (1944)

* * *

In Walker v. Steffes, 139 Ga. 520(9), 77 S.E. 580, 581, it is said: 'The rule requiring continuity of possession is one of substance, and not of absolute mathematical continuity, provided there is no break, so as to make a severance of two possessions.'

In 17 Am.Jur. 972, § 60, it is said: '* * * The uninterrupted and continuous enjoyment of a right of way necessary to constitute adverse possession does not require the use thereof every day for the statutory period, but simply the exercise of the right more or less frequently according to the nature of the use.' See, also, 2 C.J. 100, § 134, note 7; 2 C.J.S., Adverse Possession, p. 681, § 125. In Park v. Powers, 2 Cal.2d 590, 42 P.2d 75(3), it was said: 'Where enclosed land suitable for grazing and pasturage is occupied each year during the entire season therefor, as from May until late October or November, possession is 'continuous' within adverse possession statute.' Adverse possession includes: the use of an irrigation ditch 'during the cropping season,' Hesperia Land & Water Co. v. Rogers, 83 Cal. 10, 23 P. 196(1), 17 Am.St.Rep. 209; 'whenever needed * * * during the irrigation season,' Glantz v. Gabel, 66 Mont. 134, 212 P. 858(3); use of a right of way 'whenever it is needed,' Myers v. Berven, 166 Cal. 484, 137 P.

260(7); use of a fishery 'every year at the proper season,' McLellan v. McFadden, 114 Me. 242, 95 A. 1025(15), 1029; raising a dam 'during the months of April, May, and June in each year, for the purpose of sluicing logs,' Swan v. Munch, 65 Minn. 500, 67 N.W. 1022, 1023, 35 L.R.A. 743, 60 Am.St.Rep. 491. Where a lake covered land of adjoining owner, 'the occasional letting off the water' did not constitute such interruption as would break its continuity, Alcorn v. Sadler, 71 Miss. 634, 14 So. 444, 445, 42 Am.St.Rep. 484; as to use of irrigation ditch 'whenever necessary', it was said, 'what constitutes continuity of use will depend altogether upon the nature and character of the right claimed.' Hays v. De Atley, 65 Mont. 558, 212 P. 296. 298.

In 9 R.C.L. 774, § 34, it is said: 'The correct rule as to continuity of user, and what shall constitute such continuity, can be stated only with reference to the nature and character of the right claimed. An omission to use when not needed does not disprove a continuity of use, shown by using it when needed, for it is not required that a person shall use the easement every day for the prescriptive period. It simply means that he shall exercise the right more or less frequently according to the nature of the use to which its enjoyment may be applied.'

* * *

Kay v. Biggs
13 Ariz.App. 172 (1970)

The plaintiffs claimed ownership by adverse possession of certain beachfront property, which they occupied for several weeks for each of thirty summers. Is the occupation continuous? The court holds in the affirmative.

* * *

In the similar factual case to the one at bar of Cowan v. Hatcher, 59 S.W. 689 (Tenn. Ch.App., 1900), the court held that the adverse possession element of continuous use was proven where the evidence established that the claimant went upon the land to make personal use of a mineral spring, built a cabin, cleared one and one-half acres of land, fenced it, planted fruit trees, constructed a stable and spent two to four weeks each summer at the cabin with his family for the statutory period. See the cases collected in 24 A.L.R.2d 632 (annotation: Adverse Possession, sufficiency as regards continuity of seasonal possession other than Agricultural or logging purposes), and in 3 Am.Jur.2d, Adverse Possession, §§ 56, 57, pp. 145, 146. See also Kraus v. Mueller, 12 Wis.2d 430, 107 N.W.2d 467 (1961) where the continuous occupancy of a hunting shack during hunting season was sufficient exclusive possession; Nechtow v. Brown, 369 Mich. 460, 120 N.W.2d 251 (1963) where the use of property for a summer home for recreational purposes was sufficient adverse possession; Mahoney v. Heebner, 343 Mass. 770, 178 N.E.2d 26 (1961) where even seasonal physical absence from a summer residence did not break the chain of continuous peaceable possession for the purpose of establishing adverse user; and Booten v. Peterson, 4 Wash.2d 565, 288 P.2d 1084 (1955) where weekend summer use of a beach place was held sufficient to establish peaceable adverse possession to an adjacent parcel of real property used for a recreation center and camping.

Under the facts of this case, it cannot be said that the plaintiffs failed to treat the disputed parcel of land 'as would an ordinary owner of the same type of land.' They built a summer home in an area where there were other such homes and used it exclusively as such for almost thirty years. They physically erected a fence and buildings and dealt with the disputed parcel as if they were the owners. These facts satisfy the early requirements of 'actual' and 'visible' possession discussed in Costello v. Muheim, 9 Ariz. 422, 428, 84 P. 906 (1906). In the Costello case the Supreme Court accepted as the law in Arizona the proposition that neither actual occupancy nor cultivation nor residency was necessary to constitute actual possession, and that the acts necessary to constitute peaceful possession were necessarily varied depending upon the circumstances of each case. Holding that the facts were insufficient in Costello to apply the rule, the court did apply it, however, in Spillsbury v. School District No. 19, supra, by affirming the school district's acquisition of an acre of real property by such adverse possession.

Under the facts and circumstances of this case we hold that the evidence establishing two or three weeks continuous physical presence coupled with the other facts in this case is sufficient to establish the 'continuous peaceable possession' and the 'adverse' claim element required by the statute. Consequently, the evidence is sufficient to support both judgments.

* * *

§ 2.8.2 Tacking

"Tacking" means that an adverse possessor can "tack on," that is, add to his period of possession the possession of his predecessor to satisfy the period of limitations. Thus, for example, if AP1 occupies the land for 6 years and AP2 occupies the land for 5 years, assuming a 10-year limitations period, AP2 has satisfied the element of continuity of possession. The cases that follow provide further elucidation.

Worm v. Crowell
165 Neb. 713 (1958)

In Worm v. Crowell, *after explaining the concept of continuity of possession, the court discusses tacking. In this regard, pay attention to especially the last paragraph of the opinion.*

* * *

'The claim of title to land by adverse possession must be proved by actual, open, exclusive, and continuous possession under a claim of ownership for the statutory period of 10 years.' Purdum v. Sherman, 163 Neb. 889, 81 N.W.2d 331, 332. See, also, McDermott v. Boman, supra.

The possession is sufficient if the land is used continuously for the purpose to which it may be in its nature adapted. See, James v. McNair, supra; Walker v. Bell, 154 Neb. 221, 47 N.W.2d 504, 506. As stated in Walker v. Bell, supra: "* * * Ordinarily the law does not undertake to specify the particular acts of occupation by which alone title by adverse possession may be acquired since the existence and establishment of the continuity must necessarily depend greatly on the circumstances of each case, and the use to which the property is adapted, the actual manner of its use, the circumstances of the occupant, and to some extent his intention must be considered. * * *.' 2 C.J.S. Adverse Possession § 125, p. 681.'

'It is the established rule in this state that when a fence is constructed as a boundary line fence between two properties, and where the parties claim ownership of the land up to the fence for the full statutory period and are not interrupted in their possession or control during that time, they will, by adverse possession, gain title to such land as may have been improperly enclosed with their own.' James v. McNair, supra [164 Neb. 1, 81 N.W.2d 815]. See, also, Horbach v. Miller, 4 Neb. 31; Levy v. Yerga, 25 Neb. 764, 41 N.W. 773, 13 Am.St.Rep. 525; Tourtelotte v. Pearce, 27 Neb. 57, 42 N.W. 915. '* * * taxation of the land for a series of years to the person claiming it, and the payment of taxes by him are competent evidence tending to show ownership.' Horbach v. Miller, supra. See, also, Walker v. Bell, supra.

'The title to land becomes complete in the adverse occupant when he and his grantors have maintained an actual, continued, notorious, and adverse possession thereof, claiming title to the same against all persons, for 10 years.' Lantry v. Wolff, 49 Neb. 374, 68 N.W. 494. See, also, Walker, v. Bell, supra; James v. McNair, supra.

A person claiming title by adverse possession must establish it. Hehnke v. Starr, supra; McDermott v. Boman, supra. As held in Hehnke v. Starr, supra [158 Neb. 575, 64 N.W.2d 69]: 'One claiming ownership of real estate by adverse possession must recover upon the strength of his title and not because of a possible weakness in the title of his adversary.' And: 'A person claiming title by adverse possession must to establish it prove open, notorious, exclusive, continuous, and adverse possession of the real estate, claiming title to the same against all persons for the full period of 10 years.' See, also, McDermott v. Boman, supra. * * *

'If the adverse possession of the occupant is a continuation of the possession of a prior adverse possessor claiming title, and such occupant claims title from such prior possessor, then the possession of the occupant may be tacked to that of such prior possessor.' Walker v. Bell, supra.

* * *

Waller v. Dansby
224 S.W. 615 (Ark. 1920)

A son sought to tack onto his possession the possession of his father. The court will state when tacking is allowed.

HART, J. * * *
It is claimed by counsel for appellant that Marshall Dansby had no color of title[5] to the 40 acres involved in this appeal, and therefore could only acquire title by adverse

---

[5] [Color of title is discussed in the next section.]

possession to the 10 acres of land which he had cleared and actually had in his possession. In making this contention counsel have not taken into consideration the fact that Marshall Dansby could tack his possession to that of his father, Jacob Dansby. The record shows that Jacob Dansby originally owned the land and had a deed thereto. According to the testimony of Amanda Dansby they paid taxes on the land and claimed it as their own until the year 1907. Marshall Dansby said that he entered the land at that time under a parol agreement from his father and mother, and has continuously occupied it ever since, claiming it as his own, and either himself or his father paid the taxes thereon. This created a privity between him and his father, and he had the right to avail himself of the occupancy of his father. In order to create the privity requisite to enable the subsequent occupant to tack to his possession that of the prior occupant, it is not necessary that there be a conveyance in writing. It is sufficient if it is shown that the prior occupant transferred his possession to him, even though by parol. The authorities agree that privity between successive possessors is all that is necessary to render them continuous, if the possession be in fact actual and adverse. The privity may be created in any way that will prevent a break in the adverse possession and refer the several possessions to the original entry, and it may be created either by parol or otherwise from vendor to vendee. Memphis & Little Rock Rd. Co. as Reorganized v. Organ, 67 Ark. 84, 55 S. W. 952; Wilson v. Rogers, 97 Ark. 369, 134 S. W. 318; St. L. S. W. Ry. Co. v. Mulkey, 100 Ark. 71, 139 S. W. 643, Ann. Cas. 1913C, 1339. From these authorities it is apparent that the court was justified in finding from the testimony that Marshall Dansby had been in adverse possession of the land for more than 7 years under color of title.

* * *

§ 2.9 Color of Title

Color of title, not to be confused with claim of right, is when the claimant goes into possession on the basis of a deed, contract, or will—which is actually invalid.

§ 2.9.1 In General

Green v. Dixon *provides an illustration of how a claimant may come in under an invalid deed.*

Green v. Dixon
727 So.2d 781 (Ala. 1998)

  HOOPER, Chief Justice.
  Rosa Green and the estate of Lucille Green Dawsey appeal from a summary judgment declaring that they had no interest in certain real property and the underlying minerals. We reverse and remand.

Statement of Facts

In 1933, the tax collector of Choctaw County conducted a tax sale of four parcels of real estate totaling 112 acres. The land had been owned by John L. Parker. John L. Parker was never personally served with notice of the tax sale. Service was accomplished through publishing the notice for three weeks in the local newspaper and by posting it in the county courthouse. The tax sale occurred on August 7, 1933; the property was sold to John Green, Sr., for $34.03. On August 10, 1933, the probate judge of Choctaw County executed a tax deed to John Green, Sr., conveying to him Parker's interest in the property. Green recorded the deed two days later.

* * *

Void Tax Deed as Color of Title

Although the litigation between these parties is rather convoluted, the issue before this Court is a narrow one: Did the void tax deed provide the Greens with color of title under § 6-5-200? The invalidity of the tax sale and the tax deed is undisputed. The Greens have also abandoned any claim that the short statute of limitations entitles them to possession of the mineral interests.

Simply put, color of title is a writing that appears to transfer title but that in reality does not. *Bradley v. Gordon,* 240 Ala. 556, 200 So. 736 (1941); *Bowles v. Lowery,* 181 Ala. 603, 62 So. 107 (1913). Under § 6-5-200(a)(1), color of title, as opposed to a rightful claim to title, requires only that a deed or other writing purporting to convey title be recorded in the probate office of the county where the land lies and that it has been recorded for 10 years before the action is filed. *Lewis v. Hardin,* 512 So.2d 96 (Ala.1987). Color of title is only a facade-it is the appearance that matters and not what is behind it. Generally, even a defective, irregular, or void deed can constitute color of title. "Any instrument purporting to convey an interest in land may be color of title, however defective or imperfect it is, and no matter from what cause it is invalid," *Edmonson v. Colwell,* 504 So.2d 235, 236 (Ala.1987), citing *Van Meter v. Grice,* 380 So.2d 274 (Ala.1980). Moreover, void tax deeds have specifically been held to furnish color of title. *Turnham v. Potter,* 289 Ala. 685, 271 So.2d 246 (1972); *Pierson v. Case,* 272 Ala. 527, 133 So.2d 239 (1961); *Brannan v. Henry,* 142 Ala. 698, 39 So. 92 (1905). Certainly, the tax deed to John Green, Sr., appeared to convey title to the subject property. It was recorded in 1933; thus, the 10-year requirement was easily met. The tax deed, while not a valid title itself, thus appears to have the attributes necessary to constitute color of title.

* * *

* * * Therefore, we conclude that the void tax deed to John Green, Sr., provided color of title to the Greens for the purposes of § 6-5-200.

* * *

REVERSED AND REMANDED.

MADDOX, HOUSTON, KENNEDY, and LYONS, JJ., concur.

§ 2.9.2 Intent

The question we raise here is whether the intent of the claimant coming in under color of title must have a certain state of mind. In this regard, pay careful attention to the footnote in Karvonen v. Dyer.

Karvonen v. Dyer
261 F.2d 671 (Ninth Cir. 1958)

* * *

'Color of title' is a phrase of art, and its technical meaning cannot be supplied by substitution of other factors which may appear to the claimant to be just as good.[6]

The judgment of the District Court, based upon the verdicts directed against Karvonen on each of the two causes of action and against Dyer on the counterclaim, was correct.

Affirmed.

Duncan v. Gragg
242 S.W. 491 (Tex. Civ. App. 1922)

* * *

The trial court finds, and the evidence sustains the finding, that Thomas Callahan, to whom the certificate was issued and whose heirs were the grantees in the patent, was not the grandfather of A. B. Collenham, but this finding does not make the deed of A. B. Collenham a forgery, nor does it contradict the affidavits of Collingham and others to the effect that Thomas Collingham, the grandfather of A. B. Collingham, lived and died in Austin county, Tex., prior to the issuance of the patent to the land in controversy to the heirs of Thomas Collingham, and the father of A. B. Collingham often spoke of lands which his father owned in Leon county, Tex. A. B. Collingham may or may not have believed when he executed the deed to appellees that the land in controversy belonged to his grandfather, but his good faith in his claim could not affect the genuineness of his deed.

* * *

§ 2.9.3 Effect

Assuming that an adverse possessor comes in under color of title, what are the advantages? The next three cases give the answer.

Harper v. Smith
582 So.2d 1089 (Ala.1991)

* * *

In Alabama there are basically two types of adverse possession: statutory adverse possession and adverse possession by prescription. Both require common elements of

---

[6] 'One cannot make his own title.' Pacific Coast Co. v. James, 5 Alaska 180, affirmed 9 Cir., 234 F.2d 595.

open, notorious, hostile, continuous, and exclusive possession under a claim of right. In addition, statutory adverse possession requires 10 years of actual possession and requires that the possessor have held under color of title, have paid the taxes on the property for 10 years, or have derived his title by descent or devise. Ala.Code 1975, § 6-5-200. *Tidwell v. Strickler,* supra; *Downey v. North Alabama Mineral Development Co.,* 420 So.2d 68 (Ala.1982). Adverse possession by prescription requires possession characterized by all five of the standard elements, i.e., that the possession be open, notorious, hostile, continuous, and exclusive, and that the possession be under a claim of right for a period of 20 years.

* * *

Territory v. Pai-a
34 Haw. 722 (1938)

* * *

It is recognized in this jurisdiction that an oral transfer is sufficient to authorize tacking. (*Kapiolani Est.* v. *Kaneohe R. Co.,* 14 Haw. 643, 646; *Kainea* v. *Kreuger,* 31 Haw. 108, 117.) So if the occupancy of the property by both Kapahu and Kaui was hostile to the owner, by tacking to the possession of Kapahu that of her successor, the appellant, the total period of ten years required by the statute had expired before the Territory became interested in the property, it being recognized of course that prescriptive title cannot be acquired against the government and therefore the moment the Territory acquired title from the owners the running of the statute, if it in fact had been set in motion, was stayed. (*United States* v. *Nashville R'y. Co.,* 118 U. S. 120, 126.)

The trial judge held that in order to prevail over the owner of the paper title, namely, the government, the burden was upon the appellant to show affirmatively that the possession through which she claimed title was hostile to the true owners and that the evidence introduced at the trial was insufficient to establish such hostility. Thus the character of the possession relied upon by appellant, that is, whether or not such possession was hostile, becomes the controlling issue in this appeal.

The appellant does not claim that Kapahu went into possession of or occupied the property in question under any color of title. This fact is commented upon by the trial judge as having bearing upon appellant's claim of hostility of possession. The court indicated that the absence of a showing of color of title was a circumstance which detracted from the strength of appellant's attempt to show hostility. It is the rule in this jurisdiction that color of title is not indispensable to prove title by adverse possession if the other necessary elements, namely, actual, open, notorious, continuous and exclusive possession for the statutory period as the apparent owner, are shown to exist, and is not explained. (*Albertina* v. *Kapiolani Estate,* 14 Haw. 321, 325. And see also 2 C. J. 172, 173.) Color of title reflects the character of the occupant's possession and if shown to exist is unquestionably an element tending to prove hostility of possession.

* * *

Birchfield v. Thiercof
5 Ariz.App. 484 (Ct.App. 1967)

* * *

That the plaintiffs may have had some 'color of title' under their unrecorded deed is of no avail because:

'While color of title may not be necessary to give title by adverse possession, it is required to extend an *actual possession* of a part of a tract of land constructively over the rest of it. *However, color of title, without adverse possession thereunder, does not operate to give constructive possession.*' (Emphasis added.) 3 Am.Jur.2d Adverse Possession s 106, p. 190.

And see 2 C.J.S. Adverse Possession § 60 (c), p. 581.

* * *

§ 2.10 Payment of Taxes

In some jurisdictions, one of the elements for acquiring title by adverse possession is that the claimant must pay the property taxes for the property in question.

Scott v. Gubler
95 Idaho 441 (1973)

* * *

The district court found that from 1959, the year that the fence was built, until 1968, when the fence was torn down, Mrs. Scott [the one claiming title by adverse possession] and her husband had paid all the taxes levied by the Jerome County Assessor on Lot 4 [which was owned by the Scotts]. He concluded that all the requirements of I.C. § 5-210 had been met and that the payment of all the taxes levied on Lot 4 by the Jerome County Assessor constituted payment of taxes on all the land actually being occupied as Lot 4, including the disputed land. We consider this conclusion to be correct.

Only a minority of American jurisdictions have enacted statutes which require payment of taxes on adversely claimed land as a prerequisite of obtaining title by adverse possession. See Comment, Payment of Taxes as a Condition of Title by Adverse Possession: A Nineteenth Century Anachronism, 9 Santa Clara Lawyer, 244, 249-50 (1969). * * *

* * *

§ 2.11 Disabilities

If the true owner was under a "disability" at the time the actual entry was made, the period of limitations does not begin to run. The next two cases illustrate and explain this principle.

Abel v. Abel

245 Iowa 907 (1954)

Record title is in the name of John W. Abel, Sr. Plaintiff is the wife of George C. Abel, John's son. The plaintiff claims title to property on the theory of adverse possession. Importantly, John was adjudicated insane during the time that George's adverse possession began (when the actual entry was made).

* * *

II. The claim of ownership by adverse possession encounters many insurmountable obstacles. * * *

* * * [W]e think no ownership by adverse possession could have been acquired by George C. Abel while his father, the holder of the legal title, was under adjudication of insanity. A prescriptive right arises upon the theory of a grant by the title holder; that is to say, it is assumed through long and hostile possession under claim of right or color of title that the occupant holds under a grant from the former owner. But an insane person cannot make a valid grant. The reason for the theory of prescriptive rights fails when the holder of the legal title was at the time of the taking of possession by the claimant and throughout the running of the time required incompetent to make a conveyance. 1 Am.Jur., Adverse Possession, section 19, and cases cited; 2 C.J.S., Adverse Possession, § 5, pp. 514, 515; Callison v. Wabash Railway Company, 219 Mo.App. 271, 275 S.W. 965, 969.

An allied rule is that the true owner must have knowledge, actual or constructive, of the hostile possession. 2 C.J.S., Adverse Possession, § 45, pp. 558, 559. No presumption of a grant may arise when the title holder had no knowledge or means of knowledge of the possession and of the claim being made. It is evident that an insane person, confined in a state hospital some distance from the land, could not be charged with such knowledge.

The running of the statute is tolled when the owner is insane at the time of the commencement of the possession alleged to be adverse to him, at least for so long as such insanity continues uninterrupted. 44 C.J.S., Insane Persons, § 105, and cases cited in notes 75 and 76 thereunder; 1 Am.Jur., Adverse Possession, section 22.

* * *

Commercial Bank & Trust Co. v. Jordan

278 P. 832 (Mont. 1929)

The plaintiff, who claims title by adverse possession, made his actual entry during the lifetime of John Asbury, who was the holder of record title. Before the ten-year statute of limitations lapsed, John died in 1915. His heirs were his minor daughters. They did not pursue any action before the ten-year period of limitations lapsed.

* * *

The bar of the statute is here complete unless the minority of the defendants Dorothy Asbury Jordan and Elizabeth Augusta Asbury prevented the running of the statute [of limitations]. The record discloses that on July 3, 1915, Dorothy Asbury Jordan was about 15 years of age and Elizabeth Augusta Asbury was 17 years of age. The record shows that John F. Asbury died in December, 1915, and that plaintiff took adverse possession of the property during the lifetime of John F. Asbury and with his knowledge. The cause of action here pleaded by the defendants Dorothy Asbury Jordan and Elizabeth Augusta Asbury, therefore, arose during the lifetime of their ancestor, John F. Asbury, through whom they claim. The rule is that when the statute of limitations has commenced to run against a claim, its operation is not suspended by the subsequent death of the one in whose favor the cause of action accrued, because of the minority of his heirs. Thus, in 2 C. J. 118, it is said: "If an adverse possession commences in the lifetime of an ancestor it will continue to run against the heir notwithstanding any existing disability on the part of the latter, where the right accrues to him or to her. Although they are infants, married women, or persons of unsound mind, they are nevertheless bound to sue before the expiration of the statutory period just as much as their ancestor would have been had he lived." To the same effect are Scallon v. Manhattan, etc., Co., 185 N. Y. 359, 78 N. E. 284, 7 Ann. Cas. 168; Westphal v. Arnoux, 51 Cal. App. 532, 197 P. 395; Hardin v. Swinney, 214 Ky. 793, 284 S. W. 75; Huling v. Moore (Tex. Civ. App.) 194 S. W. 188; Street v. Shaddix, 197 Ala. 446, 73 So. 73; Kidd v. Browne, 200 Ala. 299, 76 So. 65; Garner v. Wingrove, 2 Ch. 233, 3 Ann. Cas. 837; McDonald v. Hovey, 110 U. S. 619, 4 S. Ct. 142, 28 L. Ed. 269.

The evidence discloses that the causes of action pleaded by the defendants Dorothy Asbury Jordan and Elizabeth Augusta Asbury are barred by the statute of limitations. Since these defendants have no right, title, or interest in the property in question, it follows that defendant Marcia E. Stocker, who by her own testimony claims but the right to repurchase from them, has no right, title, or interest therein.

The judgment is affirmed.

§ 2.12 Boundary Line Disputes

If White owns Whiteacre and Black owns adjoining Blackacre, and they have a dispute as to where their respective boundary line is, several theories are available to resolve the problem. King v. Carden *tells us what the theories are.*

King v. Carden
237 So.2d 26 (Fla. App. 1970)

* * *

In the absence of an instrument in writing, lands may sometimes be acquired through the acts and conduct of abutting property owners which require the application of an equitable estoppel. The general principles of law that have evolved under this doctrine have been characterized as (1) adverse possession, (2) boundary by agreement, and (3) boundary by acquiescence. The doctrine of adverse possession has not been invoked in the instant cause so it will not be considered. Boundary by agreement requires allegation and proof of three elements: 1. Uncertainty or dispute as to the true boundary, 2. An agreement that a certain line will be treated by the parties as the true line, and 3. Subsequent occupation by the parties in accordance with that agreement for a period of time sufficient to show a settled recognition of the line as the permanent boundary. Boundary by acquiescence involves at least two elements: 1. A dispute from which it can be implied that both parties are in doubt as to the boundary, and 2. Continued occupation and acquiescence in a line other than the true boundary for a period of more than the statute of limitations. Therefore, a salient element that requires proof for either the doctrine of boundary by agreement or boundary by acquiescence is a dispute between the abutting property owners as to the boundary line. McRae Land and Timber Co. v. Ziegler [citation omitted] held:

'It is clear that coterminous landowners cannot conclusively establish as a boundary between their lands a line which they know not to be the true one, except by an agreement in writing based on a proper consideration, and containing words of conveyance, unless a true line is uncertain or disputed.'

* * *

CHAPTER 3
SIMULTANEOUS OWNERSHIP: COTENANCIES

§ 3.1 Types of Cotenancies

In the previous chapters, we have seen how possession is an important aspect of property law. In this chapter, we learn how two or more people may own one tract of real property and how each of them has, as a fascinating characteristic of a cotenancy, a right to possess the whole of the property. (Individuals may also own an interest in other types of property, such as stock or bank accounts, as co-tenants.)

U.S. v. Craft
535 U.S. 274 (2002)

The Internal Revenue Service seized the proceeds from the sale of certain property held by a husband and wife as tenants by the entirety because the husband owed federal income taxes. In discussing whether the IRS could lawfully do this, the court examined the nature of various cotenancies: the tenancy in common, joint tenancy, and tenancy by the entirety.

* * *

III

We turn first to the question of what rights respondent's husband had in the entireties property by virtue of state law. In order to understand these rights, the tenancy by the entirety must first be placed in some context.

English common law provided three legal structures for the concurrent ownership of property that have survived into modern times: tenancy in common, joint tenancy, and tenancy by the entirety. 1 G. Thompson, Real Property § 4.06(g) (D. Thomas ed. 1994) (hereinafter Thompson). The tenancy in common is now the most common form of concurrent ownership. 7 R. Powell & P. Rohan, Real Property §51.01[3] (M. Wolf ed. 2001) (hereinafter Powell). The common law characterized tenants in common as each owning a separate fractional share in undivided property. *Id.,* § 50.01[1]. Tenants in common may each unilaterally alienate their shares through sale or gift or place encumbrances upon these shares. They also have the power to pass these shares to their heirs upon death. Tenants in common have many other rights in the property, including the right to use the property, to exclude third parties from it, and to receive a portion of any income produced from it. *Id.,* §§ 50.03-50.06.

Joint tenancies were the predominant form of concurrent ownership at common law, and still persist in some States today. 4 Thompson § 31.05. The common law characterized each joint tenant as possessing the entire estate,[1] rather than a fractional share: "[J]oint-tenants have one and the same interest . . . held by one and the same undivided possession." 2 W. Blackstone, Commentaries on the Laws of England 180 (1766). Joint tenants possess many of the rights enjoyed by tenants in common: the right to use, to exclude, and to enjoy a share of the property's income. The main difference between a joint tenancy and a tenancy in common is that a joint tenant also has a right of automatic inheritance known as "survivorship." Upon the death of one joint tenant, that tenant's share in the property does not pass through will or the rules of intestate succession; rather, the remaining tenant or tenants automatically inherit it.[2] Id., at 183; 7 Powell § 51.01[3]. Joint tenants' right to alienate their individual shares is also somewhat different. In order for one tenant to alienate his or her individual interest in the tenancy, the estate must first be severed-that is, converted to a tenancy in common with each tenant possessing an equal fractional share. Id., § 51.04[1]. Most States allowing joint tenancies facilitate alienation, however, by allowing severance to automatically accompany a conveyance of that interest or any other overt act indicating an intent to sever. Ibid.

A tenancy by the entirety is a unique sort of concurrent ownership that can only exist between married persons. 4 Thompson § 33.02. Because of the common-law fiction that the husband and wife were one person at law (that person, practically speaking, was the husband, see J. Cribbet et al., Cases and Materials on Property 329 (6th ed. 1990)), Blackstone did not characterize the tenancy by the entirety as a form of concurrent ownership at all. Instead, he thought that entireties property was a form of single ownership by the marital unity. Orth, Tenancy by the Entirety: The Strange Career of the Common-Law Marital Estate, 1997 B.Y.U.L. Rev. 35, 38-39. Neither spouse was considered to own any individual interest in the estate; rather, it belonged to the couple.

Like joint tenants, tenants by the entirety enjoy the right of survivorship. Also like a joint tenancy, unilateral alienation of a spouse's interest in entireties property is typically not possible without severance. Unlike joint tenancies, however, tenancies by the entirety cannot easily be severed unilaterally. 4 Thompson § 33.08(b). Typically, severance requires the consent of both spouses, id., § 33.08(a), or the ending of the marriage in divorce, id., § 33.08(d). At common law, all of the other rights associated with the entireties property belonged to the husband: as the head of the household, he could control the use of the property and the exclusion of others from it and enjoy all of the income produced from it. Id., § 33.05. The husband's control of the property was so extensive that, despite the rules on alienation, the common law eventually provided that he could unilaterally alienate entireties property without severance subject only to the wife's survivorship interest. Orth, supra, at 40-41.

With the passage of the Married Women's Property Acts in the late 19th century granting women distinct rights with respect to marital property, most States either abolished the tenancy by the entirety or altered it significantly. 7 Powell § 52.01[2].

---

[1] [The court actually means—amazingly—that each tenant actually owns the whole of the estate; any type of cotenancy allows any tenant to possess the whole. See also footnotes 7 and 8, infra.]

[2] [See footnotes 7 and 8, infra.]

Michigan's version of the estate is typical of the modern tenancy by the entirety. Following Blackstone, Michigan characterizes its tenancy by the entirety as creating no individual rights whatsoever: "It is well settled under the law of this State that one tenant by the entirety has no interest separable from that of the other . . . . Each is vested with an entire title." *Long v. Earle*, 277 Mich. 505, 517, 269 N.W. 577, 581 (1936). And yet, in Michigan, each tenant by the entirety possesses the right of survivorship. Mich. Comp. Laws Ann. § 554.872(g) (West Supp. 1997), recodified at § 700.2901(2)(g) (West Supp. Pamphlet 2001). Each spouse-the wife as well as the husband-may also use the property, exclude third parties from it, and receive an equal share of the income produced by it. See § 557.71 (West 1988). Neither spouse may unilaterally alienate or encumber the property, *Long v. Earle, supra*, at 517, 269 N.W., at 581; *Rogers v. Rogers*, 136 Mich.App. 125, 134, 356 N.W.2d 288, 292 (1984), although this may be accomplished with mutual consent, *Eadus v. Hunter*, 249 Mich. 190, 228 N.W. 782 (1930). Divorce ends the tenancy by the entirety, generally giving each spouse an equal interest in the property as a tenant in common, unless the divorce decree specifies otherwise. Mich. Comp. Laws Ann. § 552.102 (West 1988).

In determining whether respondent's husband possessed "property" or "rights to property" within the meaning of 26 U.S.C. § 6321, we look to the individual rights created by these state law rules. According to Michigan law, respondent's husband had, among other rights, the following rights with respect to the entireties property: the right to use the property, the right to exclude third parties from it, the right to a share of income produced from it, the right of survivorship, the right to become a tenant in common with equal shares upon divorce, the right to sell the property with the respondent's consent and to receive half the proceeds from such a sale, the right to place an encumbrance on the property with the respondent's consent, and the right to block respondent from selling or encumbering the property unilaterally.

* * *

Note

Typically, where spouses own property as tenants by the entirety, the property cannot be encumbered for the debts of one spouse. See *In re Sauders*, 365 F.Supp. 1351 (W.D. Va. 1073). Conversely, if owners, including spouses, own property as tenants in common or joint tenants, the property can be encumbered for the debts of one of the owners.

§ 3.2 Characteristics, Creation, Termination

With the introduction given in U.S. v. Craft, *we now proceed to examine in greater depth joint tenancies, tenancies in common, and tenancies by the entirety: their characteristics, how they are created, and how they may be terminated.*

§ 3.2.1 Joint Tenancies and Tenancies in Common

Simonich v. Wilt
197 Kan. 417 (1966)

This short excerpt identifies the "four unities" needed to create a joint tenancy under the common law (which still is the law today in a number of jurisdictions).

* * *

At common law and also under the law as it generally prevails at present, the creation and the continued existence of a joint tenancy depends upon the coexistence of four requisites, namely: The tenants must have one and the same interest; the interests must accrue by one and the same instrument or conveyance; they must commence at one and the same time; and the property must be held by one and the same undivided possession. In other words, there must be the following four unities: (1) unity of interest; (2) unity of title; (3) unity of time; and (4) unity of possession.[3] If any one of these elements is lacking, the estate will not be one in joint tenancy. (20 Am.Jur.2d, Cotenancy and Joint Ownership, § 4; and Baade v. Ratner, 187 Kan. 741, 359 P.2d 877.)

* * *

Note

If A, B, and C are joint tenants and C makes a conveyance to D, the conveyance will sever the joint tenancy interest of D. Thus, as between A and B, they remain joint tenants. D, however, is a tenant in common with A and B. Thus, on D's death, D's heir, E, would inherit D's interest. On A's death, B remains the owner of the joint tenancy property by right of survivorship. Thus, on A's death, B has a two-thirds ownership interest and E has a one-third ownership interest, as tenants in common.

Taylor v. Canterbury
92 P.3d 961 (Colo. 2004)

In this case, A and B own Blackacre as joint tenants with right of survivorship, and A attempted to terminate the joint tenancy (so that A and B end up as tenants in common) by unilaterally conveying to himself. Thus, A and B own Blackacre as joint tenants, and A conveys, "to A and B as tenants in common." Initially, the court examines the history of how joint tenancies could be created under the common law and then examines the modern approach. The court then examines how a joint tenancy could be terminated under the common law and then examines the modern approach—and recognizes that today one may indeed terminate a joint tenancy by unilaterally conveying to oneself.

---

[3] [The "four unities" of time, title, interest, and possession are explained in *Taylor v. Canterbury, infra.*]

Justice KOURLIS delivered the Opinion of the Court.

I. INTRODUCTION

The question we address in this case is whether one joint tenant may extinguish a joint tenancy by conveying his interest in real property back to himself as a tenant in common. In the past, courts did not honor such transactions because of two premises: one, that someone could not be both a grantor and a grantee in the same real property transaction; and two, that in order to extinguish a joint tenancy, a joint tenant had to destroy one of the "four unities" of time, title, interest, or possession.

What is not at issue in this opinion is whether a joint tenant may destroy a joint tenancy without the consent of the other joint tenant or tenants. It is indisputable under Colorado law that one joint tenant may unilaterally dissolve the survivorship interest by creating a tenancy in common in lieu of a joint tenancy. However, for a joint tenant to sever the joint tenancy yet remain an owner of the property, courts [under the common law] required the use of a "strawman" transaction whereby the joint tenant executed a deed to a third person, and then a deed back from that third person to the joint tenant--this time as a tenant in common. By transferring legal title to the property held in joint tenancy to a third party, the transferor destroyed the unities of time and title and severed the joint tenancy.

We conclude that this circuitous process is no longer required under Colorado law because the two premises undergirding it are no longer valid. In Colorado and other jurisdictions around the country, joint tenancy law has evolved. The four unities are no longer the compass; rather, the polestar by which joint tenancies are now measured is the intent of the parties. For this reason, we have recognized in recent cases that acts inconsistent with the right of survivorship operate to sever the joint tenancy. Similarly, by operation of statute, the notion that a property owner may not be both the grantor and grantee in the same transaction has evaporated. Currently, the owner of real property may create a joint tenancy by conveying real property back to himself and one or more persons as joint tenants. Hence, the common law notions that once drove the jurisprudence of joint tenancy are gone. In their place are principles that focus on the intent of the property owners.

Therefore, we find no common law or legislative support for preventing a landowner from doing directly what he can do indirectly. We hold that a joint tenant who unilaterally conveys his interest in real property back to himself, with the intent of creating a tenancy in common, effectively severs the joint tenancy as to that joint tenant and the remaining joint tenant or tenants. We reverse the court of appeals and remand the case for further proceedings consistent with this opinion.

II. FACTS AND PROCEDURAL HISTORY

Terrell Taylor (Taylor) was the owner in fee simple of a 666-acre ranch in Fremont County, Colorado.[4] The Petitioner, Noah Taylor, is the personal representative for Taylor, now deceased. On March 4, 1991, Taylor executed a warranty deed[5] that

---

[4] The facts in this case are undisputed and come to this court by stipulation of the parties.

[5] [Warranty deeds, not relevant to an understanding of this case, are discussed in chapter 7.]

conveyed that property from Taylor as sole owner to Taylor and Lucy I. Canterbury (Canterbury) as joint tenants. The validity of that deed is not in dispute.

In 1997, Taylor executed a second deed: this time a quitclaim deed[6] purporting to transfer the property back to himself and Canterbury as tenants in common. Taylor's manifest intent to sever the joint tenancy between himself and Canterbury, and to create a tenancy in common, could not have been clearer. The second deed stated: "It is my intention by this deed to sever the joint tenancy created by [the 1991 deed], and to create a tenancy in common." The deed was duly recorded on June 16, 1997--the same day it was executed. Taylor died on August 20, 1999.

Canterbury filed an action to quiet title to the property to herself as surviving joint tenant. In that complaint, she also asked the trial court to set aside the 1997 conveyance and award her damages arising out of Taylor's attempted conveyance. Following a bench trial, the trial court found that "as a matter of law, the right of survivorship interest of a joint tenant is an estate in land which vests on the creation of the joint tenancy." Relying on our decision in *Lee's Estate v. Graber,* 170 Colo. 419, 462 P.2d 492 (1969), the court concluded "that the rights of a joint tenant or joint tenants are vested and fixed at the time of the creation of the joint tenancy" and therefore the 1997 deed failed to effectively sever the joint tenancy between Canterbury and Taylor. On that basis, the court determined that "all interests which Taylor owned ... at the time of his death passed to [Canterbury] pursuant to the 1991 deed."

The court of appeals affirmed the trial court's judgment in *Canterbury v. Taylor,* 74 P.3d 457 (Colo.App.2003), holding that a joint tenant cannot effectively sever a joint tenancy by executing a deed which purports to convey title back to the two individuals as tenants in common. *Id.* at 459. Like the trial court, the court of appeals also relied on our decision in *Graber* to conclude that once a joint tenancy is created, the rights of each joint tenant are "fixed and vested." *Id.* Thus, the court concluded that Taylor's unilateral effort to sever the joint tenancy was an improper "form of dominion" over Canterbury's rights to the property. *Id.* The court also noted that Taylor's conveyance to himself was contrary to the general rule that a grantor and grantee cannot be the same person for purposes of conveying property. *Id.*

We granted certiorari to address the issue of whether it is "permissible for a joint owner of real estate to sever the joint tenancy by unilaterally conveying his interest in the property back to himself to create a tenancy in common with the other joint tenant." We answer that question in the affirmative. Therefore, we reverse the court of appeals and remand this case for further proceedings consistent with this opinion.

III. ANALYSIS

This case presents an issue of first impression in Colorado: whether the holder of an interest in joint tenancy may unilaterally sever that joint tenancy by conveying property back to himself as a tenant in common. We begin our analysis by discussing the basic characteristics of the two forms of concurrent ownership implicated in this case: tenancies in common and joint tenancies. Next, we analyze the law regarding the termination of joint tenancies in Colorado. Finally, we examine the specific subject of the validity of the transaction at issue in this case and conclude that, in light of the evolution

---

[6] [Quitclaim deeds contain no warranties. Discussion of such deeds is postponed until chapter 7.]

of joint tenancy law in Colorado and other jurisdictions throughout the country, the common law principles that once supported the prohibition against a unilateral self-conveyance no longer have vitality.

A. Tenancy in Common and Joint Tenancy

A tenancy in common is a form of ownership in which each co-tenant owns a separate fractional share of undivided property. *United States v. Craft,* 535 U.S. 274, 279-80, 122 S.Ct. 1414, 152 L.Ed.2d 437 (2002) (citing to 7 R. Powell & P. Rohan, Real Property § 50.01[1] (M. Wolf ed.2001) (hereinafter Powell)). All co-tenants share a single right to possession of the entire interest. 7 Powell, *supra,* § 50.01[1]. Each co-tenant also possesses the right to: unilaterally alienate his or her interest through sale, gift or encumbrance; to exclude third parties from the property; and to receive a portion of any income derived from the property. *Craft,* 535 U.S. at 280, 122 S.Ct. 1414.

Conversely, joint tenancy is a form of ownership in which each joint tenant possesses the entire estate,[7] rather than a fractional share. *Id.* Upon the death of one joint tenant, the remaining joint tenant or tenants automatically inherit[8] that tenant's share in the property. *Id.* ("Upon the death of one joint tenant, that tenant's share in the property does not pass through will or the rules of intestate succession; rather, the remaining tenant or tenants automatically inherit it."). This feature, called the "right of survivorship," is the principal distinction between a joint tenancy and a tenancy in common. *Bradley v. Mann,* 34 Colo.App. 135, 525 P.2d 492, 493 (1974) ("Upon the death of one of the co-tenants in joint tenancy, the entire undivided interest of the deceased passes, by operation of law, to the surviving co-tenant.").

At common law, joint tenancies were the favored form of concurrent ownership of real property. *Smith v. Greenburg,* 121 Colo. 417, 218 P.2d 514, 519 (1950). If property was conveyed to two or more persons, the law presumed that a joint tenancy was intended. 4 David A. Thomas, Thompson on Real Property § 31.06(a) (David A. Thomas ed.1994) (hereinafter Thompson). For purposes of establishing a joint tenancy, the "four unities" of time, title, interest, and possession were essential components. 7 Powell, *supra,* § 51.01[2] (citing to 2 Blackstone, Commentaries 180); *see also Tabor v. Sullivan,* 12 Colo. 136, 20 P. 437, 441 (1889) (Elliott, J., concurring) (noting that joint tenancies require the four unities of time, title, interest, and possession). This requirement meant that to create a joint tenancy, "a conveyance had to convey to two or more persons at the same time the same title to the same interest with the same right of possession." 7 Powell, *supra,* § 51.01[2]. If one of the four unities ceased to exist, a tenancy in common remained. *Riddle v. Harmon,* 102 Cal.App.3d 524, 162 Cal.Rptr. 530, 531 (1980).

---

[7] [The court here makes a mistake. While it is true that a joint tenant has a right to possess the whole (as does a tenant in common), it is critical to note that a joint tenant, unlike a tenant in common, also *owns* the whole, at least for survivorship purposes. See next footnote.]

[8] [The court again errs. The surviving joint tenant(s) does not "inherit" anything. Rather, the surviving joint tenant(s) simply remains the owner, sans the predeceased joint tenant. Inheritance is a term of art and means the people who take a decedent's estate when the decedent dies either (1) without a valid will or (2) with a valid will but the will fails to make a complete disposition of the decedent's estate. The right of survivorship of a joint tenancy cannot be defeated by a will.]

Today, in Colorado, joint tenancies are no longer the presumptive form of concurrent ownership of real property. *Greenburg*, 218 P.2d at 519. Rather, tenancies in common are favored and the very existence of the joint tenancy is circumscribed by statute. *Id*. Courts strictly construe instruments purporting to create a joint tenancy and do not recognize joint tenancies created by instruments that lack statutorily prescribed language. *In re Kwatkowski's Estate,* 94 Colo. 222, 29 P.2d 639, 640 (1934).

The requirements for establishing a joint tenancy in real property are set forth in section 38-31-101(1), 10 C.R.S. (2003). That provision states:

> No estate in joint tenancy in real property, except when conveyed or devised to executors, trustees, or fiduciaries, shall be created or established unless, in the instrument conveying the property or in the will devising the same, it is declared that the property is conveyed or devised in joint tenancy or as joint tenants. The abbreviation "JTWROS" and the phrase "as joint tenants with right of survivorship" or "in joint tenancy with right of survivorship" shall have the same meaning. Any grantor in any such instrument of conveyance may also be one of the grantees therein.

Thus, to establish a joint tenancy in Colorado, there must only be specific language evidencing the intent to create a joint tenancy. The four unities have been abolished by statute.

B. Termination of Joint Tenancies

We turn to the question of how a joint tenancy may be terminated. In that inquiry, we pause to address the notion that the interests associated with the ownership of real property held in joint tenancy are fixed and vested. That principle comes most recently from our decision in *Lee's Estate v. Graber* where we addressed the issue of whether "the gift of a joint interest in real estate held jointly with the donor is complete and irrevocable." 462 P.2d at 493. Answering that question affirmatively, we held that "[i]n the case of real property, rights under a joint tenancy are fixed and vested in the joint tenants at the time of the creation of the joint tenancy." *Id.* at 494. As a result, once a donor creates a joint tenancy, he or she may not convey or otherwise interfere with the property interests vested in the other joint tenant by virtue of the conveyance. *Id.; see also First Nat'l Bank of Southglenn v. Energy Fuels Corp.,* 200 Colo. 540, 618 P.2d 1115, 1118 (1980) ("A joint tenant cannot alienate, encumber, or transfer the interest of other joint tenants without their consent."). What *Graber* restates is the axiom that once a joint tenancy is created, each joint tenant owns a vested interest in the property, which cannot be extinguished or alienated without that particular tenant's consent.

Graber does *not* hold that the right of survivorship itself is irrevocable or "fixed and vested" and cannot be eliminated without the consent of the other joint tenant or tenants. Indeed, such a holding would fly in the face of years of precedent to the contrary. Even characterizing survivorship as a "right" is somewhat misleading. Rather, survivorship is an expectancy that is not irrevocably fixed upon the creation of the estate; it arises only upon success in the ultimate gamble--survival--and then only if the unity of the estate has not theretofore been destroyed by voluntary conveyance, by partition proceedings, by involuntary alienation under an execution, or by any other action which operates to sever the joint tenancy. *Tenhet v. Boswell,* 18 Cal.3d 150, 133 Cal.Rptr. 10, 554 P.2d 330, 334 (1976) (internal citations omitted). Thus, in order for an expectancy of a survivorship interest to become a vested right, one joint tenant must survive the death of another joint tenant during the period of time that the joint tenancy remains intact.

Hence, the right of survivorship is not fixed in such a way as to constrain a joint tenant from changing his mind and abrogating it. Rather, a joint tenant may unilaterally eliminate the survivorship element of the ownership rights, and by doing so, eliminate his own survivorship rights as well.[9] Stated otherwise, a joint tenant has the absolute right to terminate a joint tenancy unilaterally. *Carmack v. Place,* 188 Colo. 303, 535 P.2d 197, 198 (1975); *see also* 7 Powell, *supra,* § 51.04 [1].

In this case, therefore, we are not dealing with whether a joint tenant may sever the tenancy and create a tenancy in common; we are dealing with the question of how that can be accomplished. Historically, whether the severance of a joint tenancy was effective turned on the question of whether the act was sufficient to destroy any of the four unities. *Bradley,* 525 P.2d at 493. Thus, conveying the property to a third party,[10] transferring legal title into a trust,[11] executing a lien,[12] or foreclosing on a mortgage, were

---

[9] We are aware that the ability of one joint tenant to sever the tenancy risks a circumstance where a joint tenant may terminate the survivorship right of other co-tenants while retaining his or her own. For example,

> [a] joint tenant may execute an undisclosed severance, deposit the severing instrument with a third person, and instruct the third person to produce the instrument if the severing joint tenant dies first so the severed half may pass to his or her heirs or devisees. However, if the other joint tenant dies first, the secret severing instrument may be destroyed so that the surviving joint tenant will take the other half of the property by survivorship, thereby becoming owner of the entire property.

England v. Young, 233 Cal.App.3d 1, 284 Cal.Rptr. 361, 363 (1991); *see also* Samuel M. Fetters, *An Invitation to Commit Fraud: Secret Destruction of Joint Tenant Survivorship Rights,* 55 Fordham L.Rev. 173, 179 (1986). However, the possibility of such concealment exists even with the strawman requirement. We do note that after California abolished the strawman requirement in *Riddle v. Harmon,* 102 Cal.App.3d 524, 162 Cal.Rptr. 530, (1980), the California General Assembly took the opportunity to enact legislation to close this loophole. Specifically, California passed legislation requiring that all instruments purporting to unilaterally sever a joint tenancy be recorded for purposes of providing other joint tenants with constructive notice of the severance. *See England,* 284 Cal.Rptr. at 363-64; Cal. Civ.Code § 683.2 (West 2004). In the case before the court today, Taylor did record the severance deed, so we do not opine on whether the failure to do so would have made a difference.

[10] *See Carmack v. Place,* 188 Colo. 303, 535 P.2d 197, 198 (1975) ("It is well established that an owner in joint tenancy is free to convey his undivided share of property so held, and that upon conveyance by one joint tenant to a third party, the latter becomes a tenant in common with the remaining joint tenant(s).").

[11] *See Reiss v. Reiss,* 45 Cal.App.2d 740, 114 P.2d 718, 722 (1941) (holding that the transfer of legal title of property held in joint tenancy to a trust effectively severed the joint tenancy).

all considered to be effective means of severing a joint tenancy. We also specifically recognized the antiquated convention whereby the joint tenant wishing to terminate a joint tenancy would convey the property to a strawman who would in turn reconvey the property back to the former joint tenant as a tenant in common. *Alden v. Alden*, 155 Colo. 51, 393 P.2d 5, 6 (1964). The rationale underlying all of these transactions was that because legal title was transferred, the unities of time and title were destroyed, and therefore the joint tenancy, and the survivorship interest associated with it, were destroyed as well.

Along these same lines, mortgages,[13] leases, and other encumbrances[14] that did not involve the transfer of legal title were considered insufficient to sever a joint tenancy. Again, the underlying rationale was that because the grantor had not transferred title to the real property, the unities remained intact and the transaction did not sever the joint tenancy.

In stark contrast to traditional common law, "[t]he modern tendency is to not require that the act of the co-tenant be destructive of one of the essential four unities of time, title, possession or interest before a joint tenancy is terminated." *Mann v. Bradley,* 188 Colo. 392, 535 P.2d 213, 214 (1975). In *Mann,* we recognized that a joint tenancy may be terminated by mere agreement between the joint tenants, despite the fact that no property is conveyed or interests alienated. *Id.* Thus, in determining whether a joint tenancy has been created or severed, we look not to the four unities, but rather to the intent of the parties. *Id.* at 214-15; *see also Mangus v. Miller,* 35 Colo.App. 115, 532 P.2d 368, 369 (1974). Actions that are inconsistent with the right of survivorship may terminate a joint tenancy. *Mann,* 535 P.2d at 214-15.

C. Unilateral Self-Conveyance

As we have noted, historically, a joint tenant wishing to sever the joint tenancy used a strawman transaction. That method satisfied the common law proscription that "a conveyance to oneself has no legal consequence and therefore does not destroy any unities." Thompson, *supra,* § 31.08(b). This "two-to-transfer" artifice stemmed from the English common law feoffment ceremony with livery of seisin. *Riddle,* 162 Cal.Rptr. at 533. Under the livery of seisin, the grantor of property had to transfer a physical remnant of the land (such as a lump of dirt or a twig) to the grantee. Therefore, the grantor could not be both grantor and grantee simultaneously.

---

[12] *See First Nat'l Bank of Southglenn v. Energy Fuels Corp.,* 200 Colo. 540, 618 P.2d 1115, 1118 (1980) (holding that joint tenancy is severed when interest of joint tenant in real property is subject to execution and sale by a judgment creditor).

[13] Some authority supports the position that in a title theory state, the mere act of mortgaging a piece of property is sufficient to sever a joint tenancy because legal title to the property is actually transferred. 7 R. Powell & P. Rohan, Real Property § 51.04[1][c] (M. Wolf ed.2001). However, in lien theory states such as Colorado, *see* § 38-35- 117, 10 C.R.S. (2003), merely mortgaging property does not transfer legal title and is therefore insufficient to sever a joint tenancy. *See* Powell, *supra,* § 51.04[1][c]. [Mortgages are discussed in chapter 9.]

[14] *See Webster v. Mauz,* 702 P.2d 297, 298 (Colo.App.1985) (stating that merely encumbering one's own interest in joint tenancy is insufficient to sever a joint tenancy).

In light of the changes to joint tenancy law in Colorado, the justifications for prohibiting unilateral self-conveyances no longer exist. For example, section 38-31-101 expressly allows the owner of property to become both the grantor and the grantee for purposes of establishing a joint tenancy. This concept directly conflicts with the four unities doctrine and the notion that one could not be a grantor and a grantee. Further, the livery of seisin requirement has been explicitly abolished in Colorado. § 38-30-103, 10 C.R.S. (2003). In short, none of the underpinnings that led to the artifice of a third-party transfer to sever a joint tenancy have continuing vitality.

Other jurisdictions have similarly concluded that it no longer makes sense to prohibit joint tenants from doing directly what they are already able to do indirectly through a strawman transaction. For instance, in *Hendrickson v. Minneapolis Fed. Sav. & Loan Ass'n,* 281 Minn. 462, 161 N.W.2d 688 (1968), the Supreme Court of Minnesota rejected the strawman requirement. The court in that case recognized the validity of a "Declaration of Election to Sever Survivorship of Joint Tenancy" by one joint tenant for purposes of severing the joint tenancy. *Id.* at 689.

Similarly, California has rejected the strawman requirement. *Riddle,* 162 Cal.Rptr. at 534. In that case, the court addressed a unilateral self-conveyance like the one at issue here. There, the court relied heavily on the fact that California, like Colorado, allowed for the creation of a joint tenancy by a self-conveyance. *Id.* at 532. In deciding that the grantor need not make use of a strawman to sever the joint tenancy, the court stated that "[i]n view of the rituals that are available to unilaterally terminate a joint tenancy, there is little virtue in steadfastly adhering to cumbersome feudal law requirements." *Id.* at 534. Quoting Justice Holmes, the court went on to state that

> [i]t is revolting to have no better reason for a rule of law than that so it was laid down in the time of Henry IV. It is still more revolting if the grounds upon which it was laid down have vanished long since, and the rule simply persists from blind imitation of the past.

Id.

Since *Harmon,* other states addressing this issue have followed suit. *See Minonk State Bank v. Grassman,* 95 Ill.2d 392, 69 Ill.Dec. 387, 447 N.E.2d 822, 825 (1983) (holding that conveyance of a joint tenant's property back to herself effectively severed the joint tenancy); *In re Estate of Knickerbocker,* 912 P.2d 969, 976 (Utah 1996) (holding that a joint tenant may effectively sever a joint tenancy by executing and recording a unilateral self-conveyance).

The exception is Nebraska. In *Krause v. Crossley,* 202 Neb. 806, 277 N.W.2d 242, 246 (1979), the Supreme Court of Nebraska disallowed the severance of a joint tenancy by a joint tenant who attempted to reconvey property to himself as tenant in common. That court specifically relied upon the notion that in order for title of property to transfer, the grantor and grantee had to be separate individuals. *Id.*

We note, in passing, that the Nebraska General Assembly enacted legislation the year following *Krause* specifically allowing such unilateral self-conveyances. Neb.Rev.Stat. § 76-118(4) (2004).

We conclude, in light of Colorado's statutory and precedential approach to joint tenancy, that a joint tenant may sever a joint tenancy by conveying the property to himself or herself as a tenant in common, without the need for an intermediary strawman. The statute, which permits the grantor and grantee to be one and the same, and which bypasses the four unities, does not preclude such a termination of the joint tenancy. The underlying premises that gave rise to the fiction of the strawman transaction in the first place have disappeared in the law of real property; and the law does not require a futile act. *See generally Danielson v. Zoning Bd. of Adjustment,* 807 P.2d 541, 543 n. 4 (Colo.1990). The strawman transaction does not protect the other joint tenant to any greater degree than the direct transfer, and, we repeat, the overriding consideration is that the survivorship interest is *not* vested.

IV. CONCLUSION

We reverse the court of appeals and thus the trial court's conclusion that the deed from Taylor to Taylor as a tenant in common was not valid for purposes of severing the joint tenancy. Rather, we conclude that Taylor had the right to sever the joint tenancy by means of a conveyance to himself. Taylor retained an undivided one-half interest in the property as a tenant in common at the time of his death in 1999. We return this case to the court of appeals for remand to the trial court for proceedings consistent with this opinion.

Justice COATS dissents.
Justice COATS, dissenting.

* * *

The majority looks to other states for support, but even by its count, a mere handful of states have abrogated the requirement that the interest of a joint tenant be conveyed to another in order for severance of the joint tenancy to occur. Tellingly, of the extreme minority--a mere half-dozen or so-- jurisdictions abrogating the requirement, either by case law or statute, virtually all include some recording requirement to ensure that notice is at least possible, and to limit abuses. Even if I considered the majority's policy choice to be sound, and even if I considered the court free to make that choice in light of existing legislation, I would nevertheless be reluctant to strike down well-established formalities without replacing them with other protections, as the legislature has done with regard to the creation of joint tenancies.[15]

Because I believe the court's action in striking down a principle of property law accepted for scores, if not hundreds, of years and validated by our own legislature is neither wise nor the proper function of the judiciary, I respectfully dissent.

---

[15] Although permitting termination of joint tenancies by a self-conveyance comports with a preference for effectuating intention, it does permit one joint tenant to attempt to gain an advantage over the other by executing the self-conveyance and delivering it to an heir or devisee with instructions to record it, but only if, the self-conveyor dies first, in which case the severance will be effective and the interest will pass by intestacy or devise; if the self-conveyor survives the other joint tenant, the self-conveyance can be suppressed and the survivor take all by right of survivorship. In consequence, some states require recording for effectiveness of self-conveyances. Thomas, § 31.06(d), at 24.

Note

The court in *Taylor v. Canterbury* discusses whether a mortgage executed by one joint tenant alone will sever a joint tenancy. A borrower executes a mortgage to a lender to secure or collateralize the repayment of a loan. Many jurisdictions have addressed whether a mortgage given by one joint tenant unilaterally is a conveyance of that tenant's title to the property that severs the joint tenancy. The determination depends on whether the jurisdiction follows the lien theory or title theory of mortgages. Under the majority approach, a mortgage placed on property is merely a lien, and it does not sever the joint tenancy. See, e.g., *Harms v. Sprague*, 105 Ill.2d 215 (1984) (joint tenancy is not severed because a mortgage does not sever the unity of title); *Brant v. Hargrove*, 129 Ariz. 475 (Ariz. Ct. App. 1981) (title does not pass upon granting a mortgage and it does not sever the joint tenancy). Some states have statutes following the lien theory of mortgages. See, e.g., Wis. Stat. § 700.24 (2012) (survivorship rights not destroyed but the surviving joint tenant must take the property subject to the mortgage). A minority of states follow the title theory of mortgages, which deems a mortgage to be a conveyance of title. In such case, if A and B are joint tenants and A unilaterally places a mortgage on his undivided interest, the mortgage to the lender severs the joint tenancy between A and B, who become tenants in common. We cover mortgages in Chapter 9.

§ 3.2.2 Tenancies by the Entirety

Grahl v. Davis
971 S.W.2d 373 (Tenn. 1998)

Having learned what a tenancy by the entirety is from U.S. v. Craft, *this short squib gives us additional information, including the principle that there is a presumption that property held by married persons is held as tenants by the entirety. Although many states have eliminated tenancies by the entirety, the majority of states continue to recognize this form of concurrent ownership.*

* * *

* * * [W]e begin with the well-settled proposition that tenancy by the entirety is a form of property ownership which is unique to married persons. *Griffin v. Prince*, 632 S.W.2d 532, 534 (Tenn.1982). The essential characteristic of a tenancy by the entirety is that "each spouse is seized of the whole or the entirety and not of a share, moiety, or divisible part." *Sloan v. Jones*, 192 Tenn. 400, 241 S.W.2d 506, 507 (1951). Upon the death of one spouse, ownership of tenancy by the entirety property immediately vests in the survivor, and the laws of descent and distribution do not apply. *Id.* 241 S.W.2d at 509. It is well-settled in this state that personal property as well as realty may be owned by spouses by the entirety. *Griffin*, 632 S.W.2d at 535. It has also been expressly held that a tenancy by the entirety with the right of survivorship may exist in certificates of deposit and bank accounts. *White v. Watson*, 571 S.W.2d 493, 495 (Tenn.App.1978); *Smith v. Haire*, 133 Tenn. 343, 181 S.W. 161 (1915) (certificates of deposit); *Sloan, supra,* and *Griffin, supra,* (bank accounts). In fact, there is clear authority in this state that a bank account or negotiable instrument in the name of "husband or wife" will be deemed to create a tenancy by the entirety with right of survivorship, in the absence of proof to the contrary. *Griffin*, 632 S.W.2d at 536.

* * *

Beal Bank, SSB v. Almand and Associates
780 So.2d 45 (Fla. 2001)

If a bank account is held in the name of A and B but without indicating they were married or the type of tenancy, the question is whether the account presumptively is a tenancy by the entirety. The court holds in the affirmative.

* * *

III. ANALYSIS

A. TENANCIES BY THE ENTIRETIES

To understand the key legal issues in this case, we start with an overview of the different forms of legal ownership of property in the State of Florida. Property held as a tenancy by the entireties possesses six characteristics: (1) unity of possession (joint ownership and control); (2) unity of interest (the interests in the account must be identical); (3) unity of title (the interests must have originated in the same instrument); (4) unity of time (the interests must have commenced simultaneously); (5) survivorship; and (6) unity of marriage (the parties must be married at the time the property became titled in their joint names). *See First Nat'l Bank v. Hector Supply Co.,* 254 So.2d 777, 781 (Fla.1971), *cited in Sitomer v. Orlan,* 660 So.2d 1111, 1113 (Fla. 4th DCA 1995); *see also In re Estate of Lyons,* 90 So.2d 39, 41 (Fla.1955) (citing *Andrews v. Andrews,* 155 Fla. 654, 21 So.2d 205, 206 (1945)). Because of the sixth characteristic-unity of marriage-a tenancy by the entireties is a form of ownership unique to married couples. *See Quick v. Leatherman,* 96 So.2d 136, 138 (Fla.1957), *cited in Sitomer,* 660 So.2d at 1113.

Although only a married couple is legally entitled to hold property as a tenancy by the entireties, a married couple may also hold property jointly as tenants in common or as joint tenants with right of survivorship. Tenancies in common, joint tenancies, and tenancies by the entireties all share the characteristic of unity of possession; however, tenancies in common do not share the other characteristics or unities. *See Andrews,* 21 So.2d at 206. Joint tenancies and tenancies by the entireties share the characteristic of survivorship and three additional unities of interest, title, and time. *See id.* In other words, for both joint tenancies and tenancies by the entireties, the owners' interests in the property must be identical, the interests must have originated in the identical conveyance, and the interests must have commenced simultaneously.

Although a tenancy by the entireties and joint tenancy with right of survivorship share all of the same characteristics of form, there are significant differences in the legal consequences between the forms of ownership when creditors of one spouse seek to garnish these assets, when one spouse declares bankruptcy, or when one spouse attempts to recover monies transferred without his or her permission. When a married couple holds

81

property as a tenancy by the entireties, each spouse is said to hold it "per tout," meaning that each spouse holds the "whole or the entirety, and not a share, moiety, or divisible part." *Bailey v. Smith,* 89 Fla. 303, 103 So. 833, 834 (1925). Thus, property held by husband and wife as tenants by the entireties belongs to neither spouse individually, but each spouse is seized of the whole. *See Hector Supply Co.,* 254 So.2d at 780; *Wilson v. Florida Nat'l Bank & Trust Co.,* 64 So.2d 309, 313 (Fla.1953). In a joint tenancy with right of survivorship, each person has only his or her own separate share ("per my"), which share is presumed to be equal for purposes of alienation; whereas, for purposes of survivorship, each joint tenant owns the whole ("per tout"), so that upon death the remainder of the estate passes to the survivor.

Because of this distinction between each spouse owning the whole versus each owning a share, if property is held as a joint tenancy with right of survivorship, a creditor of one of the joint tenants may attach the joint tenant's portion of the property to recover that joint tenant's individual debt. *See Sitomer,* 660 So.2d at 1114. However, when property is held as a tenancy by the entireties, only the creditors of both the husband and wife, jointly, may attach the tenancy by the entireties property; the property is not divisible on behalf of one spouse alone, and therefore it cannot be reached to satisfy the obligation of only one spouse. *See Winters v. Parks,* 91 So.2d 649, 651 (Fla.1956); *Sitomer,* 660 So.2d at 1114.

Early this century, this Court adopted the common law rule that a tenancy by the entireties may exist in both real property and personal property. *See Bailey,* 103 So. at 834. In the years following *Bailey,* this Court has continued to adhere to its holding that a tenancy by the entireties in personal property constitutes a legally recognized form of ownership. *See Hector Supply Co.,* 254 So.2d at 779-80; *Winters,* 91 So.2d at 651; *In re Estate of Lyons,* 90 So.2d at 41-42; *Hagerty v. Hagerty,* 52 So.2d 432, 434 (Fla.1951).

Despite the fact that this Court has recognized the tenancy by the entireties form of ownership in both real property and personal property, this Court has adopted different standards of proof for each. Where real property is acquired specifically in the name of a husband and wife, it is considered to be a "rule of construction that a tenancy by the entireties is created, although fraud may be proven." *Hector Supply Co.,* 254 So.2d at 780. As explained in *Hector Supply Co.,* when we reaffirmed the vitality of the tenancy by the entireties form of ownership in both real property and personal property:

> Though the modern tendency is to regard the creation of an estate by the entireties as resting, not upon a rule of law arising from the supposed incapacity of husband and wife to hold in moities, but upon a rule of construction based on the presumption of intention, it may be laid down as a general proposition that, where land [and also personalty] is conveyed to both husband and wife, they become seized of the estate thus granted *per tout et non per my* ["by the whole and not by the half"], and not as joint tenants or tenants in common. The estate thus created is, however, essentially a joint tenancy, modified by the common-law doctrine that the husband and wife are one person.

Hector Supply Co., 254 So.2d at 780 (quoting *English v. English,* 66 Fla. 427, 63 So. 822, 823 (1913)); *see Bailey,* 103 So. at 834.

In the case of ownership of real property by husband and wife, the ownership in the name of both spouses vests title in them as tenants by the entireties. *See Losey v. Losey,* 221 So.2d 417, 418 (Fla.1969).[16] Thus, "[a] conveyance to spouses as husband and wife creates an estate by the entirety in the absence of express language showing a contrary intent." *In re Estate of Suggs,* 405 So.2d 1360, 1361 (Fla. 5th DCA 1981) (citing *Losey v. Losey,* 221 So.2d 417 (Fla.1969)); *see Espenship v. Carter,* 514 So.2d 1108, 1109 (Fla. 1st DCA 1987); *Dixon v. Davis,* 155 So.2d 189, 191 (Fla. 2d DCA 1963).

Unlike real property titled in the name of both spouses that is presumptively considered to be a tenancy by the entireties as long as the other unities are established, our jurisprudence has treated bank accounts and other personal property differently.

* * *

[The court, finding that different standards of proof for real property and personal property were unjustified, "receded" from *Hector Supply Company,* and went on to hold that a bank account in the name of A and B, without indicating the type of ownership nor their marital status was presumptively a tenancy by the entirety.]

§ 3.2.3 Community Property

Smith v. Smith
12 Cal. 216 (1859)

The final type of cotenancy is community property. There are eight community property states and property acquired during marriage is presumptively community property, as this short excerpt establishes.

* * *

The law of this State in relation to the rights of husband and wife, as to the common property, is similar to the law of Louisiana and Texas; and in those States it is held, by their highest tribunals, that all property acquired, by either spouse, during the existence of the community, is *presumed* to belong to it, and that this presumption can only be overcome by clear and satisfactory proof that it was acquired by the separate funds of one or the other; and that the burden of proof lies upon the party claiming the property as separate. Lott *v.* Leach, 5 Texas, 394; Houston *v.* Civil, 8 Texas, 242; Gilliard *v.* Chesney, 13 Texas, 337; Chapman *v.* Allen, 15 Texas, 278; Claiborne *v.* Tanner, 18 Texas, 69; Ford *v.* Ford, 1 Louisiana, 207; Dominguez *v.* Lee, 17 Louisiana, 290; Smalley *v.* Lawrence, 9 Rob. 214; Fisher *v.* Gordy, 2 La. Ann. 763; Webb *v.* Peck, 7 Ann. 92.

In a case decided at the present term, (Meyer *v.* Kinzer and wife) we have had occasion to consider whether the possession of property by either spouse during the existence of the community, acquired by purchase, created a presumption that the property was common; and we arrived at a conclusion similar to that of the Louisiana and

---

[16] In addition, in the case of real property, the owners do not need to be described as husband and wife in the deed and their marital relationship does not need to be referred to in the deed in order to establish a tenancy by the entireties. *See American Cent. Ins. Co. v. Whitlock,* 122 Fla. 363, 165 So. 380, 381 (1936).

Texas cases, that the presumption of the law is, that all property belongs to the community, which can be repelled only by clear and decisive proof that it was either owned before marriage, or subsequently acquired in one of the particular ways designated in the statute; that is, by gift, bequest, devise or descent, or was taken in exchange for, or in the investment, or as the price of such property, so originally owned or acquired; and that the proof rests upon the party asserting the right.

* * *

§ 3.3 Rights and Liabilities Among Cotenants

Assume that A and B are joint tenants, tenants in common, or tenants by the entirety. Because of the cotenancy, A has certain rights against B, and B has certain rights against A. These cases explore the nature of the cotenants' rights, responsibilities, and liabilities.

§ 3.3.1 Contribution for Expenditures

Suppose A and B are cotenants with respect to Blackacre. Suppose also that only A pays for certain expenditures related to the cotenancy. The problem we address in this series of cases is whether A has a claim for "contribution" (reimbursement) against B.

Meckler v. Weiss
80 So.2d 608 (Fla. 1955)

A and B own Blackacre as cotenants, and Blackacre is encumbered with a mortgage. A pays the entire mortgage (or pays more than his pro-rata share of the mortgage), and files an action for contribution against B. The question in Meckler v. Weiss *is whether A will prevail against B in A's action for contribution.*

DREW, Chief Justice.
The original plaintiff appeals from a final order dismissing with prejudice his amended complaint in equity. In substance it was alleged that appellant and appellee, as cotenants, each owned an undivided one-half interest in real estate upon which they executed jointly a note and third mortgage to evidence and secure a debt which was their equal responsibility and that after maturity of the debt appellant without reimbursement from appellee paid the entire amount due and obtained a satisfaction of the mortgage. Thereafter appellant conveyed his undivided one-half interest to a third party who is not a party to nor involved in this litigation. Appellant prayed that the security of the third mortgage be kept alive and enforced in equity as a lien against appellee's undivided one-half interest in the property for his proportionate share of the mortgage debt which had been paid by appellant.

While there is much to be desired in the draftsmanship of the complaint, the facts alleged are sufficient to establish a right to a lien on appellee's interest in the property by way of subrogation in equity. See Jones v. Carpenter, 90 Fla. 407, 414, 106 So. 127, 129,

43 A.L.R. 1409; where we noted that equitable liens are based upon the doctrine of estoppel and 'arise in cases of expenditures by one joint owner on real or other property * * *.' This result conforms to the general rule applicable to co-obligors that as between them, when one of them pays more than his proportionate share of the debt owed by both, the payer is entitled to contribution from the other; and where the entire obligation has been discharged the payor in addition to an action at law for restitution is entitled to be subrogated to the position of the creditor but his right of recovery by means of subrogation is limited to contribution if between them neither had a prior duty of performance. * * * But appellant's right of recovery in equity being 'limited to contribution,' he is not entitled to fees for services of his attorney in this suit.

The mere fact that the appellant has conveyed his undivided one-half interest to another does not deprive him of his equitable lien on the undivided one-half interest of his former cotenant because the interest of appellant's vendee is in no way affected by this suit and rights of bona fide purchasers for value and without notice are not involved. See Martin v. Carlisle, 46 Okl. 268, 148 P. 833, 6 A.L.R. 154.

Reversed.

Janik v. Janik
474 N.E.2d 1054 (Ind.App. 1985)

In Janik v. Janik, *one cotenant pays all (or more than his pro-rata share) of the property taxes and insurance payments with respect to the cotenancy property. Again, the question is whether one cotenant who pays more than his pro rata share of payments can secure contribution from the non-paying cotenant.*

* * *

It was also error for the trial court to award Margaret [one of the two cotenants who paid all of the tax and insurance payments on the property] a credit for all tax and insurance expenses incurred following emancipation of the parties' youngest child in 1978. Generally, a tenant-in-common who has paid or assumed liens or encumbrances is entitled to proportionate reimbursement * * * . *Alleman, supra.* This right includes an accounting for money advanced to discharge taxes and assessments on the property. *Hosanna et al. v. Odishoo* (1935), 208 Ind. 132, 193 N.E. 599. In this case, the trial court awarded a credit for all tax and insurance payments, whereas Margaret is entitled only to a one-half contribution.

* * *

Lewis v. Latham
224 Miss. 107 (1955)

In Lewis v. Latham, *the court correctly states that one cotenant who pays for necessary repairs has a right of contribution. On the other hand, if the expenditure made is not for a necessary repair, but for an "improvement," reimbursement will not be allowed.*

* * *

Now 'the general rule is that a tenant in common is entitled to contribution for expenditures made for repairs which were necessary, when he acted in good faith and there was a substantial benefit to the premises * * *.' 86 C.J.S., Tenancy in Common, § 68b, Repairs, page 449. See also 14 Am.Jur. 114, Section 48; and Connolly v. McLeod, 217 Miss. 231, 63 So.2d 845.

But the ditch here in question was constructed because, after the Arkabutla Dam was built, water backed up and closed the old Cow Pen Ditch. The Federal Government contributed $5,011.12 under the PMA Program. The expenditures were not incurred in cleaning out and repairing an existing ditch; but they were used for a new construction, which was permanent in character. The generally accepted rule is that 'a cotenant who, on his own motion without the consent or agreement of his cotenants, places improvements on the common property cannot compel his cotenants to contribute to his expenditures therefor, and cannot maintain an action at law for contribution against them.' 86 C.J.S., Tenancy in Common, § 68c, Improvements, pages 450-451. See also 14 Am.Jur. 115-116, Cotenancy, Section 49. Delta Cotton Oil Company v. Lovelace, 189 Miss. 113, 196 So. 644, is not in point here for the appellants because the improvement, in that instance, was made with the cotenant's acquiescence.

Consequently the court below was correct in disallowing credit for the ditch, and in that respect, the decree is affirmed.

* * *

Hermance v. Weisner
279 N.W. 608 (Wis. 1938)

We have seen in Lewis v. Latham *that a cotenant who pays for an improvement does not have a right to contribution. But does that mean that such a tenant gets no benefit at all from his expenditure? The answer is that such a tenant may get some benefit, but the benefit is postponed until some future time, as when the cotenancy is ended (what the court calls a "partition"); there is no immediate right to contribution, however. Moreover, the amount secured by the improving cotenant is not based on the cost of the improvement. Rather, the amount secured is based on the increase in value to the cotenancy property, as* Hermance v. Weisner *makes clear.*

* * *

The next question is as to her right to have allowed to her upon partition[17] the amount by which the property has been increased in value through improvements purchased and paid for by her without accounting for rents received by her. In 47 Corpus Juris 417, the rule is thus stated: "Improvements made by tenant in common in possession may also be adjusted by setting them off as against a claim for rents and profits."

* * *

---

[17] [A partition action is one to end the cotenancy. The topic is discussed in § 3.3.6 below.]

§ 3.3.2 Rents and Profits from Third Persons

If A and B own Blackacre as cotenants and A leases Blackacre to X, who pays rent to A, the question arises as to A's liability to B for the rents received: whether A has to share net rental income with B. The Faust *case addresses this matter.*

Faust v. Faust
251 Ala. 35 (1948)

* * *

'* * * It has become a settled rule in this country that a cotenant who has received money from third persons for the use of the common property becomes a trustee for the amount collected for the benefit of his cotenants, * * *.' 14 Am.Jur. pp. 99, 100. For money so received, he must account. Henderson v. Stinson, 207 Ala. 365, 92 So. 453; 27 A.L.R. page 188. In the present case W. M. Faust, Jr. and Virginia Ragsdale took charge of the real estate, which was owned by their father, in their individual capacities and as cotenants with their brothers and sisters. There was no occasion for them as administrators to intercept the possession of the real estate from the heirs. Powell v. Labry, 210 Ala. 248, 97 So. 707. Since they held the rents which they had collected as trustees, the equity court had jurisdiction to pass on their rental account on their petition for an accounting. 65 C.J. p. 897; Rhoades v. Frazier, 124 Fla. 737, 169 So. 379.

* * *

§ 3.3.3 One Tenant in Exclusive Possession

If A and B own Blackacre as cotenants, and A is in exclusive possession of Blackacre, must A pay rent to B? The next two cases address this question.

Fundaburk v. Cody
261 Ala. 25 (1954)

This first case deals with the situation where A and B are cotenants and A is in sole possession, but A's possession is, as the court puts it, "friendly." In this context, A is not depriving B of possession. Not surprisingly, the court finds that A is not liable to B for A's sole possession.

* * *

We have consistently approved the general principle that 'a friendly occupancy of the common estate by one tenant does not render him liable to account for rents and profits.' * * *

The principle is thus stated in Rehfuss v. McAndrew, supra [250 Ala. 55, 33 So.2d 17]:

'It is also well understood that a tenant in common in possession by virtue of his own title is not liable to his cotenants for use and occupation unless he actually excludes his cotenants from the premises. * * *.'

In Warner v. Warner, supra, this court stated as follows [248 Ala. 556, 28 So.2d 710]:

'The only essential to a cotenancy or tenancy in common is a unity of possession or right of possession of the property and a cotenancy may exist in every species of property, real, personal and mixed, corporeal or incorporeal. 7 R.C.L. 815-817, paragraphs 8-10. Though a cotenant may occupy the entire property, no liability for rent or use and occupation exists in the absence of express agreement between the parties or such hostile occupancy of the whole as is tantamount to ouster of the cotenants. 7 R.C.L. pp. 828 et seq., paragraphs 22, 23 and 24; Turner v. Johnson, 246 Ala. 114, 19 So.2d 397.'

In Burk v. Burk, supra [247 Ala. 91, 22 So.2d 609], it was stated as follows:

'It is, of course, a well-recognized principle that in the absence of any agreement to compensate his co-tenants, a co-tenant who has entered upon the common property without excluding the others or interfering with their rights is under no obligation to account to them for any profits that he may have made. 14 Am.Jur. p. 102; Turner v. Johnson [246] Ala. [114], 19 So.2d 397.

* * *

The following discussion and statement of the rule is from Newbold v. Smart, supra:

'Tenants in common are seized *per my et per tout*. Each has an equal right to occupy; and unless the one in actual possession denies to the other the right to enter, or agrees to pay rent, nothing can be claimed for such occupation. Such possession by one is treated as had, with the consent and approbation of the co-tenant. 'A mere participation in the profits of land, with a joint occupation, or an occupation which does not exclude the owner from possession, will not amount to a tenancy.' Taylor's Landlord and Ten. § 24. In Badger v. Holmes, 6 Gray 118, [72 Mass. 118] the court said: 'Nothing is better settled than the rule, that the mere occupation of premises owned in common, by one of the tenants in common, does not entitle his co-tenant to call him to account, or render him in any way liable to an action for the use and occupation of the estate. Each owns the estate *per my et per tout*. If a co-tenant does not see fit to come in and occupy, the other still has the right to the enjoyment of the estate; and in such case, the sole occupation of one, is not an exclusion of the other. Each tenant, being seized of each and every part and parcel of the estate, has a right to the use and enjoyment of it; and so long as he does not hold his co-tenant out, or in any way deprive him of the occupation of the estate, he exercises only a legal right, and receives nothing for which he is bound to account to his co-tenant.' * * * In 1 Washb. on Real Prop. 570, [420], is this language:

'To render one co-tenant liable to another for rent, or for use and occupation, there must be something more than an occupancy of the estate by one, and a forbearance to occupy by the other. The tenant who merely occupies the estate does no more than he has a right to do on his own account.'

Brunscher v. Reagh
164 Cal.App.2d 174 (1958)

In this next case, A "ousts" B, meaning that A's occupation is "hostile" (to use the term used by the court in Fundaburk v. Cody) *in denying B's ownership interest. In such a case, A is liable to B. In* Brunscher v. Reagh, *the court addresses the extent of A's liability. (We address ouster in greater depth in § 3.3.5)*

* * *

It is the general rule that each tenant in common has a right to occupy the common property, and, generally speaking, one such tenant cannot recover rent from the other tenant. McWhorter v. McWhorter, 99 Cal.App.2d 293, 278 P. 454; Nevarov v. Nevarov, 117 Cal.App.2d 581, 256 P.2d 330. But this rule does not apply where one cotenant wrongfully ousts the other and prevents him from enjoying joint possession. In such event, the wrongfully ousted cotenant may recover the damages resulting from the ouster, which ordinarily are his share of the value of the use and occupation of the land during the period of the ouster. Zaslow v. Kroenert, 29 Cal.2d 541, 176 P.2d 1.

* * *

§ 3.3.4 Waste

Waste is a term of art and means, in a real shorthand definition, the destruction of the premises by one of the cotenants. (Waste can arise in other situations, too. Those situations are discussed in chapters 4 and 10.) In the next case, most cotenants (but not all the cotenants) lease out the property—a coalmine—to the Chosar Corporation and the latter extracts coal. The question for the court is whether the tenants who leased out the property can be liable to the non-consenting cotenants for waste. This court holds that the tenants who leased out the coalmine are liable to the non-consenting cotenants.

Chosar Corp. v. Owens
235 Va. 660 (1988)

Present: All the Justices.
STEPHENSON, Justice.
The principal questions in this appeal are (1) whether mining of coal owned by cotenants without the consent of all owners constitutes waste and the exclusion of the interests of the nonconsenting owners entitling them to injunctive relief * * *.

In this chancery cause, Beulah Owens and others (collectively, Owens) seek to enjoin Chosar Corporation and William H. Drake (collectively, Chosar) from mining coal in which Owens owns an undivided fractional interest and from hauling coal from the land of a third party through an underground passageway created by such mining. The trial court ruled that "the mining of coal by Chosar and its lessees ..., without the consent of all cotenants, is the commission of waste, the exclusion by [Chosar] of [Owens] from their interest in the property, and an appropriation thereof to [Chosar]." The court also ruled that fewer than all cotenants could not permit the haulage of coal, produced from other lands, through underground passages carved out of the jointly-owned coal. Consequently, the trial court permanently enjoined Chosar from such mining and haulage, ordered an accounting, and referred the cause to a special commissioner. This appeal ensued pursuant to Code § 8.01-670(B).

The relevant facts are undisputed. The coal in controversy lies within a 61-acre tract of land in Dickenson County (the Willis tract). The coal is owned by the heirs and successors in title of Andrew and Crissie Willis (collectively, Willis). At present, approximately 90 persons own undivided interests in the coal.

Approximately 85 percent of the co-owners executed leases transferring to Chosar "all their right, title and interest" in all the merchantable seams of coal on the Willis tract. The leases provided for a royalty that is the greater of two dollars per 2,000 pounds of coal or eight percent of the price obtained from the coal. The leases also granted Chosar the right to transport coal from adjoining lands through underground passageways on the leased premises.

The most valuable coal on the Willis tract is the "Splashdam seam," which is several hundred feet beneath the surface of the land. Chosar subleased the right to mine the Splashdam seam to coal operators at a royalty rate of 14 percent of the selling price. Because the Splashdam seam does not outcrop on the Willis tract, access for underground mining had to be achieved from other lands. Consequently, Chosar obtained a lease from Pittston Resources, Inc. (Pittston), to mine coal from land owned by Pittston that adjoins the Willis tract. Thus, a portal was established at the outcropping of the Splashdam seam on the Pittston tract, approximately 200 feet from the Willis tract's boundary.

The mining operation proceeded from the portal to the Willis tract, thence through the Willis tract to Pittston's land on the opposite side. Thereafter, coal mined from Pittston's property was transported underground through the passageways on the Willis tract and thence to the surface. The passageways on the Willis tract were created by the mining operation.

Although a cotenant may transfer to another his undivided interest in the common property without the consent of his cotenants, *see Va. Coal and Iron Co. v. Hylton*, 115 Va. 418, 421-22, 79 S.E. 337, 338 (1913), nonconsenting cotenants are not bound by an agreement purporting to lease the entire property or any specific portion thereof, *Phillips v. Dulany*, 114 Va. 681, 683, 77 S.E. 449, 449 (1913). A lessee claiming under such a lease acquires rights no greater than those of his lessor. *See Nickels v. Miller*, 126 Va. 59, 64, 101 S.E. 68, 70 (1919). Consequently, our inquiry here necessarily focuses upon the extent of the consenting cotenants' rights in the common coal lands.

We first consider whether Chosar's mining of the coal without the consent of all owners constituted waste. Generally, waste is defined as "[a] destruction or material alteration or deterioration of the freehold, or of the improvements forming a material part thereof, by any person rightfully in possession, but who has not the fee title or the full estate." *Black's Law Dictionary* 1425 (5th ed. 1979). At common law, a cotenant was not liable to his cotenants for waste. 2 R. Minor, *The Law of Real Property* § 879 (2d ed. 1928). The common law, however, has been changed by statute: "If a tenant in common, joint tenant or parcener commit waste, he shall be liable to his cotenants, jointly or severally, for damages." Code § 55-212. Injured parties also have a remedy at law for waste committed by "any tenant of land . . . while he remains in possession." Code § 55-211.

Notwithstanding these statutory remedies, a court of equity, in a proper case, may grant an injunction to prohibit waste. *Marble Co. v. Standard Gas Co.,* 155 Va. 249, 257-58, 154 S.E. 518, 521 (1930); *Fleenor v. Sproles,* 148 Va. 503, 508, 139 S.E. 286, 288 (1927); *Harris v. Thomas,* 11 Va. (1 Hen. & M.) 17, 18 (1806). What constitutes waste sufficient to entitle the injured party to injunctive relief depends upon the circumstances of each particular case. *Findlay v. Smith,* 20 Va. (6 Munf.) 134, 142 (1818). For example, the cutting of timber in some instances may constitute waste, while in other cases it may be a benefit. *Macaulay's ex'or v. Dismal Swamp Land Co.,* 41 Va. (2 Rob.) 507, 527-28 (1843); *Findlay v. Smith,* 20 Va. (6 Munf.) at 148-49 (Roane, J., dissenting).

In the case of tenants in common, no tenant can change or alter the common property to the injury of his cotenants without their consent. *Woods v. Early,* 95 Va. 307, 312, 28 S.E. 374, 376 (1897). Injunctive relief against a cotenant is proper where the injury is material, continuing, and not adequately remedied in damages. *Id.* at 314-15, 28 S.E. at 376-77.

In the present case, the extraction of coal from the Willis tract is a material and continuing destruction of the very substance of the mineral estate. The consenting cotenants had no right to remove coal from the common property without the consent of Owens. Consequently, the consenting cotenants could not authorize Chosar to mine coal from the property without the consent of the other cotenants. We conclude, therefore, that the trial court correctly ruled that Chosar's mining within the Willis tract constituted the commission of waste. Because continued mining would cause irreparable harm to Owens, we further conclude that the trial court properly enjoined Chosar from committing further waste.

* * *

Affirmed and remanded.

* * *

§ 3.3.5 Ouster

We previously learned in Fundaburk v. Cody *and* Brunscher v. Reagh *that an ouster of B by A subjects A to monetary liability: that A will be liable to B for one-half the fair rental value of the premises. The cases in this subsection of text explore in greater depth what an ouster is and what the consequences of an ouster are.*

Howell v. Bradford
570 So.2d 643 (Ala. 1990)

The case explores the meaning of ouster, and how A may oust B (and how the ouster can ripen into adverse possession).

* * *

The Howells claim that, regardless of the boundary established by the deed, they own the land south of the field road by adverse possession. The trial court found that Anthony and May Bradford had acquired during their lifetime three parcels of land, from which they deeded a portion to the Howells and the remainder of which comprises the estate property in this action. Although the trial court did not explicitly state that it did so, it could have determined that in relation to the estate property that the Howells claim by adverse possession, the Howells and Bradford are co-tenants. See, *Porter v. Porter,* 472 So.2d 630 (Ala.1985).

In *Beard v. Bates,* 418 So.2d 862, 864 (Ala.1982), we cited *Tyson v. Jackson,* 364 So.2d 1140, 1141-42 (Ala.1978), to explain long-settled law concerning adverse possession as between tenants in common:

" 'The rule has long been established in this jurisdiction that the possession of one tenant in common is presumed to be the possession of all; and such possession does not become adverse to the cotenant until he is actually ousted or short of ouster, the adverse character of the possession of one is actually known to the other, or the possession of one is so open and notorious in its hostility and exclusiveness as to put the cotenant on notice of its adverse character. *Foshee v. Foshee,* 278 Ala. 205, 177 So.2d 99 (1965); *Barry v. Thomas,* 273 Ala. 527, 142 So.2d 918 (1962); *Markstein v. Schilleci,* 258 Ala. 68, 61 So.2d 75 (1952); *Hames v. Irwin,* 253 Ala. 458, 45 So.2d 281 (1949); *Ratliff v. Ratliff,* 234 Ala. 320, 175 So. 259 (1937).

" 'Before the possession of a cotenant may be regarded as adverse to his cotenant, he must repudiate the cotenant's interest in the property by act or declaration. *Livingston v. Livingston,* 210 Ala. 420, 98 So. 281 (1923). This means that there must be some express denial of title and right to possession of the fellow cotenant brought home to him openly and unequivocally. *Williams v. Sinclair Refining Co.,* 39 N.M. 388, 47 P.2d 910 (1935); 86 C.J.S. Tenancy in Common § 27. In *Ratliff v. Ratliff,* supra (234 Ala. at 322, 323, 175 So. at 261), this court stated the rule as follows:

" ' "The possession of a tenant in common exercising the customary acts of ownership does not alone operate as a disseisin of cotenants; but there must be positive information of the facts, however informally communicated or acquired . . . ." ' " 418 So.2d at 864.

The trial court could permissibly have determined that the Howells failed to prove such an open, unequivocal ouster. Furthermore, there is additional evidence to justify the trial court's decision that the Howells did not adversely possess the land south of the field road. We conclude that the trial court did not err in establishing the boundary line between the Howells' property and the estate property.

The judgment is due to be affirmed.

AFFIRMED.

Cummings v. Anderson
94 Wash.2d 135 (1980)

In this case of blended families, one cotenant (a wife) refuses to live with the other cotenant (her husband), because the wife is concerned about the safety of her young children from a prior marriage. Consequently, the wife moves out and claims she was ousted by the husband. The court rules in favor of the husband.

ROSELLINI, Justice.

In September 1973, the petitioner and the respondent, contemplating marriage, bought the purchaser's interest in a contract for the sale of a single-family residence in

Enumclaw and assumed the obligations of the underlying contract. They paid $2,500 for the assignment of the purchaser's interest. The contract called for monthly payments of $150, including interest, and the payment of the balance in full on or before August 1, 1975. It provided for forfeiture upon default.

The assignment was made to the petitioner and the respondent as tenants in common, and, according to the testimony of the attorney who advised them in this transaction, they intended to acquire the property as equal owners.

The evidence showed that both parties contributed to the down payment, neither of them having assets sufficient to pay for the interest which they bought from the purchaser. They used their separate funds[18] for a part of it and obtained a loan for the balance. From the circumstances, it is evident that they planned to pay the balance owed on the real estate contract, as well as the balance of the loan, with community funds which would belong to both of them. From these facts, it can be inferred that they intended to contribute equally in the purchase of the property.

The respondent in her answer to the petition tacitly acknowledges that the obligations of the parties were equal.

In February 1974, the parties were married. They lived in the residence, with the petitioner's two teenaged children and the respondent's four younger children, until August 1974, when the respondent left the home, taking her children and substantially all of the community personalty, including the cash in the joint bank account. She was granted a default dissolution in March 1975, the decree making no disposition of the property of the parties.

At the time of the respondent's departure from the residence, the parties had paid $2,828.92 toward the purchase of the property and $16,350.16 remained to be paid. They had no discussion regarding their rights in the property or their future obligations. The respondent did not communicate with the petitioner and made no offer to participate in making the payments necessary for acquisition of the property, nor did she assert a right to occupy the property or to receive rent for the petitioner's occupancy of it. He remained in possession and continued to make the payments under the contract, paying also the taxes and insurance premiums. At the time this action was brought, he had reduced the unpaid balance to $8,763.85. He had arranged with the sellers to assume their mortgage obligations instead of paying the full balance of the purchase price in August 1975.

Shortly before the final payment became due under the original contract, the respondent, who had remarried after the dissolution, offered to purchase the petitioner's interest in the contract for the sum of $1,000. This offer was rejected. She then brought this suit for partition, claiming a one-half interest in the purchaser's equity, and demanding one-half of the rental value of the premises during the period that the residence had been occupied by the petitioner alone.

At the trial, the respondent testified she had left the premises to protect her children from involvement in and observation of the sexual activities of the petitioner's son, then in his early teens. She said that she had told the petitioner that one of them would have to leave, and he had said it would have to be her. His testimony was that she

---

[18] The respondent's only source of income, at that time, insofar as the record discloses, was child support payments.

had left the home without notice and without explanation. She did not contend that her departure had been occasioned by any conduct or omission of the petitioner.

The trial court found that the respondent had not been ousted by the petitioner. * * *

The Court of Appeals, Division One, affirmed the lower court's finding that there had been no ouster of the respondent, as well as its conclusion that the petitioner was not obliged to pay rent for his exclusive occupancy of the premises. * * *

* * *

The respondent urges reversal of the Court of Appeals upon the question of her entitlement to rent. She relies upon the conduct of the petitioner's son as constituting ouster, but cites no authority which supports that contention.

It is the rule in Washington that, in the absence of an agreement to pay rent, or limiting or assigning rights of occupancy, a cotenant in possession who has not ousted or actively excluded the cotenant is not liable for rent based upon his occupancy of the premises. Fulton v. Fulton, 57 Wash.2d 331, 357 P.2d 169 (1960). In order for ouster to exist, there must be an assertion of a right to exclusive possession. See cases cited in Annot., Accountability of cotenants for rents and profits or use and occupation, 51 A.L.R.2d 388, 438 (1957); Black's Law Dictionary 1253 (4th rev. ed. 1968).

An appealing argument is made that, in a situation such as this, where the property is not adaptable to double occupancy, the mere occupation of the property by one cotenant may operate to exclude the other. See Annot., 51 A.L.R.2d at 443.

Had the respondent not abandoned her obligations under the contract of purchase at a time when over four-fifths of the purchase price remained to be paid, we would be much inclined to agree that she is entitled to receive rent. Under the circumstances as they exist, she has not demonstrated a sufficient equitable interest to warrant this extension of the rule.

* * *

In re Marriage of Maxfield
47 Wash.App. 699 (1987)

The wife is in sole possession of the family residence and seeks to require her husband to pay one-half of the mortgage and property taxes. The court finds the husband is not liable to the wife because the wife ousted the husband.

THOMPSON, Justice.

Robert Maxfield appeals a judgment entered March 22, 1985, granting Mrs. Maxfield $12,800 on her motion for summary judgment. He also appeals the trial court's denial of his motion to stay and set aside the contempt order and judgment that was the basis for granting Mrs. Maxfield the $12,800. Mrs. Maxfield cross-appeals, contending her motion for contribution for house payments, insurance and tax costs should have been granted. We affirm in part, reverse in part.

The 25-year marriage of Joann and Robert Maxfield ended October 28, 1981 * * *. The decree ordered the family home sold and the completion of certain necessary repairs.

* * *

In her cross appeal, Mrs. Maxfield contends Mr. Maxfield should be required to pay one-half of the mortgage payments, taxes, and insurance costs incurred in maintaining the home until its eventual sale. We disagree.

Following dissolution of their marriage, Mr. and Mrs. Maxfield held the family home as tenants in common. *Fritch v. Fritch,* 53 Wash.2d 496, 502, 335 P.2d 43 (1959); *Witzel v. Tena,* 48 Wash.2d 628, 632, 295 P.2d 1115 (1956). In the absence of an agreement to pay rent, or limiting or assigning rights of occupancy, a cotenant in possession who has not ousted or actively excluded the cotenant out of possession is not liable for rent based upon her occupancy of the premises. *Fulton v. Fulton,* 57 Wash.2d 331, 357 P.2d 169 (1960). However, in this case, the court found the cost of house payments and utilities to be approximately $500 per month, and ordered Mr. Maxfield to pay that sum to his wife, up to $18,000 so that she might remain in *exclusive* possession of the home. Where the exclusive occupancy of the property by Mrs. Maxfield operated to exclude Mr. Maxfield, "ouster" had occurred. *Cummings v. Anderson,* 94 Wash.2d 135, 145, 614 P.2d 1283 (1980), recognized this theory in noting: "[W]here the property is not adaptable to double occupancy, the mere occupation of the property by one cotenant may operate to exclude the other." *See also,* Annot., *Accountability of Cotenants For Rents and Profits or Use and Occupation,* 51 A.L.R.2d 388, 443 (1957); *Palmer v. Protrka,* 257 Or. 23, 476 P.2d 185, 190 (1970). Mrs. Maxfield is thus not entitled to reimbursement for one-half the mortgage, nor is she entitled to half the taxes and insurance. This is consistent with the general rule that where one cotenant's use of property in fact excludes others, the occupying cotenant will be required to reimburse the others for rental value of their property interest. *Fulton.* The court did not err when it denied Mrs. Maxfield's motion for contribution for one-half the mortgage payments, taxes, and insurance expenses incurred in maintaining the home.

Mrs. Maxfield's request for attorney fees on appeal is denied. Reversed as to Mr. Maxfield's appeal; affirmed as to Mrs. Maxfield's cross appeal.

McINTURFF, C.J., concurs.

GREEN, Justice (dissenting).
I respectfully dissent.

* * *

§ 3.3.6 Partition

If cotenants cannot agree as to the use of the property, any joint tenant or tenant in common (but not a tenant by the entirety) has an absolute right to "partition," meaning the right to end the cotenancy. As the next case explains, there are two types of partition: in kind (where the property physically is divided up between the cotenants) or by sale (where the property is sold off and the proceeds distributed between the cotenants). The case also examines which type of partition is favored by the courts and how courts can equalize a partition in kind when the two separate parcels are not of equal value.

Dewrell v. Lawrence

58 P.3d 223 (Okla. Civ. App. Div. 2002)

CARL B. JONES, Judge:

¶ 1 This action was brought by J. Ladon Dewrell and Carol A. Dewrell (Dewrells), Appellees, for partition of 45 acres of land owned in undivided interests one-half by the Dewrells and one-half by Kathleen R. Lawrence (Lawrence), Appellant. The Dewrells and Lawrence are unrelated business partners who jointly purchased significantly improved property north of Lexington, Oklahoma (Ranch) and certain personal property located thereon. The Dewrells paid $225,000.00 cash for their undivided one-half interest. Lawrence contributed $100,000.00 of her own cash and borrowed the remaining $125,000.00 from the Dewrells under a promissory note and mortgage.

¶ 2 The Ranch has approximately 743 feet of frontage on Highway 77 and is improved with a small house, a large main barn and office, a climate controlled "show barn" used for high value show horses, a hay barn, a training track, outer and inner fencing, pipe and cable working pens and arenas. Lawrence resides on the Ranch and operates a horse breeding and showing business thereon. The Dewrells are Florida residents and do not intend to live in Oklahoma.

¶ 3 Lawrence agreed to the partition. The trial court appointed three commissioners and instructed them "to make partition of the property among the parties according to their respective interests, if such partition can be made without manifest injury." The trial court further instructed "[i]f partition cannot be made, the [c]ommissioners shall make a valuation and appraisement of the property." The commissioners reported that partition in kind could not be made according to the parties respective interests without manifest injury to the parties and they appraised the property.

¶ 4 Lawrence filed her exception to the commissioners' report urging the land can be partitioned in kind, and if not so partitioned, Lawrence would suffer "grave manifest injury." Lawrence suggested the trial court resubmit the matter to the commissioners with instructions to partition the Ranch into various tracts of uneven sizes and values so the court may allot a parcel to Lawrence thereby providing her with a place to live and maintain her livelihood. The Dewrells requested the trial court to approve the commissioners' report and order the property sold "on the courthouse steps."

¶ 5 The cause was tried with both parties presenting witnesses and documentary evidence. Lawrence testified she desired 10-acres with 343 feet of frontage and the show barn and she suggested the remaining 35-acres and improvements thereon be allotted to the Dewrells. Lawrence desired that the trial court make the necessary adjustments, under the doctrine of owelty, to balance the monetary value of the property allocated to each party.

¶ 6 Mr. Dewrell testified the Ranch is a beautiful showplace and every acre is needed to facilitate the use and utility of the improvements on the Ranch. He testified he would not recover his investment from the 35-acres because this tract was located in the flood plain and had only approximately 400 feet of frontage. Mr. Dewrell testified he wanted the property sold so that the parties can equally profit or suffer their proportionate loss on the Ranch.

¶ 7 All three commissioners testified that based on their instructions to partition according to the parties respective one-half interests and the character, location, frontage and improvements of the ranch, it could not be partitioned in kind without manifest injury. * * *

¶ 8 Upon conclusion of trial, the trial court found the Ranch was overbuilt with tremendous improvements and any attempt to equalize the partition value by cutting out a piece of the Ranch would diminish the value of the whole property. The trial court also openly questioned whether it was legally possible to instruct the commissioners to specifically appraise to partition in kind without the parties agreeing to it and prior to the commissioners rendering an initial report and opinion that the property can be partitioned in kind. The trial court announced it must place great factual deference on the opinion of the commissioners that the ranch could not be partitioned in kind. The trial court denied Lawrence's exception, approved the commissioners' report and ordered the land sold. Lawrence filed a motion for new trial which was denied and this appeal ensued.

¶ 9 We begin with an analysis of the applicable law. Partition proceedings are governed by 12 O.S.2001 § 1501.1 et seq. The right to partition is absolute and the proceeding is one of equitable cognizance; therefore, equitable principals apply. *Chesmore v. Chesmore,* 1971 OK 49, ¶ 6, 484 P.2d 516, 518. "The prevailing rule is that as between partition in kind or a sale of the land and division of the proceeds, the courts and statutes favor a partition in kind, if it can be accomplished without manifest injury to the parties." *Diehl v. Hieronymus,* 1967 OK 79, ¶ 10, 426 P.2d 368, 370-371.

* * *

¶ 12 Our standard of review in a partition action is whether the trial court's decision is either against the clear weight of the evidence, or is contrary to law. *Cain v. Christie,* 1997 OK CIV APP 7, ¶ 14, 937 P.2d 119, 122. After reviewing the evidence in the record, we find the trial court erred when it failed to exercise its authority and consider re-submitting this matter to the commissioners under new instructions to allot unequal portions of the Ranch to the parties and invoke the doctrine of owelty. *Id.* at ¶ 13.

¶ 13 Title 12 O.S.2001 § 1507 specifically authorizes that "[f]or good and sufficient reasons appearing to the court, the commissioners may be directed to allot particular portions to any one of the parties." In such event, the doctrine of owelty is available to the trial court in the exercise of its equitable powers, and the party who sought owelty is entitled to a judicial consideration of her application for same. *Chesmore,* 1971 OK 49 at ¶ 8, 484 P.2d at 519. The Oklahoma Supreme Court explained:

> I[n] making divisions along natural and practical lines the allotments cannot always be made of equal area or value, and, when an allotment is made to a party which is in excess of his share, the court may require him to pay such excess, which is called owelty, to the other co-tenants. It would seem more equitable, in a proper case, to require the payment or receipt of a reasonable sum of money than to require lands to be sold as a whole, where a proportionately small sum is required to equalize the shares. The object of partition is a division of the property; a sale of the lands is justified only when partition in kind, with or without owelty, is impractical.

Chesmore at ¶ 6, 484 P.2d at 518-519 (citations omitted).

¶ 14 The trial court was concerned that it could not resubmit this matter for appraisal of unequal allotments *unless the parties agreed*. *Chesmore* explains the trial court's error:

> The general rule of equity requiring the payment of owelty does not give defendants an absolute right to receive a share of the land set off to them in kind and pay owelty to equalize the shares awarded to plaintiffs. The rule does give the court the power to consider the application of owelty, without regard to an agreement between the parties that he may do so. Owelty, like a division of the lands in kind, is within the broad equitable powers of the court in partition proceedings. The court will not be denied the exercise of its equitable powers in partition proceedings by the failure of all parties to agree that its inherent power may be so exercised.

Id. at ¶ 7, 484 P.2d at 519 (citations omitted).

¶ 15 The commissioners should have been instructed by the trial court to consider whether an allotment of a particular portion of the ranch to Lawrence along with owelty could be accomplished without manifest injury to the parties. The trial court still has the discretion to determine Lawrence's desired 10-acre allotment along with owelty is not practicable or equitable. Accordingly, we reverse and remand to the trial court for further proceedings consistent with this opinion.

JOPLIN, V.C.J., and BUETTNER, J., concur.

§ 3.4 Looking Forward

Sims v. Sims
502 So.2d 722 (Ala. 1987)

This case does not deal with cotenancies. Rather, it serves to introduce you to another type of simultaneous ownership and as an introduction to estates in land, a subject we take up in depth in the next chapter.

* * *

The trial court having found that T.W. Sims owned the real property in question at his death, could his widow, Fannie Sims, hold adversely to the children of T.W. and Daisy Sims? Although the trial court did not make an express finding on this issue, it is nevertheless implicit in its order that Fannie Sims, as the widow of T.W. Sims, could have, under the law at the time of his death, only a life estate in his lands. Code of 1975, § 43-5-1(1) (subsequently repealed). *Worley v. Worley,* 388 So.2d 502 (Ala.1980). Defendants here, the children of T.W. and Daisy Sims and holders of a three-elevenths interest in the land of their father, were remaindermen. There can be no adverse possession by a life tenant against a remainderman. *Lucas v. Brown,* 396 So.2d 63 (Ala.1981). Thus, Fannie Sims could not have acquired title to the interests of the children of T.W. and Daisy Sims by adverse possession.

CHAPTER 4
SIMULTANEOUS OWNERSHIP: ESTATES AND FUTURE INTERESTS

§ 4.1 Introduction

In chapter 3, we learned how two or more people can own Blackacre simultaneously and how each of them has a right to possess Blackacre simultaneously (unity of possession). In this chapter, we learn that A and B own Blackacre simultaneously, but only A has a right to possess Blackacre now; while B owns Blackacre, too, B does not have a right to immediate possession. Rather, B's right of possession is postponed until sometime in the future (and, as you will see, B may never have the right to possess Blackacre).

§ 4.1.1 The Meaning of "Estates"

This chapter is going to introduce you to terms that you almost certainly never heard of before. One of these terms is "estate." In the area of property law, we often refer to X as owning an estate in Blackacre, rather than X owning Blackacre. The reason for this will become clear as we progress.

Black v. Sylvania Producing Co.
105 Ohio St. 346 (1922)

Initially, this short squib tells us what an estate denotes: the nature of the ownership right or the degree of ownership in Blackacre.

* * *

The same authority [Cyc.] (volume 16, p. 599) summarizing the definitions and applications of the term 'estate,' as used in the statute, says:

'An estate in land is the degree, quantity, nature, or extent of interest which a person has in it. While in its primary and technical sense the term 'estate' refers only to an interest in land, yet by common usage it has acquired a much wider import and application, being applied to personal property as well as realty, and in its most extreme sense signifying everything of which riches or fortune may consist. In many cases therefore its precise meaning can only be ascertained from the context, or the circumstances under which it is used. As applied to land it does not necessarily import a fee or even a freehold, but merely the quantity of interest a person has from absolute ownership to naked possession, and is applied to rights in land, both in possession. * * *'

And numerous cases are cited in support of the doctrine.

Liberty Cent. Trust Co. of St. Louis, Mo., v. Gilliland Oil Co.
297 F. 494 (D.C. Tex. 1924)

This case tells us how long an estate in land can endure. Note that this "estate," curiously, seems to have a life unto itself, separate and apart from the land.

* * *

We must not lose sight of the fact that an estate in land may vary in its duration. It may be forever; it may be for life, or for a term of years, or at will. Its duration has nothing to do with its character, it is an estate nevertheless.

In the report of the master, which is a very satisfactory one, I find the following citations which may be preserved as interesting lights which the bar may care to make use of in studying this question: De Witt's Estate, 266 Pa. 548, 109 Atl. 699; Blackstone's Commentaries, book 2, p. 1, and book 2, p. 2; note 24 Am.St.Rep. 554; 8 R.C.L. 1071; Caldwell v. Fulton, 31 Pa. 475, 72 Am.Dec. 760; Coke on Littleton, 4 b; Barnsdall v. Gas Co., 225 Pa. 338, 74 Atl. 207, 26 L.R.A.(N.S.) 614; Transcontinental Oil Co. v. Emerson, 298 Ill. 394, 131 N.E. 645, 16 A.L.R. 507; Michigan Law Review, vol. 18, p. 749; Wolfe County v. Beckett, 127 Ky. 252, 105 S.W. 447, 17 L.R.A. (N.S.) 688; Stoughton's Appeal, 88 Pa. 198; Blakley v. Marshall, 174 Pa. 425, 34 Atl. 564; Bruner v. Hicks, 230 Ill. 536, 82 N.E. 888, 120 Am.St.Rep. 332; Ohio Oil Co. v. Daughetee, 240 Ill. 361, 88 N.E. 818, 36 L.R.A.(N.S.) 1108.

From the authorities and a study of the lease itself we conclude that the lease is a conveyance of the land as well as the right to use it for an indeterminable period of time. The lessee, by reason of the instrument, has exclusive dominion over the oil and gas therein found, and this dominion and ownership is as effective as though the oil was described in gallons, texture, fineness, and color, and the gas in cubic feet and volatility.

In re Estate of Van Den Boom
590 N.W.2d 350 (Minn. App. 1999)

This short squib emphasizes that an incident of ownership of an estate in land is the right to possess the underlying realty.

* * *

An estate in possession is one in which the owner has an immediate right to possession of the real estate. * * *

* * *

U. S. ex rel. Hill v. Deegan
268 F.Supp. 580 (D.C.N.Y. 1967)

Previously we noted that an estate in land seems to have a life all unto itself—as though it is apart from the land. This next short excerpt reinforces that point.

* * *

'If you think you can think about something which is attached to something else without thinking about what it is attached to, then you have what is called a legal mind.' Thomas Reed Powell, in an unpublished manuscript, as quoted by Arnold, Criminal Attempts--The Rise and Fall of an Abstraction, 40 Yale L.J. 53, 58 (1930).

* * *

§ 4.1.2 The Meaning of "Future Interest"

When A owns an estate in land, unless A owns a "fee simple" (which is all rights to the land; we discuss the fee simple in §4.3), there always is a concomitant "future interest," too. Thus, A will own some estate in land (there are various types of estates) and B will own some future interest in land (there are various types of future interests). The material that follows explores the term "future interest."

Commissioner of Internal Revenue v. Wells
132 F.2d 405 (6th Cir. 1942)

One of the issues presented in this case was whether the grantor was entitled to a statutory dollar exemption for the beneficiaries of a trust, who received "future interests." The court, in addressing the problem, explained what future interests are. It will be helpful to keep in mind what we stated earlier: that a future interest gives the owner a right to possess the land, not in the present, but in the future. The court restates this point and provides still further information on the characteristics of a future interest.

* * *

* * * [T]here arose the question of whether the beneficiary had received a present or future interest; and if the latter were the case, no exemptions would be allowable to the donor.

To raise this question, it was necessary to amend the answer conforming to the rule that two exemptions--instead of one--were allowable for the two beneficiaries unless they had received future interests, but countering affirmatively that their interests were, in fact, of this nature, and, therefore, no exemptions were allowable.

The contention of the Commissioner that the interests, received by the beneficiaries of the trust in the instant case, were future interests is based upon the fact that the distribution of any principal or interest from the trust rests entirely within the discretion of the trustee, according to the provisions of the trust instrument.

In considering this question, it is necessary to put aside conceptions of 'estates in futuro' as understood by Blackstone and the classic commentators on the common law.[1] For future estates, as the term is used in the statute, are not to be understood as interests similarly designated in the law of conveyancing. They are, rather, interests in land or other things, in which the privilege of possession or of enjoyment is future and not present; and the one essential is the possibility of future enjoyment. See Helvering v. Hutchings, supra; Paul, Federal Estate and Gift Taxation, Sec. 15.11.

'The term 'future interests in property' refers to any interest or estate, whether vested or contingent,[2] limited to commence in possession or enjoyment at a future date. The exemption being available only in so far as the donees are ascertainable, the denial of the exemption in the case of gifts of future interests is dictated by the apprehended difficulty, in many instances, of determining the number of eventual donees and the values of their respective gifts.' H. Rep. No. 708, 72d Cong., 1st Sess., page 29; S. Rep. No. 665, 72d Cong., 1st Sess., p. 41.

A future interest was defined in Treasury Regulations, 79, in effect at the time of the hearing before the Board, as follows: 'A future interest in property is any interest or estate in property, whether vested or contingent, which is limited to commence in use, possession, or enjoyment at some future date or time.' (Article 11, 1933 Ed.)

In United States v. Pelzer, 312 U.S. 399, 61 S.Ct. 659, 85 L.Ed. 913, the Supreme Court held that where beneficiaries had no right to the present enjoyment of the corpus or the income of a trust, and could only receive it after they survived a ten-year period, the use, possession, and enjoyment of each donee was postponed to the happening of a future uncertain event, and was a future interest. In Ryerson v. United States, 312 U.S. 405, 61 S.Ct. 656, 85 L.Ed. 917, the court held that where gifts of separate equal shares of the corpus of a trust were payable to each of the two trustees in the event of their joint request that the trust be terminated, the gifts depended upon the contingency of both trustees' joining in the exercise of the power of disposition, which might never happen, and that in such a case the gifts were future interests.

In Welch v. Paine, 1 Cir., 120 F.2d 141, where a taxpayer created a trust, with himself as trustee, to hold and pay over net income from trust property to his wife and minor children, in such proportions and at such times as the trustee might, in his sole discretion, determine, or to accumulate it for their benefit until the termination, at his death, of the trust, when it would be distributed to the donees, it was held that none of the beneficiaries had a right to the immediate beneficial enjoyment of the income of the trust; and that such gifts were clearly gifts of future interests.

We are of the opinion that the proposed amended answer of the Commissioner raised a meritorious question of liability for an increase of deficiency.

* * *

---

[1] [Although the court indicates that the definition that it is going to give is different from common law "law of conveyancing," in fact, the definition that it gives is the same as under the common law.]

[2] [The difference between vested and contingent future interests is discussed in depth later in this chapter.]

§ 4.1.3 Future Interest Distinguished from "Mere Expectancy"

One should not think that a future interest is not a property interest; it is very much an interest in property. On the other hand, a "mere expectancy" is not an interest in property. In the next two excerpts, Robinson v. Eagle-Picher Lead Co. *and* California Civil Code section 700, *we learn what a "mere expectancy" is.*

Robinson v. Eagle-Picher Lead Co.
297 P. 697 (Kan. 1931)

* * *

As to the first proposition, stating a rule to which appellants have very properly made the exception of its not being enforceable against the landlord, we think further exceptions or modifications are necessary, unless they are impliedly embodied in the word "expectancy" which is a "contingency as to possession, that which is expected or hoped for." Bouv. Law Dict. Vol. 1, page 1156. At most it is a mere hope or expectation, contingent upon the will and pleasure of the landowner, and hardly reaches the height of a property right, much less a vested right, because where there is no obligation there is no right. It is a possibility for which a party may under certain circumstances properly hope. Words and Phrases, First, Second and Third Series, "expectancy"; Robinson v. Jewett, 116 N. Y. 40, 22 N. E. 224.

California Civil Code § 700
Future interests; possibilities

SAME. A mere possibility, such as the expectancy of an heir apparent, is not to be deemed an interest of any kind.

§ 4.2 Freehold Estates

In Matter of Estate of Stroh *and* Pacific Southwest Realty Co. v. County of Los Angeles, *we learn two important points. The first point is that under the broad category of "estates in land," there are two subcategories: one of these subcategories is "freehold estates"; the other is "non-freehold estates" (more commonly known as leaseholds, a subject we take up in depth in chapter 10). The second point is that under the subcategory of freehold estates, we learn that there are a number of different types of freehold estates.*

Matter of Estate of Stroh
151 Mich.App. 513 (1986)

* * *

* * * A freehold is an estate for life or in fee. Black's Law Dictionary (5th ed.), p. 598. * * *

Pacific Southwest Realty Co. v. County of Los Angeles

1 Cal.4th 155 (1991)

* * *

It is undisputed that plaintiff transferred the entire fee to Metropolitan Life. An estate in fee simple is a freehold estate. (Civ.Code, §§ 762, 765.) A freehold estate is distinguished from other forms of estates in that it is of indeterminate duration (*Millsap v. Quinn* (Mo.1990) 785 S.W.2d 82, 84 [appointed officeholder qualification case]; *Board of Transp. v. Turner* (1978) 37 N.C.App. 14, 245 S.E.2d 223, 225 ["the true test of a freehold is its indeterminate tenure"]), and carries with it title to land (see *Cohn v. Litwin* (1941) 311 Ill.App. 55, 35 N.E.2d 410, 413). But an estate for years--in this case, a nonperiodic tenancy under a lease--is not a freehold estate. (Civ.Code, § 765.) Indeed, under California law an estate for years is not real property at all but rather a chattel real-- a form of personalty--even though the substance of the estate, being land, is real property. (*Id.,* §§ 761, 765; *Dabney v. Edwards* (1935) 5 Cal.2d 1, 11, 53 P.2d 962, 103 A.L.R. 822; see also *Weaver v. Superior Court* (1949) 93 Cal.App.2d 729, 734, 209 P.2d 830 ["The sale of a lease for a term of years is not the sale of real property."]; *Parker v. Superior Court* (1970) 9 Cal.App.3d 397, 400, 88 Cal.Rptr. 352 [although a leasehold is not real property, it is nevertheless an estate in land].)

Notwithstanding the fact that a lease is a present possessory interest in land, there is no question that as a nonfreehold estate it is a different species of interest from a freehold estate in fee simple. Any other conclusion would be contrary to centuries of English and American common law and its codification, as modified, in our Civil Code. A leasehold is not an ownership interest, unlike the possession of land in fee simple even when encumbered by a mortgage, for in the latter situation the mortgagor acquires equity over time through periodic payments. It is for that reason that common parlance refers to the "owner" of a freehold estate, encumbered or unencumbered, but to the "holder" of a lease; the freeholder is seised of land,[3] whereas the leaseholder is not.

Thus plaintiff's contention that it did not convey a present interest in real property is simply incorrect and cannot forestall a conclusion that a transfer of a present interest in real property occurred. Plaintiff did not retain the same interest when it sold its fee and reserved an estate for years.* * *

§ 4.3 The Fee Simple

The first type of freehold estate is the fee simple. If you have a family member who bought a house, he or she almost certainly owns it in fee simple.

---

[3] [What does "seised of the land" or "seisin" mean? See *Robins Island Preservation Fund, Inc. v. Southold Development Corp.*, infra. As you will learn, seisin is difficult to define. For our purposes right now, however, we may state that seisin is ownership. That said, does not a leaseholder "own" the lease?]

4.3.1 Characteristics

The characteristics of a fee simple are really quite "simple." In short, a fee simple is all ownership rights to the land. As such, there is no future interest in another person. The next four case excerpts explore the characteristics of a fee simple in greater depth.

Sterner v. Nelson
210 Neb. 358 (1982)

* * *

An absolute title estate or property is a fee simple estate;[4] it is an estate without end or limitations and the largest estate a person can possibly have. See, Long v. Kyte, 340 S.W.2d 623 (Mo.1960); Middleton v. Dudding, 183 S.W. 443 (Mo.1916).

* * *

Wray v. Wymer
77 Ohio App.3d 122 (1991)

* * *

The term "fee simple title" is undefined in R.C. Chapter 5529. Accordingly, this phrase must be read in context and construed according to rules of grammar and common usage, unless it has acquired a particular meaning. R.C. 1.42. In Ohio, the phrase "fee simple" has acquired a particular meaning as a result of case law. A fee simple is the highest right, title and interest that one can have in land; it is the full and absolute estate in all that can be granted. *Masheter v. Diver* (1969), 20 Ohio St.2d 74, 49 O.O.2d 350, 253 N.E.2d 780, paragraph one of the syllabus; *Waldock v. Unknown Heirs* (June 7, 1991), Erie App. No. E-89-53, unreported, 1991 WL 97317. * * * [A] fee can be of unlimited duration. *Myers v. East Ohio Gas Co.* (1977), 51 Ohio St.2d 121, 5 O.O.3d 103, 364 N.E.2d 1369; *Zelch v. Samonte* (Mar. 21, 1991), Cuyahoga App. No. 58283, unreported, 1991 WL 39698.

* * *

Bryant v. Palmer Coking Coal Co.
86 Wash.App. 204 (1997)

* * *

Bryant commenced this action to quiet title. That is a claim to fee ownership, the most comprehensive type of ownership under Washington law. The fee simple estate includes "all possible rights and privileges with respect to land."[5] This necessarily

---

[4] [Hence, a fee simple is also sometimes called, a "fee simple absolute."]
[5] 2 *Thompson on Real Property,* Thomas Edition, § 17.07, at 453 (David A. Thomas ed. 1994).

includes a claim to mineral rights as well as all other rights incidental to ownership of the fee.

* * *

Sullivan v. U.S.
461 F.Supp. 1040, (D.C.Pa. 1978)

* * *

We must remember the fee in real estate is the total bundle of rights held by the owner with respect to the land. Rothensies v. Fidelity Philadelphia Trust Co., 112 F.2d 758 (3d Cir. 1940). The purchaser of the fee gets the leases and rents arising from the property whether specified or not. It is of course possible to break up this bundle of rights into innumerable other bundles such as the land, the buildings erected on the land, easements under, on or over the same, and numerous leases and subleases. There should be no obstacle to separating the right to receive rents from the ownership of the land so that one party owns all the leases covering the land without owning any of the land if that is clearly specified. Such a situation raises various practical obstacles but there is nothing theoretically which cannot be done in this respect.

* * *

§ 4.3.2 Creation

Recognizing that a fee simple is the largest degree of ownership recognized in law, the next question is how one can create a fee simple. Thus, for example, if O owns a fee simple in Blackacre, and O wants to transfer his fee simple to A, what words must O use in the deed to A to transfer O's fee simple? In the next case, you will learn that under the ancient common law, O had to use some very specific words to transfer a fee simple to A—and if O did not, A did not receive a fee simple. You also will learn that modernly, O does not have to use these very special words.

Penienskice v. Short
194 A. 409 (Del. Super. 1937)

RODNEY, J., sitting.

This was an * * * action to recover a deposit made in connection with an agreement for the sale of real estate. The defendant, by the agreement, undertook to convey a marketable fee simple title to the premises mentioned and especially "all the right, title and claim whatsoever in law and equity held by the aforesaid Caroline Wedderburn Gates (a former owner) in said lots." The land had been sold by John S. Isaacs, former County Treasurer and Receiver of Taxes for Sussex County, as the property of Caroline Wedderburn Gates who, in the agreement is conceded to have had a fee simple title. The purchaser at the tax sale was William J. Mustard, a predecessor in title of the defendant. The County Treasurer and Receiver of Taxes made a deed to Mustard, which deed recited the regularity of all proceedings and is included in the statement of facts. This deed, however, both in the granting clause and in the habendum conveyed the property to William J. Mustard "its successors and assigns" and the usual words "his heirs and assigns" were entirely omitted.

The whole controversy arose from this language of the deed and its validity is the sole question considered by the Court.

RODNEY, J., delivering the opinion of the Court:

It may readily be conceded that the word "heirs" was a necessary word at common law in a conveyance, inter vivos, between individuals in order to grant a fee simple title. Statutes of most states have changed this rule and some slight consideration will later be given to the pertinent Delaware statute. This modification of the Common Rule is but an application of the almost universal modern rule that in the construction of deeds, like all other instruments, the real intention of the parties is to be sought and carried out unless such intention is in conflict with some fixed canon of construction, settled rule of property, or is repugnant to the terms of the grant. 8 R.C.L. 1037.

It has been said that the estate intended to be conveyed is the main thing and the conveyance is the instrument by which the transfer is effected (McWilliams v. Nisly, 2 Serg. & R. [Pa.] 507, 7 Am.Dec. 654), and where the intention of the grantor clearly appears from the face of the deed effect must be given thereto, however unusual the form of the deed unless the repugnancy is such that the intention cannot be carried out.

In the construction of the deed, presently involved, there are three aspects in which it should be considered (1) as conveying no estate whatever and being an entire nullity (2) as conveying merely a life estate in William J. Mustard and (3) as conveying a fee simple interest notwithstanding the lack of appropriate words of inheritance.

(1) Every deed, otherwise valid, will be considered to have intended to convey some estate of some nature (Pelletier v. Langlois, 130 Me. 486, 157 A. 577) and since all proceedings are recited and admitted to have been regular it is difficult to see how the deed could be so construed as to show an intent to convey no interest whatever.

The (2) and (3) aspects of the deed are closely connected and will be considered together. Counsel for the plaintiff argues that a conveyance to "A, his successors and assigns" was a recognized method of conveying a life estate at common law and that the present deed should be construed as evidencing a like intention. I do not so understand the authorities. At common law the word "heirs" was necessary to carry a fee simple and with this word "heirs" absent the estate was construed as a life estate because that was the largest estate that could be granted without proper words of inheritance. A deed at common law to "A, his successors and assigns" conveyed merely a life estate not because that was a recognized method of such conveyances but the life estate was the largest estate that could be vested in the absence of the word "heirs."

* * *

We have seen that the intent of the parties is to be sought and, if possible, given effect. I am of the opinion that the Collector could formulate no legal intent contrary to the express language of the statute that the deed "shall convey the title of the taxable." He could never have intended to grant a life estate by the deed when the taxable actually had a fee simple estate as is here conceded.

That the Collector did not intend to grant a life estate in the premises may be affirmatively gathered from the fact that in his deed he not only recited the statute making it obligatory for him to convey the title of the taxable, but also in the deed he used the following language indicative of his compliance with the statute. The deed conveyed to "William J. Mustard, its successors and assigns forever, all the right, title and claim whatsoever in law and equity of the said Caroline Wedderburn Gates to" the premises in question.

In 1 Thompson on Real Property, § 671, it is said:

"A sale by an officer of the law, under an order of Court may operate to pass an estate in fee without the use of the word 'heirs': as where a Sheriff on an execution sale of real estate owned by the judgment debtor in fee executes to the purchaser at such sale a deed of 'all the estate, title and interest' which the judgment debtor had in such land, the deed passes the fee in the land though the word 'heirs' is omitted. The Sheriff had no authority to sell less than the debtor's entire estate which was an estate in fee."

See, also, Carolina Sav. Bank v. McMahon, 37 S.C. 309, 16 S.E. 31.

* * *

The statute required that the deed of the Collector should convey the title of the taxable and the deed in fact did, in ipsissimis verbis ["word for word"], grant all the "right, title and claim whatsoever in law and equity" of the taxable. The taxable, concededly, had a fee simple title. This fee simple title then passed to the purchaser by the deed and the Collector could not limit the extent of the title. In view of the language of the act and of the deed I cannot conclude that the deed is a nullity.

I am of the opinion that the deed of John S. Isaacs, the Collector, conveyed to William J. Mustard a fee simple title to the property, notwithstanding the omission of the word "heirs" from such deed, it having been conceded that the taxable whose property was sold had a fee simple title therein. It is quite arguable that the word "heirs" in a deed like the present is not only not necessary but not desirable. The word "heirs" could properly have been included in the present deed because the taxable had a fee simple interest, but if the taxable had less than a fee simple interest then all that would be sold would be that lesser interest, and the Collector could not sell or convey a fee simple interest, and the inclusion of the word "heirs" in such deed would be misleading. The Collector can not be expected to examine the title of every taxable to ascertain the extent of his interest.

Strengthening inferences as to the correctness of the conclusion that the word "heirs" is not necessary in a deed of a Collector of Taxes under the statute now considered may be drawn from the fact that since 1923 the word "heirs" has not been necessary in Delaware in a deed between individuals to grant a fee simple title. By vol. 33, p. 604, c. 207 (Rev.Code 1935, § 3659) a short form of deed was set out which did not include any words of inheritance and it was provided:

"A deed in the above form, duly executed and acknowledged, unless otherwise restricted or limited, or a contrary intention appear therein, shall be construed to pass and convey to the grantee therein and to his heirs and assigns the fee simple title or other the whole estate or interest which the grantor could lawfully convey in and to the property therein described."

Under this act the intent of the grantor using the statutory form is to be given effect and in the absence of a contrary showing he will be presumed to have intended to grant the largest estate or interest that he could grant.

Pursuant to the agreed statement of facts, judgment will be entered for the defendant.

§ 4.4 Defeasible Fees: In General

We have seen that one type of freehold estate is the fee simple (or fee simple absolute), an estate "without end" (per Sterner v. Nelson*), an estate that will endure forever. We also have seen that the owner of a fee simple can break up his fee simple into smaller parts* (Sullivan v. U.S.). *In this regard, if O owns a fee simple absolute, O can transfer something less than a fee simple absolute to A: O can transfer one of several "defeasible fees" to A.* Elmore v. Austin *lists the types of defeasible fees. Note that all of these estates are still "fees" because they may (although do not have to) endure forever. But they are "defeasible" because they may come to an end at some time in the future if some prohibited event happens.*

Elmore v. Austin
232 N.C. 13 (1950)

* * *

An estate in fee simple defeasible may be either (1) an estate in fee simple determinable, or (2) an estate in fee simple subject to a condition subsequent, or (3) an estate in fee simple subject to an executory limitation. Am.Law Inst. Restatement, Property, Vol. 1, sections 44, 45, 46.

* * *

Note
Yet another type of defeasible fee, a fourth type, is a fee simple determinable subject to an executory limitation. We begin our study of the four types of defeasible fees immediately below.

§ 4.5 Defeasible Fees: The Fee Simple Determinable

The first type of defeasible fee we cover is the fee simple determinable, meaning that the fee will endure until the occurrence of some event stated in the deed or will in the future.

§ 4.5.1 Characteristics and Creation

Board of County Comm'rs of Van Wert County v. Consolidated Rail Corp.
14 Ohio Misc.2d 4 (Ohio Com.Pl. 1983)

As you will learn from Board of County Comm'rs of Van Wert County v. Consolidated Rail Corp.*, the key characteristic of a fee simple determinable is that if the prohibited* *event does ever occur, the fee will end automatically; the grantor need not do anything to end the fee simple determinable. As for creation of a fee simple determinable, you will learn that the grantor must use "words of duration" to create a fee simple determinable. As to what constitutes words of duration, that, too, will be addressed in* Board of County Comm'rs of Van Wert County.

WALTERS, Judge.

Plaintiff, Van Wert County Board of Commissioners, filed its complaint on November 30, 1982 alleging that a piece of property located adjacent to the Van Wert County Courthouse was deeded on August 7, 1881 to the Pittsburgh, Ft. Wayne and Chicago Railway Co., which conveyance was subject to a reversion[6] in that said transfer was "so long as said strip may be required or used for passenger station purposes only; but in the event that said strip shall be finally vacated and abandoned for passenger station purposes, then, and in that event the same shall revert to Van Wert County"; and that the real estate has been vacated and abandoned for such purposes; and praying for a declaratory judgment ordering the property reverted to the county. The defendant, Consolidated Rail Corporation ("Conrail"), the successor in interest to the Pittsburgh, Ft. Wayne and Chicago Railway Co., admits that on or about April 30, 1971, passenger trains ceased stopping at the property in question for the purpose of permitting passengers to enter or leave passenger trains.

* * *

R.C. 5302.04 provides that a conveyance of an estate shall be deemed to include all rights, easements, privileges and appurtenances unless the contrary is stated in the deed. An estate which descends as a fee simple but which may or will terminate is generally known as a "qualified fee." Among qualified fees, there are generally three types, the classification of which depends upon the manner in which the estate may or will terminate. A "fee simple determinable" is created by an instrument providing that the estate shall automatically terminate upon the happening of a stated event. 41 Ohio Jurisprudence 3d (1983) 443, Estates, Section 15.

In determining whether the present conveyance is a fee simple determinable, we must first ascertain the intent of the parties at the time of the conveyance, for it is an accepted principle of construction that all doubts will be resolved against a finding that such an estate exists.[7] In the present case, the deed in question states in the habendum clause, in very plain language, that the defendant's title will be defended "for so long as said strip may be required or used for passenger station purposes *only*" (emphasis added) and then continues with the reverter language stating, "but in the event that said strip shall be finally vacated and abandoned for passenger station purposes, then, and in that event the same shall revert to Van Wert County." The court finds that this language alone would sufficiently express the intent to convey a determinable fee; however, there is further evidence presented to support this intent. Prior to the grant in question, the commissioners journalized a resolution which speaks of the grant as a "lease" to the

---

[6] [The future interest involved here is *not* a reversion. Rather, the interest is a possibility of reverter, as the material that follows makes clear. What's this? Courts actually make mistakes? Can this be?]

[7] [Why is it that the fee simple determinable is not favored?]

railroad and further states, "said ground to be used solely for [passenger] depot purposes and to revert to county when said Pittsburgh, Ft. Wayne and Chicago Rail Road Company cease [*sic*] to so use it."

Therefore, having found that a fee simple determinable was in fact intended, we must determine whether it was properly created. It is generally accepted that a bare statement within a deed specifying a use and nothing more will fail to create a qualified fee.[8] Generally, the usage of the magic words "so long as" will be sufficient to create a determinable fee; however, in Ohio, a much cited case, *In re Copps Chapel Methodist Episcopal Church* (1929), 120 Ohio St. 309, 166 N.E. 218, has held otherwise. The syllabus of *Copps Chapel* states that the usage of these words in the habendum clause, "without any provision for forfeiture or reversion," will not serve to limit or qualify the grant. Thus, in Ohio, it is necessary, in order to create a fee simple determinable, that there must be the limiting words, such as "so long as," and if these words are contained in the habendum clause rather than in the granting clause, then there must also be a provision for forfeiture or reversion.[9] The court finds that both exist in the present case and that, therefore, there exists a fee simple determinable.

The next consideration is whether the qualifying event recited in the limiting phrase has occurred. The two phrases used in the deed in question are: "so long as said strip may be required or used for passenger station purposes only" and "in the event that said strip shall be finally vacated and abandoned for passenger station purposes." The defendant argues that the property has not been finally vacated and abandoned for passenger station purposes because it stands ready, willing and able to use the property for such purposes. This argument is fatuous since by defendant's own admission no passenger trains have stopped at the depot since April 30, 1971, or nearly thirteen years ago. The court further takes notice that Conrail is not in the passenger transportation business and it is not anywhere argued that Conrail stands ready to reinstitute such business. * * * The court therefore finds that the event specified in the deed, being the abandonment of the premises for passenger station purposes, has occurred and that the forfeiture provisions contained in the deed should now be enforced.

* * *

Judgment for plaintiff.

Riggs v. City of New Castle
229 Pa. 490 (1911)

In the Riggs *case, you will understand the difference between a durational limitation (a characteristic of a fee simple determinable) and a mere statement of purpose (which is fully consistent with a fee simple absolute and cannot transform a fee simple into a fee simple determinable).*

---

[8] [For an example of this, see *Riggs v. City of New Castle*, the next case.]
[9] [The court errs again. The court should have stated here, and again, four lines up, "forfeiture or reverter." We discuss reversions later in this chapter.]

MOSCHZISKER, J.

The proper construction of a written instrument is the essential point for determination in this case.

In 1856 the land in controversy was owned by certain ancestors of the present plaintiffs. * * * This writing provides: 'The parties of the first part upon consideration of the premises hereinafter expressed, hereby agree that the said party of the second part, its lessees and assigns, may and shall occupy forever for purposes of wharf all that strip of land lying on the west side of Neshannock creek (describing the land in controversy) in consideration whereof said borough hereby agrees that said parties of the first part may and shall occupy from and after the date hereof without let, hindrance, or interference from the said borough to the sole use, benefit, and behoof [sic] of said parties of the first part, their heirs and assigns forever and for whatever purpose the said parties of the first part may see proper' (here follows a description of a piece of land then owned by the borough). The plaintiffs contend that this instrument only gave to the borough an easement in gross which has since been terminated by operation of law. The defendant contends that it created a fee absolute.

* * *

The writing stipulates that the borough of New Castle, its lessees and assigns, may and shall occupy forever certain land of the grantors, and that the grantors may and shall occupy forever certain land belonging to the borough. This was a mutual grant, and it seems plain that it must have been the intention of the parties that the words 'may and shall occupy forever' should have the same meaning in both instances. This language was sufficient to pass a fee absolute, and the additional words, 'for the purposes of wharf,' used in connection therewith, should not be taken to diminish the estate so created. As noted by the court below, the words of the grant 'are not preceded or followed by any words of condition or limitation. The instrument does not state that the grant is made upon condition or provided that a wharf be built or maintained, nor does it say that the grant is to continue 'so long as' or during such time as the premises are used for the purposes of a wharf, nor are there any other words of condition or limitation used.'

In Slegel v. Lauer, 148 Pa. 236, 23 Atl. 996, 15 L. R. A. 547, it is said: 'The mere expression of a purpose will not of and by itself debase a fee. Thus a grant in fee simple to county commissioners of land 'for the use of the inhabitants of Delaware county to accommodate the public service of the county' was held not to create a base fee; * * * as also a grant to county commissioners and their successors in office of a tract of land with a brick courthouse thereon erected 'in trust for the use of said county, in fee simple,' the statute under which the purchase was made authorizing the acquisition of the property for the purpose of a courthouse, jail, and office for the safe-keeping of the records. * * * Similarly a devise of land to a religious body in fee 'there to build a meeting house upon' was held to pass an unqualified estate; * * * as also a grant to a congregation 'for the benefit, use and behoof of the poor of * * * the congregation * * * forever, and for a place to erect a house of religious worship, for the use and service of said congregation, and if occasion shall require a place to bury their dead. * * *'

* * * As was said, in the case of Griffitts v. Cope, 17 Pa. 96: 'The use to which the granting clause declares that this land is to be applied is of the character which the law requires. * * * The presumption would therefore appear fair and obvious, that by that declaration, the devisor merely meant to make the grant lawful upon its face;' * * *

* * *

The assignments of error are all overruled and the judgment is affirmed.

§ 4.5.2 Concomitant Future Interest: Possibility of Reverter

In every fee simple determinable, O retains a future interest. This future interest is called a "possibility of reverter." But who owns the possibility of reverter? The answer is, it depends on whether O transfers the fee simple determinable by deed or by will, as the next two cases explain.

Mount Olivet Cemetery Ass'n v. Salt Lake City
164 F.3d 480 (10th Cir. 1998)

The Mount Olivet Cemetery Ass'n *case tells you who owns the possibility of reverter when O conveys (that is, transfers by deed) a fee simple determinable to A.*

* * *

Congress unambiguously conveyed ownership of the land to the Association through the 1909 Act and the subsequently issued deed. The deed "grants and conveys" the cemetery land to the Association *until* the land is no longer used as a cemetery, at which point it reverts to the government. [Emphasis added.] Under well-settled rules of property law, the Association obtained a fee simple determinable via this conveyance, while the government retained a possibility of reverter. *See* Chester H. Smith & Ralph E. Boyer, *Survey of the Law of Property* 8 (2d ed.1971). "A fee simple determinable is a fee simple created to continue until the happening of a stated event." *Id.* A possibility of reverter is merely the interest retained by a grantor after conveyance of a determinable fee. *See Helvering v. Hallock,* 309 U.S. 106, 118 n. 6, 60 S.Ct. 444, 84 L.Ed. 604 (1940). It is a future contingent interest in real property, and, at best, a future estate in land. *See* Roger A. Cunningham et al., *The Law of Property* 39 (2d ed.1993).

* * *

Elmore v. Austin
232 N.C. 13 (1950)

This case tells you who owns the possibility of reverter when O transfers the fee simple determinable by will (and you should note that a will takes effect only at the death of the transferor, called the "testator").

* * *

When the owner of land in fee simple absolute devises it in fee simple determinable, a possibility of reverter, which is a reversionary interest subject to a condition precedent, springs up. It arises without being created by any specific words in the will, and exists in the eligible heirs of the devisor while the fee simple determinable is outstanding in the devisee or his successors in interest, that is to say, until that estate ends by the happening of the stated event on which it is limited, or until that estate is converted into a fee simple absolute. Am.Law Inst. Restatement, Property, Vol. 1, sections 44, 58, and Vol. 2, section 154; Simes: Law of Future Interests, sections 177, 187; 19 Am.Jur., Estates, section 31. The term, 'eligible heirs' does not refer to the heirs of the devisor in general. It embraces only those persons who would answer the description of heirs of the devisor at a particular time if the stated event terminating the fee simple determinable were then to occur. It necessarily follows that where an estate in fee simple determinable created by will is ended by the happening of the stated event limiting it, the property reverts in fee simple absolute to those who are heirs of the testator at the time when the estate terminates, and not to those who were heirs of the testator at any other time. Burden v. Lipsitz, 166 N.C. 523, 82 S.E. 863; Church of Henderson v. Young, 130 N.C. 8, 40 S.E. 691.

* * *

Note

It also has been said, to be as technically correct as possible, that a possibility of reverter is the interest left in the grantor, or in the successor in interest of the testator, when a grantor or testator transfers a "vested" estate of the "same quantum." See *Williams v. Watt*, 668 P.2d 620 (Wyo. 1983). What does "vested" mean here? It simply means a possessory estate. What does "same quantum" mean? The answer lies in the common law's quantification of estates: Defeasible fees were deemed to be of the same quantum as a fee simple absolute. The quantum of estates, in descending order, is: fee simple (or defeasible fee), fee tail (see below), life estate (see below), and leasehold (see chapter 10).

Shelby Contracting Co. v. Pizitz
285 Ala. 301 (1970)

Most interests in property can be transferred by deed during the owner's lifetime (what we call a "conveyance") or by will at the owner's death (what we call a "devise"). This was not the case with a possibility of reverter, however, at least not under the common law, as Shelby Contracting Co. *makes clear.*

* * *

'A possibility of reverter is, at common law, not an estate, and does not require the existence, at the time of its retention, of an ascertained person, natural or artificial, to take as grantee. It is not a present or future right, or a vested interest in land; it is merely a possibility of acquiring an estate. . . .

'A possibility of reverter at common law is inalienable, not assignable . . . or devisable . . . although it may be made so by statute. However . . . it is descendible, and may be released to the tenant in possession. In some jurisdictions, even in the absence of statute, a possibility of reverter has been held capable of transmission by the grantor to his grantee, and will pass to the latter under a conveyance of the reversion.' 31 C.J.S. Estates § 105, pages 204, 205.

* * *

Walton v. City of Red Bluff
2 Cal.App.4th 117 (1991)

Under the common law, as we have seen, if O conveys, "To A so long as liquor is never sold," A has a fee simple determinable and O has a possibility of reverter. Modernly, however, in some jurisdictions, A does not have a fee simple determinable (and O does not have a possibility of reverter), as the Walton *case explains.*

* * *

Section 885.020 [of the California Civil Code], enacted in 1982, provides: "Fees simple determinable and possibilities of reverter are abolished. Every estate that would be at common law a fee simple determinable is deemed to be a fee simple subject to a restriction in the form of a condition subsequent.[10] Every interest that would be at common law a possibility of reverter is deemed to be and is enforceable as a power of termination."[11] (Stats.1982, ch. 1268, § 1, p. 4678.) Walton's interest was a power of termination. Such a power must be exercised: Instead of an immediate right to the property, Walton had to reenter. (See 5 Miller & Starr, *op. cit. supra,* § 11:8, pp. 13-14.)

Walton makes an undeveloped argument that the conversion of his interest into a right of reentry following a fee simple on condition subsequent violates due process: "The provision is declared to be retrospective, subject to a grace period.... [¶] Due process questions are thus raised which cannot be briefed in the prescribed time frame. [¶] Could the Legislature, for example, enact that estates in fee simple will be 'deemed' to be tenancies at will, or licenses to enter, after five years?" Walton misconstrues the import of the statute. Walton's possibility of reverter was not abolished; it was transformed into a power of termination. Walton does not explain how this has harmed him. As the Law Review Commission explained, the two are essentially the same. "The possibility of reverter is an unnecessary estate in property law. It serves the same functions as the right of entry and there is no practical difference of any substance between the two." (Recommendations relating to Marketable Title of Real Property (Nov.1981) 16 Cal.Law Revision Com.Rep. p. 416. See Cal.Law Revision Com. com., Deering's Ann.Civ.Code, § 885.020 (1990) p. 111.) Walton does not articulate how his interest has been harmed by what is essentially a name change; we therefore reject his contention.

* * *

§ 4.6 Defeasible Fees: The Fee Simple on Condition Subsequent

The next defeasible fee we cover is the fee simple on condition subsequent. Like a fee simple determinable, it is a fee because it may endure forever. It is defeasible, however, because it can end. It will end when the prohibited event materializes. Of course, this last statement makes the fee simple on condition subsequent seem identical to a fee simple

---

[10] [The fee simple on condition subsequent is discussed immediately below.]
[11] [The power of termination is discussed below.]

determinable. It is not the same, however, as the Department of Transportation v. Knight *case explains.*

§ 4.6.1 Characteristics and Creation

Department of Transportation v. Knight
238 Ga. 225 (1977)

After you read this case, you might be tempted to say, "So, it is all in the wording!" My answer to this statement is, absolutely! Take note that that is all that lawyers in every area of practice do: deal with words. When lawyers deal with any statute, contract, deed, will, trust, jury instruction, etc., "all" they deal with is words. Indeed, it is always—always!—in the wording.

* * *

* * * The only basic difference between an estate upon conditional limitation and upon condition subsequent is that upon the stated event the former determines automatically and the latter requires re-entry. Franks v. Sparks, 217 Ga. 117, 121, 121 S.E.2d 27, 31 (1961). 'No precise technical words are required to create a limitation or a condition subsequent and the construction must always be founded upon the intention of the parties as disclosed in the conveyance. However, the words used may serve as guides to construction. Words of time such as 'so long as,' 'while,' 'until,' 'during,' usually denote limitation. Words of qualification or condition such as 'provided,' 'upon condition,' are most often used to create conditions subsequent.' Id. E.g., Atlanta Consolidated Street Ry. Co. v. Jackson, 108 Ga. 634, 34 S.E. 184 (1898) ('so long as'); Lawson v. Georgia S. & F. Ry. Co., 142 Ga. 14, 16, 82 S.E. 233, 234 (1914) ('to have and to hold . . . for railroad purposes only, and for the time that they shall so use it'). See generally Code Ann. Ch. 85-9. No such words appear in the deed before us.

* * *

Note
If O conveys, "to A so long as liquor is never sold," A has a fee simple determinable. If, on the other hand, O conveys, "to A on the condition that liquor is never sold," A has a fee simple on condition subsequent. Yes, it is all in the words.

Mountain Brow Lodge No. 82, Independent Order of Odd Fellows v. Toscano
257 Cal.App.2d 22 (1967)

Suppose O conveys, "To A, but A can never sell the property." On the face of the deed, A has a fee simple, subject to a so-called direct restraint on alienation (a provision prohibiting the sale of the property). What happens in such case is that A takes a fee simple and the restriction, that A can never sell the property, is stricken. This is so because in a free-market economy, it is important to allow property to be freely transferrable. Hence, the restriction on sale is void. In the Mountain Brow Lodge *case, the court has to decide whether a deed with a restriction "for use by the lodge only," with an express reverter (determinable fee not recognized, for reasons discussed in the case) is a valid fee simple on condition subsequent—or an invalid de facto direct restraint on alienation.*

GARGANO, Associate Justice.

This action was instituted by appellant, a non-profit corporation, to quiet its title to a parcel of real property which it acquired on April 6, 1950, by gift deed from James V. Toscano and Maria Toscano, both deceased. Respondents are the trustees and administrators of the estates of the deceased grantors and appellant sought to quiet its title as to their interest in the land arising from certain conditions contained in the gift deed.

* * *

The controversy between the parties centers on the language contained in the habendum clause of the deed of conveyance which reads as follows:

'Said property is restricted for the use and benefit of the second party [the Mountain Brow Lodge No. 82], only; and in the event the same fails to be used by the second party or in the event of sale or transfer by the second party of all or any part of said lot, the same is to revert to the first parties herein, their successors, heirs or assigns.'

Respondents maintain that the language creates a fee simple subject to a condition subsequent and is valid and enforceable. On the other hand, appellant contends that the restrictive language amounts to an absolute restraint on its power of alienation and is void. It apparently asserts that, since the purpose for which the land must be used is not precisely defined, it may be used by appellant for any purpose and hence the restriction is not on the land use but on who uses it. Thus, appellant concludes that it is clear that the reversionary clause was intended by grantors to take effect only if appellant sells or transfers the land.

Admittedly, the condition of the habendum clause which prohibits appellant from selling or transferring the land under penalty of forfeiture is an absolute restraint against alienation and is void. The common law rule prohibiting restraint against alienation is embodied in Civil Code section 711 which provides:

'Conditions restraining alienation, when repugnant to the interest created, are void.'

However, this condition and the condition relating to the use of the land are in the disjunctive and are clearly severable. In other words, under the plain language of the deed the grantors, their successors or assigns may exercise their power of termination 'if the land is not used by the second party' or 'in the event of sale or transfer by second party.' Thus, the invalid restraint against alienation does not necessarily affect or nullify the condition on land use (Los Angeles Investment Company v. Gary, 181 Cal. 680, 186 P. 596, 9 A.L.R. 115).

The remaining question, therefore, is whether the use condition created a defeasible fee as respondents maintain or whether it is also a restraint against alienation and nothing more as appellant alleges. Significantly, appellant is a non-profit corporation organized for lodge, fraternal and similar purposes. Moreover, decedent, James V. Toscano, was an active member of the lodge at the time of his death. In addition, the term 'use' as applied to real property can be construed to mean a 'right which a person has to use or enjoy the property of another according to his necessities' (Mulford v. LeFranc (1864), 26 Cal. 88, 102). Under these circumstances it is reasonably clear that when the grantors stated that the land was conveyed in consideration of 'love and affection' and added that it 'is restricted for the use and benefit of the second party' they simply meant to say that the land was conveyed upon condition that it would be used for lodge, fraternal and other purposes for which the nonprofit corporation was formed. Thus, we conclude that the portion of the habendum clause relating to the land use, when construed as a whole and in light of the surrounding circumstances, created a fee subject to a condition subsequent with title to revert to the grantors, their successors or assigns if the land ceases to be used for lodge, fraternal and similar purposes for which the appellant is formed.[12] No formal language is necessary to create a fee simple subject to a condition subsequent as long as the intent of the grantor is clear. It is the rule that the object in construing a deed is to ascertain the intention of the grantor from words which have been employed and from surrounding circumstances (Brannan v. Mesick, 10 Cal. 95; Aller v. Berkeley Hall School Foundation, 40 Cal.App.2d 31, 103 P.2d 1052; Schofield v. Bany, 175 Cal.App.2d 534, 346 P.2d 891).

It is of course arguable, as appellant suggests, that the condition in appellant's deed is not a restriction on land use but on who uses it. Be this as it may, the distinction between a covenant which restrains the alienation of a fee simple absolute and a condition which restricts land use and creates a defeasible estate was long recognized at common law and is recognized in this state. Thus, conditions restricting land use have been upheld by the California courts on numerous occasions even though they hamper, and often completely impede, alienation. A few examples follow: Mitchell v. Cheney Slough Irrigation Co., 57 Cal.App.2d 138, 134 P.2d 34 (irrigation ditch); Aller v. Berkeley Hall School Foundation, 40 Cal.App.2d 31, 103 P.2d 1052 (exclusively private dwellings); Rosecrans v. Pacific Electric Railway Co., 21 Cal.2d 602, 134 P.2d 245 (to maintain a train schedule); Schultz v. Beers, 111 Cal.App.2d 820, 245 P.2d 334 (road purposes); Firth v. Marovich, 160 Cal. 257, 116 P. 729 (residence only).

Moreover, if appellant's suggestion is carried to its logical conclusion it would mean that real property could not be conveyed to a city to be used only for its own city purposes, or to a school district to be used only for its own school purposes, or to a church to be used only for its own church purposes. Such restrictions would also be restrictions upon who uses the land. And yet we do not understand this to be the rule of this state. For example, in Los Angeles Investment Company v. Gary, supra, 181 Cal. 680, 186 P. 596 land had been conveyed upon condition that it was not to be sold, leased, rented or occupied by persons other than those of Caucasian race. The court held that the condition against alienation of the land was void, but upheld the condition restricting the land use. Although a use restriction compelling racial discrimination is no longer consonant with constitutional principles under more recent decisions, the sharp distinction that the court drew between a restriction on land use and a restriction on alienation is still valid. For further example, in the leading and often cited case of Johnston v. City of Los Angeles, 176 Cal. 479, 168 P. 1047, the land was conveyed to the

---

[12] It is arguable that the gift deed created a fee simple determinable. However, in doubtful cases the preferred construction is in favor of an estate subject to a condition subsequent (2 Witkin, Summary Calif.Law., Real Prop. § 97, pp. 949--50).

City of Los Angeles on the express condition that the city would use it for the erection and maintenance of a dam, the land to revert if the city ceased to use it for such purposes. The Supreme Court held that the condition created a defeasible estate, apparently even though it was by necessity a restriction on who could use the land.

Our independent research indicates that the rule is the same in other jurisdictions.

* * *

* * *

For the reasons herein stated, the first paragraph of the judgment below is amended and revised to read:

'1. That at the time of the commencement of this action title to the parcel of real property situated in the City of Los Banos, County of Merced, State of California, being described as:

Lot 20 Block 72 according to the Map of the Town of Los Banos was vested in the MOUNTAIN BROW LODGE NO. 82, INDEPENDENT ORDER OF ODD FELLOWS, subject to the condition that said property is restricted for the use and benefit of the second party only; and in the event the same fails to be used by the second party the same is to revert to the first parties herein, their successors, heirs or assigns.'

As so modified the judgment is affirmed. Respondents to recover their costs on appeal.

The petition for rehearing is denied.

STONE, Associate Justice.

I dissent. I believe the entire habendum clause which purports to restrict the fee simple conveyed is invalid as a restraint upon alienation within the ambit of Civil Code section 711. It reads:

'Said property is restricted for the use and benefit of the second party, only; and in the event the same fails to be used by the second party or in the event of sale or transfer by the second party of all or any part of said lot the same is to revert to the first parties herein, their successors, heirs or assigns.'

If the words 'sale or transfer,' which the majority find to be a restraint upon alienation, are expunged, still the property cannot be sold or transferred by the grantee because the property may be used by only the I.O.O.F. Lodge No. 82, upon pain of reverter. This use restriction prevents the grantee from conveying the property just as effectively as the condition against 'sale or transfer * * * of all or any part of said lot.' (Los Angeles Investment Co. v. Gary, 181 Cal. 680, 682, 186 P. 596; Property Restatement, s 404 et seq.; 2 Witkin, Summary of Cal. Law, Real Property, p. 1004; Simes, Perpetuities in California since 1951; 18 Hastings L.J., p. 248.)

Certainly, if we are to have realism in the law, the effect of language must be judged according to what it does. When two different terms generate the same ultimate legal result, they should be treated alike in relation to that result.

* * *

* * * I would hold the property free from restrictions, and reverse the judgment.

Notes

1. Direct restraints on alienation are of three types: First, there is the disabling restraint, which simply prohibits the grantee from selling or otherwise transferring the property. The second type is a forfeiture restraint. In such a restraint, the grantee loses or forfeits

the property if he even attempts to transfer the property. This is the type of direct restraint that was probably involved in the *Mountain Brow Lodge* (with reverter clause). The third type of direct restraint on alienation is a promissory restraint. With such a restraint, the deed provides that the grantee promises or agrees not to transfer the property. In the event that the grantee does transfer the property with such a restraint, the grantee is liable for damages. Any type of absolute direct restraint on alienation with respect to a fee is invalid because, it is said, that such a restraint is in derogation of the fee. See *Vinson v. Johnson*, 931 So.2d 245 (Fla.App. 2006). If a restraint is reasonable, however, the restriction may be recognized. See, e.g., *Melton v. Melton*, 221 S.W.3d 391 (Ky.App. 2007) (agreement entered into by six siblings and their spouses restricting sale of property for twenty-one years held reasonable). Promissory restraints and forfeiture restraints typically are allowed, however, with respect to life estates (see below for discussion of life estates).

2. Notwithstanding everything just said, direct restraints on alienation *are* allowed with respect to trusts that have so-called spendthrift provisions. The subject of trusts is discussed more fully in the next chapter.

3. There also are *indirect* restraints on alienation. An indirect restraint on alienation arises when the grantor or testator does not intend to restrain alienation, but the effect is to restrain alienation nonetheless. Examples of indirect restraints on alienation include defeasible fees and restrictions as to use. The question in these cases is whether such an indirect restraint is actually a de facto direct restraint, as the *Mountain Brow Lodge* case illustrates.

Skinner v. Shepard
130 Mass.180 (1880)

In this case, O will convey to A, land, "subject to the condition that no building shall ever be placed" on the property. It would seem that this creates a fee simple on condition subsequent. Nonetheless, the court ultimately holds that A has a fee simple absolute. How can this be? The answer lies not in the law of property, but as you will see, in the law of contracts.

MORTON, J.

On April 16, 1859, Willis Bucknam, now deceased, conveyed the land in question to Harris Munroe and others by a deed, which bounded it on one side by Green Street and on another side by the Woburn Branch Railroad, and which, after the description and before the habendum, contained this provision: "Said premises are hereby conveyed subject to the condition that no building shall ever be placed on that part of the same lying within twenty-five feet of said Green Street, and also that the present occupant of a part of the premises near said railroad for a lumber-yard shall be allowed the time until the first day of October next after the date hereof to remove his lumber and evacuate the premises, but no longer without the consent of said grantees." The land by mesne conveyances came into the possession of the defendants, who conveyed it to the plaintiffs by a warranty deed containing the usual covenants.

The words in the deed of Bucknam, above quoted, are sufficient to create a condition, the breach of which would forfeit the estate, if such clearly appears to have been the intention of the grantor; but they are not to have that effect, if his intention from the whole deed appears to have been otherwise.

We think that the last clause of the conditional paragraph could not have been intended as a technical condition. It relates merely to an occupation of a part of the premises for a short time, and is in its nature a personal stipulation of the grantees to permit such occupation, rather than a condition by a breach of which the estate should be wholly forfeited. The words "subject to the condition" apply equally to both clauses of the paragraph, and there is no reason for giving them a more technical or a different meaning when applied to the first clause than that which they have as applied to the second. We are of opinion that both clauses can have effect only as restrictions. *Episcopal City Mission v. Appleton,* 117 Mass. 326.

Undoubtedly Willis Bucknam might have enforced the first restriction while he lived; but there is nothing in the deed which shows that the parties intended that the restriction as to building within twenty-five feet of Green Street should create a servitude or easement in the granted land, which should attach to and be an appurtenance to any neighboring land.

* * *

We are therefore of opinion, that the restriction as to building must be construed, not as a condition which the heirs of the grantor can enforce, but as a personal covenant merely with the grantor; and that, after his death, it created no encumbrance or servitude upon the estate for which the plaintiffs can maintain this action.

Judgment for the defendants.

§ 4.6.2 Concomitant Future Interest: Right of Entry

Whenever O creates a fee simple on condition subsequent, O retains the future interest called a right of entry. The next several cases in this subsection explore the characteristics of this future interest.

Ludington & Northern Ry. v. Epworth Assembly
188 Mich.App. 25 (1991)

We have learned that when O conveys a fee simple determinable, O retains a possibility of reverter. Similarly, when O creates a fee simple on condition subsequent, O retains a right of entry. Besides the fact that a possibility of reverter always follows a fee simple determinable and a right of entry always follows a fee simple on condition subsequent, it seems that there is no real difference between the possibility of reverter and right of entry. But there is a big difference, as the Ludington & Northern Ry. *case explains.*

* * *

Traditionally, a "possibility of reverter" refers to the type of future interest remaining in a grantor where there has been created a fee simple determinable, 28 Am.Jur.2d, Estates, § 182, p. 319, whereas a "right of entry"[13] refers to the interest remaining in the grantor[14] where an estate on condition subsequent has been created. *Id.*, § 188, p. 328. The distinction between the two interests is that in the former the estate reverts at once on the occurrence of the event by which it is limited, while in the latter the estate in fee does not terminate until entry by the person having the right. *Id.*, § 183, p. 323.

* * *

Gray v. Blanchard
25 Mass. 284 (1829)

If O conveys, "to A on the condition that liquor is never sold, but if it is ever sold, O shall have the right to reenter," A has a fee simple on condition subsequent and O has a right of reentry. This is clear. Suppose now, however, that O conveys, "to A on the condition that liquor is never sold." On such facts, A still has a fee simple on condition subsequent and O still has a right of entry. That O still has a right of entry, even when O did not expressly create it, is explained in Gray v. Blanchard.

* * *

The demandant, being owner of a parcel of land with a dwelling house thereon, adjoining on the north to land with a dwelling house thereon belonging to his sister, facing to the south, conveys to the tenant's grantor in fee simple, "provided, however, this conveyance is upon the condition, that no windows shall be placed in the north wall of the house aforesaid, or of any house to be erected on the premises, within thirty years from the date hereof." After the sister has conveyed her land to a stranger, the tenant mortgages by a deed reciting the foregoing provision, and afterward, while remaining in possession, makes windows in the north wall. *Held,* that the above clause * * * gave the demandant a right to re-enter.

PARKER C. J.
The tenant moves to have the verdict set aside, on several grounds.
* * *
The last point made in the argument for the tenant is, that there being no clause of re-entry for breach of condition in the deed, the provision is not strictly a condition going to the forfeiture of the estate, but may for this reason be construed into a covenant. But here again the law seems to be clear the other way.

A clause of re-entry is not necessary to make a condition. *Proviso, ita quod, sub conditione,* make the estate conditional.[15] Com. Dig. *Condition, A* 2. Other words, such as

---

[13] [A right of entry is also commonly referred to as a power of termination or right of re-entry. Use of any of these terms is proper.]

[14] [Or in the successor in interest of a testator.]

[15] [The words, "proviso," "ita quod," and "sub conditione" mean, respectively, "provided," "so as," and "upon condition," and traditionally were words used to create a conditional estate.]

si, si contingat,[16] do not make a condition, which will work a forfeiture, without clause of re-entry Lit. § 331; Shep. Touch. 121.

* * *

Franks v. Sparks
217 Ga. 117 (1961)

In this case, the grantor, after having conveyed a fee simple on condition subsequent to a school board, conveyed his right of entry—called a right of reentry by the court—to a bank. The question is whether the grantor could so transfer his interest.

* * *

'The general rule at common law is well settled that the right of reentry is not alienable or assignable. No stranger can take advantage of the condition. It is sometimes held or stated that upon the conveyance of a fee subject to a condition subsequent, there remains in the grantor no estate or interest in the land which can be transferred, which seems to be only another way of stating the general rule.' 33 Am.Jur. 690, 'Life Estates, Remainders, etc.,' § 209. See also, in this connection, 31 C.J.S. Estates § 20, p. 32; 26 C.J.S. Deeds § 148, pp. 1052-1054; Thompson, Real Property, Vol. 4, p. 687.

In this State this question seems never to have been expressly ruled upon. However, those cases which have enunciated the distinction between conditions subsequent and limitations, in stressing that the former can only be reserved for the grantor and his heirs, also state that a stranger cannot take advantage of a condition subsequent. Norris v. Milner, 20 Ga. 563, 566, supra; Atlanta Consolidated Street Ry. Co. v. Jackson, 108 Ga. 634, 637, 34 S.E. 184, supra. It is this restriction of reservation, as old as condition subsequent itself, which prevents alienation to a stranger, rather than the right of re-entry being a 'bare contingency or possibility,' not the subject of sale under Code, § 96-102.

The decisions of this court cited by the plaintiff as supporting the alienability of C. L. Alexander's right or re-entry do not support him.

* * *

Note

In some jurisdictions, not only is a right of entry not capable of being transferred, but the mere attempt to transfer it extinguishes it. See, for example, *Rice v. Boston & W.R. Corp.*, 94 Mass. 141 (1866). The modern and majority view, however, is that a right of entry may be transferred inter-vivos by deed or at death by will. See, for example, *Shell Petroleum v. Hollow*, 70 F.2d 811 (10th Cir. 1934).

---

[16] [The words, "si, si contingat," mean, "if, if it happen."]

§ 4.7 Defeasible Fees: The Fee Simple Subject to an Executory Limitation

The third defeasible fee that we cover is the fee simple subject to an executory limitation.

§ 4.7.1 Characteristics and Creation

The classical formulation to create a fee simple subject to an executory limitation is O conveys, "to A, but if liquor is ever sold, then to B." A has a fee simple subject to an executory limitation and B has the future interest called an executory interest. Thus, a fee simple subject to an executory limitation looks very similar to a fee simple on condition subsequent but with one important distinction: if liquor is ever sold, O's intent, as manifested by the deed (or will) is that B (via B's executory interest) will become the owner of the property, not O.

Slowey v. Jenkins
408 S.W.2d 452 (Ky. 1966)

In this case, we do not have a grantor conveying by deed, but a testator devising her property by will. That is of no consequence; all of the preceding principles applicable to deeds also are applicable to wills. That said, the testator in Slowey v. Jenkins *essentially devises her property, "to my husband, but if my husband does not survive my daughter, to my daughter." From the introduction of this topic, we can say that the husband has a fee simple subject to an executory limitation and the daughter has an executory interest.* Slowey v. Jenkins *explains why this was not possible under the common law, but why it is possible now.*

HILL, Judge.

By this opinion, we undertake to construe Item III of the will of Anna Carroll Jenkins, first wife of Allen L. Jenkins. The controversy is between Katie Jenkins (the second wife of Allen L. Jenkins and appellee herein) and appellant Frances Perkins Slowey, the adopted daughter of Anna Carroll and Allen L. Jenkins.

Allen L. Jenkins died shortly after his second marriage, which was to appellee Katie Jenkins.

We quote 'Item III' in its entirety:

'ITEM III: I give, devise and bequeath all of my remaining estate, of whatever kind and nature, that I may own at my death to my husband, Allen L. Jenkins. * * *

'In the event my husband, Allen L. Jenkins, predeceases my adopted daughter, Frances Perkins Castleman, then in that event all of my estate shall go to my adopted daughter, Frances Perkins Castleman.'

It was the opinion and judgment of the circuit court that Allen L. Jenkins took an absolute fee simple title 'without any limitation, restriction or encumbrance.' Under this judgment, appellee Katie Jenkins inherited from Allen L. Jenkins, who has since departed this life. Appellant Frances Perkins Slowey contends that her adoptive parent, Allen L.

Jenkins, took a life estate, or 'defeasible fee,' under Item III of the will of her adoptive mother. We agree and reverse the judgment.

Of course, the fundamental rule in will construction directs that the intention of the testator be determined from the contents of the will. Greenway v. White, 196 Ky. 745, 246 S.W. 137, 32 A.L.R. 1385 (1922); and Phelps v. Stoner's Adm'r, 184 Ky. 466, 212 S.W. 423 (1919).

* * *

At common law, an absolute fee simple title with power of disposition or appointment could not be followed by or converted into a remainder or executory interest because the two estates were considered repugnant and impossible as the entitle estate had already vested in the holder of the fee simple title. We quote an interesting comment by J. J. Dukeminier, Jr., from the Minnesota Law Review, Vol. 43:13, p. 28 (1958--59):

'Out of a dictum of Chancellor Kent grew a rule that an executory interest limited after a fee was void if the owner of the fee had the absolute power to dispose of the property. The typical situation in which this rule may be invoked is a devise of property 'to my wife absolutely, to do with as seems best for her, but if any of the property remains undisposed of at her death, then to A.' The remnant gift over to A, an executory interest, is void if the rule is applied. The rule can not be applied to a contingent remainder, since the rule presupposes the prior estate is a fee, and a remainder by definition cannot follow a fee.

'*The rule is entirely illogical as a matter of theory. There is no reason why a valid executory interest cannot be limited subject to being destroyed by the exercise by another of a power of disposition.*' (Emphasis ours.)

A suitable definition of the estates created in the present case may be found in Restatement of the Law, Property, section 46, p. 147, from which we quote:

'(1) Except as stated in Subsection (2) (no application here), an estate in fee simple subject to an executory limitation exists when any limitation, in an otherwise effective conveyance of land,

(a) creates an estate in fee simple in a conveyee, or leaves an estate in fee simple in the conveyor or his successor in interest; and

(b) provides that the estate subject thereto, upon the occurrence of a stated event is to be divested, before the normal expiration thereof, in favor of another interest in a person other than the conveyor, or his successor in interest.'

Allen Jenkins had a defeasible fee simple title . . . . That is, his fee simple title was subject to being defeated by the contingency of his predeceasing Frances. . . . . Frances had a contingent future interest denominated as an executory interest, or an estate upon a conditional limitation. That is, the fee simple title to whatever Allen Jenkins had not . . . consumed during his lifetime was limited to shift from him to her if and when he died and she survived. Though not recognized by the common law of medieval times, this cutting off and transference of a fee simple title, called a shifting use,[17] was legitimated in law as well as equity by the Statute of Wills (1540) and the Statute of Uses (1536).

The judgment is reversed with directions to enter another consistent herewith.

---

[17] [Executory interests can "shift." They also can "spring." When they shift, they are called "shifting executory interests." When they spring, they are called "springing executory interests." Shifting and springing executory interests are explored in the materials in the next section.]

§ 4.7.2 Concomitant Future Interest: Executory Interest

You have already learned that when O creates a fee simple subject to an executory limitation in A, B has an executory interest, the concomitant future interest. In this subsection, we explore the characteristics of an executory interest.

Presbyterian Church of Carlyle v. St. Louis Union Trust Co.
18 Ill.App.3d 713 (1974)

This two-sentence excerpt tells you several important points. The first sentence will tell you who can own an executory interest. The second sentence will tell you how it vests (that is, how it can become a possessory interest).

* * *

An executory interest is a future interest created in one other than the grantor which is not a remainder.[18] An executory interest vests upon the happening of a condition or event and in derogation of a vested freehold estate. * * *

* * *

Miller v. Miller
136 P. 953 (Kan. 1913)

You have previously learned that an executory interest can exist when O creates a fee simple subject to an executory limitation in A (and B has the executory interest). But an executory interest can exist in another scenario, too. Here is how that can happen: Suppose that O owns Blackacre in fee simple and conveys, "to A if A marries B." The court in Miller v. Miller *discussed how a grantor or testator could not create an estate to arise in the future under the ancient common law—and why this was so—but why it is now possible.*

* * *

* * * The purpose of the grantor was to create freehold estates in remainder to commence at a future time. Under the common law this could not be done without the grant of a precedent particular estate to support them, and under the common law, whenever the particular estate is void at its inception, or for any reason does not come into being, remainders limited upon it are defeated.

This court is of the opinion that the common-law rules referred to have been abrogated by statute.

The territorial Legislature of 1855 passed an act relating to conveyances * * *.

* * *

In 1859 the act of 1855 regulating conveyances was revised, and section 9 was condensed and restated as follows: "Estates may be created, to commence at a future

---

[18] [Remainders are discussed later in this chapter.]

day." Kansas Statutes 1859, c. 30, § 6. This act remained in force until repealed in 1868, when another revision occurred. In this revision section 6 of the act of 1859 was omitted, and the subject was covered by a declaration as general as it was possible to make.

"Conveyances of land, or of any other estate or interest therein, may be made by deed, executed by any person having authority to convey the same, or by his agent or attorney, and may be acknowledged and recorded as herein directed, without any other act or ceremony whatever." Gen. Stat. 1868, c. 22, § 3.

The words "conveyances of land" mean, of course, the land itself in fee simple absolute. The words "any other estate or interest therein" include estates of freehold and less than freehold, of inheritance and not of inheritance, absolute and limited, present and future, vested and contingent, and any other kind a grantor may choose to invent consistent, of course, with public policy.

The doctrine of the particular estate arose from the necessity under the feudal system of always having a tenant to fulfill feudal duties, defend the estate, and represent it so that other claimants might maintain their rights. The only way to pass a freehold estate was by livery of seisin which operated immediately or not at all, and, if the freehold became vacant, the lord had an immediate right of entry, and all limitations of the tenancy came to an end. The result was that, in order to create a freehold estate, the enjoyment of which was to be postponed to a future time, it was necessary to support it by a precedent particular estate taken out of the inheritance, and to make livery of seisin to the particular tenant, which by fiction inured to the remainderman or remaindermen.[19] A much more liberal and equitable doctrine applied to the transmission of estates by will.

"An executory devise of lands is such a disposition of them by will that thereby no estate vests at the death of the devisor, but only on some future contingency. It differs from a remainder in three very material points: (1) That it needs not any particular estate to support it; (2) that by it a fee-simple or other less estate may be limited after a fee-simple; (3) that by this means a remainder may be limited of a chattel interest, after a particular estate for life created in the same."[20] 2 Bl. Com. p. 172.

The Legislature of 1855 placed conveyances by deed on the same footing as wills so far as the creation of future estates was concerned; but, following the lead of the Legislatures of some of the older states, the Kansas Legislature of 1868 undertook not only to permit the granting of future estates but to abolish other common-law restrictions on alienation not suited to allodial tenures and modern conveyancing, and to make transfers of interests in land as free as possible. The concluding portion of section 3 of the act of 1868, quoted above, expressly abolishes the common-law ceremony of livery of seisin which stood as an insuperable bar to the creation of freeholds to begin in futuro unless supported by a particular estate. The language was adapted from statutes of other states which usually provided that deeds duly acknowledged and recorded should be valid and pass estates in land "without livery of seisin, attornment, or other ceremony whatever."

* * *

---

[19] [A remainder is a future interest in a grantee. It is discussed later in this chapter.]

[20] [Estates for life, or life estates, are discussed later in this chapter.]

Notes

1. In light of *Slowey v. Jenkins*, we can say that if O conveys, "to A, but if such and such happens, to B," A has a fee simple subject to an executory limitation, and B has a *shifting executory interest* in fee simple (meaning that if B's executory interest vests, it will divest A's fee and B will own the fee simple absolute). In light of *Miller v. Miller*, we can say that if O conveys, "to A if such and such happens," O has a fee simple subject to an executory limitation and A has a *springing executory interest* in fee simple (meaning that when the stated event happens, the fee simple will "spring" out of O into A).

2. As stated in the *Slowey* and *Miller* cases, under the ancient common law, a fee simple could not be divested by a future interest in a third person. Thus, under the ancient common law, if O wanted to convey, "to A, but when B returns from New York, to B," this simply was not possible. Further, under the ancient common law, an estate could not spring up at some time in the future. Thus, if O wanted to convey, "to A if A marries B," this, too, was not possible. Why was this? Because of the ancient ritual of livery of seisin: to transfer an estate the grantor had to go onto the land in question and give the grantee some symbolic part of the land such as a twig or clump of dirt. But all that changed as a consequence (an indirect one at that) of the enactment of the English Statute of Uses. See chapter 5, § 5.1.1, "History of Trusts."

§ 4.8 Defeasible Fees: The Fee Simple Determinable Subject to an Executory Limitation

The fourth and last type of defeasible fee is the fee simple determinable subject to an executory limitation. At first blush, it seems identical to a fee simple subject to an executory limitation. There is a difference, however. In a fee simple determinable subject to an executory limitation, durational language ("until") is used; in a fee simple subject to an executory limitation, conditional language ("but if") is used.

§ 4.8.1 Characteristics and Creation

To create a fee simple determinable subject to an executory limitation, O conveys, "to A so long as liquor is never sold, then to B." Note the durational language that O uses ("so long as"). Note also that B holds the executory interest: if the prohibited event occurs, A will lose his estate and B's executory interest will become a fee simple absolute. That said, there is a problem with this conveyance and the conveyance in Institution For Savings in Roxbury v. Roxbury Home For Aged Women. *That problem is addressed in the note following the case.*

Institution For Savings in Roxbury v. Roxbury Home For Aged Women
244 Mass. 583 (1923)

The grantor conveyed property to the Institution For Savings in Roxbury, "for their use as long as the present institution shall continue to exist" and "when the institution shall cease to exist the trustees shall convey the whole estate to the then authorized managers of the Old Ladies' Home in Roxbury for the sole benefit of that worthy institution . . . ." (The name of the home later was changed to the Roxbury Home For Aged Women.) One question for the court was what estate the Institution For Savings in Roxbury took.

CARROLL, J.

* * *

The land court decided that the petitioner took a determinable or qualified fee, * * *

Such an estate in land as a qualified or determinable fee is recognized in this commonwealth. The question whether this form of estate was done away with by the statute quia emptores was considered in First Universalist Society v. Boland, 155 Mass. 171, 29 N. E. 524, 15 L. R. A. 231; and it was decided that a qualified or determinable fee may exist in this commonwealth.

* * *

The conveyance by the order of the probate court was to conform with the meaning and intent of the donor and was for the uses and upon the trust expressed in his letter to the Institution for Savings. The institution was to continue to hold the estate 'as long as the present institution shall continue to exist.' These words create a qualified or determinable fee. They indicate that the grantee was to own the estate as long as it continued to exist and that its ownership was to cease on the happening of that event. The petitioner owned a fee, as the land court decided, because it might last forever; but as the estate would end when the circumstance mentioned occurred, the fee was not absolute but was qualified or determinable.

In First Universalist Society v. Boland, supra, the plaintiff was to hold the estate-- "so long as said real estate shall by said society or its assigns be devoted to the uses' * * * as specified. 'And when * * * diverted from the uses * * * then the title of said society * * * shall forever cease, and be forever vested in the following named persons."

And it was held that these words did not create an absolute fee, nor an estate on condition, but an estate to continue till the happening of a certain event and then to cease; that the grant was not upon a condition subsequent and a re-entry would be unnecessary; that the estate was terminated by its own limitations when it was no longer devoted to the specified uses. That case is decisive of the case at bar. The land court was right in deciding that the petitioner had a qualified or determinable fee. See Easterbrook v. Tillinghast, 5 Gray, 17.

* * *

The decision of the land court was right. The petitioner took a qualified or determinable fee. * * *

Exceptions overruled.

Note

A second issue decided by the court, but not reproduced in the edited case in your text, was whether the future interest of the Old Ladies' Home in Roxbury (which interest is an executory interest, as the next section of text explains) violated the "Rule Against Perpetuities," and was therefore void. The court held that the executory interest did indeed violate the Rule Against Perpetuities, a subject addressed in depth in chapter 6.

§ 4.8.2 Concomitant Future Interest: Executory Interest

When O conveys, "To A until the property ceases to be used as a savings and loan, then to B," as we have seen, A has a fee simple determinable subject to an executory limitation and B has the executory interest in fee simple. Yet, this result is conceptually troubling and not technically correct. Why is this so? Consider this: An executory interest, as we have seen earlier in this chapter, at § 4.7.2, either (a) causes the underlying freehold estate, the fee, to spring out from the grantor at some time in the future or (b) divests another transferee. Clearly, there is no springing out in a fee simple determinable subject to an executory limitation. Further—and this is the critical point here—there is no divesting. This is because a fee simple determinable simply expires "naturally" when the event in question materializes—"to A until such and such happens." In fact, the concomitant future interest should be a remainder—yet another future interest in a transferee (we discuss remainders in the materials that follow). Nevertheless, it is not a remainder due to the case of Pells v. Brown, Cro. Jac. 590 *(King's Bench 1620). That case held that a remainder cannot follow any type of fee (except a fee tail, discussed infra). Thus, when O conveys, "To A until such and such happens, then to B," we had to call B's future interest something. But what is it? It could not be a remainder based on precedent, and it could not be an executory interest based on doctrine. In the words of songwriter Johnny Mercer, "Something's Gotta Give," and it did (doctrine). For further elucidation, see* Proprietors of the Church in Brattle Square v. Grant, *infra.*

§ 4.9 The Fee Tail

A fee tail is created when O conveys, "to A and the heirs of his body." A has a fee tail, a fee that descends to the grantee's issue, in perpetuity. It is a fee because it has the ability to endure forever (so long as A has lineal descendants).

§ 4.9.1 Characteristics and Creation

When O conveys a fee tail to A, upon A's death, the fee tail descends to A's issue (lineal descendants). Thus, if A has a child, A1, upon A's death, A1 owns a fee tail. Upon A1's death, if A1 has issue surviving him, e.g. A2, A2 has a fee tail. The Robins Island *case provides further elucidation on the fee tail.*

Robins Island Preservation Fund, Inc. v. Southold Development Corp.
959 F.2d 409 (2nd Cir. 1992)

In this case, a fee tail held by O was confiscated by New York State under an act of attainder during the Revolutionary War. New York thereafter abolished the fee tail, providing that in all cases, anyone seized of a fee tail shall be seized of a fee simple. The ultimate question is whether New York owned a fee simple. The court will hold in the affirmative. In the opinion, the court gives the history of the development of the fee tail— and why it was abolished by many states after the United States became an independent nation.

ALTIMARI, Circuit Judge:
This appeal stems from a property dispute encompassing events which took place over two centuries ago when the State of New York seized land belonging to individuals who refused to support the American Revolution. The property at issue is Robins Island, an island of approximately 445 acres in the Peconic Bay of Long Island. In 1779, Parker Wickham, then the owner of Robins Island, was stripped of title to this property as punishment for his continued allegiance to the British monarchy.

Plaintiff-appellant Robins Island Preservation Fund ("RIPF"), is a non-profit corporation dedicated to the preservation of Robins Island in its natural state. RIPF alleges that it is the rightful owner of an approximate 75 percent undivided interest in Robins Island, which it claims as successor-in-interest to Parker Wickham, whom RIPF charges was unlawfully deprived of title and possession. Specifically, RIPF claims that New York's Act of Attainder of 1779, pursuant to which the State of New York confiscated and sold the island, was invalid, because at the time of its passage New York had no sovereignty over Robins Island, which was then under British control. RIPF further argues that even if the Act of Attainder were valid in general, it was invalid with regard to Robins Island because New York took physical possession of Robins Island only after the enactment of the Treaty of Peace of 1783 between Great Britain and the United States, which prohibited future confiscations of British and loyalist property. As an alternative theory, RIPF contends that the Act of Attainder of 1779 seized only a life estate and not a fee simple interest in Robins Island, title to which passed on Parker Wickham's death to his son, Joseph Parker Wickham.

* * *

BACKGROUND
This action brought by RIPF requires us to revisit the events surrounding our nation's birth in revolution. However, the events of the American Revolution which we must consider are not widely celebrated today. These events relate to the systematic confiscation of property belonging to those Americans who refused to join the Revolution. We are asked to examine the property rights of persons as they existed over two hundred years ago-when the newly formed states were fighting both British troops and British sympathizers, when individuals could be convicted without trials, and when ancient doctrines controlled the laws of property. Because the underlying action is deeply rooted in historical events, we begin by examining the circumstances surrounding the ownership and confiscation of Robins Island in the eighteenth century.

A. *Parker Wickham's Inheritance*

In 1715, Joseph Wickham, Sr. purchased Robins Island. In 1734, he devised the island to his son Joseph Wickham, Jr. "and to the male heirs of his body lawfully begotten or to be begotten forever." This devise created an "estate tail" by which the devisee, and subsequently his male heirs, would hold only a "fee tail" interest in the property, which would pass at death to the next directly descended male heir. Using this means of conveyance, Joseph Wickham, Sr. intended to pass title to Robins Island from generation to generation in a direct and perpetual line of descent.

At the death of his father, Joseph Wickham, Jr. took possession of the estate. Upon his death in 1749, the land passed to his eldest son, Parker Wickham.

B. *The Act of Attainder*

Parker Wickham was a "loyalist" during the American Revolution. Loyalists were those colonists who maintained their allegiance to the King of Great Britain. This was not unusual in New York which, among the original thirteen colonies, had the largest number of inhabitants sympathetic to the British monarchy. The pro-Crown sympathies of New York's large loyalist population facilitated the capture and occupation by British troops of most of the southern portion of the state, including Long Island, in 1776. Consequently, Robins Island remained under British control for the remainder of the war.

Perceiving a threat to the Revolution, American patriots clamored for measures to punish loyalists. In response, the Continental Congress declared on June 24, 1776, that the property of all adherents to the Crown would be liable to confiscation. *See* Allan Nevins, *The American States During and After the Revolution 1775-1789,* at 268 (1969). Following this declaration, New York, under intense pressure from patriot citizens, enacted a series of similar measures resulting in the seizure of loyalist and British property and the disenfranchisement of all persons who either had refused to recognize the authority of the revolutionary government or had aided the British. *See id.*

These measures did not, however, satisfy the more zealous patriots, many of whom were members of the newly convened New York State Legislature. Bowing to intensified popular pressure, the New York State Legislature on October 22, 1779 passed "An Act for the forfeiture and sale of the estates of persons who have adhered to the enemies of this state" ("Act of Attainder"), commonly known as the Confiscation Act, which declared Parker Wickham and fifty-eight other individuals *ipso facto* convicted of "adherence" to the British. *See* Act of Attainder of October 22, 1779, 1779 N.Y.Laws 3rd Sess., ch. 25 at art. 1. As punishment, all property owned by the "attainted" individuals was declared to be immediately forfeited to the State of New York. *See id.*

C. *The Act to Abolish Entails of 1782*

As the war drew to a close, the American states turned their attention toward eradicating the more offensive vestiges of aristocracy brought to the colonies by wealthy British settlers. An early target was the "estate tail." The estate tail, or "fee tail," was a freehold estate in which there was a permanently fixed line of inheritable succession, strictly limited to the natural children of the grantee or devisee. The use of the estate tail to keep ancestral lands in one family had provided landed British aristocracy with a basis of social and political power seen as incompatible with either the ideals underlying the American Revolution or the social conditions in the new states. *See* Cornelius J.

Moynihan, *Introduction to the Law of Real Property* § 6, at 37 (2d ed. 1988) ("Moynihan"); Gregory S. Alexander, *Time and Property in the American Republican Legal Culture,* 66 N.Y.U. L.Rev. 273, 295-302 (1991).

The New York State Legislature abolished the estate tail in 1782. In so doing, the Legislature provided:

> That in all cases, wherein any person or persons would, if this law had not been made, had been seized in fee-tail, of any lands tenements heriditaments, such person or persons shall, in future, be deemed to be seized of the same in fee-simple.

Act to Abolish Entails of July 12, 1782, 1782 N.Y.Laws 6th Sess., ch. 2 at art. 1. The effect of this Act was to convert all estates tail into estates in fee simple. In 1786, New York passed an almost identical "Act to Abolish Entails" whose only difference lay in curing ambiguities created by omission in the former enactment. *See* Act to Abolish Entails of February 23, 1786, 1786 N.Y.Laws 9th Sess., ch. 12.

* * *

Before turning to the underlying action, we set forth a time line of pertinent events:

> 1715 Joseph Wickham, Sr. purchases Robins Island.
>
> 1734 Joseph Wickham wills Robins Island to his oldest son, Joseph Wickham, Jr. in fee tail.
>
> 1749 Joseph Wickham, Jr. dies. His oldest son Parker Wickham survives and takes title to Robins Island.
>
> 1754 Joseph Parker Wickham, first son of Parker Wickham, is born.
>
> July 4, 1776 The Declaration of Independence is signed.
>
> July 9, 1776 The Provincial Congress of the State of New York approves the Declaration of Independence.
>
> July 16, 1776 The Provincial Congress of the State of New York resolves that all persons within the state owe allegiance to its laws.
>
> Aug. 1776 American revolutionary forces leave Long Island.
>
> Apr. 20, 1777 New York adopts its first state constitution.
>
> Oct. 22, 1779 Parker Wickham and others are attainted under New York's Act of Attainder; Robins Island is declared confiscated.
>
> July 12, 1782 The New York State Legislature abolishes the estate tail.
>
> Nov. 30, 1782 The Provisional Treaty of Peace is signed.
>
> Apr. 15, 1783 The Provisional Treaty of Peace is ratified by Congress.
>
> Sept. 3, 1783 The Definitive Treaty of Peace is concluded.
>
> Nov. 1783 British forces commence evacuation of Long Island.
>
> May 12, 1784 The New York State Legislature passes the Speedy Sales Act, expediting the sale of confiscated estates.
>
> Aug. 5, 1784 Robins Island is sold to Benjamin Tallmedge and Caleb Brewster pursuant to the Speedy Sales Act.
>
> May 22, 1785 Parker Wickham dies.

1791 Parker Wickham's oldest son, Joseph Parker Wickham, returns to Southold, Long Island after receiving compensation from Great Britain for the loss of his father's estate.

See Dwight Holbrook, *The Wickham Claim* 14-15 (1986) ("Holbrook").

F. *The Underlying Action*

RIPF initiated this action against SDC seeking, among other things, title and possession to Robins Island. RIPF claims title based on various quitclaim deeds it holds from the successors-in-interest to Parker Wickham. In total, RIPF has accounted for approximately a 75 percent undivided interest in Robins Island. Both RIPF and SDC moved for partial summary judgment on the issue of ownership. In support of its motion, RIPF offered several theories of recovery, which it again offers on appeal.

[After concluding that the Act of Attainder of 1779 was valid and the confiscation lawful, the court continued:]

* * *

DISCUSSION

* * *

II. *The Estate Seized By New York*

RIPF next contends that even if the seizure were valid, New York seized and sold only the interest held by the attainted Parker Wickham which was, in essence, a life estate.[21] Specifically, RIPF argues that because Parker Wickham had a son before the passage of the Act to Abolish Entails of 1782, Parker Wickham's son received at birth a vested remainder in fee tail.[22] This remainder, according to RIPF, was not reached by New York's Act of Attainder of 1779, and was subsequently transformed into a remainder in fee simple by the Act to Abolish Entails of 1782. Thus, because New York had seized only the estate of Parker Wickham, RIPF argues this remainder in fee simple was left undisturbed by the sale of Robins Island. That is, the purchasers of Robins Island acquired only a life estate for the life of Parker Wickham. According to RIPF, upon Parker Wickham's death, Robins Island passed in fee simple to his son Joseph Parker Wickham.

This argument rests on an interpretation of the nature of the estate held by Parker Wickham, the reach of the Act of Attainder, and the effect of New York's Act to Abolish Entails. We examine these issues in turn.

a. *The Estate Tail*

Prior to 1285, a gift or devise of real property to a man "and the heirs of his body" constituted a fee simple conditional. The fee was conditioned on the donee having heirs of his body. When this condition was satisfied, the donee had full power of alienation. *See* 2 Richard Powell, *The Law of Real Property* ¶ 193, at 62 (Patrick J. Rohan ed., 1990) ("Powell"). Upon the birth of issue to the donee, the only significant distinction between what the donee held and a fee simple estate was that in the event the donee died without

---

[21] [The life estate is covered more fully in § 4.11.]

[22] [A remainder is a future interest in a transferee. It is discussed in depth later in this chapter.]

leaving surviving issue and without having alienated the land, the property then reverted to the donor, regardless of the survivorship of collateral heirs. *See generally* Moynihan § 5, at 34. The power of alienation in the donee was the product of judicial construction which favored the free alienability of lands. However, the landed nobility of England grew dissatisfied with the result of this judicial construction which permitted the transfer of lands out of their families. Pressure by the nobility resulted in the enactment of the Statute De Donis Conditionalibus in 1285, which declared, contrary to prior judicial interpretation, that conveyances to a donee and "the heirs of his body" should be strictly construed to convey an estate which would without exception pass to the heirs of the donee's body. *See* Statute De Donis Conditionalibus, 13 Edw. I (1285).

Under the Statute De Donis Conditionalibus, the donee was said to hold an estate in fee tail (from the Latin *talliatum* or "cut out of the fee"). * * *

* * *

b. *The Estate Confiscated Pursuant to the Act of Attainder of 1779*

When New York confiscated the estate of Parker Wickham, it seized his fee tail ownership of Robins Island. RIPF contends that New York's seizure and sale of the land affected only the life interest held by Parker Wickham and did not destroy the future interest left to his heirs. RIPF characterizes the interest seized as a "life estate." In contrast, SDC argues that by seizing and selling Robins Island, New York exercised its right as tenant in tail to "bar the entail" of Parker Wickham's heirs. In essence, SDC contends that New York's confiscation of Parker Wickham's interest in Robins Island, pursuant to the Act of Attainder, cut off the future interest of Joseph Parker Wickham. We reject both arguments as misconstructions of the effect of the Act of the Attainder. By its terms, the Act of Attainder stripped the attainted individuals of any and all title, ownership or interest in real property existing in the State of New York. The property interests of the offenders were then vested, absolutely and immediately, in New York. Because Parker Wickham owned Robins Island in fee tail, it was ownership in fee tail that was assumed by New York.

Since an attainder was a criminal conviction, it did not affect the rights of future generations. Indeed, it is axiomatic that the Act of Attainder "vest[ed] in the state . . . . the 'estates' only of the offenders." *Carver*, 29 U.S. at 57. It is well-settled that solely by virtue of an attainder, a sovereign did not destroy the future interests of heirs to an estate tail. *See* 4 James Kent, *Commentaries on American Law* * 13 (4th ed. 1830) ("[E]states tail were not liable to forfeiture for treason or felony. . . . "); Moynihan § 5, at 35 (At early English common law, "[t]he estate in fee tail was not subject (beyond the tenant's lifetime) to forfeiture for treason or attainder for felony."). Thus, contrary to SDC's assertion, Parker Wickham's attainder for adherence to the British did not, in itself, "disentail" Parker Wickham's heirs. *See Borland v. Dean*, 3 F.Cas. 905, 908 (C.C.D.Mass.1826) (Story, *J.*) ("The power of barring the entail was personal to the tenant in tail" and a seizure of property by attainder appropriated the attainted party's tenancy in tail but did not extinguish the estate tail); *see also Carver*, 29 U.S. at 57 ("[P]owers and conditions, personal to the parties, did not, by an attainder, pass to the crown.").

We cannot conclude, however, that because a confiscation by attainder of an estate tail did not disentail an offender's heirs, the estate confiscated was something less than full ownership in fee tail. In contrast to a life estate, an estate tail was, by definition, an estate in which the tenant in tail held virtually unfettered ownership rights to use the property as the tenant saw fit during his or her lifetime.

The rights of a tenant in tail were thus far broader than those of the holder of a life estate. *See* Harold G. Aron, *Aron's Digest of New York Real Property Law* 22 (1923) ([B]efore, [the invention of the common recovery] or after, provided it was not taken advantage of, [the tenant in tail] had the fee for life; this is not at all the same as saying [the tenant] had a life estate in the fee. . . ."); 4 James Kent, *Commentaries on American Law* * 18-* 19 (John M. Gould ed., 14th ed. 1896) ("Kent (14th ed.)") (discussing the differences in rights and duties between a tenant in tail and the holder of a life estate). For example, the holder of a life estate was liable to the owner of the future estate for waste. *See* Moynihan § 12, at 52-54. In contrast, "[t]he tenant in tail was not chargeable with waste." Kent (14th ed.) at * 12.

Simply stated, there is no evidence that in seizing Robins Island, New York changed the nature of the estate from an estate tail into a mere life estate. In short, when New York confiscated Robins Island, it stepped into Parker Wickham's shoes for the duration of Parker Wickham's life. We therefore conclude that the Act of Attainder of 1779 fully and completely confiscated Parker Wickham's fee tail ownership of Robins Island, which-in the absence of any further enactments-would have passed by inheritance to Joseph Parker Wickham, just as it would have passed had Parker Wickham remained owner.

c. *The Effect on Robins Island of the Act to Abolish Entails*

In 1782, New York passed an "Act to Abolish Entails." *See* Act to Abolish Entails of July 12, 1782, 1782 N.Y.Laws, 6th Sess., ch. 2; *see also* N.Y. Est.Powers & Trusts Law § 6-1.2 (McKinney 1979). The Act to Abolish Entails of 1782 provided:

> That in all cases, wherein any person or persons would, if this law had not been made, had been *seized in fee-tail,* of any lands tenements heriditaments, such person or persons shall, in future, be deemed to be *seized of the same in fee-simple.*

Act to Abolish Entails of July 12, 1782, 1782 N.Y.Laws 6th Sess. ch. 2 at art. 1 (emphasis added). In 1786, New York promulgated an almost identical "Act to Abolish Entails," which superceded the 1782 Act. *See* Act to Abolish Entails of February 23, 1786, 1786 N.Y.Laws 9th Sess., ch. 12.

New York's purpose in promulgating the 1782 and 1786 Acts was to remove the estate tail and the restraints on alienation it engendered. * * *The Acts accomplished this reform by invoking the feudal concept of "seisin." Any person, "seized in fee tail" of an interest in land, was held to have an equivalent interest in fee simple. In other words, seisin of an estate in fee tail gave an individual seisin of an estate in fee simple.

In the present case, Robins Island already existed as an estate in fee tail prior to the enactment of New York's 1782 Act to Abolish Entails. Because an estate tail was already in operation, the 1782 Act vested an estate in fee simple in whomever was "seized in fee tail" of the property.

* * *

"Seisin," a concept of vast and fundamental importance in early English law, connoted peaceful possession. Moynihan § 1, at 98. "The man who is seized is the man who is sitting on land; when he was put in seisin he was set there and made to sit there." *Id.* (quoting 2 Pollack and Maitland, *History of English Law* 30 (2d ed. 1899)). From its feudal roots, the concept gradually evolved to encompass a claim of title as well as one of possession. By the eighteenth century, seisin came to mean "possession under claim of a freehold estate therein." *Id.* Therefore, a tenant for a term of years had possession, but not seisin, of a freehold estate. A tenant in fee tail, however, had seisin as the owner of the property in possession of the land.

Significantly, seisin did not require actual physical possession of the property, but merely an immediate legal right to possess and enjoy it. Where there was actual or constructive possession by an owner, this was deemed actual seisin or seisin in fact. *See Vanderheyden v. Crandall,* 2 Denio 9, 21 (N.Y.Sup.Ct.1846), *aff'd sub nom., Wendell v. Crandall,* 1 N.Y. (1 Comstock) 491 (1848); 1 Alfred G. Reeves, *A Treatise on the Law of Real Property* 379 (1909) ("Reeves"). Yet even absent an act of physical dominion, "[w]here the law casts the freehold upon a person[,] he has before exercising any act of ownership over it, what is called a sei[s]in in law." *Vanderheyden v. Crandall,* 2 Denio at 21; *see also* Reeves, at 379.

Under the common law there must always be someone seized of a freehold estate. *See* Earl P. Hopkins, *Handbook on the Law of Real Property* § 10, at 34 (1896). Moreover, there could be only one seisin of a freehold just as today there can be only one title deed to a piece of property. *See* 1 Emory Washburn, *A Treatise on the American Law of Real Property* 61 (Joseph Willard and Simon G. Coswell, eds. 5th ed. 1887). With regard to Robins Island, it is undisputed that until his attainder, Parker Wickham held both title and possession, and thus seisin, of Robins Island. By his 1779 attainder, Parker Wickham was stripped of his title and, consequently, of legal seisin of Robins Island. The Act of Attainder vested complete and absolute title in New York, and with title went legal seisin. Thus, by virtue of the Act of Attainder, New York obtained legal seisin of Robins Island which, following the withdrawal of the British in 1783, became actual seisin. Consequently, by virtue of the Act of Attainder, New York was "seized of an estate in fee tail." We therefore hold, that under the 1782 Act to Abolish Entails, New York's seisin of Robins Island as owner in fee tail was transformed into seisin as owner in fee simple.

Indeed, the result could not be otherwise. Joseph Parker Wickham, as issue in tail, had neither possession nor ownership of the property. In short, Joseph Parker Wickham did not hold seisin of Robins Island.

* * *

We therefore hold that by operation of the Act to Abolish Entails of 1782, Joseph Parker Wickham's future interest in Robins Island was extinguished. * * *

* * *

Note

As the *Robins Development Corporation* case shows, in many jurisdictions what would be a fee tail under the common law is now a fee simple. In other jurisdictions, what would be a common law fee tail now is a life estate. Still other jurisdictions provide that a fee tail may be created in the transferee, but that any issue of the transferee takes a fee simple (see *Long v. Long,* infra). There are only a few jurisdictions today where a common law fee tail may be created. Nonetheless, where the common law fee tail still is recognized, if the owner of the fee tail conveys a fee simple absolute, the transferee has a full-blown fee simple absolute. Abracadabra.

§ 4.9.2 Concomitant Future Interest: Reversion

When O conveys, "to A and the heirs of his body," if the jurisdiction in question recognizes the fee tail, then O has a reversion (which will become a fee simple absolute if A's line of lineal descendants cease).

Long v. Long
45 Ohio St.2d 165 (1976)

In Long v. Long, *the grantor conveyed a fee tail. Recalling that we must always account for the full fee simple absolute, the question for the court was what future was left in the grantor. The trial court erroneously found it to be a possibility of reverter. The appellate court correctly finds it is a reversion. The court then explains what a reversion is.*

* * *

The Probate Court determined that a possibility of reverter is not an estate of inheritance and that, upon the happening of the contingency, the grantee's death without issue, the property passes to the next of kin and heirs at law of the grantor then living-in the present case the appellees, Howard Long and Paul Olinger.

The Court of Appeals affirmed the judgment of the Probate Court, one judge dissenting.

The cause is now before this court pursuant to the allowance of appellant's motion to certify the record.

J. J. P. CORRIGAN, Justice.

I.

The unique issue in this case concerns the nature of the interest remaining in the grantor, Henry Long, after the creation by deed of a fee tail estate which was conveyed by the grantor to his son 'Jesse S. Long, and the children of his body begotten, and their heirs and assigns forever.'

The parties agree that the estate created by the grantor was a fee tail. Pollock v. Speidel (1867), 17 Ohio St. 439.

* * *

II.

Considerable confusion exists in the present case because of the term used to designate the nature of the grantor's future interest in the property conveyed. * * *

* * *

A reversion is the residue of an estate left in the grantor or other transferor, to commence in possession after the determination of some particular estate transferred by him. A reversion arises only by operation of law and is a vested right. Ohio Jurisprudence, supra, at page 356; 33 American Jurisprudence 668, Life Estates, Remainders, and Reversions, Section 194.

A reversion arises whenever a person having a vested estate transfers to another a lesser vested estate. Since the reversion is the undisposed of portion of a vested estate, it follows that all reversions are vested interests. A reversion is said to be vested because there is no condition precedent to the taking effect in possession other than the termination of the preceding estates. This does not mean, however, that every reversion is certain to take effect in possession and enjoyment. The distinguishing feature of the reversion is that it is not subject to a condition precedent to its taking effect in possession, and all other conditions defeating a reversion are regarded as conditions subsequent. 1 Simes & Smith, Law of Future Interests (2 Ed.), Reversions, Sections 82, 90; 2 Restatement on Property 525, Section 154.

A reversion is historically distinguishable from a possibility of reverter in that a reversion arises when the estate transferred is of a lesser quantum than the transferor owns. A possibility of reverter arises when the estate conveyed is of the same quantum as the transferor owns. Simes, supra, at page 329, Section 282.

III.

* * *

* * *The important point in this discussion is that the future interest remaining in the grantor of a common-law fee tail estate is an estate designated a reversion and not a possibility of reverter or right of entry.

The only remaining issue to consider is whether the Ohio enactment of 1811 (10 Ohio Laws 7),[23] modifying fee tail estates, has had any effect on the reversionary interest in the grantor.

In Pollock v. Speidel, supra [17 Ohio St. 439], this court recognized the continued existence of estates tail in Ohio, subject to the statutory modification enacted in 1811, and now embodied in R.C. 2131.08, which converted estates tail into fees simple in the hands of the issue of the first donee in tail. * * *

* * *

In accordance with the undisputed authority that the interest created in the grantor of a common-law fee tail estate is a vested reversion, and in view of the decisions to the effect that the Ohio enactment restricting fee tail estates does not alter the fundamental nature of the estate tail in the first donee in tail, we hold that such reversions are vested estates fully descendible, devisable and alienable inter vivos.

* * *

Judgment reversed.

---

[23]'AN ACT to restrict the entailment of real estate.

'Sect, 1 Be it enacted by the General Assembly of the state of Ohio. That from and after the taking effect of this act, no estate in fee simple, fee tail, or any lesser estate in lands or tenements, lying within this state, shall be given or granted by deed or will to any person or persons, but such as are in being, or to the immediate issue or descendants of such as are in being at the time of making such deed or will, and that all estates given in tail shall be and remain an absolute estate in fee simple to the issue of the first donee in tail.

'This act to take effect and be in force from and after the first day of June next.
'* * *

'December 17, 1811.'

§ 4.9.3 Concomitant Future Interest: Remainder

We have just seen that if O creates a fee tail in A, O has a reversion in fee simple. But what if O does not want the property back upon A's bloodline running out? Suppose that O desires B to get the property when A's bloodline runs out. Is it possible, in that event, for O to convey, "to A and the heirs of his body, and then to B"? The answer is, yes. In such case, B has a remainder. The materials that follow explore this future interest.

§ 4.10 Remainders

Initially, it is important to keep in mind that a remainder is a future interest created in a third person; it is not an interest retained by the grantor or the heirs of a testator (as is the case with a reversion, possibility of reverter, or power of termination).

§ 4.10.1 In General

The next two cases will provide you with further elucidation as to what a remainder is.

Commercial Bldg. Co. v. Parslow
93 Fla. 143 (1927)

* * *

In Myers v. Adler, 6 Mackey (17 D. C.) 515, 1 L. R. A. 432,[24] a remainder is defined as an estate [in a third person] limited to take effect in possession immediately after the expiration of a prior estate created at the same time and by the same instrument.* * *

* * *

Proprietors of Church in Brattle Square v. Grant
69 Mass. 142(1855)

In the first paragraph of this case, you are told a key characteristic of a remainder: that it does not become possessory until the prior estate ends by its own terms. The second paragraph gives a basic example of what a remainder is and how this future interest can become a possessory estate. The third and last paragraph of the opinion tells you why a remainder cannot ever follow any type of defeasible fee (fee simple determinable, fee simple determinable subject to an executory limitation, etc.).

---

[24] [*Myers v. Adler* is reproduced below.]

* * *

* * * The essence of a remainder is, that it is to arise immediately on the termination of the particular estate by lapse of time or other determinate event, and not in abridgment of it. Thus a devise to A for twenty years, remainder to B in fee, is the most simple illustration of a particular estate and a remainder. The limitation over does not arise and take effect until the expiration of the period of twenty years, when the particular estate comes to an end by its own limitation.

So a gift to A until C returns from Rome,[25] and then to B in fee, constitutes a valid remainder, because the particular estate, not being a fee, is made to determine upon a fixed and definite event, upon the happening of which it comes to its natural termination.

But if a gift be to A and his heirs till C returns from Rome, then to B in fee, the limitation over is not good as a remainder, because the precedent estate, being an estate in fee, is abridged and brought to an abrupt termination by the gift over on the prescribed contingency. One of the tests, therefore, by which to distinguish between estates in remainder and other contingent and conditional interests in real property, is, that where the event, which gives birth to the ulterior limitation, determines and breaks off the preceding estate before its natural termination, or operates to abridge it, the limitation over does not create a remainder, because it does not wait for the regular expiration of the preceding estate. 1 Jarman on Wills, 780. 4 Kent Com. 197. Besides; wherever the gift is of a fee, there cannot be a remainder, although the fee may be a qualified or determinable one. The fee is the whole estate. When once granted, there is nothing left in the donor but a possibility or right of reverter, which does not constitute an actual estate. 4 Kent Com. 10, *note. Martin v. Strachan,* 5 T. R. 107, *note.* 1 Jarman on Wills, 792. All the estate vests in the first grantee, notwithstanding the qualification annexed to it. If, therefore, the prior gift or grant be of a fee, there can be neither particular estate nor remainder; there is no particular estate, which is an estate less than a fee; and no remainder, because, the fee being exhausted by the prior gift, there is nothing left of it to constitute a remainder. Until the happening of the contingency, or a breach of the condition by which the precedent estate is determined, it retains all the characteristics and qualities of an estate in fee. Although defeasible, it is still an estate in fee. The prior estate may continue forever, it being an estate of inheritance, and liable only to determine on an event which may never happen. For this reason, the rule of the common law was established, that a remainder could not be limited after a fee. In the present case, the devise was, as we have already stated, a gift to the deacons and their successors forever; and they being by statute a quasi corporation, empowered to take and hold grants in fee, it vested in them, *ex vi termini* ["by the force of the term"], an estate in fee, qualified and determinable by a failure to comply with the prescribed condition. * * *

* * *

---

[25] [Why is this not a fee simple subject to an executory limitation? Because A's estate did not include words of inheritance ("and his heirs"), and during this period of time, such words were required. Thus, A has a life estate. Life estates are discussed below.]

§ 4.10.2 Classification of Remainders

There are two types of remainders, as Myers v. Adler *states.*

Myers v. Adler
6 Mackey 515 (D.C. Sup. 1888)

* * *

We all know that the definition of a remainder is "an estate limited to take effect in possession immediately after the expiration of a prior estate created by the same instrument." We also know, from the elementary works, that remainders are vested and contingent * * * .

* * *

§ 4.10.3 Contingent Remainders: Creation and Characteristics

In re Marriage of Meeks
276 Mont. 237 (1996)

In re Marriage of Meeks *states two important principles. The first is when a remainder is a contingent remainder. The other principle is that contingent remainders are traditionally not favored in law; as between construing a remainder as contingent or vested, it is construed as vested (which we have yet to define; see infra).*

* * *

A contingent remainder is a right to property which may or may not vest in possession at some future date. Generally, a remainder will be considered contingent if the recipient is unknown or if the interest will only vest upon the occurrence of an event which is not certain to happen. A remainder will not be considered contingent if it can fairly be construed to be vested. 23 Thompson on Real Property, Thomas Edition (David A. Thomas, ed., 1994), 314 (citations omitted).

* * *

In re Ferry's Estate
55 Cal.2d 776 (1961)

In re Ferry's Estate *explains that remainders, whether contingent or vested, are fully alienable.*

* * *

Furthermore, it is clear that by virtue of Civil Code section 699,[26] an interest, whether vested, contingent or of an executory nature, may be transferred inter vivos, devised, or be the subject of intestate succession. Although in some respects the distinction between the types of further interests is important, upon the attribute of alienability and descendibility there is no distinction. Therefore, aside from the question whether there is an implied condition in the language of the decree of distribution that Mary Silva need survive Joseph in order to take a transmissible interest, Mary Silva's interest is descendible. See Estate of Zuber, supra, 146 Cal.App.2d 584, 591-593, 304 P.2d 247.

* * *

Notes

1. If O conveys, "to A for ten years, then to A's heirs," what interest do A's heirs have? A's heirs have a contingent remainder because a living person (A in this case) does not have heirs; a living person has only heirs apparent. Thus, when O makes the aforementioned conveyance, we cannot identify who the remaindermen are. Consequently, these remaindermen are contingent remaindermen.

2. If O conveys, "to A for ten years, then to B if B returns to New York within the next twelve months," B has a contingent remainder. Although B is identifiable, B's interest is a contingent remainder because B's interest is subject to a condition precedent: for B to take, B must first return to New York within twelve months.

3. If O conveys to A for life, "then to B if B is not convicted of a felony before obtaining age 30, but if B is so convicted of a felony, to C," B and C have "alternative contingent remainders." This means that if B's remainder vests, C's cannot; and if C's remainder vests, B's cannot. See *Summers v. Garland*, 352 Ark. 29 (2003).

4. Note that under the common law, vested remainders are preferred over contingent remainders. See *In re Marriage of Meeks*, supra. Why is this? Contingent remainders are not as marketable as vested remainders. This subject is more fully discussed in the next chapter.

5. Finally, note that if O conveys to A in fee tail, for life, or for a term of years, and B has a contingent remainder in fee simple, then O must have a reversion in fee simple. Why is this? The answer is that you must always account for the entire fee simple absolute. Thus, if the last interest in the conveyance is a contingent remainder, O must always have a reversion. But what if A has a fee tail or a life estate and B and C have alternative contingent remainders? Must O still have a reversion? After all, it is guaranteed that either B's contingent remainder will vest, or C's contingent remainder will vest. The answer is that even where B and C have alternative contingent remainders, O must have a

[26] Civil Code, section 699: 'Future interests pass by succession, will, and transfer, in the same manner as present interests.'

reversion. The reason for this is that under the common law, contingent remainders could be destroyed. (We cover the destructibility of contingent remainders in chapter 5.) As such, O must be prepared to take seisin. Hence, O always has a reversion when the last interest is a contingent remainder.

§ 4.10.4 Vested Remainders: In General

We have learned that a contingent remainder is one given to unascertainable beneficiaries or subject to a condition precedent. A vested remainder is the opposite, as In re Marriage of Meeks *explains.*

In re Marriage of Meeks
276 Mont. 237 (1996)

* * *

[A] vested remainder is one which is limited to an ascertained person in being, whose right to the estate is fixed and certain, and does not depend on the happening of any future event, but whose enjoyment and possession is postponed to some future time. . . . [A] vested remainder is not rendered contingent by the fact that it may never vest in possession.

23 Thompson on Real Property, 325-26 (citations omitted).

* * *

§ 4.10.5 Vested Remainders: Classifications, Creation, and Characteristics

In re Wher's Trust
36 Wis.2d 154 (1967)

In re Wher's Trust, *quoting from the Restatement, states that there are three types of vested remainders: (1) indefeasibly vested; (2) vested subject to open; and (3) vested subject to complete or total defeasance. The footnotes to the text provide further explanation.*

* * *

2 Restatement, Property [(First)], p. 541, sec. 157, classifies remainders as follows:

'A remainder can be

'(a) indefeasibly vested;[27] or
'(b) vested subject to open;[28] or
'(c) vested subject to complete defeasance;[29] or
'(d) subject to a condition precedent.'[30]

* * *

§ 4.10.6 Distinguishing Between Conditions Precedent and Subsequent

We have seen that a remainder that is subject to a condition precedent is a contingent remainder. We also have seen that a remainder subject to condition subsequent (called a vested remainder subject to complete defeasance, above) is a vested remainder. Thus, it becomes important to distinguish a condition precedent (which will create a contingent remainder) from a condition subsequent (which will create a vested remainder subject to total defeasance). The next case explains how we distinguish between conditions precedent and subsequent.

Baker v. Bates
76 Ill.App.2d 30 (1966)

Baker v. Bates *initially tells us that the distinction is—language! It is all in the words (again)! Indeed! The case goes on to teach us that to distinguish between conditions*

---

[27] [An illustration of an indefeasibly vested remainder is, O conveys, "to A for life, then to B." B has an indefeasibly vested remainder in fee simple. An indefeasibly vested remainder is certain to become a possessory estate.]

[28] [An illustration of a vested remainder subject to open (also called a vested remainder subject to partial defeasance) is, O conveys, "to A for life, then to the children of B." At the time of the conveyance, B has one child. Of course, B can have more children (under the common law, everyone is presumed capable of procreating, as you will see in chapter 6). Thus, if at the time of the conveyance B has one child, B1, B1 has a vested remainder subject to open. This means that B1 may have his share cut down if B has more children. For example, if B has twins, B2 and B3, then all of B's children have vested remainders subject to open, each owning an undivided 1/3 interest. Thus, with a vested remainder subject to open, the share of the remainderman may be decreased but it can never be totally wiped out. Upon B's death, the class closes. At that time B1, B2, and B3 would own an indefeasibly vested remainder in fee simple. A significant point to keep in mind here is that future interests change with births, deaths, and materializing of conditions (precedent and subsequent, as you will see).]

[29] [A basic illustration would be, O conveys, "to A for life, then to B, but if C returns to New York to C." A has a life estate, B has a vested remainder in fee simple subject to complete defeasance, and C has a shifting executory interest in fee simple. Why does C have a shifting executory interest? Only a shifting executory interest can defease or cut off a prior estate or prior vested remainder.]

[30] [A remainder subject to a condition precedent is a contingent remainder. See supra.]

precedent and subsequent, we need to see if the condition is part of the gift or if the condition follows the gift.

* * *

Carey and Schuyler, Illinois Law of Future Interests, Sec. 291, at page 398, says:

'Today it is accepted as axiomatic that the law favors the vesting of estates and that remainders will be construed to vest at the earliest possible moment. It is conceivable, and in fact very likely, that the root of this rule of construction was the unwillingness of judges to subject remainders to the harsh doctrine of destructibility[31] except when absolutely necessary.'

The classic definition of a vested remainder and the distinction between a vested remainder or a contingent remainder has been precisely stated by Professor Gray in Gray, The Rule Against Perpetuities (4th Ed.), Sec. 108, p. 95, as follows:

'Whether a remainder is vested or contingent depends upon the language employed. If the conditional element is incorporated into the description of, or into the gift to, the remainderman, then the remainder is contingent; but if, after words giving a vested interest, a clause is added divesting it, the remainder is vested. Thus on a devise to A. for life, remainder to his children, but if any child dies in the lifetime of A. his share to go to those who survive, the share of each child is vested, subject to be divested by its death. But on a devise to A. for life, remainder to such of his children as survive him, the remainder is contingent.'

Gray's classic exposition has been frequently quoted and approved by the Illinois Court. Smith v. Chester, 272 Ill. 428, 112 N.E. 325; Lachenmyer v. Gehlbach, 266 Ill. 11, 107 N.E. 202; Brechbeller v. Wilson, 228 Ill. 502, 81 N.E. 1094.

* * *

§ 4.10.7 Distinguishing Between Vested and Contingent Remainders: In General

Having established that it is important to distinguish vested remainders from contingent remainders, we need to ask, why? Why do we care if a remainder is contingent versus vested? The answer is simple: There are a number of reasons why it is important to distinguish between vested remainders and contingent remainders. First, contingent remainders are subject to the Rule Against Perpetuities; vested remainders are not. Second, only contingent remainders are subject to the rule of destructibility. We cover these topics in the next chapter. Other reasons now follow.

§ 4.10.8 Distinguishing Between Vested and Contingent Remainders: Waste

We have previously learned in chapter 3 what waste is and how one cotenant may be liable to the other cotenant(s) for waste, that is, for destroying the cotenancy property.

---

[31] [Destructibility of contingent remainders is discussed in chapter 6.]

We now come across waste again: in the context of remaindermen. The Federal Deposit Ins. Corp. *case tells us what waste is and which type of remainderman can state a cause of action for waste.*

Federal Deposit Ins. Corp. v. Mars
821 P.2d 826 (Colo. App. 1991)

* * *

At common law, "waste" referred to any unauthorized destruction or severance of improvements, trees, minerals, or other corporeal hereditaments on or from the land belonging to another by one who did not have title, but who was rightfully in possession. *Wingard v. Lee,* 287 S.C. 57, 336 S.E.2d 498 (S.C.App.1985); *Oldham v. Keaton,* 597 S.W.2d 938 (Tex.Civ.App.1980).

This concept has evolved and broadened into a legal means by which any concurrent non-possessory holders of an interest in land are enabled to prevent or restrain harm to land committed by persons in possession. *Smith v. Cap Concrete,* 133 Cal.App.3d 769, 184 Cal.Rptr. 308 (1982). However, the existence of a vested interest in the property, such as a remainder or a reversion, is a vital prerequisite to maintenance of an action for waste. *Saxon v. Johnson,* 393 So.2d 1007 (Ala.Civ.App.1980).

* * *

Notes

1. There is also authority for the proposition that a contingent remainderman has the right to seek equitable relief by way of an injunction to prevent the life tenant from committing waste. See *Pedro v. January*, 261 Or. 582 (1972).

2. What if the life tenant tears down a house in very poor condition so, that as a result, the underlying land is worth more without the house? Is the life tenant liable? The answer is, no. This is called "ameliorative waste" and, in the U.S., the life tenant is not liable in an action for waste. See *Pynchon v. Stearns*, 52 Mass. 304 (Mass. 1846).

§ 4.10.9 Distinguishing Between Vested and Contingent Remainders: Acceleration

A black-letter rule of law is that vested remainders "accelerate" into possession, whenever and however possible. Trust Co. of New Jersey v. Lange *explains what "acceleration" means.*

Trust Co. of New Jersey v. Lange
123 N.J. Eq. 1 (1938)

The testator gave a life estate to his sister,[32] with a vested remainder to a hospital. The sister died before the testator, and the question was whether the vested remainderman's

---

[32] [Life estates are discussed in the next major section of text.]

interest "accelerated"—immediately went into possession upon the death of the testator (which is when a will becomes effective). The court held that the vested remainder did indeed accelerate into possession. The court explained:

* * *

In 23 R.C.L., § 103, is the following: 'It is the general rule that, in the absence of a controlling equity or of an express or implied provision in the will to the contrary, where an estate is given to a person for life, with a vested remainder in another, the remainder takes effect in possession whenever the prior gift ceases or fails in whatever manner. The death of the life tenant before that of the testator simply accelerates the time when the devise over becomes operative, as does also the revocation by the testator of the bequest of the life estate. * * * If the estate for life is void from its inception, it is as if it had never been made and the remainderman is at once entitled to the possession of his estate.'

To the same purport is the opinion in Ryder v. Myers, 113 N.J.Eq. 360, 367, 167 A. 22, affirmed in 115 N.J.Eq. 169, 169 A. 691.

The death of the decedent's sister before his demise had the effect of accelerating the gift to the North Hudson Hospital. The bequest to that institution is, plainly, words of substitution. In this state 'distribution to vested remainderman will be accelerated by termination of precedent estate by any event removing it.' Anthony v. Camden Safe Deposit & Trust Co., 106 N.J.Eq. 41, 149 A. 822.

This court has said that: 'It is familiar law that a legacy lapses by the death of the legatee in the lifetime of the testator, unless there be words of substitution or other provision in the will, or by the statute, against a lapse.' Schoen v. Siegmund, 119 N.J.Eq. 524, 183 A. 292, 294. It may be observed that if the courts can so construe a will as to avoid the lapsing of legacies, that they will do so. Cowley v. Knapp, 42 N.J.L. 297; Peer v. Jenkins, 102 N.J.Eq. 235, 140 A. 413; Fisch v. Fisch, 105 N.J.Eq. 746, 155 A. 146; Roe v. Doe ex dem., 5 Boyce, Del., 545, 93 A. 373; In re Feeney's Estate, 293 Pa. 273, 142 A. 284. Julia Lange Stock died without issue; consequently, section 22 of the statute of wills, 4 Comp.St.1910, p. 5866, § 22, will not apply to the instant case. It is my opinion that the North Hudson Hospital is entitled to the said bequest, and I shall so instruct.

* * *

Application of Wolfsohn
339 N.Y.S.2d 755 (1973)

While vested remainders accelerate into possession, contingent remainders do not, as Application of Wolfsohn *explains:*

* * *

Case law is explicit that the excision of an intermediate estate will not permit the acceleration of remainders unless such remainders are vested. That is to say, no contingent remainder will be permitted to accelerate.

* * *

The cases hold without exception that a contingent remainder cannot be accelerated.

'The law does not accelerate [contingent] remainders * * * .' (Matter of Durand, 250 N.Y. 45, 55, 164 N.E. 737, 740; Kalish v. Kalish, 166 N.Y. 368, 59 N.E. 917.)' Matter of Maloney, 8 A.D.2d 756, 757, 185 N.Y.S.2d 588, 590-591,affd. 7 N.Y.2d 863, 196 N.Y.S.2d 996, 164 N.E.2d 867.)

* * *

§ 4.10.10 Distinguishing Between Vested and Contingent Remainders: Creditors' Claims

The traditional view is that while vested remainders can be attached by creditors, contingent remainders, being too ephemeral, cannot. See, e.g. Patterson v. Caldwell, *124 Pa. 455 (1889). Nonetheless, the more modern approach is that a contingent remainder is still a property interest and, as such, irrespective of whether it actually ever vests in possession, may be attached by creditors. See, e.g.* Wood v. Watson, *20 R.I. 223 (1897).*

§ 4.11 The Life Estate

The life estate is the last freehold estate that we visit. Its creation and its characteristics are discussed in the material that follows.

§ 4.11.1 Creation and Characteristics

In re Felker
211 B.R. 165 (Bkrtcy. M.D.Pa. 1997)

If O conveys, "to A for life," A has a life estate. A discussion of the rights that A has as a life tenant follows. One of the rights that a life tenant has is the right to transfer his life estate. Thus, if A owns a life estate and transfers his estate to B, it is necessary to determine what B owns. In re Felker explains B's interest, as well as other aspects of the characteristics of a life tenant's ownership interest.

* * *

While the pleadings are somewhat convoluted, succinctly stated the issues are (1) whether a life estate was created by the deed of June 30, 1983; (2) if a life estate was created, what is its value * * *

DISCUSSION

Property interests in bankruptcy are typically determined under state law. *Jason Realty, L.P. v. First Fidelity Bank, NA.,* 59 F.3d 423, 427 (3rd Cir.1995). This is so to prevent forum shopping between the state and the federal courts. *Butner v. United States,* 440 U.S. 48, 55, 99 S.Ct. 914, 918, 59 L.Ed.2d 136 (1979).

Black's Law Dictionary defines life estate as "[a]n estate whose duration is limited to the life of the party holding it, or some other person." *Cited, with approval, in Estate of Kinert v. Pennsylvania Dept. of Revenue,* 693 A.2d 643 (Pa.Cmwlth.1997).

The holder of a life estate, i.e., a life tenant, is entitled to both the possession and the use of the property to the exclusion of the remainderman. *Deffenbaugh v. Hess,* 225 Pa. 638, 641, 74 A. 608 (1909). This would include the right of the life tenant to the rents, issues, and profits generated by the parcel during the tenant's life. 51 Am.Jur.2d *Life Tenants and Remaindermen,* § 32 (1970). That a life tenant is entitled to the income from the corpus, is well-established in Pennsylvania. *In re Nirdlinger's Estate,* 290 Pa. 457, 461, 139 A. 200, 202 (1927).

Implicit, of course, to the life tenant's rights to rent is the life tenant's power to "underlease" the property for a lesser term. ("At common law, . . . it was the established doctrine that a tenant for life, with a general power to make leases, could make only leases in possession, and not leases in reversion or in futuro.") *United States v. Noble,* 237 U.S. 74, 82, 35 S.Ct. 532, 535-36, 59 L.Ed. 844 (1915).

Furthermore, the life tenant generally has the power to transfer the estate to such extent no greater than he or she has.[33] Restatement of Property § 124 (1936). It is even possible, under some circumstances, for a life tenant to consume or deplete the estate, if such is consistent with the conveyance. *Allen v. Hirlinger,* 219 Pa. 56, 59, 67 A. 907, 908 (1907).

The life tenant is empowered to mortgage the life estate, and that interest may be sold through foreclosure. 51 Am.Jur.2d *Life Tenants and Remaindermen,* § 99 (1970). * * *.

This package of rights possessed by a life tenant is not without the corresponding duties and obligations the tenant may owe to the successor remaindermen.

> A life tenant is entitled to possession and enjoyment of the property as long as the estate endures. He may convey or lease his interest, but he may not disregard the rights of those who take when his life estate ends. So, he is responsible for ordinary course of business repairs and maintenance; but improvements of a permanent nature, without the acquiescence of the remaindermen, are at his own expense even though the property is thereby made more valuable. The life tenant must pay the taxes, municipal assessments for sidewalk paving, and mortgage interest accruing during his ownership. [Furthermore], the life tenant must not commit or permit waste.

P. Nicholson Wood, *Ladner on Conveyancing in Pennsylvania* § 1:05, at 8 (3rd ed.1961).

With this legal background, I draw the parties' attention to the specific facts of this case.

The conveyance from Joseph Felker, Sr. and Marie F. Felker (Felkers, Sr.) to Joseph M. Felker and Margaret A. Felker (Felkers, Jr.) by deed dated June 30, 1983 is

---

[33] [This is called a life estate "pur autre vie," that is, a life estate measured "by the life of another." Thus, if O conveys "to A for life," and A transfers A's interest to B, B has a life estate pur autre vie, a life estate measured by the life of A. Upon A's death, B's estate ends.]

claimed by the Debtors to have reserved a life estate. The specific language relied upon by the Debtors reads as follows: "EXCEPTING AND RESERVING to the Grantors herein and each of them, the right and privilege to live upon the property herein conveyed for the remainder of their natural lives."

The threshold issue is whether language, such as found in this deed, can support the reservation of a life estate as that term is understood in Pennsylvania jurisprudence. This finding is critical to the Debtors' case. The attributes associated with a life estate are quite different from those flowing from a tenancy less than freehold or a personal license or privilege. (*See, for example, Baldesberger v. Baldesberger,* 378 Pa. 113, 105 A.2d 713 (1954)).

A life estate, along with a fee simple, is a freehold estate. Chester Smith, *Real Property Survey,* at 3 (1956). A freehold estate is typically characterized by the right of possession as well as title. Title is the right of ownership of the property. *P. Nicholson Wood, Ladner on Conveyancing in Pennsylvania* § 1:01 at 2 (3rd ed.1961). A less than freehold estate, such as a tenancy at will, can be identified by the right to possession but not title. (*See id.* at 11). This can be further distinguished from a license where possession remains in the licensor and the licensee has a mere privilege of being on the land without being treated as a trespasser. (Chester Smith, *Real Property Survey,* at 102.) A license is an authority to do an act or a series of acts on the property of another without possessing an estate therein. *Baldwin v. Taylor,* 166 Pa. 507, 31 A. 250 (1895), *In re Shipley's Estate,* 45 Pa.Super. 570, 573 (1911).

* * *

White v. Brown
559 S.W.2d 938 (Tenn. 1977)

If O conveys by deed or devises by will, "to A for life," A has a life estate. That is fundamental. In White v. Brown, *however, T devises, "I give A my home to live in and not to be sold." The issue that the court will have to resolve is whether A took a life estate or a fee simple (with an invalid direct restraint on alienation).*

BROCK, Justice.

This is a suit for the construction of a will. The Chancellor held that the will passed a life estate, but not the remainder, in certain realty, leaving the remainder to pass by inheritance to the testatrix's heirs at law. The Court of Appeals affirmed.

Mrs. Jessie Lide died on February 15, 1973, leaving a holographic will which, in its entirety, reads as follows:

"April 19, 1972

"I, Jessie Lide, being in sound mind declare this to be my last will and testament. I appoint my niece Sandra White Perry to be the executrix of my estate. I wish Evelyn White to have my home to live in and not to be sold.

"I also leave my personal property to Sandra White Perry. My house is not to be sold.

Jessie Lide"

(Underscoring by testatrix).

Mrs. Lide was a widow and had no children. Although she had nine brothers and sisters, only two sisters residing in Ohio survived her. These two sisters quitclaimed any interest they might have in the residence to Mrs. White. The nieces and nephews of the testatrix, her heirs at law, are defendants in this action.

Mrs. White, her husband, who was the testatrix's brother, and her daughter, Sandra White Perry, lived with Mrs. Lide as a family for some twenty-five years. After Sandra married in 1969 and Mrs. White's husband died in 1971, Evelyn White continued to live with Mrs. Lide until Mrs. Lide's death in 1973 at age 88.

Mrs. White, joined by her daughter as executrix, filed this action to obtain construction of the will, alleging that she is vested with a fee simple title to the home. The defendants contend that the will conveyed only a life estate to Mrs. White, leaving the remainder to go to them under our laws of intestate succession. The Chancellor held that the will unambiguously conveyed only a life interest in the home to Mrs. White and refused to consider extrinsic evidence concerning Mrs. Lide's relationship with her surviving relatives. Due to the debilitated condition of the property and in accordance with the desire of all parties, the Chancellor ordered the property sold with the proceeds distributed in designated shares among the beneficiaries.

I.

Our cases have repeatedly acknowledged that the intention of the testator is to be ascertained from the language of the entire instrument when read in the light of surrounding circumstances. See, e.g., Harris v. Bittikofer, 541 S.W.2d 372, 384 (Tenn.1976); Martin v. Taylor, 521 S.W.2d 581, 584 (Tenn.1975); Hoggatt v. Clopton, 142 Tenn. 184, 192, 217 S.W. 657, 659 (1919). But, the practical difficulty in this case, as in so many other cases involving wills drafted by lay persons, is that the words chosen by the testatrix are not specific enough to clearly state her intent. Thus, in our opinion, it is not clear whether Mrs. Lide intended to convey a life estate in the home to Mrs. White, leaving the remainder interest to descend by operation of law, or a fee interest with a restraint on alienation. Moreover, the will might even be read as conveying a fee interest subject to a condition subsequent (Mrs. White's failure to live in the home).

In such ambiguous cases it is obvious that rules of construction, always yielding to the cardinal rule of the testator's intent, must be employed as auxiliary aids in the courts' endeavor to ascertain the testator's intent.

In 1851 our General Assembly enacted two such statutes of construction, thereby creating a statutory presumption against partial intestacy.

Chapter 33 of the Public Acts of 1851 (now codified as T.C.A. §§ 64-101 and 64-501) reversed the common law presumption[34] that a life estate was intended unless the

---

[34] Because the feudal lord granted land solely as compensation for personal services, the grant was for no longer than the life of the grantee. Later the grant was extended to the sons and other issue of the grantee under the designation of "heirs." Heirs were thus entitled to stand in the place of their ancestor after his death if mentioned in the grant but only if specifically mentioned. Thereafter, the word "heirs," when used in a conveyance to a man "and his heirs," came to include collateral as well as lineal heirs, ultimately indicating that such grantee took an estate which would pass to his heirs or the heirs of anyone to whom he aliened it. That is, "heirs" ceased

intent to pass a fee simple was clearly expressed in the instrument. T.C.A. § 64-501 provides:

"Every grant or devise of real estate, or any interest therein, shall pass all the estate or interest of the grantor or devisor, unless the intent to pass a less estate or interest shall appear by express terms, or be necessarily implied in the terms of the instrument."

Chapter 180, Section 2 of the Public Acts of 1851 (now codified as T.C.A. § 32-301) was specifically directed to the operation of a devise. In relevant part, T.C.A. § 32-301 provides:

"A will . . . shall convey all the real estate belonging to (the testator) or in which he had any interest at his decease, unless a contrary intention appear by its words and context."

Thus, under our law, unless the "words and context" of Mrs. Lide's will clearly evidence her intention to convey only a life estate to Mrs. White, the will should be construed as passing the home to Mrs. White in fee. " 'If the expression in the will is doubtful, the doubt is resolved against the limitation and in favor of the absolute estate.' " Meacham v. Graham, 98 Tenn. 190, 206, 39 S.W. 12, 15 (1897) (quoting Washbon v. Cope, 144 N.Y. 287, 39 N.E. 388); Weiss v. Broadway Nat'l Bank, 204 Tenn. 563, 322 S.W.2d 427 (1959); Cannon v. Cannon, 182 Tenn. 1, 184 S.W.2d 35 (1945).

Several of our cases demonstrate the effect of these statutory presumptions against intestacy by construing language which might seem to convey an estate for life, without provision for a gift over after the termination of such life estate, as passing a fee simple instead. In Green v. Young, 163 Tenn. 16, 40 S.W.2d 793 (1931), the testatrix's disposition of all of her property to her husband "to be used by him for his support and comfort during his life" was held to pass a fee estate. Similarly, in Williams v. Williams, 167 Tenn. 26, 65 S.W.2d 561 (1933), the testator's devise of real property to his children "for and during their natural lives" without provision for a gift over was held to convey a fee. And, in Webb v. Webb, 53 Tenn.App. 609, 385 S.W.2d 295 (1964), a devise of personal property to the testator's wife "for her maintenance, support and comfort, for the full period of her natural life" with complete powers of alienation but without provision for the remainder passed absolute title to the widow.

II.

Thus, if the sole question for our determination were whether the will's conveyance of the home to Mrs. White "to live in" gave her a life interest or a fee in the home, a conclusion favoring the absolute estate would be clearly required. The question, however, is complicated somewhat by the caveat contained in the will that the home is "not to be sold" a restriction conflicting with the free alienation of property, one of the most significant incidents of fee ownership. We must determine, therefore, whether Mrs. Lide's will, when taken as a whole, clearly evidences her intent to convey only a life estate in her home to Mrs. White.

Under ordinary circumstances a person makes a will to dispose of his or her entire estate. If, therefore, a will is susceptible of two constructions, by one of which the testator disposes of the whole of his estate and by the other of which he disposes of only a part of

---

to be a word of purchase and became a word of limitation. 1 Tiffany, Real Property § 28 (3d ed. 1939).

his estate, dying intestate as to the remainder, this Court has always preferred that construction which disposes of the whole of the testator's estate if that construction is reasonable and consistent with the general scope and provisions of the will. See Ledbetter v. Ledbetter, 188 Tenn. 44, 216 S.W.2d 718 (1949); Cannon v. Cannon, supra ; Williams v. Williams, supra; Jarnagin v. Conway, 21 Tenn. 50 (1840); 4 Page, Wills s 30.14 (3d ed. 1961). A construction which results in partial intestacy will not be adopted unless such intention clearly appears. Bedford v. Bedford, 38 Tenn.App. 370, 274 S.W.2d 528 (1954); Martin v. Hale, 167 Tenn. 438, 71 S.W.2d 211 (1934). It has been said that the courts will prefer any reasonable construction or any construction which does not do violence to a testator's language, to a construction which results in partial intestacy. Ledbetter, supra.

The intent to create a fee simple or other absolute interest and, at the same time to impose a restraint upon its alienation can be clearly expressed. If the testator specifically declares that he devises land to A "in fee simple" or to A "and his heirs" but that A shall not have the power to alienate the land, there is but one tenable construction, viz., the testator's intent is to impose a restraint upon a fee simple. To construe such language to create a life estate would conflict with the express specification of a fee simple as well as with the presumption of intent to make a complete testamentary disposition of all of a testator's property. By extension, as noted by Professor Casner in his treatise on the law of real property:

"Since it is now generally presumed that a conveyor intends to transfer his whole interest in the property, it may be reasonable to adopt the same construction, (conveyance of a fee simple) even in the absence of words of inheritance, if there is no language that can be construed to create a remainder." 6 American Law of Property s 26.58 (A. J. Casner ed. 1952).

In our opinion, testatrix's apparent testamentary restraint on the alienation of the home devised to Mrs. White does not evidence such a clear intent to pass only a life estate as is sufficient to overcome the law's strong presumption that a fee simple interest was conveyed.

Accordingly, we conclude that Mrs. Lide's will passed a fee simple absolute in the home to Mrs. White. Her attempted restraint on alienation must be declared void as inconsistent with the incidents and nature of the estate devised and contrary to public policy. Nashville C & S.L. Ry. v. Bell, 162 Tenn. 661, 39 S.W.2d 1026 (1931). The decrees of the Court of Appeals and the trial court are reversed and the cause is remanded to the chancery court for such further proceedings as may be necessary, consistent with this opinion. Costs are taxed against appellees.

COOPER and FONES, JJ., concur.

HARBISON, J., dissents.
HENRY, C. J., joins in dissent.
HARBISON, Justice, dissenting.

With deference to the views of the majority, and recognizing the principles of law contained in the majority opinion, I am unable to agree that the language of the will of Mrs. Lide did or was intended to convey a fee simple interest in her residence to her sister-in-law, Mrs. Evelyn White.

The testatrix expressed the wish that Mrs. White was "to have my home to live in and not to be sold ". The emphasis is that of the testatrix, and her desire that Mrs. White was not to have an unlimited estate in the property was reiterated in the last sentence of the will, to wit: "My house is not to be sold."

The testatrix appointed her niece, Mrs. Perry, executrix and made an outright bequest to her of all personal property.

The will does not seem to me to be particularly ambiguous, and like the Chancellor and the Court of Appeals, I am of the opinion that the testatrix gave Mrs. White a life estate only, and that upon the death of Mrs. White the remainder will pass to the heirs at law of the testatrix.

* * *

§ 4.11.2 Concomitant Future Interests: Reversion or Remainder

Whenever a transferor conveys or devises a life estate, a reversion remains in the grantor or in the successors in interest of a testator, unless a vested remainder is created in a third person. Everything stated in the material regarding the concomitant future interest for the fee tail applies to life estates.

CHAPTER 5
HINDERING AND HELPING ALIENATION

§ 5.1 Introduction

In this chapter, we cover rules that both hinder and help alienation (that is, transferability) of property. More specifically, we will learn how a so-called spendthrift trust can hinder alienation property. We will also cover doctrines that historically have helped further alienation: destructibility of contingent remainders, the Rule in Shelley's Case, and the Doctrine of Worthier Title. Before we cover these subjects, however, we need to explain briefly the development and history of trusts.

§ 5.2 Introduction to Trusts

Although you will learn much about trusts in the course, "Wills & Trusts," it is important to learn something about the subject now. The reason is that virtually all future interests in this country are created in the context of trusts. But what is a trust? The materials that follow explain.

§ 5.2.1 History of Trusts

The history of modern day trusts began in the late middle ages with the common law "use." For example, O would convey, "to X, for the use of A for life, then for the use of B." X would be the legal owner while A would use the property for the lifetime of A. At A's death, X would make certain that B would have use of the property. Thus, X not only owned the fee simple, but also was charged with carrying out O's intent. This arrangement worked well, until X tried to keep the land for himself. When that happened, if O or A went to a court of law to seek a remedy to compel X to comply with the terms of the conveyance, a court of law would dismiss the complaint: a "use" was not a legally recognized property interest. Nonetheless, the new, separate, and competing courts of equity would give relief to O or A on equitable grounds: O trusted (hence the word, "trust") X to comply and equity would enforce the use. Hence, we have the beginning of the modern trust.

Of course, the question must be asked: why would someone even want to structure ownership in this manner? There were several reasons. This arrangement—the common law use—often was employed for lawful reasons (to provide for a minor child or an incapacitated relative), but it also was employed by those who did not want others to know that they had a property interest.

For example, members of the clergy who took a vow of poverty could not own property, so they employed the use to escape these vows: such vows did not prohibit them from using the property of the legal owner. Similarly, debtors who sought to evade their creditors would have title to their property put in the name of another, thus making themselves judgment proof if they defaulted on loans. Others employed the use to defeat inheritance taxes.

Overall, the so-called use was quite popular in England. In fact, it was so popular that by the early part of the sixteenth century, virtually all land in England was held by the use. Nonetheless, the use presented many problems for King Henry: the clergy were gaining great financial power; creditors were becoming hesitant about extending credit; and, perhaps most importantly, the royal treasury was going broke from evasion of inheritance taxes.

In 1536, Parliament, at Henry's urging, enacted the Statute of Uses. In short, the statute "executed the use," meaning that the person who had beneficial use of the property received legal title by operation of law. The Statute of Uses, reproduced immediately below, first delineated the problems in the realm and then provided for the solution—the execution of the use:

> *Where, by the common laws of this realm, lands, tenements, and hereditaments be not devisable by testament, nor ought to be transferred from one to another but by solemn livery and seisin . . . , yet, nevertheless, divers and sundry imaginations, subtle inventions, and practices have been used whereby the hereditaments of this realm have been conveyed from one to another by fraudulent feoffments, fines, recoveries, and other assurances craftily made to secret uses, intents, and trusts, and also by wills and testaments sometime made by . . . words, sometime by signs and tokens, and sometime by writing . . . . , for the extirping and extinguishment of all such . . . , and to the intent that the king's highness or any other his subjects of this realm shall not in any wise hereafter . . . be deceived, damaged, or hurt by reason of such trusts, uses, or confidences . . . . : it may please the king's most royal majesty that it may be enacted by his highness, by the assent of the lords spiritual and temporal and the commons in this present parliament assembled, and by authority of the same . . . , that, where any person or persons stand or be seised or at any time hereafter shall happen to be seised of and in any honours, castles, manors, lands, tenements, rents, services, reversions, remainders, or other hereditaments, to the use, confidence, or trust of any other person or persons, or of any body politic, by reason of any bargain, sale, feoffment, fine, recovery, covenant, contract, agreement, will, or otherwise . . . , in every such case all and every such person and persons and bodies politic . . . shall from henceforth stand and be seised, deemed, and adjudged in lawful seisin, estate, and possession of and in the same honours [etc.] . . . to all intents, constructions, and purposes in the law . . . . ; and that the estate, right, title, and possession that was in such person*

or persons that were or shall be hereafter seised of any lands, tenements, or hereditaments to the use, confidence, or trust of any such person or persons, or of any body politic, be from henceforth clearly deemed and adjudged to be in him or them that have or hereafter shall have such use, confidence, or trust. . . .

Statute of Uses, 27 Hen. 8 c. 10 (1536).

Subsequent legislation was enacted to carry out the Statute of Uses.

Two consequences flowed from the Statute of Uses. The first was that a new future interest was recognized in law: the executory interest (the interest that "executed the use"). Because Parliament did not require the ritual of livery of seisin to transfer a property interest, the courts of law no longer did, either. The second consequence was that spurious uses (or trusts) came to an end. But—and this is the big qualification—uses that were not passive but active (meaning that the trustee had real management-like duties) survived the Statute of Uses. It is for this reason that the Statute of Uses did not put an end to all trusts. The Statute of Uses ended only passive (that is, fraudulent) trusts of real property. The Statute of Uses had no application to so-called active trusts and to trusts of personal property.

§ 5.2.2 Modern-Day Trusts

California-Nevada Annual Conference of United Methodist Church v. St. Luke's United Methodist Church
121 Cal.App.4th 754 (2004)

Now that you have some idea of how trusts evolved, it is time to provide you with a concrete definition of a so-called private express trust, the type of trust that lawyers use with respect to creating estates in land and future interests. (There are other types of trusts, too: charitable trusts, constructive trusts, and resulting trusts. You will learn about these other types of trusts in the course, "Wills & Trusts.")

* * *

A trust is "a fiduciary relationship with respect to property, subjecting the person by whom the title to the property is held to equitable duties to deal with the property for the benefit of another person, which arises as a result of a manifestation of an intention to create it." (Rest.2d Trusts, § 2, p. 6.) "A trust is created by a manifestation of intention of the settlor to create a trust, trust property, a lawful trust purpose, and an identifiable beneficiary." (*Chang v. Redding Bank of Commerce* (1994) 29 Cal.App.4th 673, 684, 35 Cal.Rptr.2d 64.) "An express trust is generally created in one of two ways: (1) a *declaration of trust,* by which the owner of property declares that he holds it as trustee for some beneficiary; (2) a *transfer in trust,* by which the owner transfers to another as trustee for some beneficiary, either by *deed* or other transfer *inter vivos,* or by will." (11 Witkin, Summary of Cal. Law (9th ed. 1990) Trusts, § 26(a), p. 911; see also Prob.Code, § 15200; Rest.2d Trusts, § 17.)

* * *

§ 5.2.3 Spendthrift Trusts

A spendthrift trust is simply a private express trust with a so-called spendthrift provision: a prohibition against voluntary alienation (preventing a trust beneficiary from transferring his right to receive payment from the trust in the future) and involuntary alienation (preventing a creditor of the beneficiary from attaching the beneficiary's right to receive payment from the trust in the future). So states Brosamer v. Mark.

Brosamer v. Mark
540 N.E.2d 652 (Ind.App. 1989)

* * *

In general, a spendthrift trust is one in which the beneficiary is unable to transfer, assign, or alienate his right to future payments of income or principal, and which provides the beneficiary's creditors are unable to subject the beneficiary's interest to the payment of their claims while in the hands of the trustee. *See* Bogert, *Trusts* § 40 (6th ed.1987); 76 Am.Jur.2d *Trusts* § 148 (1975); 89 C.J.S. *Trusts* § 22 (1955).* * * .

When funds from a spendthrift trust are paid to a beneficiary, those funds are no longer protected by the trust. As Professor Bogert observed:

"Such a trust does not involve any restraint on alienability or creditors rights with respect to property after it is received by the beneficiary from the trustee, but rather is merely a restraint with regard to his rights to future payments under the trust." Bogert, *Trusts* § 40 at 148-49 (6th ed. 1987). *See also* 76 Am.Jur.2d *Trusts* § 173 (1975); 90 C.J.S. *Trusts* § 198 (1955).

* * *

Sherman v. Skuse
166 N.Y. 345 (1901)

Skuse was the beneficiary of a spendthrift trust. As such, the trust restricted voluntary and involuntary alienation. Sherman was a physician who had provided medical services to Skuse and sought compensation directly from the trustee.

WERNER, J.

This action is brought to compel the defendant trustees to account for the property, effects, income, and interest received by them to which the defendant Frank Skuse has title, or in which he has an interest, under the will of Francis N. Skuse, and to account for all payments made therefrom by said trustees, and out of any balance remaining in their hands to pay the plaintiff's claim against said Frank Skuse for medical services rendered by the former to the latter. * * * The reason for * * * [the restriction on alienation] provision for the benefit of Frank is found in the undisputed testimony that he is addicted to periodic and excessive indulgence in intoxicants, which renders him at times incapable of prudently managing himself or his affairs.

The history of the plaintiff's claim is embraced in the following facts: At various times between May 4, 1894, and August, 1896, the plaintiff, who is a physician, furnished medicines and rendered medical services to the defendant Frank. Under this head the trial court has found 'that the services and medicines so rendered and furnished by the plaintiff for the defendant Frank Skuse were rendered and furnished to him for his personal bodily ailments, and were such services and medicines as were proper and necessary to be rendered by the plaintiff to the defendant Frank Skuse as his physician; that such services were partly rendered at the house of the defendant Richard Skuse, who had knowledge thereof; and that they were so rendered upon the request of the defendant Frank Skuse.' There were further findings to the effect that the defendant Frank Skuse was insolvent, and that the defendants James, Thomas, and Richard, as such trustees, have in their hands unexpended income applicable to the support of the defendant Frank. These findings were not disturbed by the appellate division, and are therefore binding upon this court.

* * *

* * * It is one of the fundamental maxims of equity that 'equity looks upon that as done which should be done.' Under the testator's direction referred to, these trustees may be regarded as the mere custodians of any income in their hands which should properly be applied to the payment of necessaries furnished to them for the beneficiary, or to the beneficiary himself with their knowledge and consent. In theory of equity, it is already applied. The court simply directs the formal payment out of said fund, which the trustees should have made without such direction. It seems, therefore, that, in any view which may be taken of the nature of this case, it is the duty of equity to interpose in aid of the plaintiff. If we should hold, as the appellants contend, that this is an action to enforce the trust, there would be no obstacle to the further conclusion that the plaintiff has such an interest in that portion of the trust fund applicable to the payment of necessaries as to give him standing in a court of equity. * * * In Virginia it has been held that a guardian's bond may be subjected in equity to the payment of a creditor's claim for necessaries furnished to the ward. Barnum v. Frost's Adm'r, 17 Grat. 398. In Georgia it has been decided that a creditor for necessaries furnished to a trustee for his cestui que trust upon the faith of the estate may file a bill in equity to obtain payment for such necessaries to the extent of the income. Hatcher v. Massey, 71 Ga. 794. A similar case is Kupferman v. McGehee, 63 Ga. 251. These cases are all so different from the one at bar that they are useful only for the purpose of showing that where similar questions have arisen in other states the courts have found some way of doing justice. The order of the appellate division should therefore be affirmed, and judgment absolute rendered for the plaintiff, upon appellants' stipulation, with costs.

PARKER, C. J., and GRAY, O'BRIEN, HAIGHT, LANDON, and CULLEN, JJ., concur.

§ 5.3 Destructibility of Contingent Remainders

Contingent remainders are not marketable. Who, for example, would buy a contingent remainder, on the condition that "A survive B" or "if A reaches age 35" or "if A is not arrested for a felony within the next 20 years"? All of these are gambles, of which no serious investor would partake. As such, contingent remainders were seen as impeding alienation. Hence, the common law created several doctrines to eliminate these impediments to marketability. One of these was the doctrine of destructibility of contingent remainders. This doctrine holds that if a contingent remainder does not become a vested remainder or a possessory estate (e.g. life estate) upon the termination of the preceding estate, the contingent remainder is destroyed. Ryan v. Monaghan *provides us with an illustration of the problem as well as a statement of the doctrine.*

Ryan v. Monaghan
99 Tenn. 338 (1897)

Testator devised, "to my wife for life, then to the heirs of my son." Note that a living person has no heirs. Thus, when the wife died, the son was still alive. Therefore, the heirs of the son (the contingent remaindermen) were unascertainable. The contingent remainder could not vest when the life tenant died. The destructibility of contingent remainders thus came into play, as the court explains.

BEARD, J.

James Monaghan died, leaving a will, which was duly probated. The seventh and eighth clauses of this will are as follows: "Art 7. To my beloved wife, Margaret, I give during her natural life all other real and personal property I may die seised and possessed of, to be used by her for her own separate use and benefit, without being controlled or interfered with under any circumstances by any one, except that she may pay fifty dollars each month to my son, James P., for his maintenance, provided it does not exceed one-third of the income of the estate. Art 8. At the death of my wife, I direct, will, and bequeath to the heirs of my son, James P. Monaghan, all of the real estate which I did seised and possessed of, to be for their use and benefit, under the direction of the probate court of Shelby county, Tennessee * * * ."

The testator left surviving him his wife, Margaret, and James P. Monaghan, his only child and heir at law, who was at the death of testator, and continues to be, an unmarried man. The life tenant having subsequently died, this bill was filed by the brothers and the sister of the testator, asking primarily for a construction of the eighth clause of the will, and alleging that upon a proper interpretation of it James P. Monaghan, the son, is without interest in the property covered by this clause; and that, as the life estate has fallen in[1], they are entitled to be let into its possession and enjoyment as owners in fee. There is no doubt of the intention of the testator as it is expressed in clause or article 7 of the will. He intended that his wife, Margaret, should take a life estate in all his real and personal property, save the lot named in his eighth clause as No. 23 Alabama street, which he had disposed of in an earlier article of his will. For some reason, undisclosed in the record, the father made no provision for his son taking an interest in his realty. He did not disinherit him, but he simply failed to provide for him, so far as his real estate was concerned. While omitting to make provision for him in this respect, he did not disregard his heirs, but devised to them, on the falling in of the life estate, all of

---

[1] [That is, the life estate ended.]

the realty which, by the preceding article, had been given to the wife for the term of her natural life. This estate thus devised to the "heirs of" the son was a contingent remainder; and as this son was then alive, and as nemo est haeres viventis,[2] this remainder estate, not being able to take effect on the termination of the particular or supporting estate, fell to the ground.[3] In the meantime, where rests the inheritance of this property? In whom is it lodged? * * * By accident or design the testator failed to dispose of the inheritance, and by operation of law it passed to his son and only heir, James P. Monaghan. Clopton v. Clopton, 2 Heisk. 31; Bigley v. Watson, 98 Tenn. 353, 39 S. W. 525.

* * *

Note

The doctrine of destructibility applies only to legal contingent remainders of real property. The doctrine has no application to equitable interests.

Johnson v. Amstutz

101 N.M. 94 (1984)

This case takes the majority view: that the doctrine of destructibility of contingent remainders is not generally followed today.

OPINION

RIORDAN, Justice.

George I. and Geraldine Johnson (Johnsons) were among several plaintiffs in a quiet title action against numerous defendants. The district court found for the Johnsons, and on appeal we reversed. *Abo Petroleum Corp. v. Amstutz,* 93 N.M. 332, 600 P.2d 278 (1979). We held in pertinent part that the contingent remainders in the heirs of the grantors in the Johnsons' chain of title were not destroyed by the 1916 deed. Thereafter, the Johnsons brought an action for declaratory judgment to determine their rights in and to certain real property and the value of improvements made to such real property. The district court granted defendants' motion to dismiss Count I, which is the subject of this appeal. The Johnsons appeal. We affirm.

The sole issue we address is whether the doctrine of destructibility of contingent remainders has ever been the law in New Mexico.

In *Abo,* we recognized that even though New Mexico adopted the common law of England, pursuant to NMSA 1978, Section 38-1-3, if the common law is not applicable to our condition and circumstances, we will not give it effect. Therefore, we declined to apply the doctrine of destructibility of contingent remainders because the doctrine "is but a relic of the feudal past, which has no justification or support in modern society[.]" *Abo,* 93 N.M. at 335, 600 P.2d at 281.

---

[2] ["No one is the heir of a living person."]
[3] [That is to say, it was destroyed.]

In this appeal, the Johnsons argue that until the decision in *Abo,* the doctrine of destructibility of contingent remainders was the law in New Mexico. In other words, they argue that *Abo* did not declare that the doctrine has never been the law in New Mexico, but simply declared that the doctrine would not be applied in modern New Mexico society. We disagree with the Johnsons' argument.

In *Abo,* 93 N.M. at 334, 600 P.2d at 280, we stated that:

> The doctrine of destructibility of contingent remainders has been almost universally regarded to be obsolete by legislatures, courts and legal writers. *See, e.g., Whitten v. Whitten,* 203 Okl. 196, 219 P.2d 228 (1950); 1 L. Simes and A. Smith, *Law of Future Interests* § 209 (2d ed. 1956). It has been renounced by virtually all jurisdictions in the United States, either by statute or judicial decision, and *was abandoned in the country of its origin over a century ago.* Section 240 of the *Restatement of Property* (1936) takes the position that the doctrine is based in history, not reason. Comment (d) to § 240 states that "complexity, confusion, unpredictability and frustration of manifested intent" are the demonstrated consequences of adherence to the doctrine of destructibility. Furthermore, because operation of the doctrine can be avoided by the use of a trust to support the contingent remainder, the doctrine places a premium on the drafting skills of the lawyer. 49 Mich.L.Rev. 762, 764 (1951). (emphasis added).

In analyzing the reception of the English common law doctrine of destructibility of contingent remainders in American states, we look to the cited authority relied upon in *Abo,* and again find ourselves in agreement with *Restatement of Property* Section 240 comment c (1936), that provides in pertinent part:

The English rule as to the "destructibility of contingent remainders" originated in the then already outmoded feudal concepts of seisin * * *. Its unsuitability to the circumstances of its country of origin is evidenced by the quick development in England of conveyancing devices and construction tendencies narrowing its significance close to the vanishing point * * *. The conditions of the New World were even less appropriate for an acceptance of this anachronism. During the colonial period the colonial law was supposed to agree with the common law, but after the revolution when courts were deciding the extent of reception of the English common law the doctrine was settled that only those rules of the common law appropriate to the conditions obtaining in the New World were intended by the so-called reception statutes. The English rule as to the "destructibility of contingent remainders" was not, and is not, thus appropriate. Consequently *that rule can reasonably be declared never to have become a part of the law of an American state, by the reception of the English common law.* (emphasis added). Therefore, we specifically hold that the doctrine is not now and has never been the law in New Mexico.

In light of this determination, the other issue raised in this appeal is moot.

The decision by the district court is affirmed.

IT IS SO ORDERED.

STOWERS and WALTERS, JJ., concur.

§ 5.4 The Rule in Shelley's Case

The Rule in Shelley's Case is yet another ancient doctrine whose purpose was to make property more marketable by destroying certain contingent interests. The rule essentially provides that when O conveys (or T devises), "to A for life, then to the heirs of A," A's heirs take nothing; rather, A takes a remainder. Unlike the destructibility doctrine, the Rule in Shelley's Case applies to legal and equitable interests.

City Bank and Trust Co. in Dixon v. Morrissey
118 Ill.App.3d 640 (1983)

A will provided for the establishment of a trust, for William Tyne for his life, then to "the heirs [of William Tyne] who survive him." In determining the distribution of the trust assets, the court applies and explains the Rule in Shelley's Case.

* * *

* * * The sole issue on appeal is whether the Rule in Shelley's Case applies to the fifth paragraph of Margaret Tyne's will which created the Trust.

Initially, we note that although the Rule was abolished by statute in 1953 (Ill.Rev.Stat.1981, ch. 30, par. 186), the statute has no retroactive application and the rule must be given effect to instruments executed and delivered prior to the enactment of the statute. (Ill.Rev.Stat.1981, ch. 30, par. 187; *Arnold Baker* (1962), 26 Ill.2d 131, 134, 185 N.E.2d 844, 846; *Orme v. Northern Trust Co.* (1962), 25 Ill.2d 151, 160, 183 N.E.2d 505, 510; *See also, Evans v. Giles* (1980), 83 Ill.2d 448, 47 Ill.Dec. 349, 415 N.E.2d 354.) The Rule in Shelley's Case provides that if an estate of freehold is granted by any instrument and the remainder is limited by the same instrument, either mediately or immediately, to the heir or heirs of the body of the person taking the freehold as a class, without explanation, the person taking the freehold also takes the remainder, thus vesting him with a fee simple interest. (*Churchill v. Marr* (1921), 300 Ill. 302, 308, 133 N.E. 335, 337; *Seymour v. Heubaum* (1965), 65 Ill.App.2d 89, 95-96, 211 N.E.2d 897, 900, *leave to appeal denied.*) There are three requisites for the application of the Rule: (1) a freehold estate must be granted to the ancestor; (2) a remainder must be limited to his heirs, general or special; and (3) the two estates, freehold and remainder, must both be of the same quality, either legal or equitable. (*Sutliff v. Aydelott* (1940), 373 Ill. 633, 636, 27 N.E.2d 529, 531; *Seymour v. Heubaum* (1965), 65 Ill.App.2d 89, 95-96, 211 N.E.2d 897, 900, *leave to appeal denied.*) The Rule has been applied to the equitable interests in trusts (*Sutliff v. Aydelott* (1940), 373 Ill. 633, 636, 27 N.E.2d 529, 531; *Wilson v. Harrold* (1919), 288 Ill. 388, 393-94, 123 N.E. 563, 565), however, it does not apply to trusts insofar as the trust contains personal property.[4] *Sutliff v. Aydelott* (1940), 373 Ill. 633,

---

[4] [In other jurisdictions, the Rule in Shelley's Case has been applied to personal property. See, for example, *In re Thorne's Estate*, 344 Pa. 503 (1942) (rule applied by analogy).]

638, 27 N.E.2d 529, 532; *Lord v. Comstock* (1909), 240 Ill. 492, 505, 88 N.E. 1012, 1018.

The Rule in Shelley's Case is a rule of law and not of construction. (*Lord v. Comstock* (1909), 240 Ill. 492, 499, 88 N.E. 1012, 1015; *McFall v. Kirkpatrick* (1908), 236 Ill. 281, 296, 86 N.E. 139, 143; Restatement of Property § 312, comment (k) at 1759 (1940, 1982 Supp.).) Thus, if the requirements for the application of the Rule are present, the Rule will be applied regardless of the intent of the grantor. (*Cahill v. Cahill* (1949), 402 Ill. 416, 421, 84 N.E.2d 380, 384; *Lord v. Comstock* (1909), 240 Ill. 492, 499, 88 N.E. 1012, 1015.) When applied the Rule operates on the remainder alone, taking it from the heirs and vesting it in the ancestor thus giving the ancestor, through the doctrine of merger, a fee simple interest. *Lydick v. Tate* (1942), 380 Ill. 616, 623, 44 N.E.2d 583, 589; *Seymour v. Heubaum* (1965), 65 Ill.App.2d 89, 96-97, 211 N.E.2d 897, 900-01, *leave to appeal denied.*

When the foregoing authority is applied to the instrument before us, it is clear that the trial court correctly applied the Rule in Shelley's Case. The appellants do not contest that the first two elements necessary for the application of the Rule are present in the instant case, *i.e.,* that William Tyne received a freehold estate and that the remainder was to his heirs at law. No contrary conclusion is possible since the word "heirs" is a technical word which is presumed to have been used in its strict legal sense absent clear and affirmative language to the contrary. (*Lydick v. Tate* (1942), 380 Ill. 616, 625, 44 N.E.2d 583, 589; *Seymour v. Heubaum* (1965), 65 Ill.App.2d 89, 97, 211 N.E.2d 897, 901, *leave to appeal denied.*) Since no such language is used in the Margaret Tyne will, the first two elements for the application of the Rule are satisfied.

[The court also found the third element of the Rule in Shelley's Case satisfied.]

As a result of the foregoing, all three of the elements necessary for the application of the Rule are present and once the Rule is applied it does not matter that the quality or nature of one of the estates is altered at a later date. (*Seymour v. Heubaum* (1965), 65 Ill.App.2d 89, 103- 04, 211 N.E.2d 897, 904, *leave to appeal denied;* Restatement of Property § 312, comment (h) at 1756 (1940, 1982 Supp.).) Thus, William Tyne received a fee simple interest in the realty of the Trust at the time of its original conveyance and that interest continued even though the realty may later have been converted into personalty. Accordingly, the trial court was correct in applying the Rule to the realty of the Trust and its proceeds and distributing them to the appellees as legatees of William Tyne's will. The court was also correct in not applying the Rule to the personalty which was ordered distributed to the appellants and appellees as William Tyne's heirs at law. For the foregoing reasons the judgment of the circuit court of Lee County is affirmed.

Affirmed.

SEIDENFELD, P.J., and VAN DUESEN, J., concur.

Note

Modernly, where the Rule in Shelley's Case is not applicable (the vast majority of jurisdictions), the life tenant does not take a remainder; rather, the grantee's heirs or the devisee's heirs take a contingent remainder.

§ 5.5 The Doctrine of Worthier Title

The Doctrine of Worthier Title is yet another doctrine to eliminate contingent interests. The doctrine applies when O, who owns Blackacre, reserves a life estate for himself (or transfers a life estate to a third person) and conveys the remainder, "to O's heirs." In such case, under the Doctrine of Worthier Title, the heirs of O take nothing. Rather, O takes a reversion in fee simple.

Bixby v. California Trust Co.
33 Cal.2d 495 (1949)

The plaintiff created an irrevocable spendthrift trust whereby he owned the equitable life estate and his "heirs" owned the equitable remainder. He now seeks to end the trust (he needs the money). The only way he can end it is if he also owns the future interest. The only way he can own the future interest is if the Doctrine of Worthier Title is applied.

GIBSON, Chief Justice.

Plaintiff is seeking to terminate a spend-thrift trust established by him and declared to be irrevocable. The trial court construed the trust instrument as creating remainder interests in his heirs at law and denied termination. Plaintiff has appealed contending that he is the sole beneficiary and is entitled to the relief sought.

The trust instrument provided that plaintiff settlor was to receive the income for life, and his interest was stated to be inalienable and inaccessible to creditors. It also provided that 'Upon the death of said trustor and beneficiary * * * all of the residue and remainder of said Trust Estate shall be * * * distributed and delivered to the heirs at law (of the trustor) in accordance with the laws of sucession of the State of California then in effect. * * *'

Where the trustor is the sole beneficiary no problem arises of defeating the trust against the trustor's wishes, and it has been held that, even where the trust instrument contains spendthrift provisions, he can compel termination in the absence of a showing of incapacity or other reason why he should not be permitted to exercise control over his property. See Weymouth v. Delaware Trust Co., Del.Ch., 45 A.2d 427; Burton v. Boren, 308 Ill. 440, 139 N.E. 868; Fidelity & Columbia Trust Co. v. Williams, 268 Ky. 671, 105 S.W.2d 814; Stephens v. Moore, 298 Mo. 215, 249 S.W. 601; Wade v. McKeown, 193 Okl. 415, 145 P.2d 951; O'brien v. Holden, 104 Vt. 338, 160 A. 192; Rest., Trusts, § 339; 3 Scott on Trusts (1939) § 339; Griswold, Spendthrift Trusts (1947) pp. 576, 577; 37 Yale L.J. (1927) 1076. In the present case plaintiff was under no disability, and there was no showing of any facts which would justify a refusal to determinate if he was the sole beneficiary. On the other hand, if remainder interests were created in plaintiff's heirs, they were also beneficiaries, and the court could not terminate the trust without their consent. Eakle v. Ingram, 142 Cal. 15, 75 P. 566, 100 Am.St.Rep. 99; Scrivner v. Dietz, 84 Cal. 295, 297, 24 P. 171; Hellman v. McWilliams, 70 Cal. 449, 453, 11 P. 659; see In re Estate of Madison, 26 Cal.2d 453, 465, 159 P.2d 630; Fidelity & Columbia Trust Co. v. Gwynn, 206 Ky. 823, 268 S.W. 537, 38 A.L.R. 937, 941; Rehr v. Fidelity Philadelphia Trust Co., 310 Pa. 301, 165 A. 380, 91 A.L.R. 99, 102; Garneau v. Garneau, 63 R.I. 416,

9 A.2d 15, 131 A.L.R. 450, 457. Accordingly, the question presented for decision is whether the trust instrument created remainder interests in the heirs at law.

When the trust instrument specifies that the income shall be paid to the trustor for life and provides that on his death the trust property shall be distributed to his heirs at law, it is generally held that no remainder interests are created and that the trustor is the sole beneficiary and retains a reversionary interest in the trust corpus. Doctor v. Hughes, 225 N.Y. 305, 122 N.E. 221; Burton v. Boren, 308 Ill. 440, 139 N.E. 868; Bottimore v. First & Merchants Nat. Bank, 170 Va. 221, 196 S.E. 593; Stephens v. Moore, 298 Mo. 215, 249 S.W. 601; Dunnett v. First Nat. Bank & Trust Co. of Tulsa, 184 Okl. 82, 85 P.2d 281; Fidelity Union Trust Co. v. Parfner, 135 N.J.Eq. 133, 37 A.2d 675; Fidelity & Columbia Trust Co. v. Williams, 268 Ky. 671, 105 S.W.2d 814; see Note 125 A.L.R. 548-590; 1 Scott on Trusts (1939) p. 656; Rest., Trusts, § 127, Comment a.

The rule established by the above decisions has been justified upon the theory that such a result carries out the usual intention of the trustor, and it applies unless a contrary intent is manifested. See Doctor v. Hughes, 225 N.Y. 305, 122 N.E. 221, 223; Fidelity Union Trust Co. v. Parfner, 135 N.J.Eq. 133, 37 A.2d 675, 678; Dunnett v. First Nat. Bank & Trust Co. of Tulsa, 184 Okl. 82, 85 P.2d 281, 283, 284; Rest., Property, s 314, Comment a; Rest., Trusts, § 127, Comment a; 1 Scott on Trusts (1939) pp. 656, 657; cf. 1 Simes, The Law of Future Interests (1936) § 147; see also cases collected in 125 A.L.R. 555-558. It is said that where a person creates a life estate in himself with a gift over to his heirs he ordinarily intends the same thing as if he had given the property to his estate; that he does not intend to make a gift to any particular person but indicates only that upon his death the residue of the trust property shall be distributed according to the general laws governing succession; and that he does not intend to create in any persons an interest which would prevent him from exercising control over the beneficial interest. See Rest., Property, § 314, Comment a; 1 Scott on Trusts (1939) p. 657. Moreover, this rule of construction is in accord with the general policy in favor of the free alienability of property, since its operation tends to make property more readily transferable. See Rest., Property, § 314, Comment a; 1 Simes, The Law of Future Interests (1936) p. 265. The same result was reached in the early common law as an outgrowth of the doctrine of 'worthier title,' which, for reasons based on feudal law and having no counterpart in the modern law of property, preferred passage of title to heirs by descent rather than by purchase. See 125 A.L.R. 553; 1 Scott on Trusts (1939) p. 657; 1 Simes, The Law of Future Interests (1936) § 147.

In the present case there is nothing which shows an intent on the part of plaintiff to create remainder interests in his heirs at law or to justify a departure from the usual rule of construction. Accordingly, the trial court erred in construing the trust instrument as creating such interests.

* * *

The judgment is reversed.

* * *

Note

There is some authority for the proposition that the Doctrine of Worthier Title also applies to wills. See *City National Bank of Birmingham v. Andrews*, 355 So.2d 341 (Ala. 1978).

§ 5.6 The Rule Against Perpetuities

While the destructibility of contingent remainders doctrine, the Rule in Shelley's Case, and the Doctrine of Worthier Title are nowhere near as viable as they once were, the Rule Against Perpetuities is still a potent force, either in its common law form or in its modern statutory form. As such, we must grapple with it. Due to its complexities, however, we do so in a separate chapter.

CHAPTER 6
THE RULE AGAINST PERPETUITIES

§ 6.1 Statement of the Rule

The Rule Against Perpetuities is a rule that is designed to prevent contingent remainders and executory interests from vesting too far in the future. That, in essence, is the purpose of the rule.

Pace v. Culpepper
347 So.2d 1313 (Miss. 1977)

The rule itself is just one sentence in length (28 words) and is stated in its classical form in Pace v. Culpepper. *Note, too, the last paragraph of this excerpt, which explains the purpose of the rule.*

* * *

The rule against perpetuities is the law limiting [the vesting of remote contingent interests]. Gray, The Rule Against Perpetuities, Fourth Edition, Sec. 4, p. 4. It is stated as follows: * * * 'No interest is good unless it must vest, if at all, not later than twenty-one years after some life in being at the creation of the interest.' Sec. 201, p. 191, ibid. But, a true vested interest is never obnoxious to that Rule, while a contingent interest not only may be, but often is, violative of the Rule. Sec. 99, p. 88, ibid. And again, 'A vested interest is not subject to the Rule against Perpetuities.' Sec. 205, p. 194, ibid. See also 70 C.J.S. Perpetuities § 10, p. 585. (243 Miss. at 343, 136 So.2d at 875-876).

The rule against perpetuities is a rule invalidating interests which vest too remotely. * * *

* * *

§ 6.2 Meaning of "Vest"

The purpose of the rule, as we have seen, is to invalidate "interests which vest too remotely." What does it mean for an interest to "vest"? The Rich, Rich & Nance *case explains the meaning of this important term.*

Rich, Rich & Nance v. Carolina Const. Corp.
144 N.C.App. 303 (2001)

* * *

The rule against perpetuities applies only to non-vested or contingent future interests. *Thornhill v. Riegg,* 95 N.C.App. 532, 536, 383 S.E.2d 447, 449 (1989). "A future interest is vested 'when there is either an immediate right of present enjoyment or a present fixed right of future enjoyment.' " *Id.* (quoting *Joyner v. Duncan,* 299 N.C. 565, 569, 264 S.E.2d 76, 82 (1980)). A future interest is contingent, or has yet to vest, when it is "*either* subject to a condition precedent (in addition to the natural expiration of prior estates), *or* owned by unascertainable persons, *or both.*" *Rawls v. Early,* 94 N.C.App. 677, 680, 381 S.E.2d 166, 168 (1989) (quoting T. Bergin & P. Haskell, *Preface to Estate in Land and Future Interests* at 73 (1984) (emphasis in original)).

* * *

§ 6.3 Commencement of the Perpetuities Period and the Measuring Life

Recall the statement of the rule: "No interest is good unless it must vest, if at all, not later than twenty-one years after some life in being at the creation of the interest." Thus, the contingent interest (contingent remainder or executory interest) must vest—or terminate ("if at all")—not more than 21 years after the death of someone who was alive at the time the interest was created. What is important to know, therefore, is when an interest is deemed to be created. The next two subsections explain this.

§ 6.3.1 Transfer by Will

An interest is created in a will at the time the testator dies. This is because a will has no legal significance during the testator's lifetime.

Joyner v. Duncan
299 N.C. 565 (1980)

Joyner v. Duncan *explains a fundamental principle: Because a will goes into effect only upon testator's death, it is at that time that we look for a "life in being," that is, a person who can be a measuring life to validate the gift of the contingent interest. Thus, if someone was alive when testator died, that person is a "life in being" at the time the interest was created. If the contingent interest must vest or fail no later than 21 years after such a person's death, that person is a "measuring life" (and there is no violation of the Rule Against Perpetuities).*

* * *

The essence of the rule in a will case is the search for an answer to the following question: Must the contingent future interest in question vest (if it ever does vest) within the lifetime of some one or more people who were alive at testator's death (plus the 21 year period and any period of gestation)? These lives in being at testator's death are referred to as the measuring life or lives for the interest in question. Frequently the measuring life or lives will be the beneficiary or beneficiaries of an interest in the trust or will that precedes the interest in question. If there is any possibility that the gift will vest in interest in the lifetime of someone who was not a life in being at testator's death and more than 21 years after the death of all possible measuring lives plus any period of gestation, then the interest vests too remotely and is void because it is in violation of the rule against perpetuities.

* * *

§ 6.3.2 Transfer by Deed

When the contingent interest is created by deed, the lives in being are those people who were alive when the deed was delivered by the grantor to the grantee, as Crockett v. Scott *explains.*

Crockett v. Scott
199 Tenn. 90 (1955)

* * * Counsel for the appellants argue very forcefully that there is quite a difference between the two cases, primarily because of the difference between a deed, in the Hassell v. Sims case, and the will in the instant case. As we gather from reading the authorities the difference only comes about in the computation of time, since the deed becomes effective at delivery, while the will takes effect at the death of the testator. * * *

* * *

Note
When the transfer is by irrevocable trust, the perpetuities period begins when the trust instrument is delivered to the trustee. The measuring life, if any, is a person alive at the time the trust instrument is delivered. In the case of a revocable trust, however, the perpetuities period does not begin until the trust becomes irrevocable. In such case, the measuring life, if any, is a person alive at the time the trust becomes irrevocable.

§ 6.4 Legal Possibilities, Class Gifts, and Further Elucidation

Jee v. Audley *is a classic and in every property casebook. What happens here is the testator, in essence, executes a will that provides a gift of money, "to Mary Hall and the issue of her body, and in default of such issue, to the daughters of John and Elizabeth Jee." Mary Hall has a fee simple subject to an executory limitation (a fee tail could not be created in personal property at this time in England). The daughters of John and Elizabeth Jee have an executory interest. The court finds that the gift of the executory interest to the daughters is in violation of the Rule Against Perpetuities. In the process, the court states several principles that have become firm doctrine for application of the rule.*

Jee v. Audley

1 Cox 324 (Chancery 1787)

Testator gave £1000 to M. and the issue of her body, and in default of such issue he gave the said £1000 to be equally divided between the daughters *then* living of J. and E. his wife. This devise takes in daughters of J. and E. born after the testator's death, and therefore the limitation is too remote.

Edward Audley, by his will, bequeathed as follows, "Also my will is that £1000 shall be placed out at interest during the life of my wife, which interest I give her during her life, and at her death I give the said £1000 unto my niece Mary Hall and the issue of her body lawfully begotten, and to be begotten, and in default of such issue I give the said £1000 to be equally divided between the daughters *then* living of my kinsmen John Jee and his wife Elizabeth Jee."

It appeared that John Jee and Elizabeth Jee were living at the time of the death of the testator, had four daughters and no son, and were of a very advanced age. Mary Hall was unmarried and of the age of about 40; the wife was dead. The present bill was filed by the four daughters of John and Elizabeth Jee to have the £1000 secured for their benefit upon the event of the said Mary Hall dying without leaving children. And the question was, whether the limitation to the daughters of John and Elizabeth Jee was not void as being too remote; and to prove it so, it was said that this was to take effect on a general failure of issue of Mary Hall;[1] and though it was to the daughters of John and Elizabeth Jee, yet it was not confined to the daughters living at the death of the testator, and consequently it might extend to after-born daughters, in which case it would not be within the limit of a life or lives in being and 21 years afterwards, beyond which time an executory devise is void.

On the other side it was said, that though the late cases had decided that on a gift to children generally, such children as should be living at the time of the distribution of the fund should be let in, yet it would be very hard to adhere to such a rule of construction so rigidly, as to defeat the evident intention of the testator in this case, especially as there was no real possibility of John and Elizabeth Jee having children after the testator's death, they being 70 years old; that if there were two ways of construing words, that should be adopted which would give effect to the disposition made by the testator; that the cases, which had decided that after-born children should take, proceeded

---

[1] [*General* failure of issue means if the beneficiary's bloodline ever runs out. In this case, general failure of issue means whenever Mary Hall's bloodline runs out. This is to be contrasted with *definite* failure of issue, meaning if the beneficiary dies without having issue surviving. In this case, definite failure of issue means if Mary Hall dies without issue surviving.]

on the implied intention of the testator, and never meant to give an effect to words which would totally defeat such intention.

* * *

Master of the Rolls [Sir Lloyd Kenyon]. Several cases determined by Lord *Northington*, Lord *Camden*, and the present *Chancellor*, have settled that children born after the death of the testator shall take a share in these cases; the difference is, where there is an immediate devise, and where there is an interest in remainder; in the former case the children living at the testator's death only shall take; in the latter those who are living at the time the interest vests in possession; and this being now a settled principle, I shall not strain to serve an intention at the expense of removing the land marks of the law; it is of infinite importance to abide by decided cases, and perhaps more so on this subject than any other. The general principles which apply to this case are not disputed: the limitations of personal estate are void, unless they necessarily vest, if at all, within a life or lives in being and 21 years or 9 or 10 months afterwards. This has been sanctioned by the opinion of judges of all times, from the time of the Duke of Norfolk's case to the present: it is grown reverend by age, and is not now to be broken in upon; I am desired to do in this case something which I do not feel myself at liberty to do, namely to suppose it impossible for persons in so advanced an age as John and Elizabeth Jee to have children; but if this can be done in one case it may in another, and it is a very dangerous experiment, and introductive of the greatest inconvenience to give a latitude to such sort of conjecture.

Another thing pressed upon me, is to decide on the events which have happened; but I cannot do this without overturning very many cases. The single question before me is, not whether the limitation is good in the events which have happened, but whether it was good in its creation; and if it were not, I cannot make it so. Then must this limitation, if at all, *necessarily* take place within the limits prescribed by law? The words are "in default of such issue I give the said £1000 to be equally divided between the daughters *then* living of John Jee and Elizabeth his wife." If it had been to "daughters now living," or "who should be living at the time of my death," it would have been very good; but as it stands, this limitation may take in after-born daughters; this point is clearly settled by *Ellison v. Airey*, and the effect of law on such limitation cannot make any difference in construing such intention. If then this will extended to after-born daughters, is it within the rules of law? Most certainly not, because John and Elizabeth Jee might have children born ten years after the testator's death, and then Mary Hall might die without issue 50 years afterwards; in which case it would evidently transgress the rules prescribed. I am of opinion therefore though the testator might possibly mean to restrain the limitation to the children who should be living at the time of death, I cannot, consistently with decided cases, construe it in such restrained sense, but must intend it to take in after-born children. This therefore not being within the rules of law, and as I cannot judge upon subsequent events, I think the limitation void. Therefore dismiss the bill, but without costs.

§ 6.5 Effect of Violation

When a contingent interest violates the Rule Against Perpetuities, the contingent interest is stricken. The next two cases provide further elucidation.

Wedel v. American Elec. Power Service Corp.
681 N.E.2d 1122 (Ind.App.1997)

The Wedel *case tells us that when an interest violates the rule, the interest is stricken and void* ab initio *(from its inception).*

* * *

Under the rule against perpetuities, for an interest in property to be valid, it *must* vest not later than twenty-one years after a life in being. Any conceivable scenario in which the interest will not vest within the required period will void the interest entirely. "A limitation of an interest or estate in property which will not necessarily become vested within or at the end of the period prescribed by the rule against perpetuities is wholly void ab initio."

* * *

Brown v. Independent Baptist Church of Woburn
325 Mass. 645 (1950)

The testator's will provided a gift to a church, "so long as" the church exists, at which time the property is to go to certain named individuals in the will. The court holds that the gift is a fee simple determinable subject to an executory limitation and that the executory interest in these named individuals violates the Rule Against Perpetuities. Thus, their interest is stricken and what is left is a possibility of reverter. The issue is, who gets that possibility of reverter? Does it go to the heirs of the decedent, or does it go to the residuary devisees? Initially, it is helpful for you to know what a residuary devise is: a catchall for all property not otherwise disposed of in the will. For example, the will might state, "I devise Blackacre to A; Greenacre to B; Whiteacre to C; and the residue of my estate to D." The residuary devise is a gift of all other property that testator owned at death that is not otherwise disposed of in the will. The residue may be worth $1 or $1 billion. That said, the court states that the possibility of reverter goes to the residuary devisees.

QUA, Chief Justice.

* * *

Sarah Converse died seised of the land on July 19, 1849, leaving a will in which she specifically devised it 'to the Independent Baptist Church of Woburn, to be holden [sic] and enjoyed by them so long as they shall maintain and promulgate their present religious belief and faith and shall continue a Church; and if the said Church shall be dissolved, or if its religious sentiments shall be changed or abandoned, then my will is that this real estate shall go to my legatees hereinafter named, to be divided in equal portions between them. * * * ' Then followed ten money legacies in varying amounts to different named persons, after which there was a residuary clause in these words, 'The rest and residue of my estate I give and bequeath to my legatees above named, saving and except therefrom the Independent Baptist Church; * * *'

* * * The church named by the testatrix ceased to 'continue a church' on October 19, 1939.

The parties apparently are in agreement, and the single justice ruled, that the estate of the church in the land was a determinable fee. We concur. First Universalist Society of North Adams v. Boland, 155 Mass. 171, 174, 29 N.E. 524, 15 L.R.A. 231; Institution for Savings in Roxbury and its Vicinity v. Roxbury Home for Aged Women, 244 Mass. 583, 585-586, 139 N.E. 301; Dyer v. Siano, 298 Mass. 537, 540, 11 N.E.2d 451. The estate was a fee, since it might last forever, but it was not an absolute fee, since it might (and did) 'automatically expire upon the occurrence of a stated event.' Restatement: Property, § 44. It is also conceded, and was ruled, that the specific executory devise over to the persons 'hereinafter named' as legatees was void for remoteness. This conclusion seems to be required by Proprietors of Church in Brattle Square v. Grant, 3 Gray 142, 152, 155-156, 63 Am.Dec. 725; First Universalist Society of North Adams v. Boland, 155 Mass. 171, 173, 29 N.E. 524, 15 L.R.A. 231, and Institution for Savings in Roxbury and its Vicinity v. Roxbury Home for Aged Women, 244 Mass. 583, 587, 139 N.E. 301. See Restatement: Property, § 44, illustration 20. The reason is stated to be that the determinable fee might not come to an end until long after any life or lives in being and twenty-one years, and in theory at least might never come to an end, and for an indefinite period no clear title to the entire estate could be given.

Since the limitation over failed, it next becomes our duty to consider what became of the possibility of reverter which under our decisions remained after the failure of the limitation. First Universalist Society of North Adams v. Boland, 155 Mass. 171, 175, 29 N.E. 524, 15 L.R.A. 231; Institution for Savings in Roxbury and its Vicinity v. Roxbury Home for Aged Women, 244 Mass. 583, 587, 139 N.E. 301. Restatement: Property, § 228, illustration 2, and Appendix to Volume II, at pages 35-36, including note 2. A possibility of reverter seems, by the better authority, to be assignable inter vivos (Restatement: Property, § 159; Simes, Future Interests, § 715; see Tiffany, Real Property, 3d Ed., § 314, note 31, and must be at least as readily devisable as the other similar reversionary interest known as a right of entry for condition broken, which is devisable, though not assignable. Dyer v. Siano, 298 Mass. 537, 539, 11 N.E.2d 451; Hayden v. Inhabitants of Stoughton, 5 Pick. 528, 535-540; Brigham v. Shattuck, 10 Pick. 306; Austin v. Cambridgeport Parish, 21 Pick 215, 223-224; Clapp v. Wilder, 176 Mass. 332, 337, 57 N.E. 692, 50 L.R.A. 120. Battistone v. Banulski, 110 Conn. 267, 147 A. 820; G.L.(Ter.Ed.) c. 191, §§ 1, 24; Restatement: property, § 165 (see comment f). Simes, Future Interests, § 732. See Tiffany, Real Property, 3d Ed., § 314, note 34; Steel v. Cook, 1 Metc. 281. It follows that the possibility of reverter passed under the residuary clause of the will to the same persons designated in the invalid executory devise. It is of no consequence that the persons designated in the two provisions were the same. * * *

* * *

We cannot accept the contention made in behalf of Mrs. Converse's heirs * * *

* * *

Note

The court is correct that the will of Mrs. Converse created a fee simple determinable subject to an executory limitation in the church and an executory interest in the named legatees, which interest violated the Rule Against Perpetuities. The court also was correct in holding that the executory interest was to be stricken, leaving a fee simple determinable in the church and a possibility of reverter (the future interest that remains when testator devised, "To the church, so long as the church continues to exist"). The court, however, is fully wrong in holding that the possibility of reverter went to the residuary devisees. Why? A will can only transfer property the testator owned at death. In *Brown*, the testator did not own a possibility of reverter at death (she owned a fee simple absolute). Thus, the residuary clause of the will could not have disposed of the possibility of reverter, which should have gone to Mrs. Converse's heirs.

§ 6.6 Examples of Violations of the Rule

§ 6.6.1 Open-Ended Contingencies

If O conveys or testator devises property to someone, "when such and such happens," be warned: it may well be 1000 years until "such and such" happens—and we have a definite violation of the Rule Against Perpetuities. The next case illustrates this problem.

Johnson v. Preston
226 Ill. 447 (1907)

The testator devised certain property to her executor, as trustee; importantly, the devise to the executor as trustee was to commence only after the probate of testator's will was completed. (Probate is the court proceeding to validate the document in question as the testator's last will.) The court found that the devise to the executor violated the Rule Against Perpetuities.

VICKERS, J.

* * *

* * * No interest subject to a condition precedent is good unless the condition must be fulfilled, if at all, within 21 years after some life in being at the execution of the instrument, or, in case of wills, at the death of the testator. Gray on Perpetuities, § 201; Howe v. Hodge, supra; Lawrence v. Smith, 163 Ill. 149, 45 N. E. 259. It is not enough that a contingent event may happen, or even that it will probably happen within the limits of the rule against perpetuities. If it can possibly happen beyond those limits, an interest conditioned on it is too remote. Gray on Perpetuities, § 214; Lawrence v. Smith, supra; Eldred v. Meek, 183 Ill. 26, 55 N. E. 536, 75 Am. St. Rep. 86; Owsley v. Harrison, 190 Ill. 235, 60 N. E. 89; Chapman v. Cheney, 191 Ill. 574, 61 N. E. 363; Schuknecht v. Schultz, 212 Ill. 43, 72 N. E. 37. It would seem to result necessarily from the rule laid down in the above authorities that the condition precedent upon which the estate of the executor was to vest--that is, the probate of the will--brings the estate of the trustee directly within the rule against perpetuities.

* * *

It is clear, from the language of the will itself, that whatever interest the executor took under it could not vest in him until the probate of the will, and while this event would, in the ordinary and usual course of events, probably occur within a few months, or at most a few years, after the death of the testatrix, yet it cannot be said that it is a condition that must inevitably happen within 21 years from the death of the testatrix. Since a bare possibility that the condition upon which the estate is to vest may not happen within the prescribed limits is all that is necessary to bring the devise in conflict with the rule, we see no escape from the conclusion that the devise to the executor offends the rule against perpetuities, and is therefore void. The devise to the executor is not saved from the effect of this rule by reason of the fact that it is merely a term of years, instead of an estate in fee simple or other freehold interest. Terms of years may be created to commence in futuro; but if the condition upon which they are to arise is uncertain, and may not happen within the limits fixed by the rule against perpetuities, such terms are void. 1 Washburn on Real Property, § 468.

* * *

§ 6.6.2 Gifts to Unborn Widows

Suppose testator devises, "To A for life, then to A's widow for life, then to A's issue." The question is whether such a devise to the issue violates the Rule Against Perpetuities.

Dickerson v. Union Nat. Bank of Little Rock
268 Ark. 292 (1980)

In a somewhat simplification of facts, testator's will provided: "To my sons Cecil and Martin for life, then to Martin's widow for life, then to Martin's issue." The court held that this devise to Martin's issue violates the Rule Against Perpetuities. (Note, too, the second paragraph, first sentence of the opinion.)

GEORGE ROSE SMITH, Justice.

* * *

Second, the trust is void because there is a possibility that the estate will not vest within a period measured by a life or lives in being at the testatrix's death, plus 21 years. A bare possibility is enough. "The interest must vest within the time allowed by the rule. If there is any possibility that the contingent event may happen beyond the limits of the rule, the transaction is void." Comstock v. Smith, 255 Ark. 564, 501 S.W.2d 617 (1973).

The terms of this trust present an instance of the "unborn widow," a pitfall that is familiar to every student of the rule against perpetuities. This trust is not to terminate until the deaths of Cecil, Martin, and Martin's widow, but the identity of Martin's widow cannot be known until his death. Martin might marry an 18-year-old woman twenty years after his mother's death, have additional children by her, and then die. Cecil also might die. Martin's young widow, however, might live for another 40 or 50 years, after which the interests would finally vest. But since Cecil and Martin would have been the last measuring lives in being at the death of the testatrix, the trust property would not vest until many years past the maximum time allowed by the rule. The rule was formulated to prevent just such a possible uncertainty about the title to real or personal property for an unreasonably long time in the future.

The violation of the rule, except for the interposition of a trust, is actually so clear that the appellee does not argue the point. * * *

§ 6.6.3 Options to Purchase Property

An option contract gives the option holder the right to enter into a binding contract with the other party to the option to buy the underlying property. More specifically, as stated by the court in Symphony Space, Inc. v. Pergola Properties, Inc., *the next case, "An option grants to the holder the power to compel the owner of property to sell it whether the owner is willing to part with ownership or not." As a general rule, options must be exercised within the perpetuities period, as the next case illustrates.*

Symphony Space, Inc. v. Pergola Properties, Inc.
88 N.Y.2d 466 (1996)

Broadwest sold a building to Symphony, who leased it back to Broadwest (Pergola is a successor to Broadwest). In addition to the lease, in 1978, the parties entered into an option contract: Broadwest (Pergola) could exercise an option to purchase the building for $10 if executed within certain timeframes: 1987, 1993, 1998 or 2003. In 1987, Pergola attempted to exercise the option. Symphony refused to honor the contract on the ground that the option contract violated the Rule Against Perpetuities. The court will agree with Symphony.

OPINION OF THE COURT

KAYE, Chief Judge.

This case presents the novel question whether options to purchase commercial property are exempt from the prohibition against remote vesting embodied in New York's Rule against Perpetuities (EPTL 9-1.1[b]).[2] Because an exception for commercial options finds no support in our law, we decline to exempt all commercial option agreements from the statutory Rule against Perpetuities.

Here, we agree with the trial court and Appellate Division that the option defendants seek to enforce violates the statutory prohibition against remote vesting and is therefore unenforceable.

I. FACTS

---

[2] [EPTL in New York stands for Estate, Powers, and Trust Laws.]

The subject of this proceeding is a two-story building situated on the Broadway block between 94th and 95th Streets on Manhattan's Upper West Side. In 1978, Broadwest Realty Corporation owned this building, which housed a theater and commercial space. Broadwest had been unable to secure a permanent tenant for the theater--approximately 58% of the total square footage of the building's floor space (*see, Matter of Symphony Space v. Tishelman,* 60 N.Y.2d 33, 35, n. 1, 466 N.Y.S.2d 677, 453 N.E.2d 1094). Broadwest also owned two adjacent properties, Pomander Walk (a residential complex) and the Healy Building (a commercial building). Broadwest had been operating its properties at a net loss.

Plaintiff Symphony Space, Inc., a not-for-profit entity devoted to the arts, had previously rented the theater for several one-night engagements. In 1978, Symphony and Broadwest engaged in a transaction whereby Broadwest sold the entire building to Symphony for the below-market price of $10,010 and leased back the income-producing commercial property, excluding the theater, for $1 per year. Broadwest maintained liability for the existing $243,000 mortgage on the property as well as certain maintenance obligations. As a condition of the sale, Symphony, for consideration of $10, also granted Broadwest an option to repurchase the entire building. Notably, the transaction did not involve Pomander Walk or the Healy Building.

The purpose of this arrangement was to enable Symphony, as a not-for-profit corporation, to seek a property tax exemption for the entire building--which constituted a single tax parcel--predicated on its use of the theater. The sale-and-leaseback would thereby reduce Broadwest's real estate taxes by $30,000 per year, while permitting Broadwest to retain the rental income from the leased commercial space in the building, which the trial court found produced $140,000 annually. The arrangement also furthered Broadwest's goal of selling all the properties, by allowing Broadwest to postpone any sale until property values in the area increased and until the commercial leases expired. Symphony, in turn, would have use of the theater at minimal cost, once it received a tax exemption.

Thus, on December 1, 1978, Symphony and Broadwest--both sides represented by counsel--executed a contract for sale of the property from Broadwest to Symphony for the purchase price of $10,010. The contract specified that $10 was to be paid at the closing and $10,000 was to be paid by means of a purchase-money mortgage.

The parties also signed several separate documents, each dated December 31, 1978: (1) a deed for the property from Broadwest to Symphony; (2) a lease from Symphony to Broadwest of the entire building except the theater for rent of $1 per year and for the term January 1, 1979 to May 31, 2003, unless terminated earlier; (3) a 25-year, $10,000 mortgage and mortgage note from Symphony as mortgagor to Broadwest as mortgagee, with full payment due on December 31, 2003; and (4) an option agreement by which Broadwest obtained from Symphony the exclusive right to repurchase all of the property, including the theater.

It is the option agreement that is at the heart of the present dispute. Section 3 of that agreement provides that Broadwest may exercise its option to purchase the property during any of the following "Exercise Periods":

"(a) at any time after July 1, 1979, so long as the Notice of Election specifies that the Closing is to occur during any of the calendar years 1987, 1993, 1998 and 2003; * * * "

Section 1 states that "Broadwest may exercise its option at any time during any Exercise Period." That section further specifies that the notice of election must be sent at least 180 days prior to the closing date if the option is exercised pursuant to section 3(a) and at least 90 days prior to the closing date if exercised pursuant to any other subdivision.

* * *

Importantly, the option agreement specifies in section 5 that "Broadwest's right to exercise the option granted hereby is * * * unconditional and shall not be in any way affected or impaired by Broadwest's performance or nonperformance, actual or asserted, of any obligation to be performed under the Lease or any other agreement or instrument by or between Broadwest and Symphony," other than that Broadwest was required to pay Symphony any unpaid rent on the closing date. Finally, section 6 established that the option constituted "a covenant running with the land, inuring to the benefit of heirs, successors and assigns of Broadwest."

Symphony ultimately obtained a tax exemption for the theater. In the summer of 1981, Broadwest sold and assigned its interest under the lease, option agreement, mortgage and mortgage note, as well as its ownership interest in the contiguous Pomander Walk and Healy Building, to defendants' nominee for $4.8 million. The nominee contemporaneously transferred its rights under these agreements to defendants Pergola Properties, Inc., Bradford N. Swett, Casandium Limited and Darenth Consultants as tenants in common.

* * *

Thereafter, the parties cross-moved for summary judgment in the instant declaratory judgment proceeding. The trial court granted Symphony's motion while denying that of defendants. In particular, the court concluded that the Rule against Perpetuities applied to the commercial option contained in the parties' agreement, that the option violated the Rule and that Symphony was entitled to exercise its equitable right to redeem the mortgage. The trial court also dismissed defendants' counterclaim for rescission of the agreements underlying the transaction based on the parties' mutual mistake.

In a comprehensive writing by Justice Ellerin, the Appellate Division likewise determined that the commercial option was unenforceable under the Rule against Perpetuities and that rescission was inappropriate. The Appellate Division certified the following question to us: "Was the order of the Supreme Court, as affirmed by this Court, properly made?" We conclude that it was and now affirm.

II. STATUTORY BACKGROUND

The Rule against Perpetuities evolved from judicial efforts during the 17th century to limit control of title to real property by the dead hand of landowners reaching into future generations. Underlying both early and modern rules restricting future dispositions of property is the principle that it is socially undesirable for property to be inalienable for an unreasonable period of time. These rules thus seek "to ensure the productive use and development of property by its current beneficial owners by simplifying ownership, facilitating exchange and freeing property from unknown or embarrassing impediments to alienability" (*Metropolitan Transp. Auth. v. Bruken Realty*

Corp., 67 N.Y.2d 156, 161, 501 N.Y.S.2d 306, 492 N.E.2d 379, citing *De Peyster v. Michael,* 6 N.Y. 467, 494).

The traditional statement of the common-law Rule against Perpetuities was set forth by Professor John Chipman Gray: "No interest is good unless it must vest, if at all, not later than twenty-one years after some life in being at the creation of the interest" (Gray, The Rule Against Perpetuities § 201, at 191 [4th ed. 1942]).

* * *

III. VALIDITY OF THE OPTION AGREEMENT

Defendants proffer three grounds for upholding the option: that the statutory prohibition against remote vesting does not apply to commercial options; that the option here cannot be exercised beyond the statutory period; and that this Court should adopt the "wait and see" approach to the Rule against Perpetuities.[3] We consider each in turn.

A. Applicability of the Rule to Commercial Options

Under the common law, options to purchase land are subject to the rule against remote vesting (*see,* Simes, Future Interests § 132 [2d ed 1966]; Simes and Smith, Future Interests § 1244 [2d ed]; Leach, *Perpetuities in a Nutshell,* 51 Harv.L.Rev. 638, 660; *see also, London & S.W. Ry. Co. v. Gomm,* 20 ChD 562). Such options are specifically enforceable and give the option holder a contingent, equitable interest in the land (Dukeminier, *A Modern Guide to Perpetuities,* 74 Cal.L.Rev. 1867, 1908; Leach, *Perpetuities in Perspective: Ending the Rule's Reign of Terror,* 65 Harv.L.Rev. 721, 736-737). This creates a disincentive for the landowner to develop the property and hinders its alienability, thereby defeating the policy objectives underlying the Rule against Perpetuities (*see,* Dukeminier, *A Modern Guide to Perpetuities,* 74 Cal.L.Rev. 1908; 5A Powell, Real Property ¶ 771[1]).

Typically, however, options to purchase are part of a commercial transaction. For this reason, subjecting them to the Rule against Perpetuities has been deemed "a step of doubtful wisdom" (Leach, *Perpetuities in Perspective: Ending the Rule's Reign of Terror,* 65 Harv.L.Rev. 737; *see also,* Dukeminier, *A Modern Guide to Perpetuities,* 74 Cal.L.Rev. 1908; Note, *Options and the Rule Against Perpetuities,* 13 U.Fla.L.Rev. 214, 214-215). As one vocal critic, Professor W. Barton Leach, has explained,

"[t]he Rule grew up as a limitation on family dispositions; and the period of lives in being plus twenty-one years is adapted to these gift transactions. The pressures which created the Rule do not exist with reference to arms-length contractual transactions, and neither lives in being nor twenty-one years are periods which are relevant to business men and their affairs" (Leach, *Perpetuities: New Absurdity, Judicial and Statutory Correctives,* 73 Harv.L.Rev. 1318, 1321-1322).

Professor Leach, however, went on to acknowledge that, under common law, "due to an overemphasis on concepts derived from the nineteenth century, we are stuck with the application of the Rule to options to purchase," urging that "this should not be extended to other commercial transactions" (*id.,* at 1322; *see also,* Simes and Smith, Future Interests § 1244).

It is now settled in New York that, generally, EPTL 9-1.1(b) [the Rule Against Perpetuities] applies to options.

---

[3] [The wait and see approach is discussed later in this chapter.]

* * *

Our decision in *Metropolitan Transp. Auth. v. Bruken Realty Corp.*, 67 N.Y.2d 156, 501 N.Y.S.2d 306, 492 N.E.2d 379, *supra*) is not to the contrary. In *Bruken,* we held that EPTL 9-1.1(b) did not apply to a preemptive right in a "commercial and governmental transaction" that lasted beyond the statutory perpetuities period. In doing so, we explained that, *unlike options,* preemptive rights (or rights of first refusal) only marginally affect transferability:

"An option grants to the holder the power to compel the owner of property to sell it whether the owner is willing to part with ownership or not. A preemptive right, or right of first refusal, does not give its holder the power to compel an unwilling owner to sell; it merely requires the owner, when and if he decides to sell, to offer the property first to the party holding the preemptive right so that he may meet a third-party offer or buy the property at some other price set by a previously stipulated method" (*id.,* at 163, 501 N.Y.S.2d 306, 492 N.E.2d 379).

* * *

Here, the option agreement creates precisely the sort of control over future disposition of the property that we have previously associated with purchase options and that the common-law rule against remote vesting--and thus EPTL 9-1.1(b)--seeks to prevent. As the Appellate Division explained, the option grants its holder absolute power to purchase the property at the holder's whim and at a token price set far below market value. This Sword of Damocles necessarily discourages the property owner from investing in improvements to the property. Furthermore, the option's existence significantly impedes the owner's ability to sell the property to a third party, as a practical matter rendering it inalienable.

That defendants, the holder of this option, are also the lessees of a portion of the premises does not lead to a different conclusion here.

Generally, an option to purchase land that originates in one of the lease provisions, is not exercisable after lease expiration, and is incapable of separation from the lease is valid even though the holder's interest may vest beyond the perpetuities period (*see,* Berg, *Long-Term Options and the Rule Against Perpetuities,* 37 Cal.L.Rev. 1, 21; Leach, *Perpetuities: New Absurdity, Judicial and Statutory Correctives,* 73 Harv.L.Rev. 1320; Simes and Smith, Future Interests § 1244). Such options--known as options "appendant" or "appurtenant" to leases--encourage the possessory holder to invest in maintaining and developing the property by guaranteeing the option holder the ultimate benefit of any such investment. Options appurtenant thus further the policy objectives underlying the rule against remote vesting and are not contemplated by EPTL 9-1.1(b) (*see, Metropolitan Transp. Auth. v. Bruken Realty Corp.,* 67 N.Y.2d at 165, 501 N.Y.S.2d 306, 492 N.E.2d 379, *supra; see also, Buffalo Seminary v. McCarthy,* 86 A.D.2d at 441, n. 5, 451 N.Y.S.2d 457, *supra*).

To be sure, the option here arose within a larger transaction that included a lease. Nevertheless, not all of the property subject to the purchase option here is even occupied by defendants. The option encompasses the entire building--both the commercial space and the theater--yet defendants are leasing only the commercial space. With regard to the theater space, a disincentive exists for Symphony to improve the property, since it will eventually be claimed by the option holder at the predetermined purchase price.

Furthermore, the option is not contained in the lease itself, but in a separate agreement. Indeed, section 5 of the option agreement specifies that the right to exercise the option is wholly independent from the lease, stating that it "shall not be in any way affected or impaired by * * * performance or nonperformance, actual or asserted, of any obligation to be performed under the Lease or any other agreement." The duration of the option, moreover, exceeds the term of the lease. Consequently, defendants could compel Symphony to sell them the property even after they have ceased possession as lessee. Put simply, the option here cannot qualify as an option appurtenant and significantly deters development of the property. If the option is exercisable beyond the statutory perpetuities period, refusing to enforce it would thus further the purpose and rationale underlying the statutory prohibition against remote vesting.

* * *

We therefore conclude that the option agreement is invalid under EPTL 9-1.1(b). In light of this conclusion, we need not decide whether the option violated Symphony's equitable right to redeem the mortgage.

* * *

Accordingly, the order of the Appellate Division should be affirmed, with costs, and the certified question answered in the affirmative.

§ 6.7 Amelioration

That the Rule Against Perpetuities can cause havoc with a testator's testamentary plan is beyond dispute. Hence, a number of doctrines have evolved to ameliorate the harsh effects of this rule.

§ 6.7.1 Presumptions

Some jurisdictions have codified several presumptions to prevent an unknowing testator (or lawyer) from falling into the trap of the common law presumption that everyone is capable of procreating—even people well beyond mid-life. These and other presumptions are reproduced below.

McKinney's Estate, Powers, and Trust Law (New York) § 9-1.3
Perpetuities: Rules of Construction

(a) Unless a contrary intention appears, the rules of construction provided in this section govern with respect to any matter affecting the rule against perpetuities.
(b) It shall be presumed that the creator intended the estate to be valid.
(c) Where an estate would, except for this paragraph, be invalid because of the possibility that the person to whom it is given or limited may be a person not in being at the time of the creation of the estate, and such person is referred to in the instrument creating such

estate as the spouse of another without other identification, it shall be presumed that such reference is to a person in being on the effective date of the instrument.

(d) Where the duration or vesting of an estate is contingent upon the probate of a will, the appointment of a fiduciary, the location of a distributee, the payment of debts, the sale of assets, the settlement of an estate, the determination of questions relating to an estate or transfer tax or the occurrence of any specified contingency, it shall be presumed that the creator of such estate intended such contingency to occur, if at all, within twenty-one years from the effective date of the instrument creating such estate.

(e)(1) Where the validity of a disposition depends upon the ability of a person to have a child at some future time, it shall be presumed * * * that a male can have a child at fourteen years of age or over, but not under that age, and that a female can have a child at twelve years of age or over, but not under that age or over the age of fifty-five years.

* * *

(3) Where the validity of a disposition depends upon the ability of a person to have a child at some future time, the possibility that such person may have a child by adoption shall be disregarded.

(4) The provisions of subparagraphs (1) * * * and (3) shall not apply for any purpose other than that of determining the validity of a disposition under the rule against perpetuities where such validity depends on the ability of a person to have a child at some future time. A determination of validity or invalidity of a disposition under the rule against perpetuities by the application of subparagraph (1) * * * or (3) shall not be affected by the later occurrence of facts in contradiction to the facts presumed or determined or the possibility of adoption disregarded under subparagraphs (1) * * * or (3).

California Law Revision Commission Comment

[California Probate Code § 21201]

You will note that California retains the common law presumption. Perhaps the common law presumption makes some sense today—even if it made no sense 150 years ago.

* * *

2. Conclusive Presumption of Lifetime Fertility

At common law, all individuals--regardless of age, sex, or physical condition--are conclusively presumed to be able to have children throughout their entire lifetimes. This principle is not superseded by this chapter, and in view of the widely accepted rule of construction that adopted children are presumptively included in class gifts, the conclusive presumption of lifetime fertility is not unrealistic. Since even elderly individuals probably cannot be excluded from adopting children based on their ages alone, the possibility of having children by adoption is seldom extinct. See, generally, Waggoner, In re Lattouf's Will and the Presumption of Lifetime Fertility in Perpetuity Law, 20 San Diego L.Rev. 763 (1983). * * *

For a California case approving the common law rule, see Fletcher v. Los Angeles Trust & Sav. Bank, 182 Cal. 177, 184-85, 187 P. 425 (1920).

* * *

§ 6.7.2 Construction

In construction, the court construes or interprets the instrument in a manner so that the will or trust does not violate the Rule Against Perpetuities.

Singer Co. v. Makad, Inc.
213 Kan. 725 (1974)

In this case, a standard commercial lease provided that the lease was to take effect when certain preconditions were satisfied. These preconditions (obtaining of financing, etc.) could, in theory, have exceeded the perpetuities period. Nonetheless, the court finds that there was no per se violation of the Rule Against Perpetuities and construes the lease to mean that the parties contemplated a "reasonable time" for performance, a timeframe that will almost certainly avoid a perpetuities problem.

FONTRON, Justice:

This action is brought under the declaratory judgment statute, K.S.A. 60-1701. It was initiated by The Singer Company, hereafter referred to as Singer or plaintiff, which, as lessee, executed lease agreements for space in two shopping centers, one at North Platte, Nebraska, and the other at Hays, Kansas, under dates of October 17, 1967, and November 22, 1967, respectively. * * *

Two bases for relief are advanced by Singer: First, that the leases were void as violating the rule against perpetuities; * * * The trial court held that the lease agreements violated the rule against perpetuities and, accordingly, entered judgment in favor of Singer. This appeal followed.

* * *

* * * We are given to understand that the leases in question conform generally to the mold of modern shopping center leases and that the plan or method ordinarily used in the development of shopping center areas was followed in this case, which is to say: First, lease agreements are secured from prospective tenants, hopefully including at least one chain concern; second, the required finances are sought and obtained, and the leases assigned as collateral; third, construction is commenced and the project eventually completed.

* * *

Conclusions of law were formulated and entered by the trial court in the following particulars:

'2. The leasehold interest described in the leases at issue herein did not vest in the plaintiff at the time of the execution of the leases, but on the date of execution each lease created a leasehold interest for a term of years to commence in the future with the commencement of the term of each lease being dependent upon the occurrence of three uncertain and indefinite events, to-wit:

'a) The condition precedent that Landlord obtain financing acceptable to Landlord;

'b) The condition precedent that Landlord substantially erect and complete the Shopping Centers;

'c) The condition precedent that 75% of the other retail tenants of each Center are open for business.

'3. Each lease at issue herein granted a leasehold interest limited to vest upon the occurrence of certain future events. At the time of the execution of the said leases there was a possibility that these events might not occur within the period prescribed by the Rule Against Perpetuities, and therefore each lease violates the Rule Against Perpetuities and is therefore void and of no effect.'

We presume that every student of the law has been familiar at one time or another with the rule against perpetuities which has been handed down to us from the common law. Simply stated, the rule precludes the creation of any future interest in property which does not necessarily vest within twenty-one years after a life or lives presently in being, plus the period of gestation, where gestation is, in fact, taking place. (In re Estate of Freeman, 195 Kan. 190, 195, 404 P.2d 222; Lasnier v. Martin, 102 Kan. 551, 171 P. 645.) In Gray, The Rule Against Perpetuities, 4th Edition, 1942, p. 191, the author phrases the rule this way:

'No interest is good unless it must vest, if at all, not later than twenty-one years after some life in being at the creation of the interest.'

Where the twenty-one year period has no reference to a life or lives in being, it has been said to be in gross, and the devise or grant is not too remote if the contingency must happen within that time. (Keeler v. Lauer, 73 Kan. 388, 85 P. 541; Emerson v. Campbell et al., 32 Del.Ch. 178, 84 A.2d 148.)

Kansas, has long recognized the rule as part of the common law of this state. (Keeler v. Lauer, supra; Klingman v. Gilbert, 90 Kan. 545, 135 P. 682.) Moreover, it has been held that the rule applies to the creation of a term of years in an ordinary farm lease. (Ehrhart v. Spencer, 175 Kan. 227, 263 P.2d 246.) However, Kansas courts have not been called upon to consider application of the rule to a modern commercial lease of the type we have before us which, for want of a better or more descriptive name, may be designated as an 'on completion' lease.

The defendants earnestly urge that the rule was never fashioned to apply to a lease of this character; that it has no relevance to the needs of modern business; and that it is an anachronism when it comes to current leasing practices. The defendants further suggest that the recent trend among legal authorities is to relax the harsh and inflexible application of the rule and that most courts are now disposed to follow one of several tenable theories which will avoid remorseless application of the rule and give effect to the intention of the parties. A number of these theories were mentioned and discussed in the Freeman decision and need not be repeated here.

We observe a good deal of merit and common sense in the arguments advanced by the defendants. Moreover, we find them explicitly supported by respectable legal authority coming from other jurisdictions, while our own cases reflect the modern tendency to temper the rule where its rigid application would do violence to the disposition of property. (In re Estate of Freeman, supra; In re Estate of Foster, 190 Kan. 498, 376 P.2d 784; In re Estate of Showes, 207 Kan. 268, 485 P.2d 299.) * * *

* * *

While a few modern authorities would apply the rule to 'on completion' leases (Southern Airways Co. v. Dekalb County, (Southern Airways Co. v. DeKalb County, Va. Bank/Citizens & M. v. Union Oil Co. of Cal., 214 Va. 48, 197 S.E.2d 174) we believe the better and far more rational view to be the one which is forcefully expounded in the case of Wong v. Di Grazia, 60 Cal.2d 525, 35 Cal.Rptr. 241, 386 P.2d 817. The defendants refer to this rule as the 'reasonable time' rule and we deem this an apt and convenient designation.

The California case bears marked similarity to the controversy before us. The parties had executed a written agreement under which the defendant (lessor) was to construct a building and the plaintiffs (lessees) agreed to lease the same for a period of ten years, the term to commence upon the recording by the lessor of a notice of completion. Construction was to commence forthwith agreeably to the attached plans and specifications and was to continue expeditiously to final completion, subject to material or labor shortages, strikes, lockouts, governmental actions and all causes beyond lessor's control. The building was to be completed within 90 days after a building permit was obtained by lessor.

Disagreement arose over who was to pay for a sprinkling system required by the building code and the lessees filed suit to rescind the lease and to recover a down payment which had been made. The key issue was whether the agreement violated the rule against perpetuities. The California Supreme Court, in upholding the lease agreement, decided that it did not violate the rule; that the parties must have contemplated the building would be completed and the lease fully executed within a reasonable time; and that a reasonable time must necessarily be a period far less than twenty-one years.

In the course of its decision the court noted briefly The Duke of Norfolk's case, 3 Ch.Cas. 1, decided in 1682, from which the rule originally stemmed (Simes & Smith, The Law of Future Interests, 2d Ed., 1956, § 1211) and pointed out that its basic purpose was to limit family dispositions of property. The court also observed, quite sagely, that the rule does not 'facilely operate as to commercial agreements in today's dynamic economy' and thence proceeded to quote from Leach, Perpetuities in a Nutshell (1938), 51 Harv.L.Rev. 638, 660:

'The period of lives in being and 21 years, which works admirably with regard to gift transactions for family purposes, has no significance in the world of commercial affairs.'

Elaborating on the concept that the rule bears little relationship to contemporary business practices or to 'the world of commercial affairs,' the court went on to say:

'Certainly our function is not to interpret the rule so as to create commercial anomalies. A lease to commence upon completion of the leased building is a common business arrangement. Such a clause is a standard provision of leases in shopping centers, which have been and are being constructed throughout the country; the parties to such transactions do not suspect that the rule will be extended to invalidate their agreements; even the attorneys who draw the leases may excusably not anticipate such application. Surely the courts do not seek to invalidate bona fide transactions by the imported application of esoteric legalisms. Our task is not to block the business pathway but to clear it, defining it by guideposts that are reasonably to be expected. As was pointed out in (1959) 47 Cal.L.Rev. 197, 200: '(A) strict and literal application of the Rule Against Perpetuities to a lease of this nature can do little to serve the basic purpose behind the rule and can result only in placing an unnecessary burden on the parties to an accepted commercial transaction.' We therefore do not propose to apply the rule in the rigid or remorseless manner characterized by some past decisions; instead we shall seek to interpret it reasonably, in the light of its objectives and the economic conditions of modern society.' (pp. 533, 534, 35 Cal.Rptr. 247, 386 P.2d 823.)

* * *

It seems generally to be agreed, as our own cases may be said to witness, that the rule against perpetuities should not be applied where it is possible for the court to give an instrument a construction leading to its validity. The rule is phrased in Wong v. Di Grazia, supra, in these words:

'. . . Both the California cases, and those of a majority of other states, hold that a document should be interpreted if feasible to avoid the conclusion that it violates the rule against perpetuities.' (60 Cal.2d pp. 539, 540, 35 Cal.Rptr. p. 251, 386 P.2d p. 827.) Supporting this principle of construction, see Restatement, Property, § 375, Belfield v. Booth, 63 Conn. 299, 27 A. 585; Edgerly v. Barker, 66 N.H. 434, 31 A. 900; Plummer v. Roberts, 315 Mo. 627, 287 S.W. 316.

We think it not unreasonable to assume that in the hurried, competitive atmosphere of today's commercial world, experienced business people dealing at arm's length for rental space in any modern shopping area would not contemplate entering into a lease arrangement contingent on events which might not transpire until twenty-one years had gone by.

The conclusion at which we arrive in this case is consistent with past decisions of this court to the effect that where no time has been stated for performing an act which is to be done, the law will imply that performance is to be accomplished within a reasonable time, and the want of a stipulation as to time does not necessarily render the agreement void. (Leis v. Sinclair, 67 Kan. 748, 74 P. 261; Eakin v. Wycoff, 118 Kan. 167, 171, 234 P. 63; Price v. Brodrick, 183 Kan. 71, 325 P.2d 387.)

In Campbell v. Warnberg, 133 Kan. 246, 299 P. 583, the principle was expressed with respect to the exercise of an option. There, the will executed by the testator provided essentially that his sons, in specified priority, should have the right to purchase their sisters' interest in the real estate, but no time was fixed for exercising the options. The holding of the court on that point is encompassed in Syllabus 1:

'Where a person has an option to purchase property at a specified figure, and no time is fixed for the exercise of the option, a reasonable time is implied, and what length of time is reasonable is governed by the circumstances of the particular case.'

* * *

In our opinion this case must be reversed and returned to the trial court for its determination of whether the lessors' performance was within a reasonable time, and should the court find in favor of Singer then to decide what relief should be afforded in the light of all the circumstances.

It is so ordered.

§ 6.7.3 Wait and See Doctrine

The next doctrine that has been adopted by some jurisdictions is "wait and see." The court will wait for a perpetuities-like period to see if, in hindsight, there was a violation of the rule. If, in hindsight, there was no violation of the rule, the gift stands.

Hansen v. Stroecker

699 P.2d 871 (Alaska 1985)

In Hansen v. Stroecker, *we have an option to purchase (again). The option contract itself did not state when the option could be exercised. Consequently, there was a violation of the Rule Against Perpetuities under the classical "what might happen" approach of the* Jee *case. Nonetheless, because the holder of the option tried to exercise the option well within the perpetuities period, the court found, using the wait and see approach, that there was no violation of the rule.*

OPINION

MATTHEWS, Justice.

On December 31, 1971, James B. Hansen and W.G. Stroecker signed an agreement entitled "Option to Purchase." Under the terms of the agreement, Stroecker paid $1,500.00 to Hansen in exchange for an option to purchase some seven parcels. Two river fronting parcels were priced at $500.00 each, two other lots were priced at $250.00 each, one parcel was priced at $0.0333 per square foot, another parcel was priced at $0.1667 per square foot, and the seventh parcel was to be conveyed without additional consideration. The total purchase price could only be calculated after the area of the parcels being conveyed at square footage rates was calculated, and this could not be done until a survey was completed.

The agreement does not state when the option was to be exercised. Further, it does not state who was to have the property surveyed so that the parcels' price per square foot could be calculated.

There is a disputed factual issue as to who was to complete the survey. Mary Hansen and her daughter Irene Mead claim that it was Stroecker's duty. Stroecker testified that he thought that Hansen would take care of the survey.

Hansen died on June 20, 1976. Stroecker had the property surveyed in July of 1980 and on August 25, 1980, he sent a check for the balance of the purchase price, $1,028.00, to the attorney for Mrs. Hansen. Mrs. Hansen refused to deliver to Stroecker a deed to the property. Stroecker brought this action for specific performance of the agreement.

Stroecker moved for summary judgment. Mrs. Hansen opposed on the grounds that the agreement was void because it violated the rule against perpetuities and that the agreement could not be enforced because Stroecker had unreasonably delayed his exercise of the option. The superior court granted Stroecker's motion and ordered Mrs. Hansen to deliver to Stroecker a deed for the property. Stroecker moved, as the prevailing party, for an award of attorney's fees. The court, without explanation, denied this motion. Both parties appealed. Hansen seeks to have this court reverse the decision on the merits, while Stroecker urges a remand on the issue of attorney's fees.

* * *

The rule against perpetuities, in its general common law form, is this: "No interest is good unless it must vest, if at all, not later than twenty-one years after some life in being at the creation of the interest." Gray, *Rule Against Perpetuities* § 201 (4th Ed.1942). The interest in question must be examined as of the time of its creation; it must be certain to vest within the period of perpetuities.[4] Leach, *Perpetuities in a Nutshell,* 51 Harv.L.Rev. 638, 642 (1938). Thus, if anything might happen, no matter how unlikely, which would cause the interest to vest later than twenty-one years after the death of all lives in being at the creation of the interest, the interest is void. *Id.* at 643.

Under this traditional approach, it is clear that options "in gross"[5] to purchase real estate violate the rule against perpetuities when the time for their exercise is not limited to the period of perpetuities. *See* Restatement of Property § 393 (1944); 5 *Powell on Real Property* ¶ 771 [2], at 73 (1980); Annot., 66 A.L.R.3d 1294, 1296 (1975). In this case the agreement, viewed most favorably to Mrs. Hansen, creates an option in gross which was not by its terms required to be exercised within the period of perpetuities. It therefore would be void under the traditional conception of the rule against perpetuities.

Stroecker urges us, however, to apply AS 34.27.010. This provision, enacted in 1983, provides:

> In determining if an interest would violate the rule against perpetuities, the period of perpetuities shall be measured by actual rather than possible events. However, the period of perpetuities may not be measured by a life whose continuance does not have a causal relationship to the vesting or failure of the interest. An interest that would violate the rule against perpetuities as modified by this section shall be reformed, within the limits of that rule, to approximate most closely the intention of the creator of the interest.

The first two sentences of this statute adopt an approach to the rule commonly referred to as "wait-and-see." The last sentence gives the court the power to reform interests, which is known as "cy pres."[6] The wait-and-see approach requires the court to judge an interest's validity by what actually happens, rather than what might happen. Thus, if AS 34.27.010 applies to this case, the option will not violate the rule, since it was actually exercised in 1980, well within the period of perpetuities.

However, AS 34.27.010 does not apply here because of AS 01.10.090,[7] which prohibits retrospective application of a statute unless clearly provided for by the statute. * * * Even though the statutory wait-and-see approach does not apply to this case, this does not mean that the general common law approach must. * * *

Several courts from other states have adopted or used wait-and-see in at least a limited sense. *Merchant's Nat. Bank v. Curtis,* 98 N.H. 225, 97 A.2d 207, 212 (1953); * *

---

[4] [This statement actually is not correct. The court should have stated the rule as follows: "The interest in question must be examined as of the time of its creation; it must be certain to vest *or fail* within the period of perpetuities."]

[5] An option "in gross" is one which is not connected with a present interest in the questioned property. 5 *Powell on Real Property* ¶ 771[2] (1980). Options in gross should be distinguished from other types of options which are connected to an estate in land. An example would be an option to purchase real property at the end of a leasehold estate. Such options are generally held not to violate the rule against perpetuities. *See* Restatement of Property § 395 (1944).

[6] [Cy pres is discussed in the next section.]

[7] AS 01.10.090 states: "No statute is retrospective unless expressly declared therein."

* In *Curtis,* the New Hampshire Supreme Court could see no harm in the wait-and-see approach:

> There is no logical justification for deciding the problem as of the date of the death of the testator on facts that might have happened rather than facts which actually happened. It is difficult to see how the public welfare is threatened by a vesting that might have been postponed beyond the period of perpetuities but actually was not.

97 A.2d at 212.

* * *

* * * Further, bad limitations easily can be made "good" by a skilled draftsman who includes a savings clause providing that all limitations in the instrument must vest within twenty-one years after the death of the lives in being at the creation of the instrument. Thus, all the general rule does is to put a premium on skilled draftsmanship, while unfairly trapping and punishing the uninitiated.

> The adoption of the wait-and-see approach in this Restatement is largely motivated by the equality of treatment that is produced by placing the validity of all non-vested interests on the same plane, whether the interest is created by a skilled draftsman or one not so skilled.

Id., introductory note at 13.

We are persuaded by these authorities that the wait-and-see approach should be adopted as the common law rule against perpetuities in Alaska. Therefore, the agreement in this case is not void, because Stroecker exercised his option well within the period of perpetuities. The superior court's conclusion that the agreement was not void is therefore sustained.

* * *

The award of specific performance is AFFIRMED. The case is REMANDED to the superior court for an explanation of its refusal to award attorney's fees. Jurisdiction of this appeal is retained pending the explanation.

§ 6.7.4 Cy Pres

Cy pres is French and means "as nearly as possible." In cy pres, the court modifies the gift that runs afoul of the Rule Against Perpetuities as nearly as possible, consistent with the transferor's intent, so that the rule is not violated.

In re Chun Quan Yee Hop's Estate
52 Haw. 40 (1970)

The case explains the origin of cy pres and its application to the Rule Against Perpetuities. The case also applies the doctrine to a trust, the terms of which clearly violate the rule.

LEVINSON, Justice.

This case presents the question whether the orthodox common law Rule Against Perpetuities will be strictly applied to nullify a testamentary trust which violates the Rule or whether some part of the trust or all of it will be allowed to take effect. We choose to resolve this issue by applying the doctrine of equitable approximation (also known as the cy pres doctrine) so that the trust will not violate the Rule or its underlying policies and the testator's expressed desires will be satisfied.

The facts have been stipulated by the parties. The testator, Chun Quan Yee Hop, died on August 11, 1954, leaving a will executed on September 28, 1953. His wife, who is still living, his four sons, and twelve daughters survived him. When this action was filed in 1967 his issue including children, grandchildren, and great grandchildren numbered 135, of whom not less than 85 were living when the testator died.

The portion of the testator's will in question provided that: 'This trust shall cease and determine upon the death of my wife, Chun Lai Shee, or thirty (30) years from the date of my death, whichever shall last occur, * * *.' At the termination of the trust, the trust estate including principal and accumulated income was to vest in and be transferred to the beneficiaries with three-fourths of the trust estate going to the survivors of the four sons and the lawful issue of any deceased son, and the remaining one-fourth of the trust estate going to the survivors of the twelve daughters and the lawful issue of any deceased daughter.

* * *

In resolving an issue which has bedeviled lawyers and engaged legal scholars since Lord Nottingham began it all in the Duke of Norfolk's Case in 1682,[8] we are aided by the very able briefs of counsel and a wealth of law review articles and treatises on the subject. Fortunately, we are not confronted by some of the more chimerical characters and situations [of the rule]. We are simply dealing with a testamentary trust which might ultimately vest in the residuary legatees at a time beyond a specified life in being (the testator's widow) and twenty-one years thereafter. Since the Testator's wife might have died within nine years after his death, there was no assurance at the time of his death that the trust estate would vest within the life of his wife or 21 years thereafter. The will expressly says that the trust is to cease and determine on the death of the testator's wife or thirty years from his death, whichever shall last occur. The trust, therefore, violated the orthodox Rule Against Perpetuities.

* * *

The policy against tying up of property in future estates has a number of important aspects. One is the freeing of wealth so that it can be channeled into open commerce without subjecting it to the limited discretion of a trustee. Another aspect is that the rule is conducive to giving the ultimate recipient complete power of management and disposition over that which is to be his. He may then sink or swim on his own rather than be subordinated to the paternalistic control of a trustee. The last and most important policy is that of letting the living control the wealth here on earth, rather than allowing those who once owned it and have since passed away to retain some powers over that wealth. These reasons all support the proposition that it is wise policy to loosen the dead hand's grip upon the wealth passed from one generation to the next. Dukeminier,

---

[8] 3 Ch.Cas. 1, 49, 22 Eng.Rep. 931, 960 (1682).

Perpetuities Revision in California: Perpetual Trusts Permitted, 55 Calif.L.Rev. 678, 691 (1967); L. Simes, Public Policy and the Dead Hand 58 (1955).

The policy against the tying up of property in future estates is not inconsistent with the application of the doctrine of equitable approximation of a testamentary trust. Limiting an invalid term of thirty years to the twenty-one year period prescribed by the rule does no violence to any of the above policies or to the testator's general intent. The judicial recognition of a decedent's general testamentary intent has been recognized in an analogous body of law which applies the doctrine of equitable approximation to a charitable trust which would otherwise fail. If it is impossible, impractical or illegal to carry out the specific terms of a charitable trust in which the settlor has indicated a general charitable purpose, many courts will authorize the substitution of another charitable scheme within the testator's general purposes. Restatement (Second) of Trusts § 399 (1959). We should also keep in mind the analogies mentioned by Chief Justice Doe in Edgerly v. Barker, 66 N.H. 434, 462, 31 A. 900, 909-910 (1891): 'The feudal doctrine of forfeiture for and by a conveyance of a larger interest than the grantor has is no part of our common law. * * * A lease for 40 years, made under a power to lease for 21 years, is good for 21. * * * Under a statute restricting to a term not exceeding 21 years the time for which a tenant for life can be empowered to lease, a testamentary gift to a tenant for life of a power to lease for 63 years is not void. If he makes a lease for more than 21 years, it is void for the excess, and no more.' (citations omitted.)

Our decision should not be influenced by the fact that it was the testator's intent to distribute his estate among his children and their issue according to a plan which may appear to some as lopsidedly favoring his male progeny. This was, of course, his right. The wishes of the testator could have been accomplished exactly as he wished without violating the Rule if the attorney who drafted the will had specified that the trust was to continue until 21 years after the death of the last survivor of his wife and all of his issue living at the time of his death but not to exceed 30 years from the date of his death. Without the last mentioned limitation the trust could have continued for nearly 100 years from the date of his death without violating the Rule.

We are not alone in judicially adopting the doctrine of equitable approximation. The courts of New Hampshire and Mississippi have applied this doctrine in varying degrees and circumstances. The adoption of the rule of equitable approximation is further recommended by an overwhelming number of commentators[9] and, although the doctrine has judicial origins, it has been adopted by a number of state legislatures. We therefore hold that any interest which would violate the Rule Against Perpetuities shall be reformed within the limits of that rule to approximate most closely the intention of the creator of the interest. In the present case, where the testamentary trust violated the rule

---

[9] The cy pres doctrine was advanced by Judge James Quarles in 1946 in The Cy Pres Doctrine: Its Application to Cases Involving the Rule Against Perpetuities and Trusts for Accumulation, 21 N.Y.U.L.Rev. 384 (1946). This was a revision of his earlier article in 1904, The Cy Pres Doctrine with Reference to the Rule Against Perpetuities-An Advocation of Its Adoption in All Jurisdictions, 38 Am.L.Rev. 683 (1904). A current exposition can be found in Professor Browder's article, Construction, Reformation, and the Rule Against Perpetuities, 62 Mich.L.Rev. 1 (1963). See also Fletcher, A Rule of Discrete Invalidity: Perpetuities Reform without Waiting, 20 Stan.L.Rev. 459 (1968).

by providing that the trust 'shall cease and determine upon the death of my wife, Chun Lai Shee, or thirty (30) years from the date of my death, whichever shall last occur, * * *', the thirty year period need only be reduced to twenty-one years in order to bring the trust within the rule. In response to the questions reserved to this court we may then answer that the trust is valid in its entirety and all provisions are to be carried out in accordance with the language of the will with the exception that the trust shall cease and determine upon the death of the testator's wife, Chun Lai Shee, or twenty-one years from the date of the testator's death whichever shall last occur.

It is so ordered.

* * *

§ 6.7.5 Uniform Statutory Rule Against Perpetuities Act

Many states have adopted the Uniform Statutory Rule Against Perpetuities Act ("USRAP"), California being just one. The act, as you will see, does several things. It codifies the common law Rule Against Perpetuities but also provides for an alternative rule—a 90-year in-gross period. If the contingent interest will vest or terminate within either period (the common law perpetuities period or the 90-years in-gross period), the contingent interest is valid. If, on the other hand, the interest violates both of these rules, the court can use wait and see and, if necessary, cy pres, to save the gift.

California Probate Code § 21205

A nonvested property interest is invalid unless one of the following conditions is satisfied:
(a) When the interest is created, it is certain to vest or terminate no later than 21 years after the death of an individual then alive.
(b) The interest either vests or terminates within 90 years after its creation.

California Probate Code § 21220

On petition of an interested person, a court shall reform a disposition in the manner that most closely approximates the transferor's manifested plan of distribution and is within the 90 years allowed by the applicable provision in Article 2 (commencing with Section 21205), if any of the following conditions is satisfied:
(a) A nonvested property interest or a power of appointment becomes invalid under the statutory rule against perpetuities provided in Article 2 (commencing with Section 21205).
(b) A class gift is not but might become invalid under the statutory rule against perpetuities provided in Article 2 (commencing with Section 21205), and the time has arrived when the share of any class member is to take effect in possession or enjoyment.

(c) A nonvested property interest that is not validated by subdivision (a) of Section 21205 can vest but not within 90 years after its creation.

California Law Revision Commission, Comment
[California Probate Code § 21220]

Section 21220 is the same in substance as Section 3 of the Uniform Statutory Rule Against Perpetuities (1990). Section 21220 supersedes Civil Code Section 715.5 (reformation or construction to avoid violation of rule against perpetuities).

Background (adapted from Prefatory Note to Uniform Statute). Section 21220 directs a court, on petition of an interested person, to reform a disposition within the limits of the allowable 90-year period, in the manner deemed by the court most closely to approximate the transferor's manifested plan of distribution, in three circumstances: (1) when a nonvested property interest or a power of appointment becomes invalid under the statutory rule; (2) when a class gift has not but still might become invalid under the statutory rule and the time has arrived when the share of a class member is to take effect in possession or enjoyment; and (3) when a nonvested property interest can vest, but cannot do so within the allowable 90-year waiting period. It is anticipated that the circumstances requisite to reformation under this section will rarely arise, and consequently that this section will seldom need to be applied. [20 Cal.L.Rev.Comm.Reports 2501 (1990).]

Background (adapted from official comments to Uniform Statutory Rule Against Perpetuities)

1. Reformation

This section requires a court, on petition of an interested person, to reform a disposition whose validity is governed by the wait-and-see element of Section 21205(b) * * * so that the reformed disposition is within the limits of the 90-year period allowed by those sections, in the manner deemed by the court most closely to approximate the transferor's manifested plan of distribution, in three circumstances: First, when (after the application of the statutory rule) a nonvested property interest or a power of appointment becomes invalid under the statutory rule; second, when a class gift has not but still might become invalid under the statutory rule and the time has arrived when the share of one or more class members is to take effect in possession or enjoyment; and third, when a nonvested property interest can vest, but cannot do so within the allowable 90-year period under the statutory rule.

It is anticipated that the circumstances requisite to reformation will seldom arise, and consequently that this section will be applied infrequently. If, however, one of the three circumstances arises, the court in reforming is authorized to alter existing interests or powers and to create new interests or powers by implication or construction based on the transferor's manifested plan of distribution as a whole. * * * The court is also urged not to reduce an age contingency in excess of 21 unless it is absolutely necessary, and if it is deemed necessary to reduce such an age contingency, not to reduce it automatically to 21 but rather to reduce it no lower than absolutely necessary. See Example (3) below; Waggoner, Perpetuity Reform, 81 Mich.L.Rev. 1718, 1755-59 (1983); Langbein &

Waggoner, Reformation of Wills on the Ground of Mistake: Change of Direction in American Law?, 130 U.Pa.L.Rev. 521, 546-49 (1982).

§ 6.7.6 Abolition

A few states, Delaware included, have simply abolished the Rule Against Perpetuities. This means that a trust established in such a jurisdiction, in shades of the old fee tail, may endure forever.

25 Del. Code Annotated

§ 503 Rule against perpetuities.
(a) No interest created in real property held in trust shall be void by reason of the common law rule against perpetuities and no interest created in personal property held in trust shall be void by reason of any rule against perpetuities, whether the common law rule or otherwise.

* * *

§ 6.7.7 Perpetuities Savings Clauses

With the exception of states that have abolished the Rule Against Perpetuities, everything that we have discussed so far deals with a doctrine designed to minimize or eliminate the adverse consequences from violating the rule. In short, all of these doctrines (construction, wait and see, cy pres) are employed after the will or trust becomes effective and a violation of the rule is determined to exist. In the material that follows, we see how a smart drafter will not rely on these remedial measures. Rather, he or she will adopt prophylactic measures—a so-called perpetuities savings clause in the trust or will itself—to ensure that there is no violation in the first place.

Bank of America, N.A. v. Carpenter
401 Ill.App.3d 788 (2010)

* * *

I. BACKGROUND

Hartley Harper died in December 1932. His 14–page typed will, which he had executed in April 1932, left the residue of his estate to a trust created for the benefit of a certain group of individuals, the income beneficiaries, to receive income until the trust's termination and thereafter for another group, the remainder beneficiaries, to receive the corpus of the trust upon its termination. Questions, however, arose among the parties about the correct termination date of the trust given the effect of a provision that arguably violated the common law rule against perpetuities. The common law perpetuities rule provides "that an interest sought to be devised to be good must vest, if at all, not later than twenty-one years and nine months after some life or lives in being at the creation of the interest." *Johnston v. Cosby,* 374 Ill. 407, 410, 29 N.E.2d 608 (1940). See also *First National Bank of Joliet v. Hampson,* 88 Ill.App.3d 1057, 1061, 44 Ill.Dec. 17, 410 N.E.2d 1109 (1980), quoting Moynihan, Real Property 204 (1962) (" 'a future interest which, by any possibility, may not vest within twenty-one years after a life or lives in being at the time of its creation is void at its inception' ").

Relevant to this appeal, subparagraphs (1) and (2) of article three of the will provided that the trustee pay annual annuities to Hartley Harper's two sisters and his brother, Frederick C. Harper, and then the balance of the net income arising from the trust to his wife, Alice D. Harper, for life. Subparagraph (3) provided that, upon the death of the wife Alice, the trustee would pay Hartley Harper's stepdaughter Mary Foster a specific bequest and then pay the entire income of the trust to his brother Frederick for life. When brother Frederick died, the trustee would split the trust income equally between Frederick's two children and then to their descendants *per stirpes.* Frederick's two children were Hartley Harper's nephew, Frederick H. Harper, and niece, Alice L. Harper.

The trust would terminate according to the following provisions (for clarity, we have italicized the terms that are specifically contested by the parties in this appeal):

> (4) Upon the death of the last survivor of my said wife, my said brother, my said niece, my said nephew, *all descendants of my said nephew, and all descendants of my said niece,* I direct that all of the estate then remaining in the hands of the Trustee * * * shall be then distributed by my Trustee as follows: [in equal thirds to the group comprised of Hartley Harper's stepdaughter Mary Foster, stepgrandson Henry Foster, and sister-in-law Flora Casterline. If, upon termination of the trust, either of those three beneficiaries was deceased but had any descendants, then the deceased ancestor's share would pass *per stirpes* to such descendants. If none of stepdaughter Mary, stepgrandson Henry, sister-in-law Flora and their descendants were living, then the trust principal would be distributed to the heirs-at-law of the last survivor of stepdaughter Mary, stepgrandson Henry, and sister-in-law Flora.]
>
> (5) No trust hereby created shall in any event continue for a period longer than twenty-one (21) years after the death of the last survivor *of all the beneficiaries herein named or described* who are living at the date of my death, at the end of which said twenty-one year period this trust shall terminate and distribution shall be made in the manner in the paragraph last hereinabove provided (being subparagraph 4 of Article THIRD) without regard to, and notwithstanding, any provisions hereof which otherwise might postpone distribution beyond such time. (Emphasis added.)

The parties' dispute centers on the subparagraph (4) phrase "all descendants of my said nephew, and all descendants of my said niece," which arguably presents a perpetuities problem. Ultimately, the trustee took the position that the trust would terminate 21 years after the death of Elizabeth Sperry Rodman (born in 1918), William Casterline (born in 1924), and Burnham Casterline (born in 1929), who are the last three beneficiaries named or described in the entire will who were living at the time of Hartley Harper's death in 1932. The trustee's position was based on its determination that the will was unambiguous and must be applied as written. Accordingly, when the termination provision in subparagraph (4) was read together with the savings clause in subparagraph (5), the will on its face cured any perpetuities problem by requiring termination at the earlier of either (1) the death of all the descendants of Hartley Harper's nephew and niece, or (2) 21 years after the death of the last of all the beneficiaries named or described in the entire will who were living at the time of Hartley Harper's death.

* * *

Our review of Hartley Harper's will and trust reveals that when it is read in its entirety, the intent of Hartley Harper is clear and unambiguous. Subparagraph (4) cannot be read properly in isolation, and savings provisions like subparagraph (5) are a standard practice among estate planners and a common and effective way to avoid perpetuities problems. A savings clause operates to save a trust in the event that any of the prior termination provisions of a will or trust run afoul of the perpetuities rule. See *Hampson,* 88 Ill.App.3d at 1063, 44 Ill.Dec. 17, 410 N.E.2d 1109; *In re Estate of Reeve,* 393 Ill. 272, 65 N.E.2d 815 (1946). Hartley Harper's use of the savings clause clearly indicates that he intended to measure the maximum duration of the trust in the event that it might violate the rule against perpetuities. When subparagraphs (4) and (5) are read together, any perpetuities problem is cured by requiring the termination of the trust at the earlier of either (1) the death of all the descendants of Hartley Harper's nephew Fred and niece Alice, or (2) 21 years after the death of the last of the beneficiaries who were named or described in the entire will and were living at the time of Hartley Harper's death, *i.e.,* his sister-in-law Flora's three descendants: Elizabeth Sperry Rodman, William Casterline, and Burnham Casterline.

* * *

§ 6.7.8 Lawyer Liability

A lawyer who violates the Rule Against Perpetuities and thereby frustrates his client's intent subjects himself to a possible malpractice suit—or does he? See Lucas v. Hamm, *infra.*

Lucas v. Hamm
56 Cal.2d 583 (1961)

A lawyer drafted a testamentary trust that allegedly violated the Rule Against Perpetuities. The intended beneficiaries in the will consequently sued the attorney for negligence in drafting the instrument. The court initially held that privity of contract between the beneficiaries and the lawyer was not necessary for the beneficiaries to state a cause of action against the lawyer. Nonetheless, the court held that even if the provision in the will violated the Rule Against Perpetuities, the lawyer was not negligent. Why this is so is explained in the case.

* * *

We conclude that intended beneficiaries of a will who lose their testamentary rights because of failure of the attorney who drew the will to properly fulfill his obligations under his contract with the testator may recover as third-party beneficiaries.

However, an attorney is not liable either to his client or to a beneficiary under a will for errors of the kind alleged in the first and second causes of action.

The general rule with respect to the liability of an attorney for failure to properly perform his duties to his client is that the attorney, by accepting employment to give legal advice or to render other legal services, impliedly agrees to use such skill, prudence, and diligence as lawyers of ordinary skill and capacity commonly possess and exercise in the performance of the tasks which they undertake. Estate of Kruger, 130 Cal. 621, 626, 63 P. 31; Moser v. Western Harness Racing Ass'n, 89 Cal.App.2d 1, 7, 200 P.2d 7; Armstrong v. Adams, 102 Cal.App. 677, 684, 283 P. 871; see Wade, The Attorney's Liability for Negligence (1959) 12 Vanderbilt Law Rev. 755, 762- 765; 5 Am.Jur. 336. The attorney is not liable for every mistake he may make in his practice; he is not, in the absence of an express agreement, an insurer of the soundness of his opinions or of the validity of an instrument that he is engaged to draft; and he is not liable for being in error as to a question of law on which reasonable doubt may be entertained by well-informed lawyers. See Lally v. Kuster, 177 Cal. 783, 786, 171 P. 961; Savings Bank v. Ward, 100 U.S. 195, 198, 25 L.Ed. 621; 5 Am.Jur. 335; 7 C.J.S. Attorney and Client § 143, p. 980. These principles are equally applicable whether the plaintiff's claim is based on tort or breach of contract.

The complaint, as we have seen, alleges that defendant drafted the will in such a manner that the trust was invalid because it violated the rules relating to perpetuities and restraints on alienation. These closely akin subjects have long perplexed the courts and the bar. Professor Gray, a leading authority in the field, stated: 'There is something in the subject which seems to facilitate error. Perhaps it is because the mode of reasoning is unlike that with which lawyers are most familiar. * * * A long list might be formed of the demonstrable blunders with regard to its questions made by eminent men, blunders which they themselves have been sometimes the first to acknowledge; and there are few lawyers of any practice in drawing wills and settlements who have not at some time either fallen into the net which the Rule spreads for the unwary, or at least shuddered to think how narrowly they have escaped it.' Gray, The Rule Against Perpetuities (4th ed. 1942) p. xi; see also Leach, Perpetuities Legislation (1954) 67 Harv.L.Rev. 1349 (describing the rule as a 'technicality-ridden legal nightmare' and a 'dangerous instrumentality in the hands of most members of the bar'). Of the California law on perpetuities and restraints it has been said that few, if any, areas of the law have been fraught with more confusion or concealed more traps for the unwary draftsman; that members of the bar, probate courts, and title insurance companies make errors in these matters; that the code provisions adopted in 1872 created a situation worse than if the matter had been left to the common law, and that the legislation adopted in 1951 (under which the will involved here was drawn), despite the best of intentions, added further complexities. (See 38 Cal.Jur.2d 443; Coil, Perpetuities and Restraints; A Needed Reform (1955) 30 State Bar J. 87, 88-90.)

In view of the state of the law relating to perpetuities and restraints on alienation and the nature of the error, if any, assertedly [sic] made by defendant in preparing the instrument, it would not be proper to hold that defendant failed to use such skill, prudence, and diligence as lawyers of ordinary skill and capacity commonly exercise. The provision of the will quoted in the complaint, namely, that the trust was to terminate five years after the order of the probate court distributing the property to the trustee, could cause the trust to be invalid only because of the remote possibility that the order of distribution would be delayed for a period longer than a life in being at the creation of the interest plus 16 years (the 21-year statutory period less the five years specified in the will). Although it has been held that a possibility of this type could result in invalidity of a bequest (Estate of Johnston, 47 Cal.2d 265, 269-270, 303 P.2d 1; Estate of Campbell, 28 Cal.App.2d 102, 103 et seq., 82 P.2d 22), the possible occurrence of such a delay was so remote and unlikely that an attorney of ordinary skill acting under the same circumstances might well have 'fallen into the net which the Rule spreads for the unwary' and failed to recognize the danger. We need not decide whether the trust provision of the will was actually invalid or whether, as defendant asserts, the complaint fails to allege facts necessary to enable such a determination, because we have concluded that in any event an error of the type relied on by plaintiffs does not show negligence or breach of constract on the part of defendant. It is apparent that plaintiffs have not stated and cannot state causes of action with respect to the first two counts, and the trial court did not abuse its discretion in denying leave to amend as to these counts.

* * *

CHAPTER 7
ACQUISITION OF REAL PROPERTY BY GIFT OR PURCHASE

§ 7.1 Introduction

Suppose that Oscar owns Blackacre and wants to make a gift of Blackacre to Abel. What must Oscar do in such case? Oscar will have to execute a deed that complies with the "Statute of Frauds" and "deliver" the deed to Abel. But what does the Statute of Frauds require, and what exactly does delivery mean? The materials that follow explore these concepts.

On the other hand, suppose that Oscar wants to sell Blackacre to Abel, not make a gift of Blackacre to Abel. What must Oscar and Abel do? Here, the process is more complex. First, Oscar and Abel will execute a contract that complies with the Statute of Frauds. Again, we are concerned with what the Statute of Frauds requires. Second, very soon thereafter (the next day in all probability), escrow "opens." This means that a disinterested third party is designated by Oscar and Abel to hold in a fiduciary capacity any deposit paid by Abel, as well as funds representing the balance of the purchase price. To come up with the balance of the purchase price, Abel probably will have to secure financing from a bank or other financial institution. In any event, even if Abel has cash to pay Oscar for Blackacre, Abel will use this time (from the time that escrow opens until escrow closes—what we call the "executory period" of the contract) to check the public records in the office of the county recorder to make sure that Oscar has "marketable title." Finally, after some reasonable period of time (60 days or 90 days is most common), from the time that the contract for sale was entered into and escrow opened, and assuming that all conditions of the contract have been fulfilled, escrow will close. This means that Oscar executes all necessary paper work—including a deed (which either will be a "special warranty deed" or a "general warranty deed") and the escrow agent executes a check (after the money deposited by Abel has cleared) in favor of Oscar. Thus, at the end of escrow, if all goes well, Oscar gets his money and Abel gets Blackacre.

The materials that follow go into these and other related matters.

§ 7.2 Contracts and the Statute of Frauds Requirement

Every contract for the sale of land must comply with the Statute of Frauds. Below, we reproduce the English Statute of Frauds of 1677, upon which all modern statutes are based.

St. 29 Car. II, c. 3, § 4 (1677)
[English Statute of Frauds]

* * * no action shall be brought * * * upon any contract or sale of lands, tenements or hereditaments or any interest in or concerning them * * * unless the agreement upon which such action shall be brought or some memorandum or note thereof shall be in writing, and signed by the party to be charged therewith, or some other person thereunto by him lawfully authorized.

A. B. C. Auto Parts, Inc. v. Moran
359 Mass. 327 (1971)

In every state, the Statute of Frauds requires that there be (1) a "writing" (2) that is "signed by the party to be charged"(3) that states all the "material terms" of the contract. What can constitute a writing, who is the party to be charged, and what constitutes the material terms are addressed in this case.

Before TAURO, C.J., and SPALDING, SPIEGEL, REARDON and BRAUCHER, JJ.

REARDON, Justice.

The plaintiff appeals from a final decree in the Superior Court denying specific performance of an alleged oral contract to sell property in Cambridge and ordering the return to the plaintiff with interest of the deposit it paid to the defendant concurrent with the alleged making of the contract. We have before us findings and rulings of the judge and a transcript of the evidence.

The facts are as follows. After some months conversation relative to purchase, the plaintiff, by its president David Kagan, agreed on December 7, 1968, to buy land and a commercial garage at 227 Prospect Street in Cambridge from the defendant. Kagan gave the defendant the plaintiff corporation's check for $3,500 made out at the defendant's request to 'Prospect Realty Trust Ed Moran, trustee,' and endorsed at the defendant's request on the back of the check the following words: 'Deposit on property at 227 Prospect St.--Subject to approval of trust. Total price of 40 thousand dollars.' The defendant held the property as trustee under an instrument recorded in 1964 which by its terms provided for its termination on the death of either the defendant or his brother Roger, who had died in April of 1968. Nonetheless, the defendant testified that he considered the trust to be in existence and fully operative. Subsequently, on December 16, 1968, the defendant endorsed the check 'Prospect Realty, Moran Bros., Edward

Moran,' and deposited it to the account of Moran Bros. in a bank. The foregoing facts are generally agreed to.

* * *

On January 27, 1969, the plaintiff brought this bill in equity against the defendant who, at or about the time of receiving notice of the suit, sent the plaintiff a letter dated January 31, 1969, by certified mail stating that he would hold the property for the plaintiff until February 15 at a price of $60,000, which he represented at the trial was the figure previously agreed upon.

The judge ruled that the endorsements on the back of the check were sufficient to satisfy the statute of frauds, G.L. c. 259, § 1, and that 'to the extent that an agreement to buy and sell was reached between the parties,' it was enforceable. * * *

1. The trial judge was correct in ruling that the endorsement on the plaintiff's check was sufficient to satisfy the statute of frauds. Des Brisay v. Foss, 264 Mass. 102, 109, 162 N.E. 4; Michelson v. Sherman, 310 Mass. 774, 775, 39 N.E.2d 633; Cousbelis v. Alexander, 315 Mass. 729, 730, 54 N.E.2d 47; Epdee Corp. v. Richmond, 321 Mass. 673, 675, 75 N.E.2d 238; Pino v. Yenof, 353 Mass. 775, 235 N.E.2d 48. The endorsement clearly indicates the nature of the transaction, the parties, the locus of the property, and the purchase price. No essential element of a contract for the sale of land was omitted. The fact that the memorandum is on the back of a check is immaterial (Cousbelis v. Alexander, supra, 315 Mass. at 730, 54 N.E.2d 47), as is its silence as to when final papers will pass. In such circumstances the law will imply a reasonable time. Atwood v. Cobb, 16 Pick. 227, 231; Tzitzon Realty Co. v. Mustonen, 352 Mass. 648, 654, 227 N.E.2d 493. Nor is it material that no terms of payment are specified, for an agreement to pay cash is implied. Ryan v. Hall, 13 Metc. 520, 523; Pearlstein v. Novitch, 239 Mass. 228, 232, 131 N.E. 853; Epdee Corp. v. Richmond, 321 Mass. 673, 675, 75 N.E.2d 238; compare Grace v. Denison, 114 Mass. 16.

Having so ruled the judge was precluded from further ruling, as he did, that there was no contract between the parties. * * *

* * *

The decree is reversed and a new decree shall enter ordering the defendant to convey the premises at 227 Prospect Street, Cambridge, to the plaintiff for a price of $40,000 in cash within a period of thirty days after the entry of such decree.

So ordered.

§ 7.3 Exceptions to the Statute of Frauds Requirement

Even if the requirements of the Statute of Frauds are not satisfied, that does not necessarily mean that the transaction cannot be enforced. Even if the parties do not comply with the Statute of Frauds, it may well be that the buyer still can force the seller to go ahead with the sale or that the seller can secure damages from a buyer who backs out of the transaction. The theories that will take the case out of the Statute of Frauds are the doctrines of part performance and equitable estoppel. We discuss each in turn.

§ 7.3.1 Part Performance

The heart of part performance is that the conduct of the parties is evidence of a completed contract. The difficult question is, what conduct is probative to establish a contract? The next case gives us the basic rule for part performance—and tells us what does not qualify as part performance.

Bradshaw v. Ewing
297 S.C. 242 (1989)

The plaintiffs (Dutchland) claim that there was an oral modification to a written contract. To get past the Statute of Frauds defense of the defendant (Ewing), the plaintiffs claim part performance. The court states what part performance is and then finds that the actions of the parties do not satisfy the rule.

TOAL, Justice:

The partners of Dutchland Investments (Dutchland) brought this action to enforce an oral contract to convey real estate. The Honorable Frank P. McGowan directed a verdict for the defendant, Ewing, on Dutchland's causes of action for breach of contract, conversion, and breach of trust. Additionally, the trial judge granted a voluntary nonsuit to Dutchland on its cause of action against Ewing for unjust enrichment. At the same time, the judge granted a voluntary nonsuit to Ewing on its counterclaim against Dutchland for consequential damages allegedly suffered as a result of Dutchland's breach of the written contract. Dutchland appeals the directed verdict, voluntary nonsuit and the failure of the judge to realign the parties. We affirm the directed verdict for Ewing and affirm as modified the terms of the voluntary nonsuit.

I. BACKGROUND

Dutchland contracted on September 1, 1976 to buy from Ewing three acres of land in Irmo, South Carolina. The parties executed a written contract. The contract provided for a purchase price of $60,000, with a down payment of $13,000. The principal balance of $47,000 plus interest was due in five annual installments beginning in 1977 and ending in 1981.

Dutchland asserts that the written contract was orally modified on or about March, 1979. Dutchland claims that Linder, one of its partners, discussed the contract and its modifications with Ewing during a basketball tournament. Subsequently, Linder testified that he telephoned Ewing to modify the contract. The alleged modifications reduced the original acreage to be purchased from three to two, and proportionately reduced the purchase price from $60,000 to $40,000. Dutchland claimed that the consideration for the modification was that the partnership would pay the 1979 taxes and forgive whatever debt Ewing owed to Dutchland.

A. *Statute of Frauds*

The Statute of Frauds, codified at S.C.Code Ann. § 32-3-10, requires, in pertinent part, that a contract for the sale of land must be in writing. To remove an oral contract to convey real estate from the Statute of Frauds, Dutchland must show part performance of the oral contract. *Beckham v. Short,* 294 S.C. 415, 365 S.E.2d 42 (Ct.App.1988). Performance may be proved by evidence of the following: (1) improvements to the real estate; (2) possession of the real estate; (3) payment of the purchase price. *Stackhouse v. Cook,* 271 S.C. 518, 248 S.E.2d 482 (1978). Actual possession and improvements to the property are the strongest evidence to show part performance. *Scurry v. Edwards,* 232 S.C. 53, 100 S.E.2d 812 (1957). Payment of the purchase price is the weakest evidence of part performance and will not suffice on its own to remove a contract from the Statute of Frauds. *McMillan v. McMillan,* 77 S.C. 511, 58 S.E. 431 (1907). In order to overcome the Statute of Frauds, Dutchland must establish the parol contract "by competent and satisfactory proof, such as is clear, definite and certain." *Aust v. Beard,* 230 S.C. 515, 96 S.E.2d 558 (1957).

Dutchland presented evidence that they had improved the real estate in the following ways: (1) a large ranch house was moved on to the property; (2) the property was partially cleared and graded; (3) trash was picked up; and (4) wood was cut.

The first two improvements claimed by Dutchland were made at the direction of a third party, Ms. Shealy,[1] who temporarily stored her house on the property. For improvements to constitute part performance, they must be made by the purchaser with his own means and upon the faith of the vendor's promise. 73 Am.Jur.2d *Statute of Frauds* § 434 (1974). Since the house was moved on to the property and the property was graded at the direction of a third party, we hold that Ms. Shealy's actions may not be used by Dutchland to prove part performance. Dutchland, accordingly, may only rely on its evidence of cleaning trash off the property, and cutting wood.

We have previously held that in order for improvements to establish part performance, the improvements must be permanent or of such a character as to enhance substantially the value of the property. *Aust v. Beard,* 230 S.C. 515, 96 S.E.2d 558, 563 (1957). In *Aust,* the plaintiff presented evidence that they had removed some heavy undergrowth, planted some grass, and erected two large electric signs. There, we found that the plaintiff's evidence was not sufficient to establish improvements to the land. Likewise, Dutchland has not presented sufficient evidence to demonstrate that the improvements were permanent or such that they substantially enhanced the value of the land. Accordingly, we find that Dutchland cannot satisfy the first element of part performance.

Second, Dutchland claims that it performed several acts indicating possession. Evidence presented of possession was that Linder lobbied the Irmo City Council to extend a road through the property and directed that plats be created in order to sell the property. We hold that the evidence of possession was insufficient to establish part performance. Even though Linder lobbied the Irmo City Council to extend the road, he conceded that his efforts began prior to the alleged oral contract and were not solely on behalf of Dutchland. Even if we assume that the plats were developed in order to sell the property, Dutchland still has not proved part performance of the oral contract because the creation of the plats was consistent with the terms of the written contract.

Finally, Dutchland asserts that it paid the $40,000 purchase price pursuant to the oral contract. However, on reviewing the record, we do not find any evidence that the

---

[1] [Who is this person? Her identity and relationship to the case are a mystery.]

$40,000 Dutchland paid clearly and unequivocally refers to the oral contract. *See, Scurry v. Edwards,* 232 S.C. 53, 100 S.E.2d 812 (1957).

Because Dutchland failed to prove any of the elements of part performance, we hold that the Statute of Frauds bars the enforcement of the oral contract. We, thus, affirm the lower court's directed verdict for Ewing.

* * *

Burns v. McCormick
233 N.Y. 230 (1922)

One Halsey, an old man, asked two relatives, the plaintiffs, to live with him and take care of him, promising them that he would execute and deliver to them a deed to his house if they did. The plaintiffs sold their business in another city, moved in with Halsey, and took care of him. Halsey, however, never executed the deed. The plaintiffs sued Halsey's estate on the basis of part performance. The estate's executor pleaded the Statute of Frauds. The executor prevailed and the case makes clear that the actions of the buyer must, as per Bradshaw v. Ewing, *supra, "clearly and unequivocally refer to the oral contract."*

CARDOZO, J.

* * *

We think the defense must be upheld. Not every act of part performance will move a court of equity, though legal remedies are inadequate, to enforce an oral agreement affecting rights in land. There must be performance 'unequivocally referable' to the agreement, performance which alone and without the aid of words of promise is unintelligible or at least extraordinary unless as an incident of ownership, assured, if not existing.

'An act which admits of explanation without reference to the alleged oral contract or a contract of the same general nature and purpose is not, in general, admitted to constitute a part performance.' Woolley v. Stewart, 222 N. Y. 347, 351, 118 N. E. 847, 848.

* * *

We hold, then, that the acts of part performance are not solely and unequivocally referable to a contract for the sale of land. Since that is so, they do not become sufficient because part of the plaintiffs' loss is without a remedy at law. * * * The peril of perjury and error is latent in the spoken promise. Such, at least, is the warning of the statute, the estimate of policy that finds expression in its mandate. Equity, in assuming what is in substance a dispensing power, does not treat the statute as irrelevant, nor ignore the warning altogether. It declines to act on words, though the legal remedy is imperfect, unless the words are confirmed and illuminated by deeds. A power of dispensation, departing from the letter in supposed adherence to the spirit, involves an assumption of jurisdiction easily abused, and justified only within the limits imposed by history and precedent. The power is not exercised unless the policy of the law is saved. Pound, Equity and the Statute of Frauds, 33 Harvard Law Review, 933, 944.

In conclusion, we observe that this is not a case of fraud. No confidential relation has been abused. Goldsmith v. Goldsmith, 145 N. Y. 313, 39 N. E. 1067; Wood v. Rabe, 96 N. Y. 414, 48 Am. Rep. 640. * * *

The judgment of the Appellate Division and that entered on the report of the referee should be reversed, and the complaint dismissed, with costs in all courts.

HISCOCK, C. J., and HOGAN, POUND, McLAUGHLIN, CRANE, and ANDREWS, JJ., concur.

Judgments reversed, etc.

§ 7.3.2 Equitable Estoppel

The second theory that takes a case out of the Statute of Frauds is equitable estoppel. Typically, the key to this doctrine is detrimental reliance by the buyer and some wrongful conduct by the seller.

Baliles v. Cities Service Co.
578 S.W.2d 621 (Tenn. 1979)

One Newman, a contractor, was given a loan by a bank (Cities Service Co.) to construct a house on a certain vacant lot. The bank assured Newman that when the house's construction was well under way, the bank would execute a deed to the property in favor of Newman. Newman complied with the terms of this oral agreement, but the bank failed to execute a deed. Newman's assignee, Baliles, filed an action for specific performance to require the bank to execute the deed. The bank pleaded the Statute of Frauds as an affirmative defense. The court rejected the bank's position.

OPINION

COOPER, Justice.

* * *

"Equitable estoppel, in the modern sense, arises from the 'conduct' of the party, using that word in its broadest meaning, as including his spoken or written words, his positive acts, and his silence or negative omission to do any thing. Its foundation is justice and good conscience. Its object is to prevent the unconscientious and inequitable assertion or enforcement of claims or rights which might have existed, or been enforceable by other rules of law, unless prevented by an estoppel; and its practical effect is, from motives of equity and fair dealing, to create and vest opposing rights in the party who obtains the benefit of the estoppel." Evans v. Belmont Land Co., 92 Tenn. 348, 365, 21 S.W. 670, 673-674 (1893).

We think this is such a case. In dealing with Mr. Newman, respondent not only placed him in possession and permitted him to construct improvements on lot 100, but took affirmative action thereafter to aid Mr. Newman [to] secure a $5,000.00 loan this latter action being taken with the knowledge that the proceeds of the loan were to be used in the construction of a dwelling on lot 100. In the face of this affirmative action by respondent, to allow it to set up the statute of frauds as bar to enforcement of the agreement to sell lot 100 to Mr. Newman, and thus secure to itself the improvements on lot 100 would be a gross injustice and moral fraud on Mr. Newman.

§ 7.4 Marketable Title

Unless otherwise stated, implied in every contract for the sale of real property is the covenant of "marketable title." The meaning of marketable title is discussed in the material below.

§ 7.4.1 "Marketable Title" Defined

Lohmeyer v. Bower
170 Kan. 442 (1951)

The plaintiff entered into a contract to buy the defendant's house and now seeks rescission on the ground that the defendant could not tender marketable title. More specifically, the house was subject to a neighborhood covenant that required each house to have two stories; the house in question had only one story. Further, the house violated a local ordinance. After explaining what marketable title is, the court found the defendant could not deliver marketable title to the plaintiff and granted the plaintiff rescission.

PARKER, Justice.

This action originated in the district court of Lyon county when plaintiff filed a petition seeking to rescind a contract in which he had agreed to purchase certain real estate on the ground title tendered by the defendants was unmerchantable.[2] The defendants Bower and Bower, husband and wife, answered contesting plaintiff's right to rescind and by cross-petition asked specific performance of the contract. * * *

* * *

Plaintiff's petition alleges execution of the contract whereby he agreed to purchase Lot 37 in Berkley Hills Addition in the city of Emporia and makes such contract a part of that pleading. It avers that after execution of the agreement it came to his attention that the house on the real estate therein described had been placed there in violation of Section 5-224 of the Ordinances of the city of Emporia in that the house was located within approximately 18 inches of the north line of such lot in violation of the ordinance providing that no frame building should be erected within 3 feet of a side or rear lot line. It further avers that after execution of the agreement it came to plaintiff's knowledge the dedication[3] of the Berkley Hills Addition requires that only a two story house should be erected on the lot described in the contract whereas the house located

---

[2] [That is, "unmarketable."]

[3] [The court here means a restrictive covenant, which is a private land use arrangement. In short, the landowners in this subdivision agreed that all houses would be two stories. Restrictive covenants are discussed in chapter 12.]

thereon is a one story house. It then states the violations of the city ordinance and the dedication restrictions were unknown to the plaintiff when he entered into the contract and that he would not have entered into such agreement if he had known thereof. It next alleges that after becoming aware of such violations plaintiff notified the defendants in writing thereof, demanded that he be released from his contract and that defendants refused such demand. Finally it charges that such violations made the title unmerchantable and asks that the agreement be cancelled and set aside and that all moneys paid by plaintiff under its terms be refunded.

* * *

Pertinent provisions of the contract, entered into between the parties, essential to disposition of the issues raised by the pleadings, read:

'Witnesseth, That in consideration of the stipulations herein contained, and the payments to be made by the second party as hereinafter specified, the first party hereby agrees to sell unto the second party for following described real estate, situated in the County of Lyon, State of Kansas, to-wit:

'Lot numbered Thirty-seven (37) on Berkley Road in Berkley Hills Addition to the City of Emporia, according to the recorded plat thereof and to convey the above described real estate to the second party by Warranty Deed with an abstract of title, certified to date showing good merchantable title[4] or an Owners Policy of Title Insurance in the amount of the sale price, guaranteeing said title to party of the second part, free and clear of all encumbrances except special taxes subject, however, to all restrictions and easements of record applying to this property, it being understood that the first party shall have sufficient time to bring said abstract to date or obtain Report for Title Insurance and to correct any imperfections in the title if there be such imperfections.[']

* * *

There can be no doubt regarding what constitutes a marketable or merchantable title in this jurisdiction. This court has been called on to pass upon that question on numerous occasions. See our recent decision in Peatling v. Baird, 168 Kan. 528, 213 P.2d 1015, 1016, and cases there cited, wherein we held:

'A marketable title to real estate is one which is free from reasonable doubt, and a title is doubtful and unmarketable if it exposes the party holding it to the hazard of litigation.

'To render the title to real estate unmarketable, the defect of which the purchaser complains must be of a substantial character and one from which he may suffer injury. Mere immaterial defects which do not diminish in quantity, quality or value the property contracted for, constitute no ground upon which the purchaser may reject the title. Facts must be known at the time which fairly raise a reasonable doubt as to the title; a mere possibility or conjecture that such a state of facts may be developed at some future time is not sufficient.' (Syl ¶¶1, 2)

Under the rule just stated, and in the face of facts such as are here involved, we have little difficulty in concluding that the violation of section 5-224 of the ordinances of the city of Emporia as well as the violation of the restrictions imposed by the dedication declaration so encumber the title to Lot 37 as to expose the party holding it to the hazard of litigation and make such title doubtful and unmarketable. It follows, since, as we have

---

[4] [The traditional term is, "marketable title."]

indicated, the appellees had contracted to convey such real estate to appellant by warranty deed with an abstract of title showing good merchantable title, free and clear of all encumbrances, that they cannot convey the title contracted for and that the trial court should have rendered judgment rescinding the contract. This, we may add is so, notwithstanding the contract provides the conveyance was to be made subject to all restrictions and easements of record, for, as we have seen, it is the violation of the restrictions imposed by both the ordinance and the dedication declaration, not the existence of those restrictions, that renders the title unmarketable. The decision just announced is not without precedent or unsupported by sound authority.

* * *

To the same effect is 66 C.J. 912 § 592, where the following statement appears:

'Existing violations of building restrictions imposed by law warrant rejection of title by a purchaser contracting for a conveyance free of encumbrances. The fact that the premises to be conveyed violate tenement house regulations is ground for rejection of title where the contract of sale expressly provided against the existence of such violations, * * *.' See, also, Moran v. Borrello, 132 A. 510, 4 N.J.Misc. 344.

With respect to covenants and restrictions similar to those involved in the dedication declaration, notwithstanding the agreement--as here--excepted restrictions of record, see Chesebro v. Moers, 233 N.Y. 75, 134 N.E. 842, 21 A.L.R. 1270, holding that the violation by a property owner of covenants restricting the distance from front and rear lines within which buildings may be placed renders the title to such property unmarketable.

* * *

Finally appellees point to the contract which, it must be conceded, provides they shall have time to correct imperfections in the title and contend that even if it be held the restrictions and the ordinance have been violated they are entitled to time in which to correct those imperfections. Assuming, without deciding, they might remedy the violation of the ordinance by buying additional ground the short and simple answer to their contention with respect to the violation of the restrictions imposed by the dedication declaration is that any changes in the house would compel the purchaser to take something that he did not contract to buy.

Conclusions heretofore announced require reversal of the judgment with directions to the trial court to cancel and set aside the contract and render such judgment as may be equitable and proper under the issues raised by the pleadings.

It is so ordered.

§ 7.4.2 Time For Performance: In General

We have seen that a seller must deliver marketable title to the buyer. The question is, when must the seller so deliver?

Risse v. Thompson
471 N.W.2d 853 (Iowa 1991)

This short squib tells us when marketable title must be furnished: on the date escrow is set to close. (As we discussed early on in this chapter, when escrow closes, the buyer gets the deed to the house and the seller gets the money.)

* * *

The general rule is that merchantable title, which a vendor must furnish under an executory contract for the sale of land, must be furnished on the date required under the contract. *Wemer v. Long,* 185 N.W.2d 243, 247 (Iowa 1971); *McCubbin v. Urban,* 247 Iowa 862, 864-65, 77 N.W.2d 36, 38 (1956). Consequently, a vendee may not support a breach of contract claim by relying on a defect in a vendor's title prior to the closing time provided in the contract, especially if the defect can be removed. *Wemer,* 185 N.W.2d at 247.

* * *

Kimball v. West
82 U.S. 377 (1872)

In Kimball v. West, *we learn what happens if the seller cannot deliver marketable title on the date that escrow is set to close, but can deliver it thereafter. We also learn of the remedy that the buyer has against the seller in such a case.*

APPEAL from the Circuit Court for the District of Missouri.

Kimball and Trask brought their bill in chancery against West, to rescind a contract for the sale of land of which they were purchasers from him. The contract was an executed one, West having conveyed the land--about four hundred acres in quantity--to the complainants' agent, who had conveyed to them, and the purchase-money ($22,000) having been paid. The deed of West, the defendant, contained a clause of general warranty.

The allegation mainly relied on by the bill to set aside the contract was that the defendant represented to the agent of the complainants, that the title to the land was good; that there was no encumbrance on it, nor adverse claim to it; when in truth and in fact an action of ejectment was then pending for one hundred and eighty-four acres of it against the defendant, in which judgment was afterwards rendered against him; that the land so recovered in the suit against the defendant was the most valuable part of the [tract], and without which the complainants would not have made the purchase; and that the defendant fraudulently concealed the existence of this suit, and represented the title to the whole to be perfect. On the question of concealment and fraudulent representation testimony was taken on both sides, which did not leave the matter free from doubt. This part of the matter, however, was unimportant in the view which this court took of the case.

It appeared from the record that before the cause in the court below came to a final hearing, the defendant purchased the outstanding and conflicting title to the one hundred and eighty-four acres, and tendered to the complainants such conveyances as made their title perfect. The court, therefore, dismissed the bill, but decided that the defendant should pay the costs of the suit.

From this decree of dismissal the complainants appealed.

Mr. Justice MILLER delivered the opinion of the court.

We are of opinion that the decree of the court below was clearly right. The plaintiffs had paid their money and accepted of the defendant his deed with a clause warranting the title. For any defect in that title the law gave them a remedy by an action on the covenant. But when, declining to pursue that remedy, they apply to a court of equity to rescind the whole contract, thereby compelling the defendant to repay the sum of $22,000, and receive back the title which he had conveyed to the plaintiffs, the necessity of such a decree to obtain the ends of justice must be very clear before it will be given. When, therefore, it appears that at the time of the hearing the defendant is able to remedy the supposed defect in his title, and in point of fact secures and makes good to the complainants, at his own cost, all that he conveyed to them originally, the complainants must show some loss, injury, or damage by the delay in perfecting the title before they can claim a rescission of the contract. And even if this could be shown, which is not attempted in this case, the court, as a general rule, would not be authorized to decree a rescission, if compensation could be made for the injury arising from the delay in making good the original defect in the title.

DECREE AFFIRMED.

§ 7.4.3 Time For Performance: Time Is Of the Essence Contracts

A buyer who wishes to make certain that marketable title is delivered on a date certain should insert a "time is of the essence" clause in the contract for sale. Grace v. Nappa, *infra, provides further elucidation, explaining exactly what a "time is of the essence" clause is.*

Grace v. Nappa
46 N.Y.2d 560 (1979)

* * *

When a provision that time is to be of the essence is inserted in a real property contract, the date established as the law day[5] takes on especial significance. Ordinarily, the law will allow the vendor and vendee a reasonable time to perform their respective obligations, regardless of whether they specify a particular date for the closing of title (see, e. g., Cohen v. Kranz, 12 N.Y.2d 242, 238 N.Y.S.2d 928, 189 N.E.2d 473; Taylor v. Goelet, 208 N.Y. 253, 101 N.E. 867). When there is a declaration that time is of the essence, however, each party must tender performance on law day unless the time for performance is extended by mutual agreement (see, e. g., Rhodes v. Astro-Pac, Inc., 41 N.Y.2d 919, 394 N.Y.S.2d 623, 363 N.E.2d 347, affg. 51 A.D.2d 656, 378 N.Y.S.2d 195;

---

[5] [By "law day," the court means the date scheduled by the parties to close escrow.]

Kotcher v. Edelblute, 250 N.Y. 178, 184, 164 N.E. 897, 899; Kaplan v. Scheiner, 1 A.D.2d 329, 330, 149 N.Y.S.2d 868, 869). In the instant case, therefore, plaintiff [the buyer] was well within his rights when he refused to consent to an adjournment of the closing and instead insisted upon immediate performance of defendant's obligations. Once the closing was aborted, moreover, it was not necessary for plaintiff to entertain further proposals from defendant, for if defendant had failed to satisfy a material element of the contract, he was already in default (see Isse Realty Corp. v. Trona Realty Corp., 17 N.Y.2d 763, 270 N.Y.S.2d 422, 217 N.E.2d 144, affg. 24 A.D.2d 1000, 266 N.Y.S.2d 19).

* * *

In sum, since defendant materially breached the contract of sale, he may not be awarded specific performance, and plaintiff is entitled to prevail in his action for return of the down payment. This result flows from the provisions which the parties included in their compact.

* * *

§ 7.5 Risk of Loss

§ 7.5.1 Introduction

Suppose Buyer and Seller enter into a contract whereby Buyer agrees to pay Seller $100,000 for Blackacre, Seller's office building. Suppose also that before escrow closes, a lightning strike destroys the building. Who, in such case, bears the risk of loss? If the risk is borne by Buyer, the deal goes through. Consequently, Seller gets the full $100,000 and Buyer gets Blackacre, sans the building. On the other hand, if the risk of loss is borne by Seller, rescission is ordered. In such case, Buyer gets all consideration returned and Seller retains Blackacre, again sans the structure.

§ 7.5.2 Theories to Allocate Risk

In the case that follows, two different approaches are examined in determining who bears the risk of loss, one of which is called "equitable conversion."

Ross v. Bumstead
65 Ariz. 61 (1946)

* * *

The early case of Paine v. Meller, 6 Ves. Jr. 349, 31 Eng.Reports 1088, first announced the majority rule, and it has been followed by a long line of cases both in England and America. 22 A.L.R. 575. The courts which have followed this rule have done so either upon the theory of an equitable conversion, whereby the vendor's interest in the property has been converted by the contract from realty into personalty and the vendor holds merely the bare legal title in trust for the vendee, who holds the equitable title; or upon the theory that the beneficial incidents of ownership are in the vendee. Op.Cit., also Anno. Anderson v. Yaworski, 120 Conn. 390, 181 A. 205, 101 A.L.R. 1241.

The minority rule proceeds upon the theory that a contract for sale of realty contains an implied condition that since the vendee could not acquire all that he had bargained for by reason of the destruction of a portion of the premises, he should not be required to assume the loss. See cases cited in the Anno. 22 A.L.R. 575, at page 578, and also Hawkes v. Kehoe, 193 Mass. 419, 79 N.E. 766, 10 L.R.A.,N.S., 125, 9 Ann.Cas. 1053; Anno., 41 A.L.R. 1272.

In this jurisdiction, both reason and authority require our reaffirmance of the majority rule as stated in Kresse v. Ryerson, supra. * * *

The authorities are numerous in holding that the rule placing the risk of loss on the vendee was the rule at common law. Sewell v. Underhill, 197 N.Y. 168, 90 N.E. 430, 27 L.R.A.,N.S., 233, 134 Am.St. Rep. 863, 18 Ann.Cas. 795; Ashford v. Reese, 132 Wash. 649, 233 P. 29, at page 31. Our statutes require the adoption of the common law as the rule of decision of the courts of this state, in so far as it is consistent with and adapted to the natural and physical conditions of this state and the necessities of the people thereof, and not repugnant to, or inconsistent with the Constitution of the United States, or the constitution and laws of this state, or established customs of the people of this state. Sec. 1-106, A.C.A. 1939. As a corollary of that premise it follows that the common-law rule, until changed by statute, is the rule this court must follow.

For the reasons stated the judgment of the lower court is in all respects affirmed.

STANFORD, C. J., and MORGAN, J., concurring.

§ 7.6 Deeds

§ 7.6.1 Introduction

When escrow closes, the deed to the buyer must comply with the Statute of Frauds. That is, the deed must identify the parties, describe the property, and be signed by the grantor (it is not required in this country for the grantee to sign the deed). The deed also must be "delivered" to the grantee and be "accepted" by the grantee. In this section, we will consider these issues, as well as the types of deeds that are in use today: general warranty deeds, special warranty deeds, and quitclaim deeds.

§ 7.6.2 Statute of Frauds: Description of the Property

The Statute of Frauds requires that the property be sufficiently described. Typically, the description is a legal description based on the county tax records. The description also may be based on the house number and city. These are not the only ways to describe the property, however, as the next case illustrates.

Snyder v. Bridewell
167 Ark. 8 (1924)

In Snyder v. Bridewell, *the grantor executes a deed "of all land" owned by the grantor in certain described counties. The court addresses whether this is a sufficient description for purposes of the Statute of Frauds.*

HUMPHREYS, J.

* * *

The record herein reveals the following undisputed facts: The land in question was formerly owned by the Nashville Lumber Company. This company executed a mortgage on all of its property in Howard and several other counties in Arkansas to the Lesser-Goldman Cotton Company for a large sum. The land in question was described in the mortgage, if at all, as "all property owned by the Nashville Lumber Company or afterwards acquired by it in Howard and other counties in Arkansas." * * *

The instant suit was brought on March 28, 1923, and at that time appellants had been in actual possession of the land in question for several years, having moved upon same a short time after they purchased it on the 10th day of June, 1919. The only questions arising on the appeal for determination by this court are: First, whether the general description contained in the Goldman mortgage, and the foreclosure proceedings thereunder, was sufficient in law to convey a title to the land; and, second, whether appellants were in a position to interpose a defect or failure of the title as a defense to a recovery of the unpaid purchase money.

1. The general rule as to the sufficiency of a description to pass title to land under deed or mortgage in this state is that it shall be described with sufficient certainty to identify it. If not particularly and certainly described in the deed, the deed itself must make reference to something tangible by which the land can be located. Doe ex dem. Phillips' Heirs v. Benjamin A. Porter, 3 Ark. 18, 36 Am. Dec. 448; Tolle v. Curley, 159 Ark. 175, 251 S. W. 377. The deed itself must furnish a key by which the land sought to be conveyed may be identified, and the real question in this case is whether the reference to ownership of lands in a certain county and state will accomplish this purpose. It will be observed that the description in the mortgage and foreclosure proceedings in the instant case embraces all the property owned by the Nashville Lumber Company in Howard and certain other counties in Arkansas. Of course a reference to a part of the lands owned by said company in said counties would be too indefinite and uncertain to pass title to any lands, but we think the description covering all the lands owned by said company in said counties is definite enough to satisfy our registration laws and was constructive notice to all parties dealing with lands owned by said company in said counties. This exact point has never been decided by this court, but the rule thus announced is in accord with the weight of authority and follows the rule laid down by the Supreme Court of the United States. Wilson v. Boyce, 92 U. S. 325, 23 L. Ed. 608; Harmon v. James, 7 Smedes & M. (Miss.) 111; 45 Am. Dec. 296; Roehl v. Haumesser, 114 Ind. 314, 15 N. E. 345; Higgins v. Higgins, 121 Cal. 489, 53 P. 1081, 66 Am. St. Rep. 57; Strouse v. Cohen, 113 N. C.

349, 18 S. E. 323; Smith v. Westall, 76 Tex. 509, 13 S. W. 540; 2 Devlin on Deeds Sec. 1013; 8 R. C. L. 1076.

* * *

§ 7.6.3 Statute of Frauds: Signature of the Grantor

In this country, it is only the grantor who must sign the deed; the grantee need not sign. That said, it would seem to be a simple matter to determine if the grantor complied with the signature requirement of the Statute of Frauds: either the grantor signed the deed or did not. The next case illustrates that this "simple" requirement of signing may not be that simple after all.

McAbee v. Gerarden
187 Wis. 399 (1925)

The grantor, who was quite sick, had her brother sign the deed for her in her presence and at her direction. What the brother should have done was to sign the grantor-sister's name and his name. Instead, the brother signed only his name. Nonetheless, the court found that the signature requirement of the Statute of Frauds had been satisfied.

JONES, J.

* * *

The question here involved is whether there was such a signature by the plaintiff as complies with the statutory requirement. It is plain that there was not a literal compliance since the name of the grantor does not appear * * *

* * *

* * * Should it be held that the ridiculous mistake of the agent in signing his own name instead of that of his principal was such a failure to comply with the statute as to defeat the undoubted intention of the parties?

It is well settled that where a grantor is present and authorized another expressly or impliedly to sign his name to a deed, it is then the deed of the grantor * * *.

* * *

There are numerous cases in which it has been held that irregularities in writing the signature of the grantor, when made by mark or otherwise, do not necessarily vitiate a deed or will. Tustin v. Faught, 23 Cal. 237; Middleton v. Findla, 25 Cal. 76; Agurs v. Belcher, 111 La. 378, 35 So. 607, 100 Am. St. Rep. 485; Bailey's Heirs v. Bailey's Executor, 35 Ala. 687; Devereux v. McMahon, 108 N. C. 134, 12 S. E. 902, 12 L. R. A. 205; Timber v. Desparois, 18 S. D. 587, 101 N. W. 879.

In some of these cases the signatures at the end and in the body of the deed were dissimilar and in others entirely unlike. The cases proceed on the theory that, if a person is designated by his proper name in the body of the deed and in the certificate of acknowledgment, the deed is not invalidated by the fact that, by some mistake, he signs it by the wrong name. Devlin on Real Estate, §§ 237, 240. In case of such irregularities, it may of course be necessary to identify the grantor or grantee in case of variance in the names and to show the real intention of the parties. In a case which came to this court, it was claimed that the deed was ineffective because the grantee designated in the deed was dead. In the decision, it was said by Mr. Justice Dodge:

"If the grant, in the intention of the parties, is attempted to be made to some person who has no existence, it cannot take effect. Neal v. Nelson, 117 N. C. 393, 23 S. E. 428, 53 Am. St. Rep. 590. Many technical rules, however, have yielded to more rational views in modern times. The real intention of the parties is to be sought and effectuated by courts when possible. If it was the intention both of grantor and grantee that the grant should be to some person or persons in existence, that intent may be effectuated by ascertaining under proper rules of evidence the intention of the parties, although such person be not designated by his legal or usual name. * * * Again it is recognized in a multitude of cases that, if the court can find that a certain person was intended as grantee, it matters not what name is given him in the deed." City Bank of Portage v. Plank, 141 Wis. 653, 124 N. W. 1000, 135 Am. St. Rep. 62, 18 Ann. Cas. 869.

If we were compelled to hold that the intentions of the parties were defeated by the mistake it would work palpable injustice to the plaintiff. We do not so hold. When the grantor guided the pen of her agent, supposing that he was signing her name, and, when the deed was duly sealed and acknowledged, it became her deed, notwithstanding the mistake.

Other questions were discussed in the brief which it becomes unnecessary to decide.

Judgment affirmed.

§ 7.6.4 Delivery: In General

If O wants to transfer title of Blackacre to A, O, as we have previously seen, must execute a deed that complies with the requirements of the Statute of Frauds. Further, O must "deliver" the deed to A. Delivery is a term of art and means that title passes immediately. For a layperson, "giving" or "handing over" the deed to A would be synonymous with delivery. In the law of real property, however, such a handing over may be probative of a delivery, but not conclusive. The next case illustrates this point.

Johnson v. Ramsey
307 Ark. 4 (1991)

Alice Ramsey executed a deed in favor of one Allen Walters (and, implicitly, handed the deed over to Walters). The deed was thereafter recorded. Presumptively, on such facts, there was a delivery. Nonetheless, the court will find that there was no delivery.

HAYS, Justice.

This is an appeal from a declaratory judgment entered in the Mississippi Chancery Court. The facts are not in dispute. On July 15, 1970, the appellee, Alice Ramsey, purchased from D.S. and Elizabeth Laney a lot in Osceola, Arkansas, on Poplar Street. Ramsey executed a note and deed of trust to the Laneys for the purchase price in the sum of $4,500.00 payable at $40.00 per month.

On August 10, 1970, Alice Ramsey executed a warranty deed to Allen Walters for the Poplar Street property. The warranty deed omitted one of the calls so that the property was incorrectly described.

The deed from Ramsey to Walters provided for $10.00 consideration paid by Walters "and other good and valuable consideration, including, but not limited to, the payment of all sums due D.S. Laney on a Promissory Note dated July 15, 1970 . . ."

On April 2, 1990, the appellant, Robert Johnson, obtained a default judgment against Allen Walters arising from a motor vehicle collision. Thereafter, the Mississippi Circuit Court issued a writ of execution commanding the sheriff to recover from Allen Walters the amount of the judgment granted in favor of Johnson. The sheriff returned the writ *nulla bona,* however, when it was discovered that Allen Walters had record title to the Poplar Street property; a second writ of execution was issued.

On June 22, 1990, Walters executed a quitclaim deed to Alice Ramsey for the Poplar Street property. The deed recited that Allen Walters was reconveying the property that was "held in trust" by Walters on behalf of Alice Ramsey. Because of the reconveyance to Alice Ramsey the sheriff declined to execute the second writ of execution.

In August of 1990 Alice Ramsey filed a suit for declaratory judgment, naming Robert Johnson and the sheriff as defendants. Ramsey asked that she be declared the owner in fee simple of the Poplar Street property and for an injunction to prevent a sale of the property. The sheriff was subsequently released from the suit.

Robert Johnson filed a counter-claim against Alice Ramsey and a third party complaint against Allen Walters and his wife, Hattie Walters, alleging that he obtained a default judgment against Allen Walters and after the judgment was served on him, Walters transferred all his real and personal property to Hattie Walters or Alice Ramsey with the intent to hinder, delay or defraud Johnson. Johnson requested that all the transfers of real and personal property be void and that the sheriff be ordered to levy on all assets transferred by Allen Walters to Hattie Walters or Alice Ramsey or any proceeds derived from the transfers.

After a hearing the court found that certain real property belonging to Allen Walters was fraudulently conveyed to Hattie Walters and that Alice Ramsey was the owner in fee simple of the Poplar Street property. Robert Johnson appeals the finding regarding the ownership of the Poplar Street property.

In a letter opinion, the chancellor made the following findings: Allen Walters had no interest in the Poplar Street property because the property description in the deed from Ramsey to Walters is faulty; Walters does not seek reformation of the deed and Robert Johnson lacks standing to seek that relief; if the litigation was between Ramsey, the grantor, and Walters, the grantee, the court would find that the erroneous description in the deed should be reformed, and Walters had no interest in the Poplar Street property because there has been a total lack of consideration.

Johnson challenges the chancellor's findings, arguing that consideration was not relevant to the deed's validity and reformation was not necessary because the August 10th deed made specific reference to the deed of trust executed to Laney which contained a correct legal description of the property. Johnson insists that all essential elements of a deed were proven and the court should have found that Allen Walters owned the Poplar Street property.

We agree with Johnson that consideration and reformation are not necessary for the validity of this deed, however, the requirement of delivery of the deed is lacking, thus, the chancellor did not err in finding that the Poplar Street property did not belong to Allen Walters.

* * *

The chancellor's findings on reformation and consideration do not warrant reversal because there was no delivery of the deed. A deed is inoperative unless there has been delivery to the grantee and an essential element of a valid delivery is the grantor's intention to pass title immediately, thus, giving up dominion and control of the property. *Parker v. Lamb,* 263 Ark. 681, 567 S.W.2d 99 (1978). Even though a presumption of delivery of a deed attaches when the deed is recorded, as occurred here, that presumption may be rebutted by other factors pertaining to the deed. *See Crowder v. Crowder,* 303 Ark. 562, 798 S.W.2d 425 (1990).

Alice Ramsey testified that in August of 1970 she became ill and did not think she was going to live. At that time she had several children living at home and decided Allen Walters would be the person who would maintain her property for her children. Speaking about the execution of the warranty deed to Walters, Ramsey stated, ". . . I didn't mean to give it to him then, I just meant for him to see after it so my kids could have somewhere to stay because there wasn't nobody . . . I didn't have no relatives around and the kids was small." Ramsey further testified that she paid all payments on the property as well as the property taxes. At trial the following exchange took place between Ramsey's attorney and Allen Walters:

Q. Well, did you claim that you owned the property?
A. Well, I didn't own it because I didn't pay nothing on it. All I know is that she just put it over into my name on account of she was sick, she was having this problem.
Q. And you never have claimed to own the property?
A. No, sir. Never have claimed to own it. I haven't paid nothing on it.

The testimony of Alice Ramsey corroborated by Allen Walters showed that Ramsey did not intend to give up dominion of her property. This testimony sufficiently rebuts the presumption of delivery of the deed. Consequently, Allen Walters did not receive any interest in the Poplar Street property.

Johnson argues next that the Chancellor erred in establishing Alice Ramsey as owner of the real property because she participated in a fraudulent transfer of the property. This argument fails because of the finding that delivery of the deed was lacking, therefore, there was no transfer of the Poplar Street property.

Johnson also raises an issue concerning laches, but, finding no reference at the trial level to this argument, we do not address it on appeal.

* * *

AFFIRMED.

Kopp v. Reiter
146 Ill. 437 (1893)

One would imagine that, in light of Johnson v. Ramsey, *an undelivered deed is a complete nullity and has no legal significance whatsoever. But that is not necessarily true. In* Kopp v. Reiter, *one Mrs. Reiter owned a parcel of land. She and her husband* *signed the deed (although only she owned the property) naming one Kopp as grantee, who had put down $250 as "earnest money" as a down payment for the purchase price. The contract for sale was never reduced to a writing and the deed was never delivered. Ultimately, Mrs. Reiter prevails: she could successfully raise the Statute of Frauds as an affirmative defense to avoid the sale. See § 7.2, supra. Note, however, the court's analysis: that under certain circumstances, an undelivered deed may be used to satisfy the Statute of Frauds requirement.*

MAGRUDER, J., (after stating the facts.)

    Under the facts, did Mrs. Reiter, the owner of the lot, make any such contract for its sale and conveyance as a court of equity will compel her to perform? Section 2 of the statute of frauds provides as follows: 'No action shall be brought to charge any person upon any contract for the sale of lands, etc., * * * unless such contract or some memorandum or note thereof shall be in writing, and signed by the party to be charged therewith, or some other person thereunto by him lawfully authorized in writing, signed by such party.' 1 Starr & C. Ann. St. c. 59, § 2, p. 1192. It cannot be contended here that there has been any such part performance of a parol contract by payments, possession, and improvements as will take the case out of the statute of frauds. The purchaser, Kopp, never took possession of the lot, nor made any improvements upon it. * * * We have held in a number of cases that, in order to ascertain what sort of writing is sufficient to meet the requirements of the statute as above quoted no form of language is necessary, if only the intention can be gathered, and that any kind of writing, from a solemn deed down to mere hasty notes or memoranda in books, papers, or letters, will suffice, but that the writings, notes, or memoranda must contain on their face, or by reference to others, the names of the parties, vendor and vendee, a sufficiently clear and explicit description of the property to render it capable of being identified from other property of like kind, together with the terms, conditions, (if there be any,) and price to be paid, or other consideration to be given; and such writing, note, or memorandum must be signed by the party to be charged, or, if signed by an agent, the authority of such agent must be in writing, signed by the party to be charged, and the contract or memorandum or note thereof made by the agent must also be in writing, and signed by him. McConnell v. Brillhart, 17 Ill. 354; Cossitt v. Hobbs, 56 Ill. 231; Wood v. Davis, 82 Ill. 311; Albertson v. Ashton, 102 Ill. 50; Chappell v. McKnight, 108 Ill. 570; Lasher v. Gardner, 124 Ill. 441, 16 N. E. Rep. 919. The only writing ever signed by Mrs. Reiter in this case was the warranty deed which she executed on or about January 7, 1891, and which remained in the hands of her husband, and was never delivered to Kopp * * *. We do not think that this deed can be regarded, under the facts disclosed by the record, as such a memorandum or note of a contract for the sale of the land as is sufficient to take the case out of the statute of frauds. * * * The deed simply purported to convey the premises from the grantors to the grantee for a consideration of $5,000, but it did not recite the terms of the contract, or in any manner refer to the contract. Counsel for appellant [Kopp] disclaim any reliance upon the undelivered deed as a conveyance of title, but contend that it is such written evidence of the contract of sale as satisfies the statute of frauds, whose object and meaning 'is to reduce contracts to a certainty, in order to avoid perjury on the one hand, (by the setting up of parol evidence, which is easily fabricated,) and fraud on the other,' (Welford v. Beazely, 3 Atk. 503;) that the nondelivery of the deed, regarded as such written evidence, is immaterial; that it is immaterial whether Mrs. Reiter did, or did not, intend to charge herself thereby; and that the deed was an admission in writing of what the contract was. It is true that an undelivered deed is sometimes resorted to in order to help out the requirements of the statute of frauds, but it can hardly be said that the circumstances under which such a deed can be so used are disclosed by the facts in the present record. The language of the statute is, 'some memorandum or note thereof.' The word 'thereof' refers back to the word 'contract.' There must be some memorandum or note in writing of the contract. Hence, if an undelivered deed executed by the owner can be regarded as meeting the requirements of the statute, it must be a memorandum or note of the contract, or, in other words, must refer to the terms and conditions of the contract.

In Cagger v. Lansing, 43 N. Y. 550, it is said: 'The counsel * * * insists that the deed executed by the intestate, and delivered in escrow, is a contract for the sale of the land executed by the intestate. This position cannot be sustained. The deed purports to be a conveyance of all the intestate's interest in the premises, for a consideration therein expressed of $1,000, but is wholly silent as to the terms of the contract pursuant to which it was made.' * * * In Swain v. Burnette, 89 Cal. 564, 26 Pac. Rep. 1093, it was held that an undelivered deed, executed in pursuance of an oral agreement of sale, cannot be regarded as a sufficient memorandum to satisfy the statute of frauds, unless it is shown to have contained a memorandum of the oral agreement. Freeland v. Charmley, 80 Ind. 132; Parker v. Parker, 1 Gray, 409; Overman v. Kerr, 17 Iowa, 485; Cannon v. Cannon, 26 N. J. Eq. 316; Johnston v. Jones, 85 Ala. 286, 4 South. Rep. 748. Many of the cases cited as authority for the position that a deed executed by an owner of land, but not delivered, is a sufficient memorandum of a contract of sale, under the statute, will thus be found, upon examination, to refer to deeds containing the terms of the contract. In the case at bar, however, as has already been stated, the deed executed by Mrs. Reiter and her husband was a simple conveyance of the lot for a consideration of $5,000, and was silent as to the terms of the contract of December 27, 1890. Where the owner of land has signed a written contract of sale, or some writing amounting to such a contract, but has failed therein to properly describe the property, a deed executed by him, but not yet delivered, may be looked to as a part of the transaction, and may be made to aid the prior agreement, and secure its enforcement, by supplying the defect in such description. Thus, in Jenkins v. Harrison, 66 Ala. 345, to which reference is made by counsel for appellant, a memorandum in writing, purporting to contain the terms of a contract for the sale of land, and signed by both of the parties, failed to describe the property with the certainty and definiteness required to a specific performance, but deeds, inoperative for want of delivery, were executed by the parties a few days afterwards, which did correctly describe the land; and it was held that such undelivered deeds, and the memorandum signed by the parties, might, when taken together, satisfy the requisitions of the statute of frauds, the court saying: 'When the memorandum * * * is taken and read, as it must be, in connection with the deeds subsequently executed, there is no doubt or uncertainty as to the terms of the contract for the sale of the lands. True, the deeds do not expressly refer to the memorandum, but they were all executed as parts of a single transaction, between the same parties, having reference to the same subject-matter.' In Work v. Cowhick, 81 Ill. 317, property was struck off to appellant as the highest bidder at an administrator's sale, and the administrator's deed of the land, and a note signed by the purchaser, in which she promised to pay to the administrator the purchase money 'for land purchased by

Elizabeth Worth this day at administrator's sale,' were left with a third person to be held until the purchaser should obtain personal security on the note, and execute a mortgage, at which time the deed was to be delivered. It was held, in a suit by the administrator against the purchaser for a failure to carry out the sale, that the making of the deed and the signing of the note might be regarded as one transaction, and that together they constituted such proof as amounted to a compliance with the statute of frauds; the description in the deed indicating what land was referred to by the imperfect description in the note. * * *

It is manifest, however, that all these cases differ from the case at bar. Here, the undelivered deed executed by Mrs. Reiter cannot be used to supplement, or supply any defect in, a prior contract of sale, or a prior note or memorandum of a contract of sale, because there was no prior contract or note or memorandum which she had signed, or to which she was a party, or which she had authorized to be made. * * * Nor can her undelivered deed * * * because it was not made in pursuance of that agreement, or to carry it out, but without any reference to it. * * * A deed which has not been delivered is not, by its own force, and aside from any contract to which it may be related, a sufficient writing to meet the requirements of the statute of frauds. For these reasons we think that the decree of the circuit court was right, and the same is accordingly affirmed.

Womack v. Stegner
293 S.W.2d 124 (Tex.Civ.App. 1956)

The question raised in Womack v. Stegner *is simple: What is the legal significance of a deed executed and delivered by the grantor to the grantee, but the name of the grantee is left blank, and the grantor authorized the grantee to fill in a name (his own or the name of another) at the time of delivery?*

HAMILTON, Chief Justice.
* * *

The plaintiff claimed title to the premises involved in a deed executed and delivered to him by his brother, W. B. Womack, dated and acknowledged on December 17, 1951, and alleged to have been delivered to plaintiff in February 1952, complete in every respect except that the name of the grantee was not filled in. * * *

Testimony was offered by D. R. Womack, appellant, that at the time of delivery of said deed by W. B. Womack to D. R. Womack, W. R. Womack authorized D. R. Womack to fill his name or any name he desired in the blank as grantee. * * *
* * *

* * * It appears to be well settled in Texas that when a deed with the name of the grantee is blank is delivered by the grantor with the intention that the title shall vest in the person to whom the deed is delivered, and that person is expressly authorized at the time of delivery to insert his own or any other name as grantee, title passes with the delivery. Threadgill v. Butler, 60 Tex. 599; Fennimore v. Ingham, Tex.Civ.App., 181 S.W. 513; Schleicher v. Runge, Tex.Civ.App., 37 S.W. 982; Id., 90 Tex. 456, 39 S.W. 279. 14-B Tex.Jur. 514-515.

In Threadgill v. Butler, supra, the court said that the effect of such a transaction is to vest an irrevocable power coupled with an interest in the person to whom the deed is delivered. It appears that where there is failure to fill in the blank, the instrument coupled with the power, that is, the authority, to fill in the blank, is sufficient to vest equitable title in a person to whom the deed is delivered. Schleicher v. Runge, supra.

It is contended by appellee that since the grantor, W. B. Womack, died before the grantee, D. R. Womack, exercised his authority by filling in the blank that the authority given D. R. Womack ended with the death of the grantor, as is the case with an ordinary power of attorney. We cannot agree with appellee's contention, because if the authority given by the grantor to fill in the blank is an irrevocable power, coupled with an interest, it does not terminate with the death of the grantor. The equitable title passed at the time of the delivery of the deed, and the subsequent death of W. B. Womack before the authority was exercised is immaterial.

* * *

§ 7.6.5 Delivery: Revocable Deeds

Huber v. Backus
79 S.D. 342 (1961)

The grantor (referred to as the "decedent" by the court) executed several deeds during his lifetime in favor of his sister, the defendant. After the grantor died, grantor's other siblings, the plaintiffs in this action, claimed that because the grantor retained the power to revoke the deeds, there was no delivery to the sister during the grantor's lifetime. As such, the plaintiffs continued, the grantor died owning these properties and, consequently, all of the siblings would share in the grantor's property as his heirs at law. If the sister-defendant were to prevail, all of the properties would be hers, to the exclusion of the other siblings. The court holds that the grantor delivered the properties to the sister-defendant, notwithstanding the grantor's power to revoke the deeds during his lifetime.

RENTTO, Judge.

* * *

It is a general rule that delivery is essential to the effectiveness of a deed. In this state it is required by statute. SDC 51.1304 provides: 'A grant takes effect so as to vest the interest intended to be transferred only upon its delivery by the grantor.' To constitute a delivery the grantor must part with the legal possession of the deed and of all right to retain it. Cassidy v. Holland, 27 S.D. 287, 130 N.W. 771. The fact that a deed has been duly executed, acknowledged, and recorded is prima facie evidence of its delivery. 26A C.J.S. Deeds § 187; Wolf v. Wolf, 59 S.D. 418, 240 N.W. 349. Whether there was a delivery is a question of intent to be found from all the facts surrounding the transaction. McGillivray v. Wipf, 64 S.D. 367, 266 N.W. 724; McKenzie v. Birkholtz, 74 S.D. 173, 50 N.W.2d 95. On this record we think the trial court was warranted in concluding that these deeds had been legally delivered by the decedent to the defendant.

* * *

As supporting his contention of nondelivery the administrator points to the numerous acts of ownership that the decedent exercised over the property after the dates of the deeds and continuing until shortly before his death. During that time some of the properties were sold through decedent's efforts under contracts for deed. In most instances these were signed by defendant, but in one instance it was executed by decedent himself and on another by him as her agent. All of these sales were consummated by deeds from the defendant except where the contract had been executed by decedent. He signed that deed. In 1957 when decedent wanted to mortgage some of the conveyed property to assist a nephew in getting a Land Bank loan, the defendant executed the required deeds, but on an occasion in 1958 he executed a mortgage in his own name on one of the conveyed premises without a conveyance from her. In his application for the Land Bank loan he indicated that he was the owner of some of the properties previously conveyed to defendant. * * *

* * *

The administrator also argues that under the arrangement entered into the decedent reserved the right to recall any of the deeds involved. We do not share this view. It did not relate to the deeds that had been delivered and recorded but concerned only decedent's rights in the property thereby conveyed during the remainder of his life. Under this arrangement his reserved right to sell the properties was to be effectuated by a conveyance from defendant which would seem to confirm rather than deny the delivery of these deeds to her. If he had intended that title was not to vest immediately in the defendant then there would be no reason for their oral understanding.

In this connection he also urges that there was no valid delivery of the deeds because it was not intended thereby to make an irrevocable transfer of a present estate in the property. Under our statutes that is not necessary. A future interest is subject to present transfer by deed. SDC 51.0220. The author of the annotation in 11 A.L.R. 23 at page 36 writes:

'As is pointed out above, the term 'interest,' as used in this note, is not to be confused with 'estate.' A deed may pass a present interest in property, the estate in which is a future one. One has an interest in property when he presently owns or holds some property rights therein, regardless of the time at which the estate comes into enjoyment.' See also 76 A.L.R. 636; 11 A.L.R.2d 532.

In respect to the time of enjoyment, an interest in realty is either present or future. A future interest entitles the owner to possession of the property only at a future period. SDC 51.0215. A future interest is a vested interest when there is a person in being who will have a right, defeasible or indefeasibile, to the immediate possession of the property when the intermediate estate or interest ceases. SDC 51.0217. * * * Such interests may be transferred in the same manner as present interests. SDC 51.0220. SDC 51.0228 is as follows: 'A future interest may be defeated in any manner, or by any act or means, which the party creating such interest provided for or authorized in the creation thereof; nor is a future interest, thus liable to be defeated, to be on that ground adjudged void in its creation.' The preceding portion of this paragraph is the language and logic of the California court in Tennant v. John Tennant Memorial Home, 167 Cal. 570, 140 P. 242, 243 with our code sections substituted for identical provisions of their statutes.

In that case the court had under consideration a deed which in addition to creating a life estate in the grantor also reserved to her 'The right to revoke this deed as to the said property above described or as to any portion thereof, and further reserving to her, the said grantor, the right during her natural life to sell any of the above described property, and to sign and execute deeds therefor in her own individual name and to convey by any such deed a full, perfect and absolute title thereto to the purchaser thereof, and with right to use the proceeds arising from such sale or sales to her own use, without any liability for her or her estate to account therefor.' While this right of revocation is a part of the deed and more extensive than the oral arrangement here involved, we think the principles announced in that case are applicable here, at least in so far as the rights of the immediate parties are concerned. Clearly the reserved right to revoke the deeds does not make them invalid. See also St. Louis County Nat. Bank v. Fielder, 364 Mo. 207, 260 S.W.2d 483, 486. By these deeds decedent intended to pass to the grantee at once a vested future interest in the land, said interest being the entire fee following the termination of the reserved life estate.

* * *

In Trumbauer v. Rust, 36 S.D. 301, 154 N.W. 801, 802, 11 A.L.R. 10, this court observed that:

'There is no conflict of authority as to what distinguishes a deed from a testamentary conveyance. If it pass a present interest, or right, even though the enjoyment thereof be postponed until the death of the grantor, it is a deed; if it pass no present interest or right, but is dependent upon the death of the maker to consummate it, it is testamentary in its nature, notwithstanding it be denominated a deed and is a deed in form and in some essential characteristics.'

* * *

Note

There is contrary authority to the position taken in *Huber v. Backus*. In *Butler v. Sherwood*, 196 A.D. 603 (N.Y. 1921), the New York Court of Appeals found that where a sick woman gave her husband all of her property "on the condition . . . my husband, survive me, and the same is intended to vest and take effect only upon my decease and until said time the same shall be subject to revocation upon [my part]," nothing passed to the husband during the lifetime of the wife. The court found that the wife attempted a testamentary transfer without complying with New York's statute of wills.

§ 7.6.6 Delivery: Revocable Escrows

Escrows are used in virtually every business transaction. Here is how it works: If S wants to sell his house and B wants to buy the house, we have seen that S and B will enter into a contract for the sale of the house; the contract, of course will comply with the Statute of Frauds. Almost immediately after the contract is signed, S and B (or the real estate agents or attorneys representing S and B) will retain the services of a professional escrow company. Escrow will "open," meaning that an escrow account will be opened. The escrow company is a disinterested third person. The money that B puts aside for a down payment will be deposited into this account. Ultimately, the funds needed to purchase the property (via a bank loan or B's own personal funds) will go into the escrow account. The escrow agent will not release the funds to S until S has complied with all the terms of the contract for sale. These terms might include, for example: S establishing that he has marketable title via an abstract of title; allowing B or an agent of B to conduct a thorough inspection of the property to assure B that the property does not have any defects; or ensuring that S has complied with miscellaneous terms of the contract, such as removing unlawful improvements on the property; etc. When S has complied with all terms and B has complied with all terms (typically, for the buyer, it is the simple matter of depositing all of the purchase funds in the escrow account), the escrow agent will remit the funds to S and hand the deed that S has executed over to B. With that, escrow has now closed. Note that escrow typically is used only in a business transaction—where S is selling property and B is buying that property. In any event, deeds involving escrows are not like deeds not involving escrows. As we have seen, in about half of the jurisdictions, deeds (not involving escrows) are revocable. Escrows, on the other hand, are not revocable. Compare now with Rosengrant v. Rosengrant, *the next case.*

Rosengrant v. Rosengrant

629 P.2d 800 (Okl. App. 1981)

Jay Rosengrant was close to his aunt and uncle, Mildred and Harold Rosengrant. When their health began to fail, Mildred and Harold decided to deed their farm to Jay. To convey the farm, the Rosengrants, their banker, Mr. Vanlandingham, and Jay all met. The court explains what they did and why the intended transfer by deed to Jay failed.

BOYDSTON, Judge.

* * *

In cases involving attempted transfers such as this, it is the grantor's intent at the time the deed is delivered which is of primary and controlling importance. It is the function of this court to weigh the evidence presented at trial as to grantor's intent and unless the trial court's decision is clearly against the weight of the evidence, to uphold that finding.

The grantor and banker were both dead at the time of trial. Consequently, the only testimony regarding the transaction was supplied by the grantee, Jay. The pertinent part of his testimony is as follows:

A. (A)nd was going to hand it back to Mr. Vanlandingham [the banker] (sic), and he wouldn't take it.
Q. What did Mr. Vanlandingham (sic) say?
A. Well, he laughed then and said that "We got to make this legal," or something like that. And said, "You'll have to give it to Jay and let Jay give it back to me."
Q. And what did Harold do with the document?
A. He gave it to me.
Q. Did you hold it?

A. Yes.

Q. Then what did you do with it?

A. Mr. Vanlandingham (sic), I believe, told me I ought to look at it.

Q. And you looked at it?

A. Yes.

Q. And then what did you do with it?

A. I handed it to Mr. Vanlandingham (sic).

Q. And what did he do with the document?

A. He had it in his hand, I believe, when we left.

Q. Do you recall seeing the envelope at any time during this transaction?

A. I never saw the envelope. But Mr. Vanlandingham (sic) told me when I handed it to him, said, "Jay, I'll put this in an envelope and keep it in a vault for you until you call for it."

A. Well, Harold told me while Mildred was signing the deed that they were going to deed me the farm, but they wanted me to leave the deed at the bank with Van, and that when something happened to them that I would go to the bank and pick it up and take it to Shawnee to the court house and record it, and it would be mine.

When the deed was retrieved, it was contained in an envelope on which was typed: "J. W. Rosengrant- or Harold H. Rosengrant."

The import of the writing on the envelope is clear. It creates an inescapable conclusion that the deed was, in fact, retrievable at any time by Harold before his death. The bank teller's testimony as to the custom and usage of the bank leaves no other conclusion but that at any time Harold was free to retrieve the deed. There was, if not an expressed, an implied agreement between the banker and Harold that the grant was not to take effect until two conditions occurred: the death of both grantors and the recordation of the deed.

In support of this conclusion conduct relative to the property is significant and was correctly considered by the court. Evidence was presented to show that after the deed was filed Harold continued to farm, use and control the property. Further, he continued to pay taxes on it until his death and claimed it as his homestead.

Grantee confuses the issues involved herein by relying upon grantors' goodwill toward him and his wife as if it were a controlling factor. From a fair review of the record it is apparent Jay and his wife were very attentive, kind and helpful to this elderly couple. The donative intent on the part of grantors is undeniable. We believe they fully intended to reward Jay and his wife for their kindness. Nevertheless, where a grantor delivers a deed under which he reserves a right of retrieval and attaches to that delivery the condition that the deed is to become operative only after the death of grantors and further continues to use the property as if no transfer had occurred grantor's actions are nothing more than an attempt to employ the deed as if it were a will. Under Oklahoma law this cannot be done. The ritualistic "delivery of the deed" to the grantee and his redelivery of it to the third party for safe keeping created under these circumstances only a symbolic delivery.[6] It amounted to a pro forma attempt to comply with the legal aspects of

---

[6] [Did the court mean to use the term "symbolic delivery" as words of art, in the same manner as used in chapter 1?]

delivery. Based on all the facts and circumstances the true intent of the parties is expressed by the notation on the envelope and by the later conduct of the parties in relation to the land. Legal delivery is not just a symbolic gesture. It necessarily carries all the force and consequence of absolute, outright ownership at the time of delivery or it is no delivery at all.[7]

The trial court interpreted the envelope literally. The clear implication is that grantor intended to continue to exercise control and that the grant was not to take effect until such time as both he and his wife had died and the deed had been recorded. From a complete review of the record and weighing of the evidence we find the trial court's judgment is not clearly against the weight of the evidence. Costs of appeal are taxed to appellant.

BACON, P. J., concurs and BRIGHTMIRE, J., concurs specially.

Note

On similar facts, another court has held that the grantor did effectuate a delivery to the grantee. See *Chandler v. Chandler*, 409 So.2d 780 (Ala. 1981). As for non-commercial "death escrows," in general, see 23 Am. Jur. 2d Deeds § 124.

§ 7.6.7 Delivery: Oral Conditional Deliveries

Suppose O conveys to A by deed, with the understanding that the deed is not to become effective (that there be no delivery) until some orally stated condition is satisfied. Almost certainly, the court will not recognize the oral condition. Why is this so? The answer is simple: to recognize the oral condition would essentially destroy the integrity of the Statute of Frauds.

Sweeney v. Sweeney
126 Conn. 391 (1940)

This case presents a typical illustration of an oral conditional delivery. Maurice conveys to John. John thereafter conveys back to Maurice, but with the oral condition that the latter conveyance was to be effective only if John died first. John did not die first, however; Maurice died first. Maurice's wife now seeks her statutory share of Maurice's estate. Her share (100% in this case) is based on all assets Maurice owned at death.

---

[7] In Anderson v. Mauk, Okl., 67 P.2d 429 (1937), the court stated:

> (I)t is the established law in this jurisdiction that when the owner of land executes a deed during his lifetime and delivers the same to a third party (who acts as a depository rather than an agent of the property owner) with instructions to deliver the deed to the grantee therein named upon his death, intending at the time of delivery to forever part with all lawful right and power to retake or repossess the deed, or to thereafter control the same, the delivery to the third party thus made is sufficient to operate as a valid conveyance of real estate.

Thus, in essence, Maurice's widow claims that the conveyance from John to Maurice was absolute and that the oral condition should not be recognized. The court will agree with Maurice's widow.

JENNINGS, Judge.

Maurice Sweeney, plaintiff's intestate, hereinafter called Maurice, deeded his farm to his brother John M. Sweeney, hereinafter called John, and the deed was recorded. John deeded the property back to Maurice. This deed is unrecorded and was accidentally burned.[8] The question to be decided is whether the second deed was delivered and if so, whether or not a condition claimed to be attached to the delivery is operative. This must be determined on the finding. The following statement includes such changes therein as are required by the evidence:

The plaintiff is the widow and administratrix of Maurice but had not lived with him for the twenty years preceding his death in September, 1938, at the age of seventy-three years. Maurice lived on a tract of land of some hundred and thirty-five acres which he owned in East Hampton, where he ran a tavern. John assisted him in running the tavern to some extent. On February 2, 1937, Maurice and John went to the town clerk's office in East Hampton pursuant to an appointment made the preceding day. Maurice requested the town clerk to draw a deed of his East Hampton property to John and this was done. At the same time he requested that a deed be prepared from John to himself so that he, Maurice, would be protected if John predeceased him. Both deeds were duly executed. The first was left for recording and the second was taken away by Maurice and never recorded. A week or two later Maurice took to John the recorded deed and a week or two after that took the unrecorded deed to John's house. John kept both deeds and gave the second deed to his attorney after the institution of this action. It was destroyed when the latter's office was burned. After the execution of the deeds, Maurice continued to occupy the property, paid the fixed charges, received the rents and exercised full dominion over it until his death. In April, 1937, Maurice made a written lease to Ernest Myers of a portion of the premises and on June 18, 1938, a written lease to Frank and Esther Fricke for twenty years. The first lease is lost but the second was recorded. The defendant never collected any money from tenants or paid any fixed charges or repairs prior to the death of Maurice. On these facts the trial court concluded that there was no intention to make present delivery of John's deed to Maurice, that there was no delivery or acceptance thereof, that it was not intended to operate until John's death and rendered judgment for the defendant.

This deed was, in effect, manually delivered. Maurice continued to occupy the property and exercised full dominion over it without interference by John. It follows that all the essentials of a good delivery were present unless there is something in the contentions of John which defeats this result. He claims that there was no intention on his part to make present delivery.

It is, of course, true that physical possession of a duly executed deed is not conclusive proof that it was legally delivered. McDermott v. McDermott, 97 Conn. 31, 34, 115 A. 638. This is so under some circumstances even where there has been a manual

---

[8] [A deed that is accidentally destroyed has no bearing on the validity of the deed. Of course, in such circumstances, there may be problems of proof, but that is not at issue in this case.]

delivery. Hotaling v. Hotaling, 193 Cal. 368, 381, 224 P. 455, 56 A.L.R. 734, and note page 746. Delivery must be made with the intent to pass title if it is to be effective. Porter v. Woodhouse, 59 Conn. 568, 575, 22 A. 299, 13 L.R.A. 64, 21 Am.St.Rep. 131; McDermott v. McDermott, supra.

The deed having been in effect actually delivered to Maurice, the execution of the attestation clause was prima facie proof that the deed was delivered. New Haven Trust Co. v. Camp, 81 Conn. 539, 542, 71 A. 788. There is a rebuttable presumption that the grantee assented since the deed was beneficial to him. Moore v. Giles, 49 Conn. 570, 573. No fact is found which militates against this presumption. Where deeds are formally executed and delivered, these presumptions can be overcome only by evidence that no delivery was in fact intended. Loughran v. Kummer, 297 Pa. 179, 183, 146 A. 534; Cragin's Estate, 274 Pa. 1, 5, 117 A. 445; Stewart v. Silva, 192 Cal. 405, 409, 221 P. 191. The only purpose in making the deed expressed by either party was the statement by Maurice that it was to protect him in case John predeceased him. Since this purpose would have been defeated had there been no delivery with intent to pass title, this conclusively establishes the fact that there was a legal delivery.

The defendant next claims that if there was a delivery, it was on condition and that the condition (the death of John before that of Maurice) was not and cannot be fulfilled. This claim is not good because the delivery was to the grantee. 'A[n oral] conditional delivery is and can only be made by placing the deed in the hands of a third person to be kept by him until the happening of the event upon the happening of which the deed is to be delivered over by the third person to the grantee.' Porter v. Woodhouse, supra, 59 Conn. 574, 22 A. 300, 13 L.R.A. 64, 21 Am.St.Rep. 131; Raymond v. Smith, 5 Conn. 555, 559. [Oral] [c]onditional delivery to a grantee vests absolute title in the latter. Loughran v. Kummer, supra, 297 Pa. 185, 146 A. 534; McCarthy v. Security Trust & Savings Bank, 188 Cal. 229, 234, 204 P. 818 (grantor retained possession of the premises and gave a mortgage of it); Stewart v. Silva, supra, 192 Cal. 410, 221 P. 191; City National Bank v. Anderson, 189 Ky. 487, 225 S.W. 361 (deed surrendered to grantor): 16 Am.Jur. 506; 21 C.J. 874. As is pointed out in the Loughran case, supra, this is one of the instances where a positive rule of law may defeat the actual intention of the parties. The safety of real estate titles is considered more important than the unfortunate results which may follow the application of the rule in a few individual instances. To relax it would open the door wide to fraud and the fabrication of evidence. Although the doctrine has been criticized (2 Tiffany, Real Property [2d Ed.] p. 1764; 5 Wigmore, Evidence [2d Ed.] §§ 2405, 2408) no material change has been noted in the attitude of the courts in this country.

The finding does not support the conclusion. The finding shows a delivery and, even if a[n oral] conditional delivery is assumed, the condition is not good for the reasons stated. Since a new trial is necessary, the one ruling on evidence made a ground of appeal is noticed. The town clerk was permitted to testify to certain statements made by Maurice when the deed was drafted. Parol evidence is not admissible to vary the terms of the deed but may be received to show the use that was to be made of it. Fisk's Appeal, 81 Conn. 433, 437, 71 A. 559. The ruling was correct as showing the circumstances surrounding delivery.

There is error and a new trial is ordered.

In this opinion the other judges concurred.

Note

While the holding in *Sweeney v. Sweeney* is the norm, one can never be certain what will happen in the courtroom, as *Chillemi v. Chillemi*, 197 Md. 257 (1951), demonstrates. In that case, a war hero, going on a dangerous mission, executed a deed in favor of his wife. It was understood, however, that if he returned from the mission, the wife would execute another deed in favor of her husband. When the husband returned, the wife refused. Under highly charged "colorable facts," the court enforced the oral condition. The court stated:

> But there is actually no logical reason why a deed should not be held in escrow by the grantee as well as by any other person. The ancient rule is not adapted to present-day conditions and is entirely unnecessary for the protection of the rights of litigants. After all, conditional delivery is purely a question of intention, and it is immaterial whether the instrument, pending satisfaction of the condition, is in the hands of the grantor, the grantee, or a third person. After the condition is satisfied, there is an operative conveyance which is considered as having been delivered at the time of the conditional delivery, for the reason that it was then that it was actually delivered, although the ownership does not pass until the satisfaction of the conditions. We, therefore, hold that it is the intention of the grantor of a deed that determines whether the delivery of the deed is absolute or conditional, although the delivery is made by the grantor directly to the grantee.

§ 7.6.8 Acceptance

It is presumed that the grantee accepted the property delivered by the grantor. Of course, if the property in question is a so-called white elephant, acceptance is not presumed. For an example, see County of Worth v. Jorgenson, *253 N.W.2d 575 (Iowa 1977), where the expense of demolition and removal was more than the value of the property in question, property that no one wanted—not even the local government, to whom the owner conveyed to get rid of the property.*

§ 7.7 Warranty Deeds

There are two types of warranty deeds in use in this country: general and special warranty deeds. Although there are significant differences between general and special warranty deeds, each contains five or six traditional covenants of title. In this section, we examine these traditional covenants of title. Thereafter, we explore the differences between general and special warranty deeds. (A copy of a general warranty deed is found in the appendix.)

§ 7.7.1 Covenants of Title: In General

Colonial Capital Corp. v. Smith
367 So.2d 490 (Ala.Civ.App. 1979)

The plaintiff purchased real property from the defendant, who conveyed by a warranty deed. Later, after escrow closed, the plaintiff sued the defendant for breach of the covenant against encumbrances, because of an outstanding mortgage on the property. The court explained the various covenants of title in a warranty deed.

WRIGHT, Presiding Judge.

* * *

Defendant's liability and obligations to the plaintiffs arise from the covenants contained in the warranty deed. The language of the deed is that generally contained in a warranty deed in Alabama. Such a deed is considered to encompass five covenants. LeMaistre, George A. Legal Aspects of Real Estate Transactions, University of Alabama 1971, at 109. The covenants of [1] seisin and [2] the right to convey are basically the same and mean that the grantor owns the estate which he proposes to convey. Russell v. Belsher, 221 Ala. 360, 128 So. 452 (1930); Mackintosh v. Stewart, 181 Ala. 328, 61 So. 956 (1913). These covenants are broken at the time of conveyance if the grantor does not have good title. Wolff v. Woodruff, 258 Ala. 1, 61 So.2d 69 (1952). There is no claim that defendant did not in fact own the fee simple to the property. Therefore the covenants of seisin and right to convey are not in issue in this case.

The covenants of [3] general warranty to defend the title of grantee and his successors against the lawful claims of all persons are in substance those for possession and [4] quiet enjoyment. They are not broken so long as the grantee's enjoyment and possession are not interfered with. Chicago, Mobile Development Co. v. G. C. Coggin Co., 259 Ala. 152, 66 So.2d 151 (1953). Plaintiffs have suffered no eviction or disturbance of possession. They have suffered no breach of these covenants.

The remaining of the five covenants is [5] that against encumbrances. A covenant against encumbrances is a stipulation by the covenantor that there are no outstanding rights or interests to the estate conveyed that will diminish the value, but which are consistent with the passage of the fee. 20 Am.Jur.2d Sec. 81, Covenants, Conditions, Etc. An existing mortgage would be an encumbrance. If such covenant is broken, it is broken at the time it is made, and a cause of action arises at that time and does not pass to any subsequent grantee. Chicago, Mobile Development Co. v. G. C. Coggin Co., supra. It is not broken however, unless the alleged outstanding encumbrance is valid, legal and subsisting. 5 A.L.R. 1086. A paid mortgage, although unsatisfied of record, is not an encumbrance within the meaning of the covenant. Judevine v. Pennock, 15 Vt. 683; Boulware v. Mayfield, Fla.App., 317 So.2d 470 (1975).

* * *

Note

In many jurisdictions, there also is a sixth covenant: the covenant of further assurances. This covenant obligates the grantor to execute any other documents that the grantee may need to perfect title. The covenants of seisin, right to convey, and against encumbrances are "present covenants," meaning that they are breached, if at all, when escrow closes. The covenants of general warranty, further assurances, and quiet enjoyment are "future covenants," meaning that they are breached whenever the event in question happens (e.g. whenever someone with superior title evicts the owner, causing a breach of the covenant of quiet enjoyment). The significance between present and future covenants is explored in §§ 7.7.2 and 7.7.3, below.

§ 7.7.2 Covenants of Title: Timing of Breach

As previously stated, present covenants (seisin, right to convey, encumbrances) are breached, if at all, when escrow closes. Future covenants (general warranty, further assurances, quiet enjoyment) are breached whenever there is a breach. The next case provides further elucidation to these points.

Brown v. Lober
75 Ill.2d 547 (1979)

More than ten years after acquiring the subject property, the plaintiffs learned that they did not receive all of the mineral rights described in their deed to the property. They could not proceed against the grantor under the covenant of seisin or right to convey—present covenants—because the statute of limitations had expired. The plaintiffs, therefore, proceeded under the future covenant of quiet enjoyment.

UNDERWOOD, Justice

* * *

This court has stated on numerous occasions that, in contrast to the covenant of seisin, the covenant of warranty or quiet enjoyment is prospective in nature and is breached only when there is an actual or constructive eviction of the covenantee by the paramount titleholder. Biwer v. Martin (1920), 294 Ill. 488, 128 N.E. 518; Barry v. Guild (1888), 126 Ill. 439, 18 N.E. 759; Scott v. Kirkendall (1878), 88 Ill. 465; Bostwick v. Williams (1864), 36 Ill. 65; Moore v. Vail (1855), 17 Ill. 185.

The cases are also replete with statements to the effect that the mere existence of paramount title in one other than the covenantee is not sufficient to constitute a breach of the covenant of warranty or quiet enjoyment: "(T)here must be a union of acts of disturbance and lawful title, to constitute a breach of the covenant for quiet enjoyment, or warranty * * *." (Barry v. Guild (1888), 126 Ill. 439, 446, 18 N.E. 759, 761.) "(T)here is a general concurrence that something more than the mere existence of a paramount title is necessary to constitute a breach of the covenant of warranty." (Scott v. Kirkendall (1878), 88 Ill. 465, 467.) "A mere want of title is no breach of this covenant. There must not only be a want of title, but there must be an ouster under a paramount title." Moore v. Vail (1855), 17 Ill. 185, 189.

The question is whether plaintiffs have alleged facts sufficient to constitute a constructive eviction. They argue that if a covenantee fails in his effort to sell an interest in land because he discovers that he does not own what his warranty deed purported to convey, he has suffered a constructive eviction and is thereby entitled to bring an action against his grantor for breach of the covenant of quiet enjoyment. We think that the decision of this court in Scott v. Kirkendall (1878), 88 Ill. 465, is controlling on this issue and compels us to reject plaintiffs' argument.

In Scott, an action was brought for breach of the covenant of warranty by a grantee who discovered that other parties had paramount title to the land in question. The land was vacant and unoccupied at all relevant times. This court, in rejecting the grantee's claim that there was a breach of the covenant of quiet enjoyment, quoted the earlier decision in Moore v. Vail (1855), 17 Ill. 185, 191:

" 'Until that time (the taking possession by the owner of the paramount title), he might peaceably have entered upon and enjoyed the premises, without resistance or molestation, which was all his grantors covenanted he should do. They did not guarantee to him a perfect title, but the possession and enjoyment of the premises.' " 88 Ill. 465, 468.

Relying on this language in Moore, the Scott court concluded:

"We do not see but what this fully decides the present case against the appellant. It holds that the mere existence of a paramount title does not constitute a breach of the covenant. That is all there is here. There has been no assertion of the adverse title. The land has always been vacant. Appellant could at any time have taken peaceable possession of it. He has in no way been prevented or hindered from the enjoyment of the possession by any one having a better right. It was but the possession and enjoyment of the premises which was assured to him, and there has been no disturbance or interference in that respect. True, there is a superior title in another, but appellant has never felt 'its pressure upon him.' " 88 Ill. 465, 468-69.

* * *

Since no one has, as yet, undertaken to remove the coal or otherwise manifested a clear intent to exclusively "possess" the mineral estate, it must be concluded that the subsurface estate is "vacant." As in Scott, plaintiffs "could at any time have taken peaceable possession of it. (They have) in no way been prevented or hindered from the enjoyment of the possession by any one having a better right." (88 Ill. 465, 468.) Accordingly, until such time as one holding paramount title interferes with plaintiffs' right of possession (e. g., by beginning to mine the coal), there can be no constructive eviction and, therefore, no breach of the covenant of quiet enjoyment.

What plaintiffs are apparently attempting to do on this appeal is to extend the protection afforded by the covenant of quiet enjoyment. However, we decline to expand the historical scope of this covenant to provide a remedy where another of the covenants of title is so clearly applicable. * * *

* * *

§ 7.7.3 Covenants of Title: Suit By Remote Grantees

Suppose the following facts: O conveys to A by general warranty deed. At the time of the conveyance, O has breached a present covenant (seisin, right to convey, or encumbrances). A is not aware of the breach, however. Thereafter, A conveys to B by special warranty deed. B subsequently learns of the breach of the covenant. B cannot sue A, however, because A did not create the problem resulting in the breach of the covenant in question and A conveyed to B by special warranty deed. (The matter of special versus general warranty deeds is more fully developed in § 7.7.6.) The question is whether B can sue O. While future covenants "run with the land" so that B could sue O for breach of a "future covenant" (e.g. covenant of quiet enjoyment), present covenants do not run with the land. Does this mean that B is without a remedy? The court in Schofield v. Iowa Homestead Co., *infra, holds that B would have a cause of action against O.*

Schofield v. Iowa Homestead Co.
32 Iowa 317 (1871)

BECK, J.

I. * * * The question thus presented for our determination is this: Does the covenant of seizin run with the land?

We are fully aware of the discord of authorities upon this question, and that a great majority of the American cases hold the covenant to be *in presenti,* and that it is broken, if at all, when the deed is delivered, and that the claim for damages thereby becomes personal in its nature to the grantee, and is not transferred by a conveyance to a subsequent grantee. But in England the rule prevails that * * * recovery for a breach thereof may be had by the assignee of the grantee in the deed. *Kingdon v. Nottle,* 1 Maule & Selw. 355; 4 Id. 53; *King v. Jones,* 5 Taunt. 418; 4 Maule & Selw. 186; 1 Smith's Lead. Cases, Am. notes to *Spencer's case,* p. 150; 4 Kent's Com. 472; 1 Washburne on Real Prop. 649.

* * *

Deeds under the laws of this State have been reduced to forms of great simplicity. Intricate technicalities have been pruned away, and they are now as brief and simple in form as a promissory note. All *choses in action,* as I have just remarked, may be assigned and transferred. The covenant of seizin (if it be held that such a covenant exists in a deed of the form authorized by the laws of this State), as we have seen, is intended to secure indemnity for the deprivation of the title and enjoyment of the lands conveyed. Why not brush away the "technical scruples" gathered about the covenant of seizin, as we have the like technical and cumbrous forms of the instrument itself, and enforce it for the benefit of the party who is really injured by its breach, even though, in so doing, we find it necessary to hold that a *chose in action* is assigned and transferred by the operation of the deed?

To my mind, the position reached by this course of argument is impregnable, and I cannot be driven from it by the great weight of authorities in support of the contrary doctrine.

§ 7.7.4 Covenants of Title: Nature of Encumbrances

Suppose O conveys to A by warranty deed. After escrow closes, A determines that O constructed an illegal structure on the property. If A sues O for breach of the covenant against encumbrances, will A prevail? In Frimberger v. Anzellotti, *25 Conn.App. 401 (1991), the court held that there was no breach of the covenant against encumbrances: that a violation of law is not an encumbrance (as is an outstanding mortgage, lien, or easement). Why is this? Consider that a violation of a law will breach the implied covenant of marketable title, which gives the buyer the right to rescind the contract. On the other hand, to find that a violation of law is a breach of the covenant against encumbrances would give the buyer a right of damages against the seller (the typical remedy for breach of a covenant of title in a warranty deed). The court in* Frimberger v. Anzellotti *was unwilling to keep the sword of Damocles hanging over a seller's head for ten years (the statute of limitations for a present covenant in many jurisdictions).*

§ 7.7.5 Covenants of Title: Merger

The question that we address here is this: After escrow closes, may the buyer, if he or she chooses, sue the seller for breach of the contract (e.g., for breach of the implied covenant of marketable title) in lieu of an action based on the deed (e.g. breach of a covenant of title)? The Colorado Land & Resources, Inc. *case answers this question in the negative.*

Colorado Land & Resources, Inc. v. Credithrift of America, Inc.
778 P.2d 320 (Colo.App. 1989)

* * *

Under the doctrine of merger, a deed delivered and accepted as complete performance of a contract for the sale of land merges all prior negotiations and agreements into the deed. *Reed v. Dudley,* 35 Colo.App. 420, 533 P.2d 507 (1975).

* * *

§ 7.7.6 General and Special Warranty Deeds

In a general warranty deed, the grantor warrants that neither he nor any of his predecessors in title breached any of the covenants of title. In a special warranty deed, the grantor warrants that only he—and he alone—has not breached any of the covenants of title. For the wording of a general warranty deed, see the Appendix of this text for a copy of a general warranty deed. In contrast, in a special warranty deed, the grantor would warrant, "grantor has not placed any encumbrances on the property," or "grantor has not conveyed the property to another," or "the grantor hereby binds itself to warrant and defend the title as against all acts of the grantor herein and no other." It would seem to be clear whether the deed in question is a general warranty deed or a special warranty deed—until we come to Burton v. Price, *infra.*

Burton v. Price
105 Fla. 544 (1932)

BUFORD, C. J.

In this case declaration was filed in two counts. The first count was a conventional declaration on breach of covenant of seizin. The second count was a conventional declaration on breach of covenant of warranty. Copy of the deed of conveyance in which the covenants were contained was attached to the declaration and made a part thereof.

There was a demurrer to the declaration which was sustained as to both counts. On demurrer being sustained, plaintiff declined to amend his declaration, and judgment was entered in favor of defendant to which writ of error was sued out. The covenants in the deed of conveyance read as follows:

'And the said party of the first part does covenant with the said party of the second part that he is lawfully seized of the said premises, that they are free from all encumbrances and that he has good right and lawful authority to sell to same; and the said party of the first part does hereby fully warrant the title to said land, and will defend the same against the lawful claim of all persons whomsoever, by, through and under him.'

The demurrer was properly sustained as to the second count of the declaration because the warranty contained in the deed of conveyance was a special warranty which could not be extended to a general covenant of warranty against all persons. See Davenport v. Lamb, 13 Wall. 418, 20 L. Ed. 655; Bell v. Twilight, 26 N. H. 401; Jackson ex dem. Peek v. Peek, 4 Wend. (N. Y.) 300.

In this case the declaration shows that the incumbrance complained of was not held by one claiming the same by, through, or under the grantor in plaintiff's deed, but that such incumbrance was by reason of an outstanding adverse title existing at the time at which grantor acquired his title.

The demurrer as to the first count of the declaration should have been overruled. The covenant of a seizin contained in the deed is general and unqualified. It appears to be well established that a grantee who acquires no title by the deed of conveyance and who acquires no possession and no right of possession under such deed containing covenants of seizin may recover the purchase money paid, with interest thereon, in an action for breach of such covenant of seizin, and that the breach occurs immediately upon the execution and delivery of the conveyance. See Resser v. Carney, 52 Minn. 397, 54 N. W. 89; Blanchard v. Ellis, 1 Gray (Mass.) 195, 61 Am. Dec. 417; Nichol v. Alexander, 28 Wis. 118; McInnis v. Lyman, 62 Wis. 191, 22 N. W. 405; Burton v. Reeds, 20 Ind. 87; Abbott v. Allen, 14 Johns. (N. Y.) 248; Mackintosh v. Stewart, 181 Ala. 328, 61 So. 956; Peters v. Bowman, 98 U. S. 56, 25 L. Ed. 91; Pollard v. Dwight, 4 Cranch, 421, 2 L. Ed. 666.

The covenant of seizin may be defined to be an assurance that the grantor has the very estate in quantity and quality which he purports to convey. Brandt v. Foster, 5 Iowa, 287; Real v. Hollister, 20 Neb. 112, 29 N. W. 189.

It is not necessary that the covenant of seizin fail as to the whole of the lands conveyed that the action may be maintained, but the vendee may recover, if there be a failure of seizin as to a part of the premises described in the deed, and in such case the measure of damages is such fractional part of the whole consideration paid as the value at the time of the purchase of the part to which the title failed bears to the whole block purchased, with interest thereon during the time the plaintiff has been deprived of the use of that part to which he could not acquire possession. McLennan v. Prentice, 85 Wis. 427, 55 N. W. 764.

If plaintiff can prove the allegations of the first count of his declaration, he may recover from the defendant because of the breach of covenant of seizin, and, therefore, the judgment should be reversed, and the cause remanded for further proceedings not inconsistent with this opinion. It is so ordered.

Reversed and remanded.

ELLIS and BROWN, JJ., concur.

§ 7.8 Quitclaim Deeds

Quitclaim deeds contain no covenants of title.

Lodge v. Thorpe
120 Mont. 226 (1947)

* * *

The effect of this quitclaim deed from Roempp to Kyle was to convey only Roempp's interest in the property. Devlin on Real Estate, 3rd Ed., Vol. 1, p. 42, sec. 27, discussing the effect of quitclaim deeds, states the law as follows: 'By the use of this form of conveyance (the grantor) does not thereby affirm the possession of any title.' As was said by the court in Williams v. Reid, Mo.Sup., 37 S.W.2d 537, 540: 'Probably nothing is better understood in the law of conveyancing than that a mere quitclaim deed transfers and is designed to transfer only such title and interest as the grantor had when he delivered the deed.' To the same effect is Gibson v. Morris State Bank, 49 Mont. 60, 140 P. 76.

* * *

Note
In a quitclaim deed, the grantor essentially is stating, "I give you all that I have, and I may have nothing." Quitclaim deeds typically are used only for gratuitous transfers.

§ 7.9 Estoppel by Deed

Suppose O conveys Blackacre to A on January 1. On January 1, however, O does not own Blackacre. On March 1, O acquires title to Blackacre. Under the doctrine of estoppel by deed, A automatically owns Blackacre. Why is this? Estoppel by deed holds that when O subsequently acquires title to property that he previously conveyed, O is estopped from denying the validity of the prior deed. The next case provides further elucidation on this doctrine.

Schloeffel v. Kietzman

89 N.E.2d 477 (Ohio Prob. 1949)

* * *

* * * The author [in 13 Ohio Jurisprudence, Section 104, page 919] uses the following language: 'It is a well-established rule in Ohio that if a grantor having no title, a defective title, or an estate less than that which he assumes to grant, conveys with warranty or covenant of like import, and subsequently acquires the title or estate which he purports to convey, or perfects his title, such after acquired title or after-perfected title will inure to the benefit of the grantee by way of estoppel.'

The author then discusses various other circumstances under which this doctrine is applied, and cites many cases in support of that proposition.

The author in the article discussing Deeds, in 16 American Jurisprudence, at Section 338, page 629, uses the following language: 'It is well established that a deed may have the effect passing to the grantee a title subsequently acquired by the grantor. In other words, a grantor who executes a deed before purporting to convey land to which he has not title or to which he has a defective title at the time of the conveyance will not be permitted, when he afterwards acquires a good title to the land, to claim in opposition to his deed from the grantee or from any person claiming title under him. * * *'

The author then discusses at length circumstances under which the rule is applied, and we will not take the time to discuss the authorities quoted.

* * *

Note

The doctrine of estoppel by deed typically is not applicable with respect to quitclaim deeds.

CHAPTER 8
RECORDING STATUTES

§ 8.1 Introduction

Suppose that Oscar sells Blackacre to Abel. Suppose also that Oscar subsequently (because of either mistake or fraud) sells Blackacre to Baker. As between Abel and Baker, who owns Blackacre? Under the very logical common law rule of "first in time is first in right," Abel prevails over Baker. Why is this? The reason is straightforward: After Oscar conveyed to Abel, Oscar did not own anything to convey to Baker. Of course, Baker could sue Oscar for rescission based on either mistake or fraud, but that is not what we are concerned with here. In this chapter, we have only one concern: As between Abel and Baker, who owns Blackacre? Note that it is irrelevant at this point in our studies that Abel has not recorded. Indeed, as a rule, recordation simply is not required for a deed to transfer title.

That said, the common law rule is easy enough to understand. Now, however, it gets a little more complicated. The complication arises because every state has enacted some type of "recording statute," the consequence of which is that if Baker can come under the protection of the recording statute, Baker will prevail over Abel with respect to who owns Blackacre and, in this regard, trump the common law rule. Thus, in this chapter, we examine the different types of recording statutes that exist in this country, who can get the benefit of these statutes, and related matters.

§ 8.2 Types of Recording Statutes

There are three types of recording statutes in this country: (1) race, (2) notice, and (3) race-notice statutes. We now proceed to discuss each, in order. Note, that irrespective of which type of recording statute we are dealing with, for B to prevail over A (and trump the common law of "first in time is first is right" rule), B must be a "purchaser for value." The term is explored in greater depth later in this chapter. For the present, however, it is sufficient for you to understand that B cannot be a mere donee. A donee is not protected under any recording statute. In short, for B to prevail, at a minimum, he must be a purchaser.

§ 8.2.1 Race Statutes

In a so-called race statute jurisdiction, the one who records first prevails. (The one who wins the "race" to the courthouse or recorder's office prevails.) Thus, if O conveys to A and O later conveys to B (who, you will recall, must be a purchaser and not a donee), if B records the O-B deed before A records the O-A deed, B prevails.

Simmons v. Quick-Stop Food Mart, Inc.
307 N.C. 33 (1982)

The Simmons *case is a straightforward application of a race statute.*

* * *

Mrs. Simmons recorded her deed to the property on 5 November 1979, and the defendant recorded its options to renew the lease on 26 November 1980. It is well settled in this state that only actual prior recordation of an interest in land will serve to put a bona fide purchaser for value or a lien creditor on notice of an intervening interest or encumbrance on real property. [1] Because defendant's lease was not recorded prior to the date on which plaintiff recorded her deed, plaintiff did not take the deed subject to the lease. *Beasley v. Wilson,* 267 N.C. 95, 147 S.E.2d 577 (1966); *Bourne v. Lay & Co.,* 264 N.C. 33, 140 S.E.2d 769 (1965); N.C.Gen.Stat. § 47-18(a) (1976).[2] Therefore, Mrs. Simmons is entitled to possession, and summary judgment on the issue of summary ejectment should have been entered for the plaintiff. ***

* * *

Schuman v. Roger Baker and Associates, Inc.
70 N.C.App. 313 (1984)

The owner of the subject property gave a deed of trust to one Schuman. Later, that same owner gave a deed of trust to one Northwestern. The court first determined that

---

[1] [Is this sentence correct? More specifically, is the court correct that the subsequent transferee must be a "bona fide purchaser for value"? What exactly is a bona fide purchaser for value? Once you understand what a "BFP" is by reading the next case and the note that follows, you will conclude that the court here is not correct. See also introductory remarks to section 8.3.]

[2] [N.C. Gen. Stat. § 47-18(a) provides:

(a) No (i) conveyance of land, or (ii) contract to convey, or (iii) option to convey, or (iv) lease of land for more than three years shall be valid to pass any property interest as against lien creditors or purchasers for a valuable consideration from the donor, bargainor or lessor but from the time of registration thereof in the county where the land lies, or if the land is located in more than one county, then in each county where any portion of the land lies to be effective as to the land in that county. Unless otherwise stated either on the registered instrument or on a separate registered instrument duly executed by the party whose priority interest is adversely affected, (i) instruments registered in the office of the register of deeds shall have priority based on the order of registration as determined by the time of registration, and (ii) if instruments are registered simultaneously, then the instruments shall be presumed to have priority as determined by:

(1) The earliest document number set forth on the registered instrument.

(2) The sequential book and page number set forth on the registered instrument if no document number is set forth on the registered instrument. * * *]

Northwestern "won the race to the courthouse" and recorded first. The next question for the court was whether Northwestern could prevail when it had actual notice of the conveyance to Schuman.

* * *

Our Supreme Court has repeatedly held that no notice, however full or formal, will supply the want of registration of a deed. *Bourne v. Lay & Co.,* 264 N.C. 33, 140 S.E.2d 769 (1965); *Dulin v. Williams,* 239 N.C. 33, 79 S.E.2d 213 (1953). These cases, read (1) with those cases limiting the duty to search to the chain of title, *see Morehead v. Harris, supra,* (2) with those cases making registration of deeds defective as to material particulars ineffective, *see McClure v. Crow,* 196 N.C. 657, 146 S.E. 713 (1929), and (3) with the statutory recording and indexing requirements, *see* G.S. 47-20.1 (same county); G.S. 161-14.2 *et seq.,* clearly indicate that registration outside the chain of title has the same effect on notice as no registration. Plaintiffs, although they apparently alleged fraudulent conduct by Northwestern in their complaint, forecast no such evidence nor do they argue any fraud on Northwestern's part before this Court. Therefore, any actual notice to Northwestern is insufficient to supply the want of proper registration.

* * *

The policy behind the recording statutes supports our conclusion. The General Assembly, by enacting these laws, clearly intended that prospective purchasers should be able to safely rely on the public records. *See Hayes v. Ricard,* 245 N.C. 687, 97 S.E.2d 105 (1957); *Clark v. Butts,* 240 N.C. 709, 83 S.E.2d 885 (1954). To adopt plaintiffs' position would require prospective purchasers to search outside the chain of title in every case, and thus inject a new element of uncertainty into the process, contrary to this longstanding policy. We note also the recent adoption of G.S. 47-20.5, which requires that after-acquired property clauses in security agreements be extended or re-recorded after each subsequent purchase of real property. This indicates a legislative insistence that due recordation *in the chain of title* must remain the only effective means of protecting title.

Accordingly, we conclude that Northwestern has shown a complete defense as a matter of law. The summary judgment in its favor was properly granted and must be

Affirmed.

Notes

1. Only three states, North Carolina, Louisiana, and Delaware, employ a pure race statute. The other jurisdictions are approximately evenly split between notice and race-notice statutes, which we discuss below.

2. As the *Schuman* case makes clear, in pure race statute jurisdictions, notice of the prior conveyance is irrelevant for the subsequent purchaser to trump the prior transferee. Thus, in these states, the subsequent purchaser need only be a purchaser, not a bona fide purchaser (that is, one who takes in good faith because he does not have notice of the prior conveyance). See John H. Scheid, *Down Labyrinthine Ways: A Recording Acts Guide for First Year Law Students,* 80 U. Det. Mercy L. Rev. 91, 107 n. 115 (2002).

§ 8.2.2 Notice Statutes

In a "notice" statute jurisdiction, for B to prevail over A, B cannot have had notice or knowledge of the prior (O-A) conveyance. Again, keep in mind that B must be a purchaser. Thus, B must be a bona fide purchaser.

Smith v. Parker
67 Ark.App. 221 (1999)

* * *

The next issue concerns the effect of the lease on appellants' easement across the leased property. At the time appellants took title to their property in April 1997, the lease between Billy Jim Smith and J-Dog, Inc., had not been recorded. Generally, no instrument in writing which may affect title to real property shall be valid against a subsequent purchaser of the property unless the instrument is filed for record in the county where the real estate is situated. *See* Ark. Code Ann. § 14-15-404(b) (Repl.1998).[3] However, the instrument is valid if the subsequent purchaser had actual notice of it. *Killam v. Texas Oil & Gas Corp.*, 303 Ark. 547, 798 S.W.2d 419 (1990); *Wasp Oil, Inc. v. Arkansas Oil & Gas, Inc.*, 280 Ark. 420, 658 S.W.2d 397 (1983). Whether one buying land had notice of another's interest in the land is a question of fact. *McGill v. Grigsby*, 205 Ark. 349, 168 S.W.2d 809 (1943). We will not reverse a chancellor's finding of fact regarding whether a party is an innocent purchaser without notice unless that finding is clearly erroneous. *Malone v. Hines*, 36 Ark.App. 254, 822 S.W.2d 394 (1992).

* * *

---

[3] [The Arkansas statute referred to in the opinion, a typical notice statute, provides:

> No deed, bond, or instrument of writing for the conveyance of any real estate, or by which the title thereto may be affected in law or equity, made or executed after December 21, 1846, shall be good or valid against a subsequent purchaser of the real estate for a valuable consideration without actual notice thereof or against any creditor of the person executing such an instrument obtaining a judgment or decree which by law may be a lien upon the real estate unless the deed, bond, or instrument, duly executed and acknowledged or proved as required by law, is filed for record in the office of the clerk and ex officio recorder of the county where the real estate is situated.

[Thus, for the subsequent transferee to take, such a person must be a purchaser for valuable consideration, without actual notice, and the prior transferee cannot have recorded (thus precluding the subsequent purchaser from having constructive notice). Consequently, for the subsequent transferee to prevail, as indicated earlier, such a person must be a so-called bona fide purchaser.]

§ 8.2.3 Race-Notice Statutes

In a race-notice statute jurisdiction, B must (in addition to being a purchaser) not have notice of the O-A conveyance and must record before A records. Thus, B must be a bona fide purchaser who records first.

Miller v. Hennen
438 N.W.2d 366 (Minn. 1989)

* * *

The trial court and court of appeals' decisions are based on an application of the Minnesota Recording Act, Minn.Stat. § 507.34 (1986). The Recording Act provides, in pertinent part:

> Every conveyance of real estate shall be recorded in the office of the county recorder   * * *; and every such conveyance not so recorded shall be void as against any subsequent purchaser in good faith and for a valuable consideration of the same real estate, or any part therof, whose conveyance is first duly recorded * * *. The fact that such first recorded conveyance is in the form, or contains the terms of a deed of quitclaim and release shall not affect the question of good faith of such subsequent purchaser or be of itself notice to the subsequent purchaser of any unrecorded conveyance of the same real estate or any part thereof.

Minn.Stat. § 507.34. The goal of the statute is to protect persons who buy real estate in reliance upon the record. *Strong v. Lynn,* 38 Minn. 315, 317, 37 N.W. 448, 449 (1888). The act allows for a subsequent purchaser in good faith who records title first to obtain rights to the property as against any prior purchaser who fails to record his interest. A purchaser in good faith is one who gives valuable consideration without actual, implied or constructive notice of inconsistent outstanding rights of others. *Anderson v. Graham Investment Co.,* 263 N.W.2d 382, 384 (Minn.1978). The burden is on the party resisting the prior unrecorded title to prove that he purchased or acquired such title in good faith. *Fifield v. Norton,* 79 Minn. 264, 266, 82 N.W. 581, 581 (1900); *Mead v. Randall,* 68 Minn. 233, 236, 71 N.W. 31, 32- 33 (1897).

* * *

In addition to the requirements of providing valuable consideration without notice, a good faith subsequent purchaser under the Recording Act must also record title to the property first. In order to qualify as a valid recording, the purchaser must show record title back to the record fee owner. In the case of *Board of Education of Minneapolis v. Hughes,* 118 Minn. 404, 136 N.W. 1095 (1912), this court stated:

> The [Minnesota Recording Act] cannot be construed so as to give priority to a deed recorded before, which shows no conveyance from a record owner. It was necessary, not only that the deed to plaintiff should be recorded before the deed to [the subsequent purchaser], but also that the deed to plaintiff's grantor should be first recorded.

Id. at 410, 136 N.W. at 1097-98.[4] We agree with the trial court and the court of appeals that Miller has purchased his interest in the property (1) for valuable consideration, (2) in good faith, and (3) recorded first; therefore, under the Recording Act, he is entitled to the property free of any other outstanding interest.

* * *

Note

At this point, it may be helpful to summarize the three types of recording statutes. We use the same illustration for each type of statute: O conveys to A and O later conveys the same property to B (and in each scenario, B is a purchaser). (1) In a race statute jurisdiction, B prevails over A if B records before A. (2) In a notice statute jurisdiction, B prevails over A if B did not have notice of the prior conveyance (B must be a bona fide purchaser). (3) In a race-notice statute jurisdiction, B prevails over A if B records before A and if B did not have notice of the prior conveyance (B must be a bona fide purchaser who records first).

§ 8.3 Meaning of Notice

§ 8.3.1 Introduction

While having notice of the prior conveyance is irrelevant in a pure race jurisdiction, notice (or, more properly, lack thereof) is critical in a notice or race-notice jurisdiction. This is because the term "bona fide purchaser" (the term used to describe a grantee given protection by notice and race-notice recording acts) requires that the subsequent purchaser not have notice of the prior conveyance. What exactly does "notice" mean? The materials that follow, which includes a return to Miller v. Hennen, *explore the meaning of notice in the context of the notice and race-notice recording acts. We also explore some miscellaneous aspects of notice.*

§ 8.3.2 Actual Notice

Toupin v. Peabody
162 Mass. 473 (1895)

The state's recording statute provided: "A conveyance of an estate in fee simple, fee tail, or for life, or a lease for more than seven years from the making thereof, shall not be

---

[4] [This requirement, that in a race-notice jurisdiction not only must the subsequent purchaser record before the prior grantee but everyone that is in the subsequent purchaser's chain of title also must have recorded before the prior grantee, was decided in *Zimmer v. Sundell*, 237 Wis. 270 (1941), and adopted in *Board of Education of Minneapolis v. Hughes*, supra. Not all race-notice jurisdictions have adopted this rule.]

valid as against any person other than the grantor or lessor, and his heirs and devisees, and persons having actual notice of it, unless it is recorded in the registry of deeds for the county or district in which the real estate to which it relates is situated." Thus, if the lease is for more than seven years and is not recorded, the subsequent purchaser loses (that is, takes the property subject to the lease) only if that purchaser had actual notice. In the instant case, the subsequent purchaser did not have actual notice of the tenant's lease that exceeded seven years, but he certainly had what is referred to as "inquiry" notice (facts that would lead a reasonable person to inquire further). The court held that the subsequent purchaser was protected under the state's recording statute. (It is likely that the court would have reached a different conclusion if the statute had not expressly required actual notice.)

BARKER, J.

* * *

The plaintiff contends that it may well be claimed that the defendant had actual notice of the lease. But, while it appears from the agreed facts that the defendant knew that the plaintiff was in possession of the drug store as a tenant, it also appears that the defendant was informed and believed that the plaintiff had no written lease, and that it was not until two months after the purchase that the defendant first learned that the plaintiff had a written lease, and was informed of its terms. It is well settled that facts sufficient to put a purchaser upon inquiry are not sufficient to affect him with actual notice of an unrecorded instrument, within the meaning of the language of the statute. Pomroy v. Stevens, 11 Metc. (Mass.) 244; Parker v. Osgood, 3 Allen, 487; Lamb v. Pierce, 113 Mass. 72; Keith v. Wheeler, 159 Mass. 161, 34 N.E. 174. The only legitimate inference, from the agreed facts upon this branch of the case, is that the defendant did not have actual notice of the lease. Nor can the plaintiff rely upon the case of Cunningham v. Pattee, 99 Mass. 248, in which it was held that in equity one who purchases an estate, knowing it to be in possession of a tenant, is bound to inquire into the nature of the tenant's interest, and affected with notice of its extent, and, if the tenant has a written lease, with notice of that fact, and of the contents of the lease, including a covenant to renew. The clear distinction between that lease and the present is that in Cunningham v. Pattee the original term and the extension were together for less than seven years, and the statute now under consideration had no application. As the statute applies here, we must give it the same force in equity as at law, with the result that, as the defendant had no actual notice of the lease, it is not valid as against him, either in equity or law. Our view of the effect of the statute makes it unnecessary to consider the question whether the plaintiff's conviction of the offense of maintaining a common nuisance in the drug store during a portion of the first term of his tenancy ought to preclude him from maintaining a bill in equity for specific performance of the agreement for renewal. The case was reserved upon the pleadings and the agreed facts for the consideration of the court in banc. Let the bill be dismissed, with costs.

§ 8.3.3 Constructive Notice

Constructive notice is implied in law notice; it is a legal fiction. Constructive notice may be of one of two types: record notice (notice from the public records) or inquiry notice (knowledge of facts that would lead a reasonable owner to inquire further). The next two cases explore these types of notice.

Miller v. Hennen
438 N.W.2d 366 (Minn. 1989)

In Miller v. Hennen, *the court provides further elucidation to record notice and inquiry notice.*

* * *

This court has defined the types of notice which would take away an individual's status as a good faith purchaser. "Constructive notice is a creature of statute and, as a matter of law, imputes notice to all purchasers of any properly recorded instrument even though the purchaser has no actual notice of the record." *Anderson,* 263 N.W.2d at 384. As such, a purchaser may be held to have constructive notice of a properly recorded interest, even though he has not actually seen the recorded deed. A recorded interest is constructive notice "only of the facts appearing on the face of the record." *Id.* at 385. * * * *

Implied notice[5] has been found where one has "actual knowledge of facts which would put one on further inquiry." *Anderson,* 263 N.W.2d at 384-85. For example, if a subsequent purchaser was aware that someone other than the vendor was living on the land, the purchaser would have a duty to inquire concerning the rights of the inhabitant of the property and would be charged with notice of all facts which such an inquiry would have disclosed. *Murphy v. Anderson,* 128 Minn. 106, 111, 150 N.W. 387, 389 (1914). This court adopted the following rule for implied notice cases:

> One is not a bona fide purchaser and entitled to the protection of the recording act, though he paid a valuable consideration and did not have actual notice of a prior unrecorded conveyance from the same grantor, if he had knowledge of facts which ought to have put him on an inquiry that would have led to a knowledge of such conveyance.

Henschke v. Christian et al., 228 Minn. 142, 146-47, 36 N.W.2d 547, 550 (1949).

* * *

---

[5] [This term, "implied notice," sometimes is a synonym for inquiry notice.]

Harper v. Paradise

233 Ga. 194 (1974)

In Harper v. Paradise, *one Susan Harper conveyed to Maude Harper (Susan's daughter-in-law) for life with a remainder to Maude's children. This deed, however, became lost. Consequently, on Susan's death, Susan's heirs executed a deed conveying to Maude in fee. This latter deed expressly stated that this deed was a replacement for the previously lost deed. Through a series of conveyances emanating from this deed (the "Susan's heirs to Maude in fee," deed), Lincoln and William Paradise claimed title. The question becomes whether the recording statute in question (a race-notice statute) allows Lincoln and William Paradise to prevail over Maude's children who now claim in fee after Maude's death. The ultimate issue is whether Lincoln and William Paradise are charged with notice of the Susan-Maude deed.*

INGRAM, Justice.

This appeal involves title to land. It is from a judgment and directed verdict granted to the appellees and denied to the appellants in the Superior Court of Oglethorpe County.

Appellants claim title as remaindermen under a deed to a life tenant with the remainder interest to the named children of the life tenant. This deed was delivered to the life tenant but was lost or misplaced for a number of years and was not recorded until 35 years later.

Appellees claim title as uninterrupted successors in title to an intervening mortgagee who purchased the property at a sheriff's sale following the foreclosure of a security deed given by the life tenant to secure a loan which became in default. Prior to the execution of the security deed by the life tenant, she obtained a quitclaim deed from all but one of the then living heirs of the original grantor who died earlier. Appellees also claim prescriptive title as a result of the peaceful, continuous, open and adverse possession of the property by them and their record predecessors in title for more than 21 years.

The life tenant died in 1972 and her children and representatives of deceased children, who were named as the remaindermen, then brought the present action to recover the land. The trial court determined that appellees held superior title to the land and it is this judgment, adverse to the remaindermen, that produced the present appeal to this court.

The above condensation of the title contentions of the parties can be understood best by reciting in detail the sequential occurrence of the facts which produced these conflicting claims of title.

On February 1, 1922, Mrs. Susan Harper conveyed by warranty deed a 106.65-acre farm in Oglethorpe County to her daughter-in-law, Maude Harper, for life with remainder in fee simple to Maude Harper's named children. The deed, which recited that it was given for Five Dollars and 'natural love and affection,' was lost, or misplaced, until 1957 when it was found by Clyde Harper, one of the named remaindermen, in an old trunk belonging to Maude Harper. The deed was recorded in July, 1957.

Susan Harper died sometime during the period 1925-1927 and was survived by her legal heirs, Price Harper, Prudie Harper Jackson, Mildred Chambers and John W.

Harper, Maude Harper's husband. In 1928, all of Susan Harper's then living heirs, except John W. Harper, joined in executing an instrument to Maude Harper, recorded March 19, 1928 which contained the following language:

'Deed, Heirs of Mrs. Susan Harper, to Mrs. Maude Harper. Whereas Mrs. Susan Harper did on or about the . . . day of March, 1927, make and deliver a deed of gift to the land hereinafter more fully described to Mrs. Maude Harper the wife of John W. Harper, which said deed was delivered to the said Mrs. Maude Harper and was not recorded; and Whereas said deed has been lost or destroyed and cannot be found; and Whereas the said Mrs. Susan Harper has since died and leaves as her heirs at law the grantors herein; Now therefore for and in consideration of the sum of $1.00, in hand paid, the receipt of which is hereby acknowledged, the undersigned Mrs. Prudence Harper Jackson, Price Harper and Ben Grant as guardian of Mildred Chambers, do hereby remise, release and forever quit claim to the said Mrs. Maude Harper, her heirs and assigns, all of their right, title, interest, claim or demand that they and each of them have or may have had in and to the (described property). To have and to hold the said property to the said Mrs. Maude Harper, her heirs and assigns, so that neither the said grantors nor their heirs nor any person or persons claiming under them shall at any time hereafter by any way or means, have, claim or demand any right, title or interest in and to the aforesaid property or its appurtenances or any part thereof. This deed is made and delivered to the said Mrs. Maude Harper to take the place of the deed made and executed and delivered by Mrs. Susan Harper during her lifetime as each of the parties hereto know that the said property was conveyed to the said Mrs. Maude Harper by the said Mrs. Susan Harper during her lifetime and that the said Mrs. Maude Harper was on said property and in possession thereof.'

On February 27, 1933, Maude Harper executed a security deed, recorded the same day, which purported to convey the entire fee simple to Ella Thornton to secure a fifty dollar loan. The loan being in default, Ella Thornton foreclosed on the property, receiving a sheriff's deed executed and recorded in 1936. There is an unbroken chain of record title out of Ella Thornton to the appellees, Lincoln and William Paradise, who claim the property as grantees under a warranty deed executed and recorded in 1955. The appellees also assert title by way of peaceful, continuous, open and adverse possession by them and their predecessors in title beginning in 1940.

The appellees trace their title back through Susan Harper, but they do not rely on the 1922 deed from Susan Harper to Maude Harper as a link in their record chain of title. If appellees relied on the 1922 deed, then clearly the only interest they would have obtained would have been Maude Harper's life estate which terminated upon her death in 1972. 'No forfeiture shall result from a tenant for life selling the entire estate in lands; the purchaser shall acquire only his interest.' Code § 85-609. See Mathis v. Solomon, 188 Ga. 311, 4 S.E.2d 24; Satterfield v. Tate, 132 Ga. 256, 64 S.E. 60; New South Building & Loan Assn. v. Gann, 101 Ga. 678(3), 29 S.E. 15; McDougal v. Sanders, 75 Ga. 140.

Appellees contend that the 1928 instrument executed by three of Susan Harper's then living heirs must be treated under Code § 67-2502 as having been executed by the heirs as agents or representatives of Susan Harper, thereby making both the 1922 and 1928 deeds derivative of the same source. That Code section provides:

'All innocent persons, firms or corporations acting in good faith and without actual notice, who purchase for value, or obtain contractual liens, from distributees, devisees, legatees, or heirs at law, holding or apparently holding land or personal property by will or inheritance from a deceased person, shall be protected in the purchase of said property or in acquiring such a lien thereon as against unrecorded liens or conveyances created or executed by said deceased person upon or to said property in like manner and to the same extent as if the property had been purchased of or the lien acquired from the deceased person.'

Appellees argue that since both deeds must be treated as having emanated from the same source, the 1928 deed has priority under Code § 29-401 because it was recorded first. Code § 29-401 provides: 'Every deed conveying lands shall be recorded in the office of the clerk of the superior court of the county where the land lies. The record may be made at any time, but such deed loses its priority over a subsequent recorded deed from the same vendor, taken without notice of the existence of the first.'

* * *

In the present case, the remaindermen in the deed to the life tenant were not the heirs of the grantor. They were named children of the life tenant grantee. Therefore, after the death of the original grantor, Susan Harper, her heirs could have joined in a deed to an innocent person acting in good faith and without actual notice of the earlier deed. If such a deed had been made, conveying a fee simple interest without making any reference to a prior unrecorded lost or misplaced deed, Code § 67-2502 might well apply to place that deed from the heirs within the protection of Code § 29-401.

However, the 1928 deed relied upon by appellees was to the same person, Maude Harper, who was the life tenant in the 1922 deed. The 1928 deed recited that it was given in lieu of the earlier lost or misplaced deed from Susan Harper to Maude Harper and that Maude Harper was in possession of the property. Thus Maude Harper is bound to have taken the 1928 deed with knowledge of the 1922 deed. See King v. McDuffie, 144 Ga. 318, 320, 87 S.E. 22. The recitals of the 1928 deed negate any contention that the grantors in that deed were holding or apparently holding the property by will or inheritance from Susan Harper. Indeed, the recitals of the 1928 deed actually serve as a disclaimer by the heirs that they were so holding or apparently holding the land.

Therefore, Code § 67-2502 is not applicable under the facts of this case and cannot be used to give the 1928 deed priority over the 1922 deed under the provisions of Code § 29-401. The recitals contained in the 1928 deed clearly put any subsequent purchaser on notice of the existence of the earlier misplaced or lost deed, and, in terms of Code § 29-401, the 1928 deed, though recorded first, would not be entitled to priority. See King v. McDuffie, 144 Ga. 318(2), 87 S.E. 22, supra; Hitchcock v. Hines, 143 Ga. 377, 85 S.E. 119; Stubbs v. Glass, 143 Ga. 56, 84 S.E. 126; Holder v. Scarborough, 119 Ga. 256, 46 S.E. 93; Zorn v. Thompson, 108 Ga. 78, 34 S.E. 303.

We conclude that it was incumbent upon the appellees to ascertain through diligent inquiry the contents of the earlier deed and the interests conveyed therein. See Henson v. Bridges, 218 Ga. 6(2), 126 S.E.2d 226. Cf. Talmadge Bros. & Co. v. Interstate Building & Loan Ass'n, 105 Ga. 550, 553, 31 S.E. 618, holding that 'a deed in the chain of title, discovered by the investigator, is constructive notice of all other deeds which were referred to in the deed discovered,' including an unrecorded plat included in the deed discovered. Although the appellees at trial denied having received any information as to the existence of the interests claimed by the appellants, the transcript fails to indicate any effort on the part of the appellees to inquire as to the interests conveyed by the lost or misplaced deed when they purchased the property in 1955. 'A thorough review of the record evinces no inquiry whatsoever by the defendants, or attempt to explain why such inquiry would have been futile. Thus it will be presumed that due inquiry would have disclosed the existent facts.' Henson v. Bridges, supra, p. 10, of 218 Ga., p. 228 of 126 S.E.2d.

* * *

Judgment reversed with direction.

All the Justices concur, except JORDAN, J., who dissents.

§ 8.3.4 Miscellaneous Problems: Latent Defects

The problem that we deal with here is whether a deed with a latent defect imparts notice.

Leeds Bldg. Products, Inc. v. Sears Mortgage Corp.
267 Ga. 300 (1996)

O conveyed land to A, but the deed was improperly acknowledged because the grantor did not sign in the presence of the notary, as required by law. Thereafter, O conveyed the same land to B. B did not do a title search. B, therefore, did not have actual notice of the prior conveyance. The question before the court was whether B had constructive notice of the prior conveyance when the deed had no patent or facial defects as to attestation. The court held that the deed, even with the latent defect, provided constructive notice.

THOMPSON, Justice.

* * *

This Court has never squarely considered the effect of a recorded instrument which, although defectively acknowledged, shows no such defect on its face. However, our appellate courts have by implication determined that such a deed constitutes constructive notice. See *Glover v. Cox*, 137 Ga. 684(3), 73 S.E. 1068 (1912); *Nalley Chevrolet, Inc. v. Calif. Bank*, 100 Ga.App. 197(3)(a), 110 S.E.2d 577 (1959), overruled on other grounds, *Whitehead v. Southern Discount Co.*, 109 Ga.App. 126(2), 135 S.E.2d 496 (1964). The substance of the notice required must be sufficient to "place a [person] of ordinary prudence fully upon his guard and induce serious inquiry." *Gardner v. Granniss*, 57 Ga. 539, 557(10) (1876). "It is the published assertion, and not the truth of it, which constitutes notice. When notice is given, then the deed is good for just what it is worth according to the truth of the case." *Johnson v. Johnson*, 184 Ga. 783, 784(2), 193 S.E. 345 (1937).

A majority of jurisdictions have recognized that a defect in the acknowledgment of an instrument required for recordation, which is not apparent on the face of the instrument, does not prevent the recordation from providing constructive notice to subsequent bona fide purchasers. See Anno: Record Notice--Acknowledgment, 59 ALR2d 1316, § 25. This rule comports with Georgia's statutory recording scheme, the purpose of which is to protect third parties acting in good faith and without notice who have acquired an interest in the same property. OCGA § 44-2-2(b). The majority rule is also consistent with and better serves modern commercial practice. Thus, we conclude that in the absence of fraud, a deed which, on its face, complies with all statutory requirements is entitled to be recorded, and once accepted and filed with the clerk of court for record, provides constructive notice to the world of its existence.

* * *

Note

Leeds Bldg. Products, Inc. v. Sears Mortgage Corp. dealt with a race-notice statute. The same issue would arise, however, in a notice jurisdiction and even in a pure race jurisdiction. In a pure race jurisdiction, where notice is not relevant, a deed with a defective acknowledgment may be *deemed* recorded (if the majority position prevails) so that it, and not a subsequently filed deed, wins the race to the courthouse.

§ 8.3.5 Miscellaneous Problems: Not Recorded or Improperly Indexed Deeds

The problems we tackle here deal with a deed that the recorder's office either accidentally fails to record, or records but improperly indexes (making it virtually impossible for a title searcher to find such a deed).

Throckmorton v. Price
28 Tex. 605 (1866)

O conveyed land to A on December 15, 1858. A took the deed to the recorder's office for recordation on December 20, 1858. O then conveyed the same land to B on February 21, 1859. B previously did a title search. Only after the O-B conveyance was recorded did the county recorder record the O-A deed of December 15, 1858. The court held that as between A and B, A prevails.

MOORE, C. J.
There was no controversy as to the facts in this case.

* * *

Registration laws of a general similarity to ours have been enacted in most of the other states, yet we have been able to find no case in which the first deed has been postponed in favor of the second from the failure of the clerk to record the prior deed as directed by the statute, while the contrary has been frequently decided. In Kentucky it is emphatically declared that deeds lodged for record are valid against subsequent purchasers and creditors. Bank of Kentucky v. Hagegan, 1 A. K. Marsh. 306. And in Connecticut it is said, "If a deed, after it is received and entered up 'received for record,' remain unrecorded, through no fault of the [prior] grantee, until an attachment of said land, it shall not prejudice the [prior] grantee." Franklin v. Cannon, 1 Root; Hartmyer v. Gates, Id. 61; McDonald v. Leach, Kirby, 72; Judd v. Woodruff, 2 Root, 298. The same principle is also recognized in Alabama. McGregor v. Hill, 3 Stewt. & P. 397.

* * *

Note

There is authority contrary to *Throckmorton v. Price*. See *Failure to Properly Index Conveyance or Mortgage of Realty as Affecting Constructive Notice*, 63 A.L.R. 1057 (1929) (Westlaw).

Compiano v. Jones

269 N.W.2d 459 (Iowa 1978)

In this case, the recorder's office records the prior deed, but improperly indexes the deed, making it impossible for a title searcher to locate the deed. The court finds that a deed improperly indexed gives no notice to a subsequent purchaser. Thus, as between A and B, B prevails.

* * *

In the Iowa cases cited we deliberately adopted two rules, after recognizing opposing authority from other jurisdictions. First, we said the whole statutory scheme, not just the filing statute, must be considered in deciding how the filing and recording of instruments affecting real estate were to be accomplished. We held documents must not only be filed but must also be properly indexed. Secondly, we decided the person filing an instrument must suffer the consequences of improper indexing as he is usually the only one who can make certain it is done right. These rules have never been changed. Although it is not directly in point, the language in Fleck v. Iowa Employment Security Comm'n., 233 Iowa 67, 72-74, 8 N.W.2d 703, 706-07 (1943), is persuasive that we have not abandoned the reasoning of our earlier cases.

* * *

Note

There is authority contrary to *Compiano v. Jones*. See 76 C.J.S. Records § 16.

§ 8.3.6 Miscellaneous Problems: Idem Sonans

Idem sonans deals with two or more names that have the same pronunciation but different spellings. The question we deal with here is whether a title searcher must check all alternative spellings of a name, as the next case illustrates.

Miltonvale State Bank v. Kuhnle

50 Kan. 420 (1893)

One Johnston executed a mortgage in favor of A. The mortgage was recorded under the name "Johnson," however. Thereafter, Johnston executed another mortgage for the same property in favor of B. B did a title search under the name "Johnston" and, of course, found nothing. The issue before the court was whether B was charged with notice: did B also have a duty to check under the name "Johnson"? The court held in the affirmative.

254

GREEN, C.

* * *

* * *The contention of the plaintiff in error [that is, the subsequent transferee], that a mortgage executed by S. M. Johnson is not sufficient to impart notice of the execution of a mortgage by Samuel M. Johnston, is not well taken. This court has said that a written instrument should not be regarded as a nullity because the Christian name of any person is not mentioned therein, and has not been written in full, but only the initial letters have been used. Ferguson v. Smith, 10 Kan. 397. It is insisted that Johnston and Johnson are not even *idem sonans*. The rule has been stated: "That absolute accuracy in spelling names is not required in documents or proceedings, either civil or criminal; that if the name as spelled in the document, though different from the correct spelling thereof, conveys to the ear, when pronounced according to commonly accepted methods, a sound practically identical with the sound of the correct name, as commonly pronounced, the name as thus given is a sufficient designation of the individual referred to, and no advantage can be taken of the clerical error." 16 Amer. & Eng. Enc. Law, 122 In the pronunciation of proper names, greater latitude is indulged in than in any other class of words. Rooks v. State, 83 Ala. 79, 3 South. Rep. 720. Courts will not enforce the exact rule of lexicographers in the spelling and pronunciation of words. Indeed, it is difficult to determine when names are of the same sound, and it would take a practiced ear to detect the difference in the sound of Johnston and Johnson, as ordinarily pronounced by the generality of mankind. As previously held by this court in the case of Howard v. Bank, 44 Kan. 549, 24 Pac. Rep. 983, and Farmer's & Merchants' Bank v. Bank of Glen Elder, 46 Kan. 376, 26 Pac. Rep. 680, a subsequent mortgage, with notice of a prior mortgage, is not a subsequent mortgage in good faith, under paragraph 3905 of the General Statutes of 1889. Upon the authority of the above cases the trial court was correct in the judgment rendered.

* * *

§ 8.3.7 Miscellaneous Problems: Forged Deeds and Other Fraud

Suppose O conveys to A. Suppose also that X forges O's signature so that it appears that O conveyed to B, a bona fide purchaser for value with no notice of the prior O-A deed. The question is, as between A and B, who owns Blackacre? On the other hand, suppose that after O conveys to A, X "cons" O into executing a deed in favor of B. Again, the question is whether B prevails over A. We discuss these matters in the next case.

Diimmel v. Morse
36 Wash.2d 344 (1950)

One Mrs. Diimmel owned two properties. She was induced by a con man named Welch to convey both properties to him. Thereafter, Welch mortgaged the first property, the "Erie" property. Later still, Welch, via a bail bondsman, executed a mortgage on the Erie property and another property. The question before the court was whether Mrs. Diimmel could cancel the mortgages on both properties on the ground of fraud. Ultimately, the court distinguished a forged deed (not the case here) and fraud in the execution (also not the case here) from fraud in the inducement (what Welch engaged in).

255

The court held that Mrs. Diimmel could not cancel the deeds. The court also held that the mortgages that Welch gave on the properties were valid.

MALLERY, Justice.

This is an appeal from a judgment in which deeds from Mrs. Diimmel to one Felch were canceled as to him. Only two mortgages made by him are involved in this appeal.

Sometime prior to April 26, 1948, Mrs. Diimmel met Felch, alias Welch, as he will be designated hereafter, who represented himself to be a widower. He introduced his wife as his niece. Mrs. Diimmel was a widow, employed as a chambermaid, and was of less than average intelligence. Her acquaintance with Welch developed rapidly and soon they were engaged to be married.

Mrs. Diimmel was the owner of two pieces of real estate, referred to as the Erie street and the Hogan street properties. Each parcel had a house thereon, which was divided into apartments and rented.

Welch claimed to be a property manager, and represented to Mrs. Diimmel that certain people were trying to commit her to an asylum; that her deeds were faulty; and that if she would put her property in his name he would straighten out her title; and, also, profitably manage it for her. She trusted Welch implicitly.

On April 26, 1948, Mrs. Diimmel, accompanied by Welch, went to a notary public for the purpose of transferring her title to Welch, but this notary, for reasons unknown, refused to take her acknowledgment. They then went to the office of Welch's attorney, and he completed the transfer for them. Mrs. Diimmel did not have her glasses on and could not see well, but she testified that she knew the title to her property was being put in the name of Welch.

On May 20, 1948, Welch gave a note and mortgage to Mr. Lenzi in return for a loan of $1500 on the Erie street property. Welch and his wife were living on the property at the time. The transaction was handled through Lenzi's attorney, and Lenzi did not visit the premises. The record is silent as to whether or not the attorney was ever on the property. Lenzi did see the title insurance policy, however. He did not know Mrs. Diimmel.

On about June 1, 1948, Welch was arrested on a fugitive warrant from the state of Wisconsin, where he was wanted for forgery. Bail was set at $5,000. He called his attorney, disclosed that he had a wife, and requested him to get a bond for his release. The attorney contacted Mr. Kafflen, a bondsman, for that purpose, and they went out to look at Welch's property. Kafflen said that he would give a $2500 bond with both properties as security. Welch's attorney had the bail reduced to that amount, and a note and mortgage were given. Welch's wife joining in the conveyance. Kafflen did investigate Welch's attorney, but beyond that he relied upon the attorney without question. In so far as the record indicates, Kafflen did not check the title records; saw no title insurance policy; and was unaware of the existing prior mortgage on the Erie street property held by Lenzi. Once out of confinement, Welch and his wife left for parts unknown, and have not been heard from since. No question is raised about Kafflen's liability on the bail bond being adequate consideration for his mortgage.

During his brief tenure as manager of the property, Welch incurred several debts, and it was the attachment of the property by a creditor to satisfy one of these that precipitated this action to cancel the deeds, and to declare the mortgages invalid.

The trial court held that the Lenzi mortgage was valid, and from this judgment the plaintiff, Mrs. Diimmel, crossappeals. She contends that the deeds to Welch must be treated as forgeries, relying on the case of Horvath v. National Mortgage Co., 238 Mich. 354, 213 N.W. 202, 56 A.L.R. 578, to support her contention. In that case there was a fraudulent manipulation of papers, and the plaintiff did not realize that she was signing a deed, nor did she intend to. In the instant case, Mrs. Diimmel knew what she was signing, but did not fully realize the legal significance of her act. She did, however, understand that she was placing the title in Welch's name. There is no question that fraud was perpetrated here, and that as between Mrs. Diimmel and Welch the deeds were entitled to cancellation. See Murdoch v. Leonard, 1 Wash.2d 37, 95 P.2d 37; Kausky v. Kosten, 27 Wash.2d 721, 179 P.2d 950. However, a deed to which the grantor's signature was secured by fraud does not stand on the same footing as a forged deed, so far as concerns an innocent encumbrancer in good faith and for value. Lewis v. Kujawa, 158 Wash. 607, 291 P. 1105; 16 Am.Jur. 452.

Although Mrs. Diimmel is unquestionably of less than average intelligence, which fact was recognized by the appointment of a guardian *ad litem* by the court on its own motion, the facts remain that she was not under a general guardian; she held title to property in her own name; transacted her own business; entered the transaction in question of her own accord, however ill-advised and influenced; and she understood the general effect of a deed.

Under the circumstances, the recording acts must govern the outcome of the case. An encumbrancer, without notice of existing equities, may rely on the record chain of title, and, in the absence of notice, is not bound to go outside the records to inquire about them. Burr v. Dyer, 60 Wash. 603, 111 P. 866.

The trial court's judgment that Lenzi's mortgage is valid is affirmed.

The trial court found the facts to be that Welch's attorney acted as the agent of Kafflen, and so imputed notice to him of all of the attorney's knowledge of the facts surrounding Mrs. Diimmel's transfer of her title to Welch. Upon that factual basis the court decreed that Kafflen was not an innocent encumbrancer, and set aside his mortgage. From this judgment Kafflen appeals.

We are satisfied that the evidence in the record clearly preponderates against the finding that Welch's attorney was also the agent of Kafflen. He represented Welch only. Kafflen may have been extraordinarily credulous, but notice of things he did not know will not be imputed to him on the basis of the knowledge of Welch's attorney. Kafflen was on the premises, but he was not required to inquire of the tenants concerning the title of the property. Rehm v. Reilly, 161 Wash. 418, 297 P. 147.

Kafflen did know that Welch was wanted for forgery in another state, but inquiry there would not have led to any knowledge touching the property in question in this state. It is the general rule that one who has notice of facts sufficient to put him on inquiry is deemed to have notice of all facts which reasonable inquiry would disclose, but the rule does not impute notice of every conceivable fact, however remote, that could be learned from inquiry; it imputes notice only of those facts that are naturally and reasonably connected with the fact known, and to which the known fact can be said to furnish a clue.

Hawkes v. Hoffman, 56 Wash. 120, 105 P. 156, 24 L.R.A.,N.S., 1038; Rehm v. Reilly, supra; 39 Am.Jur. 241.

The judgment against the appellant Kafflen is reversed. In all other respects the judgment is affirmed.

SIMPSON, C. J., and ROBINSON, HILL, and HAMLEY, JJ., concur.

§ 8.4 The Consideration Requirement

As we have previously stated, to be protected under a state's recording statute, the subsequent transferee must be a purchaser; donees are not given protection. The next few cases provide further elucidation on this matter.

Valencia v. Lundgren
129 N.M. 57 (App. 2000)

In Valencia v. Lundgren, *a father conveyed property to his daughter. The father later conveyed the same property to his son. At trial, the son claimed that as between he and his sister, he owned the subject property because he came under the protection of the state recording statute (a notice statute). The trial court held in favor of the son. On appeal, the sister claimed that the trial court committed error because the court did not consider her allegation that her brother acquired the property by gift. The court explained who was protected under recording statutes and, ultimately, reversed the trial court and remanded for further proceedings.*

OPINION

PICKARD, Chief Judge.

Loretta Lundgren (Daughter) filed suit against her brother, Ernest Valencia (Son), in order to establish certain easements across his property in favor of her property. Son moved for summary judgment on the ground that he owned the property upon which Daughter resided (the Residence). Son argued he was the Residence's rightful owner pursuant to our State's recording statute because he recorded a deed purporting to transfer the Residence to him before Daughter recorded a deed purporting to transfer the Residence to her. The trial court accepted Son's argument and granted his motion for summary judgment.

Daughter claims the trial court erred on the ground that Son lacked standing to invoke the recording statute. Daughter argues she foreclosed summary judgment when she raised the factual issue of whether Son acquired the Residence by gift, because persons who have not given consideration in exchange for the title to property cannot invoke the recording statute. If we reverse the trial court's decision, Daughter asks us to construe her deed and Son's deed together, uphold her claim to the Residence, and remand to the trial court for further proceedings in regard to her claim of easements appurtenant to the Residence. We reverse the trial court's decision and remand for further proceedings consistent with this opinion.

* * *

DISCUSSION

I. RECORDING STATUTE

Son and Daughter both claimed ownership of the Residence by deed at the trial court level. Son [who received title after the daughter] recorded his deed first. Son argued that because he recorded his deed first, he was entitled to judgment as a matter of law pursuant to our State's recording statute. The recording statute states in relevant part:

> No deed, mortgage or other instrument in writing not recorded in accordance with [NMSA 1978, §] 14-9-1 [(1991)] shall affect the title or rights to, in any real estate, of any purchaser, mortgagee in good faith or judgment lien creditor, without knowledge of the existence of such unrecorded instruments.

NMSA 1978, § 14-9-3 (1990). The trial court accepted Son's argument and granted his motion for summary judgment. In its summary judgment order, the trial court found:

"Any deed to Loretta Valencia [Daughter] * * * [was] filed subsequent to that granting title to Ernest Valencia and [is] therefore void and of no legal effect."

Daughter claims the trial court erred as a matter of law because it applied the recording statute in total disregard to her factual averment that Son acquired his deed by gift. Daughter argues the trial court's legal analysis effectively and improperly reads the term "purchaser" out of the recording statute. Daughter relies on *Withers v. Board of County Commissioners,* 96 N.M. 71, 628 P.2d 316 (Ct.App.1981), and *Arias v. Springer,* 42 N.M. 350, 78 P.2d 153 (1938), in support of her argument.

In *Withers,* we addressed the issue of whether a person had standing to invoke the recording statute after he had submitted a successful bid to purchase certain real property. *See id.* at 72, 628 P.2d at 317. Answering in the negative, we reasoned that such a person had to be, but was not, a "purchaser" within the meaning of the recording statute. *See id.* In support of our holding, we relied on our Supreme Court's decision in *Arias* for the meaning of the term "purchaser." *See id.* In *Arias,* the Supreme Court stated:

> The word "purchaser" has two well-defined meanings. The common and popular meaning is that he is one who obtains title to real estate in consideration of the payment of money or its equivalent; the other is a technical meaning and includes all persons who acquire real estate otherwise than by descent. It includes acquisition by devise.
>
> It is evident that the word is used in the statute in its popular sense. . . . . The object of the statute is to prevent injustice by protecting those who, without knowledge of infirmities in the title, invest money in property or mortgage loans; and those who have acquired judgment liens without such knowledge.

Id. at 359, 78 P.2d at 159 (citations omitted).

The import of *Withers* and *Arias* is that a person can qualify as a purchaser under the recording statute if and only if he has invested money or money's worth in consideration for the title to real property. *See Withers,* 96 N.M. at 72, 628 P.2d at 317

("[T]he clear and consistent reasoning of New Mexico case law . . . holds that the object of the recording statute is to protect those who invest money in property . . . without knowledge of infirmities in title."). If a person has not made such an investment, that person cannot invoke the recording statute to invalidate a conflicting deed irrespective of the fact that the person recorded the deed first. *See id.* We hold that the trial court therefore committed reversible error by failing to consider the issue of whether Son obtained title to the Residence by gift. *See Garcia v. Sanchez,* 108 N.M. 388, 395, 772 P.2d 1311, 1318 (Ct.App.1989) (ruling that case may be remanded for application of correct principles of law when decision is based upon an error of law).

* * *

Anderson v. Anderson
435 N.W.2d 687 (N.D. 1989)

The question addressed in Anderson v. Anderson *is how much consideration must a subsequent transferee pay to be recognized as a "purchaser."*

* * *

Generally, for protection under a recording act as a good faith purchaser for value, the purchase must be for a valuable and not a nominal consideration. 6A Powell on Real Property ¶ 905[2] (1988); 5 Tiffany on Real Property § 1300 et seq. (1939); 8 Thompson on Real Property § 4319 (1963). *See* cases cited in *United States v. Certain Parcels of Land,* 85 F.Supp. 986, 1006 (S.D.Cal.1949) fn. 17. The consideration does not have to be an equivalent value in order to be valuable, but it must be substantial and not merely nominal. 6A Powell, *supra* at ¶ 905[2]; 5 Tiffany, *supra* at § 1301; 8 Thompson, *supra* at § 4319; *United States v. Certain Parcels of Land, supra.* In *Horton v. Kyburz,* 53 Cal.2d 59, 346 P.2d 399, 403 (1959), the court quoted an explanation of the rationale:

" 'The recording laws were not enacted to protect those whose ignorance of the title is deliberate and intentional, nor does a mere nominal consideration satisfy the requirement that a valuable consideration must be paid. Their purpose is to protect those who honestly believe they are acquiring a good title, and who invest some substantial sum in reliance on that belief.' "

* * *

The recital of a nominal consideration in a deed is insufficient to establish a valuable consideration or to raise a presumption of value for a good faith purchase. *E.g., United States v. Certain Parcels of Land, supra; James v. James,* 80 Cal.App. 185, 251 P. 666 (1926). Moreover, the party claiming to be a good faith purchaser has the burden of proof to establish valuable consideration from evidence other than the deed. 8 Thompson on Real Property § 4316 (1963); *United States v. Certain Parcels of Land, supra; James v. James, supra.*

In this case, the defendants relied on the abstract of title to establish that Ida and Willie paid Julia "$10.00 & OG & VC" [other good and valuable consideration] for the 1951 quit-claim deed. The defendants presented no evidence of any actual consideration. *See United States v. Certain Parcels of Land, supra; Horton v. Kyburz, supra; Croak v. Witteman,* 73 N.D. 592, 17 N.W.2d 542 (1945). We conclude, as a matter of law, that the consideration recited in the 1951 quit-claim deed was a nominal consideration and did not constitute a valuable consideration. Ida and Willie were not good faith purchasers for a valuable consideration under Section 47-19-41, N.D.C.C. Therefore, the defendants cannot claim priority over the plaintiffs by virtue of the 1951 deed.

Accordingly, we reverse the judgment and remand for entry of judgment quieting title in the plaintiffs.

Daniels v. Anderson
162 Ill.2d 47 (1994)

One Anderson conveyed to Daniels. Anderson subsequently entered into an installment land contract to convey the same land to Zografos. Zografos did not have notice of the prior conveyance to Daniels. Zografos made some installment payments to Anderson before receiving actual notice of the prior conveyance. Notwithstanding that actual notice, Zografos continued to make installment payments, eventually making full payment. The trial court awarded the property to Daniels, ordering Daniels to reimburse Zografos for the full purchase price that Zografos paid to Anderson. This court affirmed and, in the process, discussed the various lines of authority for the problem of a subsequent purchaser continuing to make installment payments after receiving actual notice of the prior conveyance.

* * *

Where a buyer receives notice of an outstanding interest subsequent to paying *some,* but prior to paying the full purchase price, authorities differ on whether the buyer is a *bona fide* purchaser. As the appellate court noted, some of the authorities state that partial payment of the consideration is insufficient to render the buyer a *bona fide* purchaser. 252 Ill.App.3d at 300-02, 191 Ill.Dec. 773, 624 N.E.2d 1151 (and authorities cited therein); 8 J. Grimes, Thompson on Real Property § 4322, at 418, 420-21 (1963). However, a majority of jurisdictions have relaxed this harsh rule. Instead, they apply a *pro tanto* rule, which protects the buyer to the extent of the payments made prior to notice, but no further. (R. Cunningham, W. Stoebuck, D. Whitman, Property 795 (1984); 8 J. Grimes, Thompson on Real Property § 4322, at 418-19 (1963); 5 B. Jones, Tiffany on Real Property § 1305 (3d ed. 1939).) This court recognized this *pro tanto* rule in *dicta* in *Redden v. Miller* (1880), 95 Ill. 336, 346.

Courts have identified at least three methods to apply this *pro tanto* protection. First, the most common method is to award the land to the holder of the outstanding interest and award the buyer the payments that he or she made. The second method is to award the buyer a fractional interest in the land proportional to the amount paid prior to notice. The third method is to allow the buyer to complete the purchase, but to pay the remaining installments to the holder of the outstanding interest. (R. Cunningham, W. Stoebuck, D. Whitman, Property 795-96 (1984); 8 J. Grimes, Thompson on Real Property § 4322, at 418 (1984).) Courts exercise considerable latitude in these cases, taking into account the relative equities of the parties. R. Cunningham, W. Stoebuck, D. Whitman, Property 796 (1984); see, *e.g.,*252 Ill.App.3d at 302-04, 191 Ill.Dec. 773, 624 N.E.2d 1151, explaining *Baldwin v. Sager* (1873), 70 Ill. 503.

In the present case, the trial court ordered Zografos to convey the [property in question to] Daniels and ordered Daniels to pay Zografos the full purchase price. The trial court also ordered Daniels to reimburse Zografos for the property taxes that Zografos had paid on the property. We agree with the appellate court that the trial court's disposition of this issue, between Daniels and Zografos, satisfied these well-settled principles of equity. (252 Ill.App.3d at 305, 191 Ill.Dec. 773, 624 N.E.2d 1151.) We cannot say that the trial court abused its discretion.

* * *

§ 8.5 Title Searches and Indexes

The material that follows explains what constitutes a "wild deed" (also known as a "stray deed"), what is a title search, and what are the types of indexes that are available in this country to do a title search..

GMAC Mortgage Corporation v. PWI Group
155 P.3d 556 (Colo.App. 2006)

We begin by explaining the term, "wild deed."

* * *

A "wild deed" is defined as "[a] recorded deed that is not in the chain of title," *Black's Law Dictionary* 446 (8th ed.2004), such as a deed "executed by a grantor with no record ownership of the interest." 11 *Thompson on Real Property* § 92.11(c) (David Thomas ed.1994); *see also* Attorneys Title Guar. Fund, Inc., *Colorado Real Estate Title Standards* 3.3.1 (2003) (an instrument that appears of record purporting to affect the title to real property that is executed by one who has no record interest in the real property on the date it is recorded is a "wild deed," which is outside the chain of title).

Here, it is undisputed that Mandalay Holdings was the grantor of the Mandalay deed of trust. It is also undisputed that Mandalay Holdings did not own any right, title, or interest in the subject properties it purported to convey to the public trustee. Thus, the Mandalay deed of trust was outside of the chain of title as disclosed in the grantor-grantee indices and constituted a "wild deed."

* * *

Bank of New York v. Nally
820 N.E.2d 644 (Ind. 2005)

This case explains the important concept of establishing a "chain of title," the key to a title search.

* * *

The purpose of recording a mortgage is to give notice to persons subsequently dealing with the property of the existence of the mortgage and to charge them with notice of what the records disclose. *Szakaly,* 544 N.E.2d at 491-92; *Keybank,* 699 N.E.2d at 327. To charge subsequent purchasers with notice, a mortgage must be recorded in the proper county, *First Nat'l Bank of Carlisle v. Coen,* 76 Ind.App. 143, 144-45, 131 N.E. 531, 532 (1921), and must contain an accurate legal description of the property, *Rinehardt v. Reifers,* 158 Ind. 675, 676-77 64 N.E. 459, 459 (1902). Both of these requirements were met by recording the Owens mortgage in the office of the Hamilton County Recorder. A third requirement, however, is disputed. We have said on a number of occasions that a recorded mortgage must be in the "chain of title." *Szakaly,* 544 N.E.2d at 492; *Sinclair v. Gunzenhauser,* 179 Ind. 78, at 117, 98 N.E. 37, at 51 (1912) ("when the record [of a mortgage] is not in the chain of title, it is almost universally held that the record is not notice"); *Meyer v. Marine Builders, Inc.,* 797 N.E.2d 760, 774 (Ind.Ct.App.2003) ("A record [of a mortgage] outside the chain of title does not provide notice to bona fide purchasers for value.").

In *Szakaly,* this Court described the concept of "chain of title" to a tract of land:

> In a title search, the prospective purchaser or his abstractor assesses the marketability of title to a tract of land by determining the "chain of title." Beginning with the person who received the grant of land from the United States, the purchaser or abstractor traces the name of the grantor until the conveyance of the tract in question. The particular grantor's name is not searched thereafter. As the process is repeated, the links in the chain of title are forged.

544 N.E.2d at 491-492 (citing Schroeder, *Title Searches and Marketable Title,* Basic Real Estate Practice I-30 (1986)). * * *

* * *

In re Hill
156 B.R. 998 (Bkrtcy.N.D.Ill. 1993)

This case informs you that there are two types of indices used in this country to perform a title search. The first (and most common) is the grantor-grantee index. The second is the tract index. Both types of indices are explained more fully in the note that follows Byrum v. Barker, *infra.*

* * *

Alternatively, the Trustee contends that if section 549 applies, Gunn and Wesav had sufficient facts to put them on notice of the avoidability of the deed because of the kind of deed used to convey the Property from Hill to Buy Right. The Court also rejects this argument as unsupported by the facts and not well founded in law. The primary means of charging any party with notice of an interest in Illinois real property is to record that interest. *See* 765 ILCS 5/30; *Smith v. Grubb,* 402 Ill. 451, 84 N.E.2d 421 (1949). A purchaser of real property in Illinois is only required to check the chain of title as shown in the grantor-grantee index search at the recorder of deeds office of the county in which the property is located in order to uncover any adverse interest on the property. *Greer v. Carter Oil Co.,* 373 Ill. 168, 25 N.E.2d 805 (1940); *Landis v. Miles Homes, Inc.,* 1 Ill.App.3d 331, 335, 273 N.E.2d 153, 155 (2d Dist.1971) (parties are "charged with knowledge of what appears in the grantor-grantee index, the legal record required to be maintained by the Recorder"). Recording outside of the grantor-grantee index, as in a tract index, is recording merely for convenience. *Landis,* 1 Ill.App.3d at 335, 273 N.E.2d at 155. If the interest is not recorded in the chain of title, it is not constructive notice to third parties. *Skidmore, Owings & Merrill v. Pathway Financial,* 173 Ill.App.3d 512, 514, 123 Ill.Dec. 395, 396-397, 527 N.E.2d 1033, 1034-1035 (3d Dist.1988).

* * *

Bynum v. Barker
39 So.3d 1013 (Ala. 2009)

Bynum v. Barker *further develops the concept of chain of title and its relationship to wild deeds and the grantor-grantee index.*

***

In establishing chain of title, a purchaser or his or her agent must search the grantor index for each name in the chain of title of the property to locate any relevant mortgages, liens, or judgments against the property. A purchaser is protected when the records do not provide notice of such an interest. As this Court stated in *Wallace v. Frontier Bank, N.A.,* 903 So.2d 792, 797 (Ala.2004):

> " 'A bona fide purchaser is one who (1) purchases legal title, (2) in good faith, (3) for adequate consideration, (4) without notice of any claim of interest in the property by any other party. *First National Bank of Birmingham v. Culberson,* 342 So.2d 347, 350 (Ala.1977). Notice sufficient to preclude a bona fide purchase may be actual or constructive or may consist of knowledge of facts which would cause a reasonable person to make an inquiry which would reveal the interest of a third party. *Hill v. Taylor,* 285 Ala. 612, 614, 235 So.2d 647, 649 (1970).' "

(Quoting *Rolling "R" Constr., Inc. v. Dodd,* 477 So.2d 330, 331-32 (Ala.1985).)

* * *

Most recently, in *First Properties, LLC v. JPMorgan Chase Bank, National Association,* 993 So.2d 438 (Ala.2008), this Court held that the assignee of a mortgage did not have constructive notice that the property had been sold in a foreclosure sale where the recorded deed did not list the correct owner. In 1998, the Forestdale fire district conducted a foreclosure sale of certain property owned by the homeowner presumably because the payment for fire-protection services was delinquent. To satisfy the delinquency, the fire district sold the property, and the fire district was the highest bidder. The business manager for the fire district executed a deed purporting to convey the property from the fire district, as grantor, to the fire district, as grantee. On October 28, 1998, the deed was properly recorded. However, "the deed was not listed in the grantor/grantee index, did not refer to [the homeowner] as the owner of record, and contained what the trial court determined was an inadequate description of the property." 993 So.2d at 440.

On November 9, 1999, the homeowner in *First Properties* secured a loan by executing a mortgage on the property in favor of First Franklin Financial Corporation.

First Franklin recorded that mortgage on January 13, 2000. On July 31, 2004, First Franklin assigned that mortgage to JPMorgan Chase Bank, and the assignment of that mortgage was recorded on June 14, 2005. On December 18, 2004, the fire district executed a quitclaim deed to the property to First Properties, LLC. The quitclaim deed listed the homeowner as owner of the property. On December 23, 2004, First Properties recorded the quitclaim deed. JPMorgan filed an action seeking a judgment declaring that it was a bona fide holder for value of the property without notice of the foreclosure sale by the fire district. The trial court held that the foreclosure-sale deed was outside the chain of title because it did not name the homeowner as the owner and, therefore, did not provide notice of the foreclosure sale of the property. First Properties argued that JPMorgan, through its assignment, was on constructive notice of all documents of record in the probate court and, therefore, had constructive notice of the foreclosure-sale deed. This Court disagreed, holding that although the foreclosure-sale deed was recorded, that deed did not list the homeowner as the record owner:

> "Thus, when the foreclosure-sale deed was indexed in the probate records the fire district was listed as both the grantor and the grantee, and the undisputed evidence before the trial court showed that a search of the grantor-grantee index in the Jefferson County Probate Office would not have uncovered the foreclosure-sale deed. Consequently, the foreclosure-sale deed is a 'wild deed,' outside the chain of title, and the fact that it was recorded did not impart constructive notice to First Franklin or to JPMorgan. As explained in *Wallace [v. Frontier Bank, NA*], 903 So.2d [792,] 797 [(Ala.2004)]: ' "A purchaser is chargeable with notice of what appears on the face of the instruments *in his or her chain of title. Ball v. Vogtner,* 362 So.2d 894, 897 (Ala.1978); *Union Oil Co. v. Colglazier,* 360 So.2d 965, 969-70 (Ala.1978). However, *an instrument outside a purchaser's chain of title does not give constructive notice.*" ' (quoting [*Rolling 'R' Constr., Inc. v.] Dodd,* 477 So.2d [330] at 332 [(Ala.1985)]) (emphasis added). *Accord Brannan v. Marshall,* 184 Ala. 375, 377, 63 So. 1007, 1007 (1913), which states:
>
> > " 'It is well settled by numerous decisions in this state that the registration of a conveyance executed by one who is a stranger to the title as it is shown by the records-that is, by a grantor who does not appear in the chain of recorded conveyances, or other title records, as one who has acquired an interest in the land in question-is not constructive notice to a subsequent purchaser in the regular chain of title. *Fenno v. Sayre,* 3 Ala. 458 [(1842)]; *Gimon v. Davis,* 36 Ala. 589 [(1860)]; *Scotch Lumber Co. v. Sage,* 132 Ala. 598, 32 South. 607, 90 Am. St. Rep. 932 [(1902)]; *Tenn. C., I. & R. Co. v. Gardner,* 131 Ala. 599, 32 South. 622 [(1902)].'

"Accordingly, First Properties' argument that the foreclosure-sale deed provided constructive notice to JPMorgan is without merit."

993 So.2d at 442-43 (footnote omitted). The Court also noted the impracticality of First Properties' argument that JPMorgan was put on constructive notice of anything of record in the probate court no matter how difficult it was to find those documents. Citing a portion of JPMorgan's brief, the Court noted:

" 'First Properties argues that all documents recorded in a probate court impart constructive notice to any buyer. Under that logic, a buyer would be required to inspect all recorded documents in searching title to property. The average number of documents recorded daily in Jefferson County is posted at the Probate Court each day, and is thus open to judicial notice. Considering both divisions, Birmingham and Bessemer, the daily number is just under 1,000, amounting to approximately 260,000 per year. A 20-year search, therefore, would require review of 5,200,000 documents. The implications of First Properties' argument do not end there. It must be considered that such a search would include a duty to look [not only] for any instrument out of the record owner, but also for any document of any nature containing the legal description of the property. Recognizing that the legal description at issue in this case does not close, First Properties would subject a title searcher to the duty of inspecting 5,200,000 documents and tracing millions of miles of calls in legal descriptions, handicapped by the even more severe burden of being subject to notice imparted by incomplete legal descriptions.' "

993 So.2d at 441-42 n. 1.

***

Note

There are two primary indices used in the public records to establish title. One such index, and the most common in use in the United States, is the grantor-grantee index. In this system, title is traced by name of owner and is arranged as follows: by grantee (in the grantee index), grantor (in the grantor index), and by year. By checking first the grantee index (which lists each grantor, too), you can also find every grantor in the "chain of title." Thus, you start by using the grantee index and go back in time as is required in your jurisdiction (usually 30-40 years). Then, having learned the name of each grantor, you check the grantor index and march forward in time until the present. In this way, you will have constructed a complete "chain of title."

Each ten years of the grantor-grantee index is placed in a decadal index. Deeds, mortgages, liens, etc. not connected in a "chain" of ownership or title are deemed wild deeds and typically do not impart notice to subsequent purchasers.

The other index system is the tract system. In such a system, all transactions relative to a particular parcel are entered with respect to that parcel. As will be seen in the next section of materials, most chain of title problems occur in jurisdictions that use the grantor-grantee index, not tract indexes. Nonetheless, few jurisdictions mandate the use of tract systems in the public record.

While computerized searches can now make a title search easier, computerized searches cannot prevent all chain of title problems, as the unedited version of *Bynum v. Barker* demonstrates (probate judge indexed mortgagor's property, "Davis & Associates, LLC," as "Davis Associates, LLC," which was the incorrect name, omitting the ampersand between "Davis" and "Associates," and resulting in the mortgage being deemed outside the chain of title). Cf. § 8.3.5, "Miscellaneous Problems: Not Recorded or Improperly Indexed Deeds," supra.

§ 8.6 Chain of Title Problems

In this section, we explore the problem of what constitutes a so-called wild deed (a deed outside the chain of title). Bear in mind, as you go through these problems, that a deed that is deemed a wild deed does not give notice in a notice jurisdiction or race-notice jurisdiction and is not deemed recorded in a race jurisdiction.

§ 8.6.1 Deed Executed By Stranger to Title

In shades of Bynum v. Barker, *supra, suppose that O conveys to A, who does not record. A then conveys to B, who records. O ultimately conveys the same property to C. On these facts, using a grantor-grantee index, without A's recordation of the O-A deed, there is no way that C could find the A-B deed. Such a deed is a wild deed. Hence, as between B and C, C's title trumps B's title. The next case is just a slight variation of this hypothetical.*

Blake v. Graham
6 Ohio St. 580 (1856)

In the first of a series of conveyances, after the death of one Dr. Lynn, his executors conveyed certain out-of-state property to one Kitner, who recorded. Kitner thereafter conveyed to one Blake (the plaintiff in this case), who recorded. In a second series of transactions, the heirs of Dr. Lynn, subsequent to the executor-Kitner conveyance, conveyed the same property to the Canal Company, which recorded. The Canal Company thereupon conveyed to Willet, who recorded. Willet then conveyed to Graham (the defendant), who also recorded. The question is, as between Blake and Graham, who owns the property. The court holds that Graham prevails.

BRINKERHOFF, J.

The plaintiffs bring their action under the code, in the nature of a bill in chancery, to quiet title to, and obtain partition of, a piece of land in Tuscarawas county described in the petition, and the possession of the defendants.

In the year 1800, Dr. Felix Lynn, of Northampton county, Pennsylvania, was the undisputed owner of the premises in controversy, and is the source of title common to both parties.

In 1807, Dr. Lynn made his last will and testament, directing the sale by his executors, of certain lands therein described, and authorizing his executors to make deeds for the same to the purchasers; but, in his will, he does not in any way refer to, or mention, specifically, his lands in Ohio, and, at the close of his will, and following immediately after the clause naming his executors, he authorizes them to make and execute all deeds of conveyance, 'according to this, my last will and testament.'

Dr. Lynn having died, on the sixteenth of January, 1809, his will was proved in Northampton county, Pennsylvania, and letters testamentary were issued; but the will was never admitted to probate in Ohio, nor were any other proceedings ever had to effectuate the same under the laws of this state.

On the first day of May, 1809, Dr. Lynn's executors executed in Northampton county, Pa., a deed in fee simple for the land in controversy to George Kintner, reciting therein that Mr. Lynn, in his lifetime, had executed to John Heckawelder a power of attorney, authorizing him to make sale of these lands; that Heckawelder had accordingly entered into contract for their sale to said Kintner, and had received a part of the purchase money thereof in the lifetime of Dr. Lynn; that they, as executors, had received the balance of said purchase money, in consideration of all which, etc., they make the deed. Under this title thus conveyed, and through sundry subsequent conveyances and descents, the plaintiffs claim.

In 1838, the New Philadelphia Lateral Canal Company, being in possession of the premises in dispute, and suspecting the invalidity of the title under which it then held them, procured from the heirs of Dr. Lynn, 'in consideration of one dollar to them in hand paid,' a deed of bargain and sale in fee simple, but without warranty, for the premises.

In January, 1842, the canal company conveyed to Fleming Willet; and in June, 1844, Willet conveyed to the defendant, Graham; and under this title the defendants claim.

Before proceeding to the consideration of the principal questions in the case, it will be proper to observe, that all the deeds above mentioned were duly recorded in the order of their dates; that the circumstances of the case, as they appear in the proofs, are not such as to give rise, on the part of either plaintiffs or defendants, to any claim under the statute of limitations; it is not claimed that the defendants had *actual* notice of plaintiffs' claim to the premises; nor is it urged, in behalf of the plaintiffs, that the conveyance by the executors of Dr. Lynn to Kintner vested in Kintner, or in those claiming under him, a perfect legal title to the premises. And if it were urged, we think it could not be maintained. The will of Dr. Lynn directed certain lands to be sold, but in no way mentioned or referred to *these* lands; it then authorized the executors to make conveyances *according to the will;* and we are of opinion that, by any proper construction of the will, the application of the powers conferred by the latter clause must be restricted by the directions of the former.

But, admitting that the will, by its terms, authorized the executors to convey these Ohio lands, still it could, being a foreign will, have, of itself, no extra-territorial force or effect. To give it effect in Ohio, it was necessary that it be admitted to probate in Ohio;

and, in order to enable the executors to carry into effect the real contracts of the testator, in respect to lands in this state, an order of the court of common pleas of the county in which the lands were situate was requisite. 1 Chase's Stat. 480, 563, 572.

It is, however, claimed by the plaintiffs, that the facts recited in the deed of the executors of Dr. Lynn to Kintner, to wit, that Dr. Lynn, in his lifetime, had authorized Heckawelder to sell these lands; that he had, prior to the death of Lynn, contracted to sell them to Kintner, and received a part of the purchase money; and that the balance of the purchase money was paid by Kintner to the executors, constitute an equitable title in favor of Kintner, and those holding under him, which may be enforced in equity against a subsequent purchaser, with notice. They furthermore claim, that the deed from the executors of Dr. Lynn to Kintner, having been duly recorded, the defendants, claiming under a subsequent deed directly from the heirs of Dr. Lynn, were bound to take notice of the recorded deed from the executors of Lynn to Kintner, and are chargeable with a knowledge of the facts stated in its recitals. And these facts being established in the proofs to our reasonable satisfaction, a question of constructive notice-decisive of this case-is presented.

Were the defendants, being purchasers without *actual* notice of the deed of Dr. Lynn's executors, bound to take notice of that deed, and are they chargeable with knowledge of its recitals?

It is well settled that the record or registry of a deed is constructive notice only to those who claim through or under the grantor by whom such deed was executed. Leiby *v.* Wolf, 10 Ohio, 83; Stuyvesant *v.* Hall, 2 Barb. Ch. 158; Murray *v.* Ballou, 1 Johns. Ch. 574, 575; Keller *v.* Nutz, 5 S. & R. 252, 254; Lightner *v.* Mooney, 10 Watts, 412; Bates *v.* Norcross, 14 Pick. 224. In the last-named case the court say: 'To hold the proprietors of land to take notice of the records of deeds, to determine whether some stranger has, without right, made conveyances of their lands, would be a most dangerous doctrine, and can not be sustained with any color of reason or authority.' 'Where a purchaser can not make out a title, but by a deed which leads him to another fact, he shall be presumed to have notice of such fact.' Fonb. Eq., book 3, ch. 3, sec. 1, note *b*.

'A purchaser of the legal title can not be affected by any latent equity of which he had not actual notice, or which does not appear on some deed necessary to the deduction of his title.' 2 Sugden on Vendors, ch. 17, note 430.

These rules rest on the obvious reason, that a searcher can be fairly supposed to be made acquainted with the contents of such deeds only as, in the process of tracing, link by link, his chain of title on the record, necessarily pass under his inspection.

Now, to apply these rules to the case before us. The grantors in the recorded deed, of which and its recitals it is claimed the defendants were bound to take notice, are the executors of Dr. Lynn; but the defendants do not claim through them; nor do they claim through that deed. They make a perfect legal title without reference to that deed, and did not, and had no occasion to, offer it in evidence. They deduce no title through it, nor from the grantors named in it. They claim title from and through the *heirs* of Dr. Lynn, and not from or through his executors; and as to them, and those under whom they claim, the executors are mere strangers and unauthorized volunteers. This application of well-settled rules is, we think, decisive of the case.

We are of opinion that the defendants are not chargeable with notice of the recitals in the deed from the executors of Dr. Lynn, nor of the latent equities therein disclosed.

Petition dismissed.

§ 8.6.2 Deed Recorded Before Grantor Secured Title

In this next chain of title problem, O conveys to A before O owns the property. A records. O later becomes the owner of the property and then conveys to B, who records. B thereupon conveys to C. The question is this: When C does a title search using the grantor-grantee index and C determines that O owned the property when O conveyed it to B, does C have a duty to continue checking in the grantor-grantee index to see if O conveyed the property previously, before O owned the property? The answer is that there is a split of authority. In some jurisdictions C has such a duty; in others, C does not on the ground that it would be too burdensome to have C check back in time before each grantor in his chain of title to determine who actually owned the property conveyed. The next case is just a slight variation of this hypothetical.

Richardson v. Atlantic Coast Lumber Corp.
93 S.C. 254 (1912)

One B. Talley Richardson conveyed to the Tilghman Lumber Company in 1899. That deed was recorded. The problem was that B. Talley did not own the property; his son, T. Monroe Richardson, owned it. In 1904, T. Monroe conveyed the subject property to B. Talley. B. Talley subsequently re-conveyed the property back to T. Monroe in 1907.

This is a case of chutzpah (Yiddish, meaning, unmitigated gall). T. Monroe—the son of the person who started this problem by conveying land he did not own—sues the defendant Atlantic Coast Lumber (who was authorized by Tilghman to cut down trees on the subject property) for damages for wood cut on the land he originally conveyed away to his father.

There is no question that estoppel by deed is applicable here: that although B Talley did not own the property when he conveyed it in 1899, when he subsequently acquired it from his son in 1904, he was estopped to deny that he previously conveyed the land to Tilghman. See text, chapter 7.

Now, however, the problem is whether T. Monroe can sue Atlantic Lumber for damages. That is to say, does Tilghman own the property? Tilghman does not own the property if the son (T. Monroe) is a subsequent purchaser who did not have constructive notice of the 1899 transaction. The court holds that T. Monroe is not charged with notice of that transaction: that T. Monroe only had to check title as far back as 1904, when B. Talley received the property—from T. Monroe! The court explains:

GARY, C. J.

* * *

The principle is thus stated in Pom. Eq. Jur. vol. 2, § 658: "If the records show a good title vested in the vendor at a certain date, and nothing done by him after that time to impair or encumber the title, it would seem that the policy of the registry acts is thereby accomplished; the purchaser is protected; he is not bound to inquire further back, and to ascertain whether the vendor has done acts which may impair his title, prior to the time at which it was vested in him, as indicated by the records. This view is supported by many decisions--it seems by the weight of authority--which hold that a purchaser need not prosecute a search for deeds or mortgages, made by his own vendor, further back than the time at which the title is shown by the records to have been vested in such vendor; or, in other words, a purchaser is not bound by the registry of deeds or mortgages from his vendor, made prior to that time."

When B. T. Richardson reconveyed the land to T. M. Richardson on the 8th of November, 1907, there was nothing upon the record indicating that B. T. Richardson had ever acquired any other title than that derived from T. M. Richardson on the 22d of October, 1904.

Section 214 of Wade on Notice is as follows: "The purchaser is not charged with notice from the record of conveyances from his grantor, prior to such grantor's acquisition of title. In such cases the subsequent purchaser would not be estopped by the record of a mortgage from his grantor prior to the date of his grantor's deed. To hold otherwise would be to impose on the purchaser the duty of examining the records indefinitely." And in section 216 the same author says: "Upon both principle and authority, it seems more consonant with the recording acts to absolve purchasers from the duty of examining the records for conveyances from their grantors prior to the time when they had a title to convey."

* * *

Note

There also is authority for the view that a subsequent purchaser is obligated to check the grantor-grantee index back in time before any grantor in the chain of title acquired the property in question. See, for example, *Bernardy v. Colonial & U.S. Mort. Co.*, 17 S.D. 637 (1904).

§ 8.6.3 Prior Deed Recorded Late

In the next chain of title problem, O conveys to A in the year 2000. A does not record until 2005. O conveys to B in 2002, who has notice of the O-A conveyance (why this is a key fact will become evident at the end of this chapter). B records immediately in 2002. In 2006, B conveys to C. The question is whether C prevails over A. That is, does C have a duty to check the grantor-grantee index for a prior deed (the O-A deed) that was recorded after the O-B deed was recorded? The answer is, yet again, there is a split of authority. In some jurisdictions, C has a duty to check for earlier deeds recorded late. In other jurisdictions, it is held that C has no such duty because the burden is deemed too great. The next case provides further elucidation.

Rolling "R" Construction, Inc. v. Dodd
477 So.2d 330 (Ala. 1985)

In Jefferson County v. Mosely, *cited and discussed in the instant case, O conveys in 1945 to Jefferson County, which records in April, 1952. In December, 1951, O conveyed the same land to one Mosely, who had notice of the O-Jefferson County conveyance; Mosely recorded in January, 1952. In May, 1952, Mosely conveyed to Peoples. The question is, as between Jefferson County and Peoples, who prevails? The court holds that Peoples prevails, and explains:*

* * *

A purchaser is chargeable with notice of what appears on the face of the instruments in his or her chain of title. *Ball v. Vogtner,* 362 So.2d 894, 897 (Ala.1978); *Union Oil Co. v. Colglazier,* 360 So.2d 965, 969-70 (Ala.1978). However, an instrument outside a purchaser's chain of title does not give constructive notice. In *Jefferson County v. Mosley,* 284 Ala. 593, 226 So.2d 652 (1969), the grantor conveyed a right of way to Jefferson County by deed executed October 18, 1945, and recorded April 2, 1952. The grantor conveyed the fee to Mosley [who had notice of the prior conveyance] by deed executed December 20, 1951, and recorded January 14, 1952. Mosley subsequently conveyed the property to [Peoples on May 26, 1952, recorded on July 7, 1952], who contended that they were bona fide purchasers without notice of Jefferson County's right of way. The court held that the deed from the grantor to Jefferson County did not give constructive notice because it was recorded after the recording of the deed from the grantor to Mosley, through whom the subsequent purchasers [Peoples] derived title. The Court quoted the following passage from American Law of Property, Vol. IV, § 17.21:

" 'If after the recording of a deed from an owner there is later recorded another deed from the same grantor to a different grantee, whether earlier or later in date, a purchaser from the * * * [second] grantee is without notice of any rights of the * * * [first] grantee unless it is by reason of some fact other than the record; the purchaser's obligation to examine the grantor's indices as to that grantor ceased at the date of the recording of the * * * [second] deed. * * *' "

Since the subsequent purchasers [Peoples] had a duty to check the grantor indices under the name of the original grantor until the recording of the deed to Mosley, the later recording of the deed to Jefferson County from the same grantor was outside their chain of title.

* * *

Note

There also is authority for the view that a prior deed recorded late is within the subsequent purchaser's chain of title. See, e.g. *Spaulding v. H.E. Fletcher Co.,* 124 Vt. 318 (1964).

§ 8.6.4 Deed Out From Common Grantor

In this last chain of title problem, O owns Blackacre and Whiteacre, two adjoining parcels. O then conveys Blackacre to A. In the deed conveying Blackacre to A, O grants to A an easement[6] to cross over Whiteacre from Blackacre. A records. Thereafter, O conveys Whiteacre to B. The question is whether the new owner of Whiteacre is burdened with the easement. More specifically, the issue is whether the O-A deed to Blackacre (in which is the grant of the easement across Whiteacre) gives notice to B. That is, does B have a duty to do a title check, not only of Whiteacre (what B purchased), but also Blackacre (the adjoining parcel)? Yet once more, there is a split of authority. The key facts in the next case are virtually identical to the facts in the hypothetical.

Moore v. Center
124 Vt. 277 (1964)

Mr. and Mrs. O own adjacent parcels, Blackacre and Whiteacre. Mr. and Mrs. O convey Blackacre to A. In the deed conveying Blackacre to A, Mr. and Mrs. O also grant to A an easement across the retained Whiteacre. The deed from O to A is recorded. Mr. and Mrs. O subsequently convey Whiteacre to B. B has no actual notice of the easement in the O-A deed. The question is whether B has a duty to do a title search, not only for Whiteacre, but also for adjacent Blackacre. If B does not have a duty, B takes Whiteacre free and clear of the easement in favor of A because B would be a bona fide purchaser for value without notice of the prior conveyance. In Moore v. Center, *however, the court held that B has such a duty. Thus, the easement created across Whiteacre in the O-A deed conveying Blackacre was in B's chain of title with respect to Whiteacre. The court explained:*

HOLDEN, Chief Justice.

* * *

* * * The record of that instrument [the O-A deed] constituted constructive notice of the true state of . . . title . . . . It afforded notice to the grantee of the servitude against the defendant's parcel, since that encumbrance was imposed by the very persons [Mr. and Mrs. O] who are the source of his grant. Flint v. Steadman, 36 Vt. 210, 217; 45 Am.Jur., Records and Recording Laws, §§ 88, 97; 28 C.J.S. Easements § 48 et seq.; 5 Thompson, Real Property § 4127.

The plaintiffs' interest [that is, A's easement] in the defendant's premises [that is, B's ownership of Whiteacre] is not impaired by the fact that the subsequent conveyance in the defendant's chain of title failed to mention it. The clause in the deed from [Mr. and Mrs. O to A] constituted notice of the easement and its corresponding burden on the land which the defendant [B] acquired. Nelson v. Bacon, 113 Vt. 161, 170, 32 A.2d 140; Sargent v. Gagne, supra, 121 Vt. at 9, 147 A.2d 892.

---

[6] [An easement is an interest in another's land allowing the owner of the easement the right to make limited use of the other's land, such as to cross the land to get to a public road. The subject is covered in depth in chapter 11.]

* * *

Note

There is authority for the opposing view: that a deed out from a common grantor does not impart notice to a subsequent purchaser of the retained servient estate (Whiteacre in the previous case). See, e.g., *Glorieux v. Lighthipe*, 96 A. 94 (N.J.Err. & App. 1915).

§ 8.7 The "Shelter Rule"

Recall that in § 8.6.3, "Prior Deed Recorded Late," we started with the introductory hypothetical: O conveyed to A in the year 2000. A did not record until 2005. O thereupon conveyed to B in 2002, who had notice of the O-A conveyance (and we stated that this is a key fact that will become evident at the end of this chapter; that time has now arrived); B recorded immediately, in 2002. In 2006, B conveyed to C. Why was it important to state that B had notice of the O-A conveyance? The reason is this: If B did not have notice of the O-A conveyance, B is a bona fide purchaser for value. Consequently, C would always trump A. Why is this so? This is because of the "shelter rule," which is explored in the next case.

Schulte v. City of Detroit
242 Mich. 152 (1928)

In 1913, one Griffin conveyed property to the City of Detroit (the defendant). The city recorded on June 22, 1914. On April 18, 1914, Griffin conveyed the same parcel to one Day. Day recorded that deed on May 5, 1914. On June 8, 1914, Day entered into a contract to sell the property to one Schulte (the plaintiff); that deed was delivered on June 22, 1914 and recorded on July 9, 1914. Note that the Griffin-City of Detroit deed was recorded before Schulte recorded. Note also that it was beyond dispute that Day was a bona fide purchaser for value. Even if Schulte had actual or constructive notice of the Griffin-City of Detroit conveyance, Schulte prevails over the City. The reason for this is the "shelter rule," which the court will explain.

FELLOWS, J.

On October 23, 1913, Michael J. Griffin and others executed a quitclaim deed to the city of Detroit of a strip of land 10 feet in width off the easterly end of lot 6 of the subdivision of John Keal, deceased, for use for alley purposes. On April 18, 1914, Griffin conveyed the lot in its entirety, and without reservation to one Oliver E. Day, who is made a defendant in this case. This conveyance was recorded May 5, 1914. On June 8th, following, Day entered into an agreement to convey the lot in its entirety to plaintiffs, and on June 22d executed to them a warranty deed thereof, which was recorded July 9, 1914. On the day the deed from Day to plaintiffs was delivered, the deed from Griffin to the city of Detroit was recorded. It is established beyond doubt that both Day and plaintiffs paid a full and adequate consideration for the entire lot, and it is likewise established beyond question that none of them had any knowledge of the deed to the city. Plaintiffs made very valuable improvements on the premises, and their basic value has materially increased. On May 25, 1926, they were served with notice to remove encroachments on the 10-foot strip; said notice being given pursuant to action of common council of defendant city. They thereupon filed this bill to restrain action by the city and its officers and to quiet title. From a decree granting such relief, the city appeals.

As we have stated, the good faith of Day and plaintiffs is established beyond doubt. While Day testifies that he noticed an alley at the rear of the lots, the blueprint attached to defendants' answer shows a 10-foot alley outside of lot 6, and we are satisfied that neither Day nor any of the plaintiffs ever knew, or had reason to know, that the city claimed any rights outside of that strip until the service of the notice in 1926. The city regularly levied general taxes on lot 6, and all special assessments were made on the basis of plaintiffs' ownership of the entire unencumbered lot.

Plaintiffs' grantor, Day, paid full consideration for the lot, bought it without knowledge or notice of any kind that the city claimed any interest in it, and recorded his deed some time before the city recorded its deed. All concede he had a perfect title as against the city. As we view the case, the sole question for our consideration is whether his deed to plaintiffs carried such title to them. The only notice it can be claimed plaintiffs had was constructive notice by reason of the recording of the deed to the city the day they purchased and before their deed was recorded. But we are satisfied that their rights do not rest on the question of notice to them, either actual or constructive. If Day had a perfect title, and all seem to concede he had, it is difficult to perceive how he can be hampered in conveying to any one he sees fit such perfect title. If he may be so hampered, his title is far from perfect and his rights of little value. Both counsel have favored us with exhaustive consideration and citation of cases from other jurisdictions, but we are satisfied our own decisions settle the question. In Godfroy v. Disbrow, Walk. Ch. (Mich.) 260, it was held (quoting from the syllabus):

'Although a party may not himself be a bona fide purchaser without notice, yet, if his grantor was such purchaser, the former is entitled to all his rights, and the protection which the law would give him.'

And in Shotwell v. Harrison, 22 Mich. 410, it was said by Mr. Justice Christiency, speaking for the majority of the court:

'But whether the defendant purchased with or without notice, and whether he paid any consideration or not, he would still hold the title, if Bacon, his grantor, could have held it as a purchaser in good faith and for a valuable consideration; for if Bacon was such purchaser, he had not only a right to hold it, but to dispose of it by sale or donation, or transmit it by descent; and the purchaser, donee, or heir, whatever notice the may have had, would take his title. But if the purchaser from Bacon paid no consideration, his rights would stand exclusively upon Bacon's title, as much as if it had come to him by descent. But a purchaser for value, though having notice of the prior unrecorded deed, would be just as clearly as purchaser in good faith within the meaning and protection of the statute, as if he had purchased without notice of it, if his grantor could have held the property as a bona fide purchaser, for value; since no injury is done by such a purchase to the holder of the prior unrecorded title.'

See, also, Title & Trust Co. v. Jaster, 241 Mich. 417, 217 N. W. 42.

The rule and the reason for the rule is thus stated with a citation of numerous authorities in 27 R. C. L. 684:

'As a general rule, if one is entitled to protection as a bona fide purchaser, he may convey a good title to a subsequent purchaser irrespective of notice on the part of the latter of defects in the title; in other words, a purchaser with notice from a bona fide purchaser without notice succeeds to the rights of the latter and occupies the position of a bona fide purchaser. The reason for this is to prevent a stagnation of property, and because the first purchaser, being entitled to hold and enjoy, must be equally entitled to sell.'

We are satisfied that, when plaintiffs received the deed from Day, they acquired the title and all the title Day had, which was a title superior to, and untrammelled by, any claim of defendant city.

The decree will be affirmed, with costs against defendant city.

SHARPE, C. J., and WIEST, CLARK, and McDONALD, JJ., concur.

CHAPTER 9
SECURITY INTERESTS IN REAL PROPERTY TRANSACTIONS

§ 9.1 Types of Security Interests and Characteristics

When property is acquired by purchase, the buyer typically does not pay cash for the property; rather, the buyer obtains a loan from a bank or other financial institution to help finance the purchase. Of course, when the bank loans the money to the borrower, the bank will insist on securing or collateralizing the loan with the underlying property. This is to protect the bank in the event the borrower defaults on the loan. In this section, you will learn about the various types of security interests that are available in real property transactions.

§ 9.1.1 Mortgages

The first type of security interest is something that everyone has heard of—the mortgage. Initially, it is important to get some basic terms out of the way. The borrower often is referred to as the mortgagor; the lender often is referred to as the mortgagee.

Land Associates, Inc. v. Becker
294 Or. 308 (1982)

Land Associates, Inc. v. Becker, *explains the history of the development of mortgage law. The case also introduces you to a term that you have probably already heard of: "foreclosure." What this term means and how it developed (as a means of stopping abuses by borrowers) is something you will have a better understanding of after you read this case.*

* * *

     In order to understand the issues in this case, it is necessary to examine the history of mortgages to some extent, even though this case is based on a land sales contract,[1] rather than a mortgage. Originally when one borrowed money on his land, he gave title to the land to the one who loaned the money. The borrower, however, could get his land back by paying the entire sum on a certain day of payment called Law Day. If he defaulted and did not pay the sum on that day, he lost all rights to his land. There were times when this absolute deadline resulted in injustices (as when the borrower was

---

[1] [We discuss land sales contracts later in this chapter.]

robbed on his way to Law Day), and the Court of Chancery conceived the idea of equitable redemption to soften this harsh rule. This allowed the borrower to come into court after default, and if he told a convincing story, he was allowed to force a reconveyance of the land. This remedy itself led to abuses, because the borrowers were allowed to reclaim their land years after they should have repaid the money. The Chancery Court, aware of the problems, then created the remedy of foreclosure.[2] Foreclosure was designed to end the period of equitable redemption so that the new owner could be sure that his title was secure and the previous owner could not redeem the land. Foreclosure, then, forecloses the previous owner from exercising the equitable right of redemption. * * *

Mortgage law continued to change; however, the theory underlying mortgages changed from the mortgage giving the lender actual title to the property subject to the right of equitable redemption to the concept that the mortgage only gives the lender a lien on the property. This theory led to foreclosure and sale, rather than the earlier strict foreclosure that was considered equitable under the title theory. Most states, including Oregon, that adopted a lien theory of mortgage also enacted statutory redemption as an additional remedy. The period for statutory redemption starts after the foreclosure and sale itself and is one last chance for the previous owner and any lien creditors to regain the property. It is important to distinguish the two types of redemption--equitable redemption only exists until the interest is foreclosed, while statutory redemption only begins after the interest is foreclosed.

* * *

§ 9.1.2 Deeds of Trust

The next type of secured interest in real property is the deed of trust. The case and the note that follow explain what this security interest is, how it is different from a mortgage—and why, from a lender's perspective, it is superior to a mortgage.

Larchmont Homes, Inc. v. Annandale Water Co., Inc.
201 Va. 178 (1959)

* * *

Black's Law Dictionary (4th ed.) p. 402 defines the term 'conveyance' as follows: 'In real property law. In the strict legal sense, a transfer of legal title to land. In the popular sense, and as generally used by lawyers, it denotes any transfer of title, legal or equitable. * * * An instrument in writing under seal * * * by which some estate or interests in lands is transferred from one person to another; such as a deed, mortgage, etc.'

---

[2] [The foreclosure referred to here is known as a "judicial foreclosure." This means that to foreclose the mortgagor's right of redemption, the mortgagee must institute a civil lawsuit. This is to be contrasted with non-judicial foreclosures, which are found in deeds of trust or power of sale mortgages. We discuss these types of security interests in the next sub-section of text.]

Black defines a deed of trust at page 503 as 'an instrument in use in many states, taking the place and serving the uses of a common law mortgage, by which the legal title to real property is placed in one or more trustees, to secure the repayment of a sum of money or the performance of other conditions.'

In *Ransome v. Watson's Admr.,* 145 Va. 669, 677, 134 S.E. 707, we quoted from Lile's Notes on Equity Jurisprudence, p. 61 wherein it is said:

'In other words, a creditor who puts out his money *specifically on a particular piece of property,* and secures from the borrower a conveyance of the legal title to the property, by way of pledge, mortgage or deed of trust as security for the loan, is, in equity, regarded as a *purchaser for value to the extent of his debt.* And rightly so, since to the extent of his debt he is the *owner,* and has legal title. * * *'

* * *

Notes

1. Modernly, a deed of trust is not a true trust. Rather, in the absence of a default by the borrower, it is a device that gives the lender a lien on (not title to) the property. What, then, is the difference between a mortgage and a deed of trust? In the former, in the event of a default, the mortgagee must resort to the judicial process to sell the property (unless the state permits a power of sale and the mortgage contains a power of sale clause). In the latter, the lender via the trustee can sell the property in a non-judicial sale. Consequently, a deed of trust provides for a more expeditious and inexpensive way of dealing with a borrower who defaults. See, e.g. *Koegel v. Prudential Mut. Sav. Bank,* 51 Wash.App. 108 (1988).

2. Some borrowers who face imminent foreclosure because they cannot pay the mortgage or deed of trust will attempt a "deed in lieu of foreclosure" remedy. In this scenario, the borrower confers with the lender and the parties agree that the borrower will transfer the deed to the lender and, thus, avoid a foreclosure. The lender gets title to the property. The advantage for the borrower is that the borrower avoids having a foreclosure on his or her credit record, is relieved from paying off the balance of the mortgage or deed of trust, and the public knows nothing of the transaction (as with a foreclosure). The advantage for the lender is that it is quick and clean—literally. It is common for the lender to insist at the closing that the property is "broom clean." Why, then, would not every lender want to accept a deed in lieu of foreclosure? The answer is that if there are junior mortgages or deeds of trust on the property (e.g. a second mortgage or second deed of trust), accepting the deed in lieu of foreclosure would result in the senior lender (e.g., the first mortgagee) taking the property subject to a junior lender (e.g., the second mortgagee). The senior lender would probably not want this lien on the property. Hence, the senior lender would opt for a foreclosure because a foreclosure would extinguish these junior liens on the property. We discuss this concept in § 9.2. Thus, the best candidate from the lender's perspective for a deed in lieu of foreclosure is a borrower who has only one mortgage or deed of trust on the property. Note, too, that while a deed in lieu of foreclosure does not have the same disastrous impact that a foreclosure has on a borrower's credit rating, it will still have a significant damaging impact on a credit report.

Murphy v. Financial Development Corp.

126 N.H. 536 (1985)

In Murphy v. Financial Development Corp., *there is a non-judicial foreclosure sale wherein the lender was the only bidder to show up for the sale. The lender, being the only bidder, acquired the property for the balance of the debt. Two days later, the lender resold the property at a substantial profit. That profit effectively represented the equity (value of the property minus the balance due on the mortgage) of the former homeowner. The homeowner sued for damages. Importantly, the lender complied with all legal requirements. Nonetheless, the court will hold the lender liable for at least part of the profit made.*

DOUGLAS, Justice.

The plaintiffs brought this action seeking to set aside the foreclosure sale of their home, or, in the alternative, money damages. The Superior Court (*Bean,* J.), adopting the recommendation of a Master (*R. Peter Shapiro,* Esq.), entered a judgment for the plaintiffs in the amount of $27,000 against two of the defendants, Financial Development Corporation and Colonial Deposit Company (the lenders).

The plaintiffs purchased a house in Nashua in 1966, financing it by means of a mortgage loan. They refinanced the loan in March of 1980, executing a new promissory note and a power of sale mortgage,[3] with Financial Development Corporation as mortgagee. The note and mortgage were later assigned to Colonial Deposit Company. In February of 1981, the plaintiff Richard Murphy became unemployed. By September of 1981, the plaintiffs were seven months in arrears on their mortgage payments, and had also failed to pay substantial amounts in utility assessments and real estate taxes. After discussing unsuccessfully with the plaintiffs proposals for revising the payment schedule, rewriting the note, and arranging alternative financing, the lenders gave notice on October 6, 1981, of their intent to foreclose.

During the following weeks, the plaintiffs made a concerted effort to avoid foreclosure. They paid the seven months' mortgage arrearage, but failed to pay some $643.18 in costs and legal fees associated with the foreclosure proceedings. The lenders scheduled the foreclosure sale for November 10, 1981, at the site of the subject property. They complied with all of the statutory requirements for notice. *See* RSA 479:25.

At the plaintiffs' request, the lenders agreed to postpone the sale until December 15, 1981. They advised the plaintiffs that this would entail an additional cost of $100, and that the sale would proceed unless the lenders received payment of $743.18, as well as all mortgage payments then due, by December 15. Notice of the postponement was posted on the subject property on November 10 at the originally scheduled time of the sale, and was also posted at the Nashua City Hall and Post Office. No prospective bidders were present for the scheduled sale.

In late November, the plaintiffs paid the mortgage payment which had been due in October, but made no further payments to the lenders. An attempt by the lenders to

---

[3] [A power of sale mortgage allows the lender to sell the property in the event of default without court proceedings. In this regard, a power of sale mortgage is similar to a deed of trust and, hence, the reason it is included in this section of the materials.]

arrange new financing for the plaintiffs through a third party failed when the plaintiffs refused to agree to pay for a new appraisal of the property. Early on the morning of December 15, 1981, the plaintiffs tried to obtain a further postponement, but were advised by the lenders' attorney that it was impossible unless the costs and legal fees were paid.

At the plaintiffs' request, the attorney called the president of Financial Development Corporation, who also refused to postpone the sale. Further calls by the plaintiffs to the lenders' offices were equally unavailing.

The sale proceeded as scheduled at 10:00 a.m. on December 15, at the site of the property. Although it had snowed the previous night, the weather was clear and warm at the time of the sale, and the roads were clear. The only parties present were the plaintiffs, a representative of the lenders, and an attorney, Morgan Hollis, who had been engaged to conduct the sale because the lenders' attorney, who lived in Dover, had been apprehensive about the weather the night before. The lenders' representative made the only bid at the sale. That bid of $27,000, roughly the amount owed on the mortgage, plus costs and fees, was accepted and the sale concluded.

Later that same day, Attorney Hollis encountered one of his clients, William Dube, a representative of the defendant Southern New Hampshire Home Traders, Inc. (Southern). On being informed of the sale, Mr. Dube contacted the lenders and offered to buy the property for $27,000. The lenders rejected the offer and made a counter offer of $40,000. Within two days a purchase price of $38,000 was agreed upon by Mr. Dube and the lenders and the sale was subsequently completed.

The plaintiffs commenced this action on February 5, 1982. The lenders moved to dismiss, arguing that any action was barred because the plaintiffs had failed to petition for an injunction prior to the sale. The master denied the motion. After hearing the evidence, he ruled for the plaintiffs, finding that the lenders had "failed to exercise good faith and due diligence in obtaining a fair price for the subject property at the foreclosure sale . . . ."

The master also ruled that Southern was a bona fide purchaser for value, and thus had acquired legal title to the house. That ruling is not at issue here. He assessed monetary damages against the lenders equal to "the difference between the fair market value of the subject property on the date of the foreclosure and the price obtained at said sale."

Having found the fair market value to be $54,000, he assessed damages accordingly at $27,000. He further ruled that "[t]he bad faith of the 'Lenders' warrants an award of legal fees." The lenders appealed.

The first issue before us is whether the master erred in denying the motion to dismiss. The lenders, in support of their argument, rely upon RSA 479:25, II, which gives a mortgagor the right to petition the superior court to enjoin a proposed foreclosure sale, and then provides: "Failure to institute such petition and complete service upon the foreclosing party, or his agent, conducting the sale prior to sale shall thereafter bar any action or right of action of the mortgagor based on the validity of the foreclosure."

If we were to construe this provision as the lenders urge us to do, it would prevent a mortgagor from challenging the validity of a sale in a case where the only claimed unfairness or illegality occurred during the sale itself-unless the mortgagor had petitioned for an injunction before any grounds existed on which the injunction could be granted.

We will not construe a statute so as to produce such an illogical and unjust result. *State v. Howland,* 125 N.H. 497, 500, 484 A.2d 1076, 1078 (1984).

The only reasonable construction of the language in RSA 479:25, II relied upon by the lenders is that it bars any action based on facts which the mortgagor knew or should have known soon enough to reasonably permit the filing of a petition prior to the sale.

The master could not have found that this was such an action, because the only unfairness referred to in his report involves the amount of the sale price. Thus, his denial of the lenders' motion to dismiss was proper.

The second issue before us is whether the master erred in concluding that the lenders had failed to comply with the often-repeated rule that a mortgagee executing a power of sale is bound both by the statutory procedural requirements *and* by a duty to protect the interests of the mortgagor through the exercise of good faith and due diligence. *See, e.g., Carrols Equities Corp. v. Della Jacova,* 126 N.H. 116, 489 A.2d 116 (1985); *Proctor v. Bank of N.H.,* 123 N.H. 395, 464 A.2d 263 (1983); *Meredith v. Fisher,* 121 N.H. 856, 435 A.2d 536 (1981); *Lakes Region Fin. Corp. v. Goodhue Boat Yard, Inc.,* 118 N.H. 103, 382 A.2d 1108 (1978); *Wheeler v. Slocinski,* 82 N.H. 211, 131 A. 598 (1926). We will not overturn a master's findings and rulings "unless they are unsupported by the evidence or are erroneous as a matter of law." *Summit Electric, Inc. v. Pepin Brothers Const., Inc.,* 121 N.H. 203, 206, 427 A.2d 505, 507 (1981).

The master found that the lenders, throughout the time prior to the sale, "did not mislead or deal unfairly with the plaintiffs." They engaged in serious efforts to avoid foreclosure through new financing, and agreed to one postponement of the sale. The basis for the master's decision was his conclusion that the lenders had failed to exercise good faith and due diligence in obtaining a fair price for the property.

This court's past decisions have not dealt consistently with the question whether the mortgagee's duty amounts to that of a fiduciary or trustee. *Compare Pearson v. Gooch,* 69 N.H. 208, 209, 40 A. 390, 390-91 (1897) *and Merrimack Industrial Trust v. First Nat. Bank of Boston,* 121 N.H. 197, 201, 427 A.2d 500, 504 (1981) (duty amounts to that of a fiduciary or trustee) *with Silver v. First National Bank,* 108 N.H. 390, 391, 236 A.2d 493, 494-95 (1967) *and Proctor v. Bank of N.H., supra* 123 N.H. at 400, 464 A.2d at 266 (duty does not amount to that of a fiduciary or trustee). This may be an inevitable result of the mortgagee's dual role as seller and potential buyer at the foreclosure sale, and of the conflicting interests involved. *See Wheeler v. Slocinski,* 82 N.H. at 214, 131 A. at 600.

We need not label a duty, however, in order to define it. In his role as a seller, the mortgagee's duty of good faith and due diligence is essentially that of a fiduciary. Such a view is in keeping with "[t]he 'trend . . . towards liberalizing the term [fiduciary] in order to prevent unjust enrichment.' " *Lash v. Cheshire County Savings Bank, Inc.,* 124 N.H. 435, 438, 474 A.2d 980, 981 (1984) (quoting *Cornwell v. Cornwell,* 116 N.H. 205, 209, 356 A.2d 683, 686 (1976)).

A mortgagee, therefore, must exert every reasonable effort to obtain "a fair and reasonable price under the circumstances," *Reconstruction &c. Corp. v. Faulkner,* 101 N.H. 352, 361, 143 A.2d 403, 410 (1958), even to the extent, if necessary, of adjourning the sale or of establishing "an upset price below which he will not accept any offer." *Lakes Region Fin. Corp. v. Goodhue Boat Yard, Inc.,* 118 N.H. at 107, 382 A.2d at 1111.

What constitutes a fair price, or whether the mortgagee must establish an upset price, adjourn the sale, or make other reasonable efforts to assure a fair price, depends on the circumstances of each case. Inadequacy of price alone is not sufficient to demonstrate bad faith unless the price is so low as to shock the judicial conscience. *Mueller v. Simmons,* 634 S.W.2d 533, 536 (Mo.App.1982); *Rife v. Woolfolk,* 289 S.E.2d 220, 223 (W.Va.1982); *Travelers Indem. Co. v. Heim,* 218 Neb. 326, 352 N.W.2d 921, 923-24 (1984).

We must decide, in the present case, whether the evidence supports the finding of the master that the lenders failed to exercise good faith and due diligence in obtaining a fair price for the plaintiffs' property.

We first note that "[t]he duties of good faith and due diligence are distinct * * * One may be observed and not the other, and any inquiry as to their breach calls for a separate consideration of each." *Wheeler v. Slocinski,* 82 N.H. at 213, 131 A. at 600. In order "to constitute bad faith there must be an intentional disregard of duty or a purpose to injure." *Id.* at 214, 131 A. at 600-01.

There is insufficient evidence in the record to support the master's finding that the lenders acted in bad faith in failing to obtain a fair price for the plaintiffs' property. The lenders complied with the statutory requirements of notice and otherwise conducted the sale in compliance with statutory provisions. The lenders postponed the sale one time and did not bid with knowledge of any immediately available subsequent purchaser. Further, there is no evidence indicating an intent on the part of the lenders to injure the mortgagor by, for example, discouraging other buyers.

There is ample evidence in the record, however, to support the master's finding that the lenders failed to exercise due diligence in obtaining a fair price. "The issue of the lack of due diligence is whether a reasonable man in the [lenders'] place would have adjourned the sale," *id.* at 215, 131 A. at 601, or taken other measures to receive a fair price.

In early 1980, the plaintiffs' home was appraised at $46,000. At the time of the foreclosure sale on December 15, 1981, the lenders had not had the house reappraised to take into account improvements and appreciation. The master found that a reasonable person in the place of the lenders would have realized that the plaintiffs' equity in the property was at least $19,000, the difference between the 1980 appraised value of $46,000 and the amount owed on the mortgage totaling approximately $27,000.

At the foreclosure sale, the lenders were the only bidders. The master found that their bid of $27,000 "was sufficient to cover all monies due and did not create a deficiency balance" but "did not provide for a return of any of the plaintiffs' equity." Further, the master found that the lenders "had reason to know" that "they stood to make a substantial profit on a quick turnaround sale." On the day of the sale, the lenders offered to sell the foreclosed property to William Dube for $40,000. Within two days after the foreclosure sale, they did in fact agree to sell it to Dube for $38,000. It was not necessary for the master to find that the lenders knew of a specific potential buyer before the sale in order to show lack of good faith or due diligence as the lenders contend. The fact that the lenders offered the property for sale at a price sizably above that for which they had purchased it, only a few hours before, supports the master's finding that the lenders had reason to know, at the time of the foreclosure sale, that they could make a substantial profit on a quick turnaround sale. For this reason, they should have taken more measures to ensure receiving a higher price at the sale.

While a mortgagee may not always be required to secure a portion of the mortgagor's equity, such an obligation did exist in this case. The substantial amount of equity which the plaintiffs had in their property, the knowledge of the lenders as to the appraised value of the property, and the plaintiffs' efforts to forestall foreclosure by paying the mortgage arrearage within weeks of the sale, all support the master's conclusion that the lenders had a fiduciary duty to take more reasonable steps than they did to protect the plaintiffs' equity by attempting to obtain a fair price for the property. They could have established an appropriate upset price to assure a minimum bid. They also could have postponed the auction and advertised commercially by display advertising in order to assure that bidders other than themselves would be present.

Instead, as Theodore DiStefano, an officer of both lending institutions testified, the lenders made no attempt to obtain fair market value for the property but were concerned *only* with making themselves "whole." On the facts of this case, such disregard for the interests of the mortgagors was a breach of duty by the mortgagees. Although the lenders *did* comply with the statutory requirements of notice of the foreclosure sale, these efforts were not sufficient in this case to demonstrate due diligence. At the time of the initially scheduled sale, the extent of the lenders' efforts to publicize the sale of the property was publication of a legal notice of the mortgagees' sale at public auction on November 10, published once a week for three weeks in the Nashua Telegraph, plus postings in public places. The lenders did not advertise, publish, or otherwise give notice to the general public of postponement of the sale to December 15, 1981, other than by posting notices at the plaintiffs' house, at the post office, and at city hall. That these efforts to advertise were ineffective is evidenced by the fact that no one, other than the lenders, appeared at the sale to bid on the property. This fact allowed the lenders to purchase the property at a minimal price and then to profit substantially in a quick turnaround sale.

We recognize a need to give guidance to a trial court which must determine whether a mortgagee who has complied with the strict letter of the statutory law has nevertheless violated his additional duties of good faith and due diligence. A finding that the mortgagee had, or should have had, knowledge of his ability to get a higher price at an adjourned sale is the most conclusive evidence of such a violation. *See Lakes Region Fin. Corp. v. Goodhue Boat Yard, Inc.,* 118 N.H. at 107-08, 382 A.2d at 1111.

More generally, we are in agreement with the official Commissioners' Comment to section 3-508 of the Uniform Land Transactions Act:

"The requirement that the sale be conducted in a reasonable manner, including the advertising aspects, requires that the person conducting the sale use the ordinary methods of making buyers aware that are used when an owner is voluntarily selling his land. Thus an advertisement in the portion of a daily newspaper where these ads are placed or, in appropriate cases such as the sale of an industrial plant, a display advertisement in the financial sections of the daily newspaper may be the most reasonable method. In other cases employment of a professional real estate agent may be the more reasonable method. It is unlikely that an advertisement in a legal publication among other legal notices would qualify as a commercially reasonable method of sale advertising." 13 Uniform Laws Annotated 704 (West 1980).

As discussed above, the lenders met neither of these guidelines.

While agreeing with the master that the lenders failed to exercise due diligence in this case, we find that he erred as a matter of law in awarding damages equal to "the difference between the fair market value of the subject property . . . and the price obtained at [the] sale."

Such a formula may well be the appropriate measure where *bad faith* is found. *See Danvers Savings Bank v. Hammer,* 122 N.H. 1, 5, 440 A.2d 435, 438 (1982). In such a case, a mortgagee's conduct amounts to more than mere negligence. Damages based upon the *fair market value,* a figure in excess of a *fair* price, will more readily induce mortgagees to perform their duties properly. A "fair" price may or may not yield a figure close to fair market value; however, it will be that price arrived at as a result of due diligence by the mortgagee.

Where, as here, however, a mortgagee fails to exercise due diligence, the proper assessment of damages is the difference between a fair price for the property and the price obtained at the foreclosure sale. We have held, where lack of due diligence has been found, that "the test is not 'fair market value' as in eminent domain cases nor is the mortgagee bound to give credit for the highest possible amount which might be obtained under different circumstances, as at an owner's sale." *Silver v. First National Bank,* 108 N.H. 390, 392, 236 A.2d 493, 495 (1967) (quoting *Reconstruction &c. Corp. v. Faulkner,* 101 N.H. 352, 361, 143 A.2d 403, 410 (1958)) (citation omitted). Accordingly, we remand to the trial court for a reassessment of damages consistent with this opinion.

Because we concluded above that there was no "bad faith or obstinate, unjust, vexatious, wanton, or oppressive conduct," on the part of the lenders, we see no reason to stray from our general rule that the prevailing litigant is not entitled to collect attorney's fees from the loser. *Harkeem v. Adams,* 117 N.H. 687, 688, 377 A.2d 617, 617 (1977). Therefore, we reverse this part of the master's decision.

Reversed in part; affirmed in part; remanded.

BROCK, J., dissented; the others concurred.

* * *

§ 9.1.3 Installment Land Sale Contracts

Suppose that A wants to purchase property from O for an agreed upon price (e.g. $90,000), but that A's credit rating is low so that A cannot obtain a loan from a bank. Consequently, O and A enter into an installment contract for the sale of O's property. Under the contract, A will pay O $750 per month for 120 months (plus an agreed upon rate of interest). After the final payment is made, O will execute and deliver a deed to A, vesting title in A. The downside of this arrangement for A is that the contract will almost invariably state that if A misses even just one payment, O may reenter and retake possession and that A will forfeit all payments made and all improvements constructed on the property. With a traditional mortgage or deed of trust, the purchaser immediately receives a deed to the property. If the purchaser defaults on the loan, the lender must resort to judicial or non-judicial foreclosure action.

Bean v. Walker

95 A.D.2d 70 (N.Y. 1983)

In Bean v. Walker, *we have a typical installment land sale contract with a default by the buyer after he made many monthly payments. What is untypical about the case is that the court treats the parties, not as promisor-promisee or vendor-vendee, but as mortgagor-mortgagee, with all of the legal consequences that flow from such a characterization.*

      DOERR, Justice.

      Presented for our resolution is the question of the relative rights between a vendor and a defaulting vendee under a land purchase contract.[4] Special Term, in granting summary judgment in favor of plaintiffs, effectively held that the defaulting vendee has no rights. We cannot agree.

      The facts may be briefly stated. In January 1973 plaintiffs agreed to sell and defendants agreed to buy a single-family home in Syracuse for the sum of $15,000.[5] The contract provided that this sum would be paid over a 15- year period at 5% interest, in monthly installments of $118.62. The sellers retained legal title to the property which they agreed to convey upon payment in full according to the terms of the contract. The purchasers were entitled to possession of the property, and all taxes, assessments and water rates, and insurance became the obligation of the purchasers. The contract also provided that in the event purchasers defaulted in making payment and failed to cure the default within 30 days, the sellers could elect to call the remaining balance immediately due or elect to declare the contract terminated and repossess the premises. If the latter alternative was chosen, then a forfeiture clause came into play whereby the seller could retain all the money paid under the contract as "liquidated" damages and "the same shall be in no event considered a penalty but rather the payment of rent."

      Defendants went into possession of the premises in January 1973 and in the ensuing years claim to have made substantial improvements on the property. They made the required payments under the contract until August 1981 when they defaulted following an injury sustained by defendant Carl Walker. During the years while they occupied the premises as contract purchasers defendants paid to plaintiff $12,099.24, of which $7,114.75 was applied to principal. Thus, at the time of their default, defendants had paid almost one-half of the purchase price called for under the agreement. After the required 30-day period to cure the default,[6] plaintiffs commenced this action sounding in ejectment seeking a judgment "that they be adjudged the owner in fee" of the property and granting them possession thereof. The court granted summary judgment to plaintiffs.

      If the only substantive law to be applied to this case was that of contracts, the result reached would be correct. However, under the facts presented herein the law with

---

[4] [A land purchase contract also is referred to as an installment land sale contract or a contract for deed.]

[5] The house now has an alleged market value of $44,000.

[6] Defendant's offer to bring the payments up-to-date and pay a higher interest rate on the balance due were unavailing.

regard to the transfer of real property must also be considered. The reconciliation of what might appear to be conflicting concepts is not insurmountable.

While there are few New York cases which directly address the circumstances herein presented, certain general principles may be observed. "It is well settled that the owner of the real estate from the time of the execution of a valid contract for its sale is to be treated as the owner of the purchase money and the purchaser of the land is to be treated as the equitable owner thereof. The purchase money becomes personal property" (*New York C. & H. R.R. Co. v. Cottle*, 187 App.Div. 131, 144, 175 N.Y.S. 178 affd. 229 N.Y. 514, 129 N.E. 896). Thus, notwithstanding the words of the contract and implications which may arise therefrom, the law of property declares that, upon the execution of a contract for sale of land, the vendee acquires equitable title.* * * The vendor holds the legal title in trust for the vendee and has an equitable lien for the payment of the purchase price * * * The vendee in possession, for all practical purposes, is the owner of the property with all the rights of an owner subject only to the terms of the contract. The vendor may enforce his lien by foreclosure or an action at law for the purchase price of the property--the remedies are concurrent.* * * The conclusion to be reached, of course, is that upon the execution of a contract an interest in real property comes into existence by operation of law, superseding the terms of the contract. An analogous result occurs in New York if an owner purports to convey title to real property as security for a loan; the conveyance is deemed to create a lien rather than an outright conveyance, even though the deed was recorded (*Schulte v. Cleri*, 39 A.D.2d 692, 332 N.Y.S.2d 518) and "one who has taken a deed absolute in form as security for an obligation, in order to foreclose the debtor's right to redeem, must institute a foreclosure, and is entitled to have the premises sold in the usual way" (14 Carmody-Wait 2d, § 92:2, p. 612).[7]

Cases from other jurisdictions are more instructive. In *Skendzel v. Marshall,* 261 Ind. 226, 301 N.E.2d 641, the court observed that while legal title does not vest in the vendee until the contract terms are satisfied, he does acquire a vested equitable title at the time the contract is consummated. When the parties enter into the contract all incidents of ownership accrue to the vendee who assumes the risk of loss and is the recipient of all appreciation of value. The status of the parties becomes like that of mortgagor-mortgagee.[8] Viewed otherwise would be to elevate form over substance (*Skendzel v. Marshall,* supra, p. 234, 301 N.E.2d 641). The doctrine that equity deems as done that which ought to be done is an appropriate concept which we should apply to the present case.

Where sale of real property is evidenced by contract only and the purchase price has not been paid and is not to be paid until some future date in accordance with the terms of the agreement, the parties occupy substantially the position of mortgagor and

---

[7] [It is a fundamental principle in the common law, not just in New York, that equity will treat a deed, absolute on its face, as a mortgage when the parties intended it to be security for a loan. See, e.g., *Helvering v. F. & R. Lazarus & Co.*, 308 U.S. 252 (1939). See also 59 C.J.S. Mortgages § 52.]

[8] New York recognizes the similarity between mortgages and contracts for sale by noting that the latter "shall be deemed to be mortgages for purposes of paying the mortgage recording tax" (Tax Law, § 250).

mortgagee at common law. In New York a mortgage merely creates a lien rather than conveying title (*Moulton v. Cornish*, 138 N.Y. 133, 33 N.E. 842), but this was not always so. At common law the mortgage conveyed title, and it was to protect the buyer from summary ejectment that Courts of Equity evolved the concept of "equitable" title as distinct from "legal" title.* * * The doctrine of equitable conversion had important consequences. The equitable owner suffered the risk of loss * * * as does a contract vendee in possession today, * * * but concomitantly, the equitable owner was also entitled to any increase in value; "since a purchaser under a binding contract of sale is in equity regarded as the owner of the property, he is entitled to any benefit or increase in value that may accrue to it." * * * Similarly, upon the parties' death, the vendor's interest is regarded as personal property (i.e., the right to receive money), while the vendee's interest is treated as real property (*Barson v. Mulligan*, supra, 191 N.Y. at p. 313-314, 84 N.E. 75).

Because the common-law mortgagor possessed equitable title, the legal owner (the mortgagee) could not recover the premises summarily, but had to first extinguish the equitable owner's equity of redemption. Thus evolved the equitable remedy of mortgage foreclosure, which is now governed by statute (RPAPL, § 1301 et seq.). In our view, the vendees herein occupy the same position as the mortgagor at common law; both have an equitable title only, while another person has legal title. We perceive no reason why the instant vendees should be treated any differently than the mortgagor at common law. Thus the contract vendors may not summarily dispossess the vendees of their equitable ownership without first bringing an action to foreclose the vendees' equity of redemption. This view reflects the modern trend in other jurisdictions. * * *

The key to the resolution of the rights of the parties lies in whether the vendee under a land sale contract has acquired an interest in the property of such a nature that it must be extinguished before the vendor may resume possession. We hold that such an interest exists since the vendee acquires equitable title and the vendor merely holds the legal title in trust for the vendee, subject to the vendor's equitable lien for the payment of the purchase price in accordance with the terms of the contract. The vendor may not enforce his rights by the simple expedient of an action in ejectment but must instead proceed to foreclose the vendee's equitable title or bring an action at law for the purchase price, neither of which remedies plaintiffs have sought.

The effect of the judgment granted below is that plaintiffs will have their property with improvements made over the years by defendants, along with over $7,000 in principal payments on a purchase price of $15,000, and over $4,000 in interest. The basic inequity of such a result requires no further comment (see, *Hudson v. Matter*, 219 App.Div. 252, 219 N.Y.S. 555; *Gerder Servs. v. Johnson*, 109 Misc.2d 216, 439 N.Y.S.2d 794).[9] If a forfeiture would result in the inequitable disposition of property and an exorbitant monetary loss, equity can and should intervene.* * *

---

[9] Some jurisdictions refuse to enforce the forfeiture provision of a land contract if the proportion of the purchase price paid is so substantial that the amount forfeited would be an invalid "penalty" (see, e.g., *Hook v. Bomar*, 320 F.2d 536 (5th Cir.1963) [applying Florida law]; *Rothenberg v. Follman*, 19 Mich.App. 383, 172 N.W.2d 845 (1969); *Morris v. Sykes*, 624 P.2d 681 [Utah 1981]; *Johnson v. Carman*, 572 P.2d 371 [Utah 1977]; *Behrendt v. Abraham*, 64

The interest of the parties here can only be determined by a sale of the property after foreclosure proceedings with provisions for disposing of the surplus or for a deficiency judgment. In arguing against this result, plaintiffs stress that in New York a defaulting purchaser may not recover money paid pursuant to an executory contract (*Lawrence v. Miller*, 86 N.Y. 131). Although we have no quarrel with this general rule of law,* * * we observe that this rule has generally been applied to cases involving down payments,* * * or to cases wherein the vendee was not in possession.[Citations omitted.]

By our holding today we do not suggest that forfeiture would be an inappropriate result in all instances involving a breach of a land contract. If the vendee abandons the property and absconds, logic compels that the forfeiture provisions of the contract may be enforced. Similarly, where the vendee has paid a minimal sum on the contract and upon default seeks to retain possession of the property while the vendor is paying taxes, insurance and other upkeep to preserve the property, equity will not intervene to help the vendee * * *. Such is not the case before us.

Accordingly, the judgment should be reversed, the motion should be denied and the matter remitted to Supreme Court for further proceedings in accordance with this Opinion.

Judgment unanimously reversed with costs, motion denied and matter remitted to Supreme Court, Onondaga County, for further proceedings, in accordance with opinion by Doerr, J.

DILLON, P.J., and DENMAN, BOOMER and SCHNEPP, JJ., concur.

Burgess v. Shiplet
230 Mont. 387 (1988)

Not all jurisdictions take the approach of New York and Bean v. Walker, *as this case demonstrates.*

HUNT, Justice.

This contract dispute is appealed to this Court from the Sixth Judicial District, Park County. Ronald Burgess, John Lake and Nick Mallas appeal the judgment of the District Court which treated respondents' purchase of land from appellants, under a contract for deed, as a mortgage. The appellants also allege error by the court in failing to award them reasonable attorney fees and damages.

We reverse and remand to the District Court.

The issues presented are as follows:

1. Did the District Court err in treating a contract for deed as an equitable mortgage?

2. * * *

3. * * *

4. * * *

5. Did the District Court err in failing to award damages?

Cal.2d 182, 49 Cal.Rptr. 292, 410 P.2d 828 (1966); *Land Development, Inc. v. Padgett*, 369 P.2d 888 [Alaska 1962]).

Respondents Robert, Jacqueline and Tami Shiplet purchased land from Shields River Bench, a partnership owned by appellants. The first tract was purchased by Robert and Jacqueline Shiplet in 1980 for $110,000. They paid $21,500 down with annual payments of $12,017. The second tract was purchased by Robert, Jacqueline and Tami (daughter) Shiplet in 1981 for $110,000. They paid $10,000 down with annual payments of $13,575. The respondents have been in possession of both tracts of land since the dates of closing on the sales. The last payment made on the 1980 contract was on May 11, 1984. The last payment made on the 1981 contract was June 27, 1983.

Appellants unsuccessfully attempted to serve default notices on the respondents, first by certified mail, then by service by the Park County Sheriff. However, respondents refused to accept the notices. Finally, after the appellants filed suit, the court ordered the respondent's attorney to accept all default notices on behalf of the Shiplets. Notices of default and continuing default were then served on the Shiplets' attorney on July 1, 1986, and September 3, 1986.

For the purposes of trial, the two causes of action, one on each contract, were consolidated. The Shiplets counterclaimed with allegations of breach of contract because appellants failed to control noxious weeds on their property; failed to establish a homeowner's association in the proposed subdivision where Shiplets purchased their land; and failed to buy gravel from the Shiplets in lieu of an annual payment under their contract.

After a bench trial, the District Court made findings of fact and conclusions of law and entered judgment against the respondents for default on the contracts for deed. The court also found that the appellants breached the contracts for not fulfilling the protective covenants and for violating their statutory obligation to control noxious weeds on their property. The court then granted the respondents one year right of redemption on the contracts beginning June 24, 1987.

Appellants contend that the District Court erred by treating the contract for deed as a mortgage.

Subsequent to the District Court's findings of fact and conclusions of law in the case now before us, this Court, in December 1987, held that "(a) contract for deed is not the same legal concept as a mortgage under Montana law." *Aveco Properties, Inc. v. Nicholson* (Mont.1987), 747 P.2d 1358, 44 St.Rep. 2098, 2102. See also *Glacier Campground v. Wild Rivers, Inc.* (1979), 182 Mont. 389, 184 Mont. 543, 597 P.2d 689, (a contract for deed and a mortgage are "distinct legal creatures.")

When a purchaser enters into a contract for deed with a seller, he or she runs the risk of defaulting on the required payments and facing the consequences of losing the property along with forfeiting the amount already paid. If this produces a harsh or unwanted result, it is for the legislature to remedy and not the job of this court to change the plain meaning of the contract.

In the case before us, the contract for deed provides that upon their default buyers have 30 days in which to correct the default or sellers are entitled to demand, within 30 days, full payment of the unpaid balance of the purchase price plus accrued interest. If the buyer fails to pay the total unpaid balance in 30 days, the agreement terminates and the property is returned to seller.

The District Court found that respondents/buyers defaulted on both contracts which they had with appellants/sellers. The default provisions under the contract for deed spells out the remedies available to appellants. Respondents cannot look to mortgage law for alternative remedies but must accept the remedies set forth in their contract with appellants. We reverse on the first issue.

* * *

Respondents had paid a total of $65,357.49 principal on the combined contracts when they stopped making payments. However, they still owed $154,642.51 on the principal plus accrued interest. Respondents lived on the property, farmed the land and kept all income from it since 1980 on one parcel and since 1981 on the other. They have continued to possess, enjoy and reap the benefits from the property without making any payments on it since June, 1983, on the first contract and May, 1984, on the second contract. Appellants, on the other hand, have been denied either payments on or possession of the property while still being responsible for their own payment obligations for the same land. We hold that the District Court * * * should have awarded forfeiture of the amount already paid by the Shiplets to appellants.

* * *

The District Court did not award attorney fees because "each party is in default." Since we held that appellants were not in default, they are entitled to attorney fees from the Shiplets pursuant to the parties' agreement. The contract provides for reasonable attorney fees to the prevailing party in the event an action is brought to enforce the terms of the contract. We remand to the District Court to make findings and award reasonable attorney fees to appellants.

The District Court found that the appellants were not entitled to damages for respondents' default on the contract. However, § 27-1-311, MCA, allows for damages arising from the breach of a contract. We remand to the District Court to determine what, if any, damages appellants may be entitled to under that statute as a result of Shiplet's breach.

Reversed and remanded to the District Court.

§ 9.2 Priority of Creditors

§ 9.2.1 In General

In discussing priorities of creditors, what we are dealing with are first and second mortgages (or deeds of trust). Thus, we need to explain first and second mortgages (or deeds of trust). In this regard, consider this hypothetical. O and A agree that A will purchase O's home for $100,000. A has $10,000 cash to put down as a down payment and gets a $90,000 loan, secured by a mortgage (or deed of trust) from Bank X. Several years after moving in, A wants to remodel his kitchen for $10,000. A, however, does not have the cash to do the remodel. Consequently, A goes to Bank Y and gets a $10,000 loan, secured by a second mortgage (or deed of trust). Thus, A now has a first mortgage for $90,000 (Bank X is the mortgagee on the first mortgage or the holder of the first deed of trust) and a second mortgage for $10,000 (Bank Y is the mortgagee on the second mortgage or the holder of the second deed of trust). What we next deal with is the situation where (1) A defaults on the first mortgage (or deed of trust) and, in the *alternative (2) A defaults on the second mortgage (or deed of trust), and the legal consequences of such defaults.*

Strobe v. Downer

13 Wis. 10 (1860)

A borrower executed a first mortgage in favor of one Weimar. This mortgage was recorded. It later was assigned but not recorded. The borrower later executed a second mortgage. This mortgage was assigned, too. What followed was an action by the assignee of the second mortgage to foreclose on the second mortgage. The first mortgagee (Weimar, not the assignee of Weimar) was made a party to the suit. The question that the court addresses is this: If the first mortgagee had still owned the mortgage to the property, what would the effect of the foreclosure action on the second mortgage be on the first mortgagee's interest? The court holds that a foreclosure action on a second mortgage has no effect on the first mortgage. The buyer in the foreclosure action of the second mortgage takes subject to the first mortgage. Thus, it is irrelevant that the first mortgagee—and not his assignee—was named as a party. The court explained:

By the Court, PAINE, J.

* * *

But we are of the opinion that the rights of Weimar [the first mortgagee] would not have been divested by the foreclosure and sale, even if he had still held the first mortgage. His mortgage was a prior encumbrance to the one being foreclosed, and of course the right under it was paramount both to the rights of the mortgagor and to those of the owner of the second mortgage. As such he was not a necessary party to the foreclosure suit on the second. And if made a party, without any allegation contesting his title, he had a right to assume that the proceeding was to be conducted upon the theory that his claim was paramount, and therefore not subject to it. * * * What was the first mortgagee called on to defend against? It was stated in the complaint that he claimed an interest, and there was no allegation against its validity which called on him to defend. He had a right to assume that, without answering his rights were not to be affected by the proceeding. This conclusion is fully sustained by the case of *Williamson vs. Probasco,* 4 Halst. Ch., 571. Assuming here that Weimar still owned the first mortgage, that case is in every respect like this, with one exception. The first mortgagee was there made a party, and his mortgage and its priority were expressly stated in the complaint. The decree, however, as in this case, barred all the parties of all right, etc., in the premises. But it was held that this had no effect upon the rights of the first mortgagee. The fact that there the priority of the first mortgage was expressly stated in the complaint, does not vary the principle. It only makes its application a little clearer. But there was really nothing more in this complaint tending to impeach or put at issue the prior right of the first mortgagee, than there was in that. Indeed, it is fairly implied from the face of the complaint, that the interest claimed by Weimar was prior and paramount to the second mortgage. * * *

Note

If a borrower defaults on a first mortgage (but not the second), the buyer at the foreclosure sale takes free and clear of any junior mortgages if the first mortgagee makes the junior mortgagees parties to the action. See, e.g., *South Bay Bldg. Enterprises, Inc. v. Riviera Lend-Lease, Inc.*, 72 Cal.App.4th 1111 (1999) (junior liens are extinguished unless bidder purchases at a price sufficiently high to pay off both senior and junior liens). Nonetheless, the borrower may still be personally liable on the debt, subject to any anti-deficiency statute. Anti-deficiency statutes are discussed in section 9.3.

§ 9.2.2 Subrogation

Subrogation, in the context of secured real property transactions, arises when a secured junior lender steps into the shoes of a secured senior lender, with all of the rights attached thereto. Why this happens, under what circumstances, and the extent of the subrogee's rights are explained in Countrywide Home Loans, Inc. v. Schmidt.

Countrywide Home Loans, Inc. v. Schmidt

306 Wis.2d 200 (2007)

BROWN, C.J.

¶ 1 Equitable subrogation is a doctrine whereby one who has paid off another's mortgage obligation is treated as the owner of that obligation. In this case, Countrywide Home Loans, Inc. lent Gary Schmidt $360,000 secured by a home mortgage. There was a problem, though-at the time Countrywide lent Schmidt the money, the house was no longer Schmidt's to mortgage. Jeanne Mayer had contracted to buy it for $300,000 and had sued Schmidt for specific performance when he tried to back out on the deal, all before Countrywide entered the picture. Eventually, realizing that Mayer's superior claim on the property rendered its $360,000 mortgage worthless, Countrywide fell back on the fact that it had paid off two prior mortgages totaling about $260,000. The circuit court allowed Countrywide to recoup the $260,000, but Countrywide claims it is entitled to more: it wants Mayer to pay interest on the old mortgages [which carried a higher rate of interest than the new Countrywide mortgage], along with taxes and insurance that it paid, all adding up to $320,000-or $20,000 more than Mayer's purchase price for the property. It claims that *Iowa County Bank v. Pittz*[10] establishes the "bright-line rule" that this is what an equitable subrogee gets. We disagree and affirm the circuit court. Equitable subrogation is a creature of equity, the object of which is to do substantial justice independent of form or contract relation between the parties. The *Pittz* court did substantial justice on the facts of the case before it, and we cannot say the circuit court here did not do the same.

¶ 2 The relevant facts are undisputed. Schmidt owned a property at 308 W. Wisconsin Ave. in Pewaukee. In 2002, Schmidt took out two loans from two different

---

[10] *Iowa County Bank v. Pittz*, 192 Wis. 83, 211 N.W. 134 (1926).

banks, one for $176,000 and one for $90,000, and issued each bank a mortgage on the property. In September 2003, Schmidt accepted Jeanne Mayer's offer to buy the property for $300,000, but in October he tried to rescind the deal and Mayer sued for specific performance. Mayer also recorded a lis pendens with the Waukesha register of deeds, and though the lis pendens correctly described the location of the property at issue, it was incorrectly captioned "Milwaukee County." Mayer later recorded a corrected lis pendens.

¶ 3 In November 2003, while Mayer's suit was pending, Schmidt obtained a loan from Countrywide for $363,750. Countrywide paid off the mortgages to the prior banks for a total of $260,275.07, with the remainder of the money going to Schmidt. Schmidt gave a mortgage to Countrywide for $363,750. This mortgage was recorded in February 2004.

¶ 4 In September 2004, Mayer won her lawsuit against Schmidt in the circuit court and was awarded specific performance. Schmidt appealed.

¶ 5 In November 2004, Countrywide began a separate action against Schmidt, seeking to foreclose on its mortgage for nonpayment. It named Mayer as a defendant by virtue of her judgment against Schmidt. Mayer answered that her interest in the property was superior to Countrywide's mortgage. She then moved for summary judgment, arguing that her lis pendens along with her specific performance judgment prevailed over Countrywide's mortgage.

¶ 6 The summary judgment motion was put on hold while the parties awaited this court's decision in the Schmidt-Mayer specific performance case. In the meantime, Countrywide amended its complaint to add its equitable subrogation claim. In November 2005, this court affirmed the grant of specific performance to Mayer.

¶ 7 On the summary judgment motion in this action, Mayer and Countrywide stipulated that Countrywide was entitled to equitable subrogation, but disputed the amount it was due. The circuit court sided with Mayer, stating that the equities were in her favor and allowing Countrywide only the $260,275.07 it had paid to the prior mortgagees. Countrywide appeals.

* * *

¶ 9 Turning to the central issue of this case, Countrywide claims that "Wisconsin law is clear that a party who is deemed the equitable subrogee of a paramount lien is entitled to 'have it maintained as it was originally.' " That is, Countrywide argues that an equitable subrogee "steps into the shoes" of the original lienholder and is entitled to receive whatever that original lienholder would have received had the original debt not been paid off. Had the banks holding the two original mortgages not been paid off, interest would have continued to accumulate after the closing date, during the pendency of the specific performance suit, and right up until the deal was done and the mortgage notes were paid. Thus, Countrywide argues, relying chiefly on *Pittz,* that it is entitled to this same interest.

¶ 10 We do not agree that *Pittz* established a "bright-line rule" that an equitable subrogee may always have interest at the rate of the prior mortgage. * * *

* * *

¶ 15 It is plain that what the court did in *Pittz* was balance the equities between the parties. * * *

* * *

¶ 18 [W]e view *Pittz* as a textbook case of balancing the equities. It is often stated that the equitable subrogation rule can only be applied to the extent that does not injure innocent third parties. *See Rock River Lumber Corp.,* 82 Wis.2d at 241, 262 N.W.2d 114; Restatement (Third) of Property: Mortgages § 7.6(b)(4) (1997) (subrogation is appropriate if it "will not materially prejudice the holders of intervening interests in the real estate"). The bank in *Pittz* was not injured by Pittz's equitable subrogation because the bank's interest remained the same as it would have been had Pittz not paid off the first mortgage and taken a second.

¶ 19 Countrywide argues that the situation here is the same: had Countrywide not paid off the two earlier mortgages, they would still be in place and accumulating interest at their old [higher] rates. Thus, Countrywide being subrogated to those loans leaves Mayer no worse off than she was before the old mortgages were refinanced. But the facts remain that the mortgages *were* refinanced, and that, until fairly recently, the total amount "due" on those mortgages has been less than Mayer's $300,000 purchase price. Because of these two facts, during Mayer's legal battles of the past four years, she has been operating under the reasonable assumption that if she were successful in her specific performance case, she could get what she bargained for.

¶ 20 Mayer filed her specific performance suit in October 2003. In November 2004, she was named in Countrywide's foreclosure action, and presumably learned that the two prior mortgages had been paid off. Looking to the record, we find that it was not until August 2005 that Countrywide first made its equitable subrogation claim, thus potentially putting the two old mortgages back in play. Not until August 2006, in its summary judgment brief, did Countrywide announce that it was seeking to enforce those old mortgages in an amount *greater* than Mayer's purchase price for the property. Mayer had little or no reason to be concerned about the old mortgages until Countrywide claimed that it had the right to enforce them for more than $300,000. She might well have conducted herself differently throughout the proceedings had she known that interest was "accumulating" on mortgages that no longer existed: for example, she could have walked away from the transaction, or asked the court to order Schmidt to make the necessary payments to preserve the status quo. It is simply not true that Mayer is no worse off if Countrywide is allowed equitable subrogation that exceeds her bargained-for purchase price.

¶ 21 Of course it is not Countrywide's fault that Schmidt delayed the sale of the property so that the original mortgages would now cost more than $300,000 to pay off, but neither is it Mayer's. Mayer's actions in this transaction and its attendant litigation are blameless, and the circuit court clearly had this in mind when it found that equity required that she be held harmless-just as the supreme court held the bank harmless for its good-faith dealings in *Pittz. See Pittz* at 92-93, 211 N.W. 134. The circuit court thus allowed Mayer to enforce her contract as written, and not pay Countrywide more than the purchase price of the property for mortgages it did not hold.[11]

¶ 22 Countrywide's last claim is that the circuit court erroneously exercised its discretion by citing "undefined equitable principles" to limit Countrywide's recovery in

---

[11] As for the difference between the $300,000 purchase price and the $260,000 the circuit court awarded Countrywide, we note along with Mayer that Countrywide may pursue Schmidt for the money that he still owes on its loan.

this case. We cannot deny that the circuit court, in giving its oral decision in this case, did not state its reasoning as clearly as it might have. Nevertheless, the circuit court did note that its role in the case was to do equity, and that the equities weighed in favor of Mayer. Each side capably put forth its factual and legal arguments below, and we are confident that the circuit court weighed them in its decision. Further, even when the circuit court does not adequately explain its reasoning, we may search the record to determine if it supports the court's discretionary decision. *Randall v. Randall,* 2000 WI App 98, ¶ 7, 235 Wis.2d 1, 612 N.W.2d 737. As our discussion above shows, we have no trouble here concluding that it does.

Judgment affirmed.

§ 9.3 Matters of Personal Liability

A borrower who has personal liability on a loan is potentially liable for a deficiency if the proceeds from the foreclosure sale are insufficient to cover the amount due on a loan in default. The issue that we deal with in this section is the legal consequences that flow from a foreclosure sale when the sale proceeds are not sufficient to pay off the mortgage or deed of trust.

§ 9.3.1 Anti-Deficiency Statutes

Many jurisdictions have so-called anti-deficiency statutes. These statutes provide that in the event that foreclosure sale proceeds are not sufficient to pay off the mortgage or deed of trust, the lender cannot look to the personal assets of the borrower to satisfy the deficiency.

Bank of Sonoma County v. Dorries
185 Cal.App.3d 1291 (1986)

The Bank of Sonoma County *case explains the history and rationale of anti-deficiency statutes, as well as its application in a non-traditional setting: application of the anti-deficiency statute to a mobile home.*

WHITE, Presiding Justice.
Respondent, Bank of Sonoma (Bank), sued appellant Norman Dorries for the balance due on a purchase money security agreement. The trial court granted the Bank's motion for summary judgment. Appellant filed a timely notice of appeal.

Statement of Facts
On November 18, 1980, appellant purchased a mobile home pursuant to a security agreement. The security agreement was subsequently assigned to respondent Bank. The agreement called for installment payments, secured by the mobile home. The agreement provided that in the event of a default by appellant, the Bank could either obtain a judgment for the balance owed, or repossess and sell the mobile home.

When appellant stopped making the payments as they became due, the Bank sued appellant for the balance owing: $32,560.57. Based upon the absence of any effort by the Bank to foreclose on the security, appellant raised as an affirmative defense the mobile home anti-deficiency statute, section 2983.8 of the California Civil Code.

The trial court rejected appellant's defense, and granted the Bank's motion for summary judgment.

DISCUSSION

The sole issue which faces this court in the present case is this: Does the anti-deficiency statute (Civ.Code, § 2983.8) bar a money judgment under a mobile home purchase money agreement? We find that it does and therefore reverse the trial court judgment.

Civil Code section 2983.8 provides in pertinent part: "Notwithstanding Section 2983.2 or any other provision of law, no deficiency judgment shall lie in any event in any of the following instances:

"(a) After any sale of any mobilehome [*sic*] * * * for failure of the purchaser to complete his conditional sale contract given to the seller to secure payment of the balance of the purchase price of such mobilehome [*sic*]."

This section appears to have been patterned after section 580b of the Code of Civil Procedure which provides in pertinent part: "No deficiency judgment shall lie in any event after any sale of real property for failure of the purchaser to complete his contract of sale * * * given to the vendor to secure payment of the balance of the purchase price of real property * * * *"

Section 580b was enacted in 1933 in response to the economic problems facing the country following the Great Depression. The major purpose of the statute is to prevent aggravation of the downturn in depression times. (*Heckes v. Sapp* (1964) 229 Cal.App.2d 549, 552, 40 Cal.Rptr. 485.) In 1972 the legislature enacted section 2983.8, an anti-deficiency statute which applies to mobile homes. The legislative history surrounding the enactment of the section reveals that similar to anti-deficiency statutes which apply to real property, the legislature intended to avoid saddling people who encounter such economic adversity as to cause them to lose their homes with the financial hardship of continuing to make payments on a mobile home in which they no longer live.

"When legislation has been judicially construed and a subsequent statute on the same or an analogous subject is framed in the identical language, it will ordinarily be presumed that the Legislature intended that the language as used in the later enactment would be given a like interpretation." (*Los Angeles Met. Transit Authority v. Brotherhood of Railroad Trainmen* (1960) 54 Cal.2d 684, 688, 8 Cal.Rptr. 1, 355 P.2d 905.)

Thus, in the instant case, since there is sparse legal interpretation of section 2983.8, and a significant amount of authority interpreting section 580b, and given the similar purpose and nearly identical wording of the statutes, we shall turn to the authority governing section 580b in deciding this issue.

Respondent Bank asserts that section 2983.8 does not apply to this case since respondent does not seek a "deficiency" (an amount of the loan not recovered due to a low resale value of the property), but rather seeks to recover the entire amount left owing on the loan. This argument has been considered and rejected by the courts interpreting section 580b. For example, in *Brown v. Jensen* (1953) 41 Cal.2d 193, 259 P.2d 425, the plaintiff urged the theory respondent proposes: that inasmuch as there had not been a sale by plaintiff within the wording of section 580b, the section did not apply. (*Id.,* at p. 196, 259 P.2d 425.) The court declined to adopt the theory, stating instead: "Indeed the purpose of section 580b is that '* * * for a purchase money mortgage or deed of trust *the security alone can be looked to for recovery of the debt.*' " (*Id.,* at p. 198, 259 P.2d 425, quoting *Mortgage Guarantee Co. v. Sampsell* (1942) 51 Cal.App.2d 180, 124 P.2d 353, emphasis added.)

Similarly, in *Venable v. Harmon* (1965) 233 Cal.App.2d 297, 43 Cal.Rptr. 490, the court commented: "Since only the land can be called upon to satisfy the debt, under *Brown* [*v. Jensen, supra,* 41 Cal.2d 193, 259 P.2d 425], the fact *that there has not been a prior sale is of no moment.*" (*Id.,* at p. 302, 43 Cal.Rptr. 490, emphasis added.) This conclusion was also reached in *Hersch and Co. v. C and W Manhattan Associates* (9th Cir.1982) 700 F.2d 476.

Respondent's argument therefore is not meritorious. Section 2983.8 of the Civil Code does not allow a lender to waive the security and sue for the balance due; rather, the lender is limited to repossession of the mobile home. The trial court erred in granting respondent's motion for summary judgment, and the judgment is therefore reversed.

SCOTT and MERRILL, JJ., concur.

§ 9.3.2 Assumption of Mortgage

Suppose A acquires Blackacre from O with a loan from Bank X, secured by a mortgage or deed of trust. Suppose also that A subsequently sells Blackacre to B with the understanding (accepted by Bank X) that B now is to pay the mortgage or deed of trust. In the event of a default by B, is B personally liable on the mortgage or deed of trust in the event that Bank X forecloses on B? The answer is dependent upon whether B "assumed" the mortgage or took "subject to" the mortgage, as the next case explains.

Burbank v. Roots
4 Colo.App. 197 (1894)

Burbank v. Roots *distinguishes between a successor to the original grantee who assumes the mortgage (which results in personal liability in the event of a default) and a successor who takes subject to the mortgage (no personal liability in the event of a default).*

REED, J.

* * *

The law of the case appears to be well settled. A recital in a deed that the property conveyed is subject to a mortgage, which forms a part of the consideration, and stops there, creates no personal liability on the part of the grantee, and the grantor and mortgagee can only look to the property. 1 Jones, Mortg. § 748; Machine Co. v. Emerson, 115 Mass. 554; Woodbury v. Swan, 58 N.H. 380; Dunn v. Rodgers, 43 Ill. 260. But when the recital or exception is, "which mortgage the grantee assumes, or assumes and agrees to pay," or the conveyance is made "subject to the payment of an outstanding mortgage," the case is different. The assumption of the mortgage makes such sum a part of the purchase money. So much of the consideration as is necessary to pay the mortgage is taken from the consideration, and appropriated to the payment of the mortgage. It was not the taking of the property subject to the mortgage, but an agreement to pay the debt as contracted by the grantor. As said in Heid v. Vreeland, 30 N.J.Eq. 591, "His retention of the vendor's money for the payment of the mortgage imposes upon him the duty of protecting the vendor against the mortgage debt." It becomes a personal obligation that may be enforced, by the vendor upon default of the vendee to pay in accordance with the contract made by his grantor. * * *The acceptance of a deed imposing upon the grantee the obligation of discharging the mortgage is sufficient. It is not necessary that he should sign the deed, or any obligation whatever. * * *

Notes

1. A mortgage or deed of trust typically includes a "due-on-sale" clause. This means that if the property is sold without the lender's consent, the balance of the mortgage or deed of trust is immediately due and owing. Thus, as a practical matter, at least when institutional lenders are involved, it is not the norm for buyers of property to either assume a mortgage or take subject to the mortgage. Generally, due-on-sale clauses are enforceable. See *Esplendido Apartments v. Metropolitan Condominium Ass'n of Arizona II*, 161 Ariz. 325 (1989) (due-on-sale clause enforceable if buyer takes subject to the mortgage or assumes the mortgage).

2. If a lender transfers the loan's note (that is, the promissory note wherein the borrower promises to repay the money loaned with interest), there is a principle in the common law that "the mortgage follows the note." See *Carpenter v. Longan*, 83 U.S. 271 (1872). This means that when security (e.g., a mortgage) is given for a negotiable promissory note, the transfer of the note by the lender to another institution or investor automatically carries with it the security, as a matter of equity, if not law. The problem, however, is that only mortgages or deeds of trust are recorded, not notes. See chapter 8. Indeed, while this is an issue that is beyond the scope of this short note, it is important to point out that this problem of banks selling their notes and physically separating the note from the mortgage or deed of trust helped create the "robo-signing" scandal that exacerbated the housing market bust of the Great Recession. See, e.g. *LaSalle Bank, N.A. v. Bialobrzeski*, 123 Conn.App. 781 (2010) and *Residential Funding Company, LLC v. Thorne*, 973 N.E.2d 294 (Ohio App. 2012). See especially *OneWest Bank, F.S.B. v. Drayton*, 910 N.Y.S.2d 857 (2010) (so-called robo signers).

CHAPTER 10
LANDLORD-TENANT RELATIONS

§ 10.1 Discrimination in Selection of Tenants

Certainly, a landlord may discriminate on the basis of credit worthiness. As between a tenant who has a good credit rating and one who has a poor credit rating, a landlord would be justified in renting to the former and rejecting the latter. What we discuss in the subsections that follow is whether a landlord may discriminate for non-economic reasons.

§ 10.1.1 In General

Kramarsky v. Stahl Management
92 Misc.2d 1030 (N.Y.Sup. 1977)

New York's version of the federal Fair Housing Act prohibits landlords from discriminating, among other categories, on the basis of race, gender, and marital status (the federal act does not include marital status). The question raised in Kramarsky v. Stahl Management *is whether a landlord can discriminate against a tenant who is black, female, and divorced, if the discrimination is not based on these categories. The court will hold that the landlord may so discriminate.*

EDWARD J. GREENFIELD, Justice.

This is an application brought on by Order to Show Cause, pursuant to § 297, Subdivision 6 of the Executive Law for an order enjoining respondents from selling, renting, leasing, or otherwise disposing of Apartment 9J at 225 West 106th Street to anyone other than petitioner until final determination of a complaint against respondent Stahl Management now pending before the State Division of Human Rights.

The application is based upon a complaint of discrimination by one Judith Pierce, a black divorced woman, who contends that Stahl Management unlawfully discriminated against her by refusing to rent an apartment because of her race, sex and marital status. In support of that contention, she points to the willingness of the respondent to rent an apartment to a later white applicant.

Respondent denies any illegal discrimination insisting that Ms. Pierce was not turned down because she was black, female or divorced, but for other reasons. In support of this contention, he demonstrates that 30% of his apartments have been rented to blacks, including the last two for which there were both black and white applicants and that 60% of the apartments have been rented to unmarried persons. The reason for her rejection, the landlord contends, is that her application indicated that in the eyes of the landlord she would be an undesirable tenant.

The application form is a one-page sheet in which Ms. Pierce indicated that she was employed as general counsel to the New York City Commission on Human Rights, that she had earned a salary of $28,000 plus a year and that she had previously been employed with the Legal Services Corporation. Under the space for repairs and remarks she had written in "Painting -- New Rulings." Mr. Stahl, the individual who operated the respondent, candidly admits that information on the application indicated that "she would be a source of trouble to me as a tenant." Rather than a lawyer attuned to her legal rights, he would have preferred, all other things being equal, a person who was likely to be less informed and more passive.

The Human Rights Law (Executive Law, Article 15) provides in subdivision 5 of section 296:

"(a) It shall be an unlawful discriminatory practice for the owner, lessee, sub-lessee, assignee, or managing agent of, or other person having the right to sell, rent or lease a housing accommodation, constructed or to be constructed, or any agent or employee thereof:

(1) To refuse to sell, rent, lease or otherwise to deny to or withhold from any person or group of persons such a housing accommodation because of the race, creed, color, national origin, sex, or disability or marital status of such person or persons.

(2) To discriminate against any person because of his race, creed, color, national origin, sex, or disability or marital status in the terms, conditions or privileges of the sale, rental or lease of any such housing accommodation or in the furnishing of facilities or services in connection therewith."

Absent a supervening statutory proscription, a landlord is free to do what he wishes with his property, and to rent or not to rent to any given person at his whim. The only restraints which the law has imposed upon free exercise of his discretion is that he may not use race, creed, color, national origin, sex or marital status as criteria. So, regrettable though it may be, a landlord can employ other criteria to determine the acceptability of his tenants occupational, physical or otherwise. He may decide not to rent to singers because they are too noisy, or not to rent to bald-headed men because he has been told they give wild parties. He can bar his premises to the lowest strata of society, should he choose, or to the highest, if that be his personal desire.

Thus, this court concludes that there is nothing illegal in a landlord discriminating against lawyers as a group, or trying to keep out of his building intelligent persons, aware of their rights, who may give him trouble in the future. A landlord has a "right to be selective and to reject a prospective tenant because of his or her failure to meet standards of acceptability other than those which concern themselves with one's race or color or standards which are otherwise proscribed by statute." State Commission for Human Rights v. Kennelly, 30 A.D.2d 310, 312, 291 N.Y.S.2d 686, 689.

Although the courts, in the interest of justice, will endeavor to facilitate to the fullest the legislative intent and public policy underlying antidiscrimination legislation, the facts and circumstances of this case do not warrant injunctive relief. The court is not persuaded that there is a reasonable likelihood that the charge of discrimination can be sustained. Accordingly, the application is denied and the temporary restraining order vacated.

§ 10.1.2 Fair Housing Act of 1968

The Fair Housing Act of 1968 generally prevents discrimination in the sale or rental of real property based on race, color, religion, sex, handicap, familial status, or national origin.

U.S. v. Starrett City Associates
840 F.2d 1096 (2nd Cir. 1988)

Starrett City is a vast complex of apartment houses in Brooklyn, New York, created with the intent to have a fully diverse community. The owners of Starrett City admittedly discriminated against blacks and Hispanics—but only to have a diverse community. Thus, Starrett City Associates practiced discrimination, but not because of animus toward any racial group. To the contrary, the discrimination was practiced in good faith and solely to ensure the community would remain diverse. Nonetheless, the court holds that the defendants violated the Fair Housing Act.

MINER, Circuit Judge:

The United States Attorney General, on behalf of the United States ("the government"), commenced this action under Title VIII of the Civil Rights Act of 1968 ("Fair Housing Act" or "the Act") against defendants-appellants Starrett City Associates, Starrett City, Inc. and Delmar Management Company (collectively, "Starrett") in the United States District Court for the Eastern District of New York (Neaher, J.). The government maintained that Starrett's practices of renting apartments in its Brooklyn housing complex solely on the basis of applicants' race or national origin, and of making apartments unavailable to black and hispanic applicants that are then made available to white applicants, violate section 804(a), (b), (c) and (d) of the Act, 42 U.S.C. § 3604(a)-(d) (1982).

* * *

BACKGROUND

Appellants constructed, own and operate "Starrett City," the largest housing development in the nation, consisting of 46 high-rise buildings containing 5,881 apartments in Brooklyn, New York. The complex's rental office opened in December 1973. Starrett has made capital contributions of $19,091,000 to the project, the New York State Housing Finance Agency has made $362,720,000 in mortgage loans, and the U.S. Department of Housing and Urban Development subsidizes Starrett's monthly mortgage interest payments. * * *

Starrett has sought to maintain a racial distribution by apartment of 64% white, 22% black and 8% hispanic at Starrett City. *Id.* at 671. Starrett claims that these racial quotas are necessary to prevent the loss of white tenants, which would transform Starrett City into a predominantly minority complex. Starrett points to the difficulty it has had in attracting an integrated applicant pool from the time Starrett City opened, despite extensive advertising and promotional efforts. Because of these purported difficulties, Starrett adopted a tenanting procedure to promote and maintain the desired racial balance.

This procedure has resulted in relatively stable percentages of whites and minorities living at Starrett City between 1975 and the present. *See id.* at 672.

* * *

DISCUSSION

Title VIII of the Civil Rights Act of 1968 ("Fair Housing Act" or "the Act"), 42 U.S.C. §§ 3601-3631 (1982), was enacted pursuant to Congress' thirteenth amendment powers, *see Williams v. Matthews Co.,* 499 F.2d 819, 825 (8th Cir.), *cert. denied,*419 U.S. 1021 & 1027, 95 S.Ct. 495 & 507, 42 L.Ed.2d 294 & 302 (1974); *United States v. Bob Lawrence Realty, Inc.,* 474 F.2d 115, 120-21 (5th Cir.), *cert. denied,*414 U.S. 826, 94 S.Ct. 131, 38 L.Ed.2d 59 (1973); *United States v. Hunter,* 459 F.2d 205, 214 (4th Cir.), *cert. denied,*409 U.S. 934, 93 S.Ct. 235, 34 L.Ed.2d 189 (1972), "to provide, within constitutional limitations, for fair housing throughout the United States." 42 U.S.C. § 3601. Section 3604 of the statute prohibits discrimination because of race, color or national origin in the sale or rental of housing by, *inter alia:* (1) refusing to rent or make available any dwelling, *id.* § 3604(a); (2) offering discriminatory "terms, conditions or privileges" of rental, *id.* § 3604(b); (3) making, printing or publishing "any notice, statement, or advertisement * * * that indicates any preference, limitation, or discrimination based on race, color * * * or national origin,"[1] *id.* § 3604(c); and (4) representing to any person "that any dwelling is not available for * * * rental when such dwelling is in fact so available," *id.* § 3604(d).

Housing practices unlawful under Title VIII include not only those motivated by a racially discriminatory purpose, but also those that disproportionately affect minorities. *See, e.g., Robinson v. 12 Lofts Realty, Inc.,* 610 F.2d 1032, 1036-37 (2d Cir.1979). Section 3604 "is designed to ensure that no one is denied the right to live where they choose for discriminatory reasons." *See Southend Neighborhood Improv. Ass'n v. County of St. Clair,* 743 F.2d 1207, 1210 (7th Cir.1984). Although "not every denial, especially a temporary denial, of low-income public housing has a discriminatory impact on racial minorities" in violation of Title VIII, *see Arthur v. City of Toledo,* 782 F.2d 565, 577 (6th Cir.1986), an action leading to discriminatory effects on the availability of housing violates the Act, *see Southend Neighborhood Improv. Ass'n,* 743 F.2d at 1209-10.

* * *

Although any racial classification is presumptively discriminatory, *see Personnel Admin. v. Feeney,* 442 U.S. 256, 272, 99 S.Ct. 2282, 2292, 60 L.Ed.2d 870 (1979), a race-conscious affirmative action plan does not necessarily violate federal constitutional or statutory provisions, *see, e.g., United States v. Paradise,* 480 U.S. 149, 107 S.Ct. 1053, 1064, 94 L.Ed.2d 203 (1987) (plurality opinion) (fourteenth amendment); *United Steelworkers v. Weber,* 443 U.S. 193, 208, 99 S.Ct. 2721, 2729, 61 L.Ed.2d 480 (1979) (Title VII). However, a race-conscious plan cannot be "ageless in [its] reach into the past, and timeless in [its] ability to affect the future." *Wygant v. Jackson Bd. of Educ.,* 476 U.S. 267, 106 S.Ct. 1842, 1848, 90 L.Ed.2d 260 (1986) (plurality opinion). A plan employing racial distinctions must be temporary in nature with a defined goal as its termination

---

[1] [The Fair Housing Act, enacted in 1968, also prohibits discrimination based on religion. By subsequent amendments, discrimination based on sex (that is, gender), and familial status (this includes whether the tenant has children), or handicap also is prohibited.]

point. *See, e.g., Johnson v. Transportation Agency,* 480 U.S. 616, 107 S.Ct. 1442, 1456, 94 L.Ed.2d 615 (1987); *Paradise,* 107 S.Ct. at 1070; *Sheet Metal Workers v. EEOC,* 478 U.S. 421, 106 S.Ct. 3019, 3053, 92 L.Ed.2d 344 (1986) (fifth amendment equal protection); *Fullilove v. Klutznick,* 448 U.S. 448, 489, 100 S.Ct. 2758, 2780, 65 L.Ed.2d 902 (1980); *Weber,* 443 U.S. at 208-09, 99 S.Ct. at 2729-30; *see also Jaimes v. Lucas Metropolitan Housing Auth.,* 833 F.2d 1203, 1208 (6th Cir.1987) (stating that affirmative integration plan for public housing authority "should end upon the [district] court's finding that its goal has been accomplished"). Moreover, we observe that societal discrimination alone seems "insufficient and over expansive" as the basis for adopting so-called "benign" practices with discriminatory effects "that work against innocent people," *Wygant,* 106 S.Ct. at 1848, in the drastic and burdensome way that rigid racial quotas do. Furthermore, the use of quotas generally should be based on some history of racial discrimination, *see id.* at 1847, or imbalance, *see Johnson,* 107 S.Ct. at 1452-53, within the entity seeking to employ them. Finally, measures designed to increase or ensure minority participation, such as "access" quotas, *see Burney,* 551 F.Supp. at 763, have generally been upheld, *see, e.g., Johnson,* 107 S.Ct. at 1456-57; *Paradise,* 107 S.Ct. at 1070-71; *Weber,* 443 U.S. at 208, 99 S.Ct. at 2729. However, programs designed to maintain integration by limiting minority participation, such as ceiling quotas, *see Burney,* 551 F.Supp. at 763, are of doubtful validity, *see Jaimes,* 833 F.2d at 1207 (invalidating public housing authority integration plan to the extent it acts as strict racial quota), because they " 'single[ ] out those least well represented in the political process to bear the brunt of a benign program,' " *Fullilove,* 448 U.S. at 519, 100 S.Ct. at 2796 (Marshall, J., concurring) (quoting *Regents v. Bakke,* 438 U.S. 265, 361, 98 S.Ct. 2733, 2784, 57 L.Ed.2d 750 (1978) (Brennan, J., concurring in part and dissenting in part)).

Starrett's use of ceiling quotas to maintain integration at Starrett City lacks each of these characteristics. First, Starrett City's practices have only the goal of integration maintenance. The quotas already have been in effect for ten years. Appellants predict that their race-conscious tenanting practices must continue for at least fifteen more years, but fail to explain adequately how that approximation was reached. In any event, these practices are far from temporary. Since the goal of integration maintenance is purportedly threatened by the potential for "white flight" on a continuing basis, no definite termination date for Starrett's quotas is perceivable. Second, appellants do not assert, and there is no evidence to show, the existence of prior racial discrimination or discriminatory imbalance adversely affecting whites within Starrett City or appellants' other complexes. On the contrary, Starrett City was initiated as an integrated complex, and Starrett's avowed purpose for employing race-based tenanting practices is to maintain that initial integration. Finally, Starrett's quotas do not provide minorities with access to Starrett City, but rather act as a ceiling to their access. Thus, the impact of appellants' practices falls squarely on minorities, for whom Title VIII was intended to open up housing opportunities. Starrett claims that its use of quotas serves to keep the numbers of minorities entering Starrett City low enough to avoid setting off a wave of "white flight." Although the "white flight" phenomenon may be a factor "take[n] into account in the integration equation," *Parent Ass'n of Andrew Jackson High School v. Ambach,* 598 F.2d 705, 720 (2d Cir.1979), it cannot serve to justify attempts to maintain integration at Starrett City through inflexible racial quotas that are neither temporary in nature nor used to remedy past racial discrimination or imbalance within the complex.

* * *

CONCLUSION
We do not intend to imply that race is always an inappropriate consideration under Title VIII in efforts to promote integrated housing. We hold only that Title VIII does not allow appellants to use rigid racial quotas of indefinite duration to maintain a fixed level of integration at Starrett City by restricting minority access to scarce and desirable rental accommodations otherwise available to them. We therefore affirm the judgment of the district court.

* * *

Fair Housing Council of San Fernando Valley v. Roommate.com, LLC
666 F.3d 1216 (9th Cir. 2012)

Several plaintiffs, non-profit organizations, sued Roommate.com, which operates an online roommate-matching website. The plaintiffs alleged that the website's questions requiring disclosure of sex, sexual orientation, and familial status, and its sorting, steering, and matching of users based on those characteristics, violated the Fair Housing Act (FHA) and the California Fair Employment and Housing Act (FEHA), which includes California's version of the Fair Housing Act. The Ninth Circuit will hold that while the non-profits have standing to sue, the term "dwelling" under the FHA meant an independent unit, thus Roommate.com could not have violated the FHA. The Ninth Circuit will also hold that FEHA was not violated either.

OPINION
KOZINSKI, Chief Judge:
There's no place like home. In the privacy of your own home, you can take off your coat, kick off your shoes, let your guard down and be completely yourself. While we usually share our homes only with friends and family, sometimes we need to take in a stranger to help pay the rent. When that happens, can the government limit whom we choose? Specifically, do the anti-discrimination provisions of the Fair Housing Act ("FHA") extend to the selection of roommates?

FACTS
Roommate.com, LLC ("Roommate") operates an internet-based business that helps roommates find each other. Roommate's website receives over 40,000 visits a day and roughly a million new postings for roommates are created each year. When users sign up, they must create a profile by answering a series of questions about their sex, sexual orientation and whether children will be living with them. An open-ended "Additional Comments" section lets users include information not prompted by the questionnaire. Users are asked to list their preferences for roommate characteristics, including sex, sexual orientation and familial status. Based on the profiles and preferences, Roommate matches users and provides them a list of housing-seekers or

available rooms meeting their criteria. Users can also search available listings based on roommate characteristics, including sex, sexual orientation and familial status.

The Fair Housing Councils of San Fernando Valley and San Diego ("FHCs") sued Roommate in federal court, alleging that the website's questions requiring disclosure of sex, sexual orientation and familial status, and its sorting, steering and matching of users based on those characteristics, violate the Fair Housing Act ("FHA"), 42 U.S.C. § 3601 et seq., and the California Fair Employment and Housing Act ("FEHA"), Cal. Gov't Code § 12955.

The district court initially dismissed the claims, holding that Roommate was immune under section 230 of the Communications Decency Act ("CDA"), 47 U.S.C. § 230. We reversed, holding that Roommate was protected by the CDA for publishing the "Additional Comments" section, but not for (1) posting questionnaires that required disclosure of sex, sexual orientation and familial status; (2) limiting the scope of searches by users' preferences on a roommate's sex, sexual orientation and familial status; and (3) a matching system that paired users based on those preferences. *Fair Hous. Council v. Roommates.com, LLC,* 521 F.3d 1157, 1166 (9th Cir.2008) (en banc).

Our opinion was limited to CDA immunity and didn't reach whether the activities, in fact, violated the FHA. On remand, the district court held that Roommate's prompting of discriminatory preferences from users, matching users based on that information and publishing these preferences violated the FHA and FEHA, and enjoined Roommate from those activities. Roommate appeals the grant of summary judgment and permanent injunction, and also the district court's order awarding the FHCs $494,714.40 in attorney's fees. The FHCs cross-appeal the amount of the attorney's fees.

STANDING

Roommate argues that the FHCs lack standing because they didn't suffer actual injury. We've held that an organization has "direct standing to sue [when] it showed a drain on its resources from both a diversion of its resources and frustration of its mission." *Fair Hous. of Marin v. Combs,* 285 F.3d 899, 905 (9th Cir.2002). However, " 'standing must be established independent of the lawsuit filed by the plaintiff.' " *Comite de Jornaleros de Redondo Beach v. City of Redondo Beach,* 657 F.3d 936, 943 (9th Cir.2011) (quoting *Walker v. City of Lakewood,* 272 F.3d 1114, 1124 n. 3 (9th Cir.2001)). An organization "cannot manufacture [an] injury by incurring litigation costs or simply choosing to spend money fixing a problem that otherwise would not affect the organization at all." *La Asociacion de Trabajadores de Lake Forest v. City of Lake Forest,* 624 F.3d 1083, 1088 (9th Cir.2010); *see also Combs,* 285 F.3d at 903 ("[A]n organization cannot, of course, manufacture the injury necessary to maintain a suit from its expenditure of resources on that very suit ...." (internal quotation marks omitted)).

Prior to commencing litigation, the FHCs investigated Roommate's alleged violations and, in response, started new education and outreach campaigns targeted at discriminatory roommate advertising. The resources spent on those campaigns were not associated with litigation. Because Roommate's conduct caused the FHCs to divert resources independent of litigation costs and frustrated their central mission, we conclude that the FHCs have organizational standing.

ANALYSIS

If the FHA extends to shared living situations, it's quite clear that what Roommate does amounts to a violation. The pivotal question is whether the FHA applies to roommates.

I

The FHA prohibits discrimination on the basis of "race, color, religion, sex, familial status, or national origin" in the "sale or rental *of a dwelling*." 42 U.S.C. § 3604(b) (emphasis added). The FHA also makes it illegal to

> make, print, or publish, or cause to be made, printed, or published any notice, statement, or advertisement, with respect to the sale or rental *of a dwelling* that indicates any preference, limitation, or discrimination based on race, color, religion, sex, handicap, familial status, or national origin, or an intention to make any such preference, limitation, or discrimination.

Id. § 3604(c) (emphasis added). The reach of the statute turns on the meaning of "dwelling."

The FHA defines "dwelling" as "any building, structure, or portion thereof which is occupied as, or designed or intended for occupancy as, a residence by one or more families." *Id.* § 3602(b). A dwelling is thus a living unit designed or intended for occupancy by a family, meaning that it ordinarily has the elements generally associated with a family residence: sleeping spaces, bathroom and kitchen facilities, and common areas, such as living rooms, dens and hallways.

It would be difficult, though not impossible, to divide a single-family house or apartment into separate "dwellings" for purposes of the statute. Is a "dwelling" a bedroom plus a right to access common areas? What if roommates share a bedroom? Could a "dwelling" be a bottom bunk and half an armoire? It makes practical sense to interpret "dwelling" as an independent living unit and stop the FHA at the front door.

There's no indication that Congress intended to interfere with personal relationships *inside* the home. Congress wanted to address the problem of landlords discriminating in the sale and rental of housing, which deprived protected classes of housing opportunities. But a business transaction between a tenant and landlord is quite different from an arrangement between two people sharing the same living space. We seriously doubt Congress meant the FHA to apply to the latter. Consider, for example, the FHA's prohibition against sex discrimination. Could Congress, in the 1960s, really have meant that women must accept men as roommates? Telling women they may not lawfully exclude men from the list of acceptable roommates would be controversial today; it would have been scandalous in the 1960s.

While it's possible to read dwelling to mean sub-parts of a home or an apartment, doing so leads to awkward results. And applying the FHA to the selection of roommates almost certainly leads to results that defy mores prevalent when the statute was passed. Nonetheless, this interpretation is not wholly implausible and we would normally consider adopting it, given that the FHA is a remedial statute that we construe broadly. Therefore, we turn to constitutional concerns, which provide strong countervailing considerations.

II

The Supreme Court has recognized that "the freedom to enter into and carry on certain intimate or private relationships is a fundamental element of liberty protected by the Bill of Rights." *Bd. of Dirs. of Rotary Int'l v. Rotary Club of Duarte,* 481 U.S. 537, 545, 107 S.Ct. 1940, 95 L.Ed.2d 474 (1987). "[C]hoices to enter into and maintain certain intimate human relationships must be secured against undue intrusion by the State because of the role of such relationships in safeguarding the individual freedom that is central to our constitutional scheme." *Roberts v. U.S. Jaycees,* 468 U.S. 609, 617–18, 104 S.Ct. 3244, 82 L.Ed.2d 462 (1984). Courts have extended the right of intimate association to marriage, child bearing, child rearing and cohabitation with relatives. *Id.* While the right protects only "highly personal relationships," *IDK, Inc. v. Clark Cnty.,* 836 F.2d 1185, 1193 (9th Cir.1988) (quoting *Roberts,* 468 U.S. at 618, 104 S.Ct. 3244), the right isn't restricted exclusively to family, *Bd. of Dirs. of Rotary Int'l,* 481 U.S. at 545, 107 S.Ct. 1940. The right to association also implies a right *not* to associate. *Roberts,* 468 U.S. at 623, 104 S.Ct. 3244.

To determine whether a particular relationship is protected by the right to intimate association we look to "size, purpose, selectivity, and whether others are excluded from critical aspects of the relationship." *Bd. of Dirs. of Rotary Int'l,* 481 U.S. at 546, 107 S.Ct. 1940. The roommate relationship easily qualifies: People generally have very few roommates; they are selective in choosing roommates; and non-roommates are excluded from the critical aspects of the relationship, such as using the living spaces. Aside from immediate family or a romantic partner, it's hard to imagine a relationship more intimate than that between roommates, who share living rooms, dining rooms, kitchens, bathrooms, even bedrooms.

Because of a roommate's unfettered access to the home, choosing a roommate implicates significant privacy and safety considerations. The home is the center of our private lives. Roommates note our comings and goings, observe whom we bring back at night, hear what songs we sing in the shower, see us in various stages of undress and learn intimate details most of us prefer to keep private. Roommates also have access to our physical belongings and to our person. As the Supreme Court recognized, "[w]e are at our most vulnerable when we are asleep because we cannot monitor our own safety or the security of our belongings." *Minnesota v. Olson,* 495 U.S. 91, 99, 110 S.Ct. 1684, 109 L.Ed.2d 85 (1990). Taking on a roommate means giving him full access to the space where we are most vulnerable.

Equally important, we are fully exposed to a roommate's belongings, activities, habits, proclivities and way of life. This could include matter we find offensive (pornography, religious materials, political propaganda); dangerous (tobacco, drugs, firearms); annoying (jazz, perfume, frequent overnight visitors, furry pets); habits that are incompatible with our lifestyle (early risers, messy cooks, bathroom hogs, clothing borrowers). When you invite others to share your living quarters, you risk becoming a suspect in whatever illegal activities they engage in.

Government regulation of an individual's ability to pick a roommate thus intrudes into the home, which "is entitled to special protection as the center of the private lives of our people." *Minnesota v. Carter,* 525 U.S. 83, 99, 119 S.Ct. 469, 142 L.Ed.2d 373 (1998) (Kennedy, J., concurring). "Liberty protects the person from unwarranted government intrusions into a dwelling or other private places. In our tradition the State is not omnipresent in the home." *Lawrence v. Texas,* 539 U.S. 558, 562, 123 S.Ct. 2472, 156 L.Ed.2d 508 (2003). Holding that the FHA applies inside a home or apartment would allow the government to restrict our ability to choose roommates compatible with our lifestyles. This would be a serious invasion of privacy, autonomy and security.

For example, women will often look for female roommates because of modesty or security concerns. As roommates often share bathrooms and common areas, a girl may not want to walk around in her towel in front of a boy. She might also worry about unwanted sexual advances or becoming romantically involved with someone she must count on to pay the rent.

An orthodox Jew may want a roommate with similar beliefs and dietary restrictions, so he won't have to worry about finding honey-baked ham in the refrigerator next to the potato latkes. Non–Jewish roommates may not understand or faithfully follow all of the culinary rules, like the use of different silverware for dairy and meat products, or the prohibition against warming non-kosher food in a kosher microwave. Taking away the ability to choose roommates with similar dietary restrictions and religious convictions will substantially burden the observant Jew's ability to live his life and practice his religion faithfully. The same is true of individuals of other faiths that call for dietary restrictions or rituals inside the home.

The U.S. Department of Housing and Urban Development recently dismissed a complaint against a young woman for advertising, "I am looking for a female christian roommate," on her church bulletin board. In its Determination of No Reasonable Cause, HUD explained that "in light of the facts provided and after assessing the unique context of the advertisement and the roommate relationship involved ... the Department defers to Constitutional considerations in reaching its conclusions." *Fair Hous. Ctr. of W. Mich. v. Tricia,* No. 05–10–1738–8 (Oct. 28, 2010) (Determination of No Reasonable Cause).
It's a "well-established principle that statutes will be interpreted to avoid constitutional difficulties." *Frisby v. Schultz,* 487 U.S. 474, 483, 108 S.Ct. 2495, 101 L.Ed.2d 420 (1988). "[W]here an otherwise acceptable construction of a statute would raise serious constitutional problems, the Court will construe the statute to avoid such problems unless such construction is plainly contrary to the intent of Congress." *Pub. Citizen v. U.S. Dep't of Justice,* 491 U.S. 440, 466, 109 S.Ct. 2558, 105 L.Ed.2d 377 (1989) (internal quotation marks omitted). Because the FHA can reasonably be read either to include or exclude shared living arrangements, we can and must choose the construction that avoids raising constitutional concerns. *See INS v. St. Cyr,* 533 U.S. 289, 299–300, 121 S.Ct. 2271, 150 L.Ed.2d 347 (2001) ("[I]f an otherwise acceptable construction of a statute would raise serious constitutional problems, and where an alternative interpretation of the statute is fairly possible, we are obligated to construe the statute to avoid such problems.") (internal citation and quotations marks omitted). Reading "dwelling" to mean an independent housing unit is a fair interpretation of the text and consistent with congressional intent. Because the construction of "dwelling" to include shared living units raises substantial constitutional concerns, we adopt the narrower construction that excludes roommate selection from the reach of the FHA.

III

Because we find that the FHA doesn't apply to the sharing of living units, it follows that it's not unlawful to discriminate in selecting a roommate. As the underlying conduct is not unlawful, Roommate's facilitation of discriminatory roommate searches does not violate the FHA. While Roommate itself has no intimate association right, it is entitled to raise the constitutional claims of its users. *See Craig v. Boren,* 429 U.S. 190, 195, 97 S.Ct. 451, 50 L.Ed.2d 397 (1976). The injunction entered by the district court precludes Roommate's members from selecting roommates unfettered by government regulation. Roommate may therefore raise these claims on their behalf.

IV

The same constitutional concerns over the right to intimate association would arise if the California Fair Employment and Housing Act ("FEHA") were applied to roommates. Accordingly, we interpret "housing accommodation" in section 12955(c) of the FEHA to exclude the sharing of living units. Similarly to how the FHA defines "dwelling," the FEHA defines "housing accommodation" as "any building, structure, or portion thereof that is occupied as, or intended for occupancy as, a residence by one or more families." Cal. Gov. Code § 12927(d). This ambiguous definition allows us to apply the canon of constitutional avoidance to find that the FEHA does not reach the selection of roommates.

* * *

§ 10.1.3 Civil Rights Act of 1866

The Civil Rights Act of 1866 (42 U.S.C. §1982) provides, "All citizens of the United States shall have the same right, in every State and Territory, as is enjoyed by white citizens thereof to inherit, purchase, lease, sell, hold, and convey real and personal property." Congress enacted the statute (passed over a veto by President Andrew Johnson) after the Civil War and at a time when the former slave states were enacting laws to limit the civil liberties of the Freedmen. The Act also declared, "all persons born in the United States not subject to any foreign power, excluding Indians not taxed," were citizens, who were "of every race and color" and "without regard to any previous condition of slavery or involuntary servitude" (14 Stat. 27).

Shaare Tefila Congregation v. Cobb
481 U.S. 615 (1987)

When a group of anti-Semites desecrated a synagogue, the synagogue and its members filed suit against the perpetrators under the Civil Rights Act of 1866. The question before the United States Supreme Court was whether Jews were a "race" for purposes of the statute. The court holds that they are.

Justice WHITE delivered the opinion of the Court.

On November 2, 1982, the outside walls of the synagogue of the Shaare Tefila Congregation in Silver Spring, Maryland, were sprayed with red and black paint and with large anti-Semitic slogans, phrases, and symbols. A few months later, the Congregation and some individual members brought this suit in the Federal District Court, alleging that defendants' desecration of the synagogue had violated 42 U.S.C. §§ 1981, 1982, 1985(3) and the Maryland common law of trespass, nuisance, and intentional infliction of emotional distress. On defendants' motion under Federal Rules of Civil Procedure 12(b)(1) and (6), the District Court dismissed all the claims. The Court of Appeals affirmed in all respects. 785 F.2d 523 (CA4 1986). Petitioners petitioned for writ of certiorari. We granted the petition, 479 U.S. 812, 107 S.Ct. 62, 93 L.Ed.2d 21 (1986), and we now reverse the judgment of the Court of Appeals.

Section 1982 guarantees all citizens of the United States, "the same right * * * as is enjoyed by white citizens * * * to inherit, purchase, lease, sell, hold, and convey real and personal property." The section forbids both official and private racially discriminatory interference with property rights, *Jones v. Alfred H. Mayer Co.,* 392 U.S. 409, 88 S.Ct. 2186, 20 L.Ed.2d 1189 (1968). Petitioners' allegation was that they were deprived of the right to hold property in violation of § 1982 because the defendants were motivated by racial prejudice. They unsuccessfully argued in the District Court and Court of Appeals that Jews are not a racially distinct group, but that defendants' conduct is actionable because they viewed Jews as racially distinct and were motivated by racial prejudice. The Court of Appeals held that § 1982 was not "intended to apply to situations in which a plaintiff is not a member of a racially distinct group but is merely *perceived* to be so by defendants." 785 F.2d, at 526 (emphasis in original). The Court of Appeals believed that "[b]ecause discrimination against Jews is not racial discrimination," *id.,* at 527, the District Court was correct in dismissing the § 1982 claim.

We agree with the Court of Appeals that a charge of racial discrimination within the meaning of § 1982 cannot be made out by alleging only that the defendants were motivated by racial animus; it is necessary as well to allege that defendants' animus was directed towards the kind of group that Congress intended to protect when it passed the statute. To hold otherwise would unacceptably extend the reach of the statute.

We agree with petitioners, however, that the Court of Appeals erred in holding that Jews cannot state a § 1982 claim against other white defendants. That view rested on the notion that because Jews today are not thought to be members of a separate race, they cannot make out a claim of racial discrimination within the meaning of § 1982. That construction of the section we have today rejected in *Saint Francis College v. Al-Khazraji,* 481 U.S., at 604, 107 S.Ct., at 2022. Our opinion in that case observed that definitions of race when § 1982 was passed were not the same as they are today, *ante,* at 609, 613, 107 S.Ct., at 2026, 2028, and concluded that the section was "intended to protect from discrimination identifiable classes of persons who are subjected to intentional discrimination solely because of their ancestry or ethnic characteristics." At 613, 107 S.Ct., at 2028. As *Saint Francis* makes clear, the question before us is not whether Jews are considered to be a separate race by today's standards, but whether, at the time § 1982 was adopted, Jews constituted a group of people that Congress intended to protect. It is evident from the legislative history of the section reviewed in *Saint Francis College,* a review that we need not repeat here, that Jews and Arabs were among the peoples then considered to be distinct races and hence within the protection of the statute. Jews are not foreclosed from stating a cause of action against other members of what today is considered to be part of the Caucasian race.

The judgment of the Court of Appeals is therefore reversed, and the case is remanded for further proceedings consistent with this opinion.

It is so ordered.

§ 10.2 Types of Tenancies

When tenant ("T") leases a residential apartment or commercial space from landlord ("L"), there are various types of leases (or "leaseholds") that T and L may enter into. This section of materials explores these different leaseholds.

Waldrop v. Siebert
286 Ala. 106 (1970)

The first type of lease is a "term for years." Note the characteristics of a term for years.

* * *

The original term of this lease created a leasehold estate in the lessee for two years. The estate granted, being one limited to endure for a definite and ascertained period, fixed in advance, is what is known as a term for years. * * *

* * *

Thompson v. Baxter
107 Minn. 122 (1909)

In Thompson v. Baxter, *L and T enter into a lease, providing that T can live on the premises "while he [T] shall wish to live in Albert Lea . . . ." The question is, what type of leasehold did L transfer to T? In resolving the problem, the court explains other types of tenancies: a tenancy at will; tenancy at sufferance; and a periodic tenancy. Ultimately, the court holds that T did not receive any leasehold. Rather, the court finds that T received a life estate determinable. (You thought you were finished with estates in land and future interests!)*

BROWN, J.

Proceedings in forcible entry and unlawful detainer, instituted in justice court, where defendant had judgment. Plaintiff appealed to the district court, where a like result followed. From the judgment of that court she appealed to this court.

The action involves the right to the possession of certain residence property in the city of Albert Lea, and was submitted to the court below upon the pleadings and a stipulation of facts. It appears that plaintiff is the owner of the premises; that she acquired title thereto by purchase from a former owner, who had theretofore entered into a contract by which he leased and demised the premises to defendant at an agreed monthly rent of $22; and plaintiff's title is subject to all rights that became vested in defendant thereby. The lease, after reciting the rental of the premises and other usual conditions, contained upon the subject of the term of the tenancy, the following stipulation: 'To have and to hold the above-rented premises unto the said party of the second part [the tenant], his heirs, executors, administrators, and assigns, for the full term of while he shall wish to live in Albert Lea, from and after the 1st day of December, 1904.' The only question involved under the stipulation is the construction of this provisions of the lease. Defendant has at all times paid the rent as it became due; but, if plaintiff has the right to terminate the tenancy and eject him, proper notice for that purpose has been given.

Appellant contends that the lease created either a tenancy at will, at sufferance, or from month to month, and that plaintiff could terminate the same at any time by proper notice. The trial court held, in harmony with defendant's contention, that the contract created a life estate in defendant, terminable only at his death or removal from Albert Lea. Appellant assigns this conclusion as error.

A determination of the question presented involves a construction of the lease and a brief examination of some of the principles of law applicable to tenancies at will, at sufferance, from month to month, and life estates. * * *

Tenancies at will may be created by express words, or they may arise by implication of law. Where created by express contract, the writing necessarily so indicates, and reserves the right of termination to either party, as where the lease provides that the tenant shall occupy the premises so long as agreeable to both parties. Richardson v. Langridge, 4 Taunt. 128; Say v. Stoddard, 27 Ohio St. 478. Such tenancies arise by implication of law where no definite time is stated in the contract, or where the tenant enters into possession under an agreement to execute a contract for a specific term and he subsequently refuses to do so, or one who enters under a void lease, or where he holds over pending negotiations for a new lease. The chief characteristics of this form of tenancy are (1) uncertainty respecting the term, and (2) the right of either party to terminate it by proper notice; and these features must exist, whether the tenancy be created by the express language of the contract or by implication of law. An accurate definition is given in 1 Wood on Landlord and Tenant, 43, in the following language: 'A tenant at will is one who enters into the possession of the lands or tenements of another, lawfully, but for no definite term or purpose, but whose possession is subject to termination by the landlord at any time he sees fit to put an end to it. He is called a tenant at will 'because he hath no certain or sure estate, for the lessor may put him out at what time it pleaseth him.' '

A tenancy at sufferance arises where the tenant wrongfully holds over after the expiration of his term, differing from the tenancy at will, where the possession is by the permission of the landlord. 4 Kent. Comm. 113; Edwards v. Hale, 9 Allen (Mass.) 462. He has a naked possession without right, and, independent of statute, is not entitled to notice to quit. 1 Wood on Landlord and Tenant, 8. It also arises where a mortgagor holds over after the expiration of the period of redemption on foreclosure. Stedman v. Gassett, 18 Vt. 346. In fact, this relation exists in all cases where a person who enters lawfully into the possession wrongfully holds possession after his estate or right has ended. Kinsley v. Ames, 2 Metc. (Mass.) 29; Jackson v. McLeod, 12 Johns. (N. Y.) 182; 2 Blackstone, 150; 1 Wood on Landlord and Tenant, 7.

A [periodic] tenancy from month to month or year to year arises where no definite time is agreed upon and the rent is fixed at so much per year or month, as the case may be, and is terminable at the expiration of any period for which rent has been paid. Finch v. Moore, 50 Minn. 116, 52 N. W. 384. This form of tenancy can never exist where the lease or contract prescribes a fixed time. The mere fact that rent is payable monthly does not alone determine the character of the tenancy. The monthly or yearly payments and an intention to limit the term to a month or year must in all cases concur to create this species of tenancy.

From these general principles of the law of tenancy it is quite clear that the lease under consideration does not come within either class mentioned. Its language does not expressly define it as a tenancy at will, and no such relation arises by implication, for the reason that the term is not indefinite, within the meaning of the law on this subject, nor is the right to terminate the lease reserved to the lessor. Indefiniteness or uncertainty as to the term of the lease is illustrated by instances where one occupies land by the naked permission of the owner (Hull v. Wood, 14 Mees. & W. 682; Williams v. Deriar, 31 Mo. 13; Larned v. Hudson, 60 N. Y. 102), or a person who holds under a void deed (Stamper v. Griffin, 20 Ga. 312, 65 Am. Dec. 628; Smith's Ex'rs v. Houston, 16 Ala. 111), or where he enters under an agreement for a lease not yet executed (Emmons v. Scudder, 115 Mass. 367), or under a lease until the premises are sold (Lea v. Hernandez, 10 Tex. 137; Ela v. Bankes, 37 Wis. 89), and under various circumstances where no time is specifically agreed upon. In the lease under consideration the tenancy is limited by the time defendant shall continue to dwell in Albert Lea, and this limitation takes the case out of the class of tenancies at will. It is equally clear that a tenancy at sufferance was not created by the contract. There has been no wrongful or unlawful holding over after the expiration of the term. Nor does the rule of tenancy from month to month apply for the reasons already pointed out.

We therefore turn to the question, the turning point in the court below, whether the instrument created a life estate in defendant within the principles of law applicable to that branch of land titles. It is thoroughly settled that a life estate may be created by a deed, lease, or devise, either with or without a stipulation for the payment of rent. This class of tenancies differs in many essential respects from tenancies at will, or from year to year, or at sufferance; the principal distinction being that the former confers a freehold upon the tenant, and the latter a mere chattel interest. The lease under consideration embodies all the essentials of a life tenancy. It contains the usual words of inheritance, necessary at common law, running to defendant, 'his heirs, executors, administrators, and assigns,' and grants the right of occupancy for the term stated therein. Life estates or life tenancies are clearly defined in the books, and the lease here involved brings it within this class of estates. 1 Taylor on Landlord and Tenant, 52, states the rule as follows: 'An estate for life may be created by express limitation or by a grant in general terms. If made to a man for a term of his own life, or for that of another person, he is called a 'life tenant.' But the estate may also be created by a general grant, without defining any specific interest, as where the grant is made to a man, or to a man and his assigns, without any limitation in point of time, it will be considered as an estate for life, and for the life of the grantee only. * * * Where made subject to be defeated by a particular event, and there is no limitation in point of time, it will be ab initio a grant for an estate for life, as much as if no such event had been contemplated. Thus, if a grant be made to a man so long as he shall inhabit a certain place, or to a woman during her widowhood, as there is no certainty that the estate will be terminated by the change of habitation or by marriage of the lessees, the estate is as much an estate for life, until the prescribed event takes place, as if it had been so granted in express terms.'

* * * [T]he trial court properly held that [the instrument] vested in defendant a life estate, terminable only at his death or his removal from Albert Lea.

Judgment affirmed.

Craig Wrecking Co. v. S.G. Loewendick & Sons, Inc.
38 Ohio App.3d 79 (1987)

This case builds on Thompson v. Baxter *and explains the consequences of finding a tenancy at sufferance—and the temporary nature of the tenancy.*

* * *

In Ohio, a tenant who holds over after the term of his lease expires is a tenant at sufferance. *Anderson v. Brewster* (1886), 44 Ohio St. 576, 580, 9 N.E. 683, 685. As such, the landlord may elect to treat the tenant as a trespasser, or hold him to a new lease term. *Gladwell v. Holcomb* (1899), 60 Ohio St. 427, 54 N.E. 473, paragraph two of the syllabus. When a tenant holds over beyond the lease term and pays rent according to the former terms, the law implies a contract on the tenant's part to hold over for an additional term under the same conditions which governed the prior term. *Bumiller v. Walker* (1917), 95 Ohio St. 344, 348-349, 116 N.E. 797, 799. Although such presumption is rebuttable, the new term may arise from the conduct of the parties regardless of the intentions of the tenant alone. *Id.* at 348-354, 116 N.E. at 799-801. The election to hold the tenant to a new term lies with the landlord and his acceptance of rent implies an election to treat the tenant as a holdover. *Baltimore & Ohio RR. Co. v. West* (1897), 57 Ohio St. 161, 165-166, 49 N.E. 344, 345. Absent any agreement to the contrary, the new lease term is governed by the provisions of the original lease. Bumiller, supra, *95 Ohio St. at 348-349, 116 N.E. at 799.*

* * *

Crechale & Polles, Inc. v. Smith
295 So.2d 275 (Miss. 1974)

In lieu of a new term, as per Craig Wrecking Co. v. S.G. Loewendick & Sons, Inc., Crechale & Polles, Inc. *provides an alternative theory: a month-to-month periodic tenancy.*

* * *

We are of the opinion that once a landlord elects to treat a tenant as a trespasser and refuses to extend the lease on a month-to-month basis, but fails to pursue his remedy of ejecting the tenant, and accepts monthly checks for rent due, he in effect agrees to an extension of the lease on a month-to-month basis. See Lally v. The New Voice, 128 Ill.App. 455 (1906); Stillo v. Pellettieri, 173 Ill.App. 104 (1912). There is authority to the contrary, but we believe this rule to be based on the best reasoned authority.

* * *

Notes
1. The key to a tenancy for years, also known as a term for years, is that it has a definite beginning and ending calendar date at the inception of the lease. Obviously, a term that is stated to be, "for the duration of the war," cannot have this definiteness. See *Michael Tuck Foundation v. Hazelcorn*, 187 Misc. 954 (N.Y.Mun.Ct. 1946).

2. A term for years can be for any fixed period of time. Thus, a term for years for one year is possible, as is a term for years for one week. For example, a lease that is "for one week, commencing January 1, 2006," is a term for years for one week. To a layperson, the terminology is certainly odd, if not confusing.

3. A term for more than one year, of course, must comply with the Statute of Frauds: the lease must be in writing, state the material terms of the lease, and be signed by the party to be charged.

4. A term for years terminates automatically; neither landlord nor tenant need give notice of termination. This is decidedly different from a tenancy at will or a periodic tenancy, which is discussed below.

5. To terminate a periodic tenancy, the common law rule is that the notice must be equal to the period, but in no event exceeding six months. Thus, for a year-to-year periodic tenancy, six months' notice must be given. In many jurisdictions today, thirty days' notice must be given, even for tenancies at will.

6. What if untimely notice is given? For example, suppose T gives L twenty days' notice to terminate a month-to-month periodic tenancy. Is the notice a nullity, or is it effective for the next period? There is authority for both views.

§ 10.3 Tenant Duties

In this section of text, we explore two duties the common law imposed on tenants: not to commit waste and to pay rent.

§ 10.3.1 Not to Commit Waste: In General

We have previously explored the concept of waste in the context of cotenancies (chapter 3) and estates in land and future interests (chapter 4). We continue the theme, now within the context of landlord-tenant relations.

Rumiche Corp. v. Eisenreich
40 N.Y.2d 174 (1976)

After briefly explaining "involuntary waste," the court explains "voluntary waste." The definition of voluntary waste in landlord-tenant law is quite similar to the definition learned in chapters 3 and 4.

* * *

Basically, at common law waste had three different definitions, each related to particular types of conduct on the part of tenants. Involuntary waste was defined as failure to prevent damage to the premises, in other words negligence. Equitable waste was defined as failure to do what a prudent owner would do and was available as a cause of action only in limited circumstances, neither of these concepts is relevant to the facts at hand.[2] But the third, voluntary waste, is. It occurs when a tenant injures the premises by an affirmative act (see 5 Powell, Real Property, par. 640; 63 N.Y.Jur., Waste, § 2, p. 109, and cases cited therein).

Voluntary waste as a concept stems from early English common law concern that the interests in land held by reversioners or remaindermen be protected from depredations by life tenants of scarce natural resources (5 Powell, Real Property, par 637). For instance, the cutting of trees or exhaustion of coal supplies were regarded as waste because their effects extended well beyond the term of the tenant's temporary interest in the land or premises. It is the impingement upon the ultimate estate of the landlord which is the keynote to the definition of waste (Rasch, New York Landlord and Tenant (2d ed.), § 455).

Its application in a modern landlord-tenant setting is well described in Pross v. Excelsior Cleaning & Dyeing Co., 110 Misc. 195, 201, 179 N.Y.S. 176, 179: '(S)uch a change as to affect a vital and substantial portion of the premises, as would change its characteristic appearance, the fundamental purpose of the erection, or the uses contemplated, or a change of such a nature, as would affect the very realty itself-extraordinary in scope and effect, or unusual in expenditure'.

Other courts have also emphasized the definition of waste as permanent or lasting damage (Wall Nut Prods. v. Radar Cent. Corp., 20 A.D.2d 125, 126-127, 244 N.Y.S.2d 827, 828-829, and cases cited therein; Agate v. Lowenbein, 57 N.Y. 604; 63 N.Y.Jur., Waste, § 1, p. 108, and cases cited therein).

Thus, not every change or alteration made by a tenant constitutes waste. For instance, prior to modern leasing developments, except as provided in tenement house legislation (see Multiple Dwelling Law, § 78), it was, and is, the tenant's and not the landlord's obligation to make repairs (Altz v. Leiberson, 233 N.Y. 16, 134 N.E. 703; Emigrant Ind. Sav. Bank v. 108 West Forty-Ninth St. Corp., 280 N.Y. 791, 21 N.E.2d 620; cf. Tonetti v. Penati, 48 A.D.2d 25, 367 N.Y.S.2d 804).

Short of waste, a tenant may also make nonstructural alterations consistent with the use of the premises contemplated by his possession of them (Diener v. Burghart, 186 N.Y.S. 565; Klein's Rapid Shoe Repair Co. v. Sheppardel Realty Co., 136 Misc. 332, 241 N.Y.S. 153, affd Sub nom. Klein's Rapid Shoe Repair Co. v. 120-122 East 14th St. Corp., 228 App.Div. 688, 239 N.Y.S. 790; Leong Won v. Snyder, 94 N.Y.S.2d 247; Rubinger v. Del Monte, 217 N.Y.S.2d 792; Andrews v. Day Button Co., 132 N.Y. 348, 30 N.E. 831; Sigsbee Holding Corp. v. Canavan, supra).

The ready removability of installations is a significant factor. For '(i)t does not follow that a tenant, by virtue of his obligation to commit no waste, may make no alterations whatsoever. Except as the tenant's rights may be limited by the terms of the lease, the tenant is at liberty to erect structures, or to make non-structural alterations, for

---

[2] [For further elucidation on the law of equitable waste, see 78 Am.Jur.2d Waste § 6.]

the purpose of carrying on legitimate business on the demised premises, and to remove them within the term, provided such structures or alterations will not do any serious injury to the realty' (Rasch, New York Landlord and Tenant (2d ed.), § 455, p. 577, citing Andrews v. Day Button Co., supra; Agate v. Lowenbein, 57 N.Y. 604, supra).

* * *

Note

In a minority of jurisdictions, a tenant who commits waste, even in the absence of provision in the lease, will have his tenancy forfeited. This is pursuant to the English Statute of Gloucester. Ignored for 300 years in England and repealed in 1879, it did not become a part of the common law of many states. See *Creekmore v. Redman Industries, Inc.*, 671 P.2d 73 (Okl.App. 1983).

§ 10.3.2 Not to Commit Waste: Relationship to Law of Fixtures

A chattel that becomes physically attached to realty in a manner so that it cannot be removed without materially damaging the underlying realty or the chattel itself is referred to as a "fixture"—personal property that becomes realty. For example, if a bathtub is attached to the realty and cannot be readily removed, it is a fixture. Upon termination of the leasehold, the fixture remains the property of the landlord. A tenant who attempts to remove such a fixture and thereby damages the realty or the fixture is liable to the landlord for waste.

What if the chattel is attached to the land but can be removed without damaging the realty or the chattel? For example, a tenant purchases a room air conditioner that is inserted in a window. In such case, it is said that the status of the personal property— whether it remains a chattel that can be removed or whether it has become a fixture that must stay with the land—depends on the intent of the parties, as evidenced by the surrounding circumstances. If the circumstances establish that the intent of the parties is that the chattel is property of the landlord and the tenant subsequently removes it, although the tenant would not be liable for waste (it can be removed easily), the tenant would nonetheless be liable for value of the fixture.

Next suppose that the tenant installs a chattel that is used in the tenant's trade or business and that is attached to the land (e.g., the owner of a pizzeria installs a pizza oven). Such a chattel is a "trade fixture" and remains the property of the tenant when the lease ends. Of course, a tenant who removes a trade fixture may still be liable to the landlord for waste for damaging the underlying realty.

For a discussion of the law of fixtures and waste, see Lehmann v. Keller, *454 Pa.Super. 42 (1996).*

§ 10.3.3 To Pay Rent

The next duty we examine is the tenant's duty to pay rent. Under the common law, the tenant's duty to pay rent was virtually absolute—but that view is no longer so, as the next case illustrates.

Albert M. Greenfield & Co., Inc. v. Kolea

475 Pa. 351 (1977)

A commercial tenant leased a building that was destroyed in a fire; neither the landlord nor the tenant was at fault. The tenant sought rescission of the lease. The court, in contradistinction with the common law view, allows rescission. The court's rationale is based, not on property law, but the law of contracts.

MANDERINO, Justice.

* * *

The general rule has been stated that in the absence of a lease provision to the contrary, a tenant is not relieved from the obligation to pay rent despite the total destruction of the leased premises. Magaw v. Lambert, 3 Pa. 444 (1846); Hoy v. Holt, 91 Pa. 88 (1879).

The reason for the rule has been said to be that although a building may be an important element of consideration for the payment of rent, the interest in the soil remains to support the lease despite destruction of the building. It has also been said that since destruction of the building is usually by accident, it is only equitable to divide the loss; the lessor loses the property and the lessee loses the term. See generally, Sum.Pa.Jur. Landlord and Tenant, § 72.

Two exceptions designed to afford relief to the tenant from the harshness of the common law principle have been created. These exceptions reflect the influence of modern contract principles as applied in the landlord-tenant relationship.

The first exception provides that where only a portion of a building is leased, total destruction of the building relieves the tenant of the obligation to pay rent. Moving Picture Co. of America v. Scottish Union & Nat'l. Ins. Co. of Edinburgh, 244 Pa. 258, 90 A. 642 (1914). See also Paxson & Comfort Co. v. Potter, 30 Pa.Super. 615 (1906). This exception recognizes that in the leasing of a part of a building there is no implication that any estate in land is granted. This Court, in other words, has recognized that in a landlord-tenant relationship with respect to an apartment, the parties have bargained for a part of a building and not the land beneath.

The influence of contract principles of bargained for exchange is also apparent in the second exception to the general common law rule. The second exception is based on the doctrine of impossibility of performance, and is stated in Greenburg v. Sun Shipbuilding Co., 277 Pa. 312, 313, 121 A. 63, 64 (1923):

"Where a contract relates to the use and possession of specific property, the existence of which is necessary to the carrying out of the purpose in view, a condition is implied by law, as though written in the agreement that the impossibility of performance arising from the destruction of the property without fault of either party, shall end all contractual obligations relating to the thing destroyed." See also Rest. Contracts, § 460, 6 Corbin on Contracts, § 1337.

As was said in West v. Peoples First Nat'l. Bank & Trust Co., 378 Pa. 275, 106 A.2d 427 (1954),

". . . where a contract relates to specific property the existence or maintenance of which is necessary to the carrying out of the purpose of the agreement, the condition is

319

implied by law, just as though it were written into the agreement, that the impossibility of performance or the frustration of purpose arising from the destruction of the property or interference with its use, without the fault of either party, ends all contractual obligations relating to the property. Moreover, impossibility in that connection means not only strict impossibility but impracticability because of extreme and unreasonable difficulty, expense, or loss involved." (footnote omitted.)

The Rest. Contracts § 454, also applies the test of impracticability rather than strict impossibility:

". . . (I)mpossibility means not only strict impossibility but impracticability because of extreme and unreasonable difficulty, expense, injury, or loss involved." (Emphasis added.)

In the instant case, it is apparent that when the building was destroyed by fire it became impossible for the appellee to furnish the agreed consideration ". . . all that one story garage building. . . ." * * * Without a building appellant could no longer carry on a used car business as contemplated by the parties at the time they entered into the lease agreement. It became extremely impracticable for the appellant to continue using the adjoining lot when his business office and repair stations were destroyed by the fire. Additionally, because of the dangerous condition created by the fire, the city required appellee to barricade the property covered by both leases, thus preventing appellant from entering the property.

* * *

In reaching a decision involving the landlord-tenant relationship, too often courts have relied on outdated common law property principles and presumptions and have refused to consider the factors necessary for an equitable and just conclusion. In this case, for example, if we applied the general rule and ignored the realities of the situation, we would bind the appellant to paying rent for barren ground when both parties to the lease contemplated that the building would be used for the commercial enterprise of repair and sale of used motor vehicles.

The trial court's decision to bind the lessee to the lease was simply an application of an outdated common law presumption. That presumption developed in a society very different from ours today: one where the land was always more valuable than the buildings erected on it. Buildings are critical to the functioning of modern society. When the parties bargain for the use of a building, the soil beneath is generally of little consequence. Our laws should develop to reflect these changes. As stated in Javins v. First Nat'l. Realty Corp., 138 U.S.App.D.C. 369, 372, 428 F.2d 1071, 1074,cert. denied, 400 U.S. 925, 91 S.Ct. 186, 27 L.Ed.2d 185 (1970):

"Courts have a duty to reappraise old doctrines in the light of the facts and values of contemporary life particularly old common law doctrines which the courts themselves created and developed. As we have said before, '(T)he continued vitality of the common law . . . depends upon its ability to reflect contemporary values and ethics.' " (Footnote omitted.)

The presumption established in Magaw and Hoy, supra, no longer has relevance to today's landlord-tenant relationships. It is no longer reasonable to assume that in the absence of a lease provision to the contrary the lessee should bear the risk of loss in the event of total destruction of the building. Where the parties do not expressly provide for such a catastrophe, the court should analyze the facts and the lease agreement as any other contract would be analyzed. Following such an analysis, if it is evident to the court that the parties bargained for the existence of a building, and no provision is made as to who bears the risk of loss if the building is destroyed, the court should relieve the parties of their respective obligations when the building no longer exists.

Accordingly, we reverse the order of the Superior Court, and remand to the trial court with directions to grant the appellant's motion for judgment n.o.v.

* * *

§ 10.4 Landlord Remedies

§ 10.4.1 Introduction

Assume that the tenant has breached a provision of the lease. Assume also that as a result of the breach, the lease allows the landlord to enter the tenant's premises and retake possession. In such case, must the landlord go through the judicial process, which can take a substantially long period of time and cost a significant amount of money? Or, is the landlord entitled to engage in so-called self-help? Further, and in any event, is the landlord required to mitigate (reduce) his damages? The materials that follow give some answers to these questions.

§ 10.4.2 Self-Help

Under the common law, if a tenant was in breach of a provision of the lease and if the lease allowed the landlord to retake possession in the event of a breach (such as failure to pay rent), a landlord could use reasonable force to evict a tenant. That is still the law in some jurisdictions today. Other jurisdictions, as illustrated in Freeman v. Muia, *infra, allow self-help by the landlord but only when the reentry is peaceable.*

Freeman v. Muia
133 Misc.2d 1097 (N.Y.City Ct. 1986)

The landlord padlocked the tenant out when the latter did not pay rent. Self-help is allowed in New York when (1) the reentry is peaceable and (2) the landlord reserves in the lease the right to reenter in the event the tenant defaults. The lease in question provided for such reentry. The tenant brought suit against the landlord for damages. The court found in favor of the landlord.

LARRY J. ROSEN, Justice.
Petitioner brings this special proceeding against respondent pursuant to Section 853 of the Real Property Actions and Proceedings Law seeking to recover treble damages

pursuant to that section. Respondent has interposed counterclaims and defenses. Trial, without jury, was held and was concluded on October 9, 1986.

The court finds that on or about September 1, 1985, the petitioner entered into a written one-year lease agreement with respondent's predecessor in title to premises commonly known as 666 State Street, Albany, New York (1st Floor). From said date the petitioner continuously remained in possession. Sometime in March 1986, respondent purchased the property, said purchase being subject to the aforementioned lease agreement. Petitioner was informed that he had a new landlord and, in fact, paid the April 1986 rental in two installments to respondent by placing said payments into respondent's mailbox at the latter's residence. On or about May 2, 1986, a note was left for petitioner by respondent (Petitioner's Exhibit 2 in evidence) stating, *inter alia,* "The full amount of rent is due by the 5th of the month * * * *."

Rental for May 1986 was not paid and on May 9, 1986, the petitioner found that the door to the apartment in question had been padlocked by the respondent. An unfortunate and escalating chain of events was thus triggered, which included a May 13, 1986 reentry by petitioner by use of a locksmith and a further note from respondent to petitioner indicating, in substance, that should petitioner attempt entry, he would be arrested. Petitioner further testified without contradiction that his personal belongings, such as they were, had been removed by respondent-landlord during this period of time from the interior of the premises to an outer enclosed porch.

Further findings of fact made by the court include that on or about May 15, 1986, petitioner was indebted to Niagara Mohawk in the amount of approximately $900.00 for the apartment in question and that telephone service to the apartment of petitioner was discontinued for nonpayment on or about May 5, 1986.

The threshold determination to be made by this court is whether the fact pattern in the instant case makes out a *prima facie* violation of Section 853 of the R.P.A.P.L. This section states,

"If a person is disseized, ejected, or put out of real property in a forcible or unlawful manner, or, after he has been put out, is held and kept out by force or by putting him in fear of personal violence or by unlawful means, he is entitled to recover treble damages in an action therefor against the wrong-doer."

Since the written lease in this case allows reentry by landlord after a rental default (said default occurring in the instant case) *Pine Hills Associates v. Malveaux,* 93 Misc.2d 63, 403 N.Y.S.2d 398 is pertinent. On page 64, 403 N.Y.S.2d 398 the applicable substantive law is stated,

"Where provided for in the lease, peaceable re-entry by landlord is permissible where the tenant has failed to pay the rent when due (see *Fults v Munro,* 202 NY 34 [95 N.E.23]; *Michaels v Fishel,* 169 NY 381 [62 N.E. 425]; *Cohen v Carpenter,* 128 App Div 862 [113 N.Y.S. 168]; *Ajax Wrecking & Lbr. Co. v Baker,* NYLJ, April 21, 1977, p 12, col 4; 2 Rasch NY Landlord and Tenant 2d ed, § 734.) However, this being a common-law right, the landlord must first make a demand for the rent."

Therefore, the further question arises as to whether notice was given petitioner. The court finds that Petitioner's Exhibit 2 in evidence, together with respondent's testimony, constitutes sufficient notice to petitioner that rental was being demanded by respondent. Petitioner never did make the payment of rent for May 1986. The court is further persuaded by the evidence that petitioner had made an independent determination, prior to the padlocking herein, to cease residing in the premises. The court finds that petitioner was in the process of vacating the premises, as evidenced by the condition of the premises and the utility arrearages, prior to the padlocking.

In the final analysis the court must conclude, however reluctantly, that petitioner's removal from the property, under the circumstances at bar, was not "forcible" or "unlawful" as such is understood by Section 853 of the RPAPL.

The court wishes to make crystal clear that it is not condoning, per se, the padlocking of a tenant from a residence by a landlord when a written lease allows such self help after a default. The holding of this court is thus strictly limited to the factual pattern found. The court specifically finds that when a landlord and tenant of relatively equal bargaining power enter into a written lease allowing reentry by landlord if a default in rent occurs and such default does occur, notice is given to tenant and the default is not cured, and prior to the default the tenant has evidenced an independent intention to vacate the premises, then in such a case a reentry and placing out of tenant cannot be held to be unlawful pursuant to Section 853 of RPAPL. This court can, however, envision situations where a padlocking would, in fact, be unlawful pursuant to Section 853 and all residential landlords would be well advised to utilize the provisions of Article VII of the RPAPL governing summary proceedings rather than self help even when authorized by a lease.

* * *

Claims and counterclaims dismissed, without costs to either party against the other.

Note

For a contrary view, and probably the prevailing view regarding self-help, see *Berg v. Wiley*, 264 N.W.2d 145 (Minn. 1978), where the court held that locking the tenant out was not peaceable because there was the potential for violence, even though no violence actually occurred, and also holding that in the future, no self-help of any kind would be sanctioned: that the judicial process is the only lawful process available henceforth.

§ 10.4.3 Mitigation Requirement

Assume that L and T have a three-year lease and that one year into the lease, T "abandons." Must L "mitigate" his damages? Must L try to get a new tenant, or can L simply sue T for the balance of the rent due? As you will see from Jordan v. Nickell *and the note that follows, there is a split of authority.*

Jordon v. Nickell
253 S.W.2d 237 (Ky.1952)

The case represents the traditional property-centered view: that a landlord does not have a duty to mitigate.

* * *

As we have indicated, the property has remained vacant continuously since appellant surrendered possession. Appellant contends that the keys have been returned, but appellee asserts he has never received them. Appellant insists that it was the duty of appellee to minimize damages by securing another tenant if possible and that in no event can recovery under the lease exceed the difference between the contract rentals and the rentals which might have been received under a new lease.

There is a difference in the rule concerning the right of a landlord to recover rental for the remainder of the term in cases where there has been a forfeiture of the lease and re-entry by the lessor on account of the breach of a covenant by the lessee, and cases in which the lessee has abandoned the leased premises. In the former case, the lessor is generally under an obligation to minimize damages, and the lessee is entitled to have any amounts received by lessor under a new lease applied toward the satisfaction of lessee's liability. However, following an abandonment by a tenant, the landlord is under no obligation to attempt to re-let the leased premises. The theory supporting the rule is that the tenant cannot by his own wrong in abandoning the premises impose a duty upon the landlord. Abraham v. Gheens, 205 Ky. 289, 265 S.W. 778, 40 A.L.R. 186; Ideal Furniture Co. v. Mazer, 234 Ky. 665, 28 S.W.2d 974; Moore v. Rogers, 240 Ky. 743, 43 S.W.2d 31; Dulworth v. Hyman, Ky., 246 S.W.2d 993, In re Dant & Dant of Ky., D.C., 39 F.Supp. 753, affirmed Kessler v. Jefferson Storage Corporation, 6 Cir., 125 F.2d 108.

* * *

Note

For an opposing, and now majority, view see *Sommer v. Kridel*, 74 N.J. 446 (1977). The court there held that when a tenant surrenders the premises ("surrender" is the tenant's offer to terminate the lease, which offer may be express, as in a letter, or implied, as by an abandonment), a landlord who does not accept the surrender nevertheless has a duty to mitigate damages. The landlord must advertise, secure a broker, etc. and otherwise add the vacant apartment to his or her existing stock. In such "mitigation" jurisdictions, if the landlord fails to mitigate, damages either will be reduced by the amount that the landlord could have secured if mitigation had been attempted or, in the alternative, the cause of action against the tenant will be totally lost. Note that in jurisdictions that require mitigation, a landlord who sues a tenant for damages for breach of lease will not sue the tenant each month for rent due. Rather, the landlord will file one action on the basis of anticipatory repudiation, a contract principle. On the other hand, a jurisdiction that follows the no-mitigation approach in *Jordon v. Nickell*, supra, will require a landlord to sue a tenant each month as the rent comes due under the lease.

One final point is in order here: Irrespective of whether a landlord is in a mitigation (*Sommer v. Kridel*) or no-mitigation (*Jordon v. Nickell*) jurisdiction, a landlord who reenters and retakes possession and attempts to relet does so with great risk. A court may find such act to be an acceptance of the surrender (the tenant's offer to terminate the lease). In such case, the tenant would be released from all future liability under the lease. Thus, a landlord who attempts to relet the apartment (especially in a *Jordon v. Nickell* jurisdiction) would be well advised to send a letter to the tenant informing the tenant that the landlord is not accepting the surrender but is merely reentering and releting on behalf of the tenant's account.

§ 10.5 Landlord Duties

§ 10.5.1 Introduction

The common law imposed relatively few duties on the landlord. These duties are covered in the material that follows. You will notice that the duty to provide habitable housing to the tenant is the last duty covered in this section. This placement at the end is neither coincidental nor arbitrary. It is at the end because the duty to provide a habitable unit is relatively new and took quite some time to develop: that until the early 1970s, rarely did landlords have such a duty, caveat lessee *being the rule. That said,* caveat lessee *still is the rule in some jurisdictions.*

§ 10.5.2 To Deliver Possession

In every jurisdiction, the landlord has a duty to deliver legal possession: that there is no legal obstacle in the way to the tenant's taking actual physical possession. An example of a legal obstacle would be where the landlord previously rented out the same premises to another tenant for the same period of time. About half of the jurisdictions require the landlord to deliver legal possession—and only legal possession. This is the so-called American rule. In the other jurisdictions, the landlord must not only deliver legal possession; he or she also must deliver actual possession: that the landlord opens up the premises to the tenant. This requirement that the landlord also deliver actual possession (in addition to legal possession) is the so-called English rule.

Where the tenant cannot take possession because there is a holdover tenant, one or the other of these two rules comes into play. In jurisdictions that adopt the American rule, the tenant who cannot take possession because of the holdover tenant has a cause of action against the holdover but not against the landlord. The rationale is that the landlord should not be held responsible for the acts of another. In jurisdictions that adopt the English rule, the tenant has a cause of action against the landlord (and can avoid liability under the lease). The rationale here is that the tenant bargained for a tenancy, not a lawsuit. For a discussion of the American rule and the English rule, see Hannan v. Dusch, *154 Va. 356 (1930).*

§ 10.5.3 To Maintain Common Areas

Under the common law (and still the law in all jurisdictions), a landlord has a duty to maintain "common areas." The meaning of the term and the consequences of failing to maintain the common areas are discussed in Pate v. Reeves.

Pate v. Reeves
719 S.W.2d 956 (Mo.App. 1986)

* * *

The mere relationship of landlord and tenant does not make the landlord liable for injuries to the tenant on the premises. *Erhardt v. Lowe,* 596 S.W.2d 489, 491

(Mo.App.1980). However, a landlord is under a duty to keep those portions of the premises which he retains in his control in a reasonably safe condition and is liable for damages resulting from his failure to do so. Id.

"Common areas" which are used by more than one tenant ordinarily would be in the control of the landlord and the landlord must maintain them in a reasonably safe condition or be liable for damage resulting from the failure to do so. See *Peterson v. Brune,* 273 S.W.2d 278, 280 (Mo.1954). A landlord is not ordinarily liable for injuries resulting from a defective condition in the part of the premises not reserved by the landlord for the common use of two or more tenants but demised to a particular tenant. *Gray v. Pearline,* 328 Mo. 1192, 43 S.W.2d 802, 805 (1931).[3]

* * *

§ 10.5.4 To Disclose Latent Defects

A latent defect is one that is hidden. The common law imposed a duty on landlords to disclose known latent defects. The next case provides further elucidation.

Anderson v. Shuman
257 Cal.App.2d 272 (1967)

A bathroom sink collapsed when the tenant leaned on it. The landlord may not have had actual knowledge of the defect in the sink in question, but the landlord knew that several similar sinks in other apartments in the same building also collapsed. The court, in holding for the tenant in her suit for damages, explains the knowledge that is necessary for a landlord to be liable for not disclosing a latent defect.

PIERCE, Presiding Justice.

The appeal is from a judgment following a jury verdict for plaintiff in an action for personal injuries. The injuries were caused by a fall. The fall resulted when a defectively installed bathroom sink in an apartment house became dislodged from the wall.

The question: Is a landlord liable to an injured tenant for the described injuries when the landlord knows and the tenant does not know that a like sink in another apartment had become dislodged and that several sinks were loose? We affirm the trial court's affirmative answer to that question.

The defendants are owners of an apartment house in Redding containing forty separate apartments. Construction of the apartment house had been completed during the latter part of 1962. On October 3, 1964, plaintiff moved into apartment number 15. Two days later, on October 5, 1964, she slipped and fell when, while cleaning her teeth and leaning on the sink with her left elbow or forearm, the sink dislodged, spilling water onto the floor. Plaintiff's elbow was fractured.

Plaintiff had had no prior knowledge or means of knowledge that the sink would become dislodged. The apartment house manager, before the accident, had acquired the

---

[3] [But see § 10.7.1 and *Sargent v. Ross* for the modern view of landlord liability in tort.]

following knowledge: Several months before the bathroom sink in apartment number 19 had similarly become dislodged, and three or four other bathroom sinks in the apartment house were discovered to be loose. Defendant landlords operated the apartment house as a partnership. The active partner was defendant Harold H. Coles. The manager, Phyllis Clay, had notified Coles of the defective conditions described and had requested authority to have all bathroom sinks inspected. That was not done. Mrs. Clay testified that as an apartment would become vacant it had been her practice to test the sinks by shaking them. She had not done this, however, in plaintiff's apartment before plaintiff moved in. She had not warned plaintiff of her experiences of the past with the dislodged and loose sinks.

A landlord is not an insurer and it has been held that, 'Subject to certain exceptions, a lessor is not subject to common law liability for harm caused to the lessee * * * by the condition of the premises * * *.' (Emphasis added.) (Finnegan v. Royal Realty Co., 35 Cal.2d 409, 428, 218 P.2d 17, 29.) He is not liable for defects which are patent, and, with respect to hidden defects, it may be said to be the settled law 'In this state, (that) a landlord is not liable to the tenant for injuries due to a defective condition or faulty construction of the demised premises, in the absence of fraud, concealment or covenant in the lease.' (Emphasis added.) (Lee v. Giosso (1965) 237 Cal.App.2d 246, 247--248, 46 Cal.Rptr. 803, 804; hear. den.)

What is concealment? We define it as being the withholding of knowledge which is material and ought to be revealed, and therefore as including the withholding of knowledge of a dangerous condition by a landlord from a tenant. There was no concealment in Lee v. Giosso, supra. The door of a wall bed had collapsed. A wrench was missing from the door's pivotal mechanism. The landlord knew the tenant had been having difficulty manipulating the bed. He knew nothing about the missing part.

Such innocence cannot be claimed here. True, when the apartment was rented to plaintiff, the landlords' agent did not know that this particular sink was about to become dislodged. But she did know that the bathroom sinks in this comparatively new apartment house were defective generally and had advised a general inspection.
* * *

Dean Prosser has stated: 'Modern ideas of social policy have given rise to a number of exceptions to * * * (the) general rules of non-liability of the lessor, which remain to be considered below. There is increasing recognition of the fact that the tenant who leases defective premises is likely to be impecunious and unable to make the necessary repairs, and that the financial burden is best placed upon the landlord, who receives a benefit from the transaction in the form of rent.

'One exception developed by the common law is that the lessor, like a vendor, is under the obligation to disclose to the lessee concealed dangerous conditions existing when possession is transferred, of which he has knowledge. There is again 'something like fraud' in a failure to give warning of a known hidden danger to one who enters upon the assumption that it does not exist; and the lessor will be liable to the lessee or to members of his family for his non-disclosure. * * *

'It is not necessary that the lessor shall believe the condition to be unsafe, or even that he have definite knowledge of its existence, before he is under any duty in regard to it. It is enough that he is informed of facts from which a reasonable man would conclude that there is danger; and the decisions run the gamut of 'reasonable notice,' 'reason to know,' or 'should have known.' If he has such information, and it would lead a reasonable man to suspect the existence of an unreasonable risk of harm, it is his duty to communicate at least that suspicion. * * *' (Prosser, Law of Torts (3d ed.) § 63, pp. 413--414.)

* * *

The judgment is affirmed.
FRIEDMAN and REGAN, JJ., concur.

§ 10.5.5 Not to Breach the Covenant of Quiet Enjoyment: Evolution of the Common Law

Under the ancient common law, a tenant had an unqualified duty to pay rent. In the event that the landlord breached a duty imposed under the lease or the law, the tenant could sue the landlord for breach of that duty—but a suit based on that breach did not excuse the tenant from performing his or her duties, such as the duty to pay rent. Why was this? Because all covenants in a lease were independent. This stemmed from the common law view that landlord-tenant relations were governed by property law and not contract law. (Cf. Albert M. Greenfield & Co., Inc. v. Kolea, *supra.) With this background, we now are able to appreciate the development of the covenant of quiet enjoyment.*

The origin of the covenant of quiet enjoyment began with a very limited fact pattern: when the landlord actually and wrongfully evicted the tenant. Thus, for example, if the landlord erroneously believed that the tenant had not paid the rent and the landlord changed the locks, thereby locking the tenant out, the landlord breached the covenant of quiet enjoyment. Moreover, because the tenant was now evicted, the tenant could not only sue the landlord for damages stemming from the wrongful eviction but also could be relieved from performing his duties under the lease. This was a major development in the common law. For the first time in landlord-tenant relations, property law witnessed a dependency of covenants: when the landlord actually and wrongfully evicted the tenant, the landlord breached the covenant of quiet enjoyment and the tenant's obligations under the lease ceased at that point. See e.g. Smith v. McEnany, *170 Mass. 26 (1897) and* Worden v. Ordway, *105 Idaho 719 (1983). But the common law did not stop there; the covenant of quiet enjoyment continued to evolve.*

It came to pass that if the landlord engaged in any affirmative act that substantially interfered with the tenant's peaceful enjoyment of the premises—not just wrongfully and actually evicting the tenant—the landlord breached the covenant of quiet enjoyment. For example, if the landlord rented out an apartment and also owned and operated a nearby brothel, the noise of which interfered with the tenant's peaceful enjoyment of the premises, the landlord breached the covenant of quiet enjoyment and the tenant could sue the landlord for damages. See Milheim v. Baxter, *46 Colo. 155 (1909). Furthermore—and this is most important—in addition to suing for damages, if the tenant vacated the premises, the tenant was deemed to have been "constructively evicted" and the tenant was no longer liable for further obligations under the lease. The lease was terminated. Thus, we again see the strengthening of the dependency of covenants in property law. Of course, for the tenant to avail himself of this remedy of constructive eviction (and it is important to keep in mind that constructive eviction is not a cause of action but a remedy for breach of the covenant of quiet enjoyment), the tenant had to move out in a timely manner. There is no hard and fast rule as to what constitutes a timely vacation of the premises; the "test" (such as it is) is dependent upon the totality of the circumstances. See* Charles E. Burt, Inc. v. Seven Grand Corp., *340 Mass. 124 (1959).*

As the covenant of quiet enjoyment continued to evolve, landlords were found to have breached the covenant of quiet enjoyment for not acting—a failure to act—if the landlord had a duty to act, which duty was found either in the lease or in the law, and that failure substantially interfered with the tenant's peaceful enjoyment of the premises. Thus, for example, if a lease provided that a landlord must deliver electrical power to a tenant and the landlord repeatedly failed to do so, the landlord breached the covenant of quiet enjoyment. See Charles E. Burt, Inc. v. Seven Grand Corp., *supra. Again, if there were a breach of the covenant of quiet enjoyment, and if the tenant moved out in a timely manner, the tenant could avail himself of the remedy of constructive eviction and be relieved of further liability under the lease.*

The next case, Reste Realty Corp. v. Cooper, *represents a revolutionary leap in the development of the covenant of quiet enjoyment—or does it?*

Reste Realty Corp. v. Cooper
53 N.J. 444 (1969)

Joy Cooper leased a basement floor of a commercial office building for her business. Because the adjacent driveway, used by all of the tenants of the building, was improperly graded, Cooper's office flooded whenever it rained. Cooper complained to the landlord on a number of occasions and the landlord attempted to solve the problem. Ultimately, however, the problem was not solved. After one particular rain, the office flooded and a staff meeting had to be adjourned and reconvened at another location. Cooper thereafter gave notice to the landlord that she was vacating and left. The landlord then sued Cooper for the rent due on the remaining term of the lease. The court will decide the case in favor of Cooper. The court will hold that the landlord breached the covenant of quiet enjoyment. What was the basis for the breach?

FRANCIS, J.

On this appeal the plaintiff-landlord claims that under the long-settled law, delivery of the leased premises to defendant-tenant was not accompanied by any implied warranty or covenant of fitness for use for commercial offices or for any other purpose. * * * *

* * * It has come to be recognized that ordinarily the lessee does not have as much knowledge of the condition of the premises as the lessor. Building code requirements and violations are known or made known to the lessor, not the lessee. He is in a better position to know of latent defects, structural and otherwise, in a building which might go unnoticed by a lessee who rarely has sufficient knowledge or expertise to see or to discover them. A prospective lessee, such as a small businessman, cannot be expected to know if the plumbing or wiring systems are adequate or conform to local codes. Nor should he be expected to hire experts to advise him. Ordinarily all this information should

be considered readily available to the lessor who in turn can inform the prospective lessee. * * *

* * * The word 'premises,' construed most favorably to the tenant, means so much of the ground floor as was leased to Mrs. Cooper for commercial offices. The driveway or its surfacing or the exterior wall or foundation under it cannot be considered included as part of the 'premises.' In any event there is nothing to show that the inspection by Mrs. Cooper of the driveway or the ground floor exterior wall and foundation under it prior to the execution of the first lease would have given or did give her notice that they were so defective as to permit rainwater to flood into the leased portion of the interior. The condition should have been and probably was known to the lessor. If known, there was a duty to disclose it to the prospective tenant. Certainly as to Mrs. Cooper, it was a latent defect, and it would be a wholly inequitable application of Caveat emptor to charge her with knowledge of it. The attempted reliance upon the agreement of the tenant in both leases to keep the 'demised premises' in repair furnishes no support for the landlord's position. The driveway, exterior ground floor wall and foundation are not part of the demised premises. Latent defects in this context, i.e., those the existence and significance of which are not reasonably apparent to the ordinary prospective tenant, certainly were not assumed by Mrs. Cooper. In fact in our judgment present day demands of fair treatment for tenants with respect to latent defects remediable by the landlord, either within the demised premises or outside the demised premises, require imposition on him of an implied warranty against such defects. See Buckner v. Azulai, 251 Cal.App.2d Supp. 1013, 59 Cal.Rptr. 806 (1967); Charles E. Burt, Inc. v. Seven Grand Corporation, 340 Mass. 124, 163 N.E.2d 4, 6, n. 2 (1959); Pines v. Perssion, supra, 111 N.W.2d at 412-413. Such warranty might be described as a limited warranty of habitability. In any event we need not at this point deal with the scope of the warranty, nor with issues of public policy that might be involved in certain types of cases where express exclusion of such warranty is contained in the lease. Cf. Henningsen v. Bloomfield Motors, Inc., 32 N.J. 358, 396-404, 161 A.2d 69, 75 A.L.R.2d 1 (1960); Michaels v. Brookchester, Inc., supra, 26 N.J. at 382-387, 140 A.2d 199; Uniform Commercial Code, N.J.S. 12A:2-302, N.J.S.A.

* * *

This brings us to the crucial question whether the landlord was guilty of a breach of a covenant which justified the tenant's removal from the premises on December 30, 1961. We are satisfied there was such a breach.

The great weight of authority throughout the country is to the effect that ordinarily a covenant of quiet enjoyment is implied in a lease. 1 American Law of Property, supra, § 3.47, pp. 271-272; Powell on Real Property, supra, §225(3), pp. 232-240; Annotation, 41 A.L.R.2d 1414, 1420 (1955). * * * Where there is such a covenant, whether express or implied,[4] and it is breached substantially by the landlord, the courts have applied the doctrine of constructive eviction as a remedy for the tenant. Under this rule any act or omission of the landlord or of anyone who acts under authority or legal right from the landlord, or of someone having superior title to that of the landlord, which renders the premises substantially unsuitable for the purpose for which they are leased, or

---

[4] [It is safe to say that today, in all jurisdictions, there is an implied covenant of quiet enjoyment in all leases.]

which seriously interferes with the beneficial enjoyment of the premises, is a breach of the covenant of quiet enjoyment and constitutes a constructive eviction of the tenant. [Citations omitted.]

Examples of constructive eviction having close analogy to the present case are easily found. Failure to supply heat as covenanted in the lease so that the apartment was 'unlivable' on cold days amounted to constructive eviction. Higgins v. Whiting, supra; Anderson v. Walker Realty Co., 1 N.J.Misc. 287 (Sup.Ct.1923). So too, when the main waste pipe of an apartment building was permitted to become and remain clogged with sewage for a long period of time causing offensive odors and danger to health, the covenant of quiet enjoyment was breached and justified the tenant's abandonment of his premises. McCurdy v. Wyckoff, supra. If a landlord lets an apartment in his building to a tenant as a dwelling and knowingly permits another part to be used for lewd purposes which use renders the tenant's premises 'unfit for occupancy by a respectable family,' his failure to terminate the use when he has the legal power to do so constitutes a constructive eviction.[5] Weiler v. Pancoast, supra. The same rule was applied in White v. Hannon, 11 N.J.L.J. 338 (Dist.Ct.1888) where it appeared that the plumbing in the rooms to the rear of the demised premises became so old and worn out as to emit strong and unhealthy odors which came through into the tenant's quarters. The tenant's removal was held justified. [Citations omitted.] * * *

* * * We reject the rule of Stewart v. Childs Co. and espouse Higgins v. Whiting as propounding the sounder doctrine. And see Groh v. Kover's Bull Pen, Inc., supra, 221 Cal.App.2d 611, 34 Cal.Rptr. at 639; Westland Housing Corp. v. Scott, supra; Stifter v. Hartman, 225 Mich. 101, 195 N.W. 673 (1923); Ingram v. Fred, supra; 39 Harv.L.Rev. 1102 (1926). Higgins v. Whiting is compatible with the sensible approach taken in Pines v. Perssion, supra, where in addition to the excerpt quoted above, the court said:

'The evidence clearly showed that the implied warranty of habitability was breached. Respondents' covenant to pay rent and appellant's covenant to provide a habitable house were mutually dependent, and thus a breach of the latter by appellant relieved respondents of any liability under the former.' 111 N.W.2d at 413. Breach of the implied warranty of habitability was held to constitute failure of consideration on the part of the landlord.

Similarly whether the landlord's default in the present case is treated as a substantial breach of the express covenant of quiet enjoyment resulting in a constructive eviction of the tenant or as a material failure of consideration, (i.e., such failure as amounts to a substantial interference with the beneficial enjoyment of the premises) the tenant's vacation was legal. Thus it is apparent from our discussion that a tenant's right to vacate leased premises is the same from a doctrinal standpoint whether treated as stemming from breach of a covenant of quiet enjoyment or from breach of any other dependent covenant. Both breaches constitute failure of consideration. The inference to be drawn from the cases is that the remedy of constructive eviction probably evolved

---

[5] [Do these acts constitute a constructive eviction, as the court states, or do they constitute a breach of the covenant of quiet enjoyment? It is the latter. The cause of action is the breach of the covenant of quiet enjoyment. A remedy that a tenant may elect is constructive eviction. It is critical to keep these two theories—one based on the cause of action and the other based on the remedy—separate and distinct, even if courts do not always do so.]

from a desire by the courts to relieve the tenant from the harsh burden imposed by common law rules which applied principles of caveat emptor to the letting, rejected an implied warranty of habitability, and ordinarily treated undertakings of the landlord in a lease as independent covenants. To alleviate the tenant's burden, the courts broadened the scope of the long-recognized implied covenant of quiet enjoyment * * * to include the right of the tenant to have the beneficial enjoyment and use of the premises for the agreed term. It was but a short step then to the rule that when the landlord or someone acting for him or by virtue of a right acquired through him causes a substantial interference with that enjoyment and use, the tenant may claim a constructive eviction. In our view, therefore, at the present time whenever a tenant's right to vacate leased premises comes into existence because he is deprived of their beneficial enjoyment and use on account of acts chargeable to the landlord, it is immaterial whether the right is expressed in terms of breach of a covenant of quiet enjoyment, or material failure of consideration, or material breach of an implied warranty against latent defects.

[The court next found that the tenant moved out in a timely manner so that she could avail herself of the remedy of constructive eviction.]

For the reasons expressed above, we hold the view that the trial court was correct in deciding that defendant had been constructively evicted from the premises in question, and therefore was not liable for the rent claimed. Accordingly, the judgment of the Appellate Division is reversed and that of the trial court is reinstated.

For reversal: Chief Justice WEINTRAUB and Justices JACOBS, FRANCIS, PROCTOR, HALL, SCHETTINO and HANEMAN-7.

For affirmance: None.

§ 10.5.6 Duty to Provide Habitable Premises: Introduction

As touched upon by the Reste Realty *court, the common law did not impose upon the landlord a duty to provide habitable premises to the tenant in a residential lease. The common law looked at a lease as a conveyance. If there were any problems with the land, it was the tenant's problem with which to deal. Nonetheless, early on, an exception was made for the short-term lease of a furnished house or apartment. Under such circumstances, there was a duty to provide habitable premises. The rationale was that for such a lease (short-term and furnished), the tenant clearly was not interested in the land. Thus, if the premises were not habitable, the tenant was justified in securing rescission of the lease and a return of any deposit. See* Ingalls v. Hobbs, *156 Mass. 348 (1892).*

§ 10.5.7 Duty to Provide Habitable Premises: Illegal Lease Theory

While the evolution of the covenant of quiet enjoyment gave tenants some relief, it was not the ideal for tenants, especially residential tenants. Why, you ask? Suppose a landlord breached the covenant of quiet enjoyment. The tenant could stay on the premises and sue the landlord for damages. But retaining counsel to prosecute a lawsuit (for amounts that typically are not substantial) is not financially feasible for most residential tenants. Of course, the tenant could avail himself of the remedy of constructive eviction. But there was risk in that, too: If a court were to find that there was no breach of the covenant of quiet enjoyment or (if there was a breach but) the tenant did not move out in a timely manner, the tenant would be in the difficult position of being liable for two leases (the old and the new). A new theory, therefore, was sought. In Brown v. Southall Realty Co., *237 A.2d 834 (D.C.Cir. 1968), it appeared that tenants secured the ideal theory: the illegal lease. The heart of the theory is that if the landlord leases a residential unit to a tenant and the unit at the beginning of the lease is in violation of the local housing code, the lease is illegal. As such, the landlord has no rights that flow from the lease. Why is this so? It is black letter law that courts do not enforce illegal contracts. Rather, in such cases, a court will leave the parties where it found them. Thus, under this illegal lease theory, if an apartment is not fit for habitation because it violates state or local housing laws, the landlord is powerless to evict the tenant for non-payment of rent due under the lease. Tenant groups finally got what they wanted: the ability to stay on the premises and not pay rent.*

The illegal lease theory did not remain at the forefront of tenant actions, however. In subsequent cases, the D.C. Circuit Court of Appeals pulled back from its novel approach in Brown. *In* Saunders v. First National Realty Corp., *245 A.2d 836 (D.C.App. 1968), the court held that the doctrine does not apply to housing code violations that develop after execution of the lease. Further, in* William J. Davis, Inc. v. Slade, 271 A.2d 412 (D.C.App. 1970), *the court held that while the landlord cannot collect rent on the basis of the lease, the landlord is nonetheless entitled to the fair rental value of the residence.*

Another theory, therefore, was needed. That theory would be the implied warranty of habitability.

§ 10.5.8 Duty to Provide Habitable Premises: Implied Warranty of Habitability

Green v. Superior Court
10 Cal.3d 616 (1974)

A tenant did not pay rent and the landlord filed an unlawful detainer action and a suit for damages. The tenant raised the affirmative defense of the landlord's breach of the implied warranty of habitability. The apartment in question was in a dilapidated state that was a threat to the tenant's health and safety. The landlord prevailed at trial and on appeal. The California Supreme Court will reverse and adopt an implied warranty of habitability in residential leases.

TOBRINER, Justice.

Under traditional common law doctrine, long followed in California, a landlord was under no duty to maintain leased dwellings in habitable condition during the term of the lease. In the past several years, however, the highest courts of a rapidly growing number of states and the District of Columbia have reexamined the bases of the old common law rule and have uniformly determined that it no longer corresponds to the realities of the modern urban landlord-tenant relationship. Accordingly, each of these jurisdictions has discarded the old common law rule and has adopted an implied warranty of habitability for residential leases. In June 1972, the California Court of Appeal reviewed this emerging out-of-state precedent in the case of Hinson v. Delis (1972) 26 Cal.App.3d 62, 102 Cal.Rptr. 661, and, persuaded by the reasoning of these decisions, held that a warranty of habitability is implied by law in residential leases in California. We granted a hearing in the instant case, and a companion case, to consider the Hinson decision and to determine whether the breach of such implied warranty may be raised as a defense by a tenant in an unlawful detainer action.

For the reasons discussed below, we have determined that the Hinson court properly recognized a common law implied warranty of habitability in residential leases in California, and we conclude that the breach of such warranty may be raised as a defense in an unlawful detainer action.

First, as the recent line of out-of-state cases comprehensively demonstrate, the factual and legal premises underlying the original common law rule in this area have long ceased to exist; continued adherence to the time-worn doctrine conflicts with the expectations and demands of the contemporary landlord-tenant relationship and with modern legal principles in analogous fields. To remain viable, the common law must reflect the realities of present day society; an implied warranty of habitability in residential leases must therefore be recognized.

Second, we shall point out that the statutory 'repair and deduct' provisions of Civil Code section 1941 et seq. do not preclude this development in the common law, for such enactments were never intended to be the exclusive remedy for tenants but have always been viewed as complementary to existing common law rights.

Finally, we have concluded that a landlord's breach of this warranty of habitability may be raised as a defense in an unlawful detainer action. Past California cases have established that a defendant in an unlawful detainer action may raise any affirmative defense which, if established, will preserve the tenant's possession of the premises. As we shall explain, a landlord's breach of a warranty of habitability directly relates to whether any rent is 'due and owing' by the tenant; hence, such breach may be determinative of whether the landlord or tenant is entitled to possession of the premises upon nonpayment of rent. Accordingly, the tenant may properly raise the issue of warranty of habitability in an unlawful detainer action.

1. *The facts of the instant case.*

We begin with a brief review of the facts of the instant case, which reveal a somewhat typical unlawful detainer action. On September 27, 1972, the landlord Jack Sumski commenced an unlawful detainer action in the San Francisco Small Claims Court seeking possession of the leased premises and $300 in back rent. The tenant admitted non-payment of rent but defended the action on the ground that the landlord had failed to maintain the leased premises in a habitable condition. The small claims court awarded possession of the premises to the landlord and entered a money judgment for $225 against the tenant.

The tenant then appealed the decision to the San Francisco Superior Court, where a de novo trial was held pursuant to section 117j of the Code of Civil Procedure. In support of his claim of uninhabitability, the tenant submitted a copy of an October 1972 inspection report of the San Francisco Department of Public Works disclosing some 80 housing code violations in the building in question, as well as an order of the department scheduling a condemnation hearing for January 19, 1973. In addition, in testimony at trial, petitioner and his roommate detailed a long list of serious defects in the leased premises which had not been repaired by the landlord after notice and which they claimed rendered the premises uninhabitable. Some of the more serious defects described by the tenants included (1) the collapse and non-repair of the bathroom ceiling, (2) the continued presence of rats, mice, and cockroaches on the premises, (3) the lack of any heat in four of the apartment's rooms, (4) plumbing blockages, (5) exposed and faulty wiring, and (6) an illegally installed and dangerous stove.[6] The landlord apparently did not attempt to contest the presence of serious defects in the leased premises, but instead claimed that such defects afforded the tenant no defense in an unlawful detainer action.

The superior court judge ultimately agreed with the landlord's contention, holding that the 'repair and deduct' provisions of Civil Code section 1941 et seq. constituted the tenant's exclusive remedy under these circumstances. Accordingly, the superior court entered judgment for the landlord, awarding him $225 and possession of the premises.

* * *

2. *The transformation of the landlord tenant relationship and developments in analogous areas of law compel the recognition of a common law implied warranty of habitability in residential leases in California.*

At common law, the real estate lease developed in the field of real property law, not contract law. Under property law concepts, a lease was considered a conveyance or sale of the premises for a term of years, subject to the ancient doctrine of caveat emptor. Thus, under traditional common law rules, the landlord owed no duty to place leased premises in a habitable condition and no obligation to repair the premises. (3 Holdsworth, A History of English Law (5th ed. 1966) pp. 122--123; see, e.g., Brewster v. DeFremery (1867) 33 Cal. 341, 345--346.) These original common law precepts perhaps suited the agrarianism of the early Middle Ages which was their matrix; at such time, the primary value of a lease lay in the land itself and whatever simple living structures may have been included in the leasehold were of secondary importance and were readily repairable by the typical 'jack-of-all-trades' lessee farmer. Furthermore, because the law of property crystallized before the development of mutually dependent covenants in contract law, a lessee's covenant to pay rent was considered at common law as independent of the lessor's covenants. Thus even when a lessor expressly covenanted to make repairs, the lessor's breach did not justify the lessee's withholding of the rent. (See 6 Williston, Contracts (3d ed. 1962) s 890, pp. 580--589; Arnold v. Krigbaum (1912) 169 Cal. 143, 145, 146 P. 423.)

In recent years, however, a growing number of courts have begun to re-examine these 'settled' common law rules in light of contemporary conditions, and, after thorough analysis, all of these courts have discarded the traditional doctrine as incompatible with

---

[6] The instant record contains no allegations--by either the landlord or tenant--that the premises were in an uninhabitable condition at the time they were first rented by petitioner. Consequently we have no occasion in the instant case to pass on the question of whether a lease of such premises constitutes an 'illegal contract' (see Shephard v. Lerner (1960) 182 Cal.App.2d 746, 6 Cal.Rptr. 433; Brown v. Southall Realty Co. (D.C.Mun.App. (1968) 237 A.2d 834) or, conversely, whether the tenant should be considered to have 'assumed the risk' of uninhabitable premises. On the present record, the case at bar involves only an allegation that the landlord failed to maintain the leased premises in a habitable condition. (Cf. Javins v. First National Realty Corp. (1970) 138 U.S.App.D.C. 369, 428 F.2d 1071, 1979.)

contemporary social conditions and modern legal values. This emerging line of decisions, along with a veritable flood of academic commentaries, demonstrates the obsolescence of the traditional common law rule absolving a landlord of any duty to maintain leased premises in a habitable condition during the term of the lease.

The recent decisions recognize initially that the geographic and economic conditions that characterized the agrarian lessor-lessee transaction have been entirely transformed in the modern urban landlord-tenant relationship. We have suggested that in the Middle Ages, and, indeed, until the urbanization of the industrial revolution, the land itself was by far the most important element of a lease transaction; this predominance explained the law's treatment of such leases as conveyances of interests in land. In today's urban residential leases, however, land as such plays no comparable role. The typical city dweller, who frequently leases an apartment several stories above the actual plot of land on which an apartment building rests, cannot realistically be viewed as acquiring an interest in land; rather, he has contracted for a place to live. As the Court of Appeal for the District of Columbia observed in Javins v. First National Realty Corp. (1970) 138 U.S.App.D.C. 369, 428 F.2d 1071, 1074: 'When American city dwellers, both rich and poor, seek, 'shelter' today, they seek a well known package of goods and services--a package which includes not merely walls and ceilings, but also adequate heat, light and ventilation, serviceable plumbing facilities, secure windows and doors, proper sanitation, and proper maintenance.' (Fn. omitted.)

In the past, California courts have increasingly recognized the largely contractual nature of contemporary lease agreements and have frequently analyzed such leases' terms pursuant to contractual principles. (See, e.g., Medico-Dental, etc., Co. v. Horton & Converse (1942) 21 Cal.2d 411, 418-- 419, 132 P.2d 457; Groh v. Kover's Bull Pen, Inc. (1963) 221 Cal.App.2d 611, 34 Cal.Rptr. 637. See generally Note, The California Lease-Contract or Coveyance? (1952) 4 Stan.L.Rev. 244.) Similarly, leading legal scholars in the field have long stressed the propriety of a more contractually oriented analysis of lease agreements. (1 American Law of Property (Casner ed. 1952) § 3.11, pp. 202--205; 2 Powell, Real Property (rev.ed.1967) 221(1), p. 179; 6 Williston, Contracts (3d ed.1962) § 890A, pp. 592--613.) Our holding in this case reflects our belief that the application of contract principles, including the mutual dependency of covenants, is particularly appropriate in dealing with residential leases of urban dwelling units.

Modern urbanization has not only undermined the validity of utilizing general property concepts in analyzing landlord-tenant relations, but it has also significantly altered the factual setting directly relevant to the more specific duty of maintaining leased premises. As noted above, at the inception of the common law rule, any structure on the leased premises was likely to be of the most simple nature, easily inspected by the lessee to determine if it fit his needs, and easily repairable by the typically versatile tenant farmer. Contemporary urban housing and the contemporary urban tenant stand in marked contrast to this agrarian model.

First, the increasing complexity of modern apartment buildings not only renders them much more difficult and expensive to repair than the living quarters of earlier days, but also makes adequate inspection of the premises by a prospective tenant a virtual impossibility; complex heating, electrical and plumbing systems are hidden from view, and the landlord, who has had experience with the building, is certainly in a much better position to discover and to cure dilapidations in the premises. Moreover, in a multiple-unit dwelling repair will frequently require access to equipment and areas solely in the control of the landlord.

Second, unlike the multi-skilled lessee of old, today's city dweller generally has a single, specialized skill unrelated to maintenance work. Furthermore, whereas an agrarian lessee frequently remained on a single plot of land for his entire life, today's urban tenant is more mobile than ever; a tenant's limited tenure in a specific apartment will frequently not justify efforts at extensive repairs. Finally, the expense of needed repairs will often be outside the reach of many tenants for '(l)ow and middle income tenants, even if they were interested in making repairs, would be unable to obtain any financing for major repairs since they have no long-term interest in the property.' (Javins v. First National Realty Corp. (1970) 138 U.S.App.D.C. 369, 428 F.2d 1071, 1078--1079.)

* * *

5. *Conclusion.*

We have concluded that a warranty of habitability is implied by law in residential leases in this state and that the breach of such a warranty may be raised as a defense in an unlawful detainer action. Under the implied warranty which we recognize, a residential landlord covenants that premises he leases for living quarters will be maintained in a habitable state for the duration of the lease. This implied warranty of habitability does not require that a landlord ensure that leased premises are in perfect, aesthetically pleasing condition, but it does mean that 'bare living requirements' must be maintained. In most cases substantial compliance with those applicable building and housing code standards which materially affect health and safety will suffice to meet the landlord's obligations under the common law implied warranty of habitability we now recognize. As the Hinson court observed: '(m)inor housing code violations standing alone which do not affect habitability must be considered de minimis and will not entitle the tenant to reduction in rent. . . .' (26 Cal.App.2d at p. 70, 102 Cal.Rptr. at p. 666.)

* * *

In summary, we have concluded that the traditional common law rule which imposed no warranty of habitability in residential leases is a product of an earlier, land-oriented era, which bears no reasonable relation to the social or legal realities of the landlord-tenant relationship of today. The United States Supreme Court has observed that 'the body of private property law . . ., more than almost any other branch, of law, has been shaped by distinctions whose validity is largely historical,' (Jones v. United States (1960) 362 U.S. 257, 266, 80 S.Ct. 725, 733, 4 L.Ed.2d 697), and on previous occasions in recent years our own court has responded to the changes wrought by modern conditions by discarding outworn common law property doctrines. (See Rowland v. Christian (1968) 69 Cal.2d 108, 70 Cal.Rptr. 97, 443 P.2d 561.) In taking a similar step today, we do not exercise a novel prerogative, but merely follow the well-established duty of common law courts to reflect contemporary social values and ethics. As Justice Cardozo wrote in his celebrated essay 'The Growth of the Law' chapter V, pages 136--137: 'A rule which in its origin was the creation of the courts themselves, and was supposed in the making to express the Mores of the day, may be abrogated by courts when the Mores have so changed that perpetration of the rule would do violence to the social conscience. . . . This is not usurpation. It is not even innovation. It is the reservation for ourselves of the same power of creation that built up the common law through its exercise by the judges of the past.'

Let a peremptory writ of mandate issue directing the superior court to vacate the San Francisco Superior Court judgment entered in the case of Sumski v. Green, S.C.A. No. 11836 on January 3, 1973, and instructing the court to proceed with the trial of the unlawful detainer action in accordance with the views expressed herein.

WRIGHT, C.J., and McCOMB, MOSK, BURKE, SULLIVAN and CLARK, JJ., concur.

Note

The vast majority of jurisdictions now recognize the implied warranty of habitability in residential leases. But of those that do, a number do not recognize it where a single family house is rented out. See e.g. *Dapkunas v. Cagle*, 42 Ill.App.3d 644 (1976). Further, the warranty typically does not apply to commercial leases, although some jurisdictions of late have recognized it in this context. See 49 Am.Jur.2d Landlord and Tenant § 565. Finally, some courts have rejected the implied warranty of habitability. See, e.g. *Bedell v. Los Zapatistas, Inc.*, 805 P.2d 1198, 1200 (Colo.App. 1991): "Plaintiff also asserts that she is entitled to an award of damages because of the breach of an implied warranty of habitability. We disagree. The trial court was correct in noting that 'an implied warranty of habitability of leased premises does not exist in this state. *Blackwell v. Del Bosco,* 191 Colo. 344, 558 P.2d 563 (1977).' "

§ 10.6 Transfer of Tenant's Interest

§ 10.6.1 Introduction

Suppose Larry (L) leases to Tina (T). Suppose also that Tina subsequently does not want the premises, so she leases to Tom (T1). The questions that arise are: Is the transfer between T and T1 an assignment or a sublease? What are the differences between an assignment and sublease? How are the legal relations among the parties (L, T, and T1) affected by characterizing the relationship as an assignment versus a sublease? These and other matters are addressed in this section.

§ 10.6.2 Assignment Versus Sublease

Siragusa v. Park
913 S.W.2d 915 (Mo.App. 1996)

In this case, in the first paragraph of the opinion, the court explains the difference between an assignment and a sublease. In the second paragraph, the court examines several legal consequences that flow from an assignment. The other legal consequences and the legal consequences that flow from a sublease are discussed in the notes that follow.

* * *

The difference between an assignment and a sublease is significant. In the former, the lessee parts with his whole term or interest as lessee, *Mutual Drug Co. v. Sewall*, 353 Mo. 375, 182 S.W.2d 575, 578 (1944), and retains no reversionary interest in the original lease. *Employees Consumer Org., Inc. v. Gorman's, Inc.*, 395 S.W.2d 162, 165 (Mo.1965). On the other hand, if there remains a reversionary interest in the estate conveyed, however small, the arrangement is a sublease. *Id.* If the transaction is an assignment, "the assignee of a lease succeeds to all the interest of the lessee and to the benefit of all the covenants and agreements of the lessor which are annexed to and run with the leasehold estate, whereas the sublessee does not acquire any right to enforce the covenants or agreements of the lessor contained in the original lease.[7] The sublessee's rights depend on the covenants or agreements in his sublease." *Id.* at 166. Furthermore, the assignee "is liable directly to the original lessor on all covenants in the original lease which run with the land, including the covenant to pay rent." *Mutual Drug Co. v. Sewall,* 182 S.W.2d at 578.

* * *

Generally, if a lease contains an express covenant to pay rent, the lessee may not escape liability on the lease merely by assigning it to another. *Jenkins v. John Taylor Dry Goods Co.*, 352 Mo. 660, 667-68, 179 S.W.2d 54, 58 (1944). A lease has a dual nature: it is both a contract and a conveyance. *Newfeld v. Chemical Dynamics, Inc.*, 784 S.W.2d 240, 242 (Mo.App.1989). As such, between the lessor and the lessee, it creates a contractual relationship, privity of contract, as well as being a conveyance of an estate in land, creating privity of estate. *Id.* Upon an assignment by the lessee, the privity of estate between the lessee and lessor is destroyed, and a new privity of estate is created between the assignee and the lessor. *Id.* However, "[p]rivity of contract, as contrasted with the more lowly privity of estate, exists and the lessee having covenanted [to pay rent] is bound even though he assign and even though the landlord receive and accept rent from the assignee." *Jenkins*, 352 Mo. at 668, 179 S.W.2d at 58.

* * *

Notes

1. The following examples will further clarify and illustrate the points made in the preceding case.

2. If L leases to T for a five-year term and T, one year into the lease, transfers the balance of his term to T1, under traditional common law theory (compare with note 6), there is an assignment. So says *Siragusa v. Parks*, as well as many other cases. But this is actually not a complete explanation. The complete explanation is a little more complex: If T transfers everything to T1, to say that there is an assignment means that "vertical privity" between T and T1 is established and, if other elements are satisfied (elements that we will cover in chapter 12), the covenants in the lease will "run with the land at law." What is

---

[7] [This statement is not totally correct. The sublessee may well be able to enforce covenants against the lessor if the benefit of the covenant runs with the land. See notes following the *Siragusa* case.]

the significance of this "running covenant"? The significance is that if L could have successfully sued T for monetary damages (a remedy at law) for breach of a covenant in the L-T lease, L can now enforce this covenant against T1, who now is primarily liable for breach of any such covenant. Thus, T1 is now burdened with this covenant. Similarly, if T could have sued L for damages for breaching a covenant in the L-T lease, T1 may now enforce such a covenant against L. (As you will see in chapter 12, however, for T1 to sue L for damages, "strict" vertical privity is not required. A loosened form of vertical privity will suffice when the benefit of a covenant runs with the land.) Consequently, T1 is now benefited by this covenant. We discuss vertical privity and other aspects of covenants that run with the land at law (also called real covenants) in greater depth in chapter 12. (See also § 7.7.3, "Covenants of Title: Suit By Remote Grantees" and *Schofield v. Iowa Homestead Co.*, supra.)

3. If there is an assignment and L sues T1 (because, as *Siragusa v. Park* states, T1 is primarily liable), does this mean that T is totally free of liability? The answer is, no. T remains secondarily liable, but liable nonetheless. The basis for T being secondarily liable is "privity of contract." This means that while L and T no longer have a relationship with respect to the land, they nevertheless continue to have a relationship based in contract—and one cannot walk away from one's contractual obligations simply by assigning to another.

4. If, on the other hand, T does not transfer all of T's interest to T1, we have under traditional common law theory (compare with note 6), a sublease. So says, again, *Siragusa v. Park* and many other decisions. But note, here, too, this actually is not a complete answer. The complete answer, yet once more, is a little more complex. If there is a sublease, vertical privity does not exist between T and T1. Consequently, under the common law, L cannot sue T1 for damages because without vertical privity, the burden of the covenant does not run with the land at law to T1. Does this mean that L cannot enforce any covenants in the L-T lease against T1? The answer is, that while L cannot sue T1 *at law* for breach of any covenant, L can sue T1 in *equity* (and seek equitable relief, such as an injunction) because vertical privity is very significantly loosened up (if needed at all) for covenants in equity. See Restatement (Third) of Property (Servitudes) § 1.4 (2000). We discuss vertical privity and covenants in equity further in chapter 12. Importantly, however, even though L cannot sue *T1* at law, T1 may be able to sue *L* at law (that is, seek monetary damages). Why is this? The reason, as stated in note 2, is that for the benefit of the covenant to run with the land at law, "strict" vertical privity is not required; a loosened form of vertical privity will suffice for the benefit of the covenant to run with the land at law. Consequently, in a sublease, the benefit of the covenant can still run with the land at law to T1 so that T1 can enforce any covenant against L. Thus, T1 can sue L for monetary damages for breach of any covenant in the L-T lease (once more, assuming the other elements for a running covenant are satisfied). Again, we take this up in greater depth in chapter 12.

5. In any event, if there is a sublease between T and T1, T is liable to L on any covenants made in the lease in any actions in law. Between T and L, there is privity of estate (a relationship with respect to the land) and, of course, privity of contract.

6. As stated in note 2, the traditional common law view (although incomplete, as discussed in note 2 above) is that if T transfers everything to T1 we have an assignment. The more modern view is that whether there is an assignment or a sublease does not depend on any mechanical test; rather the key is the intent of the parties. See e.g. *Jabar v. Miller*, 219 Ark. 59 (1951). Does this intent test really help? Is it better than the common law traditional test? Do you think that the parties even know the difference between an assignment and a sublease so that their intent is even relevant?

§ 10.6.3 Consent of Landlord Required

If a lease provides that before a tenant can assign or sublease to another, the tenant first must secure the consent of the landlord, can the landlord withhold consent for an arbitrary reason? Under the common law the answer is, yes. The landlord may withhold consent for any reason or no reason. See e.g. Vaswani v. Wohletz, *196 Ga.App. 676 (1990). Refer also to* Kramarsky v. Stahl Management, *supra. The modern view is different, however. Under this approach, the landlord can withhold consent only for a commercially objectionable reason. For example, if the proposed assignee has a lower credit rating than the tenant, the landlord's refusal to give consent would be valid. So, too, if the proposed assignee wanted to substantially change the structure of the property. What is the rationale for the modern view? The next case explains.*

Warner v. Konover
210 Conn. 150 (1989)

* * *

If a commercial lease imposes a duty of good faith and fair dealing upon a tenant, there is no reason not to impose a similar duty upon a landlord. The provisions of § 205 of the Restatement are therefore as applicable in this case as they were in *La Crepe, Inc.* Accordingly, we hold that a landlord who contractually retains the discretion to withhold its consent to the assignment of a tenant's lease must exercise that discretion in a manner consistent with good faith and fair dealing. Although this holding may well represent a minority position nationwide; see 1 M. Friedman, Leases (1978) § 7.304; a similar result has been reached in a number of other jurisdictions. See, e.g., *Homa-Goff Interiors, Inc. v. Cowden,* 350 So.2d 1035, 1038 (Ala.1977); *Fernandez v. Vazquez,* 397 So.2d 1171, 1173 (Fla.App.1981); *Arrington v. Walter E. Heller International Corporation,* 30 Ill.App.3d 631, 640-41, 333 N.E.2d 50 (1975); *Shaker Building Co. v. Federal Lime & Stone Co.,* 28 Ohio Misc. 246, 252, 277 N.E.2d 584 (1971); and compare 2 Restatement (Second), Property, Landlord and Tenant (1977) § 15.2, comment i.

§ 10.7 Landlord Liability in Tort

A tort is defined as a civil wrong not founded in contract. Thus, if A punches B, A has committed a battery and is liable for damages sustained by B. Similarly, if A drives his car carelessly and injures a pedestrian, B, B will prevail against A in a suit based on negligence. What we address here is whether a tenant who suffers injuries can recover against the landlord when the latter is negligent.

§ 10.7.1 In General

If a tenant is injured on the landlord's premises because of the landlord's negligence, can the tenant sue the landlord for damages? With few exceptions, the common law rule held that the landlord was not liable. The modern view, as exemplified by Sargent v. Ross, *infra, holds that the landlord is liable in negligence.*

Sargent v. Ross
113 N.H. 388 (1973)

KENISON, Chief Justice.

The question in this case is whether the defendant landlord is liable to the plaintiff in tort for the death of plaintiff's four-year-old daughter who fell to her death from an outdoor stairway at a residential building owned by the defendant in Nashua. The defendant resided in a groundfloor apartment in the building, and her son and daughter-in-law occupied a second story apartment serviced by the stairway from which the child fell. At the time of the accident the child was under the care of the defendant's daughter-in-law who was plaintiff's regular baby-sitter.

* * *

Claiming that there was no evidence that the defendant retained control over the stairway, that it was used in common with other tenants, or that it contained a concealed defect, defendant urges that there was accordingly no duty owing to the deceased child for the defendant to breach. This contention rests upon the general rule which has long obtained in this and most other jurisdictions that a landlord is not liable, except in certain limited situations, for injuries caused by defective or dangerous conditions in the leased premises. E.g., Black v. Fiandaca, 98 N.H. 33, 93 A.2d 663 (1953); Towne v. Thompson, 68 N.H. 317, 44 A. 492 (1895); 2 Powell, Real Property 234 (rev. ed. 1971); Prosser, Torts s 63 (4th ed. 1971); 1 Tiffany, Real Property §§ 104, 107 (3d ed. 1939). The plaintiff does not directly attack this rule of nonliability but instead attempts to show, rather futilely under the facts, defendant's control of the stairway. She also relies upon an exception to the general rule of nonliability, to wit, that a landlord is liable for injuries resulting from his negligent repair of the premises. Hunkins v. Amoskeag Mfg. Co., 86 N.H. 356, 169 A. 3 (1933); Rowan v. Amoskeag Mfg. Co., 79 N.H. 409, 109 A. 561 (1920); Prosser, supra at 410-12; 1 Tiffany, supra at § 105; Restatement (Second) of Torts § 362 (1965). The issue, as framed by the parties, is whether the rule of nonliability should prevail or whether the facts of this case can be squeezed into the negligent repair or some other exception to the general rule of landlord immunity.

* * * [W]e today discard the rule of 'caveat lessee' and the doctrine of landlord nonliability in tort to which it gave birth. We thus bring up to date the other half of landlord-tenant law. Henceforth, landlords as other persons must exercise reasonable care not to subject others to an unreasonable risk of harm. Scott v. Simons, 54 N.H. 426

(1874); Wilcox v. Hines supra; see Cummings v. Prater, 95 Ariz. 20, 386 P.2d 27 (1963); Presson v. Mountain States Properties, Inc.,18 Ariz.App. 176, 501 P.2d 17 (1972); Harkrider, Tort Liability of a Landlord, 26 Mich.L.Rev. 260 (1928). A landlord must act as a reasonable person under all of the circumstances including the likelihood of injury to others, the probable seriousness of such injuries, and the burden of reducing or avoiding the risk. See Quint v. Porietis, 107 N.H. 463, 225 A.2d 179 (1966); Flynn v. Gordon, 86 N.H. 198, 165 A. 715 (1933); Smith v. Arbaugh's Restaurant, Inc., 152 U.S.App.D.C. 86, 469 F.2d 97, 100 (1972); Conway v. O'Brien, 111 F.2d 611, 612 (2d Cir. 1940) (L. Hand, J.). See generally Note, 121 U.Pa.L.Rev. 378 (1972). We think this basic principle of responsibility for landlords as for others 'best expresses the principles of justice and reasonableness upon which our law of torts is founded.' Dowd v. Portsmouth Hosp., 105 N.H. 53, 59, 193 A.2d 788, 792 (1963) (on rehearing). The questions of control, hidden defects and common or public use, which formerly had to be established as a prerequisite to even considering the negligence of a landlord, will now be relevant only inasmuch as they bear on the basic tort issues such as the foreseeability and unreasonableness of the particular risk of harm. Cf. Clarke v. O'Connor, 140 U.S.App.D.C. 300, 435 F.2d 104, 111-113 (1970). The Massachusetts Supreme Judicial Court recently made the following pertinent remarks in a case abolishing the distinction the standards of care owed by land occupiers to licensees and invitees: 'In the absence of legislative action, we believe that this 'reasonable care in all the circumstances' standard will provide the most effective way to achieve an allocation of the costs of human injury which conforms to present community values.' Mounsey v. Ellard, Mass., 297 N.E.2d 43, 52 (1973).

The abiding respect of this court for precedent and stability in the law is balanced by an appreciation of the need for responsible growth and change in rules that have failed to keep pace with modern developments in social and juridical thought. When we abolished the tort immunity of a parent from suit by his child, another artificial and inequitable exception to the general rules of tort liability, we made the following observation which is equally pertinent to this case: 'If after thorough examination a prior judicial decision seems manifestly out of accord with modern conditions of life, it should not be followed as controlling precedent. 37 Harv.L.Rev. 409, 414. Finding to supportable rationale upon which this judicially created exception to the ordinary rules of liability can be predicated, justice demands and reason dictates that a change be made from the previous holding in such a situation.' Dean v. Smith, 106 N.H. 314, 318, 211 A.2d 410, 413 (1965); See In re Frolich Estate, 112 N.H. 320, 295 A.2d 448 (1972).

Our decision will shift the primary focus of inquiry for judge and jury from the traditional question of 'who had control?' to a determination of whether the landlord, and the injured party, exercised due care under all the circumstances. Perhaps even more significantly, the ordinary negligence standard should help insure that a landlord will take whatever precautions are reasonably necessary under the circumstances to reduce the likelihood of injuries from defects in his property. 'It is appropriate that the landlord who will retain ownership of the premises and any permanent improvements should bear the cost of repairs necessary to make the premises safe . . . .' Kline v. Burns, 111 N.H. 87, 92, 276 A.2d 248, 251 (1971).

§ 10.7.2 Exculpatory Contracts

An exculpatory contract is one where A and B agree that B will not hold A liable for injuries B suffers because of A's negligence. For example, as the court in Henrioulle v. Marin Ventures, Inc., *infra, discusses, a doctor and patient may enter into such an agreement before the doctor operates on the patient. If this sounds outrageous to you, you are in good company: In* Tunkl v. Regents of the University of California, *60 Cal.2d 92 (1963), the California Supreme Court declared exculpatory clauses in medical care scenarios invalid. The next question for the Supreme Court was whether these exculpatory clauses also were invalid in landlord-tenant relationships.*

Henrioulle v. Marin Ventures, Inc.
20 Cal.3d 512 (1978)

A tenant suffered personal injuries as a result of his landlord's negligence. The landlord defended on the ground that the tenant had signed an exculpatory contract. The California Supreme Court will hold that exculpatory clauses in residential leases are invalid, analogizing the instant facts to those in Tunkl v. Regents, *the case where the California Supreme Court held that exculpatory contracts in hospital admissions were invalid.*

BIRD, Chief Justice.

Appellant, John Henrioulle, seeks to set aside orders of the superior court granting his landlord, respondent Marin Ventures, Inc., a judgment notwithstanding the jury's verdict and a new trial. Appellant contends that the exculpatory clause in his lease could not relieve the landlord of liability for the personal injuries appellant sustained in a fall on a common stairway in the apartment building. This court agrees.

* * *

II

In Tunkl v. Regents of the University of California (1963) 60 Cal.2d 92, 32 Cal.Rptr. 33, 383 P.2d 441, this court held invalid a clause in a hospital admission form which released the hospital from liability for future negligence. This court noted that although courts have made "diverse" interpretations of Civil Code section 1668,[8] which invalidates contracts which exempt one from responsibility for certain willful or negligent acts, all the decisions were in accord that exculpatory clauses affecting the public interest are invalid. (Tunkl v. Regents of the University of California, supra, 60 Cal.2d at pp. 94-98, 32 Cal.Rptr. 33, 383 P.2d 441.)

In Tunkl, six criteria are used to identify the kind of agreement in which an exculpatory clause is invalid as contrary to public policy. "(1) It concerns a business of a type generally thought suitable for public regulation. (2) The party seeking exculpation is engaged in performing a service of great importance to the public, which is often a matter

---

[8] Civil Code section 1668 provides:

"All contracts which have for their object, directly or indirectly, to exempt anyone from responsibility for his own fraud, or willful injury to the person or property of another, or violation of law, whether willful or negligent, are against the policy of the law."

of practical necessity for some members of the public. (3) The party holds himself out as willing to perform this service for any member of the public who seeks it, or at least any member coming within certain established standards. (4) As a result of the essential nature of the service, in the economic setting of the transaction, the party invoking exculpation possesses a decisive advantage of bargaining strength against any member of the public who seeks his services. (5) In exercising a superior bargaining power the party confronts the public with a standardized adhesion contract of exculpation, and makes no provision whereby a purchaser may pay additional fees and obtain protection against negligence. (6) Finally, as a result of the transaction, the person or property of the purchaser is placed under the control of the seller, subject to the risk of carelessness by the seller or his agents." (Id., at pp. 98-101, fns. omitted, 32 Cal.Rptr. at pp. 37-38, 383 P.2d at pp. 445-446.)

The transaction before this court, a residential rental agreement, meets the Tunkl criteria. Housing in general, and residential leases in particular, are increasingly the subject of governmental regulation, the first of the Tunkl criteria. In Green v. Superior Court (1974) 10 Cal.3d 616, 627, 111 Cal.Rptr. 704, 711, 517 P.2d 1168, 1175, this court noted: "The past half century has brought the widespread enactment of comprehensive housing codes throughout the nation; in California, the Department of Housing and Community Development has established detailed, statewide housing regulations (see Health & Saf.Code, § 17921; Cal.Admin.Code, tit. 25, §§ 1000-1090), and the Legislature has expressly authorized local entities to impose even more stringent regulations. (See Health & Saf.Code, § 17951.) These comprehensive housing codes affirm that, under contemporary conditions, public policy compels landlords to bear the primary responsibility for maintaining safe, clean and habitable housing in our state." Moreover, the Legislature in 1970 enacted stricter standards of "tenantability" (see Civ.Code, s 1941.1) and has limited landlords' ability to impose waivers of tenants' rights in leases. (See, e. g., Civ.Code, ss 1942.1, 1953, 1954.)

A lessor of residential property provides shelter, a basic necessity of life, the second Tunkl criterion. Moreover, the landlord in this case offered to rent his units to all members of the public, the third Tunkl criterion.

Unequal bargaining strength, the fourth Tunkl criterion, is also present. In a state and local market characterized by a severe shortage of low-cost housing, tenants are likely to be in a poor position to bargain with landlords. As this court observed in Green, "the severe shortage of low and moderate cost housing has left tenants with little bargaining power through which they might gain express warranties of habitability from landlords . . . ." (Green v. Superior Court, supra, 10 Cal.3d at p. 625, 111 Cal.Rptr. at p. 709, 517 P.2d at p. 1173.)

Finally, the fifth and sixth Tunkl criteria are also present. Thus, it does not appear that respondent made any "provision whereby a purchaser may pay additional fees and obtain protection against negligence," (Tunkl v. Regents of the University of California, supra, 60 Cal.2d at pp. 100-101, 32 Cal.Rptr. at p. 38, 383 P.2d at p. 446) and appellant was exposed to the risk of injury through respondent's carelessness.

* * *

In holding that exculpatory clauses in residential leases violate public policy, this court joins an increasing number of jurisdictions. (See, e. g., Kuzmiak v. Brookchester, Inc. (1955), 33 N.J.Super. 575, 111 A.2d 425; Old Town Development Co. v. Langford

(Ind.App.1976) 349 N.E.2d 744; Weaver v. American Oil Co. (Ind.1971) 276 N.E.2d 144 (such clauses are void in all leases); Papakalos v. Shaka (1941) 91 N.H. 265, 18 A.2d 377, 379 (such clauses are void in all contracts); Billie Knitwear, Inc. v. New York Life Ins. Co. (N.Y.Sup.1940) 174 Misc. 978, 22 N.Y.S.2d 324, affd. (1942) 288 N.Y. 682, 43 N.E.2d 80 (such clauses invalidated by statute in all leases); see generally, Annot., Validity of Exculpatory Clause in Lease Exempting Lessor from Liability (1971) 49 A.L.R.3d 321.) * * *

Note

There is substantial authority to the contrary, the rationale resting on freedom to contract. See, e.g. *Manaster v. Gopin*, 330 Mass. 569 (1953) and *O'Callaghan v. Waller & Beckwith Realty Co.*, 15 Ill.2d 436 (1958).

§ 10.8 Retaliatory Eviction

A retaliatory eviction arises when a landlord attempts to evict a tenant because a tenant has exercised a right (e.g., reporting a housing code violation to city authorities, making use of a repair and deduct statute, etc.). As the material that follows makes clear, a retaliatory eviction is a nullity. The problem, however, is to determine when an eviction is retaliatory and when it is non-retaliatory (and, thus, quite lawful).

Uniform Residential Landlord & Tenant Act, § 5.101
[Retaliatory Conduct Prohibited]

(a) Except as provided in this section, a landlord may not retaliate by increasing rent or decreasing services or by bringing or threatening to bring an action for possession after:
(1) the tenant has complained to a governmental agency charged with responsibility for enforcement of a building or housing code of a violation applicable to the premises materially affecting health and safety; or
(2) the tenant has complained to the landlord of a violation under Section 2.104 [dealing with landlord duties, including the duty to maintain the premises in a habitable state]; or
(3) the tenant has organized or become a member of a tenant's union or similar organization.
(b) If the landlord acts in violation of subsection (a), the tenant is entitled to the remedies provided in Section 4.107 [dealing with tenant remedies for unlawful ouster, exclusion, or diminution of services] and has a defense in any retaliatory action against him for possession. In an action by or against the tenant, evidence of a complaint within [1] year before the alleged act of retaliation creates a presumption that the landlord's conduct was in retaliation. The presumption does not arise if the tenant made the complaint after notice of a proposed rent increase or diminution of services. "Presumption" means that the trier of fact must find the existence of the fact presumed unless and until evidence is introduced which would support a finding of its nonexistence.

(c) Notwithstanding subsections (a) and (b), a landlord may bring an action for possession if:

(1) the violation of the applicable building or housing code was caused primarily by lack of reasonable care by the tenant, a member of his family, or other person on the premises with his consent; or

(2) the tenant is in default in rent; or

(3) compliance with the applicable building or housing code requires alteration, remodeling, or demolition which would effectively deprive the tenant of use of the dwelling   unit.

(d) The maintenance of an action under subsection (c) does not release the landlord from liability under Section 4.101(b) [dealing with damages].

Note

For an example where a court found there was no retaliatory eviction, see *Four Seas Inv. Corp. v. International Hotel Tenants' Assn.*, 81 Cal.App.3d 604 (1978) (evidence established that the new landlord evicted all the tenants for the purpose of demolishing the building as part of a larger contemplated construction project, not because the tenants had ceased paying rent to the landlord and had filed a lawsuit).

§ 10.9 Rent Control

Rent control ordinances limit the amount of rent that a landlord can charge tenants. The question is whether such ordinances are constitutional.

Pennell v. City of San Jose
485 U.S. 1 (1988)

The city's rent control ordinance provided that a city hearing officer may consider, but is not required to consider, "tenant hardship" in determining the rent that a landlord may charge. After refusing to consider the landlord's Fifth Amendment Takings argument because the case was not yet "ripe," the court found that the ordinance does not violate the Due Process and Equal Protection Clauses of the Fourteenth Amendment.

Chief Justice REHNQUIST delivered the opinion of the Court.

* * *

Appellants also urge that the mere provision in the Ordinance that a hearing officer may *consider* the hardship of the tenant in finally fixing a reasonable rent renders the Ordinance "facially invalid" under the Due Process and Equal Protection Clauses, even though no landlord ever has its rent diminished by as much as one dollar because of the application of this provision. The standard for determining whether a state price-control regulation is constitutional under the Due Process Clause is well established: "Price control is 'unconstitutional * * * if arbitrary, discriminatory, or demonstrably irrelevant to the policy the legislature is free to adopt * * * *' " *Permian Basin Area Rate Cases,* 390 U.S. 747, 769-770, 88 S.Ct. 1344, 1361, 20 L.Ed.2d 312 (1968) (quoting

Nebbia v. New York, 291 U.S. 502, 539, 54 S.Ct. 505, 517, 78 L.Ed. 940 (1934)). In other contexts we have recognized that the government may intervene in the marketplace to regulate rates or prices that are artificially inflated as a result of the existence of a monopoly or near monopoly, see, *e.g., FCC v. Florida Power Corp.,* 480 U.S. 245, 250-254, 107 S.Ct. 1107, 1111-1113, 94 L.Ed.2d 282 (1987) (approving limits on rates charged to cable companies for access to telephone poles); *FPC v. Texaco Inc.,* 417 U.S. 380, 397-398, 94 S.Ct. 2315, 2326-2327, 41 L.Ed.2d 141 (1974) (recognizing that federal regulation of the natural gas market was in response to the threat of monopoly pricing), or a discrepancy between supply and demand in the market for a certain product, see, *e.g., Nebbia v. New York, supra,* 291 U.S., at 530, 538, 54 S.Ct., at 513, 516 (allowing a minimum price for milk to offset a "flood of surplus milk"). Accordingly, appellants do not dispute that the Ordinance's asserted purpose of "prevent[ing] excessive and unreasonable rent increases" caused by the "growing shortage of and increasing demand for housing in the City of San Jose," § 5701.2, is a legitimate exercise of appellees' police powers. Cf. *Block v. Hirsh,* 256 U.S. 135, 156, 41 S.Ct. 458, 459, 65 L.Ed. 865 (1921) (approving rent control in Washington, D.C., on the basis of Congress' finding that housing in the city was "monopolized"). They do argue, however, that it is "arbitrary, discriminatory, or demonstrably irrelevant," *Permian Basin Area Rate Cases, supra,* 390 U.S., at 769-770, 88 S.Ct. at 1361, for appellees to attempt to accomplish the additional goal of reducing the burden of housing costs on low-income tenants by requiring that "hardship to a tenant" be considered in determining the amount of excess rent increase that is "reasonable under the circumstances" pursuant to § 5703.28. As appellants put it, "[t]he objective of alleviating individual tenant hardship is * * * not a 'policy the legislature is free to adopt' in a rent control ordinance." Reply Brief for Appellants 16.

We reject this contention, however, because we have long recognized that a legitimate and rational goal of price or rate regulation is the protection of consumer welfare. See, *e.g., Permian Basin Area Rate Cases, supra,* 390 U.S., at 770, 88 S.Ct., at 1361; *FPC v. Hope Natural Gas Co.,* 320 U.S. 591, 610-612, 64 S.Ct. 281, 291-292, 88 L.Ed. 333 (1944) ("The primary aim of [the Natural Gas Act] was to protect consumers against exploitation at the hands of natural gas companies"). Indeed, a primary purpose of rent control is the protection of tenants. See, *e.g., Bowles v. Willingham,* 321 U.S. 503, 513, n. 9, 64 S.Ct. 641, 646, n. 9, 88 L.Ed. 892 (1944) (one purpose of rent control is "to protect persons with relatively fixed and limited incomes, consumers, wage earners . . . from undue impairment of their standard of living"). Here, the Ordinance establishes a scheme in which a hearing officer considers a number of factors in determining the reasonableness of a proposed rent increase which exceeds eight percent *and* which exceeds the amount deemed reasonable under either § 5703.28(a) or § 5703.28(b). The first six factors of § 5703.28(c) focus on the individual landlord-the hearing officer examines the history of the premises, the landlord's costs, and the market for comparable housing. Section 5703.28(c)(5) also allows the landlord to bring forth any other financial evidence-including presumably evidence regarding his own financial status-to be taken into account by the hearing officer. It is in only this context that the Ordinance allows tenant hardship to be considered and, under § 5703.29, "balance[d]" with the other factors set out in § 5703.28(c). Within this scheme, § 5703.28(c) represents a rational attempt to accommodate the conflicting interests of protecting tenants from burdensome rent increases while at the same time ensuring that landlords are guaranteed a fair return on their investment. Cf. *Bowles v. Willingham, supra,* at 517, 64 S.Ct., at 648 (considering, but rejecting, the contention that rent control must be established "landlord by landlord, as in the fashion of utility rates"). We accordingly find that the Ordinance, which so carefully considers both the individual circumstances of the landlord and the tenant before determining whether to allow an *additional* increase in rent over and above certain amounts that are deemed reasonable, does not on its face violate the Fourteenth Amendment's Due Process Clause.

We also find that the Ordinance does not violate the Amendment's Equal Protection Clause. Here again, the standard is deferential; appellees need only show that the classification scheme embodied in the Ordinance is "rationally related to a legitimate state interest." *New Orleans v. Dukes,* 427 U.S. 297, 303, 96 S.Ct. 2513, 2517, 49 L.Ed.2d 511 (1976). As we stated in *Vance v. Bradley,* 440 U.S. 93, 99 S.Ct. 939, 59 L.Ed.2d 171 (1979), "we will not overturn [a statute that does not burden a suspect class or a fundamental interest] unless the varying treatment of different groups or persons is so unrelated to the achievement of any combination of legitimate purposes that we can only conclude that the legislature's actions were irrational." *Id.,* at 97, 99 S.Ct., at 943. In light of our conclusion above that the Ordinance's tenant hardship provisions are designed to serve the legitimate purpose of protecting tenants, we can hardly conclude that it is irrational for the Ordinance to treat certain landlords differently on the basis of whether or not they have hardship tenants. The Ordinance distinguishes between landlords because doing so furthers the purpose of ensuring that individual tenants do not suffer "unreasonable" hardship; it would be inconsistent to state that hardship is a legitimate factor to be considered but then hold that appellees could not tailor the Ordinance so that only legitimate hardship cases are redressed. Cf. *Woods v. Cloyd W. Miller Co.,* 333 U.S. 138, 145, 68 S.Ct. 421, 425, 92 L.Ed. 596 (1948) Congress "need not control all rents or none. It can select those areas or those classes of property where the need seems the greatest"). We recognize, as appellants point out, that in general it is difficult to say that the landlord "causes" the tenant's hardship. But this is beside the point-if a landlord does have a hardship tenant, regardless of the reason why, it is rational for appellees to take that fact into consideration under § 5703.28 of the Ordinance when establishing a rent that is "reasonable under the circumstances."

For the foregoing reasons, we hold that it is premature to consider appellants' claim under the Takings Clause and we reject their facial challenge to the Ordinance under the Due Process and Equal Protection Clauses of the Fourteenth Amendment. The judgment of the Supreme Court of California is accordingly

Affirmed.

* * *

CHAPTER 11
SERVITUDES: EASEMENTS, PROFITS, AND LICENSES

§ 11.1 Easements

Easements are the first type of "servitudes" that we discuss. A servitude is simply a private land use arrangement. (Public regulation of land use is covered in chapters 14 and 15—zoning and takings, respectively.)

§ 11.1.1 Introduction

To give you an overview of the law of easements, we start with this fact pattern: Black owns Blackacre. Adjacent to Blackacre is Whiteacre, owned by White. If Black grants to White the right to walk across Blackacre to get to the public highway, Black has granted White an easement. The next two cases provide further elucidation.

C/R TV, Inc. v. Shannondale, Inc.
27 F.3d 104 (4th Cir. 1994)

This case gives a broad synopsis of what an easement is, how it may be created, and why an easement grant must comply with the Statute of Frauds.

* * *

An easement involves two separate interests in real property, the dominant estate to which the easement right belongs, and the servient estate upon which the obligation rests. *See Cottrell v. Nurnberger,* 131 W.Va. 391, 396-97, 47 S.E.2d 454, 457 (1948). The term easement usually refers to the right enjoyed by the dominant estate, and a servitude is the correlative burden imposed upon the servient estate. *Id.* The easement may be created by an express or implied grant which, because it creates an interest in land, must satisfy the statute of frauds and ordinarily be evidenced by a writing. Under an affirmative easement, as is involved in this case, the owner of the servient estate must permit "something to be done upon [the land]" or "some use to be made of it." *Id.*

* * *

Wentworth v. Sebra
829 A.2d 520 (Me. 2003)

This case explains that easements may be classified either as "appurtenant," or "in gross," and what the difference is.

* * *

[¶ 12] The law recognizes two different types of easements or rights of use over the property of another: easements appurtenant and easements in gross. *Stickney,* 2001 ME 69, ¶ 31, 770 A.2d at 605. Grantors create easements appurtenant to benefit a dominant estate and such easements run with the land. *Id.* To be appurtenant, the easement must be attached or related to a dominant estate. *Id.*

[¶ 13] In contrast, easements in gross are personal interests in land or the right to use another's land. *Id.* ¶ 32, 770 A.2d at 605. They are "not appurtenant to any estate in land" and do not belong "to any person by virtue of his ownership of an estate in other land." *Id.* (quoting *LeMay v. Anderson,* 397 A.2d 984, 987 n. 2 (Me.1979)). An easement in gross is generally not assignable and terminates upon the death of the grantee. *Id.* However, when evidence demonstrates that the parties clearly intended that an easement in gross be assignable, it is. *Id.* This policy is grounded in the general principle of property law favoring free alienability of property. *Id.*

* * *

§ 11.1.2 Creation By Express Grant

As stated in C/R TV, Inc. v. Shannondale, Inc., *supra, an easement may be created expressly. In such case, because an easement is an interest in land, the conveyance must comply with the Statute of Frauds. The next two cases provide further elucidation.*

Willard v. First Church of Christ, Scientist
7 Cal.3d 473 (1972)

If O owns Blackacre and adjacent Whiteacre and O conveys Blackacre to A, but wants to "reserve" an easement for himself over Blackacre to get to Whiteacre, such a conveyance is not a problem. In the deed conveying Blackacre to A, O simply "reserves" unto himself an easement across Blackacre. But suppose O does not want to reserve an easement for himself; rather, O wants to "reserve" an easement in favor of X (who owns adjacent Greenacre). The Willard *case explains what a "reservation" is and whether O may "reserve" an easement in favor of a third person.*

PETERS, Associate Justice.

In this case we are called upon to decide whether a grantor may, in deeding real property to one person, effectively reserve an interest in the property to another. We hold that in this case such a reservation vests the interest in the third party.

Plaintiffs Donald E. and Jennie C. Willard filed an action to quiet title to a lot in Pacifica against the First Church of Christ, Scientist (the church). After a trial judgment was entered quieting the Willards' title. The church has appealed.

Genevieve McGuigan owned two abutting lots in Pacifica known as lots 19 and 20. There was a building on lot 19, and lot 20 was vacant. McGuigan was a member of the church, which was located across the street from her lots, and she permitted it to use lot 20 for parking during services. She sold lot 19 to one Petersen, who used the building as an office. He wanted to resell the lot, so he listed it with Willard, who is a realtor. Willard expressed an interest in purchasing both lots 19 and 20, and he and Petersen signed a deposit receipt for the sale of the two lots. Soon thereafter they entered into an escrow, into which Petersen delivered a deed for both lots in fee simple.

At the time he agreed to sell lot 20 to Willard, Petersen did not own it, so he approached McGuigan with an offer to purchase it. She was willing to sell the lot provided the church could continue to use it for parking. She therefore referred the matter to the church's attorney, who drew up a provision for the deed that stated the conveyance was 'subject to an easement for automobile parking during church hours for the benefit of the church on the property at the southwest corner of the intersection of Hilton Way and Francisco Boulevard . . . such easement to run with the land only so long as the property for whose benefit the easement is given is used for church purposes.' Once this clause was inserted in the deed, McGuigan sold the property to Petersen, and he recorded the deed.

Willard paid the agreed purchase price into the escrow and received Petersen's deed 10 days later. He then recorded this deed, which did not mention an easement for parking by the church. While Petersen did mention to Willard that the church would want to use lot 20 for parking, it does not appear that he told him of the easement clause contained in the deed he received from McGuigan.

Willard became aware of the easement clause several months after purchasing the property. He then commenced this action to quiet title against the church. At the trial, which was without a jury, McGuigan testified that she had bought lot 20 to provide parking for the church, and would not have sold it unless she was assured the church could thereafter continue to use it for parking. The court found that McGuigan and Petersen intended to convey an easement to the church, but that the clause they employed was ineffective for that purpose because it was invalidated by the common law rule that one cannot 'reserve' an interest in property to a stranger to the title.

The rule derives from the common law notions of reservations from a grant and was based on feudal considerations. A reservation allows a grantor's whole interest in the property to pass to the grantee, but revests a newly created interest in the grantor.[1] (4 Tiffany, The Law of Real Property (3d ed. 1939) § 972.) While a reservation could theoretically vest an interest in a third party, the early common law courts vigorously rejected this possibility, apparently because they mistrusted and wished to limit conveyance by deed as a substitute for livery by seisin. (See Harris Reservations in Favor of strangers of the Title (1953) 6 Okla.L.Rev. 127, 132--133.) Insofar as this mistrust was the foundation of the rule, it is clearly an inapposite feudal shackle today. Consequently, several commentators have attacked the rule as groundless and have called for its abolition. (See, e.g., Harris, supra, 6 Okla.L.Rev. at p. 154; Meyers & Williams, Oil and Gas Conveyancing; Grants and Reservations by Owners of Fractional Mineral Interests (1957) 43 Va.L.Rev. 639, 650--651; Comment, Real Property: Easements: Creation by Reservation or Exception (1948) 36 Cal.L.Rev. 470, 476; Annot., Reservation or Exception in Deed in Favor of Stranger, 88 A.L.R.2d 1199, 1202; cf. 4 Tiffany, supra, § 974, at p. 54; 2 American Law of Property (Casner ed. 1952) § 8.29 at p. 254.)

---

[1] The effect of a reservation should be distinguished from an exception, which prevents some part of the grantor's interest from passing to the grantee. The exception cannot vest an interest in the third party, and the excepted interest remains in the grantor. (6 Powell, The Law of Real Property (Rohan ed. 1971) § 892.)

California early adhered to this common law rule. * * * The common law rule conflicts with the modern approach to construing deeds because it can frustrate the grantor's intent. Moreover, it produces an inequitable result because the original grantee has presumably paid a reduced price for title to the encumbered property. In this case, for example, McGuigan testified that she had discounted the price she charged Petersen by about one-third because of the easement. Finally, in some situations the rule conflicts with section 1085 of the Civil Code.[2]

In view of the obvious defects of the rule, this court has found methods to avoid it where applying it would frustrate the clear intention of the grantor. In Butler v. Gosling (1900) 130 Cal. 422, 62 P. 596, the court prevented the reserved title to a portion of the property from vesting in the grantee by treating the reservation as an exception to the grant. In Boyer v. Murphy, supra, 202 Cal. 23, 259 P. 38, the court, noting that its primary objective was to give effect to the grantor's intention (Id., at pp. 28--29, 259 P. 38), held that the rule was inapplicable where the third party was the grantor's spouse. (See Fleming v. State Bar (1952) 38 Cal.2d 341, 345, fn. 2, 239 P.2d 866.) * * *

The highest courts of two states have already eliminated the rule altogether, rather than repealing it piecemeal by evasion. In Townsend v. Cable (Ky.1964) 378 S.W.2d 806, the Court of Appeals of Kentucky abandoned the rule. It said: 'We have no hesitancy in abandoning this archaic and technical rule. It is entirely inconsistent with the basic principle followed in the construction of deeds, which is to determine the intention of grantor as gathered from the four corners of the instrument.' (Id., at p. 808.) (See also Blair v. City of Pikeville (Ky.1964) 384 S.W.2d 65, 66; Combs v. Hounshell (Ky.1961) 347 S.W.2d 550, 554.) Relying on Townsend, the Supreme Court of Oregon, in Garza v. Grayson (1970) 255 Or. 413, 467 P.2d 960, rejected the rule because it was 'derived from a narrow and highly technical interpretation of the meaning of the terms 'reservation' and 'exception' when employed in a deed' (Id., at p. 961), and did not sufficiently justify frustraing the grantor's intention. Since the rule may frustrate the grantor's intention in some cases even though it is riddled with exceptions, we follow the lead of Kentucky and Oregon and abandon it entirely.

* * *

WRIGHT, C.J., and McCOMB, TOBRINER, BURKE, and SULLIVAN, JJ., concur.

Dyer v. Dyer
275 Ga. 339 (2002)

If testator devises a fee simple to A but also devises in the same will an easement in gross across A's land to B, without specifying exactly where the easement shall exist on A's land, is the easement valid? The court must resolve that problem in Dyer v. Dyer.

---

[2] Section 1085 provides that '(a) present interest, and the benefit of a condition or covenant respecting property, may be taken by any natural person under a grant, although not named a party thereto.' * * *

HINES, Justice.

This is an appeal by co-executor Roger Dyer from the superior court's construction of certain provisions of the last will and testament of his mother, Emma Linda Dyer. For the reasons which follow, we affirm.

Worth Dyer and his wife, Emma Linda Dyer, executed a joint will dated June 4, 1981. Worth died in 1981, Emma on September 20, 1999. Roger and Sonny Dyer, sons of the decedents, were named co-executors of the estate.[3] In June 2000, Roger Dyer, as co-executor, filed a "Petition for the Construction of a Will" in the Superior Court of Union County. The petition asked the Court to interpret Items Four and Five of the will regarding the disposition of the real property owned by Emma Dyer at her death. A survey of the real property showed three tracts: Tract One consisting of 5.67 acres; Tract Two consisting of 1.15 acres and containing a one-story brick home, garden area, and asphalt drive; and Tract Three consisting of 65.34 acres.

The following provisions of the will were at issue:

ITEM FOUR
Upon the death of the Survivor, we will, devise and bequeath to our son, SONNY DYER, our farm and homeplace. * * *

ITEM FIVE
In the event any of our sons should wish to build a house on the property bequeathed to Sonny Dyer in Item Four hereof, they shall have the right to do so. * * *

* * *

1. As part of its analysis of the will provisions, the superior court found that the language in Item Five "[i]n the event any of our sons should wish to build a house on the property bequeathed to Sonny Dyer in Item Four hereof, they shall have the right to do so" was only the expression of the desire that the sons be permitted to build on the real property and did not grant them any interest in the land. Roger Dyer argues that the language was not precatory but created an easement in gross over the real property to himself and to his brothers. But the argument fails.

An easement in gross, unlike an easement appurtenant, is "a mere personal right in the land of another." *Church of the Nativity v. Whitener,* 249 Ga.App. 45, 48(2), 547 S.E.2d 587 (2001), quoting *Stovall v. Coggins Granite Co.,* 116 Ga. 376, 378, 42 S.E. 723 (1902). See also *Yaali, Ltd. v. Barnes & Noble,* 269 Ga. 695, 697(3), 506 S.E.2d 116 (1998). It "is *not* given for the purpose of ingress or egress to and from other land." *Lovell v. Anderson,* 242 Ga.App. 537, 539(2), 530 S.E.2d 233 (2000), quoting Pindar, Ga. Real Estate Law & Procedure, § 8-4 (5th ed.1998).

The language in Item Five does not mention any type of easement. See *Lovell v. Anderson,* supra at 540(2), 530 S.E.2d 233. And the superior court is not to " 'by construction reduce an estate once devised absolutely in fee, by limitations contained in subsequent parts of the will, unless the intent to limit the devise is clearly and unmistakably manifested' . . . 'An expressed devise cannot be cut down by a subsequent item of doubtful meaning.' " *Houston v. Coram,* 215 Ga. 101, 103(2), 109 S.E.2d 41

---

[3] The Dyers had seven children, five sons and two daughters.

(1959). Thus, the fee devised to Sonny Dyer could not be diminished by the questionable language in Item Five.

Moreover, even though an easement in gross is a personal right, inasmuch as it is an interest in land, its express grant should be drawn and executed with the same formalities as a deed to real estate. *Macon-Bibb County Indus. Auth. v. Central of Ga. R. Co.,* 266 Ga. 281, 283(3), 466 S.E.2d 855 (1996); *Lovell v. Anderson,* supra at 540(2), 530 S.E.2d 233. This would include language sufficient to designate with reasonable certainty the land over which the easement extends. *Macon-Bibb County Indus. Auth. v. Central of Ga. R. Co.,* supra at 383(3).

* * *

The alleged easement interest contains no limitation whatsoever with regard to time, place, or manner. Thus, the Dyer sons would have the right to build any kind and description of a structure as a "house" anywhere on the land at any time. This effectively would act as a complete restraint on the alienation of the estates granted in the will, and therefore would be repugnant to those estates. "It is the policy of the law to encourage free alienability of property, and attempts to remove either land or chattels from circulation in trade are discouraged not only by the rule against perpetuities, the abolition of fee tails, the early vesting of estates, and the doctrine of virtual representation, but by the rule against unreasonable restraints on alienation." *Leathers v. McClain,* 255 Ga. 378, 379, 338 S.E.2d 666 (1986), quoting Pindar, Ga. Real Est. Law, § 7-156 (2nd ed.). What is more, a condition which is repugnant to a granted estate is void. OCGA § 44-6-43; *Farkas v. Farkas,* 200 Ga. 886, 38 S.E.2d 924 (1, 2) (1946). Accordingly, any alleged easement in gross must fail.

* * *

Judgment affirmed.
All the Justices concur.

§ 11.1.3 Creation By Prescription

An easement also may be created by prescription—by adverse use. The elements for an easement by prescription, explained in Martin v. Proctor, *will sound familiar to you.*

Martin v. Proctor
227 Va. 61 (1984)

* * *

To acquire a prescriptive easement, a claimant must prove that his use was, *inter alia,* made under a claim of right. Proof of other characteristics of the use may suffice to raise a presumption of claim of right, but that presumption is rebuttable, and proof that the use was permissive defeats the claim.

In order to establish a private right of way over the lands of another by prescription it must appear that the use of the roadway by the claimant was adverse, under claim of right, exclusive, continuous, uninterrupted, and with knowledge and acquiescence of the owner of the land over which it passes, and that such use has continued for a period of at least twenty years. [Citations omitted].

We have said many times that "Where there has been an open, visible, continuous and unmolested use of a road across the land of another for at least twenty years, the use will be presumed to be under claim of right, and places upon the owner of the servient estate the burden of rebutting this presumption by showing that the use was permissive, and not under a claim of right." [Citations omitted]. *Craig v. Kennedy,* 202 Va. 654, 657-58, 119 S.E.2d 320, 322-23 (1961).

When the use originates by permission, it is presumed to continue with permission unless the conduct of the user is sufficient to apprise the owner of the servient tenement that the user is asserting a claim adverse and hostile to his rights.

An easement will not arise by prescription simply from permission of the owner of the servient estate, no matter how long the permissive use may continue. [Citations omitted]. And having begun by permission, it will, in the absence of some decisive act on the part of the owner of the dominant estate indicating an adverse and hostile claim, continue to be regarded as permissive, especially when the latter's use of the easement is in common with its use by others. [Citations omitted]. *Witt v. Creasey,* 117 Va. 872, 876, 86 S.E. 128, 129 (1915).

Absent such a decisive act on the part of a neighbor using a road opened by a landowner for his own use, the neighbor can never acquire a prescriptive easement. We believe it to be perfectly well settled that where the owner of land opens a way thereon for his own use and convenience, the mere use by his neighbor under circumstances which neither injures the way nor interferes with the owner's use of it, in the absence of some other circumstance indicating a claim of right, will not be considered as adverse, and will never ripen into a prescriptive right. In order to ripen into a prescriptive right, the claim to the use of the way must be adverse--that is, not accorded as a mere accommodation, but asserted under a claim of right hostile to the rights of the owner of the servient estate, so as to expose the claimant to an action if his claim is not well founded. If it be fairly shown that the use is permissive in its inception, it will never by mere lapse of time ripen into a hostile right. *Wall v. Landman,* 152 Va. 889, 895, 148 S.E. 779, 781 (1929) (citations omitted), *quoted with approval in Eagle Lodge v. Hofmeyer,* 193 Va. 864, 878, 71 S.E.2d 195, 203 (1952).

* * *

Note

The exclusivity requirement for prescriptive easements is different from the exclusivity requirement for adverse possession. For prescriptive easements, the term means that the claimant does not share the use with the public. Thus, it does not mean that the owner of the servient estate is not in possession. Nor does it mean that the owner of the servient estate does not use the land. See *Apley v. Tagert,* 584 So.2d 816 (Ala. 1991).

§ 11.1.4 Creation By Implication: Prior Use

Easements also may be created by implication. There are two types of easements by implication: by prior use and by necessity. We discuss prior use first.

Lobato v. Taylor
71 P.3d 938 (Colo. 2002)

Lobato v. Taylor *provides an overview of the elements for an easement by implication from prior use.*

* * *

An easement implied from prior use is created when 1) the servient and dominant estates were once under common ownership, 2) the rights alleged were exercised prior to the severance of the estate [often called the "quasi-easement"], 3) the use was not merely temporary, 4) the continuation of this use was reasonably necessary to the enjoyment of the parcel, and 5) a contrary intention is neither expressed nor implied. Restatement, *supra,* § 2.12; *see also Lee v. Sch. Dist. No. R-1,* 164 Colo. 326, 435 P.2d 232, 235-36 (1967); *Proper v. Greager,* 827 P.2d 591, 593 (Colo.App.1992). The rationale for this servitude is as follows:

> The rule stated in this section is not based solely on the presumed actual intent of the parties. It furthers the policy of protecting reasonable expectations, as well as actual intent, of parties to land transactions.

Restatement, *supra,* § 2.12 cmt. a.

* * *

Manitowoc Remanufacturing, Inc. v. Vocque
307 Ark. 271 (1991)

In Manitowoc Remanufacturing, Inc., *the court explains the nature of the so-called quasi-easement.*

* * *

When an owner uses a part of his or her land for the benefit of another part, a quasi-easement has been held to exist. The part of the land benefitted has been referred to as the quasi-dominant tenement, and the land utilized for the benefit of the other property has been referred to as the quasi-servient tenement. When the owner of land subject to a quasi-easement in favor of another part conveys the quasi-dominant tenement, an easement corresponding to the pre-existing quasi-easement is vested in the grantee of the land. The quasi-easement must be of an apparent, continuous, and necessary character. 3 Tiffany, *The Law of Real Property* § 781 (1920). These easements have been referred to as implied easements corresponding to pre-existing quasi-easements.

The doctrine originated in *Lampman v. Milks,* 21 N.Y. 505 (1860). A landowner diverted a stream flowing across his property through an artificial channel to benefit another portion of the property. The owner conveyed the land benefitted by the condition to the plaintiff and shortly thereafter conveyed the remaining property to the defendant. Four years later, the defendant attempted to eliminate the artificial channel which would have resulted in flooding the plaintiff's property.

The Court stated the general rule that no easement exists if there is unity of ownership. Once a severance occurs by a sale of a portion of the property, easements or servitudes are created corresponding to the benefits and burdens existing at the time of the sale. When the owner of an estate sells a portion of it, the purchaser takes the land subject to the benefits and burdens appearing at the time of the sale. If a burden is imposed upon the portion sold, the purchaser takes subject to the burden provided it was open and visible. Specifically, the Court held "[t]he parties are presumed to contract in reference to the condition of the property at the time of the sale and neither has a right, by altering arrangements then openly existing, to change materially the relative value of the respective parts."

* * *

Russakoff v. Scruggs
241 Va. 135 (1991)

In Russakoff v. Scruggs, *after introducing the facts and summarizing the law of easements, the court must decide whether a quasi-easement existed and if reasonable necessity was established. The court also will briefly address whether the easement was apparent and continuous.*

LACY, Justice.

The issue we must decide on this appeal is whether lot owners established an easement for access to and use of a lake.

In the 1960s, Richmond Real Estate Developers, Inc., which was owned by E. Carlton Wilton and his two brothers as sole stockholders, began constructing Canterbury East subdivision, located in the Tuckahoe District of Henrico County. The subdivision included a man-made lake with a waterline at the contour line of about the 136' elevation, as shown on the Canterbury East subdivision plat filed with the county. Richard L. and Diane Y. Russakoff, Edward E. Haddock, and Edwin M. Lohmann (collectively Russakoff), each own a lot in Canterbury East subdivision. Their rear lot lines abut the 140' contour, thus leaving a strip of land approximately 20 feet wide, between the lots and the lake. This strip was reserved for flood plains, sewer lines, and water lines. Richmond Real Estate Developers ceased paying taxes on the lake property, and it escheated to the Commonwealth. A tax sale was held on September 16, 1983, where Kerry I. and Doris J. Scruggs (collectively Scruggs) were the highest bidders. On May 25, 1984 the Commonwealth conveyed the lake property to Scruggs pursuant to the tax sale. Scruggs then posted "no trespassing" signs, erected a fence around the lake, and sent all homeowners surrounding the lake a letter offering them use of the lake by renting or purchasing shares. Further, Scruggs testified that, since the lake was in "bad need of repair and hadn't had anything done to it for years," as of the date of trial he had spent $8,231.53 on improvements, which included approximately $3,000 in taxes and insurance.

By bill of complaint filed February 10, 1988, Russakoff alleged that the right to use the lake had been acquired under a number of legal theories, including adverse possession. The trial court sustained Scruggs' demurrer on the adverse possession claim, but overruled the demurrer as to the other theories. In an amended bill of complaint, Russakoff alleged a right to use the lake by virtue of prescriptive easement, oral agreement, license, easement by implication, and easement by necessity. After an *ore tenus* hearing, the trial court ruled that Russakoff was not entitled to any easement or other rights to use Canterbury Lake. The court dismissed the action, and Russakoff appeals.

In the amended bill of complaint, Russakoff advanced various theories in support of the right of access to and use of Canterbury Lake. The trial judge did not relate his factual findings to any theory Russakoff identified, but characterized the claims as ones based on easements, and stated in an opinion letter and final order that Russakoff was "not entitled to any easement rights" in Canterbury Lake or "to the use of" the lake. Therefore, we must review the record to determine whether Russakoff failed to establish an easement under any of the three easement theories he pled, which were an easement created by prescription, by implication, or by necessity.

We begin by reviewing the applicable legal principles. Easements are not ownership interests in the servient tract but "the privilege to use the land of another in a particular manner and for a particular purpose." *Brown v. Haley,* 233 Va. 210, 216, 355 S.E.2d 563, 567-68 (1987). Easements are appurtenant to, and run with, the dominant tract if they benefit the owner in his use and enjoyment of that tract. *See Scott v. Moore,* 98 Va. 668, 675, 37 S.E. 342, 344 (1900).

There are a number of ways an easement can be created. "Easements may be created by express grant or reservation, by implication, by estoppel or by prescription." *Bunn v. Offutt,* 216 Va. 681, 684, 222 S.E.2d 522, 525 (1976). In the case of easements over streets and roads, we have recognized the creation of an easement by reference in the deed to a plat showing the road, even if the street or road had not been created or was not being used at the time of conveyance. *Walters v. Smith,* 186 Va. 159, 169-70, 41 S.E.2d 617, 622 (1947). Within the category of easements created by implication, we have recognized easements created by necessity, *see, e.g., Middleton v. Johnston,* 221 Va. 797, 802, 273 S.E.2d 800, 803 (1981), and by pre-existing use (also referred to as quasi-easements), *see, e.g., Brown,* 233 Va. at 218, 355 S.E.2d at 569. *See also* 1 R. Minor, *The Law of Real Property* § 99 (F. Ribble 2d ed. 1928).

Russakoff claims, *inter alia,* an easement arising by implication. Such an easement is based on the legal principle that when one conveys land, he is presumed to transfer all that is necessary to the use and enjoyment of the land conveyed. *Brown,* 233 Va. at 218, 355 S.E.2d at 569. While one cannot have an easement on land he owns, if, before severance, one part of the land was used for the benefit of another part, a "quasi-easement" exists over the "quasi-servient" portion of the land. That easement is conveyed by implication when the dominant tract is severed; the grantee of the dominant tract obtains an easement over the servient tract, based on the previous use. *See generally Sanderlin v. Baxter,* 76 Va. 299 (1882); R. Minor, *supra,* § 99.

While the extent of the easement right is determined by the circumstances surrounding the conveyance which divides the single ownership, the existence of the easement is established on a showing that (1) the dominant and servient tracts originated from a common grantor, (2) the use was in existence at the time of the severance, and that (3) the use is apparent, continuous, and reasonably necessary for the enjoyment of the dominant tract. *Brown,* 233 Va. at 219, 355 S.E.2d at 569; *Fones v. Fagan,* 214 Va. 87, 90-91, 196 S.E.2d 916, 919 (1973).

It is clear from the record before us that Russakoff's lots (dominant tracts), and the lake property (servient tract), were originally part of a single tract, thereby satisfying the first prong of the test. Next, the record is equally clear that, at the time Russakoff's predecessors in title took possession of the dominant tracts, the servient tract was a lake. Wilton testified as to the lake's existence, and the lake was reflected on the plat in the deeds conveying the dominant tracts to Russakoff's predecessors. The use of the servient tract as a lake, pre-existing the severance, was established.

Turning to the question of apparent and continuous use, the trial court identified Russakoff's use of a pump for lawn watering as the only use of the lake. This use, the trial court held, was not sufficient to establish an easement. Russakoff asserts that this holding is erroneous and that the record supports a finding that the use of the lake and strip of land to gain access to the lake was sufficient to establish an easement. We agree.

The record reflects that Russakoff and previous owners of the lots used the lake openly and continuously, through the construction of docks, piers, and sprinkler systems, and by using the lake for boating and ice skating. Mr. Lohmann, who purchased his lot in 1977, testified that he had a boat which his children used for fishing, frogging and "that type of thing," and when the lake was frozen in the winter they skated on the ice.

Haddock testified that the lake was a "big consideration" in his purchase of his property in 1968. He "bought a boat along with the house so we could use it in the lake." The boat originally belonged to Mr. Sharp, Haddock's predecessor in title. Haddock testified that he used the lake for wading, built a pier (although it had disintegrated prior to Scruggs' purchase of the lake), and bought a canoe and used it on the lake. He also testified that his family as well as neighbors skated on the lake in the winter.

Dr. Stearns, Russakoff's predecessor in title, testified that he had used the lake since 1966. He constructed a pier, a lawn irrigation system, and a retaining wall. Additionally, he observed as many as 800 people ice skating on the lake in the winter. He had used the lake for almost 20 years before Scruggs demanded that he pay $250 a year for access to and use of the lake.

Diane Russakoff testified that, in viewing the property prior to purchasing it from Stearns, she saw boats in Stearns' yard, as well as in the neighbors' yards. Mrs. Russakoff also observed that the grass was cut all the way to the water. Dr. Stearns informed her that he had made uninterrupted use of the lake since he had purchased the property. Additionally, Dr. Stearns showed the Russakoffs the sprinkler system from the lake to the lawn. Although the system was disconnected at the time of the purchase from Stearns, the Russakoffs re-connected the system and used it.

Our review of this record shows that the trial judge's finding that the only use of the lake was Russakoff's lawn sprinkler system, which he found to be insufficient to support an easement, is clearly erroneous. Rather, the record supports a contrary conclusion that use of the lake was continuous and apparent.

The third prong of the test also requires that the easement be reasonably necessary to the use and enjoyment of the dominant tract. This determination requires a showing of need which, by definition, may be less than that required for establishing an easement by necessity, but must be something more than simple convenience. We have recognized that whether this element is established "generally will depend upon the circumstances of the particular case." *Jones v. Beavers,* 221 Va. 214, 221, 269 S.E.2d 775, 779 (1980).

Here, we hold that a purchaser of a lot would have a legitimate expectation of the right to access and use the lake where a visual inspection and reference to the plat incorporated in the deed of conveyance showed the existence of a lake within 20 feet of one's lot line, and where investigation would disclose that the 20-foot strip between the lake and the lot line was retained solely for certain utility and flood plain uses. The Canterbury East developers contemplated enjoyment of the lake, as a lake, by purchasers of the lots surrounding the lake. Under these circumstances, the easement at issue was reasonably necessary to the use and enjoyment of the lakeside lots.

An easement created by implication, which, as here, is appurtenant to the land, may be vitiated if, when the servient estate is purchased by another, the purchaser of the servient tract does not have notice of the easement or the use is not apparent. Under those circumstances, the purchaser takes the land free from such easement or use. *Ricks v. Scott,* 117 Va. 370, 384, 84 S.E. 676, 681 (1915). As discussed above, the evidence in this case supports a finding of a use which was apparent, continuous, and reasonably necessary to the enjoyment of the dominant tract. The record also clearly shows Scruggs' knowledge of the use. In addition to sending a letter indicating the lot owners could *no longer* use the lake without payment of a fee, Scruggs agreed that "numerous property owners were using the lake and had pumps in the water for getting water up on their lot[s]." Furthermore, Scruggs testified that shortly after purchasing the lake, he traversed the lake in a canoe and disconnected at least two of the existing sprinkler systems which used the lake water for lawn watering purposes, and Scruggs' actions show that the use of the lake by surrounding property owners was apparent, and that he was aware of the use. At the time Scruggs purchased the lake, its use was apparent, continuous, and reasonably necessary to the enjoyment of property surrounding the lake. Therefore, we conclude that an easement by implication was established in favor of Russakoff for access to and use of Canterbury Lake.

In view of this holding, it is unnecessary to review Russakoff's claims to an easement created by prescription or by necessity.

* * *

Accordingly, we will reverse the judgment of the trial court and enter judgment in favor of the Russakoffs.

Reversed and final judgment.

Note

The quasi-easement is deemed apparent if it is visible or reasonably discoverable. *Jackson v. Nash,* 109 Nev. 1202 (1993). The use of this quasi-easement is continuous if it is permanent and not temporary. See *Wangen v. Kecskes* 256 Mont. 165 (1993). According to some authorities, the easement is reasonably necessary if another access cannot be secured at a "reasonable expense." See *Cobb v. Daugherty,* 225 W.Va. 435 (2010). Thus, if a substitute could be had but only at a substantial increase in cost, reasonable necessity would be found. See *Pendarvis v. Cook,* 391 S.C. 528 (2011).

Mitchell v. Castellaw
151 Tex. 56 (1952)

The Labato *and* Rusakoff *cases, supra, stated that "reasonable necessity" was an element for an easement by prior use. In fact, however, there is a split of authority. While some jurisdictions require reasonable necessity, others require "strict necessity" (sometimes also called "absolute necessity"). In* Mitchell v. Castellaw, *the court explains when reasonable necessity is the standard and when strict necessity is used.*

* * *

It is universally recognized that where the owner of a single area of land conveys away part of it, the circumstances attending the conveyance may themselves, without aid of language in the deed, and indeed sometimes in spite of such language, cause an easement to arise as between the two parcels thus created-not only in favor of the parcel granted ('implied grant') but also in favor of the one remaining in the ownership of the grantor ('implied reservation'). The basis of the doctrine is that the law reads into the instrument that which the circumstances show both grantor and grantee must have intended, had they given the obvious facts of the transaction proper consideration. And in the case of an implied reservation it is not necessarily a bar to its creation that the grantor's deed, into which the law reads it, actually warrants the servient tract thereby conveyed to be free of encumbrance. Restatement, Property, §§ 474-6; 28 C.J.S., Easements, §§ 30, 34; 17 * * *

On the other hand, even in the case of an implied grant, courts do not lightly hold the grantor to convey more than stated in his deed; and he being less favored in law than his grantee, the weight of authority seems still more reluctant to imply a reservation in his favor at the expense of his grantee. Restatement, supra, § 476, comments c and g; 28 C.J.S., supra, § 34; 17 Am.Jur., supra, § 45; Othen v. Rosier, State v. Black Bros., Sellers v. Texas Central Ry. Co., and other decisions, supra. Thus although various types of factual consideration may operate in a particular case to defeat the implication of intent to reserve the easement (e. g., the nonapparent character of the flood usage considered in Sellers v. Texas Central Ry. Co., supra) and while decisions of the different states are not uniform on the point, we ourselves have stated in broad terms as recently as Othen v. Rosier, supra (148 Tex. 485, 226 S.W.2d 626.), (a 'way of necessity' case) that no reservation of an easement will be implied where the claimed right of usage is not shown to be strictly necessary in order that the grantor of the alleged servient tract may enjoy his ownership of the parcel which he retained in his erstwhile single tract after making the conveyance. See also our other and somewhat earlier decision on an alleged 'way of necessity' in Bains v. Parker, supra (143 Tex. 57, 182 S.W.2d 399.). * * * As stated, the authorities are not uniform. For example, the Supreme Court of Illinois seems to have held just contrary to Bubser v. Ranguette. Bihss v. Sabolis, 322 Ill. 350, 153 N.E. 684, 53 A.L.R. 907. As indicated in the opinion below, even some of our own courts have expressly applied a rule of 'reasonable,' as distinguished from 'strict,' necessity. Scarborough v. Anderson Bros. Const. Co., Tex.Civ.App., 90 S.W.2d 305, er dism.; Missouri-Kansas-Texas Ry. Co. of Texas v. Cunningham, Tex.Civ.App., 273 S.W. 697. Neither of these decisions has been expressly overruled. The result in another Texas decision cited in the opinion below seems also in conflict with the rule of strict necessity upon a set of facts rather analogous to those of the instant case. El Paso Land Improvement Co. v. Crawford, Tex.Com.App., 292 S.W. 518. There is even some apparent conflict between the expression 'reasonably necessary' as used in Gulf, C. & S. F. Ry. Co. v. Rowland and Gulf, C. & S. F. Ry. Co. v. Ellis and the rule of strict necessity stated in Othen v. Rosier and Bains v. Parker, all supra. The American Law Institute takes the view that, while reservations of easements should indeed be less readily implied than grants thereof, the circumstance of necessity is only one of many to be considered and that a reservation may accordingly be implied in a given case even though the degree of necessity be less than 'strict.' Restatement, supra, § 476 and comments. The Institute formula, in its approach to the fundamental matter of intent of the parties, is perhaps more scientific than a doctrine, which includes the 'strict necessity' requirement. But the latter, too, has its good points. It is undoubtedly simpler of application. Moreover, as occasionally stated in the books, the whole theory of implied easements is somewhat in derogation of the registration statutes and indeed the Statute of Frauds, while even the term 'strict necessity' is not hopelessly inelastic for sensible application to varying sets of facts. On the whole, we believe the requirement of strict necessity as prerequisite to all implied reservations of easements is more in accord with our local practices and traditions than a contrary view would be.

* * *

Note

In an implied grant, the grantor retains the servient estate. Thus, the grantee obtains the easement by implication. In an implied reservation, the grantor retains the dominant estate. Thus, the grantor obtains the easement by implication.

Norken Corp. v. McGahan
823 P.2d 622 (Alaska 1991)

If necessity (whether reasonable or strict) ends, does the easement by prior use end, too? The Norken *case states that it does not.*

* * *

* * * Having once arisen, the implied easement [by prior use] is not extinguished merely because the reasonable necessity ceases to exist. *Story v. Hefner,* 540 P.2d 562, 566 (Okla.1975); *Thompson v. Schuh,* 286 Or. 201, 593 P.2d 1138, 1145 (1979). The durability of the easement comes from the fact that an implied easement is based on the theory that whenever one conveys property he includes or intends to include in the conveyance whatever is necessary for its beneficial use and enjoyment and to retain whatever is necessary for the use and enjoyment of the land retained. An easement by implication is a true easement having permanence of duration and should be distinguished from a "way of necessity" which lasts only as long as the necessity continues.

* * *

§ 11.1.5 Creation By Implication: Necessity

The second way an easement may be created by implication is by necessity. The next case states the elements for an easement by implication based on necessity.

Schwab v. Timmons
224 Wis.2d 27 (1999)

The petitioner's land is landlocked because on one side is a lake owned by the respondent, and on the other side is a bluff. Respondents will not give access across their lake to petitioner to reach the public road. As to the bluff, there is access to a public road from the bluff—but one first must reach the top of the bluff. The court, after providing the elements for an easement by necessity, denied the petitioner's easement by necessity. The court will give you an idea of what means "necessity" for an easement by necessity.

* * *

¶ 19 An easement of necessity "arises where an owner severs a landlocked portion of his [or her] property by conveying such parcel to another." *Ludke v. Egan,* 87 Wis.2d 221, 229-30, 274 N.W.2d 641 (1979). To establish an easement by necessity, a party must show common ownership of the two parcels prior to severance of the landlocked parcel, *Ruchti v. Monroe,* 83 Wis.2d 551, 556, 266 N.W.2d 309 (1978), and that the owner of the now landlocked parcel cannot access a public roadway from his or her own property, *Ludke,* 87 Wis.2d at 230, 274 N.W.2d 641. If this can be demonstrated, an easement by necessity will be implied over the land retained by the grantor. *Id.*

* * *

¶ 22 Wisconsin courts have never before recognized geographical barriers alone as circumstances warranting an easement by necessity. In fact, case law suggests otherwise. This court stated in *Backhausen* that a way of necessity is not merely one of convenience, and "the law will not imply such a way where it has provided another method for obtaining the same at a reasonable expense to the landowner." *Backhausen,* 204 Wis. at 289, 234 N.W. 904.

¶ 23 While the petitioners have provided evidence that the cost of building a road over the bluff would cost approximately $700,000--an unreasonable expense, it is apparent that they consider other methods of access--a stairway, an elevator--unacceptable. Petitioners narrowly focus on vehicular access to the lake itself as the only possible way to enjoy this property. Certainly it may be more convenient for the petitioners to seek an extension of the private road to their parcels rather than travel across the property above the bluff and navigate the bluff, but that in itself does not create the right to an easement by necessity. A grantor is not landlocked when he or she has difficulty getting from his or her land to a public road as long as he or she can get from his or her land to a public road. *See Ludke,* 87 Wis.2d at 230, 274 N.W.2d 641. *See also Sicchio v. Alvey,* 10 Wis.2d 528, 538, 103 N.W.2d 544 (1960) (Access to building at front, even though rear entry was used, does not allow for right-of-way by necessity to rear entry of store).

* * *

Finn v. Williams

376 Ill. 95 (1941)

Finn v. Williams establishes that mere non-use alone will not terminate an easement by necessity.

* * *

* * * Where an owner of land conveys a parcel thereof which has no outlet to a highway except over the remaining lands of the grantor or over the land of strangers, a way by necessity exists over the remaining lands of the grantor. 17 Am.Jur. (Easements) sec. 48; Trapp v. Gordon, 366 Ill. 102, 7 N.E.2d 869; Gilfoy v. Randall, 274 Ill. 128, 113 N.E. 88. If, at one time, there has been unity of title, as here, the right to a way by necessity may lay dormant through several transfers of title and yet pass with each transfer as appurtenant to the dominant estate and be exercised at any time by the holder of the title thereto. 17 Am.Jur. (Easements) secs. 49, 127; Logan v. Stogsdale, 123 Ind. 372, 24 N.E. 135, 8 L.R.A. 58. Plaintiffs' land is entirely surrounded by property of strangers and the land of the defendant from which it was originally severed. A right of way easement of necessity was necessarily implied in the conveyance severing the two tracts in 1895, and in 1937. The fact that the original grantee and his successors in interest have been permitted ingress to and egress from the 40 acres over the land owned by surrounding strangers is immaterial. When such permission is denied, as in the present case, the subsequent grantees may avail themselves of the dominant and servient estates.

The decree of the circuit court is right, and it is affirmed.

Decree affirmed.

§ 11.1.6 Negative Easements

Everything we have covered so far has dealt with an "affirmative" (sometimes called a "positive") easement: that O grants to A the right to go onto O's land and make a limited use thereof. What we next cover are "negative" easements. Rather than A doing something on O's land, in a negative easement, O does not do something on O's land.

U.S. v. Blackman

270 Va. 68 (2005)

Mr. and Mrs. Atkins owned a farm. In 1973, they granted a "conservation easement" to Historic Green Springs, Inc. [HSGI], a non-profit organization. The organization ultimately conveyed this easement to the United States. The easement that Mr. and Mrs. Atkins conveyed provided that the farm "will be maintained and preserved in its present state as nearly as practicable, though structural changes, alterations, additions, or improvements as would not in the opinion of the Grantee fundamentally alter its historic character or its setting may be made thereto by the owner, provided that the prior written approval of the Grantee to such change, alteration, addition, or improvements shall have been obtained. This provision applies as well to those 18th and 19th Century outbuildings located on the described property." Peter Blackman subsequently acquired the farm (the servient estate) from the Atkins and began building in a manner that would violate the terms of the easement. The United States sought to enjoin Blackman. The court holds for the United States. In doing so, the court will explain the law of easements in general and negative easements specifically.

KOONTZ, Justice.

* * *

In defense of his actions, Blackman argues that, *inter alia,* the original deed of easement granted to HGSI was invalid because at the time it was purportedly created, Virginia law did not recognize any kind of negative easement in gross, including such easements for the purpose of land conservation and historic preservation.

In its order, the district court correctly states that we have not directly addressed the issue of the validity of negative easements in gross in our prior decisions. While also correctly noting that only certain types of easements were recognized at common law, the district court references the statement in *Tardy v. Creasy,* 81 Va. (6 Hans.) 553, 557 (1886), that "there are many other easements which have been recognized, and some of them have been of a novel kind," for the proposition that prior to 1973 "*Tardy* leaves open the possibility that other easements, including negative easements related to land conservation and historic preservation, would be valid if sufficiently related to the land."

DISCUSSION

The first question certified by the district court presents the issue of law whether, in 1973, the law of Virginia permitted an individual landowner to grant a negative easement in gross to a third party for the purpose of land conservation and historic preservation. As indicated by the district court, if the law of this Commonwealth did not recognize the validity of such an easement at that time, then the purported property restrictions granted to HGSI are invalid and would be unenforceable by HGSI's transferee, the United States.

Although previously we have not addressed the issue of the validity of a negative easement in gross under the law existing in 1973, the issue is of considerable significance beyond the specific historic district involved in this case. By the brief of *amici curiae* filed in this case, we are advised that at least seven other charitable entities hold conservation or historic preservation easements, many of them easements in gross, conveyed prior to 1973. Underlying the issue is a degree of apparent conflict between the common law preference for unrestricted rights of ownership of real property and the public policy of this Commonwealth as expressed in Article XI of the Constitution of Virginia, ratified by the people of this Commonwealth in 1970, that "it shall be the policy of this Commonwealth to conserve . . . its historical sites and buildings." Accordingly, we take this opportunity to discuss in some detail the relevant law.

"An easement is 'a privilege without profit, which the owner of one tenement has a right to enjoy in respect of that tenement in or over the tenement of another person; by reason whereof the latter is obliged to suffer, or refrain from doing something on his own tenement for the advantage of the former.' " *Amstutz v. Everett Jones Lumber Corp.,* 268 Va. 551, 559, 604 S.E.2d 437, 441 (2004) (quoting *Stevenson v. Wallace,* 68 Va. (27 Gratt.) 77, 87 (1876)); *accord Brown v. Haley,* 233 Va. 210, 216, 355 S.E.2d 563, 567-68 (1987). Easements are described as being "affirmative" easements when they convey privileges on the part of one person or owner of land (the "dominant tract") to use the land of another (the "servient tract") in a particular manner or for a particular purpose. Easements are described as being "negative" when they convey rights to demand that the owner of the servient tract refrain from certain otherwise permissible uses of his own land. *Bunn v. Offutt*, 216 Va. 681, 684, 222 S.E.2d 522, 525 (1976).

Negative easements, also known as servitudes, do not bestow upon the owner of the dominant tract the right to travel physically upon the servient tract, which is the feature common to all affirmative easements, but only the legal right to object to a use of the servient tract by its owner inconsistent with the terms of the easement. In this sense, negative easements have been described as consisting solely of "a veto power." *Prospect Dev. Co. v. Bershader*, 258 Va. 75, 89, 515 S.E.2d 291, 299 (1999).

At common law, an owner of land was not permitted at his pleasure to create easements of every novel character and annex them to the land so that the land would be burdened with the easement when the land was conveyed to subsequent grantees. Rather, the landowner was limited to the creation of easements permitted by the common law or by statute. *See Tardy*, 81 Va. (6 Hans.) at 557. The traditional negative easements recognized at common law were those created to protect the flow of air, light, and artificial streams of water, and to ensure the subjacent and lateral support of buildings or land. *See* Andrew Dana & Michael Ramsey, *Conservation Easements and the Common Law*, 8 Stan. Envtl. L.J. 2, 13 (1989); *see also Tardy*, 81 Va. (6 Hans.) at 557, 563.

Easements, whether affirmative or negative, are classified as either "appurtenant" or "in gross." An easement appurtenant, also known as a pure easement, has both a dominant and a servient tract and is capable of being transferred or inherited. It frequently is said that an easement appurtenant "runs with the land," which is to say that the benefit conveyed by or the duty owed under the easement passes with the ownership of the land to which it is appurtenant. *See Greenan v. Solomon*, 252 Va. 50, 54, 472 S.E.2d 54, 57 (1996); *Lester Coal Corp. v. Lester*, 203 Va. 93, 97, 122 S.E.2d 901, 904 (1961). The four negative easements traditionally recognized at common law are, by their nature, easements appurtenant, as their intent is to benefit an adjoining or nearby parcel of land. *See* Federico Cheever, *Environmental Law: Public Good and Private Magic in the Law of Land Trusts and Conservation Easements: A Happy Present and a Troubled Future*, 73 Denv. U.L.Rev. 1077, 1081 (1996).

In contrast, an easement in gross, sometimes called a personal easement, is an easement "which is not appurtenant to any estate in land, but in which the servitude is imposed upon land with the benefit thereof running to an individual." *Lester Coal Corp.*, 203 Va. at 97, 122 S.E.2d at 904. At common law, easements in gross were strongly disfavored because they were viewed as interfering with the free use of land. Thus, the common law rule of long standing is that an easement is "never presumed to be in gross when it [can] fairly be construed to be appurtenant to land." *French v. Williams*, 82 Va. 462, 468, 4 S.E. 591, 594 (1886). For an easement to be treated as being in gross, the deed or other instrument granting the easement must plainly manifest that the parties so intended. *Prospect Dev. Co.*, 258 Va. at 90, 515 S.E.2d at 299.

Because easements in gross were disfavored by the common law, they could neither be transferred by the original grantee nor pass by inheritance. *Lester Coal Corp.*, 203 Va. at 97, 122 S.E.2d at 904. By statute, however, Virginia long ago abrogated common law restrictions on the transfer of interests in land "by declaring that any interest in or claim to real estate may be disposed of by deed or will." *Carrington v. Goddin,* 54 Va. (13 Gratt.) 587, 599-600 (1857) (internal quotation marks omitted). Pursuant to this statutory change in the common law rule, currently embodied in Code § 55-6, we have recognized that an affirmative easement in gross is an interest in land that may be disposed of by deed or will. *City of Richmond v. Richmond Sand & Gravel Co.,* 123 Va. 1, 9, 96 S.E. 204, 207 (1918). Following this Court's decision in *Lester Coal Corp.,* which in dictum made reference to the common law rule that easements in gross remained non-transferable by deed or will, 203 Va. at 97, 122 S.E.2d at 904, Code § 55-6 was amended "to make clear the transferability of easements in gross." 1962 Va. Acts ch. 169. Since 1962, Code § 55-6, in pertinent part, has expressly provided that "[a]ny interest in or claim to real estate, *including easements in gross,* may be disposed of by deed or will." (Emphasis added). We subsequently acknowledged the intent of this statutory amendment in *Corbett v. Ruben,* 223 Va. 468, 472 n. 2, 290 S.E.2d 847, 849 n. 2 (1982) and *Hise v. BARC Elec. Coop.,* 254 Va. 341, 344, 492 S.E.2d 154, 157 (1997).

Code § 55-6 unambiguously speaks to "easements in gross" as interests in real estate capable of disposition by deed or will. There is no suggestion in this language that the statute was intended to apply only to affirmative easements in gross and not to negative easements in gross. The significance of this statutory change in the common law is manifest. Easements in gross, whether affirmative or negative, are now recognized interests in real property, rather than merely personal covenants not capable of being disposed of by deed or will as was the case under common law. Moreover, as pertinent to the present inquiry, such was the case well before 1973 in this Commonwealth.

* * *

First certified question answered in the affirmative.

Notes

1. As the *Blackman* case states, "The traditional negative easements recognized at common law were those created to protect the flow of air, light, and artificial streams of water, and to ensure the subjacent and lateral support of buildings or land." A few relatively brief points for elucidation are in order with respect to water rights and support.

2. The first point relates to water rights. The common law negative easement dealt with streams of water from an *artificial* source, such as a man-made lake or an irrigation ditch. Thus, if A granted B a right that A would not interfere with the flow of water from an irrigation ditch that emanated from A's land down to B's land, this would be a valid common law negative easement. But what if A sought to impede the flow of water to B's land from a *natural* source (a natural stream, for example)—not an artificial one? Here, irrespective of any easement, the answer depends on whether the jurisdiction in question uses a riparian rights system or a prior appropriation system. See the next two notes.

3. In a riparian rights system of water usage, an upstream owner can make only reasonable use of the water. "The fundamental principle of this system is that each riparian proprietor has an equal right to make a reasonable use of the waters of the stream, subject to the equal right of the other riparian proprietors likewise to make a reasonable use." *United States v. Willow River Power Co.,* 324 U.S. 499, 505 (internal

quotations omitted). To the extent the landowner's use interferes with use by other downstream riparian owners, the unreasonable use by the upstream owner can be enjoined. The riparian rights system is used primarily by eastern, southern, and mid-western states.

4. The other system of water rights, used primarily in the western states, is the prior appropriation system. In such a system, first in time is first in right. The key to such a system is that the user must make a "beneficial use" of the water.[4] "To appropriate water means to take and divert a specified quantity thereof and put it to beneficial use in accordance with the laws of the state where such water is found, and, by so doing, to acquire under such laws, a vested right to take and divert from the same source, and to use and consume the same quantity of water annually forever. . . ." *Arizona v. California*, 283 U.S. 423, 459 (1931). Thus, the fact that a prior appropriator dries up a downstream owner's land is not actionable. What is the basis for prior appropriation? "The law of prior appropriation grew up out of the law of capture. This doctrine will only work in a frontier society with static conditions. This is clearly shown in Colorado, wherein, by constitutional provisions the right to appropriate water can never be denied." *Brasher v. Gibson*, 2 Ariz.App. 91, 98, 406 P.2d 441, 448 (Ariz.App.1965).

5. Turning now to support rights, irrespective of any negative easement for support, a landowner has a common law legal right to lateral support from an adjoining landowner. Thus, if A engages in excavation on his land causing a landslide on B's adjoining property, A is liable to B. Note that this is so even in the absence of negligence by A; A is "strictly liable" (a concept that you either have already learned, or will learn, in your course in torts). On the other hand, if A's excavation causes a building on B's land to collapse, here the rule is that A is liable for the collapse only if A did not act reasonably: that is, A is liable only if A was negligent (unless it can be shown that the land would have collapsed even in the absence of a building on B's land). Of course, if A grants to B a negative easement for support and the grant provides that A will be strictly liable for the collapse of any buildings on B's land, then B's action against A for any collapse may proceed without any showing of negligence.

6. We next explore the subject of subjacent support. Suppose that A owns only the surface rights to land, and upon which A's house is located; B owns the mineral rights underneath. What result if B removes the minerals and causes a collapse of (a) A's land, or (b) A's house? As to the first half of the question (a), irrespective of a negative easement, if B removes the subjacent support causing a collapse of A's land, B is strictly liable. "At common law, where one person owns the surface of land and another the subjacent land, the owner of the surface is entitled to have it remain in its natural condition, without subsidence by reason of the subsurface owner's withdrawal of subjacent support. (Rest., Torts, § 820; 3 Tiffany, Real Property (3d ed. 1939) § 754, p. 196; 5 Powell, Real Property (1962) § 703, p. 308; 2 Thompson, Real Property (4th ed. 1961) § 415, p. 646; VI-A Amer. Law of Property (1954) § 28.36, pp. 99-100;

---

[4] [Is there any real difference between a "reasonable use" in the riparian system and the "beneficial use" in the prior appropriation system?]

Humphries v. Brogden (1850) 12 Q.B. 739, 744-745 (116 Eng.Rep. 1048, 1050); and see Empire Star Mines Co. v. Butler (1944) 62 Cal.App.2d 466, 533-534, 145 P.2d 49.) [¶] The same authorities agree that the common law right of subjacent support is closely analogous to that of lateral support (e.g., 3 Tiffany, supra, § 754, pp. 196-197; 5 Powell, supra); each of two of the treatises concurs to the extent that each treats the two subjects together. (2 Thompson, supra, § 415, p. 640; VI-A Amer. Law of Property, supra.) Under all the authorities, also, the common law obligation of subjacent support is 'absolute.' (E.g., Rest., Torts, supra, § 820, subsec. (1), com. b; 5 Powell, supra; 2 Thompson, supra.) The authorities—California courts included—also agree that the common law obligation of lateral support is similarly 'absolute.' (Wharam v. Investment Underwriters (1943) 58 Cal.App.2d 346, 349, 136 P.2d 363; Rest., Torts, § 817, subsec. (1), com. b; 5 Powell, supra, s 699, p. 290; 2 Thompson, supra, § 415, p. 642.)" Marin Municipal Water Dist. v. Northwestern Pac. R. Co. 253 Cal.App.2d 83, 89, 61 Cal.Rptr. 520, 524 (1967).

7. As to the second half of the question (b), relating to the collapse of A's house, the answer revolves around whether subsidence still would have occurred even in the absence of a structure: "This court therefore determines that Virginia would adopt the position of the Restatement, the English courts, and the American courts which have specifically addressed the issue, that if one withdraws subjacent support for the land of another and subsidence results, if the subsidence would have occurred even in the absence of any artificial additions to the land, then he is strictly liable not only for the harm to the land caused by the subsidence, but also for any harm to the artificial additions on the land that results from the subsidence." *Breeding v. Koch Carbon, Inc.* 726 F.Supp. 645, 648 (W.D.Va.1989).

8. Finally, navigable waters, such as rivers, are owned by the public, under the "public trust" doctrine. Thus, for municipal beaches, the tides are owned by the public, as is the "wet" and "dry" sand area. Can privately owned dry sand also be held in trust by the public (which has the "appearance" of an easement for the public use)? At least one court has held yes. See *Matthews v. Bay Head Imp. Ass'n,*, 95 N.J. 306, 471 A.2d 355 (1984), which gives an excellent summary of the history of the public trust doctrine.

Petersen v. Friedman
162 Cal.App.2d 245 (1958)

While courts are hesitant to recognize new types of negative easements, they sometimes do, as Petersen v. Friedman *establishes when it recognizes an easement for a view.*

KAUFMAN, Presiding Justice.
The parties are owners of adjacent parcels of improved real estate situated on Franklin Street in San Francisco. Plaintiff's complaint sought to perpetually enjoin the defendants from violating an express easement of light, air and unobstructed view created in favor of plaintiff's property and to compel the defendants to remove certain television aerials and antennae. The trial court found all of the allegations of the complaint to be true, rendered judgment for the plaintiff, and issued both injunctions requested.

Defendants appeal.

The nature and creation of the easement appurtenant to plaintiff's property is not in dispute. On November 6, 1942, Mary Petersen, now deceased, also known as Mrs. Chris Petersen, by a grant deed duly recorded conveyed a part of her property on Franklin Street to C. A. Petersen. The deed contained the following reservation of an easement:

'Reserving, however, unto the first party, her successors and assigns, as and for an appurtenance to the real property hereinafter particularly described and designated as 'Parcel A' and any part thereof, a *perpetual easement of right to receive light, air and unobstructed view over that portion of the real property hereinabove described*, to the extent that said light, air and view will be received and enjoyed by limiting any structure, fence, trees or shrubs upon said property hereinabove described or any part thereof, to a height *not* extending above a horizontal plane *28* feet above the level of the sidewalk of Franklin Street as the sidewalk level now exists at the junction of the southern and western boundary lines of the property hereinabove described. Any obstruction of such view * * * shall be removed upon demand at the expense of second party, and his successors and assigns in the ownership of that real property described or any part thereof.'

Thereafter, the defendants, by mesne conveyances from C. A. Petersen, acquired all of the property conveyed by the deed of November 6, 1942, subject to the reservation. Plaintiff is the duly appointed and qualified executor of the estate of Mary Petersen, which is the owner of the dominant tenement.

* * *

The language of the easement is clear and leaves no room for construction or determination of the intent of the parties, as contended by the defendant. Its purpose is to avoid any type of obstruction of the light, air and view without regard to the nature thereof. The reservation was not limited to the use then being made of the servient estate, but extended to all uses to which the servient estate might thereafter be devoted. Easements of light and air may be created in this state. Civil Code, § 801; Bryan v. Grosse, 155 Cal. 132, 99 P. 499. Although we have not been able to find a California precedent on an easement of view, the weight of authority is that such an easement may be created by express grant. See 142 A.L.R. 467 and cases collected therein. It has been held in this state however that interference with an easement of light, air or view by a structure in the street is ground for an injunction. Williams v. Los Angeles R. Co., 150 Cal. 592, 89 P. 330.

* * * The record here supports the judgment.

Judgment affirmed.

§ 11.1.7 Transferability of Easements

Suppose White owns Whiteacre and Black owns Blackacre, and White grants Black an easement appurtenant across Whiteacre. Suppose also that White subsequently transfers Whiteacre to White, Jr. In such case, the burden of the easement runs with the land to White, Jr. The reason is because, assuming that the transferee is not protected under a state recording statute (see chapter 8), easements run. That is the nature of easements appurtenant. Similarly, if Black transfers Blackacre to Black, Jr., Black, Jr. gets the benefit of the easement appurtenant. Again, easements appurtenant run. It is part of their

"DNA." The questions that we now ask are: (1) Do easements in gross also run with the land? That is, to be more precise, is the transferee of the owner of the servient estate burdened by the easement? (2) Are easements in gross transferrable? Again, to be more specific, can the owner of an easement in gross transfer his easement to another? (3) If two or more persons own an easement in gross, can each use the easement however he or she chooses? The next case provides the answers to these questions.

Miller v. Lutheran Conference & Camp Ass'n
331 Pa. 241 (1938)

Frank Miller and Rufus Miller own Lake Naomi. They grant the Water Company, a corporation they own, a long-term lease to Lake Naomi. The Water Company later gives Frank an easement in gross to boat and fish in the lake, and Frank later acquires a prescriptive easement to bathe in Lake Naomi. Frank transfers part of his interest to Rufus; his executor (after Rufus' death) gives a license to the Lutheran Conference & Camp Association. The court must decide whether Frank's transfer of one-fourth of his easement to Rufus is valid (it is) and whether Frank can object to the license given to the Lutheran Conference & Camp Association (he can).

STERN, Justice.

This litigation is concerned with interesting and somewhat novel legal questions regarding rights of boating, bathing and fishing in an artificial lake.

Frank C. Miller, his brother Rufus W. Miller, and others, who owned lands on Tunkhannock Creek in Tobyhanna Township, Monroe County, organized a corporation known as the Pocono Spring Water Ice Company, to which, in September 1895, they made a lease for a term of ninety-nine years of so much of their lands as would be covered by the backing up of the water as a result of the construction of a 14-foot dam which they proposed to erect across the creek. The company was to have 'the exclusive use of the water and its privileges.' It was chartered for the purpose of 'erecting a dam * * *, for pleasure, boating, skating, fishing and the cutting, storing and selling of ice.' The dam was built, forming 'Lake Naomi,' somewhat more than a mile long and about one-third of a mile wide.

By deed dated March 20, 1899, the Pocono Spring Water Ice Company granted to 'Frank C. Miller, his heirs and assigns forever, the exclusive right to fish and boat in all the waters of the said corporation at Naomi Pines, Pa.' On February 17, 1900, Frank C. Miller (his wife Katherine D. Miller not joining), granted to Rufus W. Miller, his heirs and assigns forever, 'all the one-fourth interest in and to the fishing, boating, and bathing rights and privileges at, in, upon and about Lake Naomi * * *; which said rights and privileges were granted and conveyed to me by the Pocono Spring Water Ice Company by their indenture of the 20th day of March, A.D. 1899.' On the same day Frank C. Miller and Rufus W. Miller executed an agreement of business partnership, the purpose of which was the erection and operation of boat and bath houses on Naomi Lake and the purchase and maintenance of boats for use on the lake, the houses and boats to be rented for hire and the net proceeds to be divided between the parties in proportion to their respective interests in the bathing, boating and fishing privileges, namely, three-fourths to Frank C. Miller and one-fourth to Rufus W. Miller, the capital to be contributed and the losses to be borne in the same proportion. In pursuance of this agreement the brothers erected and maintained boat and bath houses at different points on the lake, purchased and rented out boats, and conducted the business generally, from the spring of 1900 until the death of Rufus W. Miller on October 11, 1925, exercising their control and use of the privileges in an exclusive, uninterrupted and open manner and without challenge on the part of anyone.

Discord began with the death of Rufus W. Miller, which terminated the partnership. Thereafter Frank C. Miller, and the executors and heirs of Rufus W. Miller, went their respective ways, each granting licenses without reference to the other. Under date of July 13, 1929, the executors of the Rufus W. Miller estate granted a license for the year 1929 to defendant, Lutheran Conference and Camp Association, which was the owner of a tract of ground abutting on the lake for a distance of about 100 feet, purporting to grant to defendant, its members, guests and campers, permission to boat, bathe and fish in the lake, a certain percentage of the receipts therefrom to be paid to the estate. Thereupon Frank C. Miller and his wife, Katherine D. Miller, filed the present bill in equity,[5] complaining that defendant was placing diving floats on the lake and 'encouraging and instigating visitors and boarders' to bathe in the lake, and was threatening to hire out boats and canoes and in general to license its guests and others to boat, bathe and fish in the lake. The bill prayed for an injunction to prevent defendant from trespassing on the lands covered by the waters of the lake, from erecting or maintaining any structures or other encroachments thereon, and from granting any bathing licenses. The court issued the injunction.

It is the contention of plaintiffs that, while the privileges of boating and fishing were granted in the deed from the Pocono Spring Water Ice Company to Frank C. Miller, no *bathing* rights were conveyed by that instrument. In 1903 all the property of the company was sold by the sheriff under a writ of * * * a mortgage bond which the company had executed in 1898. As a result of that sale the Pocono Spring Water Ice Company was entirely extinguished, and the title to its rights and property came into the ownership of the Pocono Pines Ice Company, a corporation chartered for 'the supply of ice to the public.' In 1928 the title to the property of the Pocono Pines Ice Company became vested in Katherine D. Miller. Plaintiffs therefore maintain that the bathing rights, never having passed to Frank C. Miller, descended in ownership from the Pocono Spring Water Ice Company through the Pocono Pines Ice Company to plaintiff Katherine D. Miller, and that Frank C. Miller could not, and did not, give Rufus W. Miller any title to them. They further contend that even if such bathing rights ever did vest in Frank C. Miller, all of the boating, bathing and fishing privileges were easements in gross which were inalienable and indivisible, and when Frank C. Miller undertook to convey a one-fourth interest in them to Rufus W. Miller he not only failed to transfer a legal title to the rights but, in attempting to do so, extinguished the rights altogether as against Katherine D. Miller, who was the successor in title of the Pocono Spring Water Ice Company. It is defendant's contention, on the other hand, that the deed of 1899 from the Pocono Spring Water Ice Company to Frank C. Miller should be construed as transferring the bathing as well as the boating and fishing privileges, but that if Frank C. Miller did not obtain them

---

[5] Plaintiffs died during the pendency of the suit and their executors were substituted as parties plaintiff.

by grant he and Rufus W. Miller acquired them by prescription, and that all of these rights were alienable and divisible even if they be considered as easements in gross, although they might more properly, perhaps, be regarded as licenses which became irrevocable because of the money spent upon their development by Frank C. Miller and Rufus W. Miller.

* * *

Coming to the merits of the controversy * * * *.

It is impossible to construe the deed of 1899 from the Pocono Spring Water Ice Company to Frank C. Miller as conveying to the latter any privileges of bathing. It is clear and unambiguous. It gives to Frank C. Miller the exclusive right to *fish and boat*. * * * * No *bathing* rights are mentioned. This omission may have been the result of oversight or it may have been deliberate, but in either event the legal consequence is the same. It is to be noted that the mortgagee to whom the company mortgaged all its property in 1898 executed in 1902 a release of the fishing and boating rights to the company and to Frank C. Miller, thus validating the latter's title to these rights under the company's deed of 1899, but in this release also the bathing rights are omitted.

But, while Frank C. Miller acquired by grant merely boating and fishing privileges, the facts are amply sufficient to establish title to the bathing rights by prescription. True, these rights, not having been granted in connection with, or to be attached to, the ownership of any land, were not easements appurtenant but in gross. There is, however, no inexorable principle of law which forbids an adverse enjoyment of an easement in gross from ripening into a title thereto by prescription. * * * *

We are thus brought to a consideration of the next question, which is whether the boating, bathing and fishing privileges were assignable by Frank C. Miller to Rufus W. Miller. What is the nature of such rights? In England it has been said that easements in gross do not exist at all, although rights of that kind have been there recognized. In this country such privileges have sometimes been spoken of as licenses, or as contractual in their nature, rather than as easements in gross. These are differences of terminology rather than of substance. We may assume, therefore, that these privileges are easements in gross, and we see no reason to consider them otherwise. It has uniformly been held that a profit in gross-for example, a right of mining or fishing-may be made assignable. Funk v. Haldeman, 53 Pa. 229; Tinicum Fishing Co. v. Carter, 61 Pa. 21, 39, 100 Am.Dec. 597; see cases cited 19 C.J. 870, note 25. In regard to easements in gross generally, there has been much controversy in the courts and by textbook writers and law students as to whether they have the attribute of assignability. There are dicta in Pennsylvania that they are non-assignable. Tinicum Fishing Co. v. Carter, supra, pages 38, 39; Lindenmuth v. Safe Harbor Water Power Corporation, 309 Pa. 58, 63, 64, 163 A. 159, 89 A.L.R. 1180; Commonwealth v. Zimmerman, 56 Pa.Super. 311, 315, 316. But there is forcible expression and even definite authority to the contrary. Tide Water Pipe Co. v. Bell, 280 Pa. 104, 112, 113, 124 A. 351, 40 A.L.R. 1516; Dalton Street Railway Co. v. Scranton, 326 Pa. 6, 12, 191 A. 133. Learned articles upon the subject are to be found in 32 Yale Law Journal 813; 38 Yale Law Journal 139; 22 Michigan Law Review 521; 40 Dickinson Law Review 46. There does not seem to be any reason why the law should prohibit the assignment of an easement in gross if the parties to its creation evidence their intention to make it assignable. Here, as in Tide Water Pipe Company v. Bell, supra, the rights of fishing and boating were conveyed to the grantee-in this case Frank C. Miller, 'his heirs and assigns,' thus showing that the grantor, the Pocono Spring Water Ice Company, intended to attach the attribute of assignability to the privileges granted. Moreover, as a practical matter, there is an obvious difference in this respect between easements for personal enjoyment and those designed for commercial exploitation; while there may be little justification for permitting assignments in the former case, there is every reason for upholding them in the latter.

The question of assignability of the easements in gross in the present case is not as important as that of their divisibility. It is argued by plaintiffs that even if held to be assignable such easements are not divisible, because this might involve an excessive user or 'surcharge of the easement' subjecting the dominant tenement to a greater burden than originally contemplated. The law does not take that extreme position. It does require, however, that if there be a division, the easements must be used or exercised as an entirety. This rule had its earliest expression in Mountjoy's Case, which is reported in Co. Litt. 164b. 165a. It was there said, in regard to the grant of a right to dig for ore, that the grantee, Lord Mountjoy, 'might assign his whole interest to one, two, or more; but then, if there be two or more, they could make no division of it, but work together with one stock.' In Caldwell v. Fulton, 31 Pa. 475, 477, 478, 72 Am.Dec. 760, and in Funk v. Haldeman, 53 Pa. 229, that case was followed, and it was held that the right of a grantee to mine coal or to prospect for oil might be assigned, but if to more than one they must hold, enjoy and convey the right as an entirety, and not divide it in severalty. There are cases in other jurisdictions which also approve the doctrine of Mountjoy's Case, and hold that a mining right in gross is essentially integral and not susceptible of apportionment; an assignment of it is valid, but it cannot be aliened in such a way that it may be utilized by grantor and grantee, or by several grantees, separately; there must be a joint user, nor can one of the tenants alone convey a share in the common right. Grubb v. Bayard, Fed.Cas.No.5,849, C.C.E.D.Pa.; Harlow v. Lake Superior Iron Co., 36 Mich. 105, 121; Stanton v. T. L. Herbert & Sons, 141 Tenn. 440, 211 S.W. 353.

These authorities furnish an illuminating guide to the solution of the problem of divisibility of profits or easements in gross. They indicate that much depends upon the nature of the right and the terms of its creation, that 'surcharge of the easement' is prevented if assignees exercise the right as 'one stock,' and that a proper method of enjoyment of the easement by two or more owners of it may usually be worked out in any given instance without insuperable difficulty.

In the present case it seems reasonably clear that in the conveyance of February 17, 1900, it was not the intention of Frank C. Miller to grant, and of Rufus W. Miller to receive, a separate right to subdivide and sub-license the boating, fishing and bathing privileges on and in Lake Naomi, but only that they should together use such rights for commercial purposes, Rufus W. Miller to be entitled to one-fourth and Frank C. Miller to three-fourths of the proceeds resulting from their combined exploitation of the privileges. They were to hold the rights, in the quaint phraseology of Mountjoy's Case, as 'one stock.' Nor do the technical rules that would be applicable to a tenancy in common of a corporeal hereditament apply to the control of these easements in gross. Defendant contends that, as a tenant in common of the privileges, Rufus W. Miller individually was entitled to their use, benefit and possession and to exercise rights of ownership in regard thereto, including the right to license third persons to use them, subject only to the limitation that he must not thereby interfere with the similar rights of his cotenant. But the very nature of these easements prevents their being so exercised, inasmuch as it is necessary, because of the legal limitations upon their divisibility, that they should be utilized in common and not by two owners severally, and, as stated, this was evidently the intention of the brothers.

Summarizing our conclusions, we are of opinion (1) that Frank C. Miller acquired title to the boating and fishing privileges by grant and he and Rufus W. Miller to the bathing rights by prescription; (2) that he made a valid assignment of a one-fourth interest in them to Rufus W. Miller; but (3) that they cannot be commercially used and licenses thereunder granted without the common consent and joinder of the present owners, who with regard to them must act as 'one stock.' It follows that the executors of the estate of Rufus W. Miller did not have the right, in and by themselves, to grant a license to defendant.

The decree is affirmed; costs to be paid by defendant.

Note

Under the Restatement (Third) of Property (Servitudes), § 5.9, easements in gross may be divisible if that is the intent of the parties and the division does not unreasonably burden the servient estate.

§ 11.1.8 Termination of Easements

We next discuss how easements can be terminated. As the material that follows explains, there are a number of ways. The Penn Bowling *case examines one way: misuse.*

Penn Bowling Recreation Center, Inc. v. Hot Shoppes, Inc.
179 F.2d 64 (D.C.Cir. 1950)

Penn Bowling Recreation Center *establishes that misuse alone will not cause the easement to terminate—with one exception, as the case makes clear.*

* * *

Misuse of an easement right is not sufficient to constitute a forfeiture, waiver, or abandonment of such right. The right to an easement is not lost by using it in an unauthorized manner or to an unauthorized extent, unless it is impossible to sever the increased burden so as to preserve to the owner of the dominant tenement that to which he is entitled, and impose on the servient tenement only that burden which was originally imposed upon it.* * *

* * *

An authorized use and an unauthorized use may be intermingled in such a way as to justify enjoining any use until the circumstances have so changed that the authorized use may be permitted without affording opportunity for the unauthorized use, which it would be difficult to discover or prove. In such a case, the issuance of an injunction may be justified restraining any use until the building is so altered or changed that that part of it which is on the dominant tenement may enjoy the easement without permitting its enjoyment by the other part of the building having no right thereto. So where it cannot be ascertained whether the easement of a right of way is being used solely for the enjoyment of the dominant tenement, or for additional property also, an injunction may be granted against further use of the easement until such time as it may be shown that only the dominant tenement is served by the easement. McCullough et al. v. Broad Exchange Company, et al., supra.

* * *

Note

Cases dealing with forfeiture of easements because of extreme misuse are fact sensitive and typically a question of fact for the trial court. See, e.g. *Stephens v. Lavitt*, 239 P.3d 634 (Wyo. 2010) (forfeiture proper as remedy as part of a sanction in a civil contempt proceeding for violating terms of permanent injunction regarding easement use).

Hudson v. Pillow
261 Va. 296 (2001)

Yet another method of terminating an easement is by abandonment by the owner of the servient estate. How the owner of the servient estate can "abandon" an easement is addressed in Hudson v. Pillow.

* * *

The party claiming abandonment of an easement, in this case the defendants, has the burden to establish such abandonment by "clear and unequivocal evidence." *Robertson v. Robertson,* 214 Va. 76, 82, 197 S.E.2d 183, 188 (1973) (citing *Lindsey v. Clark,* 193 Va. 522, 525, 69 S.E.2d 342, 344 (1952)). "Nonuse of an easement coupled with acts which evidence an intent to abandon or which evidence adverse use by the owner of the servient estate, acquiesced in by the owner of the dominant estate, constitutes abandonment."[6] *Robertson,* 214 Va. at 81, 197 S.E.2d at 188; *accord Pizzarelle v. Dempsey,* 259 Va. 521, 528, 526 S.E.2d 260, 264 (2000). If the party asserting abandonment relies upon nonuse of the easement coupled with an adverse use by the owner of the servient estate, that adverse use must continue for a period of time sufficient to establish a prescriptive right. *Lindsey,* 193 Va. at 525, 69 S.E.2d at 344 (citing *Watts v. C.I. Johnson & Bowman Real Estate Corp.,* 105 Va. 519, 525, 54 S.E. 317, 319 (1906)). However, mere nonuse will not suffice to establish an abandonment. *Id.*

* * *

* * * The chancellor * * * found that, after 1962, the gates through which anyone using the Free Hollow Road would have had to pass in order to travel over the Richeson property [the servient estate] to Free Hollow have been locked, and that individuals using the road did so only with the permission of the owners of the Richeson property. Upon our review of the record, we cannot say that the chancellor's findings are plainly wrong or without evidence to support them. Those findings establish an abandonment, i.e.,

---

[6] In the Restatement (Third) of Property § 7.7 (2000), the adverse use of an easement by a servient owner is referred to as "extinguishment by prescription."

nonuse of the easement coupled with acts by the servient owners that were "inconsistent with," or adverse to, "the future enjoyment" of the easement by the dominant owners for a period of time sufficient to create a prescriptive right. *Scott v. Moore,* 98 Va. 668, 686, 37 S.E. 342, 348 (1900); *see also Pizzarelle,* 259 Va. at 530, 526 S.E.2d at 265 (placement of fence, trees, and shrubs in easement reflect intent to adversely use easement for purpose other than ingress and egress). Thus, we will not disturb the chancellor's decision. *Rash,* 251 Va. at 283, 467 S.E.2d at 793.

* * *

Notes

1. For an abandonment, the acts manifesting an intent to abandon also may be performed by the owner of the dominant estate. For example, if a railroad has an easement and the railroad owners not only cease operations but remove the track over the servient estate, an abandonment of the right of way will be found. See, e.g. *Preseault v. United States,* 100 F.3d 1525 (Fed.Cir. 1996).

2. There are other ways that an easement can terminate. One way is by the terms of the easement. For example, if an easement is given for a term of years, then the easement will expire when the term ends. Similarly, if the easement is given until an event materializes (e.g., in fee simple determinable), then upon the occurrence of the stated event, the easement will automatically end. (See, e.g. *Willard v. First Church of Christ,* supra.) Yet another way that an easement can end is by merger of the dominant and servient estate. Thus, if the owner of the dominant estate purchases the servient estate, the easement ends (and it is not revived if the owner subsequently sells the servient estate). Finally, an easement can end by release: the owner of the dominant estate executes a writing in favor of the owner of the servient estate relinquishing the easement.

§ 11.2 Profits

The next type of servitude we discuss is a profit. What a profit is and how it is distinguished from an easement is discussed in Platt v. Pietras.

Platt v. Pietras
382 So.2d 414 (Fla.App. 1980)

A cattle rancher, Platt, owned a number of tracts. He subsequently sold off all of the tracts but acquired a so-called grazing lease for his cattle on the land he formerly owned. His cattle strayed from the leased land and grazed on neighboring land. Moreover, Platt fenced off as his own the area where his cattle strayed. Platt's neighbors sought to enjoin his use of their land. Platt claimed that he had a prescriptive easement in gross. He did not claim the land by adverse possession because Florida requires the payment of property taxes and Platt did not pay such taxes. The trial court found that Platt did not have a prescriptive easement in gross. Platt appealed. The appellate court affirms. After holding that Platt did not have an easement in gross, the court discusses the law of profits and holds that Platt also did not have a prescriptive profit. In so holding, the court explains what a profit is.

ORFINGER, Judge.

* * *

The alleged easement claimed by appellant would be an easement in gross, i. e., an easement unconnected with nor for the benefit of any dominant estate. 25 Am.Jur.2d, Easements, § 12, p. 426. However, the grazing of cattle is more than an easement it is a privilege plus a profit, the taking of forage and generally characterized by the authorities as a profit a prendre.[7]

The Florida courts have not previously been called on to determine if, through prescription one may acquire a profit a prendre in gross. This question was addressed by the Supreme Court of Utah and answered in the negative in Deseret Livestock Co. v. Sharp, 123 Utah 353, 259 P.2d 607 (1953) where it held, in a factual situation much like the one here:

> The fundamental issue in this case is: In the absence of statute, may a person through prescription acquire a profit a prendre in gross? While we reserve a general answer to the foregoing question, we think that under the facts of this case, the authorities are correct in stating that prescription will not establish such a right. In Gateward's Case, 6 Co.Rep. 59b, 77 Eng.Rep. 344, we find the initial announcement of the concept, the court reasoning that a profit allegedly acquired by custom without a dominant estate would create an interest in the land approximating a fee, the interest being transitory, altogether uncertain, in no way controlled by the needs of a dominant estate, and hence a right so unqualified cannot exist in the soil of a private landowner. (Citations omitted.) (at p. 610).

We concur with this holding and hold that under the facts here, a profit a prendre in gross could not be acquired by prescription because the appellant's claim, while characterized as an easement, is really complete possession, dominion and use of the appellees' property to the exclusion of the appellee and takes on the aspect of a fee. Since

---

[7] 25 Am.Jur.2d, Easements, § 4, p. 417, defines it as follows: "A profit a prendre, also called 'right of common,' is a right exercised by one person in the soil of another, accompanied with participation in the profits of the soil, or a right to take a part of the soil or produce of the land. It is therefore distinguishable from an easement, since one of the features of an easement is the absence of all right to participate in the profits of the soil charged with it. A profit a prendre is similar to an easement, however, in that it is an interest in land. It cannot be created by parol, but is created by grant, and may be either appurtenant to other land or in gross. If enjoyed by reason of holding certain other estate, it is regarded as appurtenant to that estate and may not be severed therefrom. On the other hand, if it belongs to an individual distinct from any ownership of other lands, it takes the character of an estate in the land itself and is assignable or inheritable.

"Examples of rights of profit a prendre are the right to take timber, gravel, coal, or minerals generally, from the land of another; the right to graze sheep on the realty of another, and the right to fish or hunt on or over the land of another."

admittedly appellant has not perfected a claim of adverse possession, we need not decide if this claim could have been perfected under the traditional doctrine of adverse possession.

With respect to the damages awarded, they appear to be supported by competent, substantial evidence, and we will not substitute our judgment for that of the trial judge.

The judgment is therefore
AFFIRMED.

§ 11.3 Licenses

The last type of servitude we discuss in this chapter (there are two more types of servitudes: real covenants and equitable servitudes; they are discussed in chapter 12) is the license.

§ 11.3.1 In General

What a license is and how it is distinguished from an easement is addressed in the Waterville Estates Association *case.*

Waterville Estates Ass'n v. Town of Campton
122 N.H. 506 (1982)

Homeowners' deeds in a planned community state that the interest they own in various common property—recreational facilities (pool, community center, etc.)—is an "easement" that "runs with the land" and does not terminate on their deaths. Additionally, the owners of this interest could "release" their rights. The town claims that the interest of the association members is a license (which would result in a higher tax assessment for the association). The association claims that the association members have an easement (which would result in a lower tax assessment for the association). The court holds that the association members own an easement in the common property. In so holding, the court explains what a license is and how it differs from an easement.

BOIS, Justice.

The defendant town appeals from a Superior Court (*Johnson*, J.) decision to abate the plaintiff's real estate taxes for 1979. We affirm.

The plaintiff, a non-profit homeowners' association, was established by the developer of Waterville Estates, a condominium development in Campton. It consists of all of the owners in Waterville Estates and holds title to several parcels of real estate, known as the common property, in the defendant town. These parcels, which are the subject of the immediate dispute, contain various recreational facilities, including a community center, an indoor swimming pool, a ski lift, a ski lodge, and other buildings. By virtue of a declaration entitled "Waterville Estates Revised Property Restrictions, Easements and Covenants," which was recorded by the developer of Waterville Estates, each owner in the condominium development has a right, in the nature of an equitable servitude, to use the common property. In addition, each owner's deed expressly includes "[a]n exclusive easement * * * as defined and described in the declaration," entitling the owner to use the common property. While the declaration provides that the homeowners' rights "shall run with the land * * * and shall remain in effect for the maximum legal period," it allows for the revocation of such rights upon an affirmative vote of two-thirds of the plaintiff's members.

In 1979, the defendant town assessed the common property for tax purposes at a valuation of $76,000. The plaintiff disputed the valuation and brought a petition in superior court for an abatement. It claimed that the homeowners' rights effectively restricted the use of the common property and that the real estate therefore did not have a value for tax purposes. The trial court agreed with the plaintiff and ordered an abatement of the assessed valuation to $100. The defendant then initiated this appeal.

The specific amount of the abatement and the sufficiency of the evidence are not in issue on this appeal. The only question which the defendant town raises is whether the trial court erred in treating the homeowners' rights as easements. The defendant readily admits that the fair market value of real property is diminished to the extent that such property is encumbered with easements. *See Gowen v. Swain*, 90 N.H. 383, 387, 10 A.2d 249, 252 (1939). It argues, however, that the homeowners' rights, which were revocable upon an affirmative vote of two-thirds of the homeowners, were not easements appurtenant, as the trial court found, but rather licenses, which generally do not diminish the fair market value of real estate.

An easement is a nonpossessory interest in realty which can only be created by prescription, written conveyance, or implication. Restatement of the Law of Property, §§ 450, 457, 467, 474, at 2901, 2923, 2953, 2972 (1944). An easement appurtenant is established for the benefit of the owner of a dominant parcel of land and entitles that landowner to a limited use or enjoyment of the servient parcel. *Burcky v. Knowles*, 120 N.H. 244, 247, 413 A.2d 585, 587 (1980); 3 R. Powell, Real Property § 405, at 34-8 to -9 and 34-19 to -20 (1981). The easement appurtenant runs with the land and is inheritable. *See Burcky v. Knowles*, 120 N.H. at 247, 413 A.2d at 587; *Duchesnaye v. Silva*, 118 N.H. 728, 734, 394 A.2d 59, 62 (1978). Although it may be released or abandoned by the owner of the dominant estate, 3 R. Powell, *supra* § 421, at 34-237, the easement appurtenant is not terminable at the will of the owner of the servient estate. Restatement of the Law of Property, § 450, at 2901 (1944).

A license, on the other hand, is a transient or impermanent interest which does not constitute an "interest in land." *See Houston v. Laffee*, 46 N.H. 505, 507 (1866); 2 G. Thompson, Real Property, § 316, at 17 (1980); 3 H. Tiffany, The Law of Real Property § 829, at 401 & n.2 (3d ed. 1939). *But see* Restatement of the Law of Property § 512 & comment c., at 3115-16 (1944). It may be created orally and is merely a revocable personal privilege to perform an act on another individual's property. *See Blaisdell v. Railroad*, 51 N.H. 483, 484-85 (1871); 3 R. Powell, *supra* § 428, at 34-293; 2 G. Thompson, *supra* § 316, at 17. As such, it terminates when the licensee attempts to assign his rights, *see Cowles v. Kidder*, 24 N.H. 364, 379 (1852); 3 R. Powell, *supra* § 428, at 34-296 to -297, or when the licensor dies or conveys the servient estate. *See Hallett v. Parker*, 68 N.H. 598, 600, 39 A. 433, 435 (1896); 3 R. Powell *supra* § 428 at 34-295 to -296.

In this case, the homeowners' rights were more than an ephemeral interest; they severely burdened the use of the common property. Although the rights were revocable upon a two-thirds affirmative vote of the homeowners, and therefore did not fall within the strict definition of easements, they resembled easements appurtenant in numerous respects. First, they were established in written instruments and permitted a limited use of the common property. Next, they were created to serve the residents of Waterville Estates-the owners of the dominant parcels. In addition, subject to the provisions for revocation, the rights were intended to run with the land and would terminate neither upon the death of the grantor nor upon the conveyance of the servient estates.

The provisions for revocation, moreover, allowed for termination only upon a two-thirds vote of the homeowners, who were also the holders of the rights. Thus the provisions essentially permitted the owners of the dominant estate to release their rights and, as previously mentioned, this procedure is a commonly accepted means for terminating an easement. Given these circumstances, especially the high percentage of owners needed to release the restrictions on the servient estate, we hold that the interest in the common area is sufficiently akin to an easement so as to justify the abatement of the plaintiff's taxes for 1979.

Affirmed.

§ 11.3.2 Irrevocable Licenses

We have just learned that licenses may be revoked at the will of the licensor. But there are several exceptions to this rule, as the next two cases explain.

Coumas v. Transcontinental Garage
68 Wyo. 99 (1951)

One way that a license can become irrevocable is by estoppel, as Coumas v. Transcontinental Garage *explains (although the court will note that not all jurisdictions recognize the doctrine).*

* * *

It is stated in 33 Am.Juris. 410: 'The courts of many of the states uphold the general rule that a parol license to do an act on the land of the licensor, while it justifies anything done by the licensee before revocation, is nevertheless revocable at the option of the licensor, and this although the intention was to confer a continuing right, and money had been expended by the licensee on the faith of the license. * * * It is asserted that the licensee is conclusively presumed, as matter of law, to know that a license is revocable at the pleasure of the licensor, and if he expends money in connection with his entry on the land of the latter he does so at his peril.'

To the same effect is 53 C.J.S., Licenses, § 90, p. 818. Massachusetts adheres to the foregoing rule. The court applied it to a wall such as involved in the case at bar, in the case of Hodgkins v. Farrington, 150 Mass. 19, 22 N.E. 73, 5 L.R.A. 209, where it held according to the syllabus in the case that: 'An oral permission given by the owner of realty to an adjoining owner to build on and let timbers into a wall standing on the former's land, of which the wall was to remain a part, passes no estate in the realty, but creates a license only, revocable at the will or by the death of the owner, or by his alienation of the land.' See similar in effect Munter v. Kobre, 107 Misc. 261, 177 N.Y.S. 393.

A different doctrine has been announced by other courts which hold that a parol license may ripen into an easement and it is said in 33 Am.Juris. 408: 'In many jurisdictions where a licensee has entered under a parol license and has expended money or its equivalent in labor, it becomes irrevocable, and the licensee acquires a right of entry on the lands of the licensor for the purpose of maintaining his structures, or, in general, his rights under his license, and the license will continue for so long a time as the nature of it calls for. * * * The cases holding to this rule as to irrevocability of certain licenses proceed on two distinct theories, one theory being that when the licensee expends large sums of money in making the improvement, and such expenditure is made without opposition by the licensor, the license becomes executed and, as such, irrevocable; and that, in fact, what was at its inception a license becomes in reality a grant. The other theory and the reason most frequently given is that after the execution of the license, it would be a fraud on the licensee to permit a revocation; and the principles of equitable estoppel are invoked to prevent what would work a great hardship in many instances.'

* * *

Laverty v. Alaska R.R. Corp.
13 P.3d 725 (Alaska 2000)

The second way a license can become irrevocable is when the license is "coupled with an interest." What this means is explained in the Laverty *case. (Pay special attention to "Illustration 3.")*

* * *

Although the * * * contract declares itself a "License Agreement," these terms do not describe a license, but a form of easement. The Restatement of Property (First) describes a license as denoting

an interest in land in the possession of another which
(a) entitles the owner of the interest to a use of the land, and
(b) arises from the consent of the one whose interest in the land used is affected thereby, and
(c) is not incident to an estate in the land, and
(d) is *not an easement.*[8]

The distinction between an easement and a license is best explained by the Restatement's illustrations:

Illustrations:
****

---

[8] Restatement (First) of Property: Servitudes § 512 (1944) (emphasis added).

2. A, the owner and possessor of Whiteacre, gives to B the privilege of entering upon Whiteacre and taking as much coal as B needs for his smelter located on Blackacre as long as the smelter remains in operation. The privilege of removing the coal is an easement[9] and is not a license.

3. A, the owner and possessor of Whiteacre, sells to B a car of coal already mined and standing on Whiteacre, which is owned and possessed by A. If there is an effective sale of the coal, B has a license coupled with an interest to go on Whiteacre to remove the coal.[10]

* * *

---

[9] Specifically a "profit." *See* Restatement (Third) of Property: Servitudes § 1.2 (2000). Where an interest in land entitles the holder to take something from the land, it is accurately described as a "profit," which the Restatement (Third) of Property would reintroduce into the Restatement:

> A profit à prendre is an easement that confers the right to enter and remove timber, minerals, oil, gas, game, or other substances from land in the possession of another. It is referred to as a "profit" in this Restatement.

Restatement (Third) of Property: Servitudes § 1.2 (2000).

[10] Restatement (First) of Property: Servitudes § 513 (1944).

CHAPTER 12
SERVITUDES: REAL COVENANTS
AND EQUITABLE SERVITUDES

§ 12.1 Real Covenants (Covenants in Law)

In chapter 11, we discussed three types of servitudes or private land use arrangements: easements, profits, and licenses. In this chapter, we discuss two more: real covenants and equitable servitudes. We begin with real covenants, sometimes called covenants in law.

§ 12.1.1. Introduction

Initially, it is important to recognize that while an easement is a grant, a covenant is a promise. To a layperson, there is no difference, but to lawyers there is a great difference. How is this so? Consider this: The benefit side of an easement appurtenant (the dominant estate) will always run to successors. As for the burden side of an easement (the servient estate), that, too, will always run so long as the successor is not protected under a state's recording statute (see chapter 8). On the other hand, as you will soon see, a covenant does not run so easily. Indeed, it is no small task for either the benefit side or the burden side (and especially for the burden side) of a covenant to run with the land, whether at law or in equity.

Flying Diamond Oil Corp. v. Newton Sheep Co.
776 P.2d 618 (Utah 1989)

We begin our discussion of real covenants with a brief overview of the elements needed for a covenant to run (whether we are discussing the burden or benefit side). Be warned, however, that errors and inconsistencies abound in this area of law. In this regard, pay attention to the first footnote of this chapter. Note that after we summarily explore the elements, we cover each of them in depth.

* * *

A covenant that runs with the land must have the following characteristics:[1] (1) The covenant must "touch and concern" the land; (2) the covenanting parties must intend

---

[1] The law of covenants running with the land has long been a source of some confusion. Covenants that run with the land have their roots in English legal history. English courts of law and courts of equity developed somewhat different requirements for covenants that run with the land. As Professor Powell has stated, "Unfortunately, the modern union of law and equity has not yet produced a unified law of covenants."

the covenant to run with the land; and (3) there must be privity of estate. *E.g., 165 Broadway Bldg., Inc. v. City Investing Co.,* 120 F.2d 813, 816 (2d Cir.), *cert. denied,* 314 U.S. 682, 62 S.Ct. 186, 86 L.Ed. 546 (1941); *Eagle Enterprises, Inc. v. Gross,* 39 N.Y.2d 505, 507, 349 N.E.2d 816, 819, 384 N.Y.S.2d 717, 718 (1976); 20 Am.Jur.2d *Covenants, Conditions, and Restrictions* § 30, at 600- 01 (1965 & Supp.1989); 5 R. Powell, *The Law of Real Property* ¶ 673[1], at 60- 37 (1988) [hereafter 5 R. Powell]. In addition, some courts require the covenant to be in writing. *Chimney Hill Owners' Assoc., Inc. v. Antignani,* 136 Vt. 446, 454-55, 392 A.2d 423, 428 (1978); 5 R. Powell, ¶ 673[1], at 60-38.

* * *

§ 12.1.2 Horizontal Privity

Sonoma Development, Inc. v. Miller
258 Va. 163 (1999)

Mr. and Mrs. Schaer own two adjacent parcels: lots 38 and 39. Lot 38 is to the left of lot 39. Lot 38 has a house on it. Lot 39 is vacant. Mr. and Mrs. Miller want to purchase lot 38 from the Schaers, but the Millers are concerned that the Schaers or their successors could build a house on lot 39 that would be too close to their lot (lot 38). Consequently, the parties agree that the Millers will buy lot 38 and, at the same time, the Schaers will execute a "Declaration of Restriction" requiring "[t]hat no improvement of any kind be constructed upon Lot 39 within three (3) feet of the north wall of the existing dwelling on Lot 38." This Declaration of Restriction was in a separate writing and not part of the Schaer-Miller deed. The Millers buy lot 38 and the Schaers execute and record the declaration. Later still, Sonoma Development purchases lot 39 and constructs a house that violates the restriction executed by the Schaers. The Millers seek an injunction to remove the improvements within three feet of the north wall. The trial court granted the injunction. This court will affirm. Note that the court will review the elements for a covenant at law and provide further explanation for these elements, especially horizontal privity.

---

5 R. Powell, *The Law of Real Property* ¶ 670[2], at 60-12 (1988) [hereafter 5 R. Powell]. One annotation states:

> The "spell of the dry grins" which a reference to covenants running with the land provoked in Mr. Justice Holmes may be taken as indicative of that great jurist's fortitude; tears of frustration might be a more characteristic reaction of less Spartan spirits attempting to investigate the subject.

Annotation, *Affirmative Covenants as Running with the Land,* 68 A.L.R.2d 1022, 1023 (1959) (footnote omitted).

The parent case for covenants running with the land is Spencer's Case, 5 Coke 16a, 77 Eng. Rep. 72 (QB 1583). The progenitor of equitable servitudes is *Tulk v. Moxhay,* 2 Phil. 774, 41 Eng.Rep. 1143 (Ch. 1848).

KINSER, Justice.

* * *

This appeal concerns the circuit court's finding that horizontal privity existed between the original covenanting parties. Because the "Declaration of Restriction" was part of a transaction that included a transfer of an interest in the land to be benefited by the restrictive covenant, we will affirm the judgment of the circuit court.

* * *

In Virginia, we recognize two types of restrictive covenants: "the common law doctrine of covenants running with the land[2] and restrictive covenants in equity known as equitable easements[3] and equitable servitudes."[4] *Sloan v. Johnson,* 254 Va. 271, 274-75, 491 S.E.2d 725, 727 (1997); *accord Mid-State Equip. Co., Inc. v. Bell,* 217 Va. 133, 140, 225 S.E.2d 877, 884 (1976). In the present case, the Millers acknowledge that the "Declaration of Restriction" does not fall within the second category of restrictive covenants. Thus, the issue is whether that document creates a valid common law restrictive covenant that runs with the land, frequently referred to as a "real covenant."[5]

To enforce a real covenant in Virginia, a party must prove the following elements: (1) privity between the original parties to the covenant (horizontal privity);[6] (2) privity between the original parties and their successors in interest (vertical privity); (3) an intent by the original covenanting parties that the benefits and burdens of the covenant will run with the land; (4) that the covenant "touches and concerns" the land; and (5) the covenant must be in writing. *Sloan,* 254 Va. at 276, 491 S.E.2d at 728.

Sonoma contends that the element of horizontal privity is absent in this case. It argues that horizontal privity did not exist between the original covenanting parties, the Schaers and the Millers, because only the Schaers were named as a party in the "Declaration of Restriction." In other words, Sonoma posits that horizontal privity must be demonstrated within the four corners of a single document.

In two of this Court's recent cases upon which Sonoma relies, we did, indeed, include horizontal privity as one of the elements of a covenant running with the land. *Waynesboro Village, L.L.C. v. BMC Properties,* 255 Va. 75, 81, 496 S.E.2d 64, 68 (1998); *Sloan,* 254 Va. at 276, 491 S.E.2d at 728. However, because the real covenants at

---

[2] [The court here means real covenants, the subject of this section of text.]

[3] [What is an "equitable easement"? Apparently, the court means a license that becomes irrevocable based upon an estoppel. See *Carpenter v. Stapleton,* 160 Va. 22 (1937). Irrevocable licenses were discussed in chapter 11. Additionally, apart from irrevocable licenses, equitable easements also exist in at least one jurisdiction. See *Tashakori v. Lakis,* 196 Cal. App.4th 1003 (2011).]

[4] [Equitable servitudes are discussed in § 12.2, infra.]

[5] Covenants affecting the use of land that run to the benefit or burden of remote successors in interest to the land came to be called "real covenants." 9 Richard R. Powell and Patrick J. Rohan, *Powell on Real Property* § 60.01[2] (1999).

[6] A number of jurisdictions have abolished the requirement of horizontal privity. 7 *Thompson on Real Property* § 61.04(a)(3) (David A. Thomas ed., 1994); 9 *Powell on Real Property* § 60.11[3]. *The Restatement (Third) of Property: Servitudes* § 2.4 (Tentative Draft No. 1, 1989), states that horizontal privity between the parties is not required to create a servitude. See *Moseley v. Bishop,* 470 N.E.2d 773, 778 n. 1 (Ind.Ct.App.1984) for a discussion regarding the status of the horizontal privity requirement.

issue in those cases were contained in deeds between named grantors and grantees, we did not focus on the essential components of horizontal privity. *Waynesboro Village*, 255 Va. at 78, 496 S.E.2d at 66; *Sloan*, 254 Va. at 277, 491 S.E.2d at 728-29. Thus, in *Waynesboro Village* and *Sloan*, we did not resolve the issue that is currently before us.

With regard to the precise issue presented in this appeal, we conclude that horizontal privity did exist between the Schaers and the Millers. We are not willing to say that, in every situation, only one document can be examined in order to determine if horizontal privity existed between the original covenanting parties. *See Cook v. Tide Water Associated Oil Co.,* 281 S.W.2d 415, 419 (Mo.Ct.App.1955) (upholding restrictive covenant that was entered into prior to deed); *Leighton v. Leonard,* 22 Wash.App. 136, 589 P.2d 279, 281 (1978) (upholding restrictive covenant created in agreement after deed conveying real estate was executed).

In order to establish horizontal privity, the party seeking to enforce the real covenant must prove that "the original covenanting parties [made] their covenant in connection with the conveyance of an estate in land from one of the parties to the other." *Runyon v. Paley,* 331 N.C. 293, 416 S.E.2d 177, 184 (1992); *accord* 7 *Thompson On Real Property* § 61.04(a)(2). The *Restatement of Property* § 534(a) (1944), provides that horizontal privity is satisfied when "the transaction of which the promise is a part includes a transfer of an interest either in the land benefited by or in the land burdened by the performance of the promise."[7] In other words, the covenant must be part of a transaction that also includes the transfer of an interest in land that is either benefited or burdened by the covenant. *Johnson v. Myers,* 226 Ga. 23, 172 S.E.2d 421, 423 (1970); *Moseley,* 470 N.E.2d at 778; *Runyon,* 416 S.E.2d at 184-85; *Bremmeyer Excavating, Inc. v. McKenna,* 44 Wash.App. 267, 721 P.2d 567, 569 (1986).

The term "transaction" is defined as "an act or agreement, or several acts or agreements having some connection with each other, in which more than one person is concerned, and by which the legal relations of such persons between themselves are altered." Black's Law Dictionary 1496 (6 th ed.1990); *cf. Virginia Housing Dev. Auth. v. Fox Run Ltd. Partnership,* 255 Va. 356, 364- 65, 497 S.E.2d 747, 752 (1998) (quoting *Richmond Postal Credit Union v. Booker,* 170 Va. 129, 134, 195 S.E. 663, 665 (1938)) (" '[N]otes and contemporaneous written agreements executed as part of the same transaction will be construed together as forming one contract.' "). In the context of the present case, we find that the transaction of which the covenant was a part commenced with the real estate contract between the Schaers and the Millers, and culminated with the deed conveying Lot 38 to the Millers. The "Declaration of Restriction" fulfilled the Schaers' contractual obligation to establish a restriction on Lot 39, which lot was being retained by the Schaers at that time, and was executed in conjunction with the deed to the Millers. Thus, it was part of a transaction that included the transfer of an interest in the land benefited by the real covenant.

* * *

For the reasons stated, we will affirm the judgment of the circuit court.
Affirmed.

---

[7] The *Restatement's* comment on clause (a) states that "[a] transfer of an interest in land as a part of a transaction in which a promise respecting the use of land is made is sufficient to create the relationship essential to the running of the burden of the promise."

§ 12.1.3 Statute of Frauds Requirement

We have previously discussed the Statute of Frauds in several other contexts: contracts for the sale of land and deeds (chapter 7) and easements (chapter 11). We now examine the Statute of Frauds requirement in the context of real covenants.

Flying Diamond Oil Corp. v. Newton Sheep Co.
776 P.2d 618 (Utah 1989)

* * *

Finally, for a covenant to run with the land, it must be in writing. Because covenants that run with the land must be based on some interest in land, the statute of frauds must be satisfied. Furthermore, a properly executed and recorded writing also serves the critical and important function of imparting notice to subsequent purchasers. The Agreement was both written and recorded.

* * *

Note

There is some authority for the view that real covenants are not interests in land and, therefore, need not comply with the Statute of Frauds. See the *Flying Diamond* case, earlier, at § 12.1.1, where the court states, "In addition, some courts require the covenant to be in writing." But even where the Statute of Frauds is a requirement, the failure to have the requisite writing does not necessarily preclude enforcement: estoppel or part performance may take the place of a writing. See Stoebuck and Whitman, THE LAW OF PROPERTY (3rd ed.) § 8.14.

§ 12.1.4 Privity (Redux), Touch and Concern, and Intent

We now proceed to explore privity, both vertical and horizontal (in somewhat greater depth than previously examined in Sonoma Development, Inc. v. Miller*), touch and concern, and the intent requirements.*

Beattie v. State ex rel. Grand River Dam Authority
41 P.3d 377 (Okla. 2002)

The concurring opinion reproduced below is an outstanding summary of the law of real covenants. The court's footnotes provide further explanation and clarification, contrasting and comparing the common law with the new Restatement of Property (Third).

* * *

OPALA, J., concurring.

¶ 1 Although I concur in the court's judgment, I would rest today's pronouncement on the law governing covenants running with the land.[8] * * *

* * *

¶ 5 A covenant is a promise that imposes a burden on the covenantor to act or refrain from acting, and confers a benefit on the covenantee consisting of the right to require the covenantor to act or not act. Covenants in deeds and other conveyances may be either real or personal. A real covenant is one which is *so connected with the underlying realty* that either the right to enforce the covenant's performance (the benefit) or the duty to perform the covenant's obligation (the burden), or both, passes to the heirs or grantees of one or both of the original covenanting parties by operation of law without express assignment or delegation.[9] A real covenant benefits or burdens remote parties

---

[8] The term covenant running with the land is used in the newly adopted Restatement (Third) of Property (Servitudes) to encompass both real covenants and equitable servitudes. RESTATEMENT (THIRD) OF PROPERTY (SERVITUDES) § 1.4 at 30 (2000).

[9] ROGER A. CUNNINGHAM ET AL., THE LAW OF PROPERTY § 8.13, at 466-469 (2nd ed.1993); *Waikiki Malia Hotel, Inc. v. Kinkai Properties Ltd. Partnership,* 75 Haw. 370, 862 P.2d 1048, 1057 (1993); C. CLARK, REAL COVENANTS AND OTHER INTERESTS WHICH "RUN WITH THE LAND" 93 (2nd ed.1947). The law governing covenants running with the land can be traced to two distinct lines of cases, both originating in England. *See* 9 R. POWELL, POWELL ON REAL PROPERTY , § 60.04[1] at 60-42 (Michael Allan Wolf, ed., Matthew Bender 2000). The first line of cases began in the sixteenth century with *Spencer's Case,* 5 Co. 16a, 77 Eng. Rep. 72 (Q.B.1583), in which a plaintiff unsuccessfully brought suit *at law* for damages for the breach of a covenant. *Id.* From this inauspicious beginning was born the concept of covenants running at law. Almost three hundred years later, an English court of equity in *Tulk v. Moxhay,* 2 Phil 774, 41 Eng. Rep. 1143 (Ch. 1848) issued an injunction to enforce *in equity* a covenant that would have been unenforceable at law due to the absence of privity between the original covenanting parties. *See* 9 R. POWELL § 60.04[1] at 60-42-43. *See also* Susan F. French, *Toward a Modern Law of Servitudes: Reweaving the Ancient Strands,* 55 S. Cal. L.Rev. 1261, 1276 (Sept.1982). From this case evolved the rules governing the running of covenants *in equity,* known as equitable restrictions. Although neither *Spencer's Case* nor *Tulk* themselves formulated rules for the running of covenants, they are considered the source for the rules that gradually developed in England and the United States governing separately the running of covenants at law and in equity. *See* 9 R. POWELL, § 60.04[1] at 60- 44. The traditional requirements for a covenant to run at law were that (1) the covenant touch and concern the land, (2) the original covenanting parties must have intended for the covenant to run, and (3) some form of privity of estate must be present. *Id.* at 60-43. The traditional requirements for a covenant to run in equity were that (1) the covenant must touch and concern the land, (2) the original covenanting parties must have intended for it to run, and (3) the successor *to the burden* must have had notice of the covenant. *Id.* at 60-44. When law and equity courts were separate, the available remedy for breach of a running covenant-- damages or injunctive relief--depended upon whether the covenant met the requirements of a real covenant or of an equitable restriction. *Id.* § 60.07 at 60-116. The present-day merger of law and equity in a single body, together with judicial confusion over the myriad technical rules governing which covenants run at law and which in equity, has resulted in the consolidation of the two separate lines of cases generated by *Spencer's Case* and *Tulk. Id.* Courts today, in general, will grant the relief appropriate to the facts regardless of the real or equitable label that might be attached to the covenant in suit. *Id.* The recently

simply "because they acquire an interest in land that carries the benefit or burden along with it, . . ." provided the covenant meets certain conditions imposed by law. While as many as five such conditions are sometimes recognized, this court has generally identified only three: (a) there must be privity of estate between the party claiming the benefit and the party upon whom the burden rests, (b) the burden or benefit must "touch and concern" the land, and (c) the original covenanting parties must have intended for the burden or benefit to pass to successors.[10] A covenant that lacks any one of these elements is merely personal, and is treated as an ordinary contractual provision that binds only the original covenanting parties. The covenant under review in this case fulfils each of these *sine qua non* conditions and hence runs with the land. Each condition is discussed below.

A.

Privity of Estate

* * *

¶ 7 Two types of privity of estate are recognized at common law, *horizontal* and *vertical.* Horizontal privity refers to the relationship between the original covenantor and covenantee. As originally conceived, horizontal privity existed only if the covenantor and covenantee created the covenant in connection with a conveyance of an estate from one to the other.[11] Vertical privity refers to the relationship between the present owner or occupier of the land and one of the original covenanting parties. It exists "when the person presently claiming the benefit, or being subjected to the burden, is a successor to the estate of the original person so benefited or burdened."[12] Many states require both

---

adopted Restatement (Third) of Property (Servitudes) has gone a step further, abandoning as anachronistic the separate treatment of real covenants and equitable restrictions, as well as of easements, and adopting a unified set of rules for the transfer, construction, and termination of all such interests in land, denominated collectively "servitudes." *Id.* § 60.11[2] at 60-162-163. The Restatement (Third) replaces the traditional rules governing these interests "with rules designed to identify more accurately the situations in which the threatened risks of harm to the general welfare justify judicial intervention to invalidate properly created transactions intended to create interests that run with the land." RESTATEMENT (THIRD) OF PROPERTY (SERVITUDES) § 3.1, Comment A at 348.

[10] *Noyes v. McDonnell, supra* * * * at ¶ 7, at 840. The other two factors commonly recognized are a writing that satisfies the Statute of Frauds and the existence of privity between the original covenanting parties. *See* ROGER A. CUNNINGHAM ET AL., *supra* note 12, § 8.13, at 469.

[11] *Flying Diamond Oil Corp. v. Newton Sheep Co.,* 776 P.2d 618, 628 (Utah 1989). Under the traditional horizontal privity rule, adjoining landowners could not enter into a covenant for their mutual benefit apart from a conveyance and have the covenant be enforceable by and against their successors. John W. Fisher, II, *The Evolution of Restrictive Covenants in West Virginia,* 100 W. Va. L.Rev. 55, 59. At English common law, only a landlord-tenant relationship between the original covenanting parties is recognized as creating horizontal privity. *Id.;* Winokur, *supra* * * * at 97 n. 43; French, *supra* * * * at 1272-1273. American courts have accepted other relationships as well, including that between grantor and grantee and between owners of easements. French, *supra* * * * at 1273.

[12] See 9 R. POWELL, *supra* * * * § 60.04[2][c] at 60-67. At one time, strict vertical privity required succession to an estate of equal duration to that of the original covenanting party. That requirement has gradually loosened to permit succession to something less than the identical estate. French, *supra* * * * at 1273.

types of privity to be present for a real covenant to run with the land.[13] Some authorities have made a distinction in the components of the privity requirement based upon whether the running of the benefit or the running of the burden is at issue, requiring both types of privity for the running of the burden, but only vertical privity for the running of the benefit.[14]

¶ 8 While this court has never expressly dispensed with horizontal privity as a condition for the running of a real covenant, the vertical aspect of privity is generally the only one identified in the few Oklahoma decisions involving the running of real covenants.[15] We have described the type of privity necessary for a covenant to run in Oklahoma as a "succession of relationship to the same thing, whether created by deed or other acts or by operation of law."[16] The conveyance to plaintiffs of fee simple title from the United States is a successive relationship which establishes privity of estate under Oklahoma law.

B.

Touch and Concern

¶ 9 Before a successor to the covenantee's estate may compel a covenant's performance, the covenant's benefit must touch and concern the land. This means that there must be a logical connection between the benefit to be derived from enforcement of the covenant and the property. * * * In none of these cases did the court explicate the meaning of the phrase other than to suggest generally that to meet this requirement, the covenant must relate to the land.[17] * * *

---

[13] William B. Stoebuck, *"Running Covenants: An Analytical Primer,"* 52 Wash. L.Rev. 861, 867 (1977). *See, e.g., Runyon, supra* note 18 at 184.

[14] The Restatement (Second) of the Law of Property, published in 1944 and superseded only last year by the Restatement (Third) of Property (Servitudes), took the position that both types of privity were necessary for the running of the burden of a real covenant, but that vertical privity alone would suffice for the running of the benefit. This distinction has been resoundingly criticized as resting on inadequate support in the case law. *See, e.g.,* C. CLARK, *supra* * * * at 137-143 and App. 1; Henry Upson Sims, *The Law of Real Covenants: Exceptions to the Restatement of the Subject by the American Law Institute,* 30 CORNELL L.Q. 1 (1944). The newly adopted Restatement (Third) of Property (Servitudes) makes no such distinction. Rather, it rejects any type of privity of estate as necessary for the creation of a servitude.

[15] Most of Oklahoma's privity of estate decisions arise out of a lessor-lessee relationship between the original covenanting parties. *See, e.g., Castle v. Double Time, Inc.,* 1986 OK 80, 737 P.2d 900. Because the landlord-tenant relationship supports horizontal privity even under the strict English common law requirement, these cases have provided no opportunity for the court to undertake a systematic discussion of the current status of the horizontal privity requirement. * * *

[16] *Macias v. Guymon Industrial Foundation,* 1979 OK 70, ¶ 5, 595 P.2d 430, 433 (privity of estate established through the relationship between successive adverse possessors).

[17] *Id.* More explicit conceptualizations of the touch-and-concern requirement are found in many treatises and scholarly articles. *See, e.g.,* C. CLARK, [adopting the test of Dean Harry Bigelow,] *supra* * * *, at 97 ("If the promisor's legal relations in respect to the land in question are lessened--his legal interest as owner rendered less valuable by the promise--the burden of the covenant touches or concerns that land; if the promisee's legal relations in respect to that land are increased--his legal interest as owner rendered more valuable by the promise--the benefit of the covenant touches or concerns that land."). *See also* Paula A. Franzese, *"Out of Touch:" The Diminished Viability of the Touch and Concern Requirement in the Law of Servitudes,* 21 SETON

C.

Intent that the Covenant Run With the Land

¶ 10 Finally, a covenant runs with the land only if the original covenanting parties intended for it to run. Their intention is to be determined from their entire agreement construed as a whole and not from any single clause or provision. No particular language is required to demonstrate an intent that a covenant run.

* * *

Note

Spencer's Case, cited in the footnotes in *Flying Diamond Oil Corp. v. Newton* and *Beattie v. State ex rel. Grand River Dam Authority*, supra, held that for the promise to run with the land at law, the promise had to touch and concern. This was and remains the prevailing law in the United States. Additionally, *Spencer's Case* also stated another rule: that with respect to something not yet in existence (e.g. a wall to be built), for the parties to have intended that the burden of the covenant runs with the land at law, the words "covenantor *and his assigns*" or "covenantor *and his successors*" had to be used. See *Bailey v. Richardson*, 66 Cal. 416 (1885). Although use of the word "assigns" or "successors" remains probative for an indication of the parties' intent as to whether they expected that the burden of the covenant should run with the land at law, the rule requiring use of these magical words as a requirement for the burden to run is generally not followed anymore in the United States. See *Ecke v. Fetzer*, 65 Wis. 55 (1886) and *Counts v. Baltimore & O.R. Co.*, 177 N.E.2d 606 (Ohio App. 1961).

§ 12.2 Equitable Servitudes (Covenants in Equity)

Having discussed real covenants (covenants at law), we are now prepared to discuss equitable servitudes (covenants in equity).

§ 12.2.1 Introduction

As we prepare to go into the realm of equitable servitudes, you will note that some of the elements for an equitable servitude are the same as for a real covenant. The question to think about is this: when are we in the realm of real covenants and when are we in the

---

HALL L.REV. 235, 238 (1991) ("[T]he 'benefit' and the 'burden' of the given promise [must] be analyzed separately. Accordingly, the benefit of a covenant will not run unless it touches and concerns the land, a condition typically construed to require that the covenant's performance render the promisee's interest in land more valuable. The rule is sometimes expressed as satisfied if the covenant confers 'a direct benefit on the owner of land by reason of his ownership,' or if, in layperson's sensibilities, the given promise would be viewed as aiding 'the promisee as landowner.' Attendantly, the burden of a covenant will not bind successors unless it too touches and concerns the land. This is generally interpreted to mean that the covenant's performance renders the promisor's interest in land less valuable." (citations omitted)).

realm of equitable servitudes? The answer depends on the remedy sought. If the remedy sought is damages, it will be treated as a real covenant enforced in law. Conversely, if injunctive relief is sought, it will be treated as an equitable servitude enforced in equity. Compare with Sonoma Development, Inc. v. Miller, *supra.*

Tulk v. Moxhay
Court of Chancery
41 Eng. Rep. 1143 (1848)

*This is the case that started the law of equitable servitudes. In 1808, one Tulk conveyed a portion of property—Leicester Square—that he owned to one Elms in fee simple with a covenant. The covenant provided, "Elms, his heirs, and assigns should, and would from time to time, and at all times thereafter at his and their own costs and charges, keep and maintain the said piece of ground and square garden, and the iron railing round the same in its then form * * * as a square garden and pleasure ground, in an open state, uncovered with any buildings, in neat and ornamental order * * *." Elms subsequently conveyed to Moxhay, who wanted to build on the land. Importantly, Moxhay had notice of the covenant in the Tulk-Elms deed at the time he acquired the property from Elms. Tulk, who still owned the retained property, sued Moxhay, seeking an injunction to prevent Moxhay from building on the land. Note that in England, horizontal privity could only be established by a landlord-tenant relationship, which did not exist between Tulk and Elms. Nonetheless, the Master of the Rolls granted the injunction. This appeal followed. The court here affirms.*

THE LORD CHANCELLOR. That this Court has jurisdiction to enforce a contract between the owner of land and his neighbour purchasing a part of it, that the latter shall either use or abstain from using the land purchased in a particular way, is what I never knew disputed. Here there is no question about the contract: the owner of certain houses in the square sells the land adjoining, with a covenant from the purchaser not to use it for any other purpose than as a square garden. And it is now contended, not that the vendee could violate the contract, but that he might sell the piece of land, and that the purchaser from him may violate it without this Court having any power to interfere. If that were so, it would be impossible for an owner of land to sell part of it without incurring the risk of rendering what he retains worthless. It is said that, the covenant being one which does not run with the land, this court cannot enforce it; but the question is, not whether the covenant runs with the land, but whether a party shall be permitted to use the land in a manner inconsistent with the contract entered into by his vendor, and with notice of which he purchased. Of course, the price would be affected by the covenant, and nothing could be more inequitable than the original purchaser should be able to sell the property the next day for a greater price, in consideration of the assignee being allowed to escape from the liability which he had himself undertaken.

That the question does not depend upon whether the covenant runs with the land is evident from this, that if there was a mere agreement and no covenant, this Court would enforce it against a party purchasing with notice of it: for if an equity is attached to the property by the owner, no one purchasing with notice of that equity can stand in a different situation from the party from whom he purchased. * * *

I think the cases cited before the Vice-Chancellor and this decision of the master of the Rolls perfect right, and therefore, that this motion [by the defendant] must be refused, with costs.

§ 12.2.2 Touch and Concern (Redux) and Vertical Privity

In the next case, we explore, yet again (although from a different perspective), the touch and concern and the vertical privity requirements.

Neponsit Property Owners' Ass'n v. Emigrant Industrial Savings Bank
278 N.Y. 248 (1938)

The court addresses two issues in the Neponsit *case. The first is whether a covenant providing that all homeowners are to pay a yearly fee of $4 to maintain common beaches and parks is one that touches and concerns the land. The second is whether the plaintiff, a homeowners association that owns no land, is a proper party to bring the suit. The court will answer both questions in the affirmative.*

LEHMAN, J.

The plaintiff, as assignee of Neponsit Realty Company, has brought this action to foreclose a lien upon land which the defendant owns. The lien, it is alleged, arises from a covenant, condition or charge contained in a deed of conveyance of the land from Neponsit Realty Company to a predecessor in title of the defendant. The defendant purchased the land at a judicial sale. The referee's deed to the defendant and every deed in the defendant's chain of title since the conveyance of the land by Neponsit Realty Company purports to convey the property subject to the covenant, condition or charge contained in the original deed. * * *

* * *

That covenant provides:

'And the party of the second part for the party of the second part and the heirs, successors and assigns of the party of the second part further covenants that the property conveyed by this deed shall be subject to an annual charge in such an amount as will be fixed by the party of the first part, its successors and assigns, not, however exceeding in any year the sum of four ($4.00) Dollars per lot 20 x 100 feet. The assigns of the party of the first part may include a Property Owners' Association which may hereafter be organized for the purposes referred to in this paragraph, and in case such association is organized the sums in this paragraph provided for shall be payable to such association. The party of the second part for the party of the second part and the heirs, successors and assigns of the party of the second part covenants that they will pay this charge to the party of the first part, its successors and assigns on the first day of May in each and every year, and further covenants that said charge shall on said date in each year become a lien on the land and shall continue to be such lien until fully paid. Such charge shall be payable to the party of the first part or its successors or assigns, and shall be devoted to the maintenance of the roads, paths, parks, beach, sewers and such other public purposes as shall from time to time be determined by the party of the first part, its successors or assigns. And the party of the second part by the acceptance of this deed hereby expressly vests in the party of the first part, its successors and assigns, the right and power to bring all actions against the owner of the premises hereby conveyed or any part thereof for the collection of such charge and to enforce the aforesaid lien therefor.

'These covenants shall run with the land and shall be construed as real covenants running with the land until January 31st, 1940, when they shall cease and determine.'

Every subsequent deed of conveyance of the property in the defendant's chain of title, including the deed from the referee to the defendant, contained, as we have said, a provision that they were made subject to covenants and restrictions of former deeds of record.

There can be no doubt that Neponsit Realty Company intended that the covenant should run with the land and should be enforceable by a property owners association against every owner of property in the residential tract which the realty company was then developing. The language of the covenant admits of no other construction. Regardless of the intention of the parties, a covenant will run with the land and will be enforceable against a subsequent purchaser of the land at the suit of one who claims the benefit of the covenant, only if the covenant complies with certain legal requirements. These requirements rest upon ancient rules and precedents. The age-old essentials of a real covenant, aside from the form of the covenant, may be summarily formulated as follows: (1) it must appear that grantor and grantee intended that the covenant should run with the land; (2) it must appear that the covenant is one 'touching' or 'concerning' the land with which it runs; (3) it must appear that there is 'privity of estate' between the promisee or party claiming the benefit of the covenant and the right to enforce it, and the promisor or party who rests under the burden of the covenant. (Clark on Covenants and Interests Running with Land, p. 74.) Although the deeds of Neponsit Realty Company conveying lots in the tract it developed 'contained a provision to the effect that the covenants ran with the land, such provision in the absence of the other legal requirements is insufficient to accomplish such a purpose.' (Morgan Lake Co. v. N. Y., N. H. & H. R. R. Co., 262 N. Y. 234, 238.) In his opinion in that case, Judge CRANE posed but found it unnecessary to decide many of the questions which the court must consider in this case.

The covenant in this case is intended to create a charge or obligation to pay a fixed sum of money to be 'devoted to the maintenance of the roads, paths, parks, beach, sewers and such other public purposes as shall from time to time be determined by the party of the first part [the grantor], its successors or assigns.' It is an affirmative covenant to pay money for use in connection with, but not upon, the land which it is said is subject to the burden of the covenant. Does such a covenant 'touch' or 'concern' the land? These terms are not part of a statutory definition, a limitation placed by the State upon the power of the courts to enforce covenants intended to run with the land by the parties who entered into the covenants. Rather they are words used by courts in England in old cases to describe a limitation which the courts themselves created or to formulate a test which the courts have devised and which the courts voluntarily apply. (Cf. Spencer's Case, Coke, vol. 3, part 5, p. 16; Mayor of Congleton v. Pattison, 10 East, 316.) In truth the test so formulated is too vague to be of much assistance and judges and academic scholars alike have struggled, not with entire success, to formulate a test at once more satisfactory and more accurate. 'It has been found impossible to state any absolute tests to determine what covenants touch and concern land and what do not. The question is one for the court to determine in the exercise of its best judgment upon the facts of each case.' (Clark, op. cit. p. 76.)

Even though that be true, a determination by a court in one case upon particular facts will often serve to point the way to correct decision in other cases upon analogous facts. Such guideposts may not be disregarded. It has been often said that a covenant to pay a sum of money is a personal affirmative covenant which usually does not concern or touch the land. Such statements are based upon English decisions which hold in effect that only covenants, which compel the covenanter to submit to some restriction on the use of his property, touch or concern the land, and that the burden of a covenant which requires the covenanter to do an affirmative act, even on his own land, for the benefit of the owner of a 'dominant' estate, does not run with his land. (Miller v. Clary, 210 N. Y. 127.) In that case the court pointed out that in many jurisdictions of this country the narrow English rule has been criticized and a more liberal and flexible rule has been substituted. In this State the courts have not gone so far. We have not abandoned the historic distinction drawn by the English courts. So this court has recently said: 'Subject to a few exceptions not important at this time, there is now in this State a settled rule of law that a covenant to do an affirmative act, as distinguished from a covenant merely negative in effect, does not run with the land so as to charge the burden of performance on a subsequent grantee [citing cases]. This is so though the burden of such a covenant is laid upon the very parcel which is the subject-matter of the conveyance.' (Guaranty Trust Co. v. N. Y. & Queens County Ry. Co., 253 N. Y. 190, 204, opinion by CARDOZO, Ch. J.)

Both in that case and in the case of Miller v. Clary (supra) the court pointed out that there were some exceptions or limitations in the application of the general rule. Some promises to pay money have been enforced, as covenants running with the land, against subsequent holders of the land who took with notice of the covenant. (Cf. Greenfarb v. R. S. K. Realty Corp., 256 N. Y. 130; Morgan Lake Co. v. N. Y., N. H. & H. R. R. Co., supra.) It may be difficult to classify these exceptions or to formulate a test of whether a particular covenant to pay money or to perform some other act falls within the general rule that ordinarily an affirmative covenant is a personal and not a real covenant, or falls outside the limitations placed upon the general rule. At least it must 'touch' or 'concern' the land in a substantial degree, and though it may be inexpedient and perhaps impossible to formulate a rigid test or definition which will be entirely satisfactory or which can be applied mechanically in all cases, we should at least be able to state the problem and find a reasonable method of approach to it. It has been suggested that a covenant which runs with the land must affect the legal relations -- the advantages and the burdens -- of the parties to the covenant, as owners of particular parcels of land and not merely as members of the community in general, such as taxpayers or owners of other land. (Clark, op. cit. p. 76. Cf. Professor Bigelow's article on The Contents of Covenants in Leases, 12 Mich. L. Rev. 639; 30 Law Quarterly Review, 319.) That method of approach has the merit of realism. The test is based on the effect of the covenant rather than on technical distinctions. Does the covenant impose, on the one hand, a burden upon an interest in land, which on the other hand increases the value of a different interest in the same or related land?[18]

* * *

Looking at the problem presented in this case from the same point of view and stressing the intent and substantial effect of the covenant rather than its form, it seems clear that the covenant may properly be said to touch and concern the land of the defendant and its burden should run with the land. True, it calls for payment of a sum of money to be expended for 'public purposes' upon land other than the land conveyed by Neponsit Realty Company to plaintiff's predecessor in title. By that conveyance the grantee, however, obtained not only title to particular lots, but an easement or right of common enjoyment with other property owners in roads, beaches, public parks or spaces and improvements in the same tract. For full enjoyment in common by the defendant and other property owners of these easements or rights, the roads and public places must be maintained. In order that the burden of maintaining public improvements should rest upon the land benefited by the improvements, the grantor exacted from the grantee of the land with its appurtenant easement or right of enjoyment a covenant that the burden of paying the cost should be inseparably attached to the land which enjoys the benefit. It is plain that any distinction or definition which would exclude such a covenant from the classification of covenants which 'touch' or 'concern' the land would be based on form and not on substance.

Another difficulty remains. Though between the grantor and the grantee there was privity of estate, the covenant provides that its benefit shall run to the assigns of the grantor who 'may include a Property Owners' Association which may hereafter be organized for the purposes referred to in this paragraph.' The plaintiff has been organized to receive the sums payable by the property owners and to expend them for the benefit of such owners. Various definitions have been formulated of 'privity of estate' in connection with covenants that run with the land, but none of such definitions seems to cover the relationship between the plaintiff and the defendant in this case. The plaintiff has not succeeded to the ownership of any property of the grantor. It does not appear that it ever had title to the streets or public places upon which charges which are payable to it must be expended. It does not appear that it owns any other property in the residential tract to which any easement or right of enjoyment in such property is appurtenant. It is created solely to act as the assignee of the benefit of the covenant, and it has no interest of its own in the enforcement of the covenant.

The arguments that under such circumstances the plaintiff has no right of action to enforce a covenant running with the land are all based upon a distinction between the corporate property owners association and the property owners for whose benefit the association has been formed. If that distinction may be ignored, then the basis of the arguments is destroyed. How far privity of estate in technical form is necessary to enforce in equity a restrictive covenant upon the use of land, presents an interesting question. Enforcement of such covenants rests upon equitable principles (Tulk v. Moxhay, 2 Phillips, 774; Trustees of Columbia College v. Lynch, 70 N. Y. 440; Korn v. Campbell, 192 N. Y. 490), and at times, at least, the violation 'of the restrictive covenant may be

---

[18] [The test, as articulated by Dean Bigelow and summarized by Judge Clark, is more fully stated in *Beattie v. State ex rel. Grand River Dam Authority*, supra.]

restrained at the suit of one who owns property, or for whose benefit the restriction was established, irrespective of whether there were privity either of estate or of contract between the parties, or whether an action at law were maintainable.' (Cheseboro v. Moers, 233 N. Y. 75, 80.) The covenant in this case does not fall exactly within any classification of 'restrictive' covenants, which have been enforced in this State (Cf. Korn v. Campbell, 192 N. Y. 490), and no right to enforce even a restrictive covenant has been sustained in this State where the plaintiff did not own property which would benefit by such enforcement so that some of the elements of an equitable servitude are present. In some jurisdictions it has been held that no action may be maintained without such elements. (But cf. Van Sant v. Rose, 260 Ill. 401.) We do not attempt to decide now how far the rule of Trustees of Columbia College v. Lynch (supra) will be carried, or to formulate a definite rule as to when, or even whether, covenants in a deed will be enforced, upon equitable principles, against subsequent purchasers with notice, at the suit of a party without privity of contract or estate. (Cf. 'Equitable Rights and Liabilities of Strangers to a Contract,' by Harlan F. Stone, 18 Columbia Law Review, 291.) There is no need to resort to such a rule if the courts may look behind the corporate form of the plaintiff.

The corporate plaintiff has been formed as a convenient instrument by which the property owners may advance their common interests. We do not ignore the corporate form when we recognize that the Neponsit Property Owners Association, Inc., is acting as the agent or representative of the Neponsit property owners. As we have said in another case: when Neponsit Property Owners Association, Inc., 'was formed, the property owners were expected to, and have looked to that organization as the medium through which enjoyment of their common right might be preserved equally for all.' (Matter of City of New York [Public Beach], 269 N. Y. 64, 75.) Under the conditions thus presented we said: 'it may be difficult, or even impossible, to classify into recognized categories the nature of the interest of the membership corporation and its members in the land. The corporate entity cannot be disregarded, nor can the separate interests of the members of the corporation' (p. 73). Only blind adherence to an ancient formula devised to meet entirely different conditions could constrain the court to hold that a corporation formed as a medium for the enjoyment of common rights of property owners owns no property which would benefit by enforcement of common rights and has no cause of action in equity to enforce the covenant upon which such common rights depend. Every reason which in other circumstances may justify the ancient formula may be urged in support of the conclusion that the formula should not be applied in this case. In substance if not in form the covenant is a restrictive covenant which touches and concerns the defendant's land, and in substance, if not in form, there is privity of estate between the plaintiff and the defendant.

We have considered the other contentions of the defendant and especially the defense that the alleged lien based upon the covenant set forth in the complaint constitutes an interest in land and is unenforceable under the provisions of sections 242 and 259 of the Real Property Law (Cons. Laws, ch. 50). We find the defense insufficient. The order should be affirmed, with costs, and the certified questions answered in the affirmative. (See 278 N. Y. 704.)

§ 12.3 Subdivisions and Implied Reciprocal Negative Easements

What we next deal with is the question of running covenants in the context of subdivisions: planned communities.

Sanborn v. McLean
233 Mich. 227 (1925)

The McLaughlins were the original owners of 91 lots. They conveyed some of the lots with restrictions in the deeds. These restrictions provided that only residences could be constructed on the properties. Christina and John McLean eventually became the owners of lot 86. Their deed and the deeds in their direct chain of title did not contain the restriction. Sanborn owns the lot next to McLean. Sanborn's deed and the deeds in her direct chain of title also apparently did not contain the restriction. Neither McLean nor Sanborn were the first to purchase in this subdivision. Some of the earlier purchasers did have the restrictions in their deeds. McLean now wants to build a gas station on her property. Sanborn seeks to enjoin such use. The court will hold for Sanborn.

WIEST, J.

* * *

This subdivision was planned strictly for residence purposes * * *. The 91 lots on Collingwood avenue were platted in 1891, designed for and each one sold solely for residence purposes, and residences have been erected upon all of the lots. Is defendants' lot subject to a reciprocal negative easement? If the owner of two or more lots, so situated as to bear the relation, sells one with restrictions of benefit to the land retained, the servitude becomes mutual, and, during the period of restraint, the owner of the lot or lots retained can do nothing forbidden to the owner of the lot sold. For want of a better descriptive term this is styled a reciprocal negative easement. It runs with the land sold by virtue of express fastening and abides with the land retained until loosened by expiration of its period of service or by events working its destruction. It is not personal to owners, but operative upon use of the land by any owner having actual or constructive notice thereof. It is an easement passing its benefits and carrying its obligations to all purchasers of land, subject to its affirmative or negative mandates. It originates for mutual benefit and exists with vigor sufficient to work its ends. It must start with a common owner. Reciprocal negative easements are never retroactive; the very nature of their origin forbids. They arise, if at all, out of a benefit accorded land retained, by restrictions upon neighboring land sold by a common owner. Such a scheme of restriction must start with a common owner; it cannot arise and fasten upon one lot by reason of other lot owners conforming to a general plan. If a reciprocal negative easement attached to defendants' lot, it was fastened thereto while in the hands of the common owner of it and neighboring lots by way of sale of other lots with restrictions beneficial at that time to it. * * *

* * *

* * * The plaintiffs run back with their title, as do defendants, to a common owner. This common owner, as before stated, by restrictions upon lots sold, had burdened all the lots retained with reciprocal restrictions. Defendants' lot and plaintiff Sanborn's lot, next thereto, were held by such common owner, burdened with a reciprocal negative easement, and, when later sold to separate parties, remained burdened therewith, and right to demand observance thereof passed to each purchaser with notice of the easement. The restrictions were upon defendants' lot while it was in the hands of the common owners, and abstract of title to defendants' lot showed the common owners, and the record showed deeds of lots in the plat restricted to perfect and carry out the general plan and resulting in a reciprocal negative easement upon defendants' lot and all lots within its scope, and defendants and their predecessors in title were bound by constructive notice under our recording acts. The original plan was repeatedly declared in subsequent sales of lots by restrictions in the deeds, and, while some lots sold were not so restricted, the purchasers thereof, in every instance, observed the general plan and purpose of the restrictions in building residences. For upward of 30 years the united efforts of all persons interested have carried out the common purpose of making and keeping all the lots strictly for residences, and defendants are the first to depart therefrom.

When Mr. McLean purchased on contract in 1910 or 1911, there was a partly built dwelling house on lot 86, which he completed and now occupies. He had an abstract of title which he examined and claims he was told by the grantor that the lot was unrestricted. Considering the character of use made of all the lots open to a view of Mr. McLean when he purchased, we think, he was put thereby to inquiry, beyond asking his grantor, whether there were restrictions. * * * He could not avoid noticing the strictly uniform residence character given the lots by the expensive dwellings thereon, and the least inquiry would have quickly developed the fact that lot 86 was subjected to a reciprocal negative easement, and he could finish his house, and, like the others, enjoy the benefits of the easement. We do not say Mr. McLean should have asked his neighbors about restrictions, but we do say that with the notice he had from a view of the premises on the street, clearly indicating the residences were built and the lots occupied in strict accordance with a general plan, he was put to inquiry, and, had he inquired, he would have found of record the reason for such general conformation, and the benefits thereof serving the owners of lot 86 and the obligations running with such service and available to adjacent lot owners to prevent a departure from the general plan by an owner of lot 86.

* * *

We notice the decree in the circuit directed that the work done on the building be torn down. If the portion of the building constructed can be utilized for any purpose within the restrictions, it need not be destroyed.

With this modification, the decree in the circuit is affirmed, with costs to plaintiffs.

§ 12.4 Covenants in Gross

In chapter 11, we discussed easements in gross: that there is no dominant estate in such an easement, only a servient estate. We now proceed to discuss covenants in gross. Again, there is no dominant estate, only a servient estate.

Caullett v. Stanley Stilwell & Sons, Inc.
67 N.J.Super. 111 (1961)

A developer-grantor placed a provision in a grantee's deed that provided for a right of first refusal: that if the grantee wanted to erect a house on the lot purchased, the grantee first had to give the developer-grantor the opportunity to construct the house. If the developer-grantor did not want the job, then the grantee could get any builder to construct the house. The grantee, however, first had to offer the construction job to the developer-grantor. Importantly, the developer-grantor retained no land in the subdivision; all of the lots had been sold off. The question before the court is whether such a restriction runs with the land in law or in equity.

FREUND, J.A.D.

This is an action in the nature of a bill to quiet title to a parcel of land in the Township of Holmdel. Defendant appeals from the entry of summary judgment in favor of plaintiffs.

Defendant, a developer, by warranty deed conveyed the subject property, consisting of a lot approximately one acre in size, to the plaintiffs for a consideration of $4,000. The deed was delivered on January 13, 1959. Following the collapse of negotiations directed towards agreement on the construction by defendant of a dwelling on the transferred premises, the present suit was instituted.

The focal point of the action is a recital in the deed, inserted under the heading of 'covenants, agreements and restrictions,' to the effect that:'(i) The grantors reserve the right to build or construct the original dwelling or building on said premises.'

The item is one of those designated in the instrument as 'covenants running with the land * * * (which) shall bind the purchasers, their heirs, executors, administrators and assigns.'

* * *

The trial judge held that the provision in question was unenforceable and should properly be stricken from the deed. He granted plaintiffs the relief demanded in their complaint, namely, an adjudication that: (1) defendant has no claim, right or interest in and to the lands by virtue of the clause in question; (2) defendant has no interest, right or cause of action against plaintiffs by virtue of the covenant; and (3) the clause in question is stricken from the deed and declared null, void and of no further force and effect.

The central issue argued on the appeal is whether the recital constitutes an enforceable covenant restricting the use of plaintiffs' land. Defendant urges that it comprises an ordinary property restriction, entered into for the benefit of the grantor and his retained lands. Plaintiff maintains that the clause is too vague to be capable of enforcement and that, in any event, it amounts to no more than a personal covenant which in no way affects or burdens the realty and has no place in an instrument establishing and delimiting the title to same.

While restrictive covenants are to be construed realistically in the light of the circumstances under which they were created, Javna v. D. J. Fredericks, Inc., 41

N.J.Super. 353, 358, 125 A.2d 227 (App.Div.1956), counter considerations, favoring the free transferability of land, have produced the rule that incursions on the use of property will not be enforced unless their meaning is clear and free from doubt, Hammett v. Rosensohn, 46 N.J.Super. 527, 535-536, 135 A.2d 6 (App.Div.1957), affirmed26 N.J. 415, 140 A.2d 377 (1958); Bruno v. Hanna, 63 N.J.Super. 282, 285, 164 A.2d 647 (App.Div.1960); Griscom v. Barcelonne, 90 N.J.Eq. 369, 107 A. 587 (Ch.1919); Grossman v. Abate, 19 N.J.Super. 516, 88 A.2d 658 (Ch.Div.1952). Thus, if the covenants or restrictions are vague or ambiguous, they should not be construed to impair the alienability of the subject property. For a concise and cogent discussion of the unenforceability of restrictive covenants because of vagueness, see Sutcliffe v. Eisele, 62 N.J.Eq. 222, 50 A. 69 (Ch.1901). Also see Fortesque v. Carroll, 76 N.J.Eq. 583, 75 A. 923 (E. & A. 1910); Newbery v. Barkalow, 75 N.J.Eq. 128, 133, 71 A. 752 (Ch.1909); Wilson v. Ocean Terrace Garden Apartments, Inc., 139 N.J.Eq. 376, 380, 51 A.2d 549 (Ch.1947).

Approached from a direction compatible with the constructional principles set forth above, it is clear that the deed item in question is incapable of enforcement and is therefore not restrictive of plaintiffs' title. The clause is descriptive of neither the type of structure to be built, the cost thereof, or the duration of the grantees' obligation. While it might conceivably have been intended to grant to defendant a right of first refusal on construction bids on the property, this is by no means its palpable design. What, for example, would be its effect were plaintiffs to erect a structure by their own hands?

It must be remembered that a restrictive covenant is in its inception a mere contract, subject to the interpretative doctrines of contract law which focus on the parties' mutual purpose. See 3 Williston, Contracts (rev. ed. 1936), § 620, pp. 1787-88, nn. 5 and 6. A purported contract so obscure that no one can be sure of its meaning is incapable of remedy at law or equity for its alleged breach, cf. Bethlehem Engineering Export Co. v. Christie, 105 F.2d 933, 125 A.L.R. 1441 (2 Cir. 1939), and therefore cannot constitute a valid impediment to title.

Moreover, assuming arguendo that the clause is sufficiently definite to give defendant a primary option to build whenever plaintiffs should decide to construct a dwelling or building on the premises, it still cannot operate either as a covenant running with the land at law, or as an equitable servitude enforceable against the original grantee and all successors, having notice, to his interest.

In the first place, it is clear to us that the item in question does not satisfy the primary requirement of covenants directly restrictive of title to land-that they 'touch and concern' the subject property. To constitute a real rather than a personal covenant, the promise must exercise direct influence on the occupation, use or enjoyment of the premises. It must be a promise 'respecting the use of the land,' that is, 'a use of identified land which is not merely casual and which is not merely an incident in the performance of the promise.' 5 Restatement, Property, Scope Note to Part III, pp. 3147-48 (1944). Furthermore, in the language of the Restatement:

'Even when the promise identifies a specific tract of land as the sphere of action contemplated by it, the use of the land may be so incidental in the performance of the promise, or the promised action may be of such a casual and temporary character, as to prevent the promise from being a 'promise respecting the use of land' * * *. The use of land involved must be a primary consideration of the undertaking of which the promise is a part and the promise must contemplate a degree of permanency in the particular use. * * * (T)he use of land involved is too casual to bring the promise of either party within the scope of promises respecting the use of land * * * (in the case of) a promise to permit the draining through the land of the promisor upon a single occasion of a pond upon the land of the promisee.'(Ibid., at pp. 3150-51).

In substantial accord with the Restatement analysis are Dunn v. Ryan, 82 N.J.Eq. 356, 88 A. 1025, 49 L.R.A.,N.S., 1015 (E. & A. 1913), and Butterhof v. Butterhof, 84 N.J.L. 285, 86 A. 394 (E. & A. 1913), holding that the breach of deed provisions, to the effect that the grantee would provide support and maintenance for the grantor during the latter's natural life, does not affect the fee conveyed but at most gives rise to an action for damages for failure to perform a collateral covenant.

Thus, to qualify as a covenant properly affecting the subject property, the deed provision must define in some measurable and reasonably permanent fashion the proscriptions of and limitations upon the uses to which the premises may be put. Typical provisions, some of them included in the deed of the parties herein, limit the property to residential purposes, provide minimum setback and acreage requirements, proscribe certain architectural forms, and limit the number of set the minimum cost of future dwellings to be constructed on the land.

The provision here in issue is not of the variety described above. It pertains to the use of plaintiffs' land only in the very incidental fashion that refusal to allow defendant to build the original structure would seemingly preclude plaintiffs from constructing at all. This is at best a personal arrangement between the two parties, designed to insure defendant a profit on the erection of a dwelling in return, allegedly, for a comparatively low sales price on the land. While there is nothing in our law precluding such an arrangement, as a contract inter partes, this form of contract, contemplating a single personal service upon the property, does not affect the title. And the stipulation between the parties in their instrument to the effect that this was a covenant running with the land cannot override the inherently personal nature of their arrangement under established legal principles.

We note, in addition, that even if the deed clause were to be construed as directly restricting plaintiffs' use of their land, i.e., prohibiting erection of a structure until such time as the owner shall permit such construction to be performed by the grantor, the clause would nonetheless comprise neither a legal restriction nor an equitable servitude upon the estate. This is so because whatever the effect of the burden of the covenant, its benefit is clearly personal to the grantor, securing to him a mere commercial advantage in the operation of his business and not enhancing or otherwise affecting the use or value of any retained lands.

Generally prerequisite to a conclusion that a covenant runs with the land at law is a finding that both burdened and benefited properties exist and were intended to be so affected by the contracting parties. Where, however, the benefit attaches to the property of one of the parties, the fact that the burden is in gross, i.e., personal, does not preclude the covenant from running with the land conveyed. National Union Bank at Dover v. Segur, 39 N.J.L. 173 (Sup.Ct.1877). There is no public policy opposed to the running of a benefit, since a continuing benefit is presumed to help rather than hinder the alienability of the property to which it is attached. 5 Powell, Real Property, § 675, p. 173; 5 Restatement, Property, supra, § 543, comment (c), pp. 3255-56. When, however, as here, the burden is placed upon the land, and the benefit is personal to one of the parties and does not extend to his or other lands, the burden is generally held not to run with the land at law. The policy is strong against hindering the alienability of one property where no corresponding enhancement accrues to surrounding lands. See 5 Restatement, Property, supra, § 537, pp. 3218-24; 2 American Law of Property, § 9.13, pp. 373-76 (1952).

Nor can the covenant be enforced as an equitable servitude where the benefit is in gross and neither affects retained land of the grantor nor is part of a neighborhood scheme of similar restrictions. Purporting to follow the case of Tulk v. Moxhay, 2 Phil. 774, 41 Eng.Rep. 1143 (Ch.1848), our courts have consistently enforced the covenantal rights of an owner of benefited property against a successor, with notice, to the burdened land, even though the covenant did not run with the land at law. De Gray v. Monnmouth Beach Club House Co., 50 N.J.Eq. 329, 24 A. 388 (Ch.1892), affirmed, 67 N.J.Eq. 731, 63 A. 1118 (E. & A. 1894); Cotton v. Cresse, 80 N.J.Eq. 540, 85 A. 600, 49 L.R.A., N.S., 357 (E. & A. 1912); Coudert v. Sayre, 46 N.J.Eq. 386, 395, 19 A. 190 (Ch.1890). However, the right to urge enforcement of a servitude against the burdened land 'depends primarily on the covenant's having been made for the benefit' of other land, either retained by the grantor or part of a perceptible neighborhood scheme. Hayes v. Waverly & Passaic R.R. Co., 51 N.J.Eq. 345, 348, 27 A. 648 (Ch.1893); Cornish v. Wiessman, 56 N.J.Eq. 610, 611-612, 35 A. 408 (Ch.1896); Roberts v. Scull, 58 N.J.Eq. 396, 401, 43 A. 583 (Ch.1899); Morrow v. Hasselman, 69 N.J.Eq. 612, 614, 61 A. 369 (Ch.1905); Lignot v. Jaekle, 72 N.J.Eq. 233, 241, 65 A. 221 (Ch.1906); Lister v. Vogel, 110 N.J.Eq. 35, 40, 158 A. 534 (E. & A. 1932). Where the benefit is purely personal to the grantor, and has not been directed towards the improvement of neighboring properties, it cannot pass as an incident to any of his retained land and therefore is not considered to burden the conveyed premises but only, at best, to obligate the grantee personally. See 2 Tiffany, Real Property, § 399, pp. 1441-42 (1920).

The latter doctrine has recently come under considerable criticism, see 2 American Law of Property, supra, § 9.32, pp. 428-30, and has even been rejected in some jurisdictions, thus permitting attachment of an equitable servitude even though the benefit is in gross. See, e.g., Pratte v. Balatsos, 99 N.H. 430, 113 A.2d 492 (Sup.Ct.1955). But the law in this jurisdiction, as last authoritatively declared, is that 'from the very nature of the equitable restriction arising from a restrictive covenant,' the 'existence of the dominant estate is * * * essential to the validity of the servitude granted * * *.'Welitoff v. Kohl, 105 N.J.Eq. 181, 189, 147 A. 390, 393, 66 A.L.R. 1317 (E. & A. 1929).

We therefore conclude that the clause in question, even were we to assume both its clarity and its direct operation upon the use of plaintiffs' land, cannot comprise an impairment of plaintiffs' title, because of the indisputably personal nature of the benefit conferred thereby. An intention to dispense broader land use benefits, in the form of a neighborhood scheme, cannot here be found, as in effect conceded by defendant and as expressly stipulated in the parties' deed.

* * *

The judgment of the trial court is affirmed.

§ 12.5 Termination of Covenants

In this section, we learn the theories available to terminate a covenant.

Peckham v. Milroy
104 Wash.App. 887 (2001)

A restrictive covenant prohibited use of the property "for business purposes of any kind whatsoever." The homeowner in question wants to run a home based daycare center. That homeowner argues that the restrictive covenant should be terminated on the basis of (1) abandonment, (2) laches, (3) estoppel, (4) changed neighborhood conditions, (5) or public policy considerations. The court explains each of these doctrines in holding that the covenant remains in force.

SWEENEY, J.

A neighborhood covenant prohibits home businesses. So, the trial court enjoined Thomas Milroy's wife from operating a home day care after neighbor complained.

The question before us is whether the trial court erred by enjoining the day-care business because the covenant was abandoned, or violated public policy. The trial court's findings are amply supported by the evidence here. And those findings amply support the court's conclusions of law that the covenant had not been abandoned through disuse. Nor does it violate public policy. We also agree that neither laches nor estoppel bars Mr. Peckham's claim here. We, therefore, affirm the court's summary dismissal.

FACTS

The material facts are not disputed. Spokane Terrace was platted in 1907. It includes the houses at issue here. The neighborhood is called the Spokane Terrace Addition (STA). The developer subjected some of the lots to restrictive covenants in 1955. One prohibited use of the property "for business purposes of any kind whatsoever . . . ." Clerk's Papers at 38.

Gordon Peckham moved into the STA in 1958. Thomas Milroy's parents moved into the STA in 1992. The Milroy property is subject to the restriction.

Mr. Milroy's mother fell and broke her hip in 1994. She required assistance after that. Mr. Milroy, his wife, and family decided to move into his mother's home in the STA.

They remodeled the home to accommodate the Milroy family, which included five children. They began to remodel in August 1995 and completed in December 1995. Mr. Peckham watched and photographed the construction. He complained to the county about the construction in November 1995. And he filed zoning complaints in February 1996. The Milroys moved into the home in December 1995. Mrs. Milroy obtained a day-care license and began running a day care.

The children are noisy. Mr. Peckham can hear them from inside his home. Parents of the children parked in front of Mr. Peckham's house. They walk across his yard. And they park in the alley behind his house.

Mr. Milroy's mother passed away in July 1996. He inherited the home. Mr. Peckham told Mrs. Milroy she was violating the covenants in July 1996. Mr. Peckham sued to enjoin the day-care operation in November 1997.

Several home businesses operated in the STA in violation of the restrictive covenant. These include a drapery business, a painting business, a small construction business, and a TV repair service.

Following a trial the court concluded that Mrs. Milroy's day care was a business. And that Mr. Peckham had an equitable right to enforce the covenant. The court enjoined the Milroys from operating the day care.

ANALYSIS

ABANDONMENT.

Mr. Milroy first argues the covenant prohibiting home businesses has been abandoned.

Abandonment requires proof that prior violations have eroded the general plan and enforcement is therefore inequitable. *Mountain Park Homeowners Ass'n v. Tydings,* 125 Wash.2d 337, 342, 883 P.2d 1383 (1994). A covenant is abandoned when it has been "habitually and substantially violated. . . ." *Id.* But a few violations do not constitute abandonment. *White v. Wilhelm,* 34 Wash.App. 763, 769-70, 665 P.2d 407 (1983).

Mr. Milroy presented evidence of four home businesses in the STA. A drapery business has been run from a home in the STA since the late 1970s. A painting business was run from 1994 to 1997. A small construction and TV repair business was operated between 1963 and 1972. And a craft business has been operated from a home for the past five to six years.

The STA covers 41 blocks and includes approximately 38 to 40 lots each. The violations are neither habitual nor substantial. *See Mountain Park Homeowners,* 125 Wash.2d at 342, 883 P.2d 1383. They comprise a very small percentage of the subdivision. A few violations do not constitute abandonment. *White,* 34 Wash.App. at 769-70, 665 P.2d 407.

Substantial evidence supports the trial court's determination that the covenant has not been abandoned.

LACHES AND ESTOPPEL.

Mr. Milroy next contends that Mr. Peckham knew Mrs. Milroy intended to operate a home day care as early as August 1995. Yet Mr. Peckham waited until November 1997 to file this action. The delay caused injury to the Milroys and was therefore unreasonable.

Laches. Laches requires: "(1) knowledge or reasonable opportunity to discover on the part of a potential plaintiff that he has a cause of action against a defendant; (2) an unreasonable delay by the plaintiff in commencing that cause of action; (3) damage to defendant resulting from the unreasonable delay." *Buell v. City of Bremerton,* 80 Wash.2d 518, 522, 495 P.2d 1358 (1972); *see Valley View Indus. Park v. City of Redmond,* 107 Wash.2d 621, 635, 733 P.2d 182 (1987).

Mr. Peckham saw the Milroys remodel. But he did not know they intended to build a day-care center until after the construction started. The Milroys incurred construction expenses before Mr. Peckham knew they intended to violate the covenant. Mr. Peckham objected to the project through early 1996. Mr. Peckham tried to enlist the aid of the county to stop the day-care operation. He told Mrs. Milroy that she was violating the covenants in July 1996.

Mr. Milroy testified that the original purpose of remodeling was to provide room for his family, not a commercial day care. Mr. Milroy stated he and his wife did not originally plan to continue the day-care service. But then they decided they needed the money. He testified the decision to operate the day care was made in late 1995, after remodeling the home.

The defense of laches requires showing all three elements. *See Buell,* 80 Wash.2d at 522, 495 P.2d 1358. The Milroys intended to remodel for reasons other than the day care. The cost of the remodel could not, then, result from Mr. Peckham's delay in bringing this action.

The court found that Mr. Peckham did not unreasonably delay the suit. That finding is amply supported by this record.

Equitable Estoppel. Equitable estoppel requires: "(1) an admission, statement or act inconsistent with the claim asserted afterward; (2) action by the other party in reasonable reliance on that admission, statement or act; and (3) injury to that party when the first party is allowed to contradict or repudiate its admission, statement or act." *Wilhelm v. Beyersdorf,* 100 Wash.App. 836, 849, 999 P.2d 54 (2000). Each element must be proven by clear, cogent, and convincing evidence. *Id.* Equitable estoppel is not favored. *Robinson v. City of Seattle,* 119 Wash.2d 34, 82, 830 P.2d 318 (1992).

Mr. Milroy has not established any of the elements of equitable estoppel. Mr. Peckham made no statements and he took no actions inconsistent with his current position--the day care violates the covenant.

Mr. Milroy argues that Mr. Peckham acquiesced to the day care through his silence. Silence can lead to equitable estoppel--"[w]here a party knows what is occurring and would be expected to speak, if he wished to protect his interest, his acquiescence manifests his tacit consent." *Bd. of Regents v. City of Seattle,* 108 Wash.2d 545, 553-54, 741 P.2d 11 (1987). Mr. Peckham was not silent. He complained to the county. He complained to Mrs. Milroy.

Neither can the Milroys show that they relied on Mr. Peckham's acquiescence. Mrs. Milroy talked to representatives of the city, county, and state about the day-care operation. She did not rely on Mr. Peckham.

CHANGED NEIGHBORHOOD CONDITIONS.

Changed conditions in a neighborhood can modify or eliminate restrictive covenants. But the changes must be material. A material change in the character of the neighborhood can defeat the object or purpose of the restriction. *St. Luke's Evangelical Lutheran Church v. Hales,* 13 Wash.App. 483, 485, 534 P.2d 1379 (1975).

Whether the character of a neighborhood has changed is a question of fact. *St. Luke's,* 13 Wash.App. at 486, 534 P.2d 1379. Again we review factual determinations for substantial evidence. *Miller v. City of Tacoma,* 138 Wash.2d 318, 323, 979 P.2d 429 (1999).

Mr. Milroy relies on *Stewart v. Jackson* [635 N.E.2d 186 (Ind.Ct.App. 1994)]. *Stewart* is not on point. There, the Indiana Court of Appeals held that an unlicensed home day care was not a business. And it did not therefore violate the restrictive covenant prohibiting commercial uses.

Washington law is clear. A licensed home day care is a business that violates covenants restricting property to residential purposes only. *Metzner v. Wojdyla*, 125 Wash.2d 445, 452, 886 P.2d 154 (1994). Mrs. Milroy operates a licensed day care. The STA is a residential neighborhood. The Milroys violate the restrictive covenant by doing so.

PUBLIC POLICY.

Mr. Milroy argues that Washington public policy makes quality child care a priority. And this public policy should override restrictive covenants preventing home day care.

Mr. Milroy cites statutes which prohibit cities, towns, and counties from prohibiting home day care in residentially zoned areas. RCW 35.63.185; RCW 36.70A.450. The regulations do not, however, limit private parties from restricting land use. Restrictive covenants in residential neighborhoods are enforceable. *Metzner*, 125 Wash.2d at 450, 886 P.2d 154.

If restrictive covenants that incidentally prohibit home day care should be repealed on public policy grounds, the decision should come from the Legislature--not this court. *See Mut. of Enumclaw Ins. Co. v. Wiscomb*, 95 Wash.2d 373, 378, 622 P.2d 1234 (1980) (determining public policy is not the judiciary's function).

Affirmed.

CHAPTER 13
NUISANCE

§ 13.1 Introduction

We have all heard of the term, "nuisance," but what exactly is it? The following excerpt, quoting Prosser's treatise, gives us an idea why the study of this topic will not be easy.

Burrows v. State
260 Cal.App.2d 29 (1968)

* * *

"There is perhaps no more impenetrable jungle in the entire law than that which surrounds the word 'nuisance.' It has meant all things to all men, and has been applied indiscriminately to everything from an alarming advertisement to a cockroach baked in a pie. There is general agreement that it is incapable of any exact or comprehensive definition. Few terms have afforded so excellent an illustration of the familiar tendency of the courts to seize upon a catchword as a substitute for any analysis of a problem; the defendant's interference with the plaintiff's interests is characterized as a 'nuisance,' and there is nothing more to be said. With this reluctance of the opinions to assign any particular meaning to the word, or to get to the bottom of it, there has been a rather astonishing lack of any full consideration of 'nuisance' on the part of legal writers. ..." (Prosser on Torts (3d ed. 1964) p. 592.)

§ 13.2 Classification of Nuisances

There are several ways to classify nuisances. We begin the classification with the distinction between public nuisances and private nuisances.

§ 13.2.1 Public and Private Nuisances

U.S. v. County Bd. of Arlington County
487 F.Supp. 137 (D.C. Va. 1979)

We start with differentiating public nuisance from private nuisance. Note how a public nuisance affects an entire community; a private nuisance, on the other hand, is more limited.

* * *

The term "nuisance" is incapable of an exhaustive definition which will fit all cases—it is very comprehensive—it includes everything that endangers life or health, gives offense to the senses, violates the laws of decency, or obstructs the reasonable and comfortable use of property.

The difference between a public and a private nuisance is that the former affects the public at large while the latter affects the individual or a limited number of individuals only.

A public nuisance has been defined as the doing of or the failure to do something that injuriously affects the safety, health, or morals of the public, or works some substantial annoyance, inconvenience or injury to the public generally—see Nuisances, 58 Am.Jur.2d.

* * *

§ 13.2.2 Nuisances *Per Se*

Private nuisances also may be classified as "per se" and "per accidens." We begin with nuisances per se.

McAndrews v. Collerd
42 N.J.L. 189 (N.J.Err. & App. 1880)

A contractor was engaged in blasting activities and maintained an explosives magazine near a residential area. The magazine blew up, damaging a number of houses. The questions before the court were (1) whether the activity of keeping explosives near a residential community is a private nuisance per se, and (2) if there is damage resulting from an explosion, is the contractor strictly liable (liable even if he had not been negligent). The court will hold in the affirmative for both issues.

The opinion of the court was delivered by THE CHANCELLOR.

The case on which the question to be considered arises, is the following: The Delaware, Lackawanna and Western Railroad Company having legislative authority to construct a tunnel for its road through Bergen Hill, contracted with McAndrews to do the work. The tunnel was driven through rock. The work was begun in 1873, and was in progress from that time until 1877, when it was completed. McAndrews constructed near the eastern end of the tunnel, and within the limits of Jersey City, a magazine for the explosive materials which he used in blasting the rock. In 1876, at night, while the magazine was maintained there by McAndrews for the purpose before mentioned, the materials exploded, doing great damage to property in the vicinity, even at the distance of about twelve hundred feet. Among the property injured were some houses belonging to Collerd, and this suit was brought to recover damages for the injury to them.

* * *

The keeping of gunpowder, nitro-glycerin, or other explosive substances, in large quantities, in the vicinity of a dwelling-house or place of business, is a nuisance *per se,* and may be abated as such by action at law or injunction in equity; and if actual injury

411

results therefrom, the person keeping them is liable therefor, even though the act occasioning the explosion is due to other persons, and is not chargeable to his personal negligence. *Wood on Nuisances*, § 142; *Cuff v. N. & N. Y. R. R. Co.*, 6 *Vroom* 17.

Our statute prohibits the keeping in store, within a quarter of a mile of any town, &c., of nitro-glycerin and of gunpowder, in larger quantity than a specified amount, making the violation of the prohibition, in either case, a misdemeanor. *Rev., pp.* 264, 466.

* * *

§ 13.2.3 Nuisances *Per Accidens*

The next type of private nuisance is a nuisance per accidens, what often is referred to as a nuisance in fact.

Hutchens v. MP Realty Group-Sheffield Square Apartments
654 N.E.2d 35 (Ind.App. 1995)

The plaintiff, who owned no property in the area, was injured by the jagged edge of a carport while playing ball. The court addresses two issues. The first issue is whether the plaintiff has standing to file an action in private nuisance. The second issue is whether a carport with a jagged edge is a nuisance per accidens. The court will assume the plaintiff has standing (when he does not) and hold that the carport is not a nuisance in fact.

RILEY, Judge.

STATEMENT OF THE CASE
Plaintiffs-Appellants David M. Hutchens and Rebecca J. Hutchens (hereinafter collectively referred to as "Hutchens") appeal from the entry of partial summary judgment in favor of the Defendant-Appellee MP Realty Group-Sheffield Square Apartments, an Indiana Limited Partnership (hereinafter "Sheffield Square") in their premises liability action.

We affirm.

ISSUE
One issue is dispositive of this appeal: Whether, considering all designated evidence in the light most favorable to Hutchens, Sheffield Square is entitled to judgment as a matter of law as to Hutchens's nuisance claim.

FACTS AND PROCEDURAL HISTORY
This is a personal injury action whereby David Hutchens (hereinafter "Dave"), the social guest of a Sheffield Square tenant, was injured on the common area playground at Sheffield Square and brought claim against Sheffield Square as the landlord/owner of the premises.

Sheffield Square Apartment complex consists of numerous multi-family apartment buildings. At the time of Dave's injuries, his parents were tenants at Sheffield Square. The playground area where Dave's injuries occurred is located across from his parents' townhouse.

The physical attributes of the area where the injury occurred are not in dispute. The playground area is a common area built and maintained by Sheffield Square, the landlord/owner of the complex. The playground area is bordered on one side by a chain-link fence which encloses an adjoining tennis court. The opposite side of the playground is bordered by a carport structure constructed of a wood frame with metal sides and a metal roof. The carport is constructed in such a way that the sheet metal roof angles downward from front to rear with the lowest point facing and immediately adjacent to the playground. The sharp exposed exterior edge of the sloping metal roof ran horizontally across the entire width of the side of the playground, approximately 18-inches from the ground.

The material facts are also not in dispute. On October 17, 1993, Dave, his children and several relatives were visiting Dave's parents at their townhouse at Sheffield Square in New Albany, Indiana. During the course of the visit, Dave took his children and several of his nieces and nephews to the common area playground to pay kickball. While chasing the kickball, Dave collided with the sharp exposed leading edge of the carport roof. He sustained personal injuries consisting of a severe cut to his knee and lacerations of his quadriceps tendon.

Hutchens filed a three count complaint against Sheffield Square based in negligence and premises liability for the injuries Dave sustained. The third count of the complaint alleged loss of services on behalf of Rebecca Hutchens due to her husband's injuries. Sheffield Square filed its answer generally denying the allegations in Hutchens's complaint and later filed a motion for partial summary judgment as to Count II of the complaint. Count II specifically alleged that the sharp exposed leading edge of the sheet metal roofing constituted a dangerous or hazardous condition on the premises injurious to health within the meaning of I.C. 34-1-52-1 *et seq.* Relying exclusively on the complaint and answer, Sheffield Square maintained that it was entitled to judgment as a matter of law as to the nuisance claim because the nuisance statute is inapplicable.

In response, Hutchens filed a copy of the incident report filed by the resident manager of Sheffield Square, which specifically states that Dave cut his leg on the edge of the metal structure situated adjacent to the east side of the playground. Hutchens also filed his opposition to Sheffield Square's motion for partial summary judgment and designated the following materials in support of the motion: the pre-pretrial entry; the affidavits of Dave Hutchens and John Schroering; the incident report; and Defendant's answers to Plaintiff's request for admissions with interrogatory.

Formal hearing on the motion was waived and the matter was submitted to the trial court for a ruling. The trial court granted Sheffield Square's motion by docket entry and did not make specific findings of fact and conclusions of law. Hutchens moved for certification of the partial summary judgment and for entry of final judgment, which the trial court granted. Hutchens appeals.

DISCUSSION AND DECISION
* * *

Nuisance

In Count II of Hutchens's complaint, he specifically alleges that the sharp exposed leading edge of the sheet metal roofing of the carport "was and is a dangerous or hazardous condition injurious to health, or an obstruction to the free use of property, so as essentially to interfere with the comfortable enjoyment of life or property, and was and is a nuisance within the definition and meaning of * * * I.C. 34-1-52-1 *et seq.*" (R. 12). In its motion for partial summary judgment, Sheffield Square essentially argues that, as a matter of law, the nuisance statute does not apply to this case. First, Sheffield Square contends that Hutchens lacks standing to bring a nuisance action. Pursuant to I.C. 34-1-52-2 (1988), only a person whose property is injured may bring an action for nuisance, and Hutchens alleges a private nuisance. Second, Sheffield Square argues that even if Hutchens is permitted to bring an action in nuisance, the facts fail to establish that a nuisance exists. Hutchens maintains that a genuine issue of material fact exists: whether the exposed sheet metal edge of the carport constitutes a nuisance *per accidens*. Hutchens does not argue that the carport constituted a nuisance *per se*.

A. Standing

Sheffield Square contends that Hutchens has no standing to bring an action based in nuisance because he had no proprietary interest in the premises on which his injuries occurred. We agree.

The tort of nuisance originated at common law and the statutory definition of nuisance has been unchanged since 1881. I.C. 34-1-52-1 (1988) defines nuisance as "[w]hatever is injurious to health, or indecent, or offensive to the senses, or an obstruction to the free use of property, so as essentially to interfere with the comfortable enjoyment of life or property, is a nuisance, and the subject of an action." I.C. 34-1-52-2 provides that "[s]uch action may be brought by any person whose property is injuriously affected, or whose personal enjoyment is lessened by the nuisance." I.C. 34-1-52-3 (1988) provides that "[w]here a proper case is made, the nuisance may be enjoined or abated, and damages recovered therefor."

Construing these statutes together, we have no hesitation in concluding that one must possess a proprietary interest in land in order to bring an action in private nuisance. Where, as here, a plaintiff has no proprietary interest in the land on which his or her injuries occur, the proper cause of action lies in premises liability and not in private nuisance.

B. Existence of a Nuisance *Per Accidens*

Although we decide that Hutchens lacks standing to bring this action, we further find that even if he were a proper party, the facts fail to support a cause of action for nuisance. Nuisance can be either public or private. A public nuisance is one which affects an entire neighborhood or community, while a private nuisance affects only a single person or a determinate number of people. *Wernke v. Halas* (1992), Ind.App., 600 N.E.2d 117, 120. We have repeatedly stated that the essence of private nuisance is the use of property to the detriment of the use and enjoyment of another's property. *Id.; Friendship Farms Camps, Inc. v. Parson* (1977), 172 Ind.App. 73, 359 N.E.2d 280, 282; *Stover v. Fechtman* (1966), 140 Ind.App. 62, 222 N.E.2d 281.

Nuisance is further sub-divided into nuisance *per se* and nuisance *per accidens*. *Wernke,* 600 N.E.2d at 120. Hutchens does not argue that the facts alleged constitute a public nuisance or a nuisance *per se,* but rather argues that they amount to an actionable private nuisance *per accidens,* or private nuisance in fact. A nuisance in fact is not a nuisance of itself, but becomes a nuisance in the manner in which it is operated. *Sand*

Creek Partners, L.P. v. Finch (1995), Ind.App., 647 N.E.2d 1149, 1152. An otherwise lawful use of land may become a nuisance *per accidens* by virtue of the circumstances surrounding the use. *Wernke,* 600 N.E.2d at 120.

In *Wernke,* in holding that the trial court erred in granting summary judgment we said that

> [t]he conclusion that something is a *per accidens* nuisance is a conclusion to be reached only after a full review of the material facts. Summary judgment, which by definition is meant to resolve only with those cases lacking material factual disputes, is therefore rarely appropriate in *per accidens* nuisance cases.

Id. at 121 (we held that a fence and toilet seat placed on a pole so as to overlook abutting neighbors land was merely aesthetically displeasing and hence not a private nuisance); *See also Sand Creek Partners, L.P.,* 647 N.E.2d at 1152.

A factually analogous case is *Stover,* 222 N.E.2d at 281. In that case, plaintiff brought an action for loss of services of his wife who, while visiting friends at their leased premises, fell and sustained injury on allegedly defective stairs. Stover brought an action in negligence against the owner of the premises alleging that he was negligent in failing to repair or warn Mrs. Stover of the defects in the stairs. The trial court granted the owner's motion for a directed verdict, and on appeal we affirmed the trial court stating that a lessor has no duty to repair leased premises in the absence of an express covenant. In addressing the plaintiff's argument that the premises were leased with an existing nuisance and thus that the owner was responsible for injuries arising from such a nuisance, we recognized the nuisance exception to *caveat lessee,*[1] but said:

> [t]he exact nature of this exception is difficult to discern. However, it can be no broader than the principles within nuisance concepts *per se.* The essence of a private nuisance is the fact that one party is using his property to the detriment of the use and enjoyment of the property of another. . . . Certainly no recovery in the facts at bar can be based on the theory of a private nuisance. The defect on the steps could not be taken as an interference with the *property* of Mrs. Stover. Consequently, there was no actionable private nuisance.

Stover, 222 N.E.2d at 284; *Demoss v. Coleman* (1966), 139 Ind.App. 346, 216 N.E.2d 861, *trans. denied.* * * *

The private nuisance cases that our research uncovers are factually similar to each other and consist of a landowner's use of his property to the detriment of the use and enjoyment of a neighboring landowner. *E.g., Wendt v. Kerkhof* (1992), Ind.App., 594 N.E.2d 795 (landowner brought nuisance action against neighboring hog farmers seeking

---

[1] The doctrine of *caveat lessee,* or let the lessee beware, essentially represents that a landlord who gives his tenant full control and possession of leased property will not be liable for the personal injury sustained by the tenant or other persons lawfully upon the leased property. *Place,* 604 N.E.2d at 674; *Dickison v. Hargitt* (1993), Ind.App., 611 N.E.2d 691, 694.

damages and injunctive relief for odor emanating from farm); *Friendship Farms Camps,* 359 N.E.2d 280 (landowner brought nuisance action against neighboring landowner to enjoin the operation of a high school band camp because of the disturbing noise); *Bagko Development Co. v. Damitz* (1994), Ind.App., 640 N.E.2d 67 (landowner brought nuisance action against adjacent landowner seeking to enjoin use of baseball practice field and bright lights); *Keane v. Pachter* (1992), Ind.App., 598 N.E.2d 1067, *reh'g denied, trans. denied* (condominium owner brought nuisance action against upstairs neighbor based on noise due to upstairs owner's installation of marble flooring); *Muehlman v. Keilman* (1991), 257 Ind. 100, 272 N.E.2d 591 (landowner brought nuisance action against adjacent property owner seeking damages and to enjoin the neighbor from racing his semi trucks and revving their engines); *Yeager & Sullivan, Inc. v. O'Neill* (1975), 163 Ind.App. 466, 324 N.E.2d 846 (landowner brought action against adjacent landowner seeking damages and to abate the nuisance due to hog feed lot); *Wernke,* 600 N.E.2d at 117 (landowner brought nuisance action against adjacent landowner due to aesthetically displeasing decoration of yard involving a toilet seat and graffiti).

As is illustrated from the aforementioned cases, private nuisance is based on one party using his or her property to the detriment of the use and enjoyment of the property of another. Generally, the subject of the nuisance is offensive to one of the senses. Frequently, the nuisance is due to a repugnant odor, unreasonable noise or unsightly aesthetics. The defect that Hutchens alleges in the carport/playground does not create a cause of action based in private nuisance. These alleged defects cannot be said to interfere with the property of Hutchens.

Based on these cases and the clear import of *Stover* and *Place,* Hutchens claim for private nuisance fails as a matter of law. Although we recognize that cases based on nuisance in fact are seldom appropriate for disposition by summary judgment, the facts here represent the rare case where summary judgment is proper. *Stover,* 222 N.E.2d 281; *Place,* 604 N.E.2d 671.

CONCLUSION

Considering all designated evidence in the light most favorable to Hutchens, the non-moving party, there is no genuine issue of material fact and Sheffield Square is entitled to judgment as a matter of law as to Count II of Hutchens's complaint. Accordingly, the trial court is affirmed.

Our holding today is in no way intended to interfere with Hutchens's claim based in negligence. We hold only that Hutchens fails to state a cause of action based in nuisance.

§ 13.3 Elements of a Private Nuisance (*Per Accidens*)

Assuming that the nuisance is a private nuisance per accidens, we now address the elements of such a nuisance.

§ 13.3.1 In General

Morgan v. High Penn Oil Co.
238 N.C. 185 (1953)

The plaintiffs, nearby landowners, alleged that the High Penn Oil Co. emitted noxious fumes from its operations, constituting a private nuisance that the plaintiffs sought to enjoin.

ERVIN, Justice.

* * *

The law of private nuisance rests on the concept embodied in the ancient legal maxim Sic utere tuo ut alienum non laedas, meaning, in essence, that every person should so use his own property as not to injure that of another. Barger v. Barringer, 151 N.C. 433, 66 S.E. 439, 25 L.R.A., N.S., 831, 19 Ann.Cas. 472; Tennessee Coal Iron & R. Co. v. Hartline, 244 Ala. 116, 11 So.2d 833; Beam v. Birmingham Slag Co., supra; G. L. Webster Co. v. Steelman, supra. As a consequence, a private nuisance exists in a legal sense when one makes an improper use of his own property and in that way injures the land or some incorporeal right of one's neighbor. King v. Ward, 207 N.C. 782, 178 S.E. 577; Holton v. Northwestern Oil Co., 201 N.C. 744, 161 S.E. 391; 39 Am.Jur., Nuisances, section 3.

Much confusion exists in respect to the legal basis of liability in the law of private nuisance because of the deplorable tendency of the courts to call everything a nuisance, and let it go at that. Moran. v. Pittsburgh-Des Moines Steel Co., supra; Taylor v. City of Cincinnati, 143 Ohio St. 426, 55 N.E.2d 724, 155 A.L.R. 44. The confusion on this score vanishes in large part, however, when proper heed is paid to the sound propositions that private nuisance is a field of tort liability rather than a single type of tortious conduct; that the feature which gives unity to this field of tort liability is the interest invaded, namely, the interest in the use and enjoyment of land; that any substantial nontrespassory invasion of another's interest in the private use and enjoyment of land by any type of liability forming conduct is a private nuisance; that the invasion which subjects a person to liability for private nuisance may be either intentional or unintentional; that a person is subject to liability for an intentional invasion when his conduct is unreasonable under the circumstances of the particular case; and that a person is subject to liability for an unintentional invasion when his conduct is negligent, reckless or ultrahazardous. See Scope and Introduction Note to Chapter 40, American Law Institute's Restatement of the Law of Torts; Moran v. Pittsburgh Des Moines Steel Co., supra; Soukoup v. Republic Steel Corp., 78 Ohio App. 87, 66 N.E.2d 334; 66 C.J.S., Nuisances, § 8.

An invasion of another's interest in the use and enjoyment of land is intentional in the law of private nuisance when the person whose conduct is in question as a basis for liability acts for the purpose of causing it, or knows that it is resulting from his conduct, or knows that it is substantially certain to result from his conduct. Restatement of the Law of Torts, section 825; Rauh & Sons Fertilizer Co. v. Shreffler, supra; Herman v. City of Buffalo, 214 N.Y. 316, 108 N.E. 451; Bohan v. Port Jervis Gas-Light Co., supra; Columbian Carbon Co. v. Tholen, supra. A person who intentionally creates or maintains a private nuisance is liable for the resulting injury to others regardless of the degree of care or skill exercised by him to avoid such injury. Judson v. Los Angeles Suburban Gas Co., 157 Cal. 168, 106 P. 581, 26 L.R.A.,N.S., 183, 21 Ann.Cas. 1247; Blackman v. Iowa Union Electric Co., 234 Iowa 859, 14 N.W.2d 721; Susquehanna Fertilizer Co. v. Spangler, 86 Md. 562, 39 A. 270, 63 Am.St.Rep. 533; Robinson v. Westman, 224 Minn. 105, 29 N. W.2d 1; Bollinger v. Mungle, Mo.App., 175 S.W.2d 912; Powell v. Brookfield Pressed Brick & Tile Mfg. Co., 104 Mo.App. 713, 78 S.W. 646; Wallace & Tiernan Co. v. U.S. Cutlery Co., 97 N.J.Eq. 408, 128 A. 872, decree affirmed, 98 N.J.Eq. 699, 130 A. 920; Monaco v. Comfort Bus Line, 134 N.J.L. 553, 49 A.2d 146; Jutte v. Hughes, 67 N.Y. 267; Whaley v. Citizens' Nat. Bank, 28 Pa. Super. 531; Western Texas Compress Co. v. Williams, Tex.Civ.App., 124 S.W. 493; Flanagan v. Gregory & Poole, Inc., supra; 39 Am.Jur., Nuisances, section 24. * * *

When the evidence is interpreted in the light most favorable to the plaintiffs, it suffices to support a finding that in operating the oil refinery the High Penn Oil Company intentionally and unreasonably caused noxious gases and odors to escape onto the nine acres of the plaintiffs to such a degree as to impair in a substantial manner the plaintiffs' use and enjoyment of their land. This being so, the evidence is ample to establish the existence of an actionable private nuisance, entitling the plaintiffs to recover temporary damages from the High penn Oil Company. Webb v. Virginia-Carolina Chemical Co., 170 N.C. 662, 87 S. E. 633, L.R.A.1916E, 971; Duffy v. E. H. & J. A. Meadows Co., 131 N.C. 31, 42 S.E. 460; Hyatt v. Myers, 71 N.C. 271; Bohan v. Port Jervis Gas-Light Co., supra; 39 Am.Jur., Nuisances, sections 58, 59; 66 C. J.S., Nuisances, §§ 23, 60. When the evidence is taken in the light most favorable to the plaintiffs, it also suffices to warrant the additional inferences that the High Penn Oil Company intends to operate the oil refinery in the future in the same manner as in the past; that if it is permitted to carry this intent into effect, the High Penn Oil Company will hereafter cast noxious gases and odors onto the nine acres of the plaintiffs with such recurring frequency and in such annoying density as to inflict irreparable injury upon the plaintiffs in the use and enjoyment of their home and their other adjacent properties; and that the issuance of an appropriate injunction is necessary to protect the plaintiffs against the threatened irreparable injury. This being true, the evidence is ample to establish the existence of an abatable private nuisance, entitling the plaintiffs to such mandatory or prohibitory injunctive relief as may be required to prevent the High Penn Oil Company from continuing the nuisance. Barrier v. Troutman, 231 N.C. 47, 55 S.E.2d 923; Pruitt v. Bethell, 174 N.C. 454, 93 S.E. 945; Hyatt v. Myers, supra; Hedrick v. Tubbs, 120 Ind.App. 326, 92 N.E.2d 561; Kepler v. Industrial Disposal Co., 84 Ohio App. 80, 85 N.E.2d 308; 39 Am.Jur., Nuisances, sections 156, 158, 172; 66 C.J.S., Nuisances, §§ 115, 116, 134.

The contention of the High Penn Oil Company that the complaint states a cause of action based solely on negligence is untenable. To be sure, the plaintiffs assert that the defendants were 'negligent and careless' in specified particulars in constructing and operating the oil refinery. When the complaint is construed as a whole, however, it alleges facts which show a private nuisance resulting from an intentional and unreasonable invasion of the plaintiffs' interest in the use and enjoyment of their land. Bohan v. Port Jervis Gas-Light Co., supra; Braun v. Iannotti, supra; Flanagan v. Gregory & Poole, Inc., supra; 39 Am. Jur., Nuisances, section 142.

For the reasons given, the evidence is sufficient to withstand the motion of the High Penn Oil Company for a compulsory nonsuit.

* * *

§ 13.3.2 Meaning of "Unreasonable"

In Morgan v. High Penn Oil Co., *the court stated that an intentional private nuisance requires "unreasonable conduct." The next two cases provide us with a definition of the term.*

Hendricks v. Stalnaker
181 W.Va. 31 (1989)

A landowner installed a well to secure a drinking water supply. Close to the well was a neighbor's septic tank. The owner of the septic tank could not get a permit to operate the tank because the governmental official charged with issuing the permit was concerned that the waste from the septic tank would contaminate the water well. The landowner seeking a permit for the septic tank filed this action to get the water well declared a nuisance. The court will hold that the water well is not a nuisance.

NEELY, Justice:

Walter S. Stalnaker, defendant below, appeals from a decision by the Circuit Court of Lewis County declaring a water well drilled on his property to be a private nuisance to Harry L. Hendricks and Mary Hendricks, plaintiffs below. The Hendrickses, owners of the property adjacent to that of Mr. Stalnaker, were refused a Health Department permit for a septic system located within 100 feet of Mr. Stalnaker's water well. The Circuit Court of Lewis County, based on a jury verdict, found the water well to be a private nuisance and ordered its abatement. On appeal, Mr. Stalnaker argues that because his water well was not an unreasonable use of his land, he is not liable for the effects on the Hendrickses' property. We agree and, therefore, reverse the decision of the circuit court.

* * *

On 15 January 1986, the county sanitarian informed Mr. Hendricks that no permit for his proposed septic system could be issued because the absorption field for his septic system was within one hundred feet of Mr. Stalnaker's water well. Mr. Hendricks did install a septic system without a permit in January 1987; however, the system was left inoperative pending the outcome of this suit.

The Hendrickses filed suit in the Circuit Court of Lewis County on 29 January 1987 requesting (1) the water well be declared a private nuisance, (2) the nuisance be abated, and (3) damages. In a bifurcated trial, the jury found that the water well was a private nuisance and the trial judge ordered it to be abated. On the issue of damages the jury found for the defendant and awarded no damages.

I

In the past we have broadly described what constitutes a nuisance:

> A nuisance is anything which annoys or disturbs the free use of one's property, or which renders its ordinary use or physical occupation uncomfortable. . . . A nuisance is anything which interferes with the rights

of a citizen, either in person, property, the enjoyment of his property, or his comfort . . . . A condition is a nuisance when it clearly appears that enjoyment of property is materially lessened, and physical comfort of persons in their homes is materially interfered with thereby. (Citations omitted).

Martin v. Williams, 141 W.Va. 595, 610-611, 93 S.E.2d 835, 844 (1956).

* * * The definition of private nuisance includes conduct that is intentional and unreasonable, negligent or reckless, or that results in an abnormally dangerous conditions or activities in an inappropriate place. *See* W. Prosser, *Handbook of the Law of Torts* § 87 at 580, § 89 at 593 (4th ed. 1971); *Restatement (Second) of Torts* §§ 821D, 821F, 822 (1979); W. Keeton, *Prosser and Keeton on the Law of Torts* § 87 (5th ed. 1984); *Frank v. Environmental Sanitation Management, Inc.,* 687 S.W.2d 876 (Mo.1985); *O'Brien v. City of O'Fallon,* 80 Ill.App.3d 841, 36 Ill.Dec. 36, 400 N.E.2d 456 (1980); *Birchwood Lakes Colony Club, Inc. v. Borough of Medford Lakes,* 90 N.J. 582, 449 A.2d 472 (1982). Recovery for a private nuisance is limited to plaintiffs who have suffered a significant harm to their property rights or privileges caused by the interference. *Restatement (Second) of Torts* §§ 821E, 821F (1979).

* * *

Because the present case concerns conduct that is not a negligent, reckless, or abnormally dangerous activity, our discussion of private nuisance is limited to conduct that is intentional and unreasonable. An interference is intentional when the actor knows or should know that the conduct is causing a substantial and unreasonable interference. *Restatement (Second) of Torts* § 825 (1979). The unreasonableness of an intentional interference must be determined by a balancing of the landowners' interests. An interference is unreasonable when the gravity of the harm outweighs the social value of the activity alleged to cause the harm. *See* W. Prosser,*supra* § 87, at 581, § 89 at 596; *Restatement (Second) of Torts* § 826 (1979); W. Keeton, *supra* § 88, at 629. *Restatement (Second) of Torts* §§ 827 and 828 (1979) list some of the factors to be considered in determining the gravity of the harm and the social value of the activity alleged to cause the harm.[2] However, this balancing to determine unreasonableness is not absolute. Additional consideration might include the malicious or indecent conduct of the actor. *Restatement (Second) of Torts* § 829.

---

[2] The *Restatement (Second) of Torts* § 827 (1979) lists the following "gravity of harm" factors:

(a) The extent of the harm involved;
(b) the character of the harm involved;
(c) the social value that the law attaches to the type of use or enjoyment invaded;
(d) the suitability of the particular use or enjoyment invaded to the character of the locality; and
(e) the burden on the person harmed of avoiding the harm.

The *Restatement (Second) of Torts* § 828 lists the following "utility of conduct" factors:

(a) the social value that the law attaches to the primary purpose of the conduct;
(b) the suitability of the conduct to the character of the locality; and
(c) the impracticability of preventing or avoiding the invasion.

Other jurisdictions applying the balancing test to determine the unreasonableness of the interference include: *Waschak v. Moffat*, 379 Pa. 441, 109 A.2d 310 (1954); *Crest Chevrolet-Oldsmobile-Cadillac, Inc. v. Willemsen*, 129 Wis.2d 129, 384 N.W.2d 692 (1986); *Robie v. Lillis*, 112 N.H. 492, 299 A.2d 155 (1972); *Sans v. Ramsey Golf & Country Club, Inc.*, 29 N.J. 438, 149 A.2d 599 (1959); *Looney v. Hindman*, 649 S.W.2d 207 (Mo. banc 1983).

In the case before us, the Hendrickses' inability to operate a septic system on their property is clearly a substantial interference with the use and enjoyment of their land. The record indicates that the installation of the water well was intentional, but there was no evidence that the installation was done so as maliciously to deprive the Hendrickses of a septic system. Mr. Stalnaker wanted to insure himself of an adequate water supply and found no alternative to the well he dug.

The critical question is whether the interference, the installation of a water well, was unreasonable. Unreasonableness is determined by balancing the competing landholders' interests. We note that either use, well or septic system, burdens the adjacent property. Under Health Department regulations, a water well merely requires non-interference within 100 feet of its location. In the case of a septic system, however, the 100 foot safety zone, extending from the edge of the absorption field, may intrude on adjacent property. Thus, the septic system, with its potential for drainage, places a more invasive burden on adjacent property. Clearly both uses present similar considerations of gravity of harm and social value of the activity alleged to cause the harm. Both a water well and a septic system are necessary to use this land for housing; together they constitute the in and out of many water systems. Neither party has an inexpensive and practical alternative. The site of the water well means quality water for Mr. Stalnaker and the Hendrickses have only one location available for their septic system.

In the case before us, we are asked to determine if the water well is a private nuisance. But if the septic system were operational, the same question could be asked about the septic system. Because of the similar competing interests, the balancing of these landowners' interests is at least equal or, perhaps, slightly in favor of the water well. Thus, the Hendrickses have not shown that the balancing of interests favors their septic system. We find that the evidence presented clearly does not demonstrate that the water well is an unreasonable use of land and, therefore, does not constitute a private nuisance.

Although questions of fact are normally for the jury, when the material facts are not disputed and only one inference may be drawn from them by reasonable minds, the factual questions at issue become questions of law for the court. *See* Syllabus Point 2, *Brake v. Cerra*, 145 W.Va. 76, 112 S.E.2d 466 (1960); Syllabus Point 4, *Walton v. Given*, 158 W.Va. 897, 215 S.E.2d 647 (1975).

We find that because the evidence is not disputed and only one interference is reasonable, the trial court should have held as a matter of law that the water well was not a private nuisance.

Accordingly, for the reasons stated above, the judgment of the Circuit Court of Lewis County is reversed and the case is remanded for entry of an order consistent with this opinion.

Reversed.

Jost v. Dairyland Power Co-op.

45 Wis.2d 164 (1969)

In Hendricks v. Stalnaker, *the court defined "unreasonable conduct" in the context of balancing. In* Jost, *the court will not balance.*

* * *

We therefore conclude that the court properly excluded all evidence that tended to show the utility of the Dairyland Cooperative's enterprise. Whether its economic or social importance dwarfed the claim of a small farmer is of no consequence in this lawsuit. It will not be said that, because a great and socially useful enterprise will be liable in damages, an injury small by comparison should go unredressed. We know of no acceptable rule of jurisprudence that permits those who are engaged in important and desirable enterprises to injure with impunity those who are engaged in enterprises of lesser economic significance. Even the government or other entities, including public utilities, endowed with the power of eminent domain—the power to take private property in order to devote it to a purpose beneficial to the public good—are obliged to pay a fair market value for what is taken or damaged. To contend that a public utility, in the pursuit of its praiseworthy and legitimate enterprise, can, in effect, deprive others of the full use of their property without compensation, poses a theory unknown to the law of Wisconsin, and in our opinion would constitute the taking of property without due process of law.

* * *

§ 13.4 Remedies and Defenses

Assuming a court declares an activity a nuisance, the question becomes the nature of the remedy. The next two cases explore the traditional remedy—and non-traditional remedies, too.

Boomer v. Atlantic Cement Co.

26 N.Y.2d 219 (1970)

In this case, a cement factory was declared a nuisance. The traditional remedy would be a permanent injunction and shut the factory down. This court does not do this, however. Instead, the remedy will be permanent damages.

BERGAN, Judge.

Defendant operates a large cement plant near Albany. These are actions for injunction and damages by neighboring land owners alleging injury to property from dirt, smoke and vibration emanating from the plant. A nuisance has been found after trial, temporary damages have been allowed; but an injunction has been denied.

The public concern with air pollution arising from many sources in industry and in transportation is currently accorded ever wider recognition accompanied by a growing sense of responsibility in State and Federal Governments to control it. Cement plants are obvious sources of air pollution in the neighborhoods where they operate.

But there is now before the court private litigation in which individual property owners have sought specific relief from a single plant operation. The threshold question raised by the division of view on this appeal is whether the court should resolve the litigation between the parties now before it as equitably as seems possible; or whether, seeking promotion of the general public welfare, it should channel private litigation into broad public objectives.

* * *

The cement making operations of defendant have been found by the court of Special Term to have damaged the nearby properties of plaintiffs in these two actions. That court, as it has been noted, accordingly found defendant maintained a nuisance and this has been affirmed at the Appellate Division. The total damage to plaintiffs' properties is, however, relatively small in comparison with the value of defendant's operation and with the consequences of the injunction which plaintiffs seek.

The ground for the denial of injunction, notwithstanding the finding both that there is a nuisance and that plaintiffs have been damaged substantially, is the large disparity in economic consequences of the nuisance and of the injunction. This theory cannot, however, be sustained without overruling a doctrine which has been consistently reaffirmed in several leading cases in this court and which has never been disavowed here, namely that where a nuisance has been found and where there has been any substantial damage shown by the party complaining an injunction will be granted.

The rule in New York has been that such a nuisance will be enjoined although marked disparity be shown in economic consequence between the effect of the injunction and the effect of the nuisance.

* * *

One alternative is to grant the injunction but postpone its effect to a specified future date to give opportunity for technical advances to permit defendant to eliminate the nuisance; another is to grant the injunction conditioned on the payment of permanent damages to plaintiffs which would compensate them for the total economic loss to their property present and future caused by defendant's operations. For reasons which will be developed the court chooses the latter alternative.

If the injunction were to be granted unless within a short period-e.g., 18 months-the nuisance be abated by improved methods, there would be no assurance that any significant technical improvement would occur.

The parties could settle this private litigation at any time if defendant paid enough money and the imminent threat of closing the plant would build up the pressure on defendant. If there were no improved techniques found, there would inevitably be applications to the court at Special Term for extensions of time to perform on showing of good faith efforts to find such techniques.

Moreover, techniques to eliminate dust and other annoying by-products of cement making are unlikely to be developed by any research the defendant can undertake within any short period, but will depend on the total resources of the cement industry nationwide and throughout the world. The problem is universal wherever cement is made.

For obvious reasons the rate of the research is beyond control of defendant. If at the end of 18 months the whole industry has not found a technical solution a court would be hard put to close down this one cement plant if due regard be given to equitable principles.

On the other hand, to grant the injunction unless defendant pays plaintiffs such permanent damages as may be fixed by the court seems to do justice between the contending parties. All of the attributions of economic loss to the properties on which plaintiffs' complaints are based will have been redressed.

* * *

The power of the court to condition on equitable grounds the continuance of an injunction on the payment of permanent damages seems undoubted. (See, e.g., the alternatives considered in McCarty v. Natural Carbonic Gas Co., Supra, as well as Strobel v. Kerr Salt Co., Supra.)

The damage base here suggested is consistent with the general rule in those nuisance cases where damages are allowed. 'Where a nuisance is of such a permanent and unabatable character that a single recovery can be had, including the whole damage past and future resulting therefrom, there can be but one recovery' (66 C.J.S. Nuisances § 140, p. 947). It has been said that permanent damages are allowed where the loss recoverable would obviously be small as compared with the cost of removal of the nuisance (Kentucky-Ohio Gas Co. v. Bowling, 264 Ky. 470, 477, 95 S.W.2d 1).

* * *

Thus it seems fair to both sides to grant permanent damages to plaintiffs which will terminate this private litigation. The theory of damage is the 'servitude on land' of plaintiffs imposed by defendant's nuisance. (See United States v. Causby, 328 U.S. 256, 261, 262, 267, 66 S.Ct. 1062, 90 L.Ed. 1206, where the term 'servitude' addressed to the land was used by Justice Douglas relating to the effect of airplane noise on property near an airport.)

The judgment, by allowance of permanent damages imposing a servitude on land, which is the basis of the actions, would preclude future recovery by plaintiffs or their grantees (see Northern Indiana Public Serv. Co. v. W. J. & M. S. Vesey, supra, p. 351, 200 N.E. 620).

* * *

The orders should be reversed, without costs, and the cases remitted to Supreme Court, Albany County to grant an injunction which shall be vacated upon payment by defendant of such amounts of permanent damage to the respective plaintiffs as shall for this purpose be determined by the court.

* * *

Spur Industries, Inc. v. Del E. Webb Development Co.
108 Ariz. 178 (1972)

A massive feedlot for cattle posed a health threat to a neighboring residential development. Importantly, the feedlot operation began before the residential development came into existence. It is also important that, through the years, the residential development moved closer and closer to the feedlot. The question before the court is whether the feedlot can be enjoined from use. The court will hold that it can be—subject to a major condition by the residential developer.

CAMERON, Vice Chief Justice.

From a judgment permanently enjoining the defendant, Spur Industries, Inc., from operating a cattle feedlot near the plaintiff Del E. Webb Development Company's Sun City, Spur appeals. Webb cross-appeals. Although numerous issues are raised, we feel that it is necessary to answer only two questions. They are:

1. Where the operation of a business, such as a cattle feedlot is lawful in the first instance, but becomes a nuisance by reason of a nearby residential area, may the feedlot operation be enjoined in an action brought by the developer of the residential area?

2. Assuming that the nuisance may be enjoined, may the developer of a completely new town or urban area in a previously agricultural area be required to indemnify the operator of the feedlot who must move or cease operation because of the presence of the residential area created by the developer?

The facts necessary for a determination of this matter on appeal are as follows.

* * *

In 1956, Spur's predecessors in interest, H. Marion Welborn and the Northside Hay Mill and Trading Company, developed feed-lots, about 1/2 mile south of Olive Avenue, in an area between the confluence of the usually dry Agua Fria and New Rivers. The area is well suited for cattle feeding and in 1959, there were 25 cattle feeding pens or dairy operations within a 7 mile radius of the location developed by Spur's predecessors. In April and May of 1959, the Northside Hay Mill was feeding between 6,000 and 7,000 head of cattle and Welborn approximately 1,500 head on a combined area of 35 acres.

In May of 1959, Del Webb began to plan the development of an urban area to be known as Sun City. For this purpose, the Marinette and the Santa Fe Ranches, some 20,000 acres of farmland, were purchased for $15,000,000 or $750.00 per acre. This price was considerably less than the price of land located near the urban area of Phoenix, and along with the success of Youngtown was a factor influencing the decision to purchase the property in question.

By September 1959, Del Webb had started construction of a golf course south of Grand Avenue and Spur's predecessors had started to level ground for more feedlot area. In 1960, Spur purchased the property in question and began a rebuilding and expansion program extending both to the north and south of the original facilities. By 1962, Spur's expansion program was completed and had expanded from approximately 35 acres to 114 acres. * * *

Accompanied by an extensive advertising campaign, homes were first offered by Del Webb in January 1960 and the first unit to be completed was south of Grand Avenue and approximately 2 1/2 miles north of Spur. By 2 May 1960, there were 450 to 500 houses completed or under construction. At this time, Del Webb did not consider odors from the Spur feed pens a problem and Del Webb continued to develop in a southerly direction, until sales resistance became so great that the parcels were difficult if not impossible to sell. * * *

* * *

By December 1967, Del Webb's property had extended south to Olive Avenue and Spur was within 500 feet of Olive Avenue to the north. * * *. Del Webb filed its original complaint alleging that in excess of 1,300 lots in the southwest portion were unfit for development for sale as residential lots because of the operation of the Spur feedlot.

Del Webb's suit complained that the Spur feeding operation was a public nuisance because of the flies and the odor which were drifting or being blown by the prevailing south to north wind over the southern portion of Sun City. At the time of the suit, Spur was feeding between 20,000 and 30,000 head of cattle, and the facts amply support the finding of the trial court that the feed pens had become a nuisance to the people who resided in the southern part of Del Webb's development. The testimony indicated that cattle in a commercial feedlot will produce 35 to 40 pounds of wet manure per day, per head, or over a million pounds of wet manure per day for 30,000 head of cattle, and that despite the admittedly good feedlot management and good housekeeping practices by Spur, the resulting odor and flies produced an annoying if not unhealthy situation as far as the senior citizens of southern Sun City were concerned. There is no doubt that some of the citizens of Sun City were unable to enjoy the outdoor living which Del Webb had advertised and that Del Webb was faced with sales resistance from prospective purchasers as well as strong and persistent complaints from the people who had purchased homes in that area.

* * *

It is noted, however, that neither the citizens of Sun City nor Youngtown are represented in this lawsuit and the suit is solely between Del E. Webb Development Company and Spur Industries, Inc.

MAY SPUR BE ENJOINED?

The difference between a private nuisance and a public nuisance is generally one of degree. A private nuisance is one affecting a single individual or a definite small number of persons in the enjoyment of private rights not common to the public, while a public nuisance is one affecting the rights enjoyed by citizens as a part of the public. To constitute a public nuisance, the nuisance must affect a considerable number of people or an entire community or neighborhood. City of Phoenix v. Johnson, 51 Ariz. 115, 75 P.2d 30 (1938).

Where the injury is slight, the remedy for minor inconveniences lies in an action for damages rather than in one for an injunction. Kubby v. Hammond, 68 Ariz. 17, 198 P.2d 134 (1948). Moreover, some courts have held, in the 'balancing of conveniences' cases, that damages may be the sole remedy. See Boomer v. Atlantic Cement Co., 26 N.Y.2d 219, 309 N.Y.S.2d 312, 257 N.E.2d 870, 40 A.L.R.3d 590 (1970), and annotation comments, 40 A.L.R.3d 601.

Thus, it would appear from the admittedly incomplete record as developed in the trial court, that, at most, residents of Youngtown would be entitled to damages rather than injunctive relief.

We have no difficulty, however, in agreeing with the conclusion of the trial court that Spur's operation was an enjoinable public nuisance as far as the people in the southern portion of Del Webb's Sun City were concerned.

* * *

It is clear that as to the citizens of Sun City, the operation of Spur's feedlot was both a public and a private nuisance. They could have successfully maintained an action to abate the nuisance. Del Webb, having shown a special injury in the loss of sales, had a standing to bring suit to enjoin the nuisance. Engle v. Clark, 53 Ariz. 472, 90 P.2d 994

(1939); City of Phoenix v. Johnson, supra. The judgment of the trial court permanently enjoining the operation of the feedlot is affirmed.

MUST DEL WEBB INDEMNIFY SPUR?

A suit to enjoin a nuisance sounds in equity and the courts have long recognized a special responsibility to the public when acting as a court of equity:

§ 104. Where public interest is involved.

'Courts of equity may, and frequently do, go much further both to give and withhold relief in furtherance of the public interest than they are accustomed to go when only private interests are involved. Accordingly, the granting or withholding of relief may properly be dependent upon considerations of public interest. * * *.' 27 Am.Jur.2d, Equity, page 626.

In addition to protecting the public interest, however, courts of equity are concerned with protecting the operator of a lawfully, albeit noxious, business from the result of a knowing and willful encroachment by others near his business.

In the so-called 'coming to the nuisance' cases, the courts have held that the residential landowner may not have relief if he knowingly came into a neighborhood reserved for industrial or agricultural endeavors and has been damaged thereby:

'Plaintiffs chose to live in an area uncontrolled by zoning laws or restrictive covenants and remote from urban development. In such an area plaintiffs cannot complain that legitimate agricultural pursuits are being carried on in the vicinity, nor can plaintiffs, having chosen to build in an agricultural area, complain that the agricultural pursuits carried on in the area depreciate the value of their homes. The area being primarily agricultural, and opinion reflecting the value of such property must take this factor into account. The standards affecting the value of residence property in an urban setting, subject to zoning controls and controlled planning techniques, cannot be the standards by which agricultural properties are judged.

'People employed in a city who build their homes in suburban areas of the county beyond the limits of a city and zoning regulations do so for a reason. Some do so to avoid the high taxation rate imposed by cities, or to avoid special assessments for street, sewer and water projects. They usually build on improved or hard surface highways, which have been built either at state or county expense and thereby avoid special assessments for these improvements. It may be that they desire to get away from the congestion of traffic, smoke, noise, foul air and the many other annoyances of city life. But with all these advantages in going beyond the area which is zoned and restricted to protect them in their homes, they must be prepared to take the disadvantages.' Dill v. Excel Packing Company, 183 Kan. 513, 525, 526, 331 P.2d 539, 548, 549 (1958). See also East St. Johns Shingle Co. v. City of Portland, 195 Or. 505, 246 P.2d 554, 560--562 (1952).

And:

'* * * a party cannot justly call upon the law to make that place suitable for his residence which was not so when he selected it. * * *.' Gilbert v. Showerman, 23 Mich. 448, 455, 2 Brown 158 (1871).

Were Webb the only party injured, we would feel justified in holding that the doctrine of 'coming to the nuisance' would have been a bar to the relief asked by Webb, and, on the other hand, had Spur located the feedlot near the outskirts of a city and had the city grown toward the feedlot, Spur would have to suffer the cost of abating the nuisance as to those people locating within the growth pattern of the expanding city:

'The case affords, perhaps, an example where a business established at a place remote from population is gradually surrounded and becomes part of a populous center, so that a business which formerly was not an interference with the rights of others has become so by the encroachment of the population * * *.' City of Ft. Smith v. Western Hide & Fur Co., 153 Ark. 99, 103, 239 S.W. 724, 726 (1922).

We agree, however, with the Massachusetts court that:

'The law of nuisance affords no rigid rule to be applied in all instances. It is elastic. It undertakes to require only that which is fair and reasonable under all the circumstances. In a commonwealth like this, which depends for its material prosperity so largely on the continued growth and enlargement of manufacturing of diverse varieties, 'extreme rights' cannot be enforced. * * *.' Stevens v. Rockport Granite Co., 216 Mass. 486, 488, 104 N.E. 371, 373 (1914).

There was no indication in the instant case at the time Spur and its predecessors located in western Maricopa County that a new city would spring up, full-blown, alongside the feeding operation and that the developer of that city would ask the court to order Spur to move because of the new city. Spur is required to move not because of any wrongdoing on the part of Spur, but because of a proper and legitimate regard of the courts for the rights and interests of the public.

Del Webb, on the other hand, is entitled to the relief prayed for (a permanent injunction), not because Webb is blameless, but because of the damage to the people who have been encouraged to purchase homes in Sun City. It does not equitably or legally follow, however, that Webb, being entitled to the injunction, is then free of any liability to Spur if Webb has in fact been the cause of the damage Spur has sustained. It does not seem harsh to require a developer, who has taken advantage of the lesser land values in a rural area as well as the availability of large tracts of land on which to build and develop a new town or city in the area, to indemnify those who are forced to leave as a result. Having brought people to the nuisance to the foreseeable detriment of Spur, Webb must indemnify Spur for a reasonable amount of the cost of moving or shutting down. It should be noted that this relief to Spur is limited to a case wherein a developer has, with foreseeability, brought into a previously agricultural or industrial area the population which makes necessary the granting of an injunction against a lawful business and for which the business has no adequate relief.

It is therefore the decision of this court that the matter be remanded to the trial court for a hearing upon the damages sustained by the defendant Spur as a reasonable and direct result of the granting of the permanent injunction. Since the result of the appeal may appear novel and both sides have obtained a measure of relief, it is ordered that each side will bear its own costs.

Affirmed in part, reversed in part, and remanded for further proceedings consistent with this opinion.

HAYS, C.J., STRUCKMEYER and LOCKWOOD, JJ., and UDALL, Retired Justice.

CHAPTER 14
ZONING

§ 14.1 Introduction

Virtually every city in the United States uses zoning. Simplified, zoning carves up a city into segments: for single-family houses; for duplexes; for apartment houses; for commercial uses; and for industrial uses. Today, there is no doubt that a city has the power to zone. It was not a foregone conclusion before 1926, however.

Village of Euclid, Ohio v. Ambler Realty Co.
272 U.S. 365 (1926)

This is the case giving cities the legal authority to zone. In this case, the Village of Euclid engaged in zoning and a landowner (developer) challenges it. The landowner asserted a Fifth Amendment Takings challenge (we discuss takings in chapter 15) and a substantive Due Process challenge. The trial court held that the ordinance was unconstitutional: "My conclusion is that the ordinance involved, as applied to plaintiff's property, is unconstitutional and void; that it takes plaintiff's property, if not for private, at least for public, use, without just compensation; that it is in no just sense a reasonable or legitimate exercise of police power. This is not to say that many of the restrictions imposed throughout the village may not be valid, nor that many of them might not be established as against plaintiff's property under the police power. But, however this may be, all the provisions of the ordinance, so far as they pertain to plaintiff's property, are so intermingled and inseparable that as to its property at least, the ordinance must be declared wholly null and void. See Hill v. Wallace, 259 U.S. 44, 70, 42 Sup.Ct. 453, 66 L.Ed. 822; Lemke v. Farmers' Grain Co., 258 U.S. 50, 42 Sup.Ct. 244, 66 L.Ed. 458." Ambler Realty Co. v. Village of Euclid, Ohio 297 F. 307, 317 (D.C.Ohio 1924). The United States Supreme Court will reverse. On what basis will the court reverse? The court will hold that zoning is a valid exercise of the police power.

Mr. Justice SUTHERLAND delivered the opinion of the Court.

The village of Euclid is an Ohio municipal corporation. It adjoins and practically is a suburb of the city of Cleveland. Its estimated population is between 5,000 and 10,000, and its area from 12 to 14 square miles, the greater part of which is farm lands or unimproved acreage. * * *

Appellee is the owner of a tract of land containing 68 acres, situated in the westerly end of the village, abutting on Euclid avenue to the south and the Nickel Plate Railroad to the north. Adjoining this tract, both on the east and on the west, there have been laid out restricted residential plats upon which residences have been erected.

On November 13, 1922, an ordinance was adopted by the village council, establishing a comprehensive zoning plan for regulating and restricting the location of trades, industries, apartment houses, two-family houses, single family houses, etc., the lot area to be built upon, the size and height of buildings, etc.

The entire area of the village is divided by the ordinance into six classes of use districts, denominated U-1 to U-6, inclusive; three classes of height districts, denominated H-1 to H-3, inclusive; and four classes of area districts, denominated A-1 to A-4, inclusive. The use districts are classified in respect of the buildings which may be erected within their respective limits, as follows: U-1 is restricted to single family dwellings, public parks, water towers and reservoirs, suburban and interurban electric railway passenger stations and rights of way, and farming, non-commercial greenhouse nurseries, and truck gardening; U-2 is extended to include two-family dwellings; U-3 is further extended to include apartment houses, hotels, churches, schools, public libraries, museums, private clubs, community center buildings, hospitals, sanitariums, public playgrounds, and recreation buildings, and a city hall and courthouse; U-4 is further extended to include banks, offices, studios, telephone exchanges, fire and police stations, restaurants, theaters and moving picture shows, retail stores and shops, sales offices, sample rooms, wholesale stores for hardware, drugs, and groceries, stations for gasoline and oil (not exceeding 1,000 gallons storage) and for ice delivery, skating rinks and dance halls, electric substations, job and newspaper printing, public garages for motor vehicles, stables and wagon sheds (not exceeding five horses, wagons or motor trucks), and distributing stations for central store and commercial enterprises; * * *

Class U-1 is the only district in which buildings are restricted to those enumerated. In the other classes the uses are cumulative-that is to say, uses in class U-2 include those enumerated in the preceding class U-1; class U-3 includes uses enumerated in the preceding classes, U-2, and U-1; and so on. In addition to the enumerated uses, the ordinance provides for accessory uses; that is, for uses customarily incident to the principal use, such as private garages. Many regulations are provided in respect of such accessory uses.

* * *

The ordinance is assailed on the grounds that it is in derogation of section 1 of the Fourteenth Amendment to the federal Constitution in that it deprives appellee of liberty and property without due process of law and denies it the equal protection of the law, and that it offends against certain provisions of the Constitution of the state of Ohio. The prayer of the bill is for an injunction restraining the enforcement of the ordinance and all attempts to impose or maintain as to appellee's property any of the restrictions, limitations or conditions. The court below held the ordinance to be unconstitutional and void, and enjoined its enforcement, 297 F. 307.

Before proceeding to a consideration of the case, it is necessary to determine the scope of the inquiry. The bill alleges that the tract of land in question is vacant and has been held for years for the purpose of selling and developing it for industrial uses, for which it is especially adapted, being immediately in the path of progressive industrial development; that for such uses it has a market value of about $10,000 per acre, but if the use be limited to residential purposes the market value is not in excess of $2,500 per acre; that the first 200 feet of the parcel back from Euclid avenue, if unrestricted in respect of use, has a value of $150 per front foot, but if limited to residential uses, and ordinary mercantile business be excluded therefrom, its value is not in excess of $50 per front foot.

* * *

It is not necessary to set forth the provisions of the Ohio Constitution which are thought to be infringed. The question is the same under both Constitutions, namely, as stated by appellee: Is the ordinance invalid, in that it violates the constitutional protection 'to the right of property in the appellee by attempted regulations under the guise of the police power, which are unreasonable and confiscatory'?

* * *

The ordinance now under review, and all similar laws and regulations, must find their justification in some aspect of the police power, asserted for the public welfare. The line which in this field separates the legitimate from the illegitimate assumption of power is not capable of precise delimitation. It varies with circumstances and conditions. A regulatory zoning ordinance, which would be clearly valid as applied to the great cities, might be clearly invalid as applied to rural communities. In solving doubts, the maxim 'sic utere tuo ut alienum non laedas,' which lies at the foundation of so much of the common law of nuisances, ordinarily will furnish a fairly helpful clue. And the law of nuisances, likewise, may be consulted, not for the purpose of controlling, but for the helpful aid of its analogies in the process of ascertaining the scope of, the power. Thus the question whether the power exists to forbid the erection of a building of a particular kind or for a particular use, like the question whether a particular thing is a nuisance, is to be determined, not by an abstract consideration of the building or of the thing considered apart, but by considering it in connection with the circumstances and the locality. Sturgis v. Bridgeman, L. R. 11 Ch. 852, 865. A nuisance may be merely a right thing in the wrong place, like a pig in the parlor instead of the barnyard. If the validity of the legislative classification for zoning purposes be fairly debatable, the legislative judgment must be allowed to control. Radice v. New York, 264 U. S. 292, 294, 44 S. Ct. 325, 68 L. Ed. 690.

There is no serious difference of opinion in respect of the validity of laws and regulations fixing the height of buildings within reasonable limits, the character of materials and methods of construction, and the adjoining area which must be left open, in order to minimize the danger of fire or collapse, the evils of overcrowding and the like, and excluding from residential sections offensive trades, industries and structures likely to create nuisances. * * *

* * *It cannot be said that the ordinance * * * 'passes the bounds of reason and assumes the character of a merely arbitrary fiat.' Purity Extract Co. v. Lynch, 226 U. S. 192, 204, 33 S. Ct. 44, 47 (57 L. Ed. 184). Moreover, the restrictive provisions of the ordinance in this particular may be sustained upon the principles applicable to the broader exclusion from residential districts of all business and trade structures, presently to be discussed.

* * *

The matter of zoning has received much attention at the hands of commissions and experts, and the results of their investigations have been set forth in comprehensive reports. These reports which bear every evidence of painstaking consideration, concur in the view that the segregation of residential, business and industrial buildings will make it easier to provide fire apparatus suitable for the character and intensity of the development in each section; that it will increase the safety and security of home life, greatly tend to prevent street accidents, especially to children, by reducing the traffic and resulting confusion in residential sections, decrease noise and other conditions which produce or intensify nervous disorders, preserve a more favorable environment in which to rear children, etc. With particular reference to apartment houses, it is pointed out that the development of detached house sections is greatly retarded by the coming of apartment houses, which has sometimes resulted in destroying the entire section for private house purposes; that in such sections very often the apartment house is a mere parasite, constructed in order to take advantage of the open spaces and attractive surroundings created by the residential character of the district. Moreover, the coming of one apartment house is followed by others, interfering by their height and bulk with the free circulation of air and monopolizing the rays of the sun which otherwise would fall upon the smaller homes, and bringing, as their necessary accompaniments, the disturbing noises incident to increased traffic and business, and the occupation, by means of moving and parked automobiles, of larger portions of the streets, thus detracting from their safety and depriving children of the privilege of quiet and open spaces for play, enjoyed by those in more favored localities-until, finally, the residential character of the neighborhood and its desirability as a place of detached residences are utterly destroyed. Under these circumstances, apartment houses, which in a different environment would be not only entirely unobjectionable but highly desirable, come very near to being nuisances.

If these reasons, thus summarized, do not demonstrate the wisdom or sound policy in all respects of those restrictions which we have indicated as pertinent to the inquiry, at least, the reasons are sufficiently cogent to preclude us from saying, as it must be said before the ordinance can be declared unconstitutional, that such provisions are clearly arbitrary and unreasonable, having no substantial relation to the public health, safety, morals, or general welfare. Cusack Co. v. City of Chicago, supra, pages 530-531 (37 S. Ct. 190); Jacobson v. Massachusetts, 197 U. S. 11, 30-31, 25 S. Ct. 358, 49 L. Ed. 643, 3 Ann. Cas. 765.

* * *

* * *Under these circumstances, therefore, it is enough for us to determine, as we do, that the ordinance in its general scope and dominant features, so far as its provisions are here involved, is a valid exercise of authority, leaving other provisions to be dealt with as cases arise directly involving them.

And this is in accordance with the traditional policy of this court. In the realm of constitutional law, especially, this court has perceived the embarrassment which is likely to result from an attempt to formulate rules or decide questions beyond the necessities of the immediate issue. It has preferred to follow the method of a gradual approach to the general by a systematically guarded application and extension of constitutional principles to particular cases as they arise, rather than by out of hand attempts to establish general rules to which future cases must be fitted. This process applies with peculiar force to the solution of questions arising under the due process clause of the Constitution as applied to the exercise of the flexible powers of police, with which we are here concerned.

Decree reversed.

Mr. Justice VAN DEVANTER, Mr. Justice McREYNOLDS, and Mr. Justice BUTLER dissent.

§ 14.2 Expansion of Zoning

In the Village of Euclid, *the Supreme Court held that zoning is a valid exercise of the police power. The question we next examine is what the outer parameters of that power are as it relates to zoning.*

§ 14.2.1 For Aesthetics

Berman v. Parker
348 U.S. 26 (1954)

Congress enacted legislation for the District of Columbia whereby the eminent domain power was used to acquire private property, redevelop it, and thereby eliminate urban blight. The plan was not just for the health of the citizenry, but for aesthetic considerations, too. The Supreme Court held that such legislation is within the scope of the police power and does not violate the Fifth Amendment's requirement that takings must be for a public use. (The public use requirement is further developed in chapter 15 in, Kelo v. City of New London, Conn.)

Mr. Justice DOUGLAS delivered the opinion of the Court.

* * *

The power of Congress over the District of Columbia includes all the legislative powers which a state may exercise over its affairs. See District of Columbia v. John R. Thompson Co., 346 U.S. 100, 108, 73 S.Ct. 1007, 1011, 97 L.Ed. 1480. We deal, in other words, with what traditionally has been known as the police power. An attempt to define its reach or trace its outer limits is fruitless, for each case must turn on its own facts. The definition is essentially the product of legislative determinations addressed to the purposes of government, purposes neither abstractly nor historically capable of complete definition. Subject to specific constitutional limitations, when the legislature has spoken, the public interest has been declared in terms well-nigh conclusive. In such cases the legislature, not the judiciary, is the main guardian of the public needs to be served by social legislation, whether it be Congress legislating concerning the District of Columbia, see Block v. Hirsh, 256 U.S. 135, 41 S.Ct. 458, 65 L.Ed. 865, or the States legislating concerning local affairs. See Olsen v. State of Nebraska, 313 U.S. 236, 61 S.Ct. 862, 85 L.Ed. 1305; Lincoln Federal Labor Union No. 19129, A.F. of L. v. Northwestern Co., 335 U.S. 525, 69 S.Ct. 251, 93 L.Ed. 212; California State Ass'n Inter-Ins. Bureau v. Maloney, 341 U.S. 105, 71 S.Ct. 601, 95 L.Ed. 788. This principle admits of no exception merely because the power of eminent domain is involved. The role of the judiciary in determining whether that power is being exercised for a public purpose is an extremely narrow one. See Old Dominion Land Co. v. United States, 269 U.S. 55, 66, 46 S.Ct. 39, 40, 70 L.Ed. 162; United States ex rel. Tennessee Valley Authority v. Welch, 327 U.S. 546, 552, 66 S.Ct. 715, 718, 90 L.Ed. 843.

Public safety, public health, morality, peace and quiet, law and order-these are some of the more conspicuous examples of the traditional application of the police power to municipal affairs. Yet they merely illustrate the scope of the power and do not delimit it. See Noble State Bank v. Haskell, 219 U.S. 104, 111, 31 S.Ct. 186, 188, 55 L.Ed. 112. Miserable and disreputable housing conditions may do more than spread disease and crime and immorality. They may also suffocate the spirit by reducing the people who live there to the status of cattle. They may indeed make living an almost insufferable burden. They may also be an ugly sore, a blight on the community which robs it of charm, which makes it a place from which men turn. The misery of housing may despoil a community as an open sewer may ruin a river.

We do not sit to determine whether a particular housing project is or is not desirable. The concept of the public welfare is broad and inclusive. See Day-Brite Lighting, Inc. v. State of Missouri, 342 U.S. 421, 424, 72 S.Ct. 405, 407, 96 L.Ed. 469. The values it represents are spiritual as well as physical, aesthetic as well as monetary. It is within the power of the legislature to determine that the community should be beautiful as well as healthy, spacious as well as clean, well-balanced as well as carefully patrolled. In the present case, the Congress and its authorized agencies have made determinations that take into account a wide variety of values. It is not for us to reappraise them. If those who govern the District of Columbia decide that the Nation's Capital should be beautiful as well as sanitary, there is nothing in the Fifth Amendment that stands in the way.

Once the object is within the authority of Congress, the right to realize it through the exercise of eminent domain is clear. For the power of eminent domain is merely the means to the end. See Luxton v. North River Bridge Co., 153 U.S. 525, 529-530, 14 S.Ct. 891, 892, 38 L.Ed. 808; United States v. Gettysburg Electric R. Co., 160 U.S. 668, 679, 16 S.Ct. 427, 429, 40 L.Ed. 576. Once the object is within the authority of Congress, the means by which it will be attained is also for Congress to determine. Here one of the means chosen is the use of private enterprise for redevelopment of the area. Appellants argue that this makes the project a taking from one businessman for the benefit of another businessman. But the means of executing the project are for Congress and Congress alone to determine, once the public purpose has been established. See Luxton v. North River Bridge Co., supra; cf. Highland v. Russell Car Co., 279 U.S. 253, 49 S.Ct. 314, 73 L.Ed. 688. The public end may be as well or better served through an agency of private enterprise than through a department of government-or so the Congress might conclude. We cannot say that public ownership is the sole method of promoting the public purposes of community redevelopment projects. What we have said also disposes of any contention concerning the fact that certain property owners in the area may be permitted to repurchase their properties for redevelopment in harmony with the overall plan. That, too, is a legitimate means which Congress and its agencies may adopt, if they choose.

In the present case, Congress and its authorized agencies attack the problem of the blighted parts of the community on an area rather than on a structure-by-structure basis. That, too, is opposed by appellants. They maintain that since their building does not imperil health or safety nor contribute to the making of a slum or a blighted area, it cannot be swept into a redevelopment plan by the mere dictum of the Planning Commission or the Commissioners. The particular uses to be made of the land in the project were determined with regard to the needs of the particular community. The experts concluded that if the community were to be healthy, if it were not to revert again to a blighted or slum area, as though possessed of a congenital disease, the area must be planned as a whole. It was not enough, they believed, to remove existing buildings that were unsanitary or unsightly. It was important to redesign the whole area so as to eliminate the conditions that cause slums-the overcrowding of dwellings, the lack of parks, the lack of adequate streets and alleys, the absence of recreational areas, the lack of light and air, the presence of outmoded street patterns. It was believed that the piecemeal approach, the removal of individual structures that were offensive, would be only a palliative. The entire area needed redesigning so that a balanced, integrated plan could be developed for the region, including not only new homes but also schools, churches, parks, streets, and shopping centers. In this way it was hoped that the cycle of decay of the area could be controlled and the birth of future slums prevented. Cf. Gohld Realty Co. v. City of Hartford, 141 Conn. 135, 141-144, 104 A.2d 365, 368-370; Hunter v. Norfolk Redevelopment Authority, 195 Va. 326, 338-339, 78 S.E.2d 893, 900-901. Such diversification in future use is plainly relevant to the maintenance of the desired housing standards and therefore within congressional power.

The District Court below suggested that, if such a broad scope were intended for the statute, the standards contained in the Act would not be sufficiently definite to sustain the delegation of authority. 117 F.Supp. 705, 721. We do not agree. We think the standards prescribed were adequate for executing the plan to eliminate not only slums as narrowly defined by the District Court but also the blighted areas that tend to produce slums. Property may of course be taken for this redevelopment which, standing by itself, is innocuous and unoffending. But we have said enough to indicate that it is the need of the area as a whole which Congress and its agencies are evaluating. If owner after owner were permitted to resist these redevelopment programs on the ground that his particular property was not being used against the public interest, integrated plans for redevelopment would suffer greatly. The argument pressed on us is, indeed, a plea to substitute the landowner's standard of the public need for the standard prescribed by Congress. But as we have already stated, community redevelopment programs need not, by force of the Constitution, be on a piecemeal basis-lot by lot, building by building.

It is not for the courts to oversee the choice of the boundary line nor to sit in review on the size of a particular project area. Once the question of the public purpose has been decided, the amount and character of land to be taken for the project and the need for a particular tract to complete the integrated plan rests in the discretion of the legislative branch. See Shoemaker v. United States, 147 U.S. 282, 298, 13 S.Ct. 361, 390, 37 L.Ed. 170; United States ex rel. Tennessee Valley Authority v. Welch, supra, 327 U.S. at page 554, 66 S.Ct. at page 718; United States v. Carmack, 329 U.S. 230, 247, 67 S.Ct. 252, 260, 91 L.Ed. 209.

The District Court indicated grave doubts concerning the Agency's right to take full title to the land as distinguished from the objectionable buildings located on it. 117 F.Supp. 705, 715-719. We do not share those doubts. If the Agency considers it necessary in carrying out the redevelopment project to take full title to the real property involved, it may do so. It is not for the courts to determine whether it is necessary for successful consummation of the project that unsafe, unsightly, or unsanitary buildings alone be taken or whether title to the land be included, any more than it is the function of the courts to sort and choose among the various parcels selected for condemnation.

The rights of these property owners are satisfied when they receive that just compensation which the Fifth Amendment exacts as the price of the taking.

The judgment of the District Court, as modified by this opinion, is affirmed.

Affirmed.

§ 14.2.2 For Low-Cost Housing

The next question is whether zoning may be used to increase low-cost housing. The next two cases provide two extremes.

Southern Burlington County NAACP v. Township of Mount Laurel
67 N.J. 151 (1975)

In the Mount Laurel *cases (there actually were three), the Supreme Court of New Jersey holds that new developments must provide for low income housing.*

* * *

The Legal Issue

The legal question before us, as earlier indicated, is whether a developing municipality like Mount Laurel may validly, by a system of land use regulation, make it physically and economically impossible to provide low and moderate income housing in the municipality for the various categories of persons who need and want it and thereby, as Mount Laurel has, exclude such people from living within its confines because of the limited extent of their income and resources. Necessarily implicated are the broader questions of the right of such municipalities to limit the kinds of available housing and of any obligation to make possible a variety and choice of types of living accommodations.

We conclude that every such municipality must, by its land use regulations, presumptively make realistically possible an appropriate variety and choice of housing. More specifically, presumptively it cannot foreclose the opportunity of the classes of people mentioned for low and moderate income housing and in its regulations must affirmatively afford that opportunity, at least to the extent of the municipality's fair share of the present and prospective regional need therefor. These obligations must be met unless the particular municipality can sustain the heavy burden of demonstrating peculiar circumstances which dictate that it should not be required so to do.

We reach this conclusion under state law and so do not find it necessary to consider federal constitutional grounds urged by plaintiffs.

* * *

Asian Americans for Equality v. Koch
128 A.D.2d 99 (N.Y.A.D. 1987)

In Asian Americans for Equality v. Koch, *New York takes the approach that there is no fundamental right to low cost housing and expressly disavows the* Mount Laurel *cases.*

ROSS, Justice.

In this matter we are presented with the issue of whether the City of New York properly exercised its zoning power in creating the Special Manhattan Bridge District, which is located in the Chinatown area, in view of the allegation that the City did not affirmatively order the construction of dwelling units for low and moderate income persons.

* * *

The Henry Street Partners (HSP) applied to the Planning Commission, in December 1981, for a special permit for development and construction of residential units on a site, now used as an open parking lot. The subject site is located at 60 Henry Street, which is within the District. The Planning Commission approved the special permit application of HSP on August 30, 1982, and, thereafter, it was approved by the Board of Estimate on April 14, 1983.

In substance, HSP proposes to construct a 21-story residential building and community facility. When completed, this building will contain approximately 87 condominium units, containing 0-4 bedrooms, which will provide housing for upper-middle income and professional residents of Chinatown, who might otherwise be forced to leave Chinatown, since it appears that there is virtually no housing presently existing in the area, which is available or suitable for their needs. Incidentally, it becomes obvious that the availability of these new apartment units will open up older housing now occupied by upper-middle income people.

* * *

In the case at bar, the plaintiffs are Asian Americans For Equality (Asian), Tai Lui Chow (Mrs. Chow), Bo Lan Tom (Mrs. Tom), Karen Chan (Mrs. Chan), Pui Ying Wong (Mrs. Wong), individually and on behalf of all others similarly situated. These plaintiffs seek to maintain a class action constitutional challenge to the zoning amendments which created the District. In their four causes of action complaint, the plaintiffs allege, in substance, that the District amendments fail to provide a realistic opportunity for the creation of low-income housing, a standard enunciated by the New Jersey Supreme Court in *Southern Burlington County N.A.A.C.P. v. Township of Mount Laurel*, 92 N.J. 158, 456 A.2d 390 (1983), and, therefore, constitutes exclusionary zoning. Furthermore, the plaintiffs also challenge in their complaint the grant of the special permit to HSP, and the potential tax abatement or exemption that might be afforded to HSP for its proposed project.

* * *

Approximately sixty years ago, the United States Supreme Court, in the landmark case of *Euclid v. Ambler Co.*, 272 U.S. 365, 387-388, 47 S.Ct. 114, 118, 71 L.Ed. 303 (1926), stated:

"The [zoning] ordinance now under review, and all similar laws and regulations, must find their justification in some aspect of the police power, asserted for the public welfare. The line which in this field separates the legitimate from the illegitimate assumption of power is not capable of precise delimitation. It varies with circumstances and conditions. . . . Thus the question whether the power exists to forbid the erection of a building of a particular kind or for a particular use, like the question whether a particular thing is a nuisance, is to be determined, not by an abstract consideration of the building or of the thing considered apart, but by considering it in connection with the circumstances and the locality. . . ." [material in brackets added]

The primary purpose of zoning is to insure the orderly rather than the haphazard development of a community, so as to promote the community "health and general welfare . . . ." (*Robert E. Kurzius, Inc. v. Incorporated Vil. of Upper Brookville*, 51

N.Y.2d 338, 343, 434 N.Y.S.2d 180, 414 N.E.2d 680 (1980), *cert. denied* 450 U.S. 1042, 101 S.Ct. 1761, 68 L.Ed.2d 240 (1981)).

* * *

Special Term relied heavily on the legal authority of two New Jersey Supreme Court decisions, when it denied the City defendants' motion to dismiss the first cause of action, which alleges the District was not established as a result of a well-considered plan; and the second cause of action, which alleges the District zoning amendments fails to provide a realistic opportunity for the construction of low income housing. *Southern Burlington County N.A.A.C.P. v. Township of Mount Laurel,* 67 N.J. 151, 336 A.2d 713 (1975), *cert. denied* and *app. dismd* 423 U.S. 808, 96 S.Ct. 18, 46 L.Ed.2d 28 (1975), which case is popularly referred to as *Mount Laurel* I; and, *Southern Burlington County N.A.A.C.P. v. Township of Mount Laurel,* 92 N.J. 158, 456 A.2d 390 (1983), which case is popularly referred to as *Mount Laurel* II. Also, as mentioned *supra,* plaintiffs specifically cite *Mount Laurel* II in their complaint, in order to support their contention that the zoning amendments creating the District allegedly do not offer a realistic opportunity for the creation of low income housing, and, therefore, constitute exclusionary zoning.

Mount Laurel is a developing suburban Township, which is located near Camden, New Jersey. It covers an area of 22 square miles, or about 14,000 acres.

In 1975, the New Jersey Supreme Court in *Mount Laurel* I held the Township's zoning ordinance violated the due process and equal protection guarantees of that State's Constitution, since the ordinance had the practical effect of excluding low and moderate income persons from living in this suburban Township. The Court found that this exclusion resulted from the fact that most of the Township's land was zoned for either single family dwellings or for industrial use, which left very little opportunity for the construction of multi-family dwellings such as garden apartments, town or row houses, and mobile park homes. Moreover, the Court's decision required developing New Jersey municipalities and/or townships, like Mount Laurel, to affirmatively use their land use regulations to provide a realistic opportunity for low and moderate income housing.

Thereafter, the Court's dissatisfaction, with the lack of encouragement given by Mount Laurel and other developing New Jersey municipalities to the construction of low and moderate income housing, resulted in its 1983 decision in *Mount Laurel* II. The Court in *Mount Laurel* II determined that, in order for developing New Jersey municipalities and/or townships to fulfill their obligation to provide low and moderate income housing, they must encourage the construction of such housing through affirmative conduct, such as mandatory set asides, density bonuses, zoning for mobile homes, and tax incentives.

Although Special Term uses the holdings in the *Mount Laurel* cases, discussed *supra,* to justify its denial of City defendants' motion to dismiss the first two causes of action contained in the complaint, it concedes in its opinion that *Mount Laurel* is not the law in New York. We go further. Not by the widest stretch of the imagination, could the fact pattern in *Mount Laurel* be applicable to New York City's record for providing for low and moderate income housing.

Legal commentators have characterized the holdings in the *Mount Laurel* cases as "the most extreme treatment of the issue of exclusionary zoning in the country. . . ." (Rice, *Zoning and Land Use,* 37 Syracuse Law Review 747, 750 (1986); and, *see also* 2

ARDEN H. RATHKOPF & DAREN A. RATHKOPF, THE LAW OF ZONING AND PLANNING § 17.04, at 17-26 and 17-27 (4th ed. 1984)).

The *Mount Laurel* holdings have been specifically rejected at the Appellate level in New York. In pertinent part, the Appellate Division, Second Judicial Department, in a unanimous decision, stated in *Suffolk Hous. v. Brookhaven,* 109 A.D.2d 323, 331, 491 N.Y.S.2d 396 (1985), that:

"[T]hese decisions [Mount Laurel I and II] go far beyond the law as declared by our own Court of Appeals, which had not, to this date, articulated any constitutional obligation on the part of our municipalities to zone for low-to-moderate-income housing . . . ." [material in brackets added].

Based upon our own review of New York case law, we join the Court in *Suffolk Hous. v. Brookhaven, supra,* in refusing to adopt the *Mount Laurel* holdings, since we find the *Mount Laurel* holdings to be essentially a legislative judgment.

We carefully note that the *Mount Laurel* holdings are solely based upon an interpretation of the provisions of the law and Constitution of the State of New Jersey, *Mount Laurel* I, *supra,* 67 N.J. at 174-175, 336 A.2d 713, and, *Mount Laurel* II, *supra,* 92 N.J. at 208-209, 456 A.2d 390.

* * *

If the plaintiffs are inclined to continue to seek the relief requested herein, they must seek same from the Legislature.

Accordingly, Order, Supreme Court, New York County (David B. Saxe, J.), entered September 26, 1985, which, *inter alia,* denied the motion of the City defendants to dismiss the first and second causes of action of the complaint, is modified, on the law and on the facts, to the extent of granting City defendants' motion to dismiss the first and second causes of action, and except as thus modified, otherwise affirmed, without costs. All concur except CARRO, J. who dissents in an Opinion and ASCH, J. who concurs in part in the dissent in a separate Opinion.

* * *

§ 14.3 Contraction of Zoning

We now examine contraction of the zoning power. We previously have seen that the zoning power is indeed quite broad. You should not believe, however, that the power is limitless, as the next two cases make clear.

§ 14.3.1 Nonconforming Uses

One such limitation of the zoning power is the so-called nonconforming use: As stated by the court in Village of Valatie v. Smith, *the next case, a nonconforming use is "a use that was legally in place at the time the municipality enacted legislation prohibiting the use." Once in place, a nonconforming use can continue; the use "runs with the land." Thus, if a commercial area is rezoned to residential, a commercial use may continue in such a rezoned area. This nonconforming use certainly is a limitation or contraction of the power of a municipality's police power. That said, does this mean that such a nonconforming use can endure forever? Must a community forever suffer a nonconforming use? The answer is that even a nonconforming use may eventually be legislated out of existence, by use of an "amortization period," a concept that the next case explains and illustrates.*

Village of Valatie v. Smith
83 N.Y.2d 396 (1994)

The court must decide whether a non-conforming use (banning mobile homes not parked in a mobile home park), whose amortization period ends with the death of the owner, violates the Substantive Due Process Clause of the Fourteenth Amendment. The court will hold that the amortization period does not offend the Constitution.

Simons, J.

This appeal challenges the facial validity of chapter 85 of the Village Code of the Village of Valatie, a local law that terminates the nonconforming use of a mobile home upon the transfer of ownership of either the mobile home or the land upon which it sits. Defendant argues that it is unconstitutional for the Village to use a change in ownership as the termination date for a nonconforming use. We conclude, however, that defendant has failed to carry her burden of showing that the local law is unreasonable on its face. Accordingly, we modify the order of the Appellate Division by denying defendant's cross motion for summary judgment.

In 1968, the Village enacted chapter 85 to prohibit the placement of mobile homes outside mobile home parks. Under the law, any existing mobile home located outside a park which met certain health standards was allowed to remain as a nonconforming use until either ownership of the land or ownership of the mobile home changed. According to the Village, six mobile homes, including one owned by defendant's father, fell within this exception at the time the law was passed.

In 1989, defendant inherited the mobile home from her father and the Village instituted this action to enforce the law and have the unit removed. Both the Village and defendant moved before the Supreme Court for summary judgment. The court granted defendant's motion and denied the Village's. The court characterized defendant's mobile home as a lawful nonconforming use--i.e., a use that was legally in place at the time the municipality enacted legislation prohibiting the use. Reasoning that the right to continue a nonconforming use runs with the land, the court held that the portion of the ordinance setting termination at the transfer of ownership was unconstitutional. The Appellate Division affirmed. The Court acknowledged that a municipality had the authority to phase out a nonconforming use with an "amortization period," but it concluded that this particular law was unreasonable, and therefore unconstitutional, because the period of time allowed "bears no relationship to the use of the land or the investment in that use". (190 AD2d 17, 20.)

Preliminarily, it is important to note that the question presented is the facial validity of the local law. The Court is not called upon to decide whether the local law *as applied* so deprived defendant of the value of her property as to constitute a governmental taking under the Fifth Amendment. Nor does defendant challenge the power of a municipality to regulate land use, including the placement of mobile homes, as a valid exercise of the police power *(see, e.g., Mobile Home Owners Protective Assoc. v Town of Chatham,* 33 AD2d 78; *see generally,* 1 Anderson, New York Zoning Law and Practice, ch 15 [3d ed]). Finally, there is no question that municipalities may enact laws reasonably limiting the duration of nonconforming uses *(see, Matter of Pelham Esplanade v Board of Trustees,* 77 NY2d 66; *Matter of Town of Islip v Caviglia,* 73 NY2d 544; *Modjeska Sign Studios v Berle,* 43 NY2d 468, *appeal dismissed* 439 US 809; *Matter of Harbison v City of Buffalo,* 4 NY2d 553; *City of Los Angeles v Gage,* 127 Cal App 2d 442, 274 P2d 34).

Thus, the narrow issue is whether the Village acted unreasonably by establishing an amortization period that uses the transfer of ownership as an end point.

The policy of allowing nonconforming uses to continue originated in concerns that the application of land use regulations to uses existing prior to the regulations' enactment might be construed as confiscatory and unconstitutional (4 Rathkopf, Zoning and Planning § 51.01 [2] [b], at 51-6 [Ziegler 4th ed]). While it was initially assumed that nonconforming uses would disappear with time, just the opposite proved to be true in many instances, with the nonconforming use thriving in the absence of any new lawful competition *(Matter of Harbison v City of Buffalo,* 4 NY2d 553, 560, *supra).* In light of the problems presented by continuing nonconforming uses, this Court has characterized the law's allowance of such uses as a "grudging tolerance", and we have recognized the right of municipalities to take reasonable measures to eliminate them *(see, Matter of Pelham Esplanade v Board of Trustees,* 77 NY2d 66, 71, *supra).*

Most often, elimination has been effected by establishing amortization periods, at the conclusion of which the nonconforming use must end. As commentators have noted, the term "amortization period" is somewhat misleading *(see, e.g.,* 4 Rathkopf, Zoning and Planning § 51B.05 [1], at 51B-44, n 3 [Ziegler 4th ed]). "Amortization" properly refers to a liquidation, but in this context the owner is not required to take any particular financial step. "Amortization period" simply designates a period of time granted to owners of nonconforming uses during which they may phase out their operations as they see fit and make other arrangements *(id.; see also, Art Neon Co. v City & County of Denver,* 488 F2d 118, 121 [5th Cir], *cert denied* 417 US 932). It is, in effect, a grace period, putting owners on fair notice of the law and giving them a fair opportunity to recoup their investment *(Modjeska Sign Studios v Berle,* 43 NY2d 468, 479, *supra; Art Neon Co. v City & County of Denver, supra,* at 121). Though the amortization period is typically discussed in terms of protecting the owners' financial interests, it serves more generally to protect "an individual's interest in maintaining the present use" of the property *(Modjeska Sign Studios v Berle, supra,* at 479).

The validity of an amortization period depends on its reasonableness *(Matter of Harbison v City of Buffalo,* 4 NY2d 553, 562-563, *supra).* We have avoided any fixed formula for determining what constitutes a reasonable period. Instead, we have held that an amortization period is presumed valid, and the owner must carry the heavy burden of overcoming that presumption by demonstrating that the loss suffered is so substantial that it outweighs the public benefit to be gained by the exercise of the police power *(Matter of Town of Islip v Caviglia,* 73 NY2d 544, 561, *supra; Modjeska Sign Studios v Berle, supra,* at 480). Using this approach, courts have declared valid a variety of amortization periods *(see,* 6 Rohan, Zoning and Land Use Controls § 41.04 [2], at 41-158). Indeed, in some circumstances, no amortization period at all is required *(see, New York State Thruway Auth. v Ashley Motor Ct.,* 10 NY2d 151; *People v Miller,* 304 NY 105). In other circumstances, the amortization period may vary in duration among the affected properties *(see, Matter of Town of Islip v Caviglia, supra).* We have also held that an amortization period may validly come to an end at the occurrence of an event as unpredictable as the destruction of the nonconforming use by fire *(see, Matter of Pelham Esplanade v Board of Trustees,* 77 NY2d 66, *supra).*

Defendant here does not challenge the local law's constitutionality under our established balancing test for amortization periods--i.e., whether the individual loss outweighs the public benefit. Instead, the challenge is a more basic due process claim: that the means of eliminating nonconforming uses is not reasonably related to the Village's legitimate interest in land use planning. More particularly, defendant makes two arguments: first, that the length of an amortization period must be related either to land use objectives or to the financial recoupment needs of the owner and, second, that the local law violates the principle that zoning is to regulate land use rather than ownership *(see, Matter of Dexter v Town Bd.,* 36 NY2d 102). Neither argument withstands analysis.

We have never required that the length of the amortization period be based on a municipality's land use objectives. To the contrary, the periods are routinely calculated to protect the rights of individual owners *at the temporary expense of* public land use objectives. Typically, the period of time allowed has been measured for reasonableness by considering whether the owners had adequate time to recoup their investment in the use *(see, e.g., Modjeska Sign Studios v Berle,* 43 NY2d 468, 474, *supra; accord, Matter of Town of Islip v Caviglia,* 73 NY2d 544, 561, *supra).* Patently, such protection of an individual's interest is unrelated to land use objectives. Indeed, were land use objectives the only permissible criteria for scheduling amortization, the law would require immediate elimination of nonconforming uses in all instances. Instead, the setting of the amortization period involves balancing the interests of the individual and those of the public. Thus, the real issue here is whether it was irrational for the Village, in striking that balance, to consider a non-financial interest of the individual owners--specifically, the individual's interest in not being displaced involuntarily.

It is significant that the six properties involved here are residential. In our previous cases dealing with amortization, we have focused almost exclusively on commercial properties, where the owner's interest is easily reduced to financial considerations. The same may not be true for the owners of residential properties, especially in instances where the property is the primary residence of the owner. Simply being able to recoup one's financial investment may be a secondary concern to staying in a neighborhood or remaining on a particular piece of land. Indeed, when mobile homes are involved, there may actually be little or no financial loss, given that the owner often will be able to relocate the structure and sell the land for legal development. Here, rather than focusing solely on financial recoupment, the Village apparently took a broader view of "an individual's interest in maintaining the present use" of the property *(see, Modjeska Sign Studios v Berle,* 43 NY2d 468, 479, *supra; see also, Matter of Taksen Liq. Store v Bonisteel,* 103 Misc 2d 34). It enacted a law that allowed owners to keep their mobile homes in place until they decided to sell, even though they may have recouped their investment long ago. By doing so, it saved the owners from a forced relocation at the end of a predetermined amortization period set by the Village. Defendant has not demonstrated why such an approach is irrational or explained why a municipality should be barred constitutionally from considering the non-financial interests of the owners in setting an amortization schedule. Thus, on this motion for summary judgment and the present record, defendant has failed to overcome the presumption of the law's validity and prove, as she must, unconstitutionality beyond a reasonable doubt *(McMinn v Town of Oyster Bay,* 66 NY2d 544, 548; *Northern Westchester Professional Park Assocs. v Town of Bedford,* 60 NY2d 492, 500).

Equally unavailing on this facial challenge is defendant's contention that the law might prevent some owners from recouping their investment. Defendant raises the hypothetical concern that in some circumstances owners might not have adequate time to recoup--for instance, if a sale took place shortly after the law's enactment. Whatever the validity of that concern, it is not relevant to this facial challenge to the law. Defendant has not claimed that she was so injured, and her argument must fall to the general principle that a litigant cannot sustain a facial challenge to a law when that law is constitutional in its application to that litigant *(see, People v Parker,* 41 NY2d 21, 24; *cf., Broadrick v Oklahoma,* 413 US 601, 610).

Defendant's second argument is premised on the "fundamental rule that zoning deals basically with land use and not with the person who owns or occupies it" *(Matter of Dexter v Town Bd.,* 36 NY2d 102, 105, *supra).* In essence, the rule is a prohibition against *ad hominem* zoning decisions. In *Dexter,* for instance, a zoning change needed to allow a supermarket was to be effective only if a certain corporation developed the site. We voided the action on the ground that the identity of the site's owner was irrelevant to its suitability for a certain type of development. Likewise, variances to accommodate the personal physical needs of the occupants have been denied on the basis that such needs are unrelated to land use *(see, Matter of Fuhst v Foley,* 45 NY2d 441). In the present case, defendant claims that the Village's amortization scheme is similarly personal in that the right to the nonconforming use is enjoyed only by those who owned the property in 1968 and cannot be transferred.

Defendant misconstrues the nature of the prohibition against *ad hominem* zoning. The hallmark of cases like *Dexter* and *Fuhst (supra)* is that an identifiable individual is singled out for special treatment in land use regulation. No such individualized treatment is involved in the present case. All similarly situated owners are treated identically. The same is true for all prospective buyers. The only preferential treatment identified by defendant is that the owner in 1968 has rights that no future owner will enjoy. But the law has long recognized the special status of those who have a preexisting use at the time land controls are adopted. Indeed, the allowance of a nonconforming use in the first instance is based on that recognition. To the extent that defendant's argument is an attack on special treatment for the owners of nonconforming uses it flies in the face of established law.

In fact, what defendant is actually arguing is that the Village should not be allowed to infringe on an owner's ability to transfer the right to continue a nonconforming use *(see, O'Connor v City of Moscow,* 69 Idaho 37, 202 P2d 401). It is true that, in the absence of amortization legislation, the right to continue a nonconforming use runs with the land *(Matter of Bexson v Board of Zoning & Appeals,* 28 AD2d 848, *affd* 21 NY2d 961; *Matter of Iazzetti v Village of Tuxedo Park,* 145 Misc 2d 78; *see also,*

4 Rathkopf, Zoning and Planning § 51.03 [1], at 51-42 [Ziegler 4th ed]). However, once a valid amortization scheme is enacted, the right ends at the termination of the amortization period. As a practical matter, that means the owner of record during the amortization period will enjoy a right that cannot be transferred to a subsequent owner once the period passes. In such circumstances, the law is not rendered invalid because the original owner no longer has a right to transfer or because the original owner and subsequent owners have received disparate treatment under the land use regulations.

Here, of course, the absence of the right at the time of transfer is not left to the happenstance of when the owner decides to sell but is an explicit part of the legislative plan. But that difference does not change the test for the validity of an amortization period. The test remains whether the period unreasonably inflicts a substantial loss on the owner or fails to comport to the reasonableness required by due process. Put simply, there is no independent requirement that the right to continue the nonconforming use be available for transfer at a given time. That is true whether the right to continue the nonconforming use is terminated by the passage of time, destruction of the use, abandonment, or as here, transfer of ownership. Thus, the mere fact that the right cannot be transferred or that later owners are treated disparately from the original owner is insufficient to sustain defendant's facial challenge to the ordinance.

Nor can we subscribe to the Appellate Division's theory that the amortization period here is unreasonable because it may be too long. In the Appellate Division's view, an open-ended amortization schedule does not reasonably advance land use objectives. The Appellate Division noted that if a corporation owned one of the mobile homes here, the amortization period would be limitless in theory. The Village answers by stating that all six mobile homes were owned by individuals, and thus amortization would end, at the latest, upon their deaths. Because the class of nonconforming users became closed at the law's enactment and will never contain more than those six, the concern about corporate ownership is unfounded, the Village argues. At this point in the litigation, defendant has not demonstrated that the Village is factually in error as to the ownership of the six units.

Of greater concern to us, the Appellate Division's rationale would seriously undermine the law of nonconforming uses. Amortization periods are the exceptions; in the absence of such schemes, owners of nonconforming uses are free to continue the uses indefinitely and transfer them to successor owners. Were the Appellate Division's rationale accepted, amortization periods would be *required* to avoid the problem of indefinite continuation of nonconforming uses. Amortization periods have never been mandatory as a matter of constitutional law, and consequently we must reject the Appellate Division's reasoning.

Thus, we conclude that defendant has failed to prevail on her facial challenge to the Village law. As to the remaining issues raised, further factual development is necessary.

Accordingly, the order of the Appellate Division should be modified, without costs, by denying defendant's cross motion for summary judgment and, as so modified, affirmed.

Chief Judge Kaye and Judges Bellacosa, Smith, Levine and Ciparick concur; Judge Titone taking no part.

Order modified, without costs, by denying defendant's cross motion for summary judgment and, as so modified, affirmed.

Note

For an opposing position, see *Pa Northwestern Distributors, Inc. v. Zoning Hearing Bd.*, 576 Pa. 186, (1991), (holding that a 90-day amortization period violated the just compensation clause of the state constitution). For a summary of cases in this area, see Jay M. Zitter, *Validity of Provisions for Amortization of Nonconforming Uses*, 8 A.L.R.5th 391 (1992).

§ 14.3.2 Fundamental Rights

Another limitation of the zoning power is when it conflicts with a challenger's fundamental rights.

Gilleo v. City of Ladue

986 F.2d 1180 (8th Cir. 1993)

A local ordinance prohibited any sign on a residence, except a sign indicating that the house was for sale. A homeowner put up a sign in the window of her home during the First Persian Gulf War. The sign stated, "For Peace in the Gulf." The court will hold that the ordinance is unconstitutional.

REAVLEY, Senior Circuit Judge.

The district court concluded that the City of Ladue's sign ordinance is unconstitutional and permanently enjoined Ladue from enforcing it, 774 F.Supp. 1564. We affirm the court's injunction * * *.

I. BACKGROUND

Ladue enacted an ordinance that prohibits most signs within the city. Ladue City Ordinance Chapter 35. The ordinance enumerates specific exceptions to the general prohibition. Ladue's stated reasons for its ordinance are: (1) to preserve the natural beauty of the community; (2) to protect the safety of residents; and (3) to maintain the value of real estate. Chapter 35, Article I ("Declaration of Findings, Policies, Interests, and Purposes").

Margaret P. Gilleo placed an 11 x 8.5 inch sign stating "For Peace in the Gulf" in the front window of her home. Gilleo was informed that her sign violated Ladue's ordinance. She filed a complaint in federal district court asserting that the ordinance violates her First Amendment right to freedom of speech. Ladue filed a counterclaim for a declaratory judgment that its ordinance is constitutional. Both parties filed motions for summary judgment. The district court entered summary judgment in favor of Gilleo, declaring the ordinance unconstitutional. The court permanently enjoined Ladue from enforcing portions of its ordinance and awarded Gilleo $74,813.25 in attorneys' fees. On appeal, Ladue challenges both the injunction and the fee award.

II. DISCUSSION

A. CONTENT-BASED RESTRICTIONS

Our method of analyzing the constitutionality of Ladue's ordinance depends on whether the ordinance is "content-neutral" or "content-based."

[The court found that the restriction was content based.]

* * *

C. CONSTITUTIONALITY OF THE CONTENT-BASED RESTRICTION

Content-based restrictions are subject to strict scrutiny. To survive strict scrutiny, content-based restrictions must be necessary to serve a compelling interest and must be narrowly drawn to achieve that end. *Simon & Schuster, Inc. v. New York Crime Victims Bd.*, 502 U.S. 105, 117, 112 S.Ct. 501, 509, 116 L.Ed.2d 476 (1991). While Ladue's interests in enacting its ordinance are substantial, *see Members of the City Council of Los Angeles v. Taxpayers for Vincent*, 466 U.S. 789, 806-07, 104 S.Ct. 2118, 2129-30, 80 L.Ed.2d 772 (1984), the interests are not sufficiently "compelling" to support a content-based restriction. With respect to the "narrowly-drawn" requirement, the content-based restriction must be the least restrictive alternative available. *See Ward*, 491 U.S. at 798 n. 6, 109 S.Ct. at 2758 n. 6. (explaining that the "narrowly-tailored" test differs according to whether the restriction is content-based or content-neutral). We have no trouble concluding that Ladue's ordinance is not the least restrictive alternative. Therefore, we affirm the district court's holding that Ladue's ordinance is unconstitutional.

* * *

D. ATTORNEYS' FEES

Pursuant to 42 U.S.C. § 1988, the district court awarded Gilleo $74,813.45 in attorneys' fees. The amount includes a 15% enhancement over the lodestar amount to compensate Gilleo's attorneys for taking the case on a contingency basis. In *City of Burlington v. Dague*, 505 U.S. 557, 565-69, 112 S.Ct. 2638, 2643-44, 120 L.Ed.2d 449 (1992), the Supreme Court held that enhancement for contingency is not permitted under certain fee-shifting statutes. Although *Dague* concerns the fee-shifting provisions of the Solid Waste Disposal Act and the Clean Water Act, the Court's analysis applies equally to § 1988. *See id.* at 562, 112 S.Ct. at 2641. We vacate the district court's 15% enhancement, thus reducing the fee award from $74,813.25 to $65,055.00.

III. CONCLUSION

Ladue's ordinance violates the First Amendment by favoring commercial speech over noncommercial * * *. We affirm the district court's permanent injunction, and reduce the court's attorneys' fee award to $65,055.00.

Note

The United States Supreme Court affirmed. *City of Ladue v. Gilleo*, 512 U.S. 43 (1994)

CHAPTER 15
TAKINGS

§ 15.1 Introduction

Our starting point for takings is the Fifth Amendment. Pay careful attention to the last clause.

Fifth Amendment, United States Constitution

No person shall be held to answer for a capital, or otherwise infamous crime, unless on a presentment or indictment of a Grand Jury, except in cases arising in the land or naval forces, or in the Militia, when in actual service in time of War or public danger; nor shall any person be subject for the same offence to be twice put in jeopardy of life or limb; nor shall be compelled in any criminal case to be a witness against himself, nor be deprived of life, liberty, or property, without due process of law; nor shall private property be taken for public use, without just compensation.

§ 15.2 Physical Takings

There are two types of takings: physical takings and regulatory takings. In physical takings, our subject at this point, the government authorizes its own agents or third persons to be on an individual's property.

§ 15.2.1 Temporary Invasions

We begin our discussion of physical takings by looking at "temporary invasions," the situation in PruneYard Shopping Center v. Robins, *below. Note that the term "temporary invasion" does not itself appear in* PruneYard. *Rather, the term is found in* Loretto v. Teleprompter Manhattan CATV Corp., *the case in the text following* PruneYard.

PruneYard Shopping Center v. Robins
447 U.S. 74 (1980)

A group of high school students attempted to distribute pro-Israel literature in a privately owned shopping mall. A mall security guard suggested the students leave, which they did.

The California Constitution, as interpreted by the California Supreme Court, Robins v. PruneYard Shopping Center, *23 Cal.3d 899 (1979), gave the public the right to come into shopping malls to exercise their free speech and petition rights. The mall owner claimed that that court decision violated his Fifth Amendment rights. The United States Supreme Court held that there was no Fifth Amendment violation.*

Mr. Justice REHNQUIST delivered the opinion of the Court.

* * *

IV

Appellants next contend that a right to exclude others underlies the Fifth Amendment guarantee against the taking of property without just compensation and the Fourteenth Amendment guarantee against the deprivation of property without due process of law.

It is true that one of the essential sticks in the bundle of property rights is the right to exclude others. *Kaiser Aetna v. United States*, 444 U.S. 164, 179-180, 100 S.Ct. 383, 392-393, 62 L.Ed.2d 332 (1979). And here there has literally been a "taking" of that right to the extent that the California Supreme Court has interpreted the State Constitution to entitle its citizens to exercise free expression and petition rights on shopping center property. But it is well established that "not every destruction or injury to property by governmental action has been held to be a 'taking' in the constitutional sense." *Armstrong v. United States*, 364 U.S. 40, 48, 80 S.Ct. 1563, 1568, 4 L.Ed.2d 1554 (1960). Rather, the determination whether a state law unlawfully infringes a landowner's property in violation of the Taking Clause requires an examination of whether the restriction on private property "forc[es] some people alone to bear public burdens which, in all fairness and justice, should be borne by the public as a whole." *Id.*, at 49, 80 S.Ct., at 1569. This examination entails inquiry into such factors as the character of the governmental action, its economic impact, and its interference with reasonable investment-backed expectations.[1] *Kaiser Aetna v. United States, supra*, at 175, 100 S.Ct., at 390. When "regulation goes too far it will be recognized as a taking." *Pennsylvania Coal Co. v. Mahon*, 260 U.S. 393, 415, 43 S.Ct. 158, 160, 67 L.Ed. 322 (1922).

Here the requirement that appellants permit appellees to exercise state-protected rights of free expression and petition on shopping center property clearly does not amount to an unconstitutional infringement of appellants' property rights under the Taking Clause. There is nothing to suggest that preventing appellants from prohibiting this sort of activity will unreasonably impair the value or use of their property as a shopping center. The PruneYard is a large commercial complex that covers several city blocks, contains numerous separate business establishments, and is open to the public at large. The decision of the California Supreme Court makes it clear that the PruneYard may restrict expressive activity by adopting time, place, and manner regulations that will minimize any interference with its commercial functions. Appellees were orderly, and they limited their activity to the common areas of the shopping center. In these

---

[1] [What exactly does the term, "reasonable investment-backed expectations," mean? The term "distinct investment backed expectations" had been used *Penn Central*. Is there a difference? See below.]

circumstances, the fact that they may have "physically invaded" appellants' property cannot be viewed as determinative.

* * *

We conclude that neither appellants' federally recognized property rights nor their First Amendment rights have been infringed by the California Supreme Court's decision recognizing a right of appellees to exercise state-protected rights of expression and petition on appellants' property. The judgment of the Supreme Court of California is therefore

Affirmed

* * *

§ 15.2.2 Permanent Occupations

We next turn to another scenario of physical takings: permanent occupations.

Loretto v. Teleprompter Manhattan CATV Corp.
458 U.S. 419 (1982)

A New York law provides that a landlord must permit a cable company to install its cable facilities on a landlord's property. In the instant case, the cable company occupied a part of the roof to install two cable boxes. Additionally, a cable wire ran down the side of the building. The landlord claimed that the law violated the Fifth Amendment. The United States Supreme Court held that there was indeed a taking.

Justice MARSHALL delivered the opinion of the Court.

* * *

When faced with a constitutional challenge to a permanent physical occupation of real property, this Court has invariably found a taking. As early as 1872, in *Pumpelly v. Green Bay Co.*, 13 Wall. (80 U.S.) 166, 20 L.Ed. 557, this Court held that the defendant's construction, pursuant to state authority, of a dam which permanently flooded plaintiff's property constituted a taking. A unanimous Court stated, without qualification, that "where real estate is actually invaded by superinduced additions of water, earth, sand, or other material, or by having any artificial structure placed on it, so as to effectually destroy or impair its usefulness, it is a taking, within the meaning of the Constitution." *Id.*, 13 Wall. (80 U.S.) at 181. * * *

Since these early cases, this Court has consistently distinguished between flooding cases involving a permanent physical occupation, on the one hand, and cases involving a more temporary invasion, or government action outside the owner's property that causes consequential damages within, on the other. A taking has always been found only in the former situation. * * *

* * *

Another recent case underscores the constitutional distinction between a permanent occupation and a temporary physical invasion. In *PruneYard Shopping Center v. Robins*, 447 U.S. 74, 100 S.Ct. 2035, 64 L.Ed.2d 741 (1980), the Court upheld a state constitutional requirement that shopping center owners permit individuals to exercise free speech and petition rights on their property, to which they had already invited the general public. The Court emphasized that the State Constitution does not prevent the owner from restricting expressive activities by imposing reasonable time, place, and manner restrictions to minimize interference with the owner's commercial functions. Since the invasion was temporary and limited in nature, and since the owner had not exhibited an interest in excluding all persons from his property, "the fact that [the solicitors] may have 'physically invaded' [the owners'] property cannot be viewed as determinative." *Id.*, at 84, 100 S.Ct., at 338.

In short, when the "character of the governmental action," *Penn Central*, 438 U.S., at 124, 98 S.Ct., at 2659, is a permanent physical occupation of property, our cases uniformly have found a taking to the extent of the occupation, without regard to whether the action achieves an important public benefit or has only minimal economic impact on the owner.

* * *

§ 15.2.3 Temporary Floodings

In PruneYard Shopping Center, *supra, the United States Supreme Court would not recognize a temporary invasion (by well-mannered high school students) as a taking. In* Loretto, *however, a permanent physical occupation was a taking. What we deal with next is whether a recurring but temporary invasion by government induced floodwaters is a taking.*

Arkansas Game and Fish Com'n v. U.S.
568 U.S. __ (2012)

The United States owns land upstream from land owned by Arkansas. At the request of farmers located downstream, the United States Army Corps of Engineers ("Corps") deviated from its own practices, set forth in its "Manual," and repeatedly and regularly over a period of six years opened a dam that it constructed and managed. Flooding and major damage to land ("Management Area") owned and managed by the Arkansas Game and Fish Commission ("Commission") ensued. Importantly, after causing damage, the floodwaters ultimately receded each time. The Commission nonetheless sued the United States for damages, alleging that the flooding was a physical taking that required compensation under the Fifth Amendment. The Supreme Court will hold that "recurrent floodings, even if of finite duration, are not categorically exempt from Takings Clause liability."

Justice GINSBURG delivered the opinion of the Court.
* * * The Commission sought compensation from the United States pursuant to the Fifth Amendment's instruction: "[N]or shall private property be taken for public use, without just compensation." The question presented is whether a taking may occur, within the meaning of the Takings Clause, when government-induced flood invasions, although repetitive, are temporary.

Ordinarily, this Court's decisions confirm, if government action would qualify as a taking when permanently continued, temporary actions of the same character may also qualify as a taking. In the instant case, the parties and the courts below divided on the appropriate classification of temporary flooding. Reversing the judgment of the Court of Federal Claims, which awarded compensation to the Commission, the Federal Circuit held, 2 to 1, that compensation may be sought only when flooding is "a permanent or inevitably recurring condition, rather than an inherently temporary situation." 637 F.3d 1366, 1378 (2011). We disagree and conclude that recurrent floodings, even if of finite duration, are not categorically exempt from Takings Clause liability.

* * *

II

The Takings Clause is "designed to bar Government from forcing some people alone to bear public burdens which, in all fairness and justice, should be borne by the public as a whole." *Armstrong v. United States,* 364 U.S. 40, 49, 80 S.Ct. 1563, 4 L.Ed.2d 1554 (1960). See also *First English Evangelical Lutheran Church of Glendale v. County of Los Angeles,* 482 U.S. 304, 318–319, 107 S.Ct. 2378, 96 L.Ed.2d 250 (1987); *Penn Central Transp. Co. v. New York City,* 438 U.S. 104, 123–125, 98 S.Ct. 2646, 57 L.Ed.2d 631 (1978). And "[w]hen the government physically takes possession of an interest in property for some public purpose, it has a categorical duty to compensate the former owner." *Tahoe–Sierra Preservation Council, Inc. v. Tahoe Regional Planning Agency,* 535 U.S. 302, 322, 122 S.Ct. 1465, 152 L.Ed.2d 517 (2002) (citing *United States v. Pewee Coal Co.,* 341 U.S. 114, 115, 71 S.Ct. 670, 95 L.Ed. 809 (1951)). These guides are fundamental in our Takings Clause jurisprudence.[2] We have recognized, however, that no magic formula enables a court to judge, in every case, whether a given government interference with property is a taking. In view of the nearly infinite variety of ways in which government actions or regulations can affect property interests, the Court has recognized few invariable rules in this area.

True, we have drawn some bright lines, notably, the rule that a permanent physical occupation of property authorized by government is a taking. *Loretto v. Teleprompter Manhattan CATV Corp.,* 458 U.S. 419, 426, 102 S.Ct. 3164, 73 L.Ed.2d 868 (1982). So, too, is a regulation that permanently requires a property owner to sacrifice all economically beneficial uses of his or her land. *Lucas v. South Carolina Coastal Council,* 505 U.S. 1003, 1019, 112 S.Ct. 2886, 120 L.Ed.2d 798 (1992).[3] But aside from the cases attended by rules of this order, most takings claims turn on situation-specific factual inquiries. See *Penn Central,* 438 U.S., at 124, 98 S.Ct. 2646. With this in mind, we turn to the question presented here—whether temporary flooding can ever give rise to a takings claim.

The Court first ruled that government-induced flooding can constitute a taking in *Pumpelly v. Green Bay Co.,* 13 Wall. 166, 20 L.Ed. 557 (1872). The Wisconsin Legislature had authorized the defendant to build a dam which led to the creation of a

---

[2] [*First English Evangelical Lutheran Church of Glendale v. County of Los Angeles, Penn Central Transp. Co. v. New York City*, and *Tahoe–Sierra Preservation Council, Inc. v. Tahoe* are reproduced later in this chapter.]

[3] [*Lucas v. South Carolina Coastal Council* is reproduced later in this chapter.]

lake, permanently submerging the plaintiff's land. The defendant argued that the land had not been taken because the government did not exercise the right of eminent domain to acquire title to the affected property. Moreover, the defendant urged, the damage was merely "a consequential result" of the dam's construction near the plaintiff's property. *Id.,* at 177. Rejecting that crabbed reading of the Takings Clause, the Court held that "where real estate is actually invaded by superinduced additions of water, earth, sand, or other material ... so as to effectually destroy or impair its usefulness, it is a taking, within the meaning of the Constitution." *Id.,* at 181.

Following *Pumpelly,* the Court recognized that seasonally recurring flooding could constitute a taking. *United States v. Cress,* 243 U.S. 316, 37 S.Ct. 380, 61 L.Ed. 746 (1917), involved the Government's construction of a lock and dam, which subjected the plaintiff's land to "intermittent but inevitably recurring overflows." *Id.,* at 328, 37 S.Ct. 380. The Court held that the regularly recurring flooding gave rise to a takings claim no less valid than the claim of an owner whose land was continuously kept under water. *Id.,* at 328–329, 37 S.Ct. 380.

Furthermore, our decisions confirm that takings temporary in duration can be compensable. This principle was solidly established in the World War II era, when "[c]ondemnation for indefinite periods of occupancy [took hold as] a practical response to the uncertainties of the Government's needs in wartime." *United States v. Westinghouse Elec. & Mfg. Co.,* 339 U.S. 261, 267, 70 S.Ct. 644, 94 L.Ed. 816 (1950). In support of the war effort, the Government took temporary possession of many properties. These exercises of government authority, the Court recognized, qualified as compensable temporary takings. See *Pewee Coal Co.,* 341 U.S. 114, 71 S.Ct. 670, 95 L.Ed. 809; *Kimball Laundry Co. v. United States,* 338 U.S. 1, 69 S.Ct. 1434, 93 L.Ed. 1765 (1949); *United States v. General Motors Corp.,* 323 U.S. 373, 65 S.Ct. 357, 89 L.Ed. 311 (1945). Notably in relation to the question before us, the takings claims approved in these cases were not confined to instances in which the Government took outright physical possession of the property involved. A temporary takings claim could be maintained as well when government action occurring outside the property gave rise to "a direct and immediate interference with the enjoyment and use of the land." *United States v. Causby,* 328 U.S. 256, 266, 66 S.Ct. 1062, 90 L.Ed. 1206 (1946) (frequent overflights from a nearby airport resulted in a taking, for the flights deprived the property owner of the customary use of his property as a chicken farm); cf. *United States v. Dickinson,* 331 U.S. 745, 751, 67 S.Ct. 1382, 91 L.Ed. 1789 (1947) (flooding of claimant's land was a taking even though claimant successfully "reclaimed most of his land which the Government originally took by flooding").

Ever since, we have rejected the argument that government action must be permanent to qualify as a taking. Once the government's actions have worked a taking of property, "no subsequent action by the government can relieve it of the duty to provide compensation for the period during which the taking was effective." *First English,* 482 U.S., at 321, 107 S.Ct. 2378. See also *Tahoe–Sierra,* 535 U.S., at 337, 122 S.Ct. 1465 ("[W]e do not hold that the temporary nature of a land-use restriction precludes finding that it effects a taking; we simply recognize that it should not be given exclusive significance one way or the other.").

Because government-induced flooding can constitute a taking of property, and because a taking need not be permanent to be compensable, our precedent indicates that government-induced flooding of limited duration may be compensable. No decision of this Court authorizes a blanket temporary-flooding exception to our Takings Clause jurisprudence, and we decline to create such an exception in this case.

III

In advocating a temporary-flooding exception, the Government relies primarily on *Sanguinetti,* 264 U.S. 146, 44 S.Ct. 264, 68 L.Ed. 608. That case involved a canal constructed by the Government connecting a slough and a river. The claimant's land was positioned between the slough and the river above the canal. The year after the canal's construction, a "flood of unprecedented severity" caused the canal to overflow onto the claimant's land; less severe flooding and overflow occurred in later years. *Id.,* at 147, 44 S.Ct. 264.

The Court held there was no taking on these facts. This outcome rested on settled principles of foreseeability and causation. The Court emphasized that the Government did not intend to flood the land or have "any reason to expect that such [a] result would follow" from construction of the canal. *Id.,* at 148, 44 S.Ct. 264. Moreover, the property was subject to seasonal flooding prior to the construction of the canal, and the landowner failed to show a causal connection between the canal and the increased flooding, which may well have been occasioned by changes in weather patterns. See *id.,* at 149, 44 S.Ct. 264 (characterizing the causal relationship asserted by the landowner as "purely conjectural"). These case-specific features were more than sufficient to dispose of the property owner's claim.

In the course of the *Sanguinetti* decision, however, the Court summarized prior flooding cases as standing for the proposition that "in order to create an enforceable liability against the Government, it is, at least, necessary that the overflow be the direct result of the structure, and constitute an actual, permanent invasion of the land." *Ibid.* The Government would have us extract from this statement a definitive rule that there can be no temporary taking caused by floods.

We do not read so much into the word "permanent" as it appears in a nondispositive sentence in *Sanguinetti*. That case, we note, was decided in 1924, well before the World War II-era cases and *First English,* in which the Court first homed in on the matter of compensation for temporary takings. That time factor, we think, renders understandable the Court's passing reference to permanence. If the Court indeed meant to express a general limitation on the Takings Clause, that limitation has been superseded by subsequent developments in our jurisprudence.

There is certainly no suggestion in *Sanguinetti* that flooding cases should be set apart from the mine run of takings claims. The sentence in question was composed to summarize the flooding cases the Court had encountered up to that point, which had unexceptionally involved permanent, rather than temporary, government-induced flooding. 264 U.S., at 149, 44 S.Ct. 264 . See *Cress,* 243 U.S., at 328, 37 S.Ct. 380; *United States v. Lynah,* 188 U.S. 445, 469, 23 S.Ct. 349, 47 L.Ed. 539 (1903). But as just explained, no distinction between permanent and temporary flooding was material to the result in *Sanguinetti.* We resist reading a single sentence unnecessary to the decision as having done so much work. In this regard, we recall Chief Justice Marshall's sage observation that "general expressions, in every opinion, are to be taken in connection with the case in which those expressions are used. If they go beyond the case, they may be respected, but ought not to control the judgment in a subsequent suit when the very point is presented for decision." *Cohens v. Virginia,* 6 Wheat. 264, 399, 5 L.Ed. 257 (1821).

***

There is thus no solid grounding in precedent for setting flooding apart from all other government intrusions on property. And the Government has presented no other persuasive reason to do so. Its primary argument is of the in for a penny, in for a pound genre: reversing the decision below, the Government worries, risks disruption of public works dedicated to flood control. "[E]very passing flood attributable to the government's operation of a flood-control project, no matter how brief," the Government hypothesizes, might qualify as a compensable taking. Brief for United States 29. To reject a categorical bar to temporary-flooding takings claims, however, is scarcely to credit all, or even many, such claims. It is of course incumbent on courts to weigh carefully the relevant factors and circumstances in each case, as instructed by our decisions. See *infra,* at 522.

***

IV

We rule today, simply and, that government-induced flooding temporary in duration gains no automatic exemption from Takings Clause inspection. When regulation or temporary physical invasion by government interferes with private property, our decisions recognize, time is indeed a factor in determining the existence *vel non* of a compensable taking. See *Loretto,* 458 U.S., at 435, n. 12, 102 S.Ct. 3164 (temporary physical invasions should be assessed by case-specific factual inquiry); *Tahoe–Sierra,* 535 U.S., at 342, 122 S.Ct. 1465 (duration of regulatory restriction is a factor for court to consider); *National Bd. of YMCA v. United States,* 395 U.S. 85, 93, 89 S.Ct. 1511, 23 L.Ed.2d 117 (1969) ("temporary, unplanned occupation" of building by troops under exigent circumstances is not a taking).

Also relevant to the takings inquiry is the degree to which the invasion is intended or is the foreseeable result of authorized government action. See *supra,* at 517; *John Horstmann Co. v. United States,* 257 U.S. 138, 146, 42 S.Ct. 58, 66 L.Ed. 171 (1921) (no takings liability when damage caused by government action could not have been foreseen).[4] See also *Ridge Line, Inc. v. United States,* 346 F.3d 1346, 1355–1356 (C.A.Fed.2003); *In re Chicago, Milwaukee, St. Paul & Pacific R. Co.,* 799 F.2d 317, 325–326 (C.A.7 1986). So, too, are the character of the land at issue and the owner's "reasonable investment-backed expectations"[5] regarding the land's use. *Palazzolo v. Rhode Island,* 533 U.S. 606, 618, 121 S.Ct. 2448, 150 L.Ed.2d 592 (2001). For example, the Management Area lies in a floodplain below a dam, and had experienced flooding in the past. But the trial court found the Area had not been exposed to flooding comparable to the 1990's accumulations in any other time span either prior to or after the construction of the Dam. See *supra,* at 516 – 517. Severity of the interference figures in the calculus as

---

[4] [One has to go back to 1921 to find foreseeability used in any Supreme Court takings case. Is the Supreme Court's reliance on foreseeability in *John Horstmann Co.* similar to the government's unpersuasive reliance on permanency in *Sanguinetti*?]

[5] [Sometimes the court uses the term "distinct investment-backed expectations," while at other times it uses the term "reasonable investment backed expectations." Is there significance to its using different terms? Are the terms the same? Is the Supreme Court itself unsure?]

well. See *Penn Central*, 438 U.S., at 130–131, 98 S.Ct. 2646; *Portsmouth Harbor Land & Hotel Co. v. United States*, 260 U.S. 327, 329–330, 43 S.Ct. 135, 67 L.Ed. 287 (1922) ("[W]hile a single act may not be enough, a continuance of them in sufficient number and for a sufficient time may prove [a taking]. Every successive trespass adds to the force of the evidence.").

The Court of Federal Claims found that the flooding the Commission assails was foreseeable. In this regard, the court noted the Commission's repeated complaints to the Corps about the destructive impact of the successive planned deviations from the Water Control Manual. Further, the court determined that the interference with the Commission's property was severe: The Commission had been deprived of the customary use of the Management Area as a forest and wildlife preserve, as the bottomland hardwood forest turned, over time, into a "headwater swamp." 87 Fed.Cl., at 610 (internal quotation marks omitted); see *supra*, at 517.

The Government, however, challenged several of the trial court's factfindings, including those relating to causation, foreseeability, substantiality, and the amount of damages. Because the Federal Circuit rested its decision entirely on the temporary duration of the flooding, it did not address those challenges. As earlier noted, see *supra*, at 521, preserved issues remain open for consideration on remand.

* * *

For the reasons stated, the judgment of the Court of Appeals for the Federal Circuit is reversed, and the case is remanded for further proceedings consistent with this opinion.

It is so ordered.

Justice KAGAN took no part in the consideration or decision of this case.

§ 15.2.4 The "Public Use" Requirement

Recall that the takings clause of the Fifth Amendment provides, "nor shall private property be taken for public use, without just compensation." We next examine what the term "public use" means.

Kelo v. City of New London, Conn.
545 U.S. 469 (2005)

The City of New London, as part of a redevelopment plan for the city, wants to use its eminent domain power to acquire a number of single-family homes in a non-blighted area. After paying the homeowners fair market value—not an issue in the litigation—the city, through a designated private nonprofit agency, would transfer the property to Pfizer, a pharmaceutical company. The homeowners claim that the taking does not satisfy the public use requirement of the Constitution because the public itself is not using the land (as it would if, for example, the land were taken for a public park or public school). The city argues that the public use requirement means not just public use, but public purpose—and the increase in jobs and tax revenues would satisfy the public purpose prerequisite. The Supreme Court holds in favor of the city.

Justice STEVENS delivered the opinion of the Court.

* * *

We granted certiorari to determine whether a city's decision to take property for the purpose of economic development satisfies the "public use" requirement of the Fifth Amendment. 542 U.S. 965, 125 S.Ct. 27, 159 L.Ed.2d 857 (2004).

III

Two polar propositions are perfectly clear. On the one hand, it has long been accepted that the sovereign may not take the property of *A* for the sole purpose of transferring it to another private party *B,* even though *A* is paid just compensation. On the other hand, it is equally clear that a State may transfer property from one private party to another if future "use by the public" is the purpose of the taking; the condemnation of land for a railroad with common-carrier duties is a familiar example. Neither of these propositions, however, determines the disposition of this case.

* * *

The disposition of this case therefore turns on the question whether the City's development plan serves a "public purpose." Without exception, our cases have defined that concept broadly, reflecting our longstanding policy of deference to legislative judgments in this field.

In *Berman v. Parker,* 348 U.S. 26, 75 S.Ct. 98, 99 L.Ed. 27 (1954), this Court upheld a redevelopment plan targeting a blighted area of Washington, D. C., in which most of the housing for the area's 5,000 inhabitants was beyond repair. Under the plan, the area would be condemned and part of it utilized for the construction of streets, schools, and other public facilities. The remainder of the land would be leased or sold to private parties for the purpose of redevelopment, including the construction of low-cost housing.

* * *

"We do not sit to determine whether a particular housing project is or is not desirable. The concept of the public welfare is broad and inclusive * * *. The values it represents are spiritual as well as physical, aesthetic as well as monetary. It is within the power of the legislature to determine that the community should be beautiful as well as healthy, spacious as well as clean, well-balanced as well as carefully patrolled. In the present case, the Congress and its authorized agencies have made determinations that take into account a wide variety of values. It is not for us to reappraise them. If those who govern the District of Columbia decide that the Nation's Capital should be beautiful as well as sanitary, there is nothing in the Fifth Amendment that stands in the way." *Id.,* at 33, 75 S.Ct. 98.

In *Hawaii Housing Authority v. Midkiff,* 467 U.S. 229, 104 S.Ct. 2321, 81 L.Ed.2d 186 (1984), the Court considered a Hawaii statute whereby fee title was taken from lessors and transferred to lessees (for just compensation) in order to reduce the concentration of land ownership. We unanimously upheld the statute and rejected the Ninth Circuit's view that it was "a naked attempt on the part of the state of Hawaii to take the property of A and transfer it to B solely for B's private use and benefit." *Id.,* at 235, 104 S.Ct. 2321 (internal quotation marks omitted). Reaffirming *Berman's* deferential approach to legislative judgments in this field, we concluded that the State's purpose of eliminating the "social and economic evils of a land oligopoly" qualified as a valid public use. 467 U.S., at 241-242, 104 S.Ct. 2321. Our opinion also rejected the contention that the mere fact that the State immediately transferred the properties to private individuals upon condemnation somehow diminished the public character of the taking. "[I]t is only the taking's purpose, and not its mechanics," we explained, that matters in determining public use. *Id.,* at 244, 104 S.Ct. 2321.

* * *

* * * For more than a century, our public use jurisprudence has wisely eschewed rigid formulas and intrusive scrutiny in favor of affording legislatures broad latitude in determining what public needs justify the use of the takings power.

IV

Those who govern the City were not confronted with the need to remove blight in the Fort Trumbull area, but their determination that the area was sufficiently distressed to justify a program of economic rejuvenation is entitled to our deference. The City has carefully formulated an economic development plan that it believes will provide appreciable benefits to the community, including-but by no means limited to-new jobs and increased tax revenue. As with other exercises in urban planning and development, the City is endeavoring to coordinate a variety of commercial, residential, and recreational uses of land, with the hope that they will form a whole greater than the sum of its parts. To effectuate this plan, the City has invoked a state statute that specifically authorizes the use of eminent domain to promote economic development. Given the comprehensive character of the plan, the thorough deliberation that preceded its adoption, and the limited scope of our review, it is appropriate for us, as it was in *Berman,* to resolve the challenges of the individual owners, not on a piecemeal basis, but rather in light of the entire plan. Because that plan unquestionably serves a public purpose, the takings challenged here satisfy the public use requirement of the Fifth Amendment.

* * *

In affirming the City's authority to take petitioners' properties, we do not minimize the hardship that condemnations may entail, notwithstanding the payment of just compensation. We emphasize that nothing in our opinion precludes any State from placing further restrictions on its exercise of the takings power. Indeed, many States already impose "public use" requirements that are stricter than the federal baseline. Some of these requirements have been established as a matter of state constitutional law, while others are expressed in state eminent domain statutes that carefully limit the grounds upon which takings may be exercised. As the submissions of the parties and their *amici* make clear, the necessity and wisdom of using eminent domain to promote economic development are certainly matters of legitimate public debate. This Court's authority, however, extends only to determining whether the City's proposed condemnations are for a "public use" within the meaning of the Fifth Amendment to the Federal Constitution. Because over a century of our case law interpreting that provision dictates an affirmative answer to that question, we may not grant petitioners the relief that they seek.

The judgment of the Supreme Court of Connecticut is affirmed.

It is so ordered.

* * *

Justice O'CONNOR, with whom THE CHIEF JUSTICE, Justice SCALIA, and Justice THOMAS join, dissenting.

* * *

* * * The logic of today's decision is that eminent domain may only be used to upgrade-not downgrade-property. At best this makes the Public Use Clause redundant with the Due Process Clause, which already prohibits irrational government action. See *Lingle,* 544 U.S. 528, 125 S.Ct. 2074. The Court rightfully admits, however, that the judiciary cannot get bogged down in predictive judgments about whether the public will actually be better off after a property transfer. In any event, this constraint has no realistic import. For who among us can say she already makes the most productive or attractive possible use of her property? The specter of condemnation hangs over all property. Nothing is to prevent the State from replacing any Motel 6 with a Ritz-Carlton, any home with a shopping mall, or any farm with a factory. Cf. *Bugryn v. Bristol,* 63 Conn.App. 98, 774 A.2d 1042 (2001) (taking the homes and farm of four owners in their 70's and 80's and giving it to an "industrial park"); *99 Cents Only Stores v. Lancaster Redevelopment Agency,* 237 F.Supp.2d 1123 (C.D.Cal.2001) (attempted taking of 99 Cents store to replace with a Costco); *Poletown Neighborhood Council v. Detroit,* 410 Mich. 616, 304 N.W.2d 455 (1981) (taking a working-class, immigrant community in Detroit and giving it to a General Motors assembly plant), overruled by *County of Wayne v. Hathcock,* 471 Mich. 445, 684 N.W.2d 765 (2004); Brief for the Becket Fund for Religious Liberty as *Amicus Curiae* 4-11 (describing takings of religious institutions' properties); Institute for Justice, D. Berliner, Public Power, Private Gain: A Five-Year, State-by-State Report Examining the Abuse of Eminent Domain (2003) (collecting accounts of economic development takings).

* * *

§ 15.3 Regulatory Takings

We now proceed to the second area of takings law: so-called regulatory takings. In these cases, the government is not physically taking anyone's property. Rather, the government is "merely" restricting the owner's use of the property. For example, the government refuses to allow a landowner to build on the land. The question in all of these cases is whether the governmental action constitutes a taking, for which the authorities must pay just compensation.

§ 15.3.1 Introduction

We begin with one of the most famous lines in takings law. Of course, the question is, when does a regulation go too far?

Pennsylvania Coal Co. v. Mahon
260 U.S. 393 (1922)

* * *

The general rule at least is that while property may be regulated to a certain extent, if regulation goes too far it will be recognized as a taking. * * *

* * *

§ 15.3.2 Economic Wipeouts of the Whole

If the government law or regulation constitutes a total economic wipeout of the landowner's property, it would be quite rational to believe that such action would amount to a taking. The next two cases examine whether this proposition is always true.

Hadacheck v. Sebastian
239 U.S. 394 (1915)

The petitioner operated a lawful brick-making business in the City of Los Angeles. Years later, with the population growing, the city enacted legislation that made it illegal to operate such a factory within the confines of the city. Notwithstanding the legislation, the petitioner continued to operate his factory. Subsequently, he was convicted of a misdemeanor for violating the ordinance. The petitioner filed a habeas corpus action in the state supreme court against the chief of police of the City of Los Angeles and argued that the city's action constituted an uncompensated taking. The United States Supreme Court will hold that the Fifth Amendment was not violated.

Mr. Justice McKenna delivered the opinion of the court:

* * *

We think the conclusion of the [state supreme] court is justified by the evidence and makes it unnecessary to review the main cases cited by petitioner in which it is decided that the police power of a state cannot be arbitrarily exercised. The principle is familiar, but in any given case it must plainly appear to apply. It is to be remembered that we are dealing with one of the most essential powers of government, one that is the least limitable. It may, indeed, seem harsh in its exercise, usually is on some individual, but the imperative necessity for its existence precludes any limitation upon it when not exerted arbitrarily. A vested interest cannot be asserted against it because of conditions once obtaining. Chicago & A. R. Co. v. Tranbarger, 238 U. S. 67, 78, 59 L. ed. 1204, 1211, 35 Sup. Ct. Rep. 678. To so hold would preclude development and fix a city forever in its primitive conditions. There must be progress, and if in its march private interests are in the way, they must yield to the good of the community. The logical result of petitioner's contention would seem to be that a city could not be formed or enlarged against the resistance of an occupant of the ground, and that if it grows at all it can only grow as the environment of the occupations that are usually banished to the purlieus.

The police power and to what extent it may be exerted we have recently illustrated in Reinman v. Little Rock, 237 U. S. 171, 59 L. ed. 900, 35 Sup. Ct. Rep. 511. The circumstances of the case were very much like those of the case at bar, and give reply to the contentions of petitioner, especially that which asserts that a necessary and lawful occupation that is not a nuisance per se cannot be made so by legislative declaration. There was a like investment in property, encouraged by the then conditions; a like reduction of value and deprivation of property was asserted against the validity of the ordinance there considered; a like assertion of an arbitrary exercise of the power of prohibition. Against all of these contentions, and causing the rejection of them all, was adduced the police power. There was a prohibition of a business, lawful in itself, there as here. It was a livery stable there; a brickyard here. They differ in particulars, but they are alike in that which cause and justify prohibition in defined localities,-that is, the effect upon the health and comfort of the community.

The ordinance passed upon prohibited the conduct of the business within a certain defined area in Little Rock, Arkansas. This court said of it: granting that the business was not a nuisance per se, it was clearly within the police power of the state to regulate it, 'and to that end to declare that in particular circumstances and in particular localities a livery stable shall be deemed a nuisance in fact and in law.' And the only limitation upon the power was stated to be that the power could not be exerted arbitrarily or with unjust discrimination. There was a citation of cases. We think the present case is within the ruling thus declared.

* * *

Judgment affirmed.

Lucas v. South Carolina Coastal Council
505 U.S. 1003 (1992)

The question before the Supreme Court is, does a governmental action that rejects a landowner's request for a building permit that consequently denies a landowner all economic or productive use constitute a regulatory taking? The court will hold that it is a taking for which the landowner must be compensated.

Justice SCALIA delivered the opinion of the Court.

In 1986, petitioner David H. Lucas paid $975,000 for two residential lots on the Isle of Palms in Charleston County, South Carolina, on which he intended to build single-family homes. In 1988, however, the South Carolina Legislature enacted the Beachfront Management Act, S.C.Code Ann. § 48-39-250 *et seq.* (Supp.1990), which had the direct effect of barring petitioner from erecting any permanent habitable structures on his two parcels. See § 48-39-290(A). A state trial court found that this prohibition rendered Lucas's parcels "valueless." App. to Pet. for Cert. 37. This case requires us to decide whether the Act's dramatic effect on the economic value of Lucas's lots accomplished a taking of private property under the Fifth and Fourteenth Amendments requiring the payment of "just compensation." U.S. Const., Amdt. 5.

* * *

III

A

* * * [O]ur decision in [*Pennsylvania Coal v. Mahon,* 260 U.S. 393, 43 S.Ct. 158, 67 L.Ed. 322 (1922)] offered little insight into when, and under what circumstances, a given regulation would be seen as going "too far" for purposes of the Fifth Amendment. In 70-odd years of succeeding "regulatory takings" jurisprudence, we have generally eschewed any " 'set formula' " for determining how far is too far, preferring to "engag [e] in * * * essentially ad hoc, factual inquiries." *Penn Central Transportation Co. v. New York City,* 438 U.S. 104, 124, 98 S.Ct. 2646, 2659, 57 L.Ed.2d 631 (1978) (quoting *Goldblatt v. Hempstead,* 369 U.S. 590, 594, 82 S.Ct. 987, 990, 8 L.Ed.2d 130 (1962)). See Epstein, Takings: Descent and Resurrection, 1987 S.Ct. Rev. 1, 4. We have, however, described at least two discrete categories of regulatory action as compensable without case-specific inquiry into the public interest advanced in support of the restraint. The first encompasses regulations that compel the property owner to suffer a physical "invasion" of his property. In general (at least with regard to permanent invasions), no matter how minute the intrusion, and no matter how weighty the public purpose behind it, we have required compensation. For example, in *Loretto v. Teleprompter Manhattan CATV Corp.,* 458 U.S. 419, 102 S.Ct. 3164, 73 L.Ed.2d 868 (1982), we determined that New York's law requiring landlords to allow television cable companies to emplace cable facilities in their apartment buildings constituted a taking, *id.,* at 435-440, 102 S.Ct., at 3175-3178, even though the facilities occupied at most only 1 1/2 cubic feet of the landlords' property, see *id.,* at 438, n. 16, 102 S.Ct., at 3177. * * *

The second situation in which we have found categorical treatment appropriate is where regulation denies all economically beneficial or productive use of land. As we have said on numerous occasions, the Fifth Amendment is violated when land-use regulation "does not substantially advance legitimate state interests *or denies an owner economically viable use of his land.*" *Agins, supra,* 447 U.S., at 260, 100 S.Ct., at 2141 (citations omitted) (emphasis added).[6]

---

[6] Regrettably, the rhetorical force of our "deprivation of all economically feasible use" rule is greater than its precision, since the rule does not make clear the "property interest" against which the loss of value is to be measured. When, for example, a regulation requires a developer to leave 90% of a rural tract in its natural state, it is unclear whether we would analyze the situation as one in which the owner has been deprived of all economically beneficial use of the burdened portion of the tract, or as one in which the owner has suffered a mere diminution in value of the tract as a whole. (For an extreme-and, we think, unsupportable-view of the relevant calculus, see *Penn Central Transportation Co. v. New York City,* 42 N.Y.2d 324, 333-334, 397 N.Y.S.2d 914, 920, 366 N.E.2d 1271, 1276-1277 (1977), aff'd, 438 U.S. 104, 98 S.Ct. 2646, 57 L.Ed.2d 631 (1978), where the state court examined the diminution in a particular parcel's value produced by a municipal ordinance in light of total value of the takings claimant's other holdings in the vicinity.) Unsurprisingly, this uncertainty regarding the composition of the denominator in our "deprivation" fraction has produced inconsistent pronouncements by the Court. Compare *Pennsylvania Coal Co. v. Mahon,* 260 U.S. 393, 414, 43 S.Ct. 158, 160, 67 L.Ed. 322 (1922) (law restricting subsurface extraction of coal held to effect a taking), with *Keystone Bituminous Coal Assn. v. DeBenedictis,* 480 U.S. 470, 497-502, 107 S.Ct. 1232, 1248-1251, 94 L.Ed.2d 472 (1987) (nearly identical law held not to effect a taking); see also *id.,* at 515-520, 107 S.Ct., at 1257-1260

* * *

Where the State seeks to sustain regulation that deprives land of all economically beneficial use, we think it may resist compensation only if the logically antecedent inquiry into the nature of the owner's estate shows that the proscribed use interests were not part of his title to begin with. This accords, we think, with our "takings" jurisprudence, which has traditionally been guided by the understandings of our citizens regarding the content of, and the State's power over, the "bundle of rights" that they acquire when they obtain title to property. It seems to us that the property owner necessarily expects the uses of his property to be restricted, from time to time, by various measures newly enacted by the State in legitimate exercise of its police powers; "[a]s long recognized, some values are enjoyed under an implied limitation and must yield to the police power." *Pennsylvania Coal Co. v. Mahon,* 260 U.S., at 413, 43 S.Ct., at 159. And in the case of personal property, by reason of the State's traditionally high degree of control over commercial dealings, he ought to be aware of the possibility that new regulation might even render his property economically worthless (at least if the property's only economically productive use is sale or manufacture for sale). See *Andrus v. Allard,* 444 U.S. 51, 66-67, 100 S.Ct. 318, 327, 62 L.Ed.2d 210 (1979) (prohibition on sale of eagle feathers). In the case of land, however, we think the notion pressed by the Council that title is somehow held subject to the "implied limitation" that the State may subsequently eliminate all economically valuable use is inconsistent with the historical compact recorded in the Takings Clause that has become part of our constitutional culture.

Where "permanent physical occupation" of land is concerned, we have refused to allow the government to decree it anew (without compensation), no matter how weighty the asserted "public interests" involved, *Loretto v. Teleprompter Manhattan CATV Corp.,* 458 U.S., at 426, 102 S.Ct., at 3171 * * * . We believe similar treatment must be accorded confiscatory regulations, *i.e.,* regulations that prohibit all economically beneficial use of land: Any limitation so severe cannot be newly legislated or decreed (without compensation), but must inhere in the title itself, in the restrictions that background principles of the State's law of property and nuisance already place upon land ownership. A law or decree with such an effect must, in other words, do no more than duplicate the result that could have been achieved in the courts-by adjacent landowners (or other uniquely affected persons) under the State's law of private nuisance, or by the State under its complementary power to abate nuisances that affect the public generally, or otherwise.

* * *

(REHNQUIST, C.J., dissenting); Rose, *Mahon* Reconstructed: Why the Takings Issue is Still a Muddle, 57 S.Cal.L.Rev. 561, 566-569 (1984). The answer to this difficult question may lie in how the owner's reasonable expectations have been shaped by the State's law of property- *i.e.,* whether and to what degree the State's law has accorded legal recognition and protection to the particular interest in land with respect to which the takings claimant alleges a diminution in (or elimination of) value. In any event, we avoid this difficulty in the present case, since the "interest in land" that Lucas has pleaded (a fee simple interest) is an estate with a rich tradition of protection at common law, and since the South Carolina Court of Common Pleas found that the Beachfront Management Act left each of Lucas's beachfront lots without economic value.

The "total taking" inquiry we require today will ordinarily entail (as the application of state nuisance law ordinarily entails) analysis of, among other things, the degree of harm to public lands and resources, or adjacent private property, posed by the claimant's proposed activities, see, *e.g.,* Restatement (Second) of Torts §§ 826, 827, the social value of the claimant's activities and their suitability to the locality in question, see, *e.g., id.,* §§ 828(a) and (b), 831, and the relative ease with which the alleged harm can be avoided through measures taken by the claimant and the government (or adjacent private landowners) alike, see, *e.g., id.,* §§ 827(e), 828(c), 830. The fact that a particular use has long been engaged in by similarly situated owners ordinarily imports a lack of any common-law prohibition (though changed circumstances or new knowledge may make what was previously permissible no longer so, see *id.,* § 827, Comment g. So also does the fact that other landowners, similarly situated, are permitted to continue the use denied to the claimant.

It seems unlikely that common-law principles would have prevented the erection of any habitable or productive improvements on petitioner's land; * * * [On remand] South Carolina must identify background principles of nuisance and property law that prohibit the uses he now intends in the circumstances in which the property is presently found. Only on this showing can the State fairly claim that, in proscribing all such beneficial uses, the Beachfront Management Act is taking nothing.

* * *

The judgment is reversed, and the case is remanded for proceedings not inconsistent with this opinion.

So ordered.

* * *

Justice BLACKMUN, dissenting.

* * *

Even more perplexing, however, is the Court's reliance on common-law principles of nuisance in its quest for a value-free takings jurisprudence. In determining what is a nuisance at common law, state courts make exactly the decision that the Court finds so troubling when made by the South Carolina General Assembly today: They determine whether the use is harmful. * * * There simply is no reason to believe that new interpretations of the hoary common-law nuisance doctrine will be particularly "objective" or "value free."[7] Once one abandons the level of generality of *sic utere tuo ut alienum non laedas, ante,* at 2901, one searches in vain, I think, for anything resembling a principle in the common law of nuisance.

* * *

---

[7] "There is perhaps no more impenetrable jungle in the entire law than that which surrounds the word 'nuisance.' It has meant all things to all people, and has been applied indiscriminately to everything from an alarming advertisement to a cockroach baked in a pie." W. Keeton, D. Dobbs, R. Keeton & D. Owen, Prosser and Keeton on The Law of Torts 616 (5th ed. 1984) (footnotes omitted). It is an area of law that "straddles the legal universe, virtually defies synthesis, and generates case law to suit every taste." W. Rodgers, Environmental Law § 2.4, p. 48 (1986) (footnotes omitted). The Court itself has noted that "nuisance concepts" are "often vague and indeterminate." *Milwaukee v. Illinois,* 451 U.S. 304, 317, 101 S.Ct. 1784, 1792, 68 L.Ed.2d 114 (1981).

§ 15.3.3 Economic Wipeouts of a Part of the Whole

Is there a taking when a law or regulation wipes out some part of the owner's property, but not the whole? That is the problem addressed in Pennsylvania Coal Co. v. Mahon.

Pennsylvania Coal Co. v. Mahon
260 U.S. 393 (1922)

Pennsylvania law recognizes three separate "estates" in land: surface rights, support rights, and mineral rights. The Pennsylvania Coal Co. sold the surface rights to Mahon, who had full knowledge that excavation by the coal company could cause his house on the land to collapse. In 1921, the state legislature enacted the Kohler Act, which prohibited removal of the support estate for mining. The question was whether this act was mere nuisance control and, thus, a valid exercise of the police power, or an uncompensated taking that violated the Fifth Amendment. The court holds it is a taking, but pay careful attention to the dissent.

        Mr. Justice HOLMES delivered the opinion of the Court.

* * *

        The statute forbids the mining of anthracite coal in such way as to cause the subsidence of, among other things, any structure used as a human habitation, with certain exceptions, including among them land where the surface is owned by the owner of the underlying coal and is distant more than one hundred and fifty feet from any improved property belonging to any other person. As applied to this case the statute is admitted to destroy previously existing rights of property and contract. The question is whether the police power can be stretched so far.

        Government hardly could go on if to some extent values incident to property could not be diminished without paying for every such change in the general law. As long recognized some values are enjoyed under an implied limitation and must yield to the police power. But obviously the implied limitation must have its limits or the contract and due process clauses are gone. One fact for consideration in determining such limits is the extent of the diminution. When it reaches a certain magnitude, in most if not in all cases there must be an exercise of eminent domain and compensation to sustain the act. So the question depends upon the particular facts. The greatest weight is given to the judgment of the legislature but it always is open to interested parties to contend that the legislature has gone beyond its constitutional power.

        This is the case of a single private house. No doubt there is a public interest even in this, as there is in every purchase and sale and in all that happens within the commonwealth. Some existing rights may be modified even in such a case. Rideout v. Knox, 148 Mass. 368, 19 N. E. 390, 2 L. R. A. 81, 12 Am. St. Rep. 560. But usually in ordinary private affairs the public interest does not warrant much of this kind of interference. A source of damage to such a house is not a public nuisance even if similar damage is inflicted on others in different places. The damage is not common or public. Wesson v. Washburn Iron Co., 13 Allen (Mass.) 95, 103, 90 Am. Dec. 181. The extent of the public interest is shown by the statute to be limited, since the statute ordinarily does not apply to land when the surface is owned by the owner of the coal. Furthermore, it is not justified as a protection of personal safety. That could be provided for by notice. Indeed the very foundation of this bill is that the defendant gave timely notice of its intent to mine under the house. On the other hand the extent of the taking is great. It purports to abolish what is recognized in Pennsylvania as an estate in land--a very valuable estate--and what is declared by the Court below to be a contract hitherto binding the plaintiffs. If we were called upon to deal with the plaintiffs' position alone we should think it clear that the statute does not disclose a public interest sufficient to warrant so extensive a destruction of the defendant's constitutionally protected rights.

But the case has been treated as one in which the general validity of the act should be discussed. The Attorney General of the State, the City of Scranton and the representatives of other extensive interests were allowed to take part in the argument below and have submitted their contentions here. It seems, therefore, to be our duty to go farther in the statement of our opinion, in order that it may be known at once, and that further suits should not be brought in vain.

It is our opinion that the act cannot be sustained as an exercise of the police power, so far as it affects the mining of coal under streets or cities in places where the right to mine such coal has been reserved. As said in a Pennsylvania case, 'For practical purposes, the right to coal consists in the right to mine it.' Commonwealth v. Clearview Coal Co., 256 Pa. 328, 331, 100 Atl. 820, L. R. A. 1917E, 672. What makes the right to mine coal valuable is that it can be exercised with profit. To make it commercially impracticable to mine certain coal has very nearly the same effect for constitutional purposes as appropriating or destroying it. This we think that we are warranted in assuming that the statute does.

It is true that in Plymouth Coal Co. v. Pennsylvania, 232 U. S. 531, 34 Sup. Ct. 359, 58 L. Ed. 713, it was held competent for the legislature to require a pillar of coal to the left along the line of adjoining property, that with the pillar on the other side of the line would be a barrier sufficient for the safety of the employees of either mine in case the other should be abandoned and allowed to fill with water. But that was a requirement for the safety of employees invited into the mine, and secured an average reciprocity of advantage[8] that has been recognized as a justification of various laws.

The rights of the public in a street purchased or laid out by eminent domain are those that it has paid for. If in any case its representatives have been so short sighted as to acquire only surface rights without the right of support we see no more authority for supplying the latter without compensation than there was for taking the right of way in the first place and refusing to pay for it because the public wanted it very much. The protection of private property in the Fifth Amendment presupposes that it is wanted for public use, but provides that it shall not be taken for such use without compensation. A similar assumption is made in the decisions upon the Fourteenth Amendment. Hairston v. Danville & Western Ry. Co., 208 U. S. 598, 605, 28 Sup. Ct. 331, 52 L. Ed. 637, 13 Ann. Cas. 1008. When this seemingly absolute protection is found to be qualified by the police power, the natural tendency of human nature is to extend the qualification more and more until at last private property disappears. But that cannot be accomplished in this way under the Constitution of the United States.

---

[8] [What does this term, "average reciprocity of advantage," mean?]

The general rule at least is that while property may be regulated to a certain extent, if regulation goes too far it will be recognized as a taking. It may be doubted how far exceptional cases, like the blowing up of a house to stop a conflagration, go-and if they go beyond the general rule, whether they do not stand as much upon tradition as upon principle. Bowditch v. Boston, 101 U. S. 16, 25 L. Ed. 980. In general it is not plain that a man's misfortunes or necessities will justify his shifting the damages to his neighbor's shoulders. Spade v. Lynn & Boston Ry. Co., 172 Mass. 488, 489, 52 N. E. 747, 43 L. R. A. 832, 70 Am. St. Rep. 298. We are in danger of forgetting that a strong public desire to improve the public condition is not enough to warrant achieving the desire by a shorter cut than the constitutional way of paying for the change. As we already have said this is a question of degree-and therefore cannot be disposed of by general propositions. But we regard this as going beyond any of the cases decided by this Court. The late decisions upon laws dealing with the congestion of Washington and New York, caused by the war, dealt with laws intended to meet a temporary emergency and providing for compensation determined to be reasonable by an impartial board. They were to the verge of the law but fell far short of the present act. Block & Hirsh, 256 U. S. 135, 41 Sup. Ct. 458, 65 L. Ed. 865, 16 A. L. R. 165; Marcus Brown Holding Co. v. Feldman, 256 U. S. 170, 41 Sup. Ct. 465, 65 L. Ed. 877; Levy Leasing Co. v. Siegel, 258 U. S. 242, 42 Sup. Ct. 289, 66 L. Ed. 595, March 20, 1922.

We assume, of course, that the statute was passed upon the conviction that an exigency existed that would warrant it, and we assume that an exigency exists that would warrant the exercise of eminent domain. But the question at bottom is upon whom the loss of the changes desired should fall. So far as private persons or communities have seen fit to take the risk of acquiring only surface rights, we cannot see that the fact that their risk has become a danger warrants the giving to them greater rights than they bought.

Decree reversed.

Mr. Justice BRANDEIS dissenting.

* * *

It is said that one fact for consideration in determining whether the limits of the police power have been exceeded is the extent of the resulting diminution in value, and that here the restriction destroys existing rights of property and contract. But values are relative. If we are to consider the value of the coal kept in place by the restriction, we should compare it with the value of all other parts of the land. That is, with the value not of the coal alone, but with the value of the whole property. The rights of an owner as against the public are not increased by dividing the interests in his property into surface and subsoil. The sum of the rights in the parts can not be greater than the rights in the whole. The estate of an owner in land is grandiloquently described as extending ab orco usque ad coelum. But I suppose no one would contend that by selling his interest above 100 feet from the surface he could prevent the state from limiting, by the police power, the height of structures in a city. And why should a sale of underground rights bar the state's power? For aught that appears the value of the coal kept in place by the restriction may be negligible as compared with the value of the whole property, or even as compared with that part of it which is represented by the coal remaining in place and which may be extracted despite the statute. * * *

* * *

Keystone Bituminous Coal Ass'n v. DeBenedictis
480 U.S. 470 (1987)

On facts that were virtually the same as Mahon, *the United States Supreme Court found that Pennsylvania's Subsidence Act does not affect a taking.*

Justice STEVENS, delivered the opinion of the Court.

In *Pennsylvania Coal Co. v. Mahon,* 260 U.S. 393, 43 S.Ct. 158, 67 L.Ed. 322 (1922), the Court reviewed the constitutionality of a Pennsylvania statute that admittedly destroyed "previously existing rights of property and contract." *Id.,* at 413, 43 S.Ct., at 159. * * *

* * *

The Public Purpose

Unlike the Kohler Act, which was passed upon in *Pennsylvania Coal,* the Subsidence Act does not merely involve a balancing of the private economic interests of coal companies against the private interests of the surface owners. The Pennsylvania Legislature specifically found that important public interests are served by enforcing a policy that is designed to minimize subsidence in certain areas. * * *

* * *

Diminution of Value and Investment-Backed Expectations

* * *

Because our test for regulatory taking requires us to compare the value that has been taken from the property with the value that remains in the property, one of the critical questions is determining how to define the unit of property "whose value is to furnish the denominator of the fraction." Michelman, Property, Utility, and Fairness: Comments on the Ethical Foundations of "Just Compensation" Law, 80 Harv.L.Rev. 1165, 1192 (1967). In *Penn Central* the Court explained:

" 'Taking' jurisprudence does not divide a single parcel into discrete segments and attempt to determine whether rights in a particular segment have been entirely abrogated. In deciding whether a particular governmental action has effected a taking, this Court focuses rather both on the character of the action and on the nature of the interference with rights *in the parcel as a whole* -here the city tax block designated as the 'landmark site.' " 438 U.S., at 130-131, 98 S.Ct., at 2662.

* * *

The judgment of the Court of Appeals is
Affirmed.

Chief Justice REHNQUIST, with whom Justice POWELL, Justice O'CONNOR, and Justice SCALIA join, dissenting.

* * *

A

The Court's conclusion that the restriction on particular coal does not work a taking is primarily the result of its view that the 27 million tons of coal in the ground "do not constitute a separate segment of property for takings law purposes." *Ante,* at 1248. This conclusion cannot be based on the view that the interests are too insignificant to warrant protection by the Fifth Amendment, for it is beyond cavil that government appropriation of "relatively small amounts of private property for its own use" requires just compensation. Instead, the Court's refusal to recognize the coal in the ground as a separate segment of property for takings purposes is based on the fact that the alleged taking is "regulatory," rather than a physical intrusion. On the facts of this case, I cannot see how the label placed on the government's action is relevant to consideration of its impact on property rights. * * *

* * *

Tahoe-Sierra Preservation Council, Inc. v. Tahoe Regional Planning Agency
535 U.S. 302 (2002)

The issue before the Supreme Court is whether a building moratorium for a period of time (32 months) constitutes a total economic wipeout for that period, thus requiring compensation under the Fifth Amendment. The court holds that it does not.

Justice STEVENS delivered the opinion of the Court.

The question presented is whether a moratorium on development imposed during the process of devising a comprehensive land-use plan constitutes a *per se* taking of property requiring compensation under the Takings Clause of the United States Constitution. This case actually involves two moratoria ordered by respondent Tahoe Regional Planning Agency (TRPA) to maintain the status quo while studying the impact of development on Lake Tahoe and designing a strategy for environmentally sound growth. The first, Ordinance 81-5, was effective from August 24, 1981, until August 26, 1983, whereas the second more restrictive Resolution 83-21 was in effect from August 27, 1983, until April 25, 1984. As a result of these two directives, virtually all development on a substantial portion of the property subject to TRPA's jurisdiction was prohibited for a period of 32 months. * * *

* * *

Contrary to the District Court, the Court of Appeals held that because the regulations had only a temporary impact on petitioners' fee interest in the properties, no categorical taking had occurred. * * *

* * *

The categorical rule that we applied in *Lucas* states that compensation is required when a regulation deprives an owner of "*all* economically beneficial uses" of his land. *Id.,* at 1019, 112 S.Ct. 2886. Under that rule, a statute that "wholly eliminated the value" of Lucas' fee simple title clearly qualified as a taking. But our holding was limited to "the extraordinary circumstance when *no* productive or economically beneficial use of land is permitted." *Id.,* at 1017, 112 S.Ct. 2886. The emphasis on the word "no" in the text of the opinion was, in effect, reiterated in a footnote explaining that the categorical rule would not apply if the diminution in value were 95% instead of 100%. *Id.,* at 1019, n. 8, 112 S.Ct. 2886. Anything less than a "complete elimination of value," or a "total loss," the Court acknowledged, would require the kind of analysis applied in *Penn Central. Lucas,* 505 U.S., at 1019-1020, n. 8, 112 S.Ct. 2886.

Certainly, our holding that the permanent "obliteration of the value" of a fee simple estate constitutes a categorical taking does not answer the question whether a regulation prohibiting any economic use of land for a 32-month period has the same legal effect. Petitioners seek to bring this case under the rule announced in *Lucas* by arguing that we can effectively sever a 32-month segment from the remainder of each landowner's fee simple estate, and then ask whether that segment has been taken in its entirety by the moratoria. Of course, defining the property interest taken in terms of the very regulation being challenged is circular. With property so divided, every delay would become a total ban; the moratorium and the normal permit process alike would constitute categorical takings. Petitioners' "conceptual severance" argument is unavailing because it ignores *Penn Central's* admonition that in regulatory takings cases we must focus on "the parcel as a whole." 438 U.S., at 130-131, 98 S.Ct. 2646. We have consistently rejected such an approach to the "denominator" question. See *Keystone,* 480 U.S., at 497, 107 S.Ct. 1232. * * *

An interest in real property is defined by the metes and bounds that describe its geographic dimensions and the term of years that describes the temporal aspect of the owner's interest. See Restatement of Property §§ 7-9 (1936). Both dimensions must be considered if the interest is to be viewed in its entirety. Hence, a permanent deprivation of the owner's use of the entire area is a taking of "the parcel as a whole," whereas a temporary restriction that merely causes a diminution in value is not. Logically, a fee simple estate cannot be rendered valueless by a temporary prohibition on economic use, because the property will recover value as soon as the prohibition is lifted. Cf. *Agins v. City of Tiburon,* 447 U.S., at 263, n. 9, 100 S.Ct. 2138 ("Even if the appellants' ability to sell their property was limited during the pendency of the condemnation proceeding, the appellants were free to sell or develop their property when the proceedings ended. Mere fluctuations in value during the process of governmental decision-making, absent extraordinary delay, are 'incidents of ownership. They cannot be considered as a "taking" in the constitutional sense' " (quoting *Danforth v. United States,* 308 U.S. 271, 285, 60 S.Ct. 231, 84 L.Ed. 240 (1939)).

* * *

More importantly, for reasons set out at some length by Justice O'CONNOR in her concurring opinion in *Palazzolo v. Rhode Island,* 533 U.S., at 636, 121 S.Ct. 2448, we are persuaded that the better approach to claims that a regulation has effected a temporary taking "requires careful examination and weighing of all the relevant circumstances." In that opinion, Justice O'CONNOR specifically considered the role that the "temporal relationship between regulatory enactment and title acquisition" should play in the analysis of a takings claim. *Id.,* at 632, 121 S.Ct. 2448. We have no occasion to address that particular issue in this case, because it involves a different temporal relationship—the distinction between a temporary restriction and one that is permanent. Her comments on the "fairness and justice" inquiry are, nevertheless, instructive:

"Today's holding does not mean that the timing of the regulation's enactment relative to the acquisition of title is immaterial to the *Penn Central* analysis. Indeed, it would be just as much error to expunge this consideration from the takings inquiry as it would be to accord it exclusive significance. Our polestar instead remains the principles set forth in *Penn Central* itself and our other cases that govern partial regulatory takings. Under these cases, interference with investment-backed expectations is one of a number of factors that a court must examine. ...

"The Fifth Amendment forbids the taking of private property for public use without just compensation. We have recognized that this constitutional guarantee is ' "designed to bar Government from forcing some people alone to bear public burdens which, in all fairness and justice, should be borne by the public as a whole." ' *Penn Central,* [438 U.S.], at 123–124[, 98 S.Ct. 2646] (quoting *Armstrong v. United States,* 364 U.S. 40, 49[, 80 S.Ct. 1563, 4 L.Ed.2d 1554] (1960)). The concepts of 'fairness and justice' that underlie the Takings Clause, of course, are less than fully determinate. Accordingly, we have eschewed 'any "set formula" for determining when "justice and fairness" require that economic injuries caused by public action be compensated by the government, rather than remain disproportionately concentrated on a few persons.' *Penn Central, supra,* at 124[, 98 S.Ct. 2646] (quoting *Goldblatt v. Hempstead,* 369 U.S. 590, 594[, 82 S.Ct. 987, 8 L.Ed.2d 130] (1962)). The outcome instead 'depends largely "upon the particular circumstances [in that] case.' " *Penn Central, supra,* at 124[, 98 S.Ct. 2646] (quoting *United States v. Central Eureka Mining Co.,* 357 U.S. 155, 168[, 78 S.Ct. 1097, 2 L.Ed.2d 1228] (1958))." *Id.,* at 633, 121 S.Ct. 2448.

In rejecting petitioners' *per se* rule, we do not hold that the temporary nature of a land-use restriction precludes finding that it effects a taking; we simply recognize that it should not be given exclusive significance one way or the other.

A narrower rule that excluded the normal delays associated with processing permits, or that covered only delays of more than a year, would certainly have a less severe impact on prevailing practices, but it would still impose serious financial constraints on the planning process. Unlike the "extraordinary circumstance" in which the government deprives a property owner of all economic use, *Lucas,* 505 U.S., at 1017, 112 S.Ct. 2886, moratoria like Ordinance 81–5 and Resolution 83–21 are used widely among land-use planners to preserve the status quo while formulating a more permanent development strategy. In fact, the consensus in the planning community appears to be that moratoria, or "interim development controls" as they are often called, are an essential tool of successful development. Yet even the weak version of petitioners' categorical rule would treat these interim measures as takings regardless of the good faith of the planners, the reasonable expectations of the landowners, or the actual impact of the moratorium on property values.

* * *

We conclude, therefore, that the interest in "fairness and justice" will be best served by relying on the familiar *Penn Central* approach[9] when deciding cases like this, rather than by attempting to craft a new categorical rule.

Accordingly, the judgment of the Court of Appeals is affirmed.

---

[9] [*Penn Central* is the next case in this text.]

It is so ordered.

Chief Justice REHNQUIST, with whom Justice SCALIA and Justice THOMAS join, dissenting.

* * *

Justice THOMAS, with whom Justice SCALIA joins, dissenting.

I join THE CHIEF JUSTICE's dissent. I write separately to address the majority's conclusion that the temporary moratorium at issue here was not a taking because it was not a "taking of 'the parcel as a whole.' " * * * While this questionable rule[10] has been applied to various alleged regulatory takings, it was, in my view, rejected in the context of *temporal* deprivations of property by *First English Evangelical Lutheran Church of Glendale v. County of Los Angeles,* 482 U.S. 304, 318, 107 S.Ct. 2378, 96 L.Ed.2d 250 (1987),[11] which held that temporary and permanent takings "are not different in kind" when a landowner is deprived of all beneficial use of his land. I had thought that *First English* put to rest the notion that the "relevant denominator" is land's infinite life. Consequently, a regulation effecting a total deprivation of the use of a so-called "temporal slice" of property is compensable under the Takings Clause unless background principles of state property law prevent it from being deemed a taking; "total deprivation of use is, from the landowner's point of view, the equivalent of a physical appropriation." *Lucas v. South Carolina Coastal Council,* 505 U.S. 1003, 1017, 112 S.Ct. 2886, 120 L.Ed.2d 798 (1992).

* * *

I would hold that regulations prohibiting all productive uses of property are subject to *Lucas' per se* rule, regardless of whether the property so burdened retains theoretical useful life and value if, and when, the "temporary" moratorium is lifted. To my mind, such potential future value bears on the amount of compensation due and has nothing to do with the question whether there was a taking in the first place. It is regrettable that the Court has charted a markedly different path today.

§ 15.3.4 An "Ad Hoc" Analysis Approach

Another approach to determining whether a regulation "goes too far" and, therefore, is a taking, is a balancing approach. The inauguration of this approach came in Penn Cent. Trasp. Co. v. City of New York, *infra. As with any balancing test, this approach is not as definitive as the test in* Loretto *or* Lucas.

---

[10] The majority's decision to embrace the "parcel as a whole" doctrine as *settled* is puzzling. See, *e.g., Palazzolo v. Rhode Island,* 533 U.S. 606, 631, 121 S.Ct. 2448, 150 L.Ed.2d 592 (2001) (noting that the Court has "at times expressed discomfort with the logic of [the parcel as a whole] rule"); *Lucas v. South Carolina Coastal Council,* 505 U.S. 1003, 1017, n. 7, 112 S.Ct. 2886, 120 L.Ed.2d 798 (1992) (recognizing that "uncertainty regarding the composition of the denominator in [the Court's] 'deprivation' fraction has produced inconsistent pronouncements by the Court," and that the relevant calculus is a "difficult question").

[11] [*First English* is reproduced, infra.]

Penn Cent. Transp. Co. v. City of New York
438 U.S. 104 (1978)

The owners of a New York City landmark—Grand Central Station—want to build vertically. A New York City ordinance prohibits such construction. The owners contend that such a law, one that prohibits expanding a building vertically, acts as a taking because their air rights will be eliminated. The United States Supreme Court will hold that there is no taking. In so holding, the court will articulate what has become known as the Penn Central Ad Hoc Analysis.

Mr. Justice BRENNAN delivered the opinion of the Court.

The question presented is whether a city may, as part of a comprehensive program to preserve historic landmarks and historic districts, place restrictions on the development of individual historic landmarks-in addition to those imposed by applicable zoning ordinances-without effecting a "taking" requiring the payment of "just compensation." Specifically, we must decide whether the application of New York City's Landmarks Preservation Law to the parcel of land occupied by Grand Central Terminal has "taken" its owners' property in violation of the Fifth and Fourteenth Amendments. [The law in question precluded building onto Grand Central Terminal, an 8-story landmark, to make it a 55-story office building.]

* * *

Although the designation of a landmark and landmark site restricts the owner's control over the parcel, designation also enhances the economic position of the landmark owner in one significant respect. Under New York City's zoning laws, owners of real property who have not developed their property to the full extent permitted by the applicable zoning laws are allowed to transfer development rights to contiguous parcels on the same city block. See New York City, Zoning Resolution Art. I, ch. 2, § 12-10 (1978) (definition of "zoning lot"). A 1968 ordinance gave the owners of landmark sites additional opportunities to transfer development rights to other parcels. Subject to a restriction that the floor area of the transferee lot may not be increased by more than 20% above its authorized level, the ordinance permitted transfers from a landmark parcel to property across the street or across a street intersection. In 1969, the law governing the conditions under which transfers from landmark parcels could occur was liberalized, see New York City Zoning Resolutions 74-79 to 74-793, apparently to ensure that the Landmarks Law would not unduly restrict the development options of the owners of Grand Central Terminal.

* * *

The issues presented by appellants are (1) whether the restrictions imposed by New York City's law upon appellants' exploitation of the Terminal site effect a "taking" of appellants' property for a public use within the meaning of the Fifth Amendment, which of course is made applicable to the States through the Fourteenth Amendment, see *Chicago, B. & Q. R. Co. v. Chicago*, 166 U.S. 226, 239, 17 S.Ct. 581, 585, 41 L.Ed. 979 (1897), and, (2), if so, whether the transferable development rights afforded appellants constitute "just compensation" within the meaning of the Fifth Amendment. We need only address the question whether a "taking" has occurred.[12]

Before considering appellants' specific contentions, it will be useful to review the factors that have shaped the jurisprudence of the Fifth Amendment injunction "nor shall private property be taken for public use, without just compensation." The question of what constitutes a "taking" for purposes of the Fifth Amendment has proved to be a problem of considerable difficulty. While this Court has recognized that the "Fifth Amendment's guarantee . . . [is] designed to bar Government from forcing some people alone to bear public burdens which, in all fairness and justice, should be borne by the public as a whole," *Armstrong v. United States*, 364 U.S. 40, 49, 80 S.Ct. 1563, 1569, 4 L.Ed.2d 1554 (1960), this Court, quite simply, has been unable to develop any "set formula" for determining when "justice and fairness" require that economic injuries caused by public action be compensated by the government, rather than remain disproportionately concentrated on a few persons. See *Goldblatt v. Hempstead*, 369 U.S. 590, 594, 82 S.Ct. 987, 990, 8 L.Ed.2d 130 (1962). Indeed, we have frequently observed that whether a particular restriction will be rendered invalid by the government's failure to pay for any losses proximately caused by it depends largely "upon the particular circumstances [in that] case." *United States v. Central Eureka Mining Co.*, 357 U.S. 155, 168, 78 S.Ct. 1097, 1104, 2 L.Ed.2d 1228 (1958); see *United States v. Caltex, Inc.*, 344 U.S. 149, 156, 73 S.Ct. 200, 203, 97 L.Ed. 157 (1952).

In engaging in these essentially ad hoc, factual inquiries, the Court's decisions have identified several factors that have particular significance. The economic impact of the regulation on the claimant and, particularly, the extent to which the regulation has interfered with distinct investment-backed expectations are, of course, relevant considerations. See *Goldblatt v. Hempstead, supra*, 369 U.S., at 594, 82 S.Ct., at 990. So, too, is the character of the governmental action. A "taking" may more readily be found when the interference with property can be characterized as a physical invasion by government, see, *e. g., United States v. Causby*, 328 U.S. 256, 66 S.Ct. 1062, 90 L.Ed. 1206 (1946), than when interference arises from some public program adjusting the benefits and burdens of economic life to promote the common good.

"Government hardly could go on if to some extent values incident to property could not be diminished without paying for every such change in the general law," *Pennsylvania Coal Co. v. Mahon*, 260 U.S. 393, 413, 43 S.Ct. 158, 159, 67 L.Ed. 322 (1922), and this Court has accordingly recognized, in a wide variety of contexts, that government may execute laws or programs that adversely affect recognized economic values. Exercises of the taxing power are one obvious example. A second are the decisions in which this Court has dismissed "taking" challenges on the ground that, while the challenged government action caused economic harm, it did not interfere with interests that were sufficiently bound up with the reasonable expectations of the claimant to constitute "property" for Fifth Amendment purposes. See, *e. g., United States v. Willow River Power Co.*, 324 U.S. 499, 65 S.Ct. 761, 89 L.Ed. 1101 (1945) (interest in high-water level of river for runoff for tailwaters to maintain power head is not property); *United States v. Chandler-Dunbar Water Power Co.*, 229 U.S. 53, 33 S.Ct. 667, 57 L.Ed.

---

[12] As is implicit in our opinion, we do not embrace the proposition that a "taking" can never occur unless government has transferred physical control over a portion of a parcel.

1063 (1913) (no property interest can exist in navigable waters); see also *Demorest v. City Bank Co.,* 321 U.S. 36, 64 S.Ct. 384, 88 L.Ed. 526 (1944); *Muhlker v. Harlem R. Co.,* 197 U.S. 544, 25 S.Ct. 522, 49 L.Ed. 872 (1905); Sax, Takings and the Police Power, 74 Yale L.J. 36, 61–62 (1964).

More importantly for the present case, in instances in which a state tribunal reasonably concluded that "the health, safety, morals, or general welfare" would be promoted by prohibiting particular contemplated uses of land, this Court has upheld land-use regulations that destroyed or adversely affected recognized real property interests. See *Nectow v. Cambridge,* 277 U.S. 183, 188, 48 S.Ct. 447, 448, 72 L.Ed. 842 (1928). Zoning laws are, of course, the classic example, see *Euclid v. Ambler Realty Co.,* 272 U.S. 365, 47 S.Ct. 114, 71 L.Ed. 303 (1926) (prohibition of industrial use); *Gorieb v. Fox,* 274 U.S. 603, 608, 47 S.Ct. 675, 677, 71 L.Ed. 1228 (1927) (requirement that portions of parcels be left unbuilt); *Welch v. Swasey,* 214 U.S. 91, 29 S.Ct. 567, 53 L.Ed. 923 (1909) (height restriction), which have been viewed as permissible governmental action even when prohibiting the most beneficial use of the property. See *Goldblatt v. Hempstead, supra,* 369 U.S., at 592–593, 82 S.Ct., at 988–989, and cases cited; see also *Eastlake v. Forest City Enterprises, Inc.,* 426 U.S. 668, 674, n. 8, 96 S.Ct. 2358, 2362 n. 8, 49 L.Ed.2d 132 (1976).

Zoning laws generally do not affect existing uses of real property, but "taking" challenges have also been held to be without merit in a wide variety of situations when the challenged governmental actions prohibited a beneficial use to which individual parcels had previously been devoted and thus caused substantial individualized harm. *Miller v. Schoene,* 276 U.S. 272, 48 S.Ct. 246, 72 L.Ed. 568 (1928), is illustrative. In that case, a state entomologist, acting pursuant to a state statute, ordered the claimants to cut down a large number of ornamental red cedar trees because they produced cedar rust fatal to apple trees cultivated nearby. Although the statute provided for recovery of any expense incurred in removing the cedars, and permitted claimants to use the felled trees, it did not provide compensation for the value of the standing trees or for the resulting decrease in market value of the properties as a whole. A unanimous Court held that this latter omission did not render the statute invalid. The Court held that the State might properly make "a choice between the preservation of one class of property and that of the other" and since the apple industry was important in the State involved, concluded that the State had not exceeded "its constitutional powers by deciding upon the destruction of one class of property [without compensation] in order to save another which, in the judgment of the legislature, is of greater value to the public." *Id.,* at 279, 48 S.Ct., at 247.

Again, *Hadacheck v. Sebastian,* 239 U.S. 394, 36 S.Ct. 143, 60 L.Ed. 348 (1915), upheld a law prohibiting the claimant from continuing his otherwise lawful business of operating a brickyard in a particular physical community on the ground that the legislature had reasonably concluded that the presence of the brickyard was inconsistent with neighboring uses. See also *United States v. Central Eureka Mining Co., supra* (Government order closing gold mines so that skilled miners would be available for other mining work held not a taking); *Atchison, T. & S. F. R. Co. v. Public Utilities Comm'n,* 346 U.S. 346, 74 S.Ct. 92, 98 L.Ed. 51 (1953) (railroad may be required to share cost of constructing railroad grade improvement); *Walls v. Midland Carbon Co.,* 254 U.S. 300, 41 S.Ct. 118, 65 L.Ed. 276 (1920) (law prohibiting manufacture of carbon black upheld); *Reinman v. Little Rock,* 237 U.S. 171, 35 S.Ct. 511, 59 L.Ed. 900 (1915) (law prohibiting livery stable upheld); *Mugler v. Kansas,* 123 U.S. 623, 8 S.Ct. 273, 31 L.Ed. 205 (1887) (law prohibiting liquor business upheld).

* * *

Pennsylvania Coal Co. v. Mahon, 260 U.S. 393, 43 S.Ct. 158, 67 L.Ed. 322 (1922), is the leading case for the proposition that a state statute that substantially furthers important public policies may so frustrate distinct investment-backed expectations as to amount to a "taking." There the claimant had sold the surface rights to particular parcels of property, but expressly reserved the right to remove the coal thereunder. A Pennsylvania statute, enacted after the transactions, forbade any mining of coal that caused the subsidence of any house, unless the house was the property of the owner of the underlying coal and was more than 150 feet from the improved property of another. Because the statute made it commercially impracticable to mine the coal, *id.,* at 414, 43 S.Ct., at 159, and thus had nearly the same effect as the complete destruction of rights claimant had reserved from the owners of the surface land, see *id.,* at 414–415, 43 S.Ct., at 159–160, the Court held that the statute was invalid as effecting a "taking" without just compensation. See also *Armstrong v. United States,* 364 U.S. 40, 80 S.Ct. 1563, 4 L.Ed.2d 1554 (1960) (Government's complete destruction of a materialman's lien in certain property held a "taking"); *Hudson Water Co. v. McCarter,* 209 U.S. 349, 355, 28 S.Ct. 529, 531, 52 L.Ed. 828 (1908) (if height restriction makes property wholly useless "the rights of property . . . prevail over the other public interest" and compensation is required). See generally Michelman, Property, Utility, and Fairness: Comments on the Ethical Foundations of "Just Compensation" Law, 80 Harv.L.Rev. 1165, 1229–1234 (1967).

* * *

B

In contending that the New York City law has "taken" their property in violation of the Fifth and Fourteenth Amendments, appellants make a series of arguments, which, while tailored to the facts of this case, essentially urge that any substantial restriction imposed pursuant to a landmark law must be accompanied by just compensation if it is to be constitutional. Before considering these, we emphasize what is not in dispute. Because this Court has recognized, in a number of settings, that States and cities may enact land-use restrictions or controls to enhance the quality of life by preserving the character and desirable aesthetic features of a city, see *New Orleans v. Dukes,* 427 U.S. 297, 96 S.Ct. 2513, 49 L.Ed.2d 511 (1976); *Young v. American Mini Theatres, Inc.,* 427 U.S. 50, 96 S.Ct. 2440, 49 L.Ed.2d 310 (1976); *Village of Belle Terre v. Boraas,* 416 U.S. 1, 9–10, 94 S.Ct. 1536, 39 L.Ed.2d 797 (1974); *Berman v. Parker,* 348 U.S. 26, 33, 75 S.Ct. 98, 102, 99 L.Ed. 27 (1954); *Welch v. Swasey,* 214 U.S., at 108, 29 S.Ct., at 571, appellants do not contest that New York City's objective of preserving structures and areas with special historic, architectural, or cultural significance is an entirely permissible governmental goal. They also do not dispute that the restrictions imposed on its parcel are appropriate means of securing the purposes of the New York City law. Finally, appellants do not challenge any of the specific factual premises of the decision below. They accept for present purposes both that the parcel of land occupied by Grand Central Terminal must, in its present state, be regarded as capable of earning a reasonable return, and that the transferable development rights afforded appellants by virtue of the Terminal's designation as a landmark are valuable, even if not as valuable as the rights to construct above the Terminal. In appellants' view none of these factors derogate from their claim that New York City's law has effected a "taking."

They first observe that the airspace above the Terminal is a valuable property interest, citing *United States v. Causby, supra.* They urge that the Landmarks Law has deprived them of any gainful use of their "air rights" above the Terminal and that, irrespective of the value of the remainder of their parcel, the city has "taken" their right to this superadjacent airspace, thus entitling them to "just compensation" measured by the fair market value of these air rights.

Apart from our own disagreement with appellants' characterization of the effect of the New York City law, see *infra,* at 2665, the submission that appellants may establish a "taking" simply by showing that they have been denied the ability to exploit a property interest that they heretofore had believed was available for development is quite simply untenable. Were this the rule, this Court would have erred not only in upholding laws restricting the development of air rights, see *Welch v. Swasey, supra,* but also in approving those prohibiting both the subjacent, see *Goldblatt v. Hempstead,* 369 U.S. 590, 82 S.Ct. 987, 8 L.Ed.2d 130 (1962), and the lateral, see *Gorieb v. Fox,* 274 U.S. 603, 47 S.Ct. 675, 71 L.Ed. 1228 (1927), development of particular parcels.[13] "Taking" jurisprudence does not divide a single parcel into discrete segments and attempt to determine whether rights in a particular segment have been entirely abrogated. In deciding whether a particular governmental action has effected a taking, this Court focuses rather both on the character of the action and on the nature and extent of the interference with rights in the parcel as a whole—here, the city tax block designated as the "landmark site."

Secondly, appellants, focusing on the character and impact of the New York City law, argue that it effects a "taking" because its operation has significantly diminished the value of the Terminal site. Appellants concede that the decisions sustaining other land-use regulations, which, like the New York City law, are reasonably related to the promotion of the general welfare, uniformly reject the proposition that diminution in property value, standing alone, can establish a "taking," see *Euclid v. Ambler Realty Co.,* 272 U.S. 365, 47 S.Ct. 114, 71 L.Ed. 303 (1926) (75% diminution in value caused by zoning law); *Hadacheck v. Sebastian,* 239 U.S. 394, 36 S.Ct. 143, 60 L.Ed. 348 (1915) (87 1/2 % diminution in value); cf. *Eastlake v. Forest City Enterprises, Inc.,* 426 U.S., at 674 n. 8, 96 S.Ct., at 2362 n. 8, and that the "taking" issue in these contexts is resolved by focusing on the uses the regulations permit. See also *Goldblatt v. Hempstead, supra.* Appellants, moreover, also do not dispute that a showing of diminution in property value would not establish a taking if the restriction had been imposed as a result of historic-district legislation, see generally *Maher v. New Orleans,* 516 F.2d 1051 (CA5 1975), but

---

[13] These cases dispose of any contention that might be based on *Pennsylvania Coal Co. v. Mahon,* 260 U.S. 393, 43 S.Ct. 158, 67 L.Ed. 322 (1922), that full use of air rights is so bound up with the investment-backed expectations of appellants that governmental deprivation of these rights invariably— *i. e.,* irrespective of the impact of the restriction on the value of the parcel as a whole—constitutes a "taking." Similarly, *Welch, Goldblatt,* and *Gorieb* illustrate the fallacy of appellants' related contention that a "taking" must be found to have occurred whenever the land-use restriction may be characterized as imposing a "servitude" on the claimant's parcel.

appellants argue that New York City's regulation of individual landmarks is fundamentally different from zoning or from historic-district legislation because the controls imposed by New York City's law apply only to individuals who own selected properties.

Stated baldly, appellants' position appears to be that the only means of ensuring that selected owners are not singled out to endure financial hardship for no reason is to hold that any restriction imposed on individual landmarks pursuant to the New York City scheme is a "taking" requiring the payment of "just compensation." Agreement with this argument would, of course, invalidate not just New York City's law, but all comparable landmark legislation in the Nation. We find no merit in it.

It is true, as appellants emphasize, that both historic-district legislation and zoning laws regulate all properties within given physical communities whereas landmark laws apply only to selected parcels. But, contrary to appellants' suggestions, landmark laws are not like discriminatory, or "reverse spot," zoning: that is, a land-use decision which arbitrarily singles out a particular parcel for different, less favorable treatment than the neighboring ones. See 2 A. Rathkopf, The Law of Zoning and Planning 26–4, and n. 6 (4th ed. 1978). In contrast to discriminatory zoning, which is the antithesis of land-use control as part of some comprehensive plan, the New York City law embodies a comprehensive plan to preserve structures of historic or aesthetic interest wherever they might be found in the city, and as noted, over 400 landmarks and 31 historic districts have been designated pursuant to this plan.

Equally without merit is the related argument that the decision to designate a structure as a landmark "is inevitably arbitrary or at least subjective, because it is basically a matter of taste," Reply Brief for Appellants 22, thus unavoidably singling out individual landowners for disparate and unfair treatment. The argument has a particularly hollow ring in this case. For appellants not only did not seek judicial review of either the designation or of the denials of the certificates of appropriateness and of no exterior effect, but do not even now suggest that the Commission's decisions concerning the Terminal were in any sense arbitrary or unprincipled. But, in any event, a landmark owner has a right to judicial review of any Commission decision, and, quite simply, there is no basis whatsoever for a conclusion that courts will have any greater difficulty identifying arbitrary or discriminatory action in the context of landmark regulation than in the context of classic zoning or indeed in any other context.[14]

Next, appellants observe that New York City's law differs from zoning laws and historic-district ordinances in that the Landmarks Law does not impose identical or similar restrictions on all structures located in particular physical communities. It follows, they argue, that New York City's law is inherently incapable of producing the fair and equitable distribution of benefits and burdens of governmental action which is characteristic of zoning laws and historic-district legislation and which they maintain is a

---

[14] When a property owner challenges the application of a zoning ordinance to his property, the judicial inquiry focuses upon whether the challenged restriction can reasonably be deemed to promote the objectives of the community land-use plan, and will include consideration of the treatment of similar parcels. See generally *Nectow v. Cambridge*, 277 U.S. 183, 48 S.Ct. 447, 72 L.Ed. 842 (1928). When a property owner challenges a landmark designation or restriction as arbitrary or discriminatory, a similar inquiry presumably will occur.

constitutional requirement if "just compensation" is not to be afforded. It is, of course, true that the Landmarks Law has a more severe impact on some landowners than on others, but that in itself does not mean that the law effects a "taking." Legislation designed to promote the general welfare commonly burdens some more than others. The owners of the brickyard in *Hadacheck*, of the cedar trees in *Miller v. Schoene*, and of the gravel and sand mine in *Goldblatt v. Hempstead*, were uniquely burdened by the legislation sustained in those cases. Similarly, zoning laws often affect some property owners more severely than others but have not been held to be invalid on that account. For example, the property owner in *Euclid* who wished to use its property for industrial purposes was affected far more severely by the ordinance than its neighbors who wished to use their land for residences.

In any event, appellants' repeated suggestions that they are solely burdened and unbenefited is factually inaccurate. This contention overlooks the fact that the New York City law applies to vast numbers of structures in the city in addition to the Terminal—all the structures contained in the 31 historic districts and over 400 individual landmarks, many of which are close to the Terminal. Unless we are to reject the judgment of the New York City Council that the preservation of landmarks benefits all New York citizens and all structures, both economically and by improving the quality of life in the city as a whole—which we are unwilling to do—we cannot conclude that the owners of the Terminal have in no sense been benefited by the Landmarks Law. Doubtless appellants believe they are more burdened than benefited by the law, but that must have been true, too, of the property owners in *Miller, Hadacheck, Euclid*, and *Goldblatt*.

Appellants' final broad-based attack would have us treat the law as an instance, like that in *United States v. Causby*, in which government, acting in an enterprise capacity, has appropriated part of their property for some strictly governmental purpose. Apart from the fact that *Causby* was a case of invasion of airspace that destroyed the use of the farm beneath and this New York City law has in nowise impaired the present use of the Terminal, the Landmarks Law neither exploits appellants' parcel for city purposes nor facilitates nor arises from any entrepreneurial operations of the city. The situation is not remotely like that in *Causby* where the airspace above the property was in the flight pattern for military aircraft. The Landmarks Law's effect is simply to prohibit appellants or anyone else from occupying portions of the airspace above the Terminal, while permitting appellants to use the remainder of the parcel in a gainful fashion. This is no more an appropriation of property by government for its own uses than is a zoning law prohibiting, for "aesthetic" reasons, two or more adult theaters within a specified area, see *Young v. American Mini Theatres, Inc.*, 427 U.S. 50, 96 S.Ct. 2440, 49 L.Ed.2d 310 (1976), or a safety regulation prohibiting excavations below a certain level. See *Goldblatt v. Hempstead*.

C

Rejection of appellants' broad arguments is not, however, the end of our inquiry, for all we thus far have established is that the New York City law is not rendered invalid by its failure to provide "just compensation" whenever a landmark owner is restricted in the exploitation of property interests, such as air rights, to a greater extent than provided for under applicable zoning laws. We now must consider whether the interference with appellants' property is of such a magnitude that "there must be an exercise of eminent domain and compensation to sustain [it]." *Pennsylvania Coal Co. v. Mahon*, 260 U.S., at 413, 43 S.Ct., at 159. That inquiry may be narrowed to the question of the severity of the impact of the law on appellants' parcel, and its resolution in turn requires a careful assessment of the impact of the regulation on the Terminal site.

Unlike the governmental acts in *Goldblatt, Miller, Causby, Griggs*, and *Hadacheck*, the New York City law does not interfere in any way with the present uses of the Terminal. Its designation as a landmark not only permits but contemplates that appellants may continue to use the property precisely as it has been used for the past 65 years: as a railroad terminal containing office space and concessions. So the law does not interfere with what must be regarded as Penn Central's primary expectation concerning the use of the parcel. More importantly, on this record, we must regard the New York City law as permitting Penn Central not only to profit from the Terminal but also to obtain a "reasonable return" on its investment.

Appellants, moreover, exaggerate the effect of the law on their ability to make use of the air rights above the Terminal in two respects. First, it simply cannot be maintained, on this record, that appellants have been prohibited from occupying *any* portion of the airspace above the Terminal. While the Commission's actions in denying applications to construct an office building in excess of 50 stories above the Terminal may indicate that it will refuse to issue a certificate of appropriateness for any comparably sized structure, nothing the Commission has said or done suggests an intention to prohibit *any* construction above the Terminal. The Commission's report emphasized that whether any construction would be allowed depended upon whether the proposed addition "would harmonize in scale, material and character with [the Terminal]." Record 2251. Since appellants have not sought approval for the construction of a smaller structure, we do not know that appellants will be denied any use of any portion of the airspace above the Terminal.

Second, to the extent appellants have been denied the right to build above the Terminal, it is not literally accurate to say that they have been denied *all* use of even those pre-existing air rights. Their ability to use these rights has not been abrogated; they are made transferable to at least eight parcels in the vicinity of the Terminal, one or two of which have been found suitable for the construction of new office buildings. Although appellants and others have argued that New York City's transferable development-rights program is far from ideal, the New York courts here supportably found that, at least in the case of the Terminal, the rights afforded are valuable. While these rights may well not have constituted "just compensation" if a "taking" had occurred, the rights nevertheless undoubtedly mitigate whatever financial burdens the law has imposed on appellants and, for that reason, are to be taken into account in considering the impact of regulation. Cf. *Goldblatt v. Hempstead*, 369 U.S., at 594 n. 3, 82 S.Ct., at 990 n. 3.

On this record, we conclude that the application of New York City's Landmarks Law has not effected a "taking" of appellants' property. The restrictions imposed are substantially related to the promotion of the general welfare and not only permit reasonable beneficial use of the landmark site but also afford appellants opportunities further to enhance not only the Terminal site proper but also other properties.

Affirmed.

Mr. Justice REHNQUIST, with whom THE CHIEF JUSTICE and Mr. Justice STEVENS join, dissenting.

Of the over one million buildings and structures in the city of New York, appellees have singled out 400 for designation as official landmarks. The owner of a building might initially be pleased that his property has been chosen by a distinguished committee of architects, historians, and city planners for such a singular distinction. But he may well discover, as appellant Penn Central Transportation Co. did here, that the landmark designation imposes upon him a substantial cost, with little or no offsetting benefit except for the honor of the designation. The question in this case is whether the cost associated with the city of New York's desire to preserve a limited number of "landmarks" within its borders must be borne by all of its taxpayers or whether it can instead be imposed entirely on the owners of the individual properties.

Only in the most superficial sense of the word can this case be said to involve "zoning." Typical zoning restrictions may, it is true, so limit the prospective uses of a piece of property as to diminish the value of that property in the abstract because it may not be used for the forbidden purposes. But any such abstract decrease in value will more than likely be at least partially offset by an increase in value which flows from similar restrictions as to use on neighboring 140 properties. All property owners in a designated area are placed under the same restrictions, not only for the benefit of the municipality as a whole but also for the common benefit of one another. In the words of Mr. Justice Holmes, speaking for the Court in *Pennsylvania Coal Co. v. Mahon*, 260 U.S. 393, 415, 43 S.Ct. 158, 160, 67 L.Ed. 322 (1922), there is "an average reciprocity of advantage."

* * *

Where a relatively few individual buildings, all separated from one another, are singled out and treated differently from surrounding buildings, no such reciprocity exists. The cost to the property owner which results from the imposition of restrictions applicable only to his property and not that of his neighbors may be substantial-in this case, several million dollars-with no comparable reciprocal benefits. And the cost associated with landmark legislation is likely to be of a completely different order of magnitude than that which results from the imposition of normal zoning restrictions. Unlike the regime affected by the latter, the landowner is not simply prohibited from using his property for certain purposes, while allowed to use it for all other purposes. Under the historic-landmark preservation scheme adopted by New York, the property owner is under an affirmative duty to *preserve* his property *as a landmark* at his own expense. To suggest that because traditional zoning results in some limitation of use of the property zoned, the New York City landmark preservation scheme should likewise be upheld, represents the ultimate in treating as alike things which are different. The rubric of "zoning" has not yet sufficed to avoid the well-established proposition that the Fifth Amendment bars the "Government from forcing some people alone to bear public burdens which, in all fairness and justice, should be borne by the public as a whole." *Armstrong v. United States*, 364 U.S. 40, 49, 80 S.Ct. 1563, 1569, 4 L.Ed.2d 1554 (1960). * * *.

* * *

Appellees in response would argue that a taking only occurs where a property owner is denied *all* reasonable value of his property.[15] The Court has frequently held that, even where a destruction of property rights would not *otherwise* constitute a taking, the inability of the owner to make a reasonable return on his property requires compensation under the Fifth Amendment. See, *e. g., United States v. Lynah*, 188 U.S., at 470, 23 S.Ct., at 357. But the converse is not true. A taking does not become a noncompensable exercise of police power simply because the government in its grace allows the owner to make some "reasonable" use of his property. "[I]t is the character of the invasion, not the amount of damage resulting from it, so long as the damage is substantial, that determines the question whether it is a taking." *United States v. Cress*, 243 U.S. 316, 328, 37 S.Ct. 380, 385, 61 L.Ed. 746 (1917); *United States v. Causby*, 328 U.S., at 266, 66 S.Ct., at 1068. See also *Goldblatt v. Hempstead*, 369 U.S., at 594, 82 S.Ct., at 990.

C

Appellees, apparently recognizing that the constraints imposed on a landmark site constitute a taking for Fifth Amendment purposes, do not leave the property owner empty-handed. As the Court notes, *ante*, at 2654–2655, the property owner may theoretically "transfer" his previous right to develop the landmark property to adjacent properties if they are under his control. Appellees have coined this system "Transfer Development Rights," or TDR's.

***

§ 15.3.5 The Late, Great, Middle-Tiered Scrutiny Approach

In a middle-tiered scrutiny approach, the government has the burden of showing that the law or regulation is substantially related to a legitimate government interest. This test, stated by the Supreme Court in a number of takings cases, was clearly articulated in Agins v. City of Tiburon.

---

[15] Difficult conceptual and legal problems are posed by a rule that a taking only occurs where the property owner is denied all reasonable return on his property. Not only must the Court define "reasonable return" for a variety of types of property (farmlands, residential properties, commercial and industrial areas), but the Court must define the particular property unit that should be examined. For example, in this case, if appellees are viewed as having restricted Penn Central's use of its "air rights," *all* return has been denied. See *Pennsylvania Coal Co. v. Mahon*, 260 U.S. 393, 43 S.Ct. 158, 67 L.Ed. 322 (1922). The Court does little to resolve these questions in its opinion. Thus, at one point, the Court implies that the question is whether the restrictions have "an unduly harsh impact upon the owner's use of the property," *ante*, at 2661; at another point, the question is phrased as whether Penn Central can obtain "a 'reasonable return' on its investment," ***; and, at yet another point, the question becomes whether the landmark is "economically viable," ***.

Agins v. City of Tiburon
447 U.S. 255 (1980)

* * *

The application of a general zoning law to particular property effects a taking if the ordinance does not substantially advance legitimate state interests, see *Nectow v. Cambridge*, 277 U.S. 183, 188, 48 S.Ct. 447, 448, 72 L.Ed. 842 (1928), or denies an owner economically viable use of his land, see *Penn Central Transp. Co. v. New York City*, 438 U.S. 104, 138, n. 36, 98 S.Ct. 2646, 2666, 57 L.Ed.2d 631 (1978). The determination that governmental action constitutes a taking is, in essence, a determination that the public at large, rather than a single owner, must bear the burden of an exercise of state power in the public interest. Although no precise rule determines when property has been taken, see *Kaiser Aetna v. United States*, 444 U.S. 164, 100 S.Ct. 383, 62 S.Ct. 332 (1979), the question necessarily requires a weighing of private and public interests. The seminal decision in *Euclid v. Ambler Co.*, 272 U.S. 365, 47 S.Ct. 114, 71 L.Ed. 303 (1926), is illustrative. In that case, the landowner challenged the constitutionality of a municipal ordinance that restricted commercial development of his property. Despite alleged diminution in value of the owner's land, the Court held that the zoning laws were facially constitutional. They bore a substantial relationship to the public welfare, and their enactment inflicted no irreparable injury upon the landowner. *Id.*, at 395-397, 47 S.Ct., at 121.

* * *

Lingle v. Chevron U.S.A. Inc.
544 U.S. 528 (2005)

In Lingle v. Chevron U.S.A. Inc., *Chevron attacked a Hawaiian statute that imposed price control on the rent charged service station operators. Chevron contended that the price control statute was a taking because the statute was not substantially related to a legitimate government interest, as per* Agins. *The United States Supreme Court will hold that the substantial relationship test is not part of takings law.*

Justice O'CONNOR delivered the opinion of the Court.

On occasion, a would-be doctrinal rule or test finds its way into our case law through simple repetition of a phrase--however fortuitously coined. A quarter century ago, in *Agins v. City of Tiburon,* 447 U.S. 255, 100 S.Ct. 2138, 65 L.Ed.2d 106 (1980), the Court declared that government regulation of private property "effects a taking if [such regulation] does not substantially advance legitimate state interests . . . ." *Id.*, at 260, 100 S.Ct. 2138. Through reiteration in a half dozen or so decisions since *Agins,* this language has been ensconced in our Fifth Amendment takings jurisprudence. See *Monterey v. Del Monte Dunes at Monterey, Ltd.,* 526 U.S. 687, 704, 119 S.Ct. 1624, 143 L.Ed.2d 882 (1999) (citing cases).

In the case before us, the lower courts applied *Agins'* "substantially advances" formula to strike down a Hawaii statute that limits the rent that oil companies may charge to dealers who lease service stations owned by the companies. The lower courts held that the rent cap effects an uncompensated taking of private property in violation of the Fifth and Fourteenth Amendments because it does not substantially advance Hawaii's asserted interest in controlling retail gasoline prices. This case requires us to decide whether the "substantially advances" formula announced in *Agins* is an appropriate test for determining whether a regulation effects a Fifth Amendment taking. We conclude that it is not.

* * *

II

A

The Takings Clause of the Fifth Amendment, made applicable to the States through the Fourteenth, see *Chicago, B. & Q.R. Co. v. Chicago,* 166 U.S. 226, 17 S.Ct. 581, 41 L.Ed. 979 (1897), provides that private property shall not "be taken for public use, without just compensation." * * *

* * *

Our precedents stake out two categories of regulatory action that generally will be deemed *per se* takings for Fifth Amendment purposes. First, where government requires an owner to suffer a permanent physical invasion of her property--however minor--it must provide just compensation. See *Loretto v. Teleprompter Manhattan CATV Corp.,* 458 U.S. 419, 102 S.Ct. 3164, 73 L.Ed.2d 868 (1982) (state law requiring landlords to permit cable companies to install cable facilities in apartment buildings effected a taking). A second categorical rule applies to regulations that completely deprive an owner of "*all* economically beneficial us[e]" of her property. *Lucas,* 505 U.S., at 1019, 112 S.Ct. 2886 (emphasis in original). We held in *Lucas* that the government must pay just compensation for such "total regulatory takings," except to the extent that "background principles of nuisance and property law" independently restrict the owner's intended use of the property. *Id.,* at 1026-1032, 112 S.Ct. 2886.

Outside these two relatively narrow categories (and the special context of land-use exactions discussed below, see *infra,* at 2085-2087), regulatory takings challenges are governed by the standards set forth in *Penn Central Transp. Co. v. New York City,* 438 U.S. 104, 98 S.Ct. 2646, 57 L.Ed.2d 631 (1978). The Court in *Penn Central* acknowledged that it had hitherto been "unable to develop any 'set formula' " for evaluating regulatory takings claims, but identified "several factors that have particular significance." *Id.,* at 124, 98 S.Ct. 2646. Primary among those factors are "[t]he economic impact of the regulation on the claimant and, particularly, the extent to which the regulation has interfered with distinct investment-backed expectations." *Ibid.* In addition, the "character of the governmental action"--for instance whether it amounts to a physical invasion or instead merely affects property interests through "some public program adjusting the benefits and burdens of economic life to promote the common good"--may be relevant in discerning whether a taking has occurred. *Ibid.* The *Penn Central* factors--though each has given rise to vexing subsidiary questions--have served as the principal guidelines for resolving regulatory takings claims that do not fall within the physical takings or *Lucas* rules. See, *e.g., Palazzolo v. Rhode Island,* 533 U.S. 606, 617- 618, 121 S.Ct. 2448, 150 L.Ed.2d 592 (2001); *id.,* at 632-634, 121 S.Ct. 2448 (O'CONNOR, J., concurring).

Although our regulatory takings jurisprudence cannot be characterized as unified, these three inquiries (reflected in *Loretto, Lucas*, and *Penn Central*) share a common touchstone. Each aims to identify regulatory actions that are functionally equivalent to the classic taking in which government directly appropriates private property or ousts the owner from his domain. Accordingly, each of these tests focuses directly upon the severity of the burden that government imposes upon private property rights. The Court has held that physical takings require compensation because of the unique burden they impose: A permanent physical invasion, however minimal the economic cost it entails, eviscerates the owner's right to exclude others from entering and using her property-- perhaps the most fundamental of all property interests. See *Dolan v. City of Tigard*, 512 U.S. 374, 384, 114 S.Ct. 2309, 129 L.Ed.2d 304 (1994); *Nollan v. California Coastal Comm'n*, 483 U.S. 825, 831-832, 107 S.Ct. 3141, 97 L.Ed.2d 677 (1987); *Loretto, supra*, at 433, 102 S.Ct. 3164; *Kaiser Aetna v. United States*, 444 U.S. 164, 176, 100 S.Ct. 383, 62 L.Ed.2d 332 (1979). In the *Lucas* context, of course, the complete elimination of a property's value is the determinative factor. See *Lucas, supra*, at 1017, 112 S.Ct. 2886 (positing that "total deprivation of beneficial use is, from the landowner's point of view, the equivalent of a physical appropriation"). And the *Penn Central* inquiry turns in large part, albeit not exclusively, upon the magnitude of a regulation's economic impact and the degree to which it interferes with legitimate property interests.

B

In *Agins v. City of Tiburon*, a case involving a facial takings challenge to certain municipal zoning ordinances, the Court declared that "[t]he application of a general zoning law to particular property effects a taking if the ordinance does not substantially advance legitimate state interests, see *Nectow v. Cambridge*, 277 U.S. 183, 188, 48 S.Ct. 447, 72 L.Ed. 842 (1928), or denies an owner economically viable use of his land, see *Penn Central Transp. Co. v. New York City*, 438 U.S. 104, 138, n. 36, 98 S.Ct. 2646, 57 L.Ed.2d 631 (1978)." 447 U.S., at 260, 100 S.Ct. 2138. Because this statement is phrased in the disjunctive, *Agins'* "substantially advances" language has been read to announce a stand-alone regulatory takings test that is wholly independent of *Penn Central* or any other test. Indeed, the lower courts in this case struck down Hawaii's rent control statute as an "unconstitutional regulatory taking," 198 F.Supp.2d, at 1193, based solely upon a finding that it does not substantially advance the State's asserted interest in controlling retail gasoline prices. See *supra*, at 2080-2081. Although a number of our takings precedents have recited the "substantially advances" formula minted in *Agins*, this is our first opportunity to consider its validity as a freestanding takings test. We conclude that this formula prescribes an inquiry in the nature of a due process, not a takings, test, and that it has no proper place in our takings jurisprudence.

There is no question that the "substantially advances" formula was derived from due process, not takings, precedents. In support of this new language, *Agins* cited *Nectow v. Cambridge*, 277 U.S. 183, 48 S.Ct. 447, 72 L.Ed. 842, a 1928 case in which the plaintiff claimed that a city zoning ordinance "deprived him of his property without due process of law in contravention of the Fourteenth Amendment," *id.*, at 185, 48 S.Ct. 447. *Agins* then went on to discuss *Village of Euclid v. Ambler Realty Co.*, 272 U.S. 365, 47 S.Ct. 114, 71 L.Ed. 303 (1926), a historic decision holding that a municipal zoning ordinance would survive a substantive due process challenge so long as it was not "clearly arbitrary and unreasonable, having no *substantial relation to the public health, safety, morals, or general welfare.*" *Id.,* at 395, 47 S.Ct. 114 (emphasis added); see also *Nectow, supra,* at 188, 48 S.Ct. 447 (quoting the same "substantial relation" language from *Euclid*).

When viewed in historical context, the Court's reliance on *Nectow* and *Euclid* is understandable. *Agins* was the Court's first case involving a challenge to zoning regulations in many decades, so it was natural to turn to these seminal zoning precedents for guidance. See Brief for United States as *Amicus Curiae* in *Agins v. City of Tiburon,* O.T.1979, No. 602, pp. 12-13 (arguing that *Euclid* "set out the principles applicable to a determination of the facial validity of a zoning ordinance attacked as a violation of the Takings Clause of the Fifth Amendment"). Moreover, *Agins'* apparent commingling of due process and takings inquiries had some precedent in the Court's then-recent decision in *Penn Central.* * * *

Although *Agins'* reliance on due process precedents is understandable, the language the Court selected was regrettably imprecise. The "substantially advances" formula suggests a means-ends test: It asks, in essence, whether a regulation of private property is *effective* in achieving some legitimate public purpose. An inquiry of this nature has some logic in the context of a due process challenge, for a regulation that fails to serve any legitimate governmental objective may be so arbitrary or irrational that it runs afoul of the Due Process Clause. See, *e.g., County of Sacramento v. Lewis,* 523 U.S. 833, 846, 118 S.Ct. 1708, 140 L.Ed.2d 1043 (1998) (stating that the Due Process Clause is intended, in part, to protect the individual against "the exercise of power without any reasonable justification in the service of a legitimate governmental objective"). But such a test is not a valid method of discerning whether private property has been "taken" for purposes of the Fifth Amendment.

In stark contrast to the three regulatory takings tests discussed above, the "substantially advances" inquiry reveals nothing about the *magnitude or character of the burden* a particular regulation imposes upon private property rights. Nor does it provide any information about how any regulatory burden is *distributed* among property owners. In consequence, this test does not help to identify those regulations whose effects are functionally comparable to government appropriation or invasion of private property; it is tethered neither to the text of the Takings Clause nor to the basic justification for allowing regulatory actions to be challenged under the Clause.

* * * A test that tells us nothing about the actual burden imposed on property rights, or how that burden is allocated cannot tell us when justice might require that the burden be spread among taxpayers through the payment of compensation. The owner of a property subject to a regulation that *effectively* serves a legitimate state interest may be just as singled out and just as burdened as the owner of a property subject to an *ineffective* regulation. It would make little sense to say that the second owner has suffered a taking while the first has not. Likewise, an ineffective regulation may not significantly burden property rights at all, and it may distribute any burden broadly and evenly among property owners. The notion that such a regulation nevertheless "takes" private property for public use merely by virtue of its ineffectiveness or foolishness is untenable.

* * *

Finally, the "substantially advances" formula is not only *doctrinally* untenable as a takings test--its application as such would also present serious practical difficulties. The

Agins formula can be read to demand heightened means-ends review of virtually any regulation of private property. If so interpreted, it would require courts to scrutinize the efficacy of a vast array of state and federal regulations--a task for which courts are not well suited. Moreover, it would empower--and might often require--courts to substitute their predictive judgments for those of elected legislatures and expert agencies. Although the instant case is only the tip of the proverbial iceberg, it foreshadows the hazards of placing courts in this role. * * *

For the foregoing reasons, we conclude that the "substantially advances" formula announced in *Agins* is not a valid method of identifying regulatory takings for which the Fifth Amendment requires just compensation. Since Chevron argued only a "substantially advances" theory in support of its takings claim, it was not entitled to summary judgment on that claim.

III

We emphasize that our holding today--that the "substantially advances" formula is not a valid takings test--does not require us to disturb any of our prior holdings. To be sure, we applied a "substantially advances" inquiry in *Agins* itself, see 447 U.S., at 261-262, 100 S.Ct. 2138 (finding that the challenged zoning ordinances "substantially advance[d] legitimate governmental goals"), and arguably also in *Keystone Bituminous Coal Assn. v. DeBenedictis,* 480 U.S. 470, 485-492, 107 S.Ct. 1232, 94 L.Ed.2d 472 (1987) (quoting " 'substantially advance[s]' " language and then finding that the challenged statute was intended to further a substantial public interest). But in no case have we found a compensable taking based on such an inquiry. Indeed, in most of the cases reciting the "substantially advances" formula, the Court has merely assumed its validity when referring to it in dicta. See *Tahoe-Sierra Preservation Council, Inc. v. Tahoe Regional Planning Agency,* 535 U.S. 302, 334, 122 S.Ct. 1465, 152 L.Ed.2d 517 (2002); *Del Monte Dunes,* 526 U.S., at 704, 119 S.Ct. 1624; *Lucas,* 505 U.S., at 1016, 112 S.Ct. 2886; *Yee v. Escondido,* 503 U.S. 519, 534, 112 S.Ct. 1522, 118 L.Ed.2d 153 (1992); *United States v. Riverside Bayview Homes, Inc.,* 474 U.S. 121, 126, 106 S.Ct. 455, 88 L.Ed.2d 419 (1985).

* * *

Twenty-five years ago, the Court posited that a regulation of private property "effects a taking if [it] does not substantially advance [a] legitimate state interes[t]." *Agins, supra,* at 260, 100 S.Ct. 2138. The lower courts in this case took that statement to its logical conclusion, and in so doing, revealed its imprecision. Today we correct course. We hold that the "substantially advances" formula is not a valid takings test, and indeed conclude that it has no proper place in our takings jurisprudence. In so doing, we reaffirm that a plaintiff seeking to challenge a government regulation as an uncompensated taking of private property may proceed under one of the other theories discussed above--by alleging a "physical" taking, a *Lucas*-type "total regulatory taking," a *Penn Central* taking, or a land-use exaction violating the standards set forth in *Nollan* and *Dolan.* Because Chevron argued only a "substantially advances" theory in support of its takings claim, it was not entitled to summary judgment on that claim. Accordingly, we reverse the judgment of the Ninth Circuit and remand the case for further proceedings consistent with this opinion.

It is so ordered.

§ 15.3.6 Timing Matters

We now address a question of timing: Does it matter when a law was enacted in determining whether the law conflicts with the Fifth Amendment's takings clause?

Palazzolo v. Rhode Island
533 U.S. 606 (2001)

Anthony Palazzolo was the sole shareholder of a corporation that owned a waterfront parcel. The corporation submitted plans for development of the parcel. The appropriate governmental agency denied the planned development. Thereafter, the state promulgated regulations that prohibited building on so-called wetlands. Later still, the corporation was dissolved and Palazzolo became the legal owner of the property in question. Palazzolo again submitted plans for development. Again, the agency declined to issue a building permit. Palazzolo subsequently filed suit alleging a regulatory taking. Ultimately, the Rhode Island Supreme Court denied his takings claim. The basis for the holding was that the regulation prohibiting building on the parcel was in effect at the time Palazzolo acquired the property from the corporation. The United States Supreme Court will hold that acquisition of title after the effective date of the regulations will not bar a regulatory takings claim.

Justice KENNEDY delivered the opinion of the Court.

* * *

II

* * *

B

We turn to the second asserted basis for declining to address petitioner's takings claim on the merits. When the Council promulgated its wetlands regulations, the disputed parcel was owned not by petitioner but by the corporation of which he was sole shareholder. When title was transferred to petitioner by operation of law, the wetlands regulations were in force. The state court held the postregulation acquisition of title was fatal to the claim for deprivation of all economic use, 746 A.2d, at 716, and to the *Penn Central* claim, 746 A.2d, at 717. While the first holding was couched in terms of background principles of state property law, see *Lucas,* 505 U.S., at 1015, 112 S.Ct. 2886, and the second in terms of petitioner's reasonable investment-backed expectations, see *Penn Central,* 438 U.S., at 124, 98 S.Ct. 2646, the two holdings together amount to a single, sweeping, rule: A purchaser or a successive title holder like petitioner is deemed to have notice of an earlier-enacted restriction and is barred from claiming that it effects a taking.

The theory underlying the argument that postenactment purchasers cannot challenge a regulation under the Takings Clause seems to run on these lines: Property rights are created by the State. See, *e.g., Phillips v. Washington Legal Foundation,* 524 U.S. 156, 163, 118 S.Ct. 1925, 141 L.Ed.2d 174 (1998). So, the argument goes, by prospective legislation the State can shape and define property rights and reasonable investment-backed expectations, and subsequent owners cannot claim any injury from lost value. After all, they purchased or took title with notice of the limitation.

The State may not put so potent a Hobbesian stick into the Lockean bundle. The right to improve property, of course, is subject to the reasonable exercise of state authority, including the enforcement of valid zoning and land-use restrictions. See *Pennsylvania Coal Co.,* 260 U.S., at 413, 43 S.Ct. 158 ("Government hardly could go on if to some extent values incident to property could not be diminished without paying for every such change in the general law"). The Takings Clause, however, in certain circumstances allows a landowner to assert that a particular exercise of the State's regulatory power is so unreasonable or onerous as to compel compensation. Just as a prospective enactment, such as a new zoning ordinance, can limit the value of land without effecting a taking because it can be understood as reasonable by all concerned, other enactments are unreasonable and do not become less so through passage of time or title. Were we to accept the State's rule, the postenactment transfer of title would absolve the State of its obligation to defend any action restricting land use, no matter how extreme or unreasonable. A State would be allowed, in effect, to put an expiration date on the Takings Clause. This ought not to be the rule. Future generations, too, have a right to challenge unreasonable limitations on the use and value of land.

Nor does the justification of notice take into account the effect on owners at the time of enactment, who are prejudiced as well. Should an owner attempt to challenge a new regulation, but not survive the process of ripening his or her claim (which, as this case demonstrates, will often take years), under the proposed rule the right to compensation may not be asserted by an heir or successor, and so may not be asserted at all. The State's rule would work a critical alteration to the nature of property, as the newly regulated landowner is stripped of the ability to transfer the interest which was possessed prior to the regulation. The State may not by this means secure a windfall for itself. See *Webb's Fabulous Pharmacies, Inc. v. Beckwith,* 449 U.S. 155, 164, 101 S.Ct. 446, 66 L.Ed.2d 358 (1980) ("[A] State, by *ipse dixit,* may not transform private property into public property without compensation"); cf. Ellickson, Property in Land, 102 Yale L.J. 1315, 1368-1369 (1993) (right to transfer interest in land is a defining characteristic of the fee simple estate). The proposed rule is, furthermore, capricious in effect. The young owner contrasted with the older owner, the owner with the resources to hold contrasted with the owner with the need to sell, would be in different positions. The Takings Clause is not so quixotic. A blanket rule that purchasers with notice have no compensation right when a claim becomes ripe is too blunt an instrument to accord with the duty to compensate for what is taken. * * *

* * *

For the reasons we have discussed, the State Supreme Court erred in * * * in ruling that acquisition of title after the effective date of the regulations barred the takings claims. The court did not err in finding that petitioner failed to establish a deprivation of all economic value, for it is undisputed that the parcel retains significant worth for construction of a residence. The claims under the *Penn Central* analysis were not examined, and for this purpose the case should be remanded.

The judgment of the Rhode Island Supreme Court is affirmed in part and reversed in part, and the case is remanded for further proceedings not inconsistent with this opinion.

It is so ordered.

Justice O'CONNOR, concurring.

* * * As the Court holds, the Rhode Island Supreme Court erred in effectively adopting the sweeping rule that the preacquisition enactment of the use restriction *ipso facto* defeats any takings claim based on that use restriction. Accordingly, the Court holds that petitioner's claim under *Penn Central Transp. Co. v. City of New York,* 438 U.S. 104, 98 S.Ct. 2646, 57 L.Ed.2d 631 (1978), "is not barred by the mere fact that title was acquired after the effective date of the state-imposed restriction." *Ante,* at 2464.

The more difficult question is what role the temporal relationship between regulatory enactment and title acquisition plays in a proper *Penn Central* analysis. Today's holding does not mean that the timing of the regulation's enactment relative to the acquisition of title is immaterial to the *Penn Central* analysis. Indeed, it would be just as much error to expunge this consideration from the takings inquiry as it would be to accord it exclusive significance. Our polestar instead remains the principles set forth in *Penn Central* itself and our other cases that govern partial regulatory takings. Under these cases, interference with investment-backed expectations is one of a number of factors that a court must examine. Further, the regulatory regime in place at the time the claimant acquires the property at issue helps to shape the reasonableness of those expectations.

* * *

§ 15.3.7 Inverse Condemnation and Remedies

Assume that government wants a particular parcel of land. Typically, the government will attempt to secure the land by purchase. If the landowner agrees to sell the property to the government, the process is relatively fast. On the other hand, if the landowner does not want to sell "voluntarily" to the government, the government will file an eminent domain action to acquire the property. Thus, in a traditional condemnation action, the government files suit against the landowner to acquire the property. In the regulatory takings area, it is the landowner filing suit against the government, claiming that the law acts as a taking (because it has gone "too far"). Hence, because the landowner initiates the litigation, we call this an "inverse condemnation suit." That said, the problem that we deal with now is: What happens if the landowner ends up prevailing in such a suit? Before First English, *the landowner had to be content with either the government revoking the regulation or repealing the law in question (or exercising its eminent domain power and acquiring the property for just compensation). Was the landowner entitled to compensation for the time during the litigation period that the landowner could not use his property? The answer was, no.* First English *changed that, however.*

First English Evangelical Lutheran Church of Glendale v. Los Angeles County
482 U.S. 304 (1987)

The First English Evangelical Lutheran Church of Glendale owned a 21-acre parcel of land, "Lutherglen," in the Angeles National Forest. Because of flooding concerns, the

County of Los Angeles promulgated regulations prohibiting building. The church filed suit in a so-called inverse condemnation action, claiming that the government action has constituted a taking. Assuming that there was a taking, the California Court of Appeal held that the church was not entitled to compensation for the period of time that the regulation was in effect. The United States Supreme Court will hold that, assuming there is a taking, when all use is denied, the government must pay compensation for the period of time that the regulation was in effect; it is not enough for the government to simply revoke the regulation.

Chief Justice REHNQUIST delivered the opinion of the Court.

* * *

In *Agins v. Tiburon, supra,* the California Supreme Court decided that a landowner may not maintain an inverse condemnation suit in the courts of that State based upon a "regulatory" taking. 24 Cal.3d, at 275-277, 157 Cal.Rptr., at 376-78, 598 P.2d, at 29-31. In the court's view, maintenance of such a suit would allow a landowner to force the legislature to exercise its power of eminent domain. Under this decision, then, compensation is not required until the challenged regulation or ordinance has been held excessive in an action for declaratory relief or a writ of mandamus and the government has nevertheless decided to continue the regulation in effect. Based on this decision, the trial court in the present case granted the motion to strike the allegation that the church had been denied all use of Lutherglen. It explained that "a careful re-reading of the *Agins* case persuades the Court that when an ordinance, even a non-zoning ordinance, deprives a person of the total use of his lands, his challenge to the ordinance is by way of declaratory relief or possibly mandamus." App. 26. Because the appellant alleged a regulatory taking and sought only damages, the allegation that the ordinance denied all use of Lutherglen was deemed irrelevant.

On appeal, the California Court of Appeal read the complaint as one seeking "damages for the uncompensated taking of all use of Lutherglen by County Ordinance No. 11,855 * * * *" App. to Juris. Statement A13-A14. It too relied on the California Supreme Court's decision in *Agins* in rejecting the cause of action, declining appellant's invitation to reevaluate *Agins* * * * .The California Supreme Court denied review.

This appeal followed, and we noted probable jurisdiction. 478 U.S. 1003, 106 S.Ct. 3292, 92 L.Ed.2d 708 (1986). Appellant asks us to hold that the California Supreme Court erred in *Agins v. Tiburon* in determining that the Fifth Amendment, as made applicable to the States through the Fourteenth Amendment, does not require compensation as a remedy for "temporary" regulatory takings-those regulatory takings which are ultimately invalidated by the courts.* * * For the reasons explained below, however, we find the constitutional claim properly presented in this case, and hold that on these facts the California courts have decided the compensation question inconsistently with the requirements of the Fifth Amendment.

Concerns with finality left us unable to reach the remedial question in the earlier cases where we have been asked to consider the rule of *Agins.* See *MacDonald, Sommer & Frates, supra,* 477 U.S., at 351, 106 S.Ct. at 2567 (summarizing cases). In each of these cases, we concluded either that regulations considered to be in issue by the state court did not effect a taking, *Agins v. Tiburon,* 447 U.S., at 263, 100 S.Ct., at 2142, or that the factual disputes yet to be resolved by state authorities might still lead to the conclusion that no taking had occurred. *MacDonald, Sommer & Frates, supra,* 477 U.S., at 351-353, 106 S.Ct. at 2567-2568; *Williamson County, supra,* 473 U.S., at 188-194, 105 S.Ct., at 3117-3120; *San Diego Gas & Electric Co., supra,* 450 U.S., at 631-632, 101 S.Ct., at 1293-1294. Consideration of the remedial question in those circumstances, we concluded, would be premature.

The posture of the present case is quite different. Appellant's complaint alleged that "Ordinance No. 11,855 denies [it] all use of Lutherglen," and sought damages for this deprivation. App. 12, 49. In affirming the decision to strike this allegation, the Court of Appeal assumed that the complaint sought "damages for the uncompensated *taking* of all use of Lutherglen by County Ordinance No. 11,855." App. to Juris. * * *

* * *

II

Consideration of the compensation question must begin with direct reference to the language of the Fifth Amendment, which provides in relevant part that "private property [shall not] be taken for public use, without just compensation." As its language indicates, and as the Court has frequently noted, this provision does not prohibit the taking of private property, but instead places a condition on the exercise of that power. See *Williamson County,* 473 U.S., at 194, 105 S.Ct., at 3120; *Hodel v. Virginia Surface Mining & Reclamation Assn., Inc.,* 452 U.S. 264, 297, n. 40, 101 S.Ct. 2352, 2371, n. 40, 69 L.Ed.2d 1 (1981); *Hurley v. Kincaid,* 285 U.S. 95, 104, 52 S.Ct. 267, 269, 76 L.Ed. 637 (1932); *Monongahela Navigation Co. v. United States,* 148 U.S. 312, 336, 13 S.Ct. 622, 630, 37 L.Ed. 463 (1893); *United States v. Jones,* 109 U.S. 513, 518, 3 S.Ct. 346, 349, 27 L.Ed. 1015 (1883). This basic understanding of the Amendment makes clear that it is designed not to limit the governmental interference with property rights *per se,* but rather to secure *compensation* in the event of otherwise proper interference amounting to a taking. Thus, government action that works a taking of property rights necessarily implicates the "constitutional obligation to pay just compensation." *Armstrong v. United States,* 364 U.S. 40, 49, 80 S.Ct. 1563, 1569, 4 L.Ed.2d 1554 (1960).

We have recognized that a landowner is entitled to bring an action in inverse condemnation as a result of " 'the self-executing character of the constitutional provision with respect to compensation * * * *' " *United States v. Clarke,* 445 U.S. 253, 257, 100 S.Ct. 1127, 1130, 63 L.Ed.2d 373 (1980), quoting 6 P. Nichols, Eminent Domain § 25.41 (3d rev. ed. 1972). As noted in Justice BRENNAN's dissent in *San Diego Gas & Electric Co.,* 450 U.S., at 654-655, 101 S.Ct., at 1305, it has been established at least since *Jacobs v. United States,* 290 U.S. 13, 54 S.Ct. 26, 78 L.Ed. 142 (1933), that claims for just compensation are grounded in the Constitution itself:

"The suits were based on the right to recover just compensation for property taken by the United States for public use in the exercise of its power of eminent domain. *That right was guaranteed by the Constitution.* The fact that condemnation proceedings were not instituted and that the right was asserted in suits by the owners did not change the essential nature of the claim. The form of the remedy did not qualify the right. It rested upon the Fifth Amendment. Statutory recognition was not necessary. A promise to pay was not necessary. Such a promise was implied because of the duty to pay imposed by the Amendment. *The suits were thus founded upon the Constitution of the United States.*" *Id.,* at 16, 54 S.Ct., at 27. (Emphasis added.)

* * *

It has also been established doctrine at least since Justice Holmes' opinion for the Court in *Pennsylvania Coal Co. v. Mahon,* 260 U.S. 393, 43 S.Ct. 158, 67 L.Ed. 322 (1922), that "[t]he general rule at least is, that while property may be regulated to a certain extent, if regulation goes too far it will be recognized as a taking." *Id.,* at 415, 43 S.Ct., at 160. While the typical taking occurs when the government acts to condemn property in the exercise of its power of eminent domain, the entire doctrine of inverse condemnation is predicated on the proposition that a taking may occur without such formal proceedings. * * *

* * * [W]e find substantial guidance in cases where the government has only temporarily exercised its right to use private property. In *United States v. Dow, supra,* at 26, 78 S.Ct., at 1046, though rejecting a claim that the Government may not abandon condemnation proceedings, the Court observed that abandonment "results in an alteration in the property interest taken-from [one of] full ownership to one of temporary use and occupation * * * * In such cases compensation would be measured by the principles normally governing the taking of a right to use property temporarily. See *Kimball Laundry Co. v. United States,* 338 U.S. 1, 69 S.Ct. 1434, 93 L.Ed. 1765 [1949]; *United States v. Petty Motor Co.,* 327 U.S. 372, 66 S.Ct. 596, 90 L.Ed. 729 [1946]; *United States v. General Motors Corp.,* 323 U.S. 373, 65 S.Ct. 357, 89 L.Ed. 311 [1945]." Each of the cases cited by the *Dow* Court involved appropriation of private property by the United States for use during World War II. Though the takings were in fact "temporary," see *United States v. Petty Motor Co.,* 327 U.S. 372, at 375, 66 S.Ct. 596, at 598, 90 L.Ed. 729 (1946), there was no question that compensation would be required for the Government's interference with the use of the property; the Court was concerned in each case with determining the proper measure of the monetary relief to which the property holders were entitled. See *Kimball Laundry Co. v. United States,* 338 U.S. 1, 4-21, 69 S.Ct. 1434, 1437-1445, 93 L.Ed. 1765 (1949); *Petty Motor Co., supra,* 327 U.S., at 377-381, 66 S.Ct., at 599-601; *United States v. General Motors Corp., supra,* 323 U.S. 373, at 379-384, 65 S.Ct. 357, at 360-362, 89 L.Ed. 311 (1945).

These cases reflect the fact that "temporary" takings which, as here, deny a landowner all use of his property, are not different in kind from permanent takings, for which the Constitution clearly requires compensation. * * *

* * *

Nothing we say today is intended to abrogate the principle that the decision to exercise the power of eminent domain is a legislative function " 'for Congress and Congress alone to determine.' " *Hawaii Housing Authority v. Midkiff,* 467 U.S. 229, 240, 104 S.Ct. 2321, 2329, 81 L.Ed.2d 186 (1984), quoting *Berman v. Parker,* 348 U.S. 26, 33, 75 S.Ct. 98, 103, 99 L.Ed. 27 (1954). Once a court determines that a taking has occurred, the government retains the whole range of options already available-amendment of the regulation, withdrawal of the invalidated regulation, or exercise of eminent domain. Thus we do not, as the Solicitor General suggests, "permit a court, at the behest of a private person, to require the * * * Government to exercise the power of eminent domain * * * *" Brief for United States as *Amicus Curiae* 22. We merely hold that where the government's activities have already worked a taking of all use of property, no subsequent action by the government can relieve it of the duty to provide compensation for the period during which the taking was effective.

We also point out that the allegation of the complaint which we treat as true for purposes of our decision was that the ordinance in question denied appellant all use of its property. We limit our holding to the facts presented, and of course do not deal with the quite different questions that would arise in the case of normal delays in obtaining building permits, changes in zoning ordinances, variances, and the like which are not before us. We realize that even our present holding will undoubtedly lessen to some extent the freedom and flexibility of land-use planners and governing bodies of municipal corporations when enacting land-use regulations. But such consequences necessarily flow from any decision upholding a claim of constitutional right; many of the provisions of the Constitution are designed to limit the flexibility and freedom of governmental authorities, and the Just Compensation Clause of the Fifth Amendment is one of them. As Justice Holmes aptly noted more than 50 years ago, "a strong public desire to improve the public condition is not enough to warrant achieving the desire by a shorter cut than the constitutional way of paying for the change." *Pennsylvania Coal Co. v. Mahon,* 260 U.S., at 416, 43 S.Ct., at 160.

Here we must assume that the Los Angeles County ordinance has denied appellant all use of its property for a considerable period of years, and we hold that invalidation of the ordinance without payment of fair value for the use of the property during this period of time would be a constitutionally insufficient remedy. The judgment of the California Court of Appeal is therefore reversed, and the case is remanded for further proceedings not inconsistent with this opinion.

It is so ordered.

* * *

Note

On remand, it was determined that the ordinance in question did not in fact preclude all use by the landowner. See 210 Cal.App.3d 1353, 258 Cal.Rptr. 893 (1989), cert.den. 493 U.S. 1056, 110 S.Ct. 866 (1990).

§ 15.4 Exactions

In everything that we have covered so far in the area of regulatory takings, the government simply prohibited the owner from building or otherwise using the property in an unrestricted manner. In exaction cases, a sub-category of regulatory takings law, the government allows the landowner to build—but only if the landowner first gives something to the government (e.g. dedicating some of the land in question for a public easement). The question involved is simple: Does the exaction comport with the Fifth Amendment's Takings Clause?

Nollan v. California Coastal Com'n
483 U.S. 825 (1987)

The Nollans own beachfront property, situated between two state beaches. The Nollans want to build on this property. The California Coastal Commission granted the Nollans permission to build, but only on the condition that they grant the public an easement to walk across their property to go from one public beach to the other. The Nollans claim that the denial of the building permit on these facts constituted an uncompensated taking. The United States Supreme Court will agree.

Justice SCALIA delivered the opinion of the Court.

* * * The California court rejected their claim that imposition of that condition violates the Takings Clause of the Fifth Amendment, as incorporated against the States by the Fourteenth Amendment. *Ibid.* We noted probable jurisdiction. 479 U.S. 913, 107 S.Ct. 312, 93 L.Ed.2d 286 (1986).

* * *

II

Had California simply required the Nollans to make an easement across their beachfront available to the public on a permanent basis in order to increase public access to the beach, rather than conditioning their permit to rebuild their house on their agreeing to do so, we have no doubt there would have been a taking. To say that the appropriation of a public easement across a landowner's premises does not constitute the taking of a property interest but rather (as Justice BRENNAN contends) "a mere restriction on its use," *post,* at 3154, n. 3, is to use words in a manner that deprives them of all their ordinary meaning. Indeed, one of the principal uses of the eminent domain power is to assure that the government be able to require conveyance of just such interests, so long as it pays for them. J. Sackman, 1 Nichols on Eminent Domain § 2.1[1] (Rev. 3d ed. 1985), 2 *id.,* § 5.01[5]; see 1 *id.,* § 1.42 [9], 2 *id.,* § 6.14. Perhaps because the point is so obvious, we have never been confronted with a controversy that required us to rule upon it, but our cases' analysis of the effect of other governmental action leads to the same conclusion. We have repeatedly held that, as to property reserved by its owner for private use, "the right to exclude [others is] 'one of the most essential sticks in the bundle of rights that are commonly characterized as property.' " *Loretto v. Teleprompter Manhattan CATV Corp.,* 458 U.S. 419, 433, 102 S.Ct. 3164, 3175, 73 L.Ed.2d 868 (1982), quoting *Kaiser Aetna v. United States,* 444 U.S. 164, 176, 100 S.Ct. 383, 391, 62 L.Ed.2d 332 (1979). In *Loretto* we observed that where governmental action results in "[a] permanent physical occupation" of the property, by the government itself or by others, see 458 U.S., at 432-433, n. 9, 102 S.Ct., at 3174-3175, n. 9, "our cases uniformly have found a taking to the extent of the occupation, without regard to whether the action achieves an important public benefit or has only minimal economic impact on the owner," *id.,* at 434-435, 102 S.Ct., at 3175-3176. We think a "permanent physical occupation" has occurred, for purposes of that rule, where individuals are given a permanent and continuous right to pass to and fro, so that the real property may continuously be traversed, even though no particular individual is permitted to station himself permanently upon the premises.[16]

---

[16] The holding of *PruneYard Shopping Center v. Robins,* 447 U.S. 74, 100 S.Ct. 2035, 64 L.Ed.2d 741 (1980), is not inconsistent with this analysis, since there the owner had already opened his property to the general public, and in addition permanent access was not required. The analysis of *Kaiser Aetna v. United States,* 444 U.S. 164, 100 S.Ct. 383, 62 L.Ed.2d 332 (1979), is not

* * *

* * * [T]he question becomes whether requiring it to be conveyed as a condition for issuing a land-use permit alters the outcome. We have long recognized that land-use regulation does not effect a taking if it "substantially advance[s] legitimate state interests" and does not "den[y] an owner economically viable use of his land," *Agins v. Tiburon,* 447 U.S. 255, 260, 100 S.Ct. 2138, 2141, 65 L.Ed.2d 106 (1980). See also *Penn Central Transportation Co. v. New York City,* 438 U.S. 104, 127, 98 S.Ct. 2646, 2660, 57 L.Ed.2d 631 (1978) ("[A] use restriction may constitute a 'taking' if not reasonably necessary to the effectuation of a substantial government purpose"). Our cases have not elaborated on the standards for determining what constitutes a "legitimate state interest" or what type of connection between the regulation and the state interest satisfies the requirement that the former "substantially advance" the latter. They have made clear, however, that a broad range of governmental purposes and regulations satisfies these requirements. See *Agins v. Tiburon, supra,* 447 U.S., at 260-262, 100 S.Ct., at 2141-2142 (scenic zoning); *Penn Central Transportation Co. v. New York City, supra* (landmark preservation); *Euclid v. Ambler Realty Co.,* 272 U.S. 365, 47 S.Ct. 114, 71 L.Ed. 303 (1926) (residential zoning); Laitos & Westfall, Government Interference with Private Interests in Public Resources, 11 Harv.Envtl.L.Rev. 1, 66 (1987). The Commission argues that among these permissible purposes are protecting the public's ability to see the beach, assisting the public in overcoming the "psychological barrier" to using the beach created by a developed shorefront, and preventing congestion on the public beaches. We assume, without deciding, that this is so-in which case the Commission unquestionably would be able to deny the Nollans their permit outright if their new house (alone, or by reason of the cumulative impact produced in conjunction with other construction) would substantially impede these purposes, unless the denial would interfere so drastically with the Nollans' use of their property as to constitute a taking. See *Penn Central Transportation Co. v. New York City, supra.*

* * *

The evident constitutional propriety disappears, however, if the condition substituted for the prohibition utterly fails to further the end advanced as the justification for the prohibition. When that essential nexus is eliminated, the situation becomes the same as if California law forbade shouting fire in a crowded theater, but granted dispensations to those willing to contribute $100 to the state treasury. While a ban on shouting fire can be a core exercise of the State's police power to protect the public safety, and can thus meet even our stringent standards for regulation of speech, adding the unrelated condition alters the purpose to one which, while it may be legitimate, is inadequate to sustain the ban. Therefore, even though, in a sense, requiring a $100 tax contribution in order to shout fire is a lesser restriction on speech than an outright ban, it would not pass constitutional muster. Similarly here, the lack of nexus between the condition and the original purpose of the building restriction converts that purpose to something other than what it was. The purpose then becomes, quite simply, the obtaining of an easement to serve some valid governmental purpose, but without payment of compensation. Whatever may be the outer limits of "legitimate state interests" in the

---

inconsistent because it was affected by traditional doctrines regarding navigational servitudes. Of course neither of those cases involved, as this one does, a classic right-of-way easement.

takings and land-use context, this is not one of them. In short, unless the permit condition serves the same governmental purpose as the development ban, the building restriction is not a valid regulation of land use but "an out-and-out plan of extortion." *J.E.D. Associates, Inc. v. Atkinson,* 121 N.H. 581, 584, 432 A.2d 12, 14-15 (1981); see Brief for United States as *Amicus Curiae* 22, and n. 20. See also *Loretto v. Teleprompter Manhattan CATV Corp.,* 458 U.S., at 439, n. 17, 102 S.Ct., at 3178, n. 17.

III

The Commission claims that it concedes as much, and that we may sustain the condition at issue here by finding that it is reasonably related to the public need or burden that the Nollans' new house creates or to which it contributes. We can accept, for purposes of discussion, the Commission's proposed test as to how close a "fit" between the condition and the burden is required, because we find that this case does not meet even the most untailored standards. The Commission's principal contention to the contrary essentially turns on a play on the word "access." The Nollans' new house, the Commission found, will interfere with "visual access" to the beach. That in turn (along with other shorefront development) will interfere with the desire of people who drive past the Nollans' house to use the beach, thus creating a "psychological barrier" to "access." The Nollans' new house will also, by a process not altogether clear from the Commission's opinion but presumably potent enough to more than offset the effects of the psychological barrier, increase the use of the public beaches, thus creating the need for more "access." These burdens on "access" would be alleviated by a requirement that the Nollans provide "lateral access" to the beach.

Rewriting the argument to eliminate the play on words makes clear that there is nothing to it. It is quite impossible to understand how a requirement that people already on the public beaches be able to walk across the Nollans' property reduces any obstacles to viewing the beach created by the new house. It is also impossible to understand how it lowers any "psychological barrier" to using the public beaches, or how it helps to remedy any additional congestion on them caused by construction of the Nollans' new house. We therefore find that the Commission's imposition of the permit condition cannot be treated as an exercise of its land-use power for any of these purposes. Our conclusion on this point is consistent with the approach taken by every other court that has considered the question, with the exception of the California state courts. [Citations omitted.]

* * * We view the Fifth Amendment's Property Clause to be more than a pleading requirement, and compliance with it to be more than an exercise in cleverness and imagination. As indicated earlier, our cases describe the condition for abridgement of property rights through the police power as a "*substantial* advanc[ing]" of a legitimate state interest. We are inclined to be particularly careful about the adjective where the actual conveyance of property is made a condition to the lifting of a land-use restriction, since in that context there is heightened risk that the purpose is avoidance of the compensation requirement, rather than the stated police-power objective.

* * *

Reversed.

* * *

Dolan v. City of Tigard
512 U.S. 374 (1994)

Dolan owns a hardware store and wants to expand. The City of Tigard granted her a building permit, but only on the condition that she dedicate some of her property as a "greenway" for flood control and dedicate another part of the subject property for a bicycle path to reduce traffic. Dolan claims that this conditional approval is an unconstitutional taking. The United States Supreme Court will agree. In the process, the court will make reference to the Nollan *"Essential Nexus" test and, append to that test a "Rough Proportionality" test.*

Chief Justice REHNQUIST delivered the opinion of the Court.

* * * We granted certiorari to resolve a question left open by our decision in *Nollan v. California Coastal Comm'n,* 483 U.S. 825, 107 S.Ct. 3141, 97 L.Ed.2d 677 (1987), of what is the required degree of connection between the exactions imposed by the city and the projected impacts of the proposed development.

I
* * *

III

In evaluating petitioner's claim, we must first determine whether the "essential nexus" exists between the "legitimate state interest" and the permit condition exacted by the city. *Nollan,* 483 U.S., at 837, 107 S.Ct., at 3148. If we find that a nexus exists, we must then decide the required degree of connection between the exactions and the projected impact of the proposed development. We were not required to reach this question in *Nollan,* because we concluded that the connection did not meet even the loosest standard. *Id.,* at 838, 107 S.Ct., at 3149. Here, however, we must decide this question.

A

We addressed the essential nexus question in *Nollan.* The California Coastal Commission demanded a lateral public easement across the Nollans' beachfront lot in exchange for a permit to demolish an existing bungalow and replace it with a three-bedroom house. *Id.,* at 828, 107 S.Ct., at 3144. The public easement was designed to connect two public beaches that were separated by the Nollan's property. The Coastal Commission had asserted that the public easement condition was imposed to promote the legitimate state interest of diminishing the "blockage of the view of the ocean" caused by construction of the larger house.

We agreed that the Coastal Commission's concern with protecting visual access to the ocean constituted a legitimate public interest. *Id.,* at 835, 107 S.Ct., at 3148. We also agreed that the permit condition would have been constitutional "even if it consisted of the requirement that the Nollans provide a viewing spot on their property for passersby with whose sighting of the ocean their new house would interfere." *Id.,* at 836, 107 S.Ct., at 3148. We resolved, however, that the Coastal Commission's regulatory authority was set completely adrift from its constitutional moorings when it claimed that a nexus existed between visual access to the ocean and a permit condition requiring lateral public access along the Nollans' beachfront lot. *Id.,* at 837, 107 S.Ct., at 3148. How enhancing the public's ability to "traverse to and along the shorefront" served the same governmental purpose of "visual access to the ocean" from the roadway was beyond our ability to countenance. The absence of a nexus left the Coastal Commission in the position of simply trying to obtain an easement through gimmickry, which converted a valid regulation of land use into " 'an out-and-out plan of extortion.' " *Ibid.,* quoting *J.E.D. Associates, Inc. v. Atkinson,* 121 N.H. 581, 584, 432 A.2d 12, 14-15 (1981).

No such gimmicks are associated with the permit conditions imposed by the city in this case. Undoubtedly, the prevention of flooding along Fanno Creek and the reduction of traffic congestion in the Central Business District qualify as the type of legitimate public purposes we have upheld. *Agins,* 447 U.S., at 260-262, 100 S.Ct., at 2141-2142. It seems equally obvious that a nexus exists between preventing flooding along Fanno Creek and limiting development within the creek's 100-year floodplain. Petitioner proposes to double the size of her retail store and to pave her now-gravel parking lot, thereby expanding the impervious surface on the property and increasing the amount of storm water runoff into Fanno Creek.

The same may be said for the city's attempt to reduce traffic congestion by providing for alternative means of transportation. In theory, a pedestrian/bicycle pathway provides a useful alternative means of transportation for workers and shoppers: "Pedestrians and bicyclists occupying dedicated spaces for walking and/or bicycling * * * remove potential vehicles from streets, resulting in an overall improvement in total transportation system flow." A. Nelson, Public Provision of Pedestrian and Bicycle Access Ways: Public Policy Rationale and the Nature of Private Benefits 11, Center for Planning Development, Georgia Institute of Technology, Working Paper Series (Jan. 1994). See also Intermodal Surface Transportation Efficiency Act of 1991, Pub.L. 102-240, 105 Stat.1914 (recognizing pedestrian and bicycle facilities as necessary components of any strategy to reduce traffic congestion).

B

The second part of our analysis requires us to determine whether the degree of the exactions demanded by the city's permit conditions bears the required relationship to the projected impact of petitioner's proposed development. * * *

The city required that petitioner dedicate "to the City as Greenway all portions of the site that fall within the existing 100-year floodplain [of Fanno Creek] * * * and all property 15 feet above [the floodplain] boundary." *Id.,* at 113, n. 3, 854 P.2d, at 439, n. 3. In addition, the city demanded that the retail store be designed so as not to intrude into the greenway area. The city relies on the Commission's rather tentative findings that increased storm water flow from petitioner's property "can only add to the public need to manage the [floodplain] for drainage purposes" to support its conclusion that the "requirement of dedication of the floodplain area on the site is related to the applicant's plan to intensify development on the site." City of Tigard Planning Commission Final Order No. 91-09 PC, App. to Pet. for Cert. G-37.

The city made the following specific findings relevant to the pedestrian/bicycle pathway:

"In addition, the proposed expanded use of this site is anticipated to generate additional vehicular traffic thereby increasing congestion on nearby collector and arterial streets. Creation of a convenient, safe pedestrian/bicycle pathway system as an alternative means of transportation could offset some of the traffic demand on these nearby streets and lessen the increase in traffic congestion." *Id.,* at G-24.

The question for us is whether these findings are constitutionally sufficient to justify the conditions imposed by the city on petitioner's building permit. Since state courts have been dealing with this question a good deal longer than we have, we turn to representative decisions made by them.

In some states, very generalized statements as to the necessary connection between the required dedication and the proposed development seem to suffice. See, *e.g., Billings Properties, Inc. v. Yellowstone County,* 144 Mont. 25, 394 P.2d 182 (1964); *Jenad, Inc. v. Scarsdale,* 18 N.Y.2d 78, 271 N.Y.S.2d 955, 218 N.E.2d 673 (1966). We think this standard is too lax to adequately protect petitioner's right to just compensation if her property is taken for a public purpose.

Other state courts require a very exacting correspondence, described as the "specifi[c] and uniquely attributable" test. The Supreme Court of Illinois first developed this test in *Pioneer Trust & Savings Bank v. Mount Prospect,* 22 Ill.2d 375, 380, 176 N.E.2d 799, 802 (1961). Under this standard, if the local government cannot demonstrate that its exaction is directly proportional to the specifically created need, the exaction becomes "a veiled exercise of the power of eminent domain and a confiscation of private property behind the defense of police regulations." *Id.,* at 381, 176 N.E.2d, at 802. We do not think the Federal Constitution requires such exacting scrutiny, given the nature of the interests involved.

A number of state courts have taken an intermediate position, requiring the municipality to show a "reasonable relationship" between the required dedication and the impact of the proposed development. Typical is the Supreme Court of Nebraska's opinion in *Simpson v. North Platte,* 206 Neb. 240, 245, 292 N.W.2d 297, 301 (1980), where that court stated:

"The distinction, therefore, which must be made between an appropriate exercise of the police power and an improper exercise of eminent domain is whether the requirement has some reasonable relationship or nexus to the use to which the property is being made or is merely being used as an excuse for taking property simply because at that particular moment the landowner is asking the city for some license or permit."

Thus, the court held that a city may not require a property owner to dedicate private property for some future public use as a condition of obtaining a building permit when such future use is not "occasioned by the construction sought to be permitted." *Id.,* at 248, 292 N.W.2d, at 302.

Some form of the reasonable relationship test has been adopted in many other jurisdictions. See, *e.g., Jordan v. Menomonee Falls,* 28 Wis.2d 608, 137 N.W.2d 442 (1965); *Collis v. Bloomington,* 310 Minn. 5, 246 N.W.2d 19 (1976) (requiring a showing of a reasonable relationship between the planned subdivision and the municipality's need for land); *College Station v. Turtle Rock Corp.,* 680 S.W.2d 802, 807 (Tex.1984); *Call v. West Jordan,* 606 P.2d 217, 220 (Utah 1979) (affirming use of the reasonable relation test). Despite any semantic differences, general agreement exists among the courts "that the dedication should have some reasonable relationship to the needs created by the [development]." *Ibid.* See generally Note " 'Take' My Beach Please!": *Nollan v. California Coastal Commission* and a Rational-Nexus Constitutional Analysis of Development Exactions, 69 B.U.L.Rev. 823 (1989); see also *Parks v. Watson,* 716 F.2d 646, 651-653 (CA9 1983).

We think the "reasonable relationship" test adopted by a majority of the state courts is closer to the federal constitutional norm than either of those previously discussed. But we do not adopt it as such, partly because the term "reasonable relationship" seems confusingly similar to the term "rational basis" which describes the minimal level of scrutiny under the Equal Protection Clause of the Fourteenth Amendment. We think a term such as "rough proportionality" best encapsulates what we hold to be the requirement of the Fifth Amendment. No precise mathematical calculation is required, but the city must make some sort of individualized determination that the required dedication is related both in nature and extent to the impact of the proposed development.[17]

* * * We turn now to analysis of whether the findings relied upon by the city here, first with respect to the floodplain easement, and second with respect to the pedestrian/bicycle path, satisfied these requirements.

It is axiomatic that increasing the amount of impervious surface will increase the quantity and rate of storm water flow from petitioner's property. Record, Doc. No. F, ch. 4, p. 4-29. Therefore, keeping the floodplain open and free from development would likely confine the pressures on Fanno Creek created by petitioner's development. In fact, because petitioner's property lies within the Central Business District, the CDC already required that petitioner leave 15% of it as open space and the undeveloped floodplain would have nearly satisfied that requirement. App. to Pet. for Cert. G-16 to G-17. But the city demanded more-it not only wanted petitioner not to build in the floodplain, but it also wanted petitioner's property along Fanno Creek for its greenway system. The city has never said why a public greenway, as opposed to a private one, was required in the interest of flood control.

The difference to petitioner, of course, is the loss of her ability to exclude others. As we have noted, this right to exclude others is "one of the most essential sticks in the bundle of rights that are commonly characterized as property." *Kaiser Aetna,* 444 U.S., at 176, 100 S.Ct., at 391. It is difficult to see why recreational visitors trampling along petitioner's floodplain easement are sufficiently related to the city's legitimate interest in reducing flooding problems along Fanno Creek, and the city has not attempted to make any individualized determination to support this part of its request.

* * *

* * * We conclude that the findings upon which the city relies do not show the required reasonable relationship between the floodplain easement and the petitioner's proposed new building.

* * *

As Justice Peterson of the Supreme Court of Oregon explained in his dissenting opinion, however, "[t]he findings of fact that the bicycle pathway system '*could* offset

---

[17] Justice STEVENS' dissent takes us to task for placing the burden on the city to justify the required dedication. * * *

some of the traffic demand' is a far cry from a finding that the bicycle pathway system *will,* or is *likely to,* offset some of the traffic demand." 317 Ore., at 127, 854 P.2d, at 447 (emphasis in original). No precise mathematical calculation is required, but the city must make some effort to quantify its findings in support of the dedication for the pedestrian/bicycle pathway beyond the conclusory statement that it could offset some of the traffic demand generated.

IV

* * *

The judgment of the Supreme Court of Oregon is reversed, and the case is remanded for further proceedings not inconsistent with this opinion.

It is so ordered.

* * *

Koontz v. St. Johns River Water Management Dist.
570 U.S. __ (2013)

Coy Koontz, Sr. (who died during the litigation and whose son, Coy Koontz, Jr., became the representative of the estate) sought to improve wetlands property that he had acquired years earlier. Pursuant to Florida law, Koontz first had to secure a permit from the St. Johns River Water Management District. In this regard, Koontz offered to mitigate the anticipated environmental effects of his development proposal by deeding to the District a conservation easement covering almost three-quarters of his property. The District rejected Koontz's proposal and informed him it would approve his project only if he deeded a larger conservation easement to the District or, alternatively, if he hired and paid contractors to make improvements to District-owned wetlands several miles away. Koontz then filed suit in state court, claiming that the District's denial of the permit constituted an unlawful taking. The trial court found the District's actions unlawful because they failed the requirements of Nollan *and* Dolan, supra. *The Florida Supreme Court reversed, however. First, it held that the petitioner's (Koontz's) claim failed because, unlike in* Nollan *or* Dolan, *the District denied the application (in* Nollan *and* Dolan, *the permits were granted on the condition that the landowners convey an easement to the public). Second, the Florida Supreme Court held that a governmental demand for money could not give rise to a takings claim under* Nollan *and* Dolan. *The United States Supreme Court, in a 5-4 decision, reverses and remands.*

Justice ALITO delivered the opinion of the Court.

Our decisions in *Nollan v. California Coastal Comm'n,* 483 U.S. 825, 107 S.Ct. 3141, 97 L.Ed.2d 677 (1987), and *Dolan v. City of Tigard,* 512 U.S. 374, 114 S.Ct. 2309, 129 L.Ed.2d 304 (1994), provide important protection against the misuse of the power of land-use regulation. In those cases, we held that a unit of government may not condition the approval of a land-use permit on the owner's relinquishment of a portion of his property unless there is a "nexus" and "rough proportionality" between the government's demand and the effects of the proposed land use. In this case, the St. Johns River Water Management District (District) believes that it circumvented *Nollan* and *Dolan* because of the way in which it structured its handling of a permit application submitted by Coy Koontz, Sr., whose estate is represented in this Court by Coy Koontz, Jr. The District did not approve his application on the condition that he surrender an interest in his land. Instead, the District, after suggesting that he could obtain approval by signing over such an interest, denied his application because he refused to yield. The Florida Supreme Court blessed this maneuver and thus effectively interred those important decisions. Because we conclude that *Nollan* and *Dolan* cannot be evaded in this way, the Florida Supreme Court's decision must be reversed.

I
A

In 1972, petitioner purchased an undeveloped 14.9–acre tract of land on the south side of Florida State Road 50, a divided four-lane highway east of Orlando. * * *

* * *

Petitioner decided to develop the 3.7–acre northern section of his property, and in 1994 he applied to the District for * * * permits. * * * To mitigate the environmental effects of his proposal, petitioner offered to foreclose any possible future development of the approximately 11-acre southern section of his land by deeding to the District a conservation easement on that portion of his property.

The District considered the 11-acre conservation easement to be inadequate, and it informed petitioner that it would approve construction only if he agreed to one of two concessions. First, the District proposed that petitioner reduce the size of his development to 1 acre and deed to the District a conservation easement on the remaining 13.9 acres. * * *

In the alternative, the District told petitioner that he could proceed with the development as proposed, building on 3.7 acres and deeding a conservation easement to the government on the remainder of the property, if he also agreed to hire contractors to make improvements to District-owned land several miles away. Specifically, petitioner could pay to replace culverts on one parcel or fill in ditches on another. Either of those projects would have enhanced approximately 50-acres of District-owned wetlands. When the District asks permit applicants to fund offsite mitigation work, its policy is never to require any particular offsite project, and it did not do so here. Instead, the District said that it "would also favorably consider" alternatives to its suggested offsite mitigation projects if petitioner proposed something "equivalent." App. 75.

Believing the District's demands for mitigation to be excessive in light of the environmental effects that his building proposal would have caused, petitioner filed suit in state court. Among other claims, he argued that he was entitled to relief under Fla. Stat. § 373.617(2), which allows owners to recover "monetary damages" if a state agency's action is "an unreasonable exercise of the state's police power constituting a taking without just compensation."

B

* * * [The Florida trial court] held the District's actions unlawful under our decisions in *Nollan* and *Dolan*.

The Florida District Court affirmed, 5 So.3d 8 (2009), but the State Supreme Court reversed, 77 So.3d 1220 (2011). A majority of that court distinguished *Nollan* and *Dolan* on two grounds. First, the majority thought it significant that in this case, unlike *Nollan* or *Dolan,* the District did not approve petitioner's application on the condition that he accede to the District's demands; instead, the District denied his application because he refused to make concessions. 77 So.3d, at 1230. Second, the majority drew a distinction between a demand for an interest in real property (what happened in *Nollan* and *Dolan*) and a demand for money. * * *

Recognizing that the majority opinion rested on a question of federal constitutional law on which the lower courts are divided, we granted the petition for a writ of certiorari, 568 U.S. ___ (2012), and now reverse.

II

A

We have said in a variety of contexts that "the government may not deny a benefit to a person because he exercises a constitutional right." *Regan v. Taxation With Representation of Wash.,* 461 U.S. 540, 545, 103 S.Ct. 1997, 76 L.Ed.2d 129 (1983). See also, *e.g., Rumsfeld v. Forum for Academic and Institutional Rights, Inc.,* 547 U.S. 47, 59–60, 126 S.Ct. 1297, 164 L.Ed.2d 156 (2006); *Rutan v. Republican Party of Ill.,* 497 U.S. 62, 78, 110 S.Ct. 2729, 111 L.Ed.2d 52 (1990). In *Perry v. Sindermann,* 408 U.S. 593, 92 S.Ct. 2694, 33 L.Ed.2d 570 (1972), for example, we held that a public college would violate a professor's freedom of speech if it declined to renew his contract because he was an outspoken critic of the college's administration. And in *Memorial Hospital v. Maricopa County,* 415 U.S. 250, 94 S.Ct. 1076, 39 L.Ed.2d 306 (1974), we concluded that a county impermissibly burdened the right to travel by extending healthcare benefits only to those indigent sick who had been residents of the county for at least one year. Those cases reflect an overarching principle, known as the unconstitutional conditions doctrine, that vindicates the Constitution's enumerated rights by preventing the government from coercing people into giving them up.

Nollan and *Dolan* "involve a special application" of this doctrine that protects the Fifth Amendment right to just compensation for property the government takes when owners apply for land-use permits. *Lingle v. Chevron U.S.A. Inc.,* 544 U.S. 528, 547, 125 S.Ct. 2074, 161 L.Ed.2d 876 (2005); *Dolan,* 512 U.S., at 385 (invoking "the well-settled doctrine of 'unconstitutional conditions' "). Our decisions in those cases reflect two realities of the permitting process. The first is that land-use permit applicants are especially vulnerable to the type of coercion that the unconstitutional conditions doctrine prohibits because the government often has broad discretion to deny a permit that is worth far more than property it would like to take. By conditioning a building permit on the owner's deeding over a public right-of-way, for example, the government can pressure an owner into voluntarily giving up property for which the Fifth Amendment would otherwise require just compensation. See *id.,* at 384; *Nollan,* 483 U.S., at 831. So long as the building permit is more valuable than any just compensation the owner could hope to receive for the right-of-way, the owner is likely to accede to the government's demand, no matter how unreasonable. Extortionate demands of this sort frustrate the Fifth Amendment right to just compensation, and the unconstitutional conditions doctrine prohibits them.

A second reality of the permitting process is that many proposed land uses threaten to impose costs on the public that dedications of property can offset. Where a building proposal would substantially increase traffic congestion, for example, officials might condition permit approval on the owner's agreement to deed over the land needed to widen a public road. Respondent argues that a similar rationale justifies the exaction at issue here: petitioner's proposed construction project, it submits, would destroy wetlands on his property, and in order to compensate for this loss, respondent demands that he enhance wetlands elsewhere. Insisting that landowners internalize the negative externalities of their conduct is a hallmark of responsible land-use policy, and we have long sustained such regulations against constitutional attack. See *Village of Euclid v. Ambler Realty Co.,* 272 U.S. 365, 47 S.Ct. 114, 71 L.Ed. 303 (1926).

Nollan and *Dolan* accommodate both realities by allowing the government to condition approval of a permit on the dedication of property to the public so long as there is a "nexus" and "rough proportionality" between the property that the government demands and the social costs of the applicant's proposal. *Dolan, supra,* at 391; *Nollan,* 483 U.S., at 837. Our precedents thus enable permitting authorities to insist that applicants bear the full costs of their proposals while still forbidding the government from engaging in "out-and-out ... extortion" that would thwart the Fifth Amendment right to just compensation. *Ibid.* (internal quotation marks omitted). Under *Nollan* and *Dolan* the government may choose whether and how a permit applicant is required to mitigate the impacts of a proposed development, but it may not leverage its legitimate interest in mitigation to pursue governmental ends that lack an essential nexus and rough proportionality to those impacts.

B

The principles that undergird our decisions in *Nollan* and *Dolan* do not change depending on whether the government *approves* a permit on the condition that the applicant turn over property or *denies* a permit because the applicant refuses to do so. We have often concluded that denials of governmental benefits were impermissible under the unconstitutional conditions doctrine. See, *e.g., Perry,* 408 U.S., at 597 (explaining that the government "*may not deny* a benefit to a person on a basis that infringes his constitutionally protected interests" (emphasis added)); *Memorial Hospital,* 415 U.S. 250, 94 S.Ct. 1076, 39 L.Ed.2d 306 (finding unconstitutional condition where government denied healthcare benefits). In so holding, we have recognized that regardless of whether the government ultimately succeeds in pressuring someone into forfeiting a constitutional right, the unconstitutional conditions doctrine forbids burdening the Constitution's enumerated rights by coercively withholding benefits from those who exercise them.

A contrary rule would be especially untenable in this case because it would enable the government to evade the limitations of *Nollan* and *Dolan* simply by phrasing its demands for property as conditions precedent to permit approval. Under the Florida Supreme Court's approach, a government order stating that a permit is "approved if" the owner turns over property would be subject to *Nollan* and *Dolan,* but an identical order that uses the words "denied until" would not. Our unconstitutional conditions cases have long refused to attach significance to the distinction between conditions precedent and conditions subsequent. See *Frost & Frost Trucking Co. v. Railroad Comm'n of Cal.,* 271

U.S. 583, 592–593, 46 S.Ct. 605, 70 L.Ed. 1101 (1926) (invalidating regulation that required the petitioner to give up a constitutional right "as a condition precedent to the enjoyment of a privilege"); *Southern Pacific Co. v. Denton,* 146 U.S. 202, 207, 13 S.Ct. 44, 36 L.Ed. 942 (1892) (invalidating statute "requiring the corporation, as a condition precedent to obtaining a permit to do business within the State, to surrender a right and privilege secured to it by the Constitution"). See also *Flower Mound,* 135 S.W.3d, at 639 ("The government cannot sidestep constitutional protections merely by rephrasing its decision from 'only if' to 'not unless' "). To do so here would effectively render *Nollan* and *Dolan* a dead letter.

The Florida Supreme Court puzzled over how the government's demand for property can violate the Takings Clause even though " 'no property of any kind was ever taken,' " 77 So.3d, at 1225 (quoting 5 So.3d, at 20 (Griffin, J., dissenting)); see also 77 So.3d, at 1229–1230, but the unconstitutional conditions doctrine provides a ready answer. Extortionate demands for property in the land-use permitting context run afoul of the Takings Clause not because they take property but because they impermissibly burden the right not to have property taken without just compensation. As in other unconstitutional conditions cases in which someone refuses to cede a constitutional right in the face of coercive pressure, the impermissible denial of a governmental benefit is a constitutionally cognizable injury.

* * *

III

We turn to the Florida Supreme Court's alternative holding that petitioner's claim fails because respondent asked him to spend money rather than give up an easement on his land.* * * Respondent and the dissent take the same position, citing the concurring and dissenting opinions in *Eastern Enterprises v. Apfel,* 524 U.S. 498, 118 S.Ct. 2131, 141 L.Ed.2d 451 (1998), for the proposition that an obligation to spend money can never provide the basis for a takings claim. See *post,* at 5–8 (opinion of KAGAN, J.).

We note as an initial matter that if we accepted this argument it would be very easy for land-use permitting officials to evade the limitations of *Nollan* and *Dolan.* Because the government need only provide a permit applicant with one alternative that satisfies the nexus and rough proportionality standards, a permitting authority wishing to exact an easement could simply give the owner a choice of either surrendering an easement or making a payment equal to the easement's value. Such so-called "in lieu of" fees are utterly commonplace, Rosenberg, The Changing Culture of American Land Use Regulation: Paying for Growth with Impact Fees, 59 S.M.U.L.Rev. 177, 202–203 (2006), and they are functionally equivalent to other types of land use exactions. For that reason and those that follow, we reject respondent's argument and hold that so-called "monetary exactions" must satisfy the nexus and rough proportionality requirements of *Nollan* and *Dolan.*

* * *

* * * The fulcrum this case turns on is the direct link between the government's demand and a specific parcel of real property.[18] Because of that direct link, this case

---

[18] Thus, because the proposed offsite mitigation obligation in this case was tied to a particular parcel of land, this case does not implicate the question whether monetary exactions must be tied

implicates the central concern of *Nollan* and *Dolan*: the risk that the government may use its substantial power and discretion in land-use permitting to pursue governmental ends that lack an essential nexus and rough proportionality to the effects of the proposed new use of the specific property at issue, thereby diminishing without justification the value of the property.

* * *

B

Respondent and the dissent argue that if monetary exactions are made subject to scrutiny under *Nollan* and *Dolan,* then there will be no principled way of distinguishing impermissible land-use exactions from property taxes. * * * We think they exaggerate both the extent to which that problem is unique to the land-use permitting context and the practical difficulty of distinguishing between the power to tax and the power to take by eminent domain.

* * *

This case does not require us to say more. We need not decide at precisely what point a land-use permitting charge denominated by the government as a "tax" becomes "so arbitrary ... that it was not the exertion of taxation but a confiscation of property." *Brushaber v. Union Pacific R. Co.,* 240 U.S. 1, 24–25, 36 S.Ct. 236, 60 L.Ed. 493 (1916). For present purposes, it suffices to say that despite having long recognized that "the power of taxation should not be confused with the power of eminent domain," *Houck v. Little River Drainage Dist.,* 239 U.S. 254, 264, 36 S.Ct. 58, 60 L.Ed. 266 (1915), we have had little trouble distinguishing between the two.

C

Finally, we disagree with the dissent's forecast that our decision will work a revolution in land use law by depriving local governments of the ability to charge reasonable permitting fees. *Post,* at 8. Numerous courts—including courts in many of our Nation's most populous States—have confronted constitutional challenges to monetary exactions over the last two decades and applied the standard from *Nollan* and *Dolan* or something like it. See, *e.g., Northern Ill. Home Builders Assn. v. County of Du Page,* 165 Ill.2d 25, 31–32, 208 Ill.Dec. 328, 649 N.E.2d 384, 388–389 (1995); *Home Builders Assn. v. Beavercreek,* 89 Ohio St.3d 121, 128, 729 N.E.2d 349, 356 (2000); *Flower Mound,* 135 S.W.3d, at 640–641. Yet the "significant practical harm" the dissent predicts has not come to pass. *Post,* at 8. * * *

* * *

We hold that the government's demand for property from a land-use permit applicant must satisfy the requirements of *Nollan* and *Dolan* even when the government denies the permit and even when its demand is for money. The Court expresses no view on the merits of petitioner's claim that respondent's actions here failed to comply with

---

to a particular parcel of land in order to constitute a taking. That is so even when the demand is considered "*outside* the permitting process." *Post,* at 8 (KAGAN, J., dissenting). The unconstitutional conditions analysis requires us to set aside petitioner's *permit application,* not his ownership of a particular parcel of real property.

the principles set forth in this opinion and those two cases. The Florida Supreme Court's judgment is reversed, and this case is remanded for further proceedings not inconsistent with this opinion.

It is so ordered.

Justice KAGAN, with whom Justice GINSBURG, Justice BREYER, and Justice SOTOMAYOR join, dissenting.
* * *

* * * The majority extends *Nollan* and *Dolan* to cases in which the government conditions a permit not on the transfer of real property, but instead on the payment or expenditure of money. That runs roughshod over *Eastern Enterprises v. Apfel,* 524 U.S. 498, 118 S.Ct. 2131, 141 L.Ed.2d 451 (1998), which held that the government may impose ordinary financial obligations without triggering the Takings Clause's protections. The boundaries of the majority's new rule are uncertain. But it threatens to subject a vast array of land-use regulations, applied daily in States and localities throughout the country, to heightened constitutional scrutiny. I would not embark on so unwise an adventure, and would affirm the Florida Supreme Court's decision.
* * *

III
* * *

The majority's errors here are consequential. The majority turns a broad array of local land-use regulations into federal constitutional questions. It deprives state and local governments of the flexibility they need to enhance their communities—to ensure environmentally sound and economically productive development. It places courts smack in the middle of the most everyday local government activity. As those consequences play out across the country, I believe the Court will rue today's decision. I respectfully dissent.

§ 15.5 Judicial Takings

The question raised here is whether the Fifth Amendment applies only to acts of the legislature and executive branches, or whether the Fifth Amendment also is applicable to judicial decisions that act as a taking of private property without just compensation.

Stop the Beach Renourishment, Inc. v. Florida Dept. of Environmental Protection
560 U.S. 702 (2010)

In an opinion written by Justice Scalia, the court held in an 8-0 decision (Justice Stevens did not participate), that when Florida, pursuant to a state statute, added sand to owners' oceanfront property, the state did not affect a taking of any rights. Justice Scalia went on to write, however, in Parts II and III, that if a court's decision denies a landowner's established rights, that court has affected a taking in violation of the

Takings Clause. Only Chief Justice Roberts, Justice Alito, and Justice Thomas joined in Parts II and III of the opinion. Those parts are reproduced, below.

* * *

II

A

Before coming to the parties' arguments in the present case, we discuss some general principles of our takings jurisprudence. The Takings Clause--"nor shall private property be taken for public use, without just compensation," U.S. Const., Amdt. 5-- applies as fully to the taking of a landowner's riparian rights as it does to the taking of an estate in land. See *Yates v. Milwaukee,* 10 Wall. 497, 504, 19 L.Ed. 984 (1871). Moreover, though the classic taking is a transfer of property to the State or to another private party by eminent domain, the Takings Clause applies to other state actions that achieve the same thing. Thus, when the government uses its own property in such a way that it destroys private property, it has taken that property. See *United States v. Causby,* 328 U.S. 256, 261-262, 66 S.Ct. 1062, 90 L.Ed. 1206 (1946); *Pumpelly v. Green Bay Co.,* 13 Wall. 166, 177-178, 20 L.Ed. 557 (1872). Similarly, our doctrine of regulatory takings "aims to identify regulatory actions that are functionally equivalent to the classic taking." *Lingle v. Chevron U.S.A. Inc.,* 544 U.S. 528, 539, 125 S.Ct. 2074, 161 L.Ed.2d 876 (2005). Thus, it is a taking when a state regulation forces a property owner to submit to a permanent physical occupation, *Loretto v. Teleprompter Manhattan CATV Corp.,* 458 U.S. 419, 425-426, 102 S.Ct. 3164, 73 L.Ed.2d 868 (1982), or deprives him of all economically beneficial use of his property, *Lucas v. South Carolina Coastal Council,* 505 U.S. 1003, 1019, 112 S.Ct. 2886, 120 L.Ed.2d 798 (1992). Finally (and here we approach the situation before us), States effect a taking if they recharacterize as public property what was previously private property. See *Webb's Fabulous Pharmacies, Inc. v. Beckwith,* 449 U.S. 155, 163-165, 101 S.Ct. 446, 66 L.Ed.2d 358 (1980)

The Takings Clause (unlike, for instance, the Ex Post Facto Clauses, see Art. I, § 9, cl. 3; § 10, cl. 1) is not addressed to the action of a specific branch or branches. It is concerned simply with the act, and not with the governmental actor ("nor shall private property *be taken*" (emphasis added)). There is no textual justification for saying that the existence or the scope of a State's power to expropriate private property without just compensation varies according to the branch of government effecting the expropriation. Nor does common sense recommend such a principle. It would be absurd to allow a State to do by judicial decree what the Takings Clause forbids it to do by legislative fiat. See *Stevens v. Cannon Beach,* 510 U.S. 1207, 1211-1212, 114 S.Ct. 1332, 127 L.Ed.2d 679 (1994) (SCALIA, J., dissenting from denial of certiorari).

Our precedents provide no support for the proposition that takings effected by the judicial branch are entitled to special treatment, and in fact suggest the contrary. *PruneYard Shopping Center v. Robins,* 447 U.S. 74, 100 S.Ct. 2035, 64 L.Ed.2d 741 (1980), involved a decision of the California Supreme Court overruling one of its prior decisions which had held that the California Constitution's guarantees of freedom of speech and of the press, and of the right to petition the government, did not require the owner of private property to accord those rights on his premises. The appellants, owners of a shopping center, contended that their private property rights could not "be denied by invocation of a state constitutional provision *or by judicial reconstruction of a State's laws of private property,*" *id.*, at 79, 100 S.Ct. 2035 (emphasis added). We held that there had been no taking, citing cases involving legislative and executive takings, and applying standard Takings Clause analysis. See *id.*, at 82-84, 100 S.Ct. 2035. We treated the California Supreme Court's application of the constitutional provisions as a regulation of the use of private property, and evaluated whether that regulation violated the property owners' "right to exclude others," *id.*, at 80, 100 S.Ct. 2035 (internal quotation marks omitted). Our opinion addressed only the claimed taking by the constitutional provision. Its failure to speak separately to the claimed taking by "judicial reconstruction of a State's laws of private property" certainly does not suggest that a taking by judicial action cannot occur, and arguably suggests that the same analysis applicable to taking by constitutional provision would apply.

Webb's Fabulous Pharmacies, supra, is even closer in point. There the purchaser of an insolvent corporation had interpleaded the corporation's creditors, placing the purchase price in an interest-bearing account in the registry of the Circuit Court of Seminole County, to be distributed in satisfaction of claims approved by a receiver. The Florida Supreme Court construed an applicable statute to mean that the interest on the account belonged to the county, because the account was "considered 'public money,' " *Beckwith v. Webb's Fabulous Pharmacies,* 374 So.2d 951, 952-953 (1979) *(per curiam).* We held this to be a taking. We noted that "[t]he usual and general rule is that any interest on an interpleaded and deposited fund follows the principal and is to be allocated to those who are ultimately to be the owners of that principal," 449 U.S., at 162, 101 S.Ct. 446. "Neither the Florida Legislature by statute, nor the Florida courts by judicial decree," we said, "may accomplish the result the county seeks simply by recharacterizing the principal as 'public money.' " *Id.*, at 164, 101 S.Ct. 446.

In sum, the Takings Clause bars *the State* from taking private property without paying for it, no matter which branch is the instrument of the taking. To be sure, the manner of state action may matter: Condemnation by eminent domain, for example, is always a taking, while a legislative, executive, or judicial restriction of property use may or may not be, depending on its nature and extent. But the particular state *actor* is irrelevant. If a legislature *or a court* declares that what was once an established right of private property no longer exists, it has taken that property, no less than if the State had physically appropriated it or destroyed its value by regulation. "[A] State, by *ipse dixit,* may not transform private property into public property without compensation." *Ibid.*

* * *

III

Respondents put forward a number of arguments which contradict, to a greater or lesser degree, the principle discussed above, that the existence of a taking does not depend upon the branch of government that effects it. First, in a case claiming a judicial taking they would add to our normal takings inquiry a requirement that the court's decision have no "fair and substantial basis." This is taken from our jurisprudence dealing with the question whether a state-court decision rests upon adequate and independent state grounds, placing it beyond our jurisdiction to review. See E. Gressman, K. Geller, S. Shapiro, T. Bishop, & E. Hartnett, Supreme Court Practice, ch. 3.26, p. 222 (9th ed.2007). To assure that there is no "evasion" of our authority to review federal questions, we insist that the nonfederal ground of decision have "fair support." *Broad*

River Power Co. v. South Carolina ex rel. Daniel, 281 U.S. 537, 540, 50 S.Ct. 401, 74 L.Ed. 1023 (1930); see also *Ward v. Board of Comm'rs of Love Cty.*, 253 U.S. 17, 22-23, 40 S.Ct. 419, 64 L.Ed. 751 (1920). A test designed to determine whether there has been an evasion is not obviously appropriate for determining whether there has been a taking of property. But if it is to be extended there it must mean (in the present context) that there is a "fair and substantial basis" for believing that petitioner's Members did not have a property right to future accretions which the Act would take away. This is no different, we think, from our requirement that petitioners' Members must prove the elimination of an established property right.

Next, respondents argue that federal courts lack the knowledge of state law required to decide whether a judicial decision that purports merely to clarify property rights has instead taken them. But federal courts must often decide what state property rights exist in nontakings contexts, see, *e.g., Board of Regents of State Colleges v. Roth,* 408 U.S. 564, 577-578, 92 S.Ct. 2701, 33 L.Ed.2d 548 (1972) (Due Process Clause). And indeed they must decide it to resolve claims that legislative or executive action has effected a taking. For example, a regulation that deprives a property owner of all economically beneficial use of his property is not a taking if the restriction "inhere[s] in the title itself, in the restrictions that background principles of the State's law of property and nuisance already place upon land ownership." *Lucas,* 505 U.S., at 1029, 112 S.Ct. 2886. A constitutional provision that forbids the uncompensated taking of property is quite simply insusceptible of enforcement by federal courts unless they have the power to decide what property rights exist under state law.

* * *

V

Because the Florida Supreme Court's decision did not contravene the established property rights of petitioner's Members, Florida has not violated the Fifth and Fourteenth Amendments. The judgment of the Florida Supreme Court is therefore affirmed.

It is so ordered.

Justice STEVENS took no part in the decision of this case.

Justice KENNEDY, with whom Justice SOTOMAYOR joins, concurring in part and concurring in the judgment.

The Court's analysis of the principles that control ownership of the land in question, and of the rights of petitioner's members as adjacent owners, is correct in my view, leading to my joining Parts I, IV, and V of the Court's opinion. As Justice BREYER observes, however, this case does not require the Court to determine whether, or when, a judicial decision determining the rights of property owners can violate the Takings Clause of the Fifth Amendment of the United States Constitution. This separate opinion notes certain difficulties that should be considered before accepting the theory that a judicial decision that eliminates an "established property right," *ante,* at ----, constitutes a violation of the Takings Clause.

The Takings Clause is an essential part of the constitutional structure, for it protects private property from expropriation without just compensation; and the right to own and hold property is necessary to the exercise and preservation of freedom. The right to retain property without the fact or even the threat of that sort of expropriation is, of course, applicable to the States under the Due Process Clause of the Fourteenth Amendment. *Chicago, B. & Q. R. Co. v. Chicago,* 166 U.S. 226, 239, 17 S.Ct. 581, 41 L.Ed. 979 (1897).

The right of the property owner is subject, however, to the rule that the government does have power to take property for a public use, provided that it pays just compensation. See *First English Evangelical Lutheran Church of Glendale v. County of Los Angeles,* 482 U.S. 304, 314-315, 107 S.Ct. 2378, 96 L.Ed.2d 250 (1987). This is a vast governmental power. And typically, legislative bodies grant substantial discretion to executive officers to decide what property can be taken for authorized projects and uses. As a result, if an authorized executive agency or official decides that Blackacre is the right place for a fire station or Greenacre is the best spot for a freeway interchange, then the weight and authority of the State are used to take the property, even against the wishes of the owner, who must be satisfied with just compensation.

In the exercise of their duty to protect the fisc, both the legislative and executive branches monitor, or should monitor, the exercise of this substantial power. Those branches are accountable in their political capacity for the proper discharge of this obligation.

To enable officials to better exercise this great power in a responsible way, some States allow their officials to take a second look after property has been condemned and a jury returns a verdict setting the amount of just compensation. See, *e.g.,* Cal.Civ.Proc.Code Ann. § 1268.510 (2007). If the condemning authority, usually acting through the executive, deems the compensation too high to pay for the project, it can decide not to take the property at all. The landowner is reimbursed for certain costs and expenses of litigation and the property remains in his or her hands. See, *e.g.,* § 1268.610(a).

This is just one aspect of the exercise of the power to select what property to condemn and the responsibility to ensure that the taking makes financial sense from the State's point of view. And, as a matter of custom and practice, these are matters for the political branches-the legislature and the executive-not the courts. See *First English, supra,* at 321, 107 S.Ct. 2378 ("[T]he decision to exercise the power of eminent domain is a legislative function").

If a judicial decision, as opposed to an act of the executive or the legislature, eliminates an established property right, the judgment could be set aside as a deprivation of property without due process of law. The Due Process Clause, in both its substantive and procedural aspects, is a central limitation upon the exercise of judicial power. And this Court has long recognized that property regulations can be invalidated under the Due Process Clause. See, *e.g., Lingle v. Chevron U.S.A. Inc.,* 544 U.S. 528, 542, 125 S.Ct. 2074, 161 L.Ed.2d 876 (2005); *Goldblatt v. Hempstead,* 369 U.S. 590, 591, 592-593, 82 S.Ct. 987, 8 L.Ed.2d 130 (1962); *Demorest v. City Bank Farmers Trust Co.,* 321 U.S. 36, 42-43, 64 S.Ct. 384, 88 L.Ed. 526 (1944); *Broad River Power Co. v. South Carolina ex rel. Daniel,* 281 U.S. 537, 539, 540-541, 50 S.Ct. 401, 74 L.Ed. 1023 (1930); *Washington ex rel. Seattle Title Trust Co. v. Roberge,* 278 U.S. 116, 121, 49 S.Ct. 50, 73 L.Ed. 210

(1928); *Nectow v. Cambridge,* 277 U.S. 183, 188, 48 S.Ct. 447, 72 L.Ed. 842 (1928); *Village of Euclid v. Ambler Realty Co.,* 272 U.S. 365, 395, 47 S.Ct. 114, 71 L.Ed. 303 (1926); see also *Pennsylvania Coal Co. v. Mahon,* 260 U.S. 393, 413, 43 S.Ct. 158, 67 L.Ed. 322 (1922) (there must be limits on government's ability to diminish property values by regulation "or the contract and due process clauses are gone"). It is thus natural to read the Due Process Clause as limiting the power of courts to eliminate or change established property rights.

The Takings Clause also protects property rights, and it "operates as a conditional limitation, permitting the government to do what it wants so long as it pays the charge." *Eastern Enterprises v. Apfel,* 524 U.S. 498, 545, 118 S.Ct. 2131, 141 L.Ed.2d 451 (1998) (KENNEDY, J., concurring in judgment and dissenting in part). Unlike the Due Process Clause, therefore, the Takings Clause implicitly recognizes a governmental power while placing limits upon that power. Thus, if the Court were to hold that a judicial taking exists, it would presuppose that a judicial decision eliminating established property rights is "otherwise constitutional" so long as the State compensates the aggrieved property owners. *Ibid.* There is no clear authority for this proposition.

When courts act without direction from the executive or legislature, they may not have the power to eliminate established property rights by judicial decision. "Given that the constitutionality" of a judicial decision altering property rights "appears to turn on the legitimacy" of whether the court's judgment eliminates or changes established property rights "rather than on the availability of compensation, ... the more appropriate constitutional analysis arises under general due process principles rather than under the Takings Clause." *Ibid.* Courts, unlike the executive or legislature, are not designed to make policy decisions about "the need for, and likely effectiveness of, regulatory actions." *Lingle, supra,* at 545, 125 S.Ct. 2074. State courts generally operate under a common-law tradition that allows for incremental modifications to property law, but "this tradition cannot justify a *carte blanch* judicial authority to change property definitions wholly free of constitutional limitations." Walston, The Constitution and Property: Due Process, Regulatory Takings, and Judicial Takings, 2001 Utah L.Rev. 379, 435.

The Court would be on strong footing in ruling that a judicial decision that eliminates or substantially changes established property rights, which are a legitimate expectation of the owner, is "arbitrary or irrational" under the Due Process Clause. *Lingle,* 544 U.S., at 542, 125 S.Ct. 2074; see *id.,* at 548-549, 125 S.Ct. 2074 (KENNEDY, J., concurring); see also *Perry v. Sindermann,* 408 U.S. 593, 601, 92 S.Ct. 2694, 33 L.Ed.2d 570 (1972) (" '[P]roperty' " interests protected by the Due Process Clauses are those "that are secured by 'existing rules or understandings' " (quoting *Board of Regents of State Colleges v. Roth,* 408 U.S. 564, 577, 92 S.Ct. 2701, 33 L.Ed.2d 548 (1972))). Thus, without a judicial takings doctrine, the Due Process Clause would likely prevent a State from doing "by judicial decree what the Takings Clause forbids it to do by legislative fiat." *Ante,* at ----. The objection that a due process claim might involve close questions concerning whether a judicial decree extends beyond what owners might have expected is not a sound argument; for the same close questions would arise with respect to whether a judicial decision is a taking. See *Apfel, supra,* at 541, 118 S.Ct. 2131 (opinion of KENNEDY, J.) ("Cases attempting to decide when a regulation becomes a taking are among the most litigated and perplexing in current law"); *Penn Central Transp. Co. v. New York City,* 438 U.S. 104, 123, 98 S.Ct. 2646, 57 L.Ed.2d 631 (1978)

("The question of what constitutes a 'taking' for purposes of the Fifth Amendment has proved to be a problem of considerable difficulty").

To announce that courts too can affect a taking when they decide cases involving property rights, would raise certain difficult questions. Since this case does not require those questions to be addressed, in my respectful view, the Court should not reach beyond the necessities of the case to announce a sweeping rule that court decisions can be takings, as that phrase is used in the Takings Clause. The evident reason for recognizing a judicial takings doctrine would be to constrain the power of the judicial branch. Of course, the judiciary must respect private ownership. But were this Court to say that judicial decisions become takings when they overreach, this might give more power to courts, not less.

* * *

These difficult issues are some of the reasons why the Court should not reach beyond the necessities of the case to recognize a judicial takings doctrine. It is not wise, from an institutional standpoint, to reach out and decide questions that have not been discussed at much length by courts and commentators. This Court's dicta in *Williamson County, supra,* at 194-197, 105 S.Ct. 3108, regarding when regulatory takings claims become ripe, explains why federal courts have not been able to provide much analysis on the issue of judicial takings. See *San Remo Hotel, L.P. v. City and County of San Francisco,* 545 U.S. 323, 351, 125 S.Ct. 2491, 162 L.Ed.2d 315 (2005) (Rehnquist, C.J., concurring in judgment) (" *Williamson County*'s state-litigation rule has created some real anomalies, justifying our revisiting the issue"). Until *Williamson County* is reconsidered, litigants will have to press most of their judicial takings claims before state courts, which are "presumptively competent ... to adjudicate claims arising under the laws of the United States." *Tafflin v. Levitt,* 493 U.S. 455, 458, 110 S.Ct. 792, 107 L.Ed.2d 887 (1990). If and when future cases show that the usual principles, including constitutional principles that constrain the judiciary like due process, are somehow inadequate to protect property owners, then the question whether a judicial decision can effect a taking would be properly presented. In the meantime, it seems appropriate to recognize that the substantial power to decide whose property to take and when to take it should be conceived of as a power vested in the political branches and subject to political control.

Justice BREYER, with whom Justice GINSBURG joins, concurring in part and concurring in the judgment.

I agree that no unconstitutional taking of property occurred in this case, and I therefore join Parts I, IV, and V of today's opinion. I cannot join Parts II and III, however, for in those Parts the plurality unnecessarily addresses questions of constitutional law that are better left for another day.

* * *

In the past, Members of this Court have warned us that, when faced with difficult constitutional questions, we should "confine ourselves to deciding only what is necessary to the disposition of the immediate case." *Whitehouse v. Illinois Central R. Co.,* 349 U.S. 366, 373, 75 S.Ct. 845, 99 L.Ed. 1155 (1955); see also *Lyng v. Northwest Indian Cemetery Protective Assn.,* 485 U.S. 439, 445, 108 S.Ct. 1319, 99 L.Ed.2d 534 (1988) ("A fundamental and longstanding principle of judicial restraint requires that courts avoid reaching constitutional questions in advance of the necessity of deciding them"); *Ashwander v. TVA,* 297 U.S. 288, 346-347, 56 S.Ct. 466, 80 L.Ed. 688 (1936) (Brandeis, J., concurring) ("The Court will not anticipate a question of constitutional law in advance of the necessity of deciding it. It is not the habit of the Court to decide questions of a constitutional nature unless absolutely necessary to a decision of the case" (citations and internal quotation marks omitted)). I heed this advice here. There is no need now to decide more than what the Court decides in Parts IV and V, namely, that the Florida Supreme Court's decision in this case did not amount to a "judicial taking."

§ 15.6 Other Types of Takings

Everything that we have covered up to this point deals with real property. The question that we now consider is whether the Fifth Amendment's Takings Clause can be applied to other scenarios.

Horne v. U.S. Dept. of Agriculture
569 U.S. __ (2013)

Pursuant to the Agricultural Marketing Agreement Act of 1937 (AMAA), any "handler" of raisins is required to surrender part of their tonnage to a governmental "reserve" to stabilize prices. Those handlers who do not comply are subject to monetary fines and penalties. The statutory scheme of the AMAA provides that those assessed a fine may contest the fine. Marvin and Laura Horne, raisin farmers, were assessed $650,000 in fines and penalties for refusing to surrender part of their tonnage. The Hornes claimed that they were producers of raisins, not handlers. Thus, they asserted, they were not subject to the law. They also claimed, as an affirmative defense, that the reserve tonnage requirement constituted an uncompensated taking. The district court affirmed the government's determination that the Hornes were handlers and the concomitant fines, while also finding no merit to the Hornes' takings defense. The Ninth Circuit, too, held that the Hornes were handlers and subject to the fines. The Ninth Circuit also held that if the Hornes wanted to raise a takings claim, they were required to first pay the fine and then bring their takings claim in the Court of Federal Claims, not raise the takings claim as an affirmative defense in the district court. Thus, the Ninth Circuit held that it lacked jurisdiction to review petitioners' takings claim. The Ninth Circuit further held that the takings claim was not ripe. The United States Supreme Court, in a unanimous decision, reverses and holds that the Hornes may raise the takings claim as an affirmative defense in a Department of Agriculture enforcement proceeding, and that the case is ripe.

Justice THOMAS delivered the opinion of the Court.

* * *

I

A

Congress enacted the AMAA during the Great Depression in an effort to insulate farmers from competitive market forces that it believed caused "unreasonable fluctuations in supplies and prices." Ch. 296, 50 Stat. 246, as amended, 7 U.S.C. § 602(4). * * *The Secretary [of the Department of Agriculture] may delegate to industry committees the authority to administer marketing orders. § 608c(7)(C).

* * * Handlers who violate the Secretary's marketing orders may be subject to civil and criminal penalties. §§ 608a(5), 608a(6), and 608c(14).

The Secretary promulgated a marketing order for California raisins in 1949.[19] See 14 Fed. Reg. 5136 (codified, as amended, at 7 CFR pt. 989 (2013)). In particular, "[t]he Raisin Marketing Order, like other fruit and vegetable orders adopted under the AMAA, [sought] to stabilize producer returns by limiting the quantity of raisins sold by handlers in the domestic competitive market." *Lion Raisins, Inc. v. United States,* 416 F.3d 1356, 1359 (C.A.Fed.2005). The Marketing Order defines a raisin "handler" as "(a) [a]ny processor or packer; (b) [a]ny person who places ... raisins in the current of commerce from within [California] to any point outside thereof; (c) [a]ny person who delivers off-grade raisins ... into any eligible non-normal outlet; or (d) [a]ny person who blends raisins [subject to certain exceptions]." 7 CFR § 989.15.

The Marketing Order also established the Raisin Administrative Committee (RAC), which consists of 47 members, with 35 representing producers, ten representing handlers, one representing the cooperative bargaining associations, and one member of the public. See § 989.26. The Marketing Order authorizes the RAC to recommend setting up annual reserve pools of raisins that are not to be sold on the open domestic market. See 7 U.S.C. § 608c(6)(E); 7 CFR §§ 989.54(d) and 989.65. Each year, the RAC reviews crop yield, inventories, and shipments and makes recommendations to the Secretary whether or not there should be a reserve pool. § 989.54. If the RAC recommends a reserve pool, it also recommends what portion of that year's production should be included in the pool ("reserve-tonnage"). The rest of that year's production remains available for sale on the open market ("free-tonnage"). § 989.54(d), (a). The Secretary approves the recommendation if he determines that the recommendation would "effectuate the declared policy of the Act." § 989.55. The reserve-tonnage, calculated as a percentage of a producer's crop, varies from year to year.

Under the Marketing Order's reserve requirements, a producer is only paid for the free-tonnage raisins. § 989.65. The reserve-tonnage raisins, on the other hand, must be held by the handler in segregated bins "for the account" of the RAC. § 989.66(f). The RAC may then sell the reserve-tonnage raisins to handlers for resale in overseas markets, or may alternatively direct that they be sold or given at no cost to secondary, noncompetitive domestic markets, such as school lunch programs. § 989.67(b). The reserve pool sales proceeds are used to finance the RAC's administrative costs. § 989.53(a). In the event that there are any remaining funds, the producers receive a pro

---

[19] The AMAA also applies to a vast array of other agricultural products, including "[m]ilk, fruits (including filberts, almonds, pecans and walnuts .., pears, olives, grapefruit, cherries, cranberries (including raspberries, blackberries, and loganberries), cranberries, ... tobacco, vegetables, ... hops, [and] honeybees." § 608c(2).

rata share. 7 U.S.C. § 608c(6)(E); 7 CFR § 989.66(h). As a result, even though producers do not receive payment for reserve-tonnage raisins at the time of delivery to a handler, they retain a limited interest in the net proceeds of the RAC's disposition of the reserve pool.

* * * A handler who violates any provision of the Order or its implementing regulations is subject to a civil penalty of up to $1,100 per day. 7 U.S.C. § 608c(14)(B); 7 CFR § 3.91(b)(1)(vii). A handler who does not comply with the reserve requirement must "compensate the [RAC] for the amount of the loss resulting from his failure to ... deliver" the requisite raisins. § 989.166(c).

B

Petitioners Marvin and Laura Horne have been producing raisins in two California counties (Fresno and Madera) since 1969. The Hornes do business as Raisin Valley Farms, a general partnership. For more than 30 years, the Hornes operated only as raisin producers. But, after becoming disillusioned with the AMAA regulatory scheme,[20] they began looking for ways to avoid the mandatory reserve program. Since the AMAA applies only to handlers, the Hornes devised a plan to bring their raisins to market without going through a traditional handler. * * *

On April 1, 2004, the Administrator of the Agriculture Marketing Service (Administrator) initiated an enforcement action against the Hornes, Raisin Valley Farms, and Lassen Vineyards (petitioners). The complaint alleged that petitioners were "handlers" of California raisins during the 2002–2003 and 2003–2004 crop years. It also alleged that petitioners violated the AMAA and the Marketing Order by submitting inaccurate forms to the RAC and failing to hold inspections of incoming raisins, retain raisins in reserve, pay assessments, and allow access to their records. Petitioners denied the allegations, countering that they were not "handlers" and asserting that they did not acquire physical possession of the other producers' raisins within the meaning of the regulations. Petitioners also raised several affirmative defenses, including a claim that the Marketing Order violated the Fifth Amendment's prohibition against taking property without just compensation.

An Administrative Law Judge (ALJ) concluded in 2006 that petitioners were handlers of raisins and thus subject to the Marketing Order. * * *

Petitioners appealed to a judicial officer who, like the ALJ, also found that petitioners were handlers and that they had violated the Marketing Order. * * *

Petitioners filed a complaint in Federal District Court seeking judicial review of the USDA's decision. See 7 U.S.C. § 608c(14)(B). The District Court granted summary judgment to the USDA. The court held that substantial evidence supported the agency's determination that petitioners were "handlers" subject to the Marketing Order, and

---

[20] The Hornes wrote the Secretary and to the RAC in 2002 setting out their grievances: "[W]e are growers that will pack and market our raisins. We reserve our rights under the Constitution of the United States ... [T]he Marketing Order Regulating Raisins has become a tool for grower bankruptcy, poverty, and involuntary servitude. The Marketing Order Regulating Raisins is a complete failure for growers, handlers, and the USDA ... [W]e will not relinquish ownership of our crop. We put forth the money and effort to grow it, not the Raisin Administrative Committee. This is America, not a communist state." App. to Pet. for Cert. 60a.

rejected petitioners' argument that they were exempt from the Marketing Order due to their status as "producers" under § 608c(13)(B). No. CV–F–08–1549LJOSMS, 2009 WL 4895362, at (E.D.Cal., Dec. 11, 2009). Petitioners renewed their Fifth Amendment argument, asserting that the reserve-tonnage requirement constituted a physical taking. Though the District Court found that the RAC takes title to a significant portion of a California raisin producer's crop through the reserve requirement, the court held that the transfer of title to the RAC did not constitute a physical taking. * * * (" '[I]n essence, [petitioners] are paying an admissions fee or toll—admittedly a steep one—for marketing raisins. The Government does not force plaintiffs to grow raisins or to market the raisins; rather, it directs that if they grow and market raisins, then passing title to their "reserve tonnage" raisins to the RAC is the admissions ticket' " (quoting *Evans v. United States,* 74 Fed.Cl. 554, 563–564 (2006))).

The Ninth Circuit affirmed. The court agreed that petitioners were "handlers" subject to the Marketing Order's provisions, and rejected petitioners' argument that they were producers, and, thus exempt from regulation. 673 F.3d 1071, 1078 (2012). The court did not resolve petitioners' takings claim, however, because it concluded that it lacked jurisdiction to do so. The court explained that "a takings claim against the federal government must be brought [in the Court of Federal Claims] in the first instance,[21] 'unless Congress has withdrawn the Tucker Act[22] grant of jurisdiction in the relevant statute.' " *Id.,* at 1079 (quoting *Eastern Enterprises v. Apfel,* 524 U.S. 498, 520, 118 S.Ct. 2131, 141 L.Ed.2d 451 (1998) (plurality opinion)). The court recognized that 7 U.S.C. § 608c(15) provides an administrative remedy to handlers wishing to challenge marketing orders under the AMAA, and it agreed that "when a handler, or a producer-handler in its capacity as a handler, challenges a marketing order on takings grounds, Court of Federal Claims Tucker Act jurisdiction gives way to section [60]8c(15)'s comprehensive procedural scheme and administrative exhaustion requirements." 673 F.3d, at 1079. But, the Ninth Circuit determined, petitioners brought the takings claim in their capacity as producers, not handlers. *Id.,* at 1080. Consequently, the court was of the view that "[n]othing in the AMAA precludes the Hornes from alleging in the Court of Federal Claims that the reserve program injures them in their capacity as producers by subjecting them to a taking requiring compensation." *Ibid.* This availability of a Federal Claims Court action thus rendered petitioners' takings claim unripe for adjudication. *Ibid.*

We granted certiorari to determine whether the Ninth Circuit has jurisdiction to review petitioners' takings claim. * * *

II

A

The Ninth Circuit's jurisdictional ruling flowed from its determination that petitioners brought their takings claim as producers rather than handlers. This determination is not correct. Although petitioners argued that they were producers—and

---

[21] [Generally, to contest an assessment made by the federal government, a person may file suit against the government in the Court of Federal Claims, but only after all assessments are first paid. Thus, under this generalization, for the Hornes to file suit in the Court of Federal Claims, they first would have to pay the $650,000 assessed.]

[22] [Under the Tucker Act, the United States waives sovereign immunity for non-tortious claims.]

thus not subject to the AMAA or Marketing Order at all—both the USDA and the District Court concluded that petitioners were "handlers." Accordingly, the civil penalty, assessment, and reimbursement for failure to reserve raisins were all levied on petitioners in their capacity as "handlers." If petitioners' argument that they were producers had prevailed, they would not have been subject to *any* of the monetary sanctions imposed on them. See 7 U.S.C. § 608c(13)(B) ("No order issued under this chapter shall be applicable to any producer in his capacity as a producer").

It is undisputed that the Marketing Order imposes duties on petitioners only in their capacity as handlers. As a result, any defense raised against those duties is necessarily raised in that same capacity. Petitioners argue that it would be unconstitutional for the Government to come on their land and confiscate raisins, or to confiscate the proceeds of raisin sales, without paying just compensation; and, that it is therefore unconstitutional to fine petitioners for not complying with the unconstitutional requirement.[23] See Brief for Petitioners 54. Given that fines can only be levied on handlers, petitioners' takings claim makes sense only as a defense to penalties imposed upon them in their capacity *as handlers*. The Ninth Circuit confused petitioners' statutory argument (*i.e.,* "we are producers, not handlers") with their constitutional argument (*i.e.,* "assuming we are handlers, fining us for refusing to turn over reserve-tonnage raisins violates the Fifth Amendment").[24]

The relevant question, then, is whether a federal court has jurisdiction to adjudicate a takings defense raised by a handler seeking review of a final agency order.

B

The Government argues that petitioners' takings-based defense was rightly dismissed on ripeness grounds. * * * According to the Government, because a takings claim can be pursued later in the Court of Federal Claims, the Ninth Circuit correctly refused to adjudicate petitioners' takings defense. In support of its position, the Government relies largely on *Williamson County Regional Planning Comm'n v. Hamilton Bank of Johnson City,* 473 U.S. 172, 105 S.Ct. 3108, 87 L.Ed.2d 126 (1985). Brief for Respondent 21–22 ("Just compensation need not 'be paid in advance of, or contemporaneously with, the taking; all that is required is that a 'reasonable, certain and

---

[23] The Ninth Circuit construed the takings argument quite differently, stating that petitioners believe the regulatory scheme "takes reserve-tonnage raisins belonging to producers." 673 F.3d 1071, 1080 (2012). When the agency brought its enforcement action against petitioners, however, it did not seek to recover reserve-tonnage raisins from the 2002–2003 and 2003–2004 crop years. Rather, it sought monetary penalties and reimbursement. Petitioners could not argue in the face of such agency action that the Secretary was attempting to take raisins that had already been harvested and sold. Instead, petitioners argued that they could not be compelled to pay fines for refusing to accede to an unconstitutional taking.

[24] The Government notes that petitioners did not own most of the raisins that they failed to reserve and argues that petitioners would have no takings claim based on those raisins. See Brief for Respondent 19. We take no position on the merits of petitioners' takings claim. We simply recognize that insofar as the petitioners challenged the imposition of monetary sanctions under the Marketing Order, they raised their takings-based defense in their capacity as handlers. On remand, the Ninth Circuit can decide in the first instance whether petitioners may raise the takings defense with respect to raisins they never owned.

adequate provision for obtaining compensation' exist at the time of the taking' " (quoting *Williamson County*, 473 U.S., at 194, 105 S.Ct. 3108)). In that case, the plaintiff filed suit against the Regional Planning Commission, claiming that a zoning decision by the Commission affected a taking of property without just compensation. *Id.*, at 182, 105 S.Ct. 3108. We found that the plaintiff's claim was not "ripe" for two reasons, neither of which supports the Government's position.

First, we explained that the plaintiff's takings claim in *Williamson County* failed because the plaintiff could not show that it had been injured by the Government's action. Specifically, the plaintiff "ha[d] not yet obtained a final decision regarding the application of the zoning ordinance and subdivision regulations to its property." *Id.*, at 186, 105 S.Ct. 3108. Here, by contrast, petitioners were subject to a final agency order imposing concrete fines and penalties at the time they sought judicial review under § 608c(14)(B). This was clearly sufficient "injury" for federal jurisdiction.

Second, the *Williamson County* plaintiff's takings claim was not yet ripe because the plaintiff had not sought "compensation through the procedures the State ha[d] provided for doing so." *Id.*, at 194, 105 S.Ct. 3108. We explained that "[i]f the government has provided an adequate process for obtaining compensation, and if resort to that process yields just compensation, then the property owner has no claim against the Government for a taking." *Id.*, at 194–195, 105 S.Ct. 3108 (internal quotation marks and alteration omitted). Stated differently, a Fifth Amendment claim is premature until it is clear that the Government has both taken property *and* denied just compensation. Although we often refer to this consideration as "prudential 'ripeness,' " *Lucas v. South Carolina Coastal Council*, 505 U.S. 1003, 1013, 112 S.Ct. 2886, 120 L.Ed.2d 798 (1992), we have recognized that it is not, strictly speaking, jurisdictional.[25] See *Stop the Beach Renourishment, Inc. v. Florida Dept. of Environmental Protection*, 560 U.S. ___, ___, and n. 10, 130 S.Ct. 2592, 2610, and n. 10, 177 L.Ed.2d 184 (2010).

Here, the Government argues that petitioners' takings claim is premature because the Tucker Act affords "the requisite reasonable, certain, and adequate provision for obtaining just compensation that a property owner must pursue." Brief for Respondent 22. In the Government's view, "[p]etitioners should have complied with the order, and, after a portion of their raisins were placed in reserve to be disposed of as directed by the RAC, ... sought compensation as producers in the Court of Federal Claims for the alleged taking." *Id.*, at 24–25. We disagree with the Government's argument, however, because the AMAA provides a comprehensive remedial scheme that withdraws Tucker Act jurisdiction over a handler's takings claim. As a result, there is no alternative "reasonable, certain, and adequate" remedial scheme through which petitioners (as handlers) must proceed before obtaining review of their claim under the AMAA.[26]

---

[25] A "Case" or "Controversy" exists once the government has taken private property without paying for it. Accordingly, whether an alternative remedy exists does not affect the jurisdiction of the federal court.

[26] That is not to say that a producer who turns over her reserve-tonnage raisins could not bring suit for just compensation in the Court of Claims. Whether a producer could bring such a claim, and what impact the availability of such a claim would have on petitioners' takings-based defense, are questions going to the merits of petitioners' defense, not to a court's jurisdiction to entertain it. We therefore do not address those issues here.

The Court of Federal Claims has jurisdiction over Tucker Act claims "founded either upon the Constitution, or any Act of Congress or any regulation of an executive department." 28 U.S.C. § 1491(a)(1). "[A] claim for just compensation under the Takings Clause must be brought to the Court of Federal Claims in the first instance, unless Congress has withdrawn the Tucker Act grant of jurisdiction in the relevant statute." *Eastern Enterprises,* 524 U.S., at 520, 118 S.Ct. 2131 (plurality opinion); see also *United States v. Bormes,* 568 U.S. ___, ___, 133 S.Ct. 12, 17, 184 L.Ed.2d 317 (2012) (where "a statute contains its own self-executing remedial scheme," a court "look[s] only to that statute"). To determine whether a statutory scheme displaces Tucker Act jurisdiction, a court must "examin[e] the purpose of the [statute], the entirety of its text, and the structure of review that it establishes." *United States v. Fausto,* 484 U.S. 439, 444, 108 S.Ct. 668, 98 L.Ed.2d 830 (1988).

Under the AMAA's comprehensive remedial scheme, handlers may challenge the content, applicability, and enforcement of marketing orders. Pursuant to § 608c(15)(A)–(B), a handler may file with the Secretary a direct challenge to a marketing order and its applicability to him. We have held that "any handler" subject to a marketing order must raise any challenges to the order, including constitutional challenges, in administrative proceedings. See *United States v. Ruzicka,* 329 U.S. 287, 294, 67 S.Ct. 207, 91 L.Ed. 290 (1946). Once the Secretary issues a ruling, the federal district court where the "handler is an inhabitant, or has his principal place of business" is "vested with jurisdiction ... to review [the] ruling." § 608c(15)(B). These statutory provisions afford handlers a ready avenue to bring takings claim against the USDA. We thus conclude that the AMAA withdraws Tucker Act jurisdiction over petitioners' takings claim. Petitioners (as handlers) have no alternative remedy, and their takings claim was not "premature" when presented to the Ninth Circuit.

C

Although petitioners' claim was not "premature" for Tucker Act purposes, the question remains whether a takings-based defense may be raised by a handler in the context of an enforcement proceeding initiated by the USDA under § 608c(14). We hold that it may. * * *

In the case of an administrative enforcement proceeding, when a party raises a constitutional defense to an assessed fine, it would make little sense to require the party to pay the fine in one proceeding and then turn around and sue for recovery of that same money in another proceeding. See *Eastern Enterprises, supra,* at 520, 118 S.Ct. 2131. * * * The grant of jurisdiction necessarily includes the power to review any constitutional challenges properly presented to and rejected by the agency. We are therefore satisfied that the petitioners raised a cognizable takings defense and that the Ninth Circuit erred in declining to adjudicate it.

III

The Ninth Circuit has jurisdiction to decide whether the USDA's imposition of fines and civil penalties on petitioners, in their capacity as handlers, violated the Fifth Amendment. The judgment of the Ninth Circuit is reversed, and the case is remanded for further proceedings consistent with this opinion.

It is so ordered.

Ex Parte Brown
393 S.C. 214 (2011)

The court appointed a lawyer, James Brown, to represent a criminal defendant. The lawyer asked for permission to withdraw as counsel because of the substantial amount of time that the case would require, coupled with the fact that the lawyer would be paid a relatively small fee, $3,500, by the court. The court denied the lawyer's petition to withdraw. Ultimately, the lawyer did represent the defendant but, at the end of the proceedings, the court would not grant the lawyer's motion for attorney's fees beyond the statutory cap of $3,500. The sole reason for denying the fees in excess of the cap was, as the trial court put it, the lawyer's "unprofessional conduct." An amicus brief asked the South Carolina Supreme Court to address the Fifth Amendment Takings Clause in the lawyer's appeal. The Supreme Court of South Carolina did so address the issue and held, "the Takings Clause of the Fifth Amendment to the United States Constitution is implicated when an attorney is appointed by the court to represent an indigent litigant. In such circumstances, the attorney's services constitute property entitling the attorney to just compensation."

* * *

Section 17–3–50 [of the South Carolina Annotated Statues] provides:

(A) *When private counsel is appointed* pursuant to this chapter, *he must be paid a reasonable fee* to be determined on the basis of forty dollars an hour for time spent out of court and sixty dollars an hour for time spent in court. The same hourly rates apply in post-conviction proceedings. *Compensation may not exceed three thousand five hundred dollars in a case in which one or more felonies is charged* and one thousand dollars in a case in which only misdemeanors are charged. Compensation must be paid from funds available to the Office of Indigent Defense for the defense of indigents represented by court-appointed, private counsel. The same basis must be employed to determine the value of services provided by the office of the public defender for purposes of Section 17–3–40.

(B) Upon a finding in ex parte proceedings that *investigative, expert, or other services are reasonably necessary for the representation of the defendant, the court shall authorize* the defendant's attorney to obtain such services on behalf of the defendant and shall order the payment, from funds available to the Office of Indigent Defense, of *fees and expenses not to exceed five hundred dollars* as the court considers appropriate.

(C) *Payment in excess of the hourly rates and limits in subsection (A) or (B) is authorized only if the court certifies, in a written order with specific findings of fact, that payment in excess of the rates is necessary to provide compensation adequate to ensure effective assistance of counsel and payment in excess of the limit is appropriate because the services provided were reasonably and necessarily incurred.*

(Emphasis added).

An award of attorney's fees in excess of the section 17–3–50 statutory cap is "within the sound discretion of the trial judge." *Bailey v. State,* 309 S.C. 455, 464, 424 S.E.2d 503, 508 (1992). An abuse of discretion occurs when the ruling lacks evidentiary support or is controlled by an error of law. *Patel v. Patel,* 359 S.C. 515, 529, 599 S.E.2d 114, 121 (2004).

Appellant presents the issue as one of law: may a trial court properly deny a request to exceed the statutory cap for attorney's fees based on the attorney's unprofessional conduct? We answer that question "yes" under the unique and compelling circumstances presented. Given the egregious level of Appellant's inexcusable conduct and persistent disregard of the trial court's orders, we find the trial court did not abuse its discretion in refusing to award fees in excess of the statutory cap.

III.

The South Carolina Bar appears Amicus Curiae. The Bar contends that the appointment of attorneys to represent indigent litigants implicates the Takings Clause of the Fifth Amendment to the United States Constitution. *See* U.S. Const. amend. V ("[N]or shall private property be taken for public use without just compensation.").[27] We agree and hold today that the Fifth Amendment Takings Clause is implicated when an attorney is appointed to represent an indigent litigant. In such circumstances, the attorney's services constitute property entitling the attorney to just compensation.

Our willingness to consider the Bar's request and our ruling today in no manner changes the nature of the practice of law in this state. Our holding is a narrow one, limited to an attorney's constitutional entitlement to compensation in appointed cases. We continue to adhere to the view that the license to practice law is a privilege and not a right. As such, the practice of law remains subject to control, regulation, and discipline— all as this Court directs.

A.

The Sixth and Fourteenth Amendments to the United States Constitution compel states to provide counsel to indigent criminal defendants. *Gideon v. Wainwright,* 372 U.S. 335, 83 S.Ct. 792, 9 L.Ed.2d 799 (1963); *see also United States v. Dillon,* 346 F.2d 633, 635 (9th Cir.1965) (stating "the obligation of the legal profession to serve indigents on court order is an ancient and established tradition...."). In South Carolina, this historic obligation of the legal profession is largely administered through Rule 608, SCACR.

Rule 608(a) requires members of the South Carolina Bar to "serve as counsel for indigent persons in the circuit and family courts pursuant to statutory and constitutional mandates." The vast majority of attorneys have commendably discharged this responsibility in a manner reflecting the highest and noblest traditions of the legal profession. Such laudable service is woven into the fabric of the legal profession, as exemplified in the lawyer's oath, in which an attorney affirms that "I will assist the defenseless or oppressed by ensuring that justice is available to all citizens and will not delay any person's cause for profit or malice." Rule 402(k)(3), SCACR.

We believe the South Carolina General Assembly recognizes the inherent fairness in providing for an award of attorney's fees and costs in appointed cases, as evidenced by

---

[27] Although not cited by the Bar, the South Carolina Constitution has a Takings Clause. S.C. Const. art. I, § 13(A) ("Except as otherwise provided in this Constitution, private property shall not be taken ... for public use without just compensation being first made for the property."). Our analysis and holding comports with the Takings Clause in our constitution.

section 17–3–50. Section 17–3–50 addresses appointment in criminal cases and post-conviction relief proceedings. Moreover, section 17–3–100 speaks more broadly to our legislature's policy favoring the payment of fees to appointed counsel: "Nothing herein contained is designed to limit the *discretionary authority of a judge to appoint counsel in any case and any such counsel shall be entitled to remuneration and reimbursement* as provided in Sections 17–3–50 and 17–3–80 hereof, so long as funds appropriated herein are available therefor." (Emphasis added.) What the legislature has recognized for statutorily authorized appointments, we now find is additionally entitled to constitutional protection. We extend the constitutional protection to all court-ordered appointments.

The Supreme Court of Kansas spoke directly to this issue:

> Attorneys make their living through their services. Their services are the means of their livelihood. We do not expect architects to design public buildings, engineers to design highways, dikes, and bridges, or physicians to treat the indigent without compensation. When attorneys' services are conscripted for the public good, such a taking is akin to the taking of food or clothing from a merchant or the taking of services from any other professional for the public good. And certainly when attorneys are required to donate funds out-of-pocket to subsidize a defense for an indigent defendant, the attorneys are deprived of property in the form of money. We conclude that attorneys' services are property, and are thus subject to Fifth Amendment protection.

State v. Smith, 242 Kan. 336, 747 P.2d 816, 842 (1987); *see also Armstrong v. United States,* 364 U.S. 40, 49, 80 S.Ct. 1563, 4 L.Ed.2d 1554 (1960) (noting that the Takings Clause was "designed to bar Government from forcing some people alone to bear public burdens which, in all fairness and justice, should be borne by the public as a whole"). We agree with the Kansas Supreme Court, with one significant caveat. A lawyer is not a merchant; the law is a regulated public service profession. While the merchant and lawyer both seek gain, "the difference between a business and a profession is essentially that while the chief end of a trade or business is personal gain, the chief end of a profession is public service." *In Re Jacobson,* 240 S.C. 436, 448, 126 S.E.2d 346, 353 (1962).

In holding that the Takings Clause is implicated in appointed cases, we revisit two cases in this state's jurisprudence. First, in *Ex parte Dibble,* 279 S.C. 592, 596, 310 S.E.2d 440, 443 (Ct.App.1983), the court of appeals understood well the Bar's concerns, acknowledging that "it is unfair to cast on [lawyers], alone, the burden of serving the needs of the whole society without compensation." While *Dibble* suggested that "[c]ourts may have the inherent power to order that appointed lawyers be compensated from public funds, thus transferring [the burden of appointed representation] to the state where it properly belongs[,]" *id.,* the court ultimately dismissed the lawyers' claim for compensation.

The lawyers in *Dibble* were appointed in a civil case to represent an indigent client who had no right to counsel. The court of appeals articulated well the role of the legal profession in society and noted that courts "have the inherent power ... to appoint lawyers to serve without compensation where it appears reasonably necessary for the court to do justice." *Id.* at 595, 310 S.E.2d at 442. Today, we hold that a court's inherent power to appoint a lawyer to serve is subject to the lawyer's entitlement to just compensation. In recognition of the burden imposed in uncompensated and discretionary appointments, *Dibble* appropriately indicated that counsel should be appointed only in "extraordinary" circumstances when "necessary to render justice." *Id.* at 597, 310 S.E.2d at 443. The appointment of counsel only when "necessary to render justice" should serve to protect the public fisc.

Next, we addressed this underlying tension in *Bailey v. State,* 309 S.C. 455, 424 S.E.2d 503 (1992). *Bailey* dealt with adequate funding in the context of capital litigation. In *Bailey,* the Court echoed *Dibble* and spoke to the legal profession's "traditional and historic role" in society. The Court then acknowledged the financial burden imposed on appointed attorneys in capital cases: "It is an understatement that the very livelihood of many attorneys appointed to death penalty trials is threatened by this burden, a result fundamentally unfair to those so impacted." *Id.* at 457, 424 S.E.2d at 505. This "burden" may well be greater in a death penalty case, but the same burden (flowing from compelled representation) exists in all appointed cases. It is a matter of degree. The *Bailey* Court avoided the takings issue by ordering compensation pursuant to statute.

Today we address the constitutional issue sidestepped in *Bailey* and hold that a court-appointed attorney's service is property for purposes of the Takings Clause.

B.

The Bar requests that we establish formulaic guidelines for the trial courts and practicing Bar in handling "the challenges of complex appointed cases." We decline to set bright-line rules, as we believe the better approach is to defer to the broad discretion of our able trial courts in addressing such claims on a case-by-case basis. The question of a taking is one of law. The question of what constitutes a fair attorney's fee under the circumstances would be one of fact, subject to an abuse of discretion standard of review. Take the case before us—Appellant's takings argument would be resolved by the payment of *some* amount as attorney's fees; whether the amount awarded is constitutionally appropriate or just under the circumstances is a question of fact, subject to an abuse of discretion standard.

We believe the case-by-case approach is in accord with the amicus curiae brief. Consider the following excerpt from the Bar's brief: "This does not mean that a lawyer is entitled to a fee which exceeds the statutory cap in *all* cases. Since takings analysis is a sliding scale, it is possible that an appointed case might require so small an allocation of a lawyer's time that a lawyer is entitled to no fee for his services." (Br. for South Carolina Bar as Amicus Curiae 4).[28]

The Bar's position reflects its recognition of the unique nature and role of the legal profession in society, thus explaining its preference for a "sliding scale" approach.

---

[28] One area of particular concern to the Bar is the general practice in our trial courts of prohibiting interim payments. As advocated in the Bar's brief, appointed attorneys should be able to request "that lower courts take an early look at the question of attorney's fees ... as opposed to postponing the decision until the end of trial." We do not foreclose a partial award of fees and costs prior to the conclusion of the appointed representation, but interim awards should be granted sparingly and only under compelling circumstances.

Bailey spoke to this in the statutory context, and we agree with the Bar that it applies in the constitutional context: "[an] appointed attorney should not expect to be compensated at *market rate,* rather, at a reasonable, but lesser rate, which reflects the unique difficulty these cases present as balanced with the attorney's obligation to defend the indigent." 309 S.C. at 464, 424 S.E.2d at 508.

C.

We thus recognize the historic obligation of an attorney to honor court-ordered appointments for the representation of indigents, while also recognizing that the attorney's service constitutes property for Fifth Amendment purposes where there is a right to counsel. We do not view these principles as mutually exclusive. In harmonizing these positions, a trial court should be guided by *Bailey*'s approach to just compensation assessed in light of the public service foundation associated with membership in the legal profession.

The Court's holding applies to all court-appointed representations commenced on or after July 1, 2012.

IV.

We find no abuse of discretion in the trial court's decision to deny Appellant's motion to exceed the $3,500 statutory cap for attorney's fees. Because of the significant public interest involved, we accept the South Carolina Bar's amicus curiae brief and hold that a court-appointed attorney's service on behalf of an indigent litigant is property for purposes of the Takings Clause of the Fifth Amendment.

AFFIRMED

* * *

Appendix

GENERAL WARRANTY DEED[1]

For good consideration, we_____
of_____, County of_____
State of_____, hereby bargain, deed and convey
to_____ of _____ County
of_____, State of_____, the following
described land in _____county, free and clear with WARRANTY
COVENANTS; to wit:

Grantor, for itself and its heirs, hereby covenants with Grantee, its heirs, and assigns, that [1] Grantor is lawfully seized in fee simple of the above-described premises; [2] that it has a good right to convey; [3] that the premises are free from all encumbrances; [4] that Grantor and its heirs, and all persons acquiring any interest in the property granted, through or for Grantor, will, on demand of Grantee, or its heirs or assigns, and at the expense of Grantee, its heirs or assigns, execute any instrument necessary for the further assurance of the title to the premises that may be reasonably required; [5] [that Grantor and its heirs and assigns will guarantee the quiet enjoyment of the premises to the Grantee, its heirs, and assigns;] [6] and that Grantor and its heirs will forever warrant and defend all of the property so granted to Grantee, its heirs, against every person lawfully claiming the same or any part thereof.

Being the same property conveyed to the Grantors by deed of
_____, dated_____19____.
WITNESS the hands and seal of said Grantors this____day of_____, 20____.

_____
Grantor

_____
Grantee

STATE   OF
COUNTY OF

On_____before me,_____, personally appeared_____, personally known to me (or proved to me on the basis of satisfactory evidence) to be the person(s) whose name(s) is/are subscribed to the within instrument and acknowledged to me that he/she/they executed the same in his/her/their authorized capacity(ies), and that by his/her/their signature(s) on the instrument the person(s), or the entity upon behalf of which the person(s) acted, executed the instrument.
WITNESS my hand and official seal.
Signature_____
Affiant _____Known _____Unknown ID Produced_____

---

[1] [The bracketed numbers within the deed make obvious the six covenants of title.]

526

Index